Lecture Notes in Artificial Intelligence   7070

Subseries of Lecture Notes in Computer Science

David L. Dowe (Ed.)

Algorithmic Probability and Friends

Bayesian Prediction and Artificial Intelligence

Papers from the Ray Solomonoff 85th Memorial Conference
Melbourne, VIC, Australia, November 30 – December 2, 2011

 Springer

Volume Editor

David L. Dowe
Monash University
Faculty of Information Technology
Clayton School of Information Technology
Bldg. 63, Wellington Road
Clayton, VIC 3800, Australia
E-mail: david.dowe@monash.edu

Cover illustration: Ray often made abstract drawings on his pages of notes.
The cover image is from 1970.
© Grace Solomonoff

ISSN 0302-9743   e-ISSN 1611-3349
ISBN 978-3-642-44957-4   e-ISBN 978-3-642-44958-1
DOI 10.1007/978-3-642-44958-1
Springer Heidelberg New York Dordrecht London

Library of Congress Control Number: 2013951870

CR Subject Classification (1998): I.2, F.1, H.3, I.4, I.5, H.4

LNCS Sublibrary: SL 1 – Theoretical Computer Science and General Issues

Typesetting: Camera-ready by author, data conversion by Scientific Publishing Services, Chennai, India

Printed on acid-free paper

Springer is part of Springer Science+Business Media (www.springer.com)

Picture of Ray taken by Grace on March 18, 1984, to accompany the 1985 article, "The Time Scale of Artificial Intelligence"

Preface

The Ray Solomonoff 85th memorial conference was held from Wednesday 30th November to Friday 2nd December 2011, to honour the work and life of Ray J. Solomonoff. Ray was not just a pioneer in computer science, artificial intelligence and machine learning, he was a visionary whose work is still today increasingly impacting on the philosophy of science. He was well aware of the human and societal implications of his work, and he will probably one day also be seen as a pioneer in statistics, econometrics and (the relatively new terms) knowledge discovery, data mining, terabyte science, data science, big data, and data management and processing, etc.

The conference was to honour Ray's 85th birthday in 2011 but, after a full life well lived (and pioneering influential research), sadly, Ray died in December 2009. The conference was held at Monash University's Clayton campus in Melbourne, Australia.

With a strong multi-disciplinary and international Program Committee including 2 Turing Award winners (and a correspondingly strong set of reviewers), there were 40 submissions (in a variety of areas of Solomonoff's work), each of which was reviewed at least twice and of which 30 were accepted as long papers and 1 as a short paper. These were accompanied by invited (talks and) papers by none less than Grace Solomonoff, Prof. Leonid Levin (Boston University, U.S.A.) and Prof. Ming Li (University of Waterloo, Canada).

There were over 40 conference delegates from countries including Australia, Brazil, Canada, China and England, Finland, France, Germany, Japan, Latvia, New Zealand, Poland, Sweden, Turkey and U.S.A., with the list of paper authors and co-authors also including Kuwait and Malaysia. (Other papers were submitted from at least two other countries.) Here and elsewhere, we thank these contributors, the sponsors [Air Force Office of Scientific Research, Asian Office of Aerospace Research & Development, Grant number FA2386-11-1-1020 AFOSR and AOARD; Faculty of Information Technology, Monash University, Australia; National ICT Australia (NICTA), Australia], the publishers (Springer) and other contributors.

Electronic computers were involved in the conference in terms of (e.g.) electronic type-setting, electronic presentations and (in some papers) rapid (faster than human) computer simulation of statistical and machine learning experiments. In the spirit of Solomonoff's work, one wonders if, when and how computers might have an increasing - and, ultimately, super-human - involvement and influence on such activities. No matter how mathematical, philosophical or otherwise, and no matter how overtly or subtly, this theme of genuine machine intelligence underlies almost all (if not all) the papers in this volume. Please enjoy the various angles and threads of this discussion throughout the conference proceedings, honouring a true pioneer who led by example, taught us so much, and gave good direction for the work now before you and work to follow.

In choosing text for the front cover (title, inter-title and sub-title), various (combinations of) terms were considered - including Universal Turing Machine (UTM). For an idea of some of the other terms and notions considered, see the back cover and also the titles - and even the contents - of the contributed papers. In addition to the front cover figure, see Ray's famous equation at http://world.std.com/~rjs, together with the link there to Ray's doodles (and perhaps also the use of parts of two of Ray's doodles by RJD to give the figure at www.csse.monash.edu.au/~dld/RaySolomonoffsVision.html or www.dowe.org/RaySolomonoffsVision.html). As well as the inside photo of Ray, see other photos of Ray in some of the contributed papers in the volume, and also photos of Ray at or linked to from http://world.std.com/~rjs.

From Ray's inaugural Kolmogorov lecture in 2003 (see end of sec. 3 of Ray's corresponding 2003 paper), following the directions Ray has given us should largely be "a never ending source of joy in discovery!". And, among other things, our work to follow (into the future) perhaps (starting now) includes the devoted thought and discussion which Ray advocated in 1967 that we have regarding the problems of the realization of artificial intelligence – before they arise.

May 2013   David L. Dowe

Organization

Organizing Committee

General and Program Chair

David L. Dowe   Monash University, Australia

Co-ordinator

Dianne Nguyen   Monash University, Australia

Program Committee

Andrew Barron	Statistics, Yale University, USA
Greg Chaitin	IBM T.J. Watson Research Center, USA
Fouad Chedid	Notre Dame University, Lebanon
Bertrand Clarke	Medical Statistics, University of Miami, USA
Peter Gacs	Boston University, USA
Alex Gammerman	Royal Holloway, University of London, UK
John Goldsmith	Linguistics, University of Chicago, USA
Marcus Hutter	Australian National University, Australia
Leonid Levin	Boston University, USA
Ming Li	Mathematics, University of Waterloo, Canada
John McCarthy (4 September 1927 - 24 October 2011)	Stanford University, USA (Turing Award winner)
Marvin Minsky	MIT, USA (Turing Award winner)
Kee Siong Ng	ANU & EMC Corp., Australia
David Paganin	Physics, Monash University, Australia
Teemu Roos	University of Helsinki, Finland
Juergen Schmidhuber	IDSIA, Switzerland
William Uther	NICTA and University of New South Wales, Australia
Farshid Vahid	Econometrics, Monash University, Australia
Paul Vitanyi	Centrum Wiskunde & Informatica (CWI), Amsterdam, The Netherlands
Vladimir Vovk	Royal Holloway, University of London, UK

Reviewers

David Albrecht	Monash University, Australia
Eric Allender	Rutgers – State University of New Jersey, USA
Luis Antunes	Porto University, Portugal
James Breen	Monash University, Australia
Mike Cameron-Jones	University of Tasmania, Australia
Douglas Campbell	University of Canterbury, New Zealand
Fouad Chedid	Notre Dame University, Lebanon
Bertrand Clarke	University of Miami, USA
Adam Day	University of California, USA
Steven De Rooij	Centrum Wiskunde & Informatica (CWI), Amsterdam, The Netherlands
Karl Friston	UCL, London, UK
Peter Gacs	Boston University, USA
Alex Gammerman	Royal Holloway, University of London, UK
Toby Handfield	Monash University, Australia
Marcus Hutter	Australian National University (ANU), Australia
Asad I. Khan	Monash University, Australia
Tor Lattimore	Australian National University, Australia
Ming Li	University of Waterloo, Canada
Kar Seng Loke	Monash University, Malaysia
Enes Makalic	University of Melbourne, Australia
Simon Musgrave	Monash University, Australia
Kee Siong Ng	ANU & EMC Corp., Australia
David Paganin	Monash University, Australia
Ronald Pose	Monash University, Australia
Teemu Roos	University of Helsinki, Finland
Daniel Schmidt	University of Melbourne, Australia
Carl Shulman	University of Oxford, UK
Martin Strauss	University of Michigan, USA
Peter Tischer	Monash University, Australia
Andrea Torsello	Ca' Foscari University of Venice, Italy
William Uther	NICTA and University of New South Wales, Australia
Farshid Vahid	Monash University, Australia
Tim van Erven	University of Paris-Sud, France
Joel Veness	University of Alberta, Canada
Gerhard Visser	Monash University, Australia
Vladimir Vovk	Royal Holloway, University of London, UK
John Woodward	University of Nottingham, Ningbo, PRC

Acknowledgements

We gratefully acknowledge our Sponsors for their support for the Ray
Solomonoff 85th Memorial Conference, thank you.

Sponsors

Air Force Office of Scientific Research (AFOSR)

Asian Office of Aerospace Research & Development (AOARD)

Faculty of Information Technology,
Monash University, Australia

National ICT Australia, Australia

A further word of gratitude to Dr Rebecca Robinson and Mrs. Genevieve Oreski
for their excellent combined efforts in proof-reading, formatting and other ad-
ministrative assistance. We further thank Rebecca for her expert assistance with
handling various LaTeX files. We also gratefully acknowledge Elke Werner and
the team at Springer for the production of these proceedings.

Table of Contents

Short Paper

Introduction to Ray Solomonoff
85th Memorial Conference

David L. Dowe

Computer Science and Software Engineering, Clayton School of Information
Technology, Monash University, Vic. 3800, Australia
david.dowe@monash.edu

Abstract. This piece is an introduction to the proceedings of the Ray
Solomonoff 85th memorial conference, paying tribute to the works and
life of Ray Solomonoff, and mentioning other papers from the conference.

Keywords: Ray Solomonoff, Solomonoff, Solomonoff memorial,
Solomonoff theory of prediction, algorithmic probability, ALP, convergence, completeness, algorithmic information theory, AIT, Kolmogorov
complexity, non-parametrics, training sequences, technological singularity, realization of artificial intelligence, dangers.

1   Introduction - and Summary

The Solomonoff 85th memorial conference was, unsurprisingly, to pay tribute
to Ray Solomonoff (1926 - 2009) in November - December 2011, in the year of
what would have been Solomonoff's 85th birthday. As we then moved from this
(2011) to 2012 and the centenary year of Alan Turing (1912 - 1954), and as
we note the (Universal) Turing machine [or (U)TM] [172] and Turing's notion
of machine intelligence (and his Imitation Game, also known as the "Turing
test") [173], if we are genuine in following Turing's legacy then it would be a sad
and unfortunate omission to neglect the influence of Solomonoff - and also his
contemporaries (e.g., [76][77, p662, col. 2 and p664, col. 1]) and successors.

As per [114], Ray Solomonoff was one of 10 researchers [118] at a conference
at Dartmouth, U.S.A. in 1956 [148, sec. 3.2]. Those in attendance included John
McCarthy (4/Sep/1927 - 24/Oct/2011, whose letter as convenor inviting the
others to the 1956 Dartmouth conference apparently coined the term "artificial
intelligence" [114, sec. 4][148, sec. 3.2]) and Marvin Minsky (who would also
- like Ray Solomonoff [147] [and [149]] - be an invited speaker at the August
1996 Information, Statistics and Induction in Science [ISIS] conference). Both
McCarthy (in 1971) and Minsky (in 1969) became Turing Award winners, and
both would much later agree to be on the Solomonoff 85th memorial Program
Committee.

(For details on so much of Ray Solomonoff's life, I can only encourage the
reader to read [114] and any other of Grace Solomonoff's writings on Ray.)

D.L. Dowe (Ed.): Solomonoff Festschrift, LNAI 7070, pp. 1–36, 2013.

1.1   Short Summary

Ray Solomonoff (25/July/1926 - 7/December/2009) was a Bayesian ahead of his time in the 1950s. He was one of 10 people present at the 1956 Dartmouth conference on artificial intelligence, 2 of whom would later win Turing Awards (the Award being inaugurated in 1966).

Ray was the original pioneer, in the early 1960s, of the use of (universal) Turing machines (using algorithmic information theory and algorithmic probability) for prediction problems in statistics, machine learning, econometrics and data mining - seeing this multi-disciplinary connection perhaps before at least half of these disciplines (not to mention the likes of terabyte science, data science, big data, data management and processing, etc.) had been named. (This [then] new area of algorithmic information theory has since become widely known as Kolmogorov complexity, despite A. N. Kolmogorov's independent work having been less general - with no study of probability and modelling data - and [slightly] later, most certainly published later than Solomonoff's technical reports from 1960 and papers from 1964.) Solomonoff shared Turing's vision of genuine machine intelligence - and, in the 1960s, described how this might occur with the use of *training sequences*, later articulating the notion of *conceptual jump size* (*CJS*). Still in the 1960s, Ray was surely one of the first to express this important sentiment: "It would be well if a large number of intelligent humans devote a lot of thought to these problems before they arise. It is my feeling that the realization of artificial intelligence will be a sudden occurrence." (Ray would later note that "Learning to train very intelligent machines should give very useful insights on how to train human students as well".)

Despite his position at one of the world's top universities (M.I.T.) relatively early in life, Ray got out of the university caper after something like only 9 months. I still remember his voice: "I ... I didn't like my lack of freedom." But, as below, throughout this survey, throughout these conference proceedings and elsewhere, his research most certainly continued.

Later (again), in the mid-1980s, Ray articulated seven stages (A to G) of machine intelligence, with what we now refer to as the "technological singularity" (sometimes also called the "infinity point", loosely when machines are as smart as humans) perhaps corresponding to somewhere between stages E and F. At about the same time (also in the mid-1980s), Ray was involved in the formation of the uncertainty in AI (UAI) "workshop", largely in response to a curious push from certain parts within the U.S.A. AI community to downplay the rôle of probability. The (so-called) UAI workshop lives on to this day.

Ray Solomonoff was a pioneer scientist ahead of his time whose work was worthy of more than a Turing Award (if not also, in time, a Nobel Prize in Economics). Perhaps more importantly, Ray was a fine human being - not just brilliant and willing to listen to the ideas of others, but also humble, fun, principled and with a firm and gentle resolve, a firm and gentle independence. His ability to live frugally, fund himself, do pioneering world-class research and be happy (see, e.g., footnote 18) is an inspiration. (If you somehow dislike his research enough to want to fund mine, please feel welcome to see the challenge from [32, end of footnote 79].)

During his life-time and since, all these various aspects of Ray Solomonoff's work have caught on and continue to do so in one place or another. There are many places one can read (of this). The best place to start that I can think of is most probably the invited talk by Grace Solomonoff [114]. Other papers in this collection of conference papers are (from) the two other invited talks [82] (by L. A. Levin, a former research student of A. N. Kolmogorov's and later close friend of Ray Solomonoff's) and [84] (by Ming Li, author of, e.g., [85]), some longer papers (in no particular order) [98, 30, 54, 67, 168, 75, 57, 89, 78, 200, 201, 5, 170, 107, 88, 87, 169, 27, 71, 53, 80, 92, 47, 166, 96, 112, 113, 50, 103, 20] and [4].

Below is a sketch of Ray's work, with some thoughts of things to come.

1.2 (Universal) Turing Machines and Prediction

Re Turing, his (Universal) Turing machine (or [U]TM) [172], his Imitation Game (or "Turing test") and (machine) intelligence [173] (and his legacy), Solomonoff [125, 126, 132] pioneered the innovative use of (Universal) Turing machines [172] for that part of intelligence [173] which pertains to predictive data analysis and prediction. If it were not for the (Bayesian) choice of which (universal) TM (of which there are infinitely many) and [172] the undecidability of the Halting problem (or Entscheidungsproblem), then − given sufficient computational resources − the universality of UTMs tells us that this gives an optimum amongst computable predictions (again, given sufficient computational resources). We follow Solomonoff in later commenting on how optimal inference and optimal prediction is inherently incomputable[1] and[2] inherently Bayesian [149, sec. 2, p4].

Many misunderstand the difference between Solomonoff's work − which involves a (typically infinite) mixture of theories for the purposes of *prediction* (see, e.g., [148, sec. 2.6]) − and the later independent Minimum Message Length (MML) work of Wallace (and co-authors) starting in 1968 [188, 195, 191, 25, 26, 187, 37, 32, 34], which involves finding a *single* theory for the purposes of induction (or inductive inference, or explanation). (See, e.g., [147][191, sec. 8][193, sec. 4][187, (sec. 4.8, p208 and) sec. 10.1][32, footnotes 223 (and surrounding text), 108 and 18][34, sec. 4.1][37, sec. 6.1.4][35, sec. 4.5, p92], and sec. 4.2.) (Readers might also wish to look at Rissanen's later[3] notion of Minimum Description Length (MDL) [100, 101, 99] (and [102, 74, 73]), or possibly also at some comparisons between MML and MDL [193, abstract][186][192, sec. 3][187, sec. 10.2][26, sec. 11.4.3, pp272-273][8][32, sec. 0.2.4 p536, sec. 0.2.5, and elsewhere][34, sec. 6.7].) The reader can decide for herself how much Solomonoff advocated the notion of taking the single best inferred theory (see, e.g., [125, 126, 133, 134] from the early 1960s, and the earlier [120, perhaps especially early sections] on

---

[1] See, e.g., [149, sec. 2, p2][153, sec. 3, p4].

[2] Via the choice of (Universal) Turing Machine.

[3] See, e.g., [148, Timeline of Papers Referenced].

inductive inference to a single theory [124, sec. 2.6 (especially top of page 10)]), before he opted to favour combining all theories for the purposes of prediction.

This work being described is – or, at least, will (when more properly noticed) become – crucial in the fields of econometrics and statistics (see, e.g., convergence result in sec. 3.1), just as it gains an ever increasing foothold in artificial intelligence and machine learning. As another way of emphasising how much this work is (still, to my mind) ahead of its time, (as per sec. 1.1) this work would have been worthy of both the Nobel Prize in Economics and the Turing Award. Quite possibly at least one of those acknowledgements will be given to a researcher lucky enough to still be living when this work catches on.

So, this (above) is at least one way in which Solomonoff took Turing's legacy to lead the way. More on this will be given in sec. 3 and beyond.

1.3   Technological Singularity (and Training Sequences)

Prior to Vernor Vinge [176] and - I am led to believe - independently of both Ulam (and von Neumann) [174] and I. J. Good [56] (and a seemingly weaker claim of C. S. Wallace's [180, pp244-245, one-sentence final paragraph][32, bullet-point from p534 (col 2) to p535 (col 1)]), Solomonoff [136, 143] anticipated a more detailed realisation of Turing's vision from Turing's ("Turing test" or) Imitation game [173]. Solomonoff [143] not only described the (infinity point or) technological singularity in 1985, but (as per sec. 1.1) also detailed it in 7 stages (A to G), where what we regard as the technological singularity occurs perhaps between stages E and F (the 5th and 6th of the 7 stages).

For some decades, I and surely others have thought that one way to advance towards the technological singularity is - or would be - via software code that continually incrementally re-writes itself. We see Solomonoff exploring a variant of this idea not only at least as far back as 1990, but also seemingly while still in typical full embrace of algorithmic information theory [94, secs. 3, 4 and perhaps especially 5][151, sec. 7.1 and perhaps elsewhere] (and perhaps [152], and possibly also elsewhere). Indeed, even back in the early 1960s (1962) and mindful of probabilities (and information theory), we see Solomonoff exploring (self-re-writing or) self-organizing systems which are guided by correct answers to select problems (or training) [131, especially secs. 1 and 2]. More specifically in 1962, we see this theoretical approach being applied to develop "training sequences", "to devise an "intelligent" machine capable of improving its own operation" [131, sec. 1, 1st page] and whose "results will be more reliable and will look just as "creative" as the results obtained using partly random choices" [131, sec. 1, 2nd page]. See also, e.g., self-improvement and "improving its own performance" [135, sec. I, p1687], and the re-write rules (and training sequences) used earlier by Solomonoff [131][135, sec. II, p1689 col. 2]. Further notes from the 1960s include "the realization of artificial intelligence will be a sudden occurrence." [136, sec. 1] and (again in the same paper) "The Problem of the Ambitious Subordinate" [136, sec. 6], and "More generally, we would like the machines to learn to improve their operation after working on a set of problems." [137, p 8, bottom half, col. 3] (the last comment of which is from 1968 [137]), etc.

Having thus briefly outlined a couple of Solomonoff's major contributions in secs. 1.1, 1.2 and 1.3, let us now attempt to go into some greater detail.

2   Papers - Beginning in 1950

Historically, in his early-to-mid 20s (from 1950 to 1952), we see Ray's writing on properties of random networks within mathematical biophysics (which might be known nowadays as biocomputing or even bioinformatics) [164, 165, 115], including mathematical genetics, epidemiology and (from artificial intelligence) neural networks.

Still in the early 1950s but in a different area of what can still be regarded as artificial intelligence, we have "An optically driven airborne chopper" [116] (and "Photoelectric chopper for guided missiles" [108]) (possibly cf. [32, sec. 0.2.4, footnote 102, p534]). And then in the mid-1950s with Ray still in his 20s, we have a captivatingly titled paper - at least partly motivated by a comment of Fano's (from the Shannon-Fano code) - showing Ray's knowledge of physics and (electrical) engineering which was perhaps the first of what would be his many published ventures into information theory: "Effects of Heisenberg's Principle on Channel Capacity" [117], beginning with the words "The limitations imposed by thermodynamics on the amount of energy necessary to transmit one bit of information ...".

Then we come to the abovementioned 1956 conference at Dartmouth, U.S.A. - perhaps the formal birthplace of the the newly-named field of *"artificial intelligence"*, with ten keen researchers [114], two of whom would later win the Turing Award. At least in hindsight, intelligence might be viewed as having several constituent parts - e.g., (i) rote learning and memory, (ii) logical, mathematical and deductive reasoning, (iii) inductive inference and predictive ability, and (iv) planning, etc. Many of Ray's contemporaries in the mid-1950s were pushing for the approach (or line) of automating logical and deductive reasoning. Ray's contribution, a privately circulated 62-page report entitled "An inductive inference machine" [118], saw his position. Later, modern theories of intelligence (mention information theory [24] and) seem to increasingly emphasise the importance of (the similar but subtly different [information-theoretic] approaches of) inductive inference and prediction [38, 39, 64, 86, 40, 58, 79][59][4][69, 70, 80, 41] and the accompanying need for probability (see also sec. 4.4), but Ray was clearly well ahead of his time. (As per sec. 1.1, even as late as the 1980s, we saw a curious push from certain parts within the U.S.A. AI community to downplay the rôle of probability. The uncertainty in AI (UAI) "workshop" was apparently born as a response to this curious push [114, sec. 6].)

Solomonoff would stay with this new-found interest in inductive inference and prediction for the rest of his life. In the ensuing years after the 1956 conference [118], he would continue with the notions of inductive learning (of grammar

---

[4] The difference between inference to the single best theory and prediction (as they pertain to intelligence) is discussed in [59, p1514], [42] and sec. 4.2.

and language), inductive inference and prediction [119, 120][5][122]. (I haven't yet found or read [9] from 1957 [although it is conceivably the same as [119]] or [121] from 1958.) In 1959, well before Bayesianism would become fashionable, trendy and (perhaps nowadays) even standard - and again before we heard much about the probabilistic approach to AI - we see Ray's work on inductive inference and prediction now introducing probability and Bayesian priors [124, sec. 2.6][6][123, Appendix I and Appendix II], including, e.g., "We will use the a priori likelihood of a language as a quantification of complexity. Simple languages have high a priori probability; complex languages have low a priori probability." [123, Appendix II, p950]. (Possibly cf. [18, sec. 4][19, Appendix] [32, sec. 0.3.1, p547, col. 2].)

The scene is now set. The presentation here is surely better read with accompaniment by [114]. Of course, the reader with sufficient inclination and time is encouraged to read the relevant Solomonoff papers herself.

Ray once told me in person - in Melbourne in August 1996 (I think) or possibly in Boston in January 1997 or January 2001 - that 1960 was the year in which his theory (of algorithmic information-theoretic [inference and] prediction) was born. And, indeed, so the internal working papers and technical reports began, with Ray's bringing what I believe was his then relatively recently acquired knowledge of Universal Turing Machines (UTMs) [172] to these problems of inductive inference and prediction.

3   Birth of the Theory in 1960 - and Onwards

So, as in sec. 1.1 and above at the end of sec. 2, Ray's general theory of (Universal) Turing Machines and prediction (as summarised in sec. 1.2) was born in 1960 [125, 126] - and, as below, would first be published in 1964 [133, 134].

In [125, sec. 14][7][126, sec. 14] on curve-fitting, we see clear mention of inductive inference to one single explanation [125, sec. 14, p21][126, sec. 14, p18][8], possibly as a precursor to Minimum Message Length (MML) [188, 189, 191, 187] later in the 1960s (and the later Minimum Description Length, or MDL, principle [100]). And, also in these works from 1960, we then see [125, sec. 15][126, sec. 15] on combining theories.

---

[5] Perhaps especially the early sections of [120] discuss inductive inference to a single theory. See also footnotes 6 and 8 (and possibly 15) and surrounding text for pointers to other places where Solomonoff considers this issue no later than 1960.

[6] [124, sec. 2.6 (especially top of page 10)] suggests inductive inference to a single theory. See also footnotes 5 and 8 (and possibly 15) and surrounding text for pointers to other places where Solomonoff considers this issue no later than 1960.

[7] Complete with hand-written annotations in the online version.

[8] Cf. the earlier [120, perhaps especially early sections] on inductive inference to a single theory [124, sec. 2.6 (especially top of page 10)]. See also footnotes 5 and 6 (and possibly 15) and surrounding text for pointers to other places where Solomonoff considers this issue no later than 1960.

In 1961, we have that [128, page 1] "The study of inductive inference gives us one way to evaluate quantitatively the size of the "conceptual jump" that is involved in the presentation of a particular new idea.". More work on conceptual jump size (CJS) would follow. This same paper makes it clear that the approach using Turing machines is Bayesian [128, sec. 1.3], using a priori probability [128, sec. 2.5 and Appendix I] (cf. [32, sec. 0.3.1 (Solomonoff) and footnote 225][34, sec. 2.4, p213 (and sec. 6.5, pp944-946)]). We also see the introduction of the notion of "significant subsequence" (of text of English or another language, music or other sequences of any other type of sequence of symbols) in information-theoretic terms [128, sec. 2.3] and the re-iteration that the "coding method defines certain special code symbols to be equivalent to certain substrings of symbols in the original sequence" [130, abstract][9]. This is done in part by using Laplace estimates for (multinomial) Bernoulli sequences [127] (cf. the later [12, 188]). The ideas are then extended and generalised in [130], where we see a discussion of "Monte Carlo music" [130, sec. VII, p16] and a "penny matching machine" [130, sec. VII, p17].

As early as 1962, we now see this theoretical approach being applied to develop "training sequences", "to devise an "intelligent" machine capable of improving its own operation" [131, sec. 1, 1st page] and whose "results will be more reliable and will look just as "creative" as the results obtained using partly random choices" [131, sec. 1, 2nd page].

A (4-page) comment relating to the mind-body problem, giving a nice analogy with theories of quantum mechanics and the easier to use consequences that are chemistry, is given in [129].

Although first written down in [125, 126], his formal theory (of algorithmic information theory and probabilistic prediction) was first published in 1964 in [133, 134][10]. The interpretation of Occam's razor mentioned in [133, sec. 2, p3 and sec. 3, p7] is that of "the more "simple" or "economical" of several hypotheses" (cf. [148, sec. 4, p13]), in the same spirit as used in Minimum Message Length (MML) [91][34, sec. 4]. The fitting of curves from [125, sec. 14][126, sec. 14] is discussed again [133, sec. 2.1, p5]. Solomonoff's formal theory includes "System in the form of a model to account for all regularities in the observable universe" [133, sec. 3.2] and "System using a universal machine with all possible input strings of a fixed length" [133, sec. 3.3]. The 1964 paper[11] [133] (1964a, which had secs. 1-3) continues into [134] (1964b, secs. 4-5) with some nice combinatorial mathematics [134, sec. 4]. This includes extending work on

---

[9] As a simple case in point, if the term "algorithmic probability" occurs frequently in a corpus of text, we can write "algorithmic probability (ALP)" the first time and then forever after on (the) subsequent occasions replace it with "ALP".

[10] See footnote 11.

[11] Ray once told me that he submitted this 1964 paper as one paper but that the journal editor at the time said that it was too long as one paper and so had to be split into two - and so became 1964a [133] and 1964b [134].

the multinomial distribution (from [127])[12], work on grammatical induction[13] from data such as (e.g.) "The Use of Phrase Structure Grammars in Coding ..." [134, sec. 4.3][14], "A Criterion for "Goodness of Fit" of a PSG to a Particular Set Of Strings" [134, sec. 4.3.2][15], "How to Find a PSG That Best "Fits" a Given Set of Strings" [134, sec. 4.3.3][16], and (indeed) "Use of the Theory for Decision Making" [134, sec. 5][17].

Solomonoff's survey [135] in 1966 "Some Recent Work in Artificial Intelligence" mentions "simulation of organic evolution" [135, sec. I, p1687, abstract], self-improvement and "improving its own performance" [135, sec. I, p1687], and the re-write rules (and training sequences) used earlier by Solomonoff [131][135, sec. II, p1689, col. 2] (and possibly also earlier in 1961). This 1966 survey [135] also mentions work by Evans ("a program for recognizing geometric analogies such as are used in "intelligence tests""[48, 49]) [135, sec. II (p1690 col. 2 and later)], which was a precursor to programs which would later pass I.Q. tests [104, 41, 167].

Following the description of [93] (1963) from [134, sec. 5], the description of [93] from [135, sec. III, p1691] suggests a difference from Minimum Message Length (MML).

Solomonoff (1967) [136] more than hints at the technological singularity (which he returns to discuss in 1985 [143]; and see also his recollection from circa 1952 as published in 1997 [148, sec. 3.2]), with the comment
"It would be well if a large number of intelligent humans devote a lot of thought to these problems before they arise. It is my feeling that the realization of artificial intelligence will be a sudden occurrence." [136, sec. 1]
and (again in the same paper).

"The Problem of the Ambitious Subordinate" [136, sec. 6], in which the machine has means such as deliberate under-performance in order to obtain control over its operator. The paper also discusses Dolphin talk [136, sec. 7], with notions following on Solomonoff's earlier works on (language learning and) grammar induction and on training sequences.

In "The search for artificial intelligence" [137] (January 1968), there is again mention of self-improvement which — given his work on (self-re-writing or) self-organizing systems which are guided by correct answers to select problems (or training) from 1962 [131, especially secs. 1 & 2] through to his last writings (e.g., [163, sec. 6]) — I think Solomonoff would join others and me [61] in

---

[12] Cf. the later [12].

[13] Perhaps cf. later independent work on grammatical inference of Probabilistic Finite State Automata (PFSAs) using MML from the 1980s [196][187, sec. 7.1].

[14] Indeed, in [150, sec. 1] in 1999, Solomonoff refers to J. Horning (1971) [66] and Solomonoff (1964b) [134] in saying that "Algorithmic probability gives a criterion for goodness of fit of such grammars" [66][134, pp 240-251].

[15] Cf. footnotes 5, 6 and 8 and surrounding text for pointers to places where Solomonoff considers the issue of inductive inference to a single theory no later than 1960.

[16] PSG is Phrase Structure Grammar.

[17] Where this last section, [134, sec. 5], mentions [93] from 1963, seemingly intimating a possible similarity between [93] and Minimum Message Length [188].

(again) relating this to the (infinity point or) technology singularity. From this January 1968 paper [137], we have: "More generally, we would like the machines to learn to improve their operation after working on a set of problems." [137, p 8, bottom half, col. 3], a section on "Minimal machine" [137, pp10-11] (the first part of which seems to suggest Occam's razor) and a section on "Complex concepts" [137, p11, col. 2] mentioning "the capacity for self improvement".

Ray had a break from publishing from the rest of 1968 until some time in 1975 (see, e.g., http://world.std.com/~rjs/pubs.html)[18]. Co-incidentally and perhaps intriguingly to some, this is exactly the same period in which the first Wallace and Boulton Minimum Message Length (MML) papers [188, 12, 13, 10, 16, 15, 14, 17, 189, 11] independently appeared — from 1968 [188] to 1975 [189, 17, 11]. Wallace and Boulton would not become aware of the work of Solomonoff, Kolmogorov [76, 77], Chaitin [22, 21] and others until about 1975 — my understanding is that this was apparently from an article (involving Greg Chaitin) in *Scientific American* in circa 1975 [23] (cf. a not unrelated comment in [114]). The first Minimum Description Length (MDL) paper would appear before the end of the 1970s in 1978 [100] (although some might contend 1976 [99]).

3.1   End of the 1970s, and Fundamental Convergence Result

Resuming in 1975, we see the claim that "Goodman's paradoxes involving various linguistic transformation of inferential data, are also easy to analyse from this point of view" [138, p20, col. 1] - a point which Ray re-iterates later regarding Goodman's "grue" paradox in [147][149, sec. 5]. For related discussion of the *grue* paradox from (algorithmic) information theory, see also, e.g., [26, sec. 11.4.4][32, footnotes 128, 184 and 227][34, sec. 7.2].

The survey in [139] mentions that Ray's approach (of algorithmic information theory and probabilistic prediction) is Bayesian [139, Introduction and sec. 1] and, then, almost in passing, mentions the key convergence result [139, sec. 1]

$$E(\textstyle\sum_{i=1}^{m}(\delta_i' - \delta_i)^2) \leq b \log \sqrt{2} = (b/2) \log 2$$

This then becomes the crucial, key, important and currently under-appreciated convergence result [140, p426, col. 1, Theorem 3 (17)] (1978)

$$E_P(\textstyle\sum_{i=1}^{n-1}(\delta_i^n - \delta_i^{n'})^2) \leq k \log \sqrt{2} = (k/2) \log 2$$

---

[18] As well as wondering about and perhaps envying Ray's work-life balance (and joie de vivre without unnecessary expense), I'm reminded of a story Ray once told me about his wanting to learn to surf. At the time, he wasn't sure whether this story was from when he was 35 (putting it at about 1961) or 45 (putting it at about 1971). He described deciding that, if one wanted to learn to surf, one should go to California, and, so, Ray being Ray, he hitch-hiked from the U.S. east coast to California. When he got to California, he apparently learnt that, if one *really* wanted to learn to surf, then one had to go to Hawai'i. As able and resourceful as so many of us know Ray was, I still sometimes wonder how he might have hitch-hiked or otherwise got across the Pacific from California to Hawai'i. I don't think he told me what happened next.

(and occurred in the same year as what many people regard as the first paper on Minimum Description Length [100]). (Perhaps see also the more recent [68].) This fundamental convergence result (which should perhaps intrigue or be core to those from statistics, econometrics, machine learning, etc.) takes us to the end of the 1970s. It also suggests connections with other convergence results pertaining to Minimum Message Length (MML) [195, sec. 2, p241][7][184][187, sec. 3.4.5] and (because of the connection that both approaches - ALP[19] and MML - have with algorithmic information theory [191][187, chap. 2]) might provide insight into at least two related conjectures (pertaining to Strict MML and approximations such as those from [32, footnotes 62-65 and surrounds]) [35, sec. 6, p93][46, sec. 5.3][191, p282][194, sec. 5, p78][26, sec. 11.3.1, p269][37, sec. 8][32, sec. 0.2.5][33, p454][34, sec. 6.5, p945].

3.2   Notes on Papers from the 1980s

Continuing with the abovementioned earlier work on training sequences ("an ordered set of problems arranged so that a student or program solving each problem becomes more able to solve subsequent problems in the set" [141, abstract]), [141] (re-)introduces the notions of conceptual jump size (CJS) ("a measure of the computational cost needed to solve a problem, given that certain information has already been acquired" [141, abstract][128, page 1], and see also [146, sec. 4][148, secs. 4.2 and 4.3][103]) and *perfect* training sequences ("having characteristics that make it particularly easy for certain kinds of machines to solve them", such as the CJS of each problem in the sequence being acceptably small [141, abstract] - perhaps cf. [61, Definitions 16 and 11]).

"Optimum Sequential Search" [142] (1984) re-visits the part of [81] pertaining to what we now know as universal Levin search, or universal Lsearch - a universal optimisation algorithm. The paper then builds on [81] to (re-)raise two issues: "Given the finite string x, how can we find in minimal time, a string p such that $M(p) = x$?" and "The problem is to find within a limited search time, τ, an input that yields the highest possible value of G." He later discusses the notions of "resource limited ALP" [147] (or resource bounded probability [RBP]) [149].

I haven't been able to locate [144], but "The Time Scale of Artificial Intelligence ..." (1985) [143] is perhaps the main paper on the technological singularity, following on [136] as discussed in sec. 1.3.

As per secs. 1.1 and 2, even as late as the 1980s, we apparently saw a curious push from certain parts within the U.S.A. AI community to downplay the rôle of probability. The uncertainty in AI (UAI) "workshop" - which lives on strong almost 3 decades later - was apparently born in 1986 as a response to this curious push [114, sec. 6]. Ray says there[20] that extreme value theory would probably be better done using algorithmic information theory: "Certain scientists have

---

[19] ALP is algorithmic probability.

[20] These papers from the 2000s [151, 152, 153] cite the 1986 paper [145] as having been in the inaugural 1986 UAI workshop - with [151] and [152] (both from the 2000s) possibly being different versions of the same paper.

expressed much confidence in their estimates of probability of catastrophic failure in nuclear reactors, national defense systems, and in public safety regulations for genetic engineering. The aforementioned considerations lead one to question this confidence." [145, sec. 1]. It would be hard to agree more with this[21]. In [145, sec. 3.3] while discussing compressing "the information in our probability distribution", regarding training sequences[22], Ray comments: "Newton's laws were much easier to discover as an outgrowth of Kepler's laws, than it would be for Newton to derive them directly from purely experimental data" and that this process of developing and pursuing training sequences "gives us the closest thing to true creativity that we can expect in a mechanized device". Still in the same paper, [145, sec. 4.3] discusses the concept of "Analogy" from intelligence tests [48, 49] in the context of algorithmic information theory (cf. [38, 39, 64, 40, 58, 86, 104] and sec. 4.4), and [145, sec. 4.4] discusses clustering in terms of algorithmic information theory (cf. [188] (especially) and other papers detailing how to do this by Minimum Message Length (MML) [181, 183, 182, 190, 185, 46, 45, 194][187, sec. 6.8][90, 178, 179]).

We see more on training sequences in [146], with "The machine starts out like a human infant ...", "A suitable training sequence of problems ...", and "The principal activity of the present research is the design of training sequences of this kind." [146, Introduction]. This paper continues: "Perhaps of most importance: If there is any describable regularity in a body of data, algorithmic probability is guaranteed to eventually describe that regularity ... [140]. It is the only definition of probability known to have this property." [146, sec. 1]. I certainly agree with the convergence results from [140, p426, col. 1, Theorem 3 (17)] referred to here, but I would also point to the MML convergence results and conjectures from the end of sec. 3.1 (at least partly because of the connection that both approaches - ALP and MML - have with algorithmic information theory [191][187, chap. 2]). Any statisticians, econometricians, machine learners, data miners, epistemologists and/or philosophers of science reading this, *please* take note.

In [146, sec. 4, "How inversion problems are solved"], Ray re-visits the notion of Conceptual Jump Size (CJS) [141][148, secs. 4.2 and 4.3][128, page 1][103] as follows. Relevant abridged notes include: "The most efficient search procedure - one whose expected time to solution is minimal - tests trial programs (i.e., strings of concepts) in order of increasing t_i/p_i. Here p_i is the probability of success of the ith trial string of concepts and t_i is the time needed to generate and test that trial. ... If p_j is the probability assigned to a particular program, A_j, that solves a problem and it takes time t_j to generate and test that program, then this entire search procedure will take a time less than $2t_j/p_j$ to discover A_j. We call t_j/p_j the "Conceptual Jump Size" (CJS) of A_j. It tells us if the machine is

---

[21] A couple of decades or so after this 1986 paper, I have seen able well-funded people collaborating with large groups of people on disaster-averting projects of extreme value theory - but whose models (last time I checked) weren't then attempting to embrace anything near the generality offered by algorithmic information theory.

[22] An idea Ray was developing in 1962 [131, especially secs. 1 & 2], as per sec. 1.3.

practically able to find a particular solution to a problem at a particular stage of its development. CJS is a critical parameter in the design of training sequences ..." [146, sec. 4]. The paper goes on [146, sec. 6, "How Training Sequences Are Written"] : "... The task of designing such sequences is very similar to writing "Top Down" computer programs or writing lesson plans for human students. ... In the early stages of its training, the machine will be given only problems of small CJS (Conceptual Jump Size) - problems that are easy for it to solve." [146, sec. 6].

3.3   Notes on Papers from the 1990s

Ray did not co-author many papers, but "Autonomous Theory Building Systems" [94] from 1990 was one of them[23], and it included [94, sec. 4, "Training plans"]. Then, as he did from 1968-1975 (as per sec. 3, and perhaps recall footnote 18), Ray took several years in the early 1990s off publishing.

As mentioned in sec. 1, Ray Solomonoff was then an invited speaker at the Information, Statistics and Induction in Science (ISIS) conference in August 1996[24], where he published [147], which was spelt out and elaborated upon into [149], entitled "Does algorithmic probability solve the problem of induction?". This includes mention of Occam's razor [149, sec. 2, p2] (see also [148, sec. 4, p13]), which then leads into a re-statement of the claim from [146, sec. 1] (recall earlier in sec. 3.2, and which we repeat later in this section) about [140] - namely, that: "ALP is the only induction technique known to be complete.

By this we mean that if there is any describable regularity in a body of data, ALP will discover it using a relatively small sample of the data[25]. As a necessary consequence of its completeness, this kind of probability must be incomputable. Conversely, any computable probability measure cannot be complete.". The comments "one cannot do prediction without a priori information" and "makes ALP very subjective" from [149, sec. 2, p4] remind one of the inherent Bayesianism of this approach (and perhaps also of Ray's Bayesianism going back to the 1950s [124, sec. 2.6] - and see also, e.g., [155, sec. 4]). Goodman's "grue" paradox from [138, p20, col. 1][147] is discussed again in [149, sec. 5, p8]. For those of us who quibble about the use - or confuse the meaning(s) - of terms such as induction, inductive inference, explanation and prediction (e.g., [34, sec. 4.1]), I think it appropriate to have a careful read of [147][149, sec. 7]. The last comment from [149, sec. 7] "Scientific laws are usually compactly expressed, enabling easy communication of good ideas" is later echoed in [42].

Solomonoff (1997), "The Discovery of Algorithmic Probability" [148], opens with the words: "This paper will describe a voyage of discovery − the discovery

---

[23] As were [164, 165, 108, 9], as might possibly have been [95], and as is [166].

[24] Also attended by Jorma Rissanen, Paul Vitanyi, Chris Wallace [184] and 1969 Turing Award winner, Marvin Minsky - see also [26, sec. 11.4.4].

[25] Here the text from [149, sec. 2, p2] goes to its [149, footnote 1], which says: "¹ See Appendix A for The Convergence Theorem, which is a more exact description of "completeness". Sol78 contains a proof of the theorem.", where Sol78 is [140].

of Algorithmic Probability". Although Ray seemed both above it and good at avoiding (or ignoring) it (cf. sec. 1.1), I can't help but notice the passing observation of "political skullduggery" [148, sec. 1][26]. Further highlights from this survey and recollection include "without explicitly considering various theories or "explanations" of the data" [148, sec. 2.6 (Carnap)], and meeting Marvin Minsky and John McCarthy (both later Turing Award winners) in 1952, persuading "Minsky that our machines would eventually go well beyond human capabilities" and "In 1956, McCarthy and Shannon organized the 'Summer Study Group in Artificial Intelligence' at Dartmouth - ..." [148, sec. 3.2 (Minsky and McCarthy)]. Also of interest is the modification of the Turing machine to have a "unidirectional output tape, a unidirectional input tape" [148, sec. 3.4 (and Appendix A.1, footnote 12)] (see also [163, sec. 1]). We also see "the idea of Occam's razor - that "simple" hypotheses are more likely to be correct" [148, sec. 4, p13], mention [148, sec. 4.2 (Levin)] that Dean, Thomas and Boddy (1988) [29] have coined the term "anytime algorithm" (as was much later used in [59]), and discussion of Conceptual Jump Size and (relatedly) T/P values [148, secs. 4.2 and 4.3]. There is further discussion of training sequences and discussion of training *environments* in [148, sec. 4.3]. The paper then goes on in [148, sec. 5.2.1] to repeat earlier claims from [146, sec. 1][149, sec. 2, p2], stating that algorithmic probability "is the only induction system we know of that is "complete". By this we mean that if there is any describable regularity in a body of data, Algorithmic Probability is guaranteed to discover it using a relative small sample of the data" [148, sec. 5.2.1]. There is further discussion in [148, sec. 5.2.2]. The reader is referred to sec. 3.1 and the results referred to from [195, sec. 2, p241][7][184][187, sec. 3.4.5] (and possibly also [34, sec. 6.5] and its conjectures, and [35, p93][46, sec. 5.3][191, p282][194, sec. 5, pp539-540][26, sec. 11.3.1, p269][37][32, sec. 0.2.5][33, sec. Statistical Consistency]) regarding the statistical consistency of Minimum Message Length (MML). The paper [148] also mentions notions of "sequential property", "process" and "monotonic machine" [148, Appendix A.1, footnote 12] and a timeline of relevant research up to 1997 [148, Timeline] (see also [77, p662, col. 2 and p664, col. 1]).

We deal with sequential prediction and sequentially ordered data in [150, secs. 1 and 2][160, sec. 1] and unordered data and unordered sets (of finite strings) of data in [150, sec. 3][160, sec. 2] - both in 1999 and again later [150, 160] (and we later [160, sec. 3] also re-visit earlier work - such as [141][152, secs. 1 and 4 and Appendix B] - on "Q, A" question and answer [training sequences and] operator learning).

3.4   Notes on Papers from the 2000s

Moving into the 2000s, as the title suggests, "Progress in incremental machine learning" (2002) [151] (revision 2.0, 30 Oct 2003, so really [152]) is something of a survey of (incremental) [machine] learning by training, with [152, secs. 1 and 4 and Appendix B] continuing the "Q,A" (question and answer) scheme from

---

[26] Cf. political observation next to footnote 28, and also text near footnote 27.

(e.g.) [141][160, sec. 3]. The paper also includes mention of (improving) universal Lsearch (universal Levin search) (e.g., [152, secs. 2.1 and 3.1]). Next, [152, sec. 3 (Time Limited Optimization Problems)] relates at least somewhat to "resource limited ALP" [147] (or resource bounded probability [RBP]) [149]. Then there is discussion of training sequences [152, sec. 5], (updating) efficiency (and problem solving techniques [PSTs]) [152, sec. 6] and a comment that Schmidhuber's OOPS [105] could do a little "edit"ing of old programs [152, sec. 7.2].

Next, in 2003, Ray had the honour of giving the inaugural Kolmogorov lecture: "The universal distribution and machine learning" [153], which brings us a survey of the notion of universal distribution, underpinning most of Ray's work since the seminal [133, 134, 125, 126]. It begins [153, sec. 1 (Universal Probability Distribution)] "I will discuss two main topics in this lecture: First, the Universal Distribution and some of its properties: its accuracy, its incomputability, its subjectivity. Secondly, I'm going to tell how to use this distribution to create very intelligent machines." The paper contains some excellent quotations, two of which [153, secs. 3 and 5] are so memorable that I've repeated them verbatim below (where the works being referred to at the end of these are [145][146][151, 152]).

From [153, sec. 3], "Many scientists are repeatedly disturbed by the need to revise their understanding of their sciences. They look forward to a "Final Theory" that will put an end to all revisions. However, the incomputability of the Universal Distribution assures us that this cannot happen. With finite computing resources, we can never be certain that we've found the best, the "Final Theory".

I, personally, am not disturbed by this state of affairs, but find it instead to be a never ending source of joy in discovery!"

And, from [153, sec. 5] about a couple of pages later, "About 1984, roughly 25 years later, at an annual meeting of the American Association for Artificial Intelligence (AAAI), a vote was taken and it was decided that probability was in no way relevant to artificial intelligence.

A protest group quickly formed at the AAAI meeting devoted to Probability and Uncertainty in A.I. ...

As part of the protest at the first workshop, I gave a paper on applying the universal distribution to problems in A.I. (Sol 86). This was an early version of the system that I've been developing since that time (Sol89, 02)."

These memorable words speak for themselves, but I'll presume to comment. We see Ray's using his work (algorithmic information theory, undecidability, prediction, inference, etc.) to show that (even in a world of ongoing and often myopic funding cuts) [and I paraphrase] even if we might hypothetically have found the "final" "best" model(s), we can never be sure, and there is a never-ending need to keep (joyously) looking. We also see (what I shall call) the technical activist[27] in him emerging when he thought the relevant community had lost the plot, and we also see some evidence of his joy.

---

[27] Cf. political observations next to footnotes 26 and 28.

In 2005, Ray gave a recorded lecture [154] at the Midwest NKS conference and two lectures at M.I.T. [155, 156].

The first M.I.T. lecture [155] mentions reasons why we haven't (yet) reached the technological singularity [155, Introduction] and the related matter of training sequences (recall sec. 1.3), as well as Levin search [155, Introduction] and the subjectivity [155, sec. 4] of algorithmic probability (ALP) (recall [149, sec. 2, p4], sec. 3.3, and [153, sec. 1]). The second M.I.T. lecture [156] makes the point about the merits of letting all theories contribute (as ALP does) [and comments that "crowds ... become very stupid in mobs or in committees in which a single person is able to strongly influence the opinions in the crowd" [28]] by discussing [156, sec. 1 (ALP and "The Wisdom of Crowds")], as well as discussing grammatical inference [156, sec. 3 (Context Free Grammar Discovery)] (recall secs. 2 and 3).

The following year, we have [157] - with discussion of conceptual jumps [157, Abstract and sec. 3] (recall [141][146, sec. 4][148, secs. 4.2 and 4.3][128, page 1]), (Prediction by Partial Matching) "PPM and Grammar Discovery" [157, Abstract] (recall secs. 2 and 3 and [156, sec. 3 (Context Free Grammar Discovery)]), the "Q, A" (question and answer) formalism [156, sec. 3 (SA, The Scientist's Assistant)] (recall [141][152, secs. 1 and 4 and Appendix B] and perhaps see [160, sec. 3]) and "How far are we from serious A.I.?" [156, sec. 5 (The future of A.I.)].

From 2007, I couldn't find [158], but [159] raises the interesting question of the probability that a UTM, given random input, will not generate any output beyond a certain point: "a probability, $P_{i+1}(u)$ that the continued random input string will not generate any output for the $i+1^{th}$ symbol" [159, Abstract]. This and related concepts have also been considered by others [187, sec. 10.1.3][20]. If we consider the halting probability (the probability that a machine given an infinite random input [with each bit having probability of 0.5 of 0 and 1, and i.i.d.] will halt), the infinite loop probability (the probability that some finite prefix of random input will cause the machine from that point on not to be able to terminate - which relates to the abovementioned $P_{i+1}(u)$ [159, Abstract]) and the universality probability [32, footnote 70][34, sec. 2.5][6][61, p181 and footnote 11], then, because any program which has gone into an infinite loop or halted has lost its universality, we have that these three probabilities add up to less than (or equal to) 1. (Related ideas are explored with a view to biological and immunological analogies with halting as (cell) death, infinite loop as cancer and (loss of) universality as (loss of) full cell function in [60, footnote 4]. This includes the possibly immunologically analogous study of sets of strings which do or don't cause halting, infinite loop[ing], loss of universality or some depletion of function[s] to a set of [universal] Turing machines[29].) The appendix [159, Appendix] also mentions (universal) "monotonic machines and associated probability distributions" (recall [148, Appendix A.1, footnote 12]).

---

[28] Cf. political observation next to footnote 26, and also text near footnote 27.

[29] With or without the notion of redundant TMs from sec. 4, footnote 31 and [32, sec. 0.2.7, p544, col. 2][59, p1514, footnote 6], one might further wonder whether a suitable analogy can be made of the reparative value of stem cells in this framework.

As in sec. 3.3 above, Solomonoff (2008) [160] follows on from [150] (including mentioning approximations [160, Introduction] in passing), but then [160, sec. 3] also re-visits earlier work - such as [141][152, secs. 1 and 4 and Appendix B] - on question and answer "Q, A" [training sequences and] operator learning.

Next is Solomonoff (2009) [161], the last of Ray's papers published before his death in December 2009. After that would follow [162], [163] and a joint paper written up after Ray's death [166]. Discussion of "Compression and ALP" is given in [161, sec. 2]. The (so-called) "elusive model paradox" [32, footnote 211][33, p455][34, sec. 7.5][110][83][42, sec. 2.2][62, footnote 9] is raised and discussed in [161, sec. 3], with the elusive model paradox's "red herring sequence" [34, sec. 7.5] also discussed in [162, Appendix B].

We also have that "This lack of an objective prior distribution makes ALP very subjective - as are all Bayesian systems." [161, sec. 4 (Subjectivity)], from which we can recall [149, sec. 2, p4], sec. 3.3 and [153, sec. 1][155, sec. 4]. We then follow [156, sec. 1 (ALP and "The Wisdom of Crowds")] (and footnote 28) with [161, sec. 5 (Diversity and Understanding)] and [161, sec. 5.1 (ALP and "The Wisdom of Crowds")]. We then follow on unordered data and unordered sets (of finite strings) of data [150, sec. 3][160, sec. 2] in [161, secs. 7.1 and 7.2], leading into [161, sec. 9 (Context Free Grammar Discovery)] (recall secs. 2 and 3 and [156, sec. 3 (Context Free Grammar Discovery)][157, Abstract], cf. [196][187, sec. 7.1]). Penultimately, following [81][142][152, secs. 2.1 and 3.1][155, Introduction], we have more discussion of universal Levin search (Lsearch) [161, sec. 10]. Finally, [161, sec. 11 (The future of ALP - some open problems)] brings many of the above issues and training sequences together, and is clearly good reading (from the proverbial horse's mouth) for budding researchers. It begins with the words "We have described ALP and some of its properties:

First, its *completeness*: Its remarkable ability to find any irregularities in an apparently small amount of data.

Second: That any *complete* induction system like ALP must be formally *incomputable*.".

Recall sec. 3.1 and [146, sec. 1][149, sec. 2, p2][148, sec. 5.2.1][140] regarding completeness of ALP, and also the likes of [195, sec. 2, p241][7][184][187, sec. 3.4.5][34, sec. 6.5][35, p93][46, sec. 5.3][191, p282][194, sec. 5, pp539-540][26, sec. 11.3.1, p269][37][32, sec. 0.2.5][33, sec. Statistical Consistency] re statistical consistency (or completeness) of Minimum Message Length (MML), whose relationship with algorithmic information theory (and undecidability and incomputability) is described in (e.g.) [191][187, chap. 2].

Ray was to present [162] in early 2010, but died in late 2009. The section heading "Subjectivity" makes familiar points (e.g., [128, sec. 1.3][128, sec. 2.5 and Appendix I][139, Introduction and sec. 1][149, sec. 2, p4], sec. 3.3 and [153, sec. 1][155, sec. 4][161, sec. 4 (Subjectivity)] and the later [163, sec. 3 (Subjectivity)]), as does the section heading "Diversity" (e.g., sec. 1.2, text near footnote 28, [156, sec. 1 (ALP and "The Wisdom of Crowds")][161, sec. 5 (Diversity and Understanding)][161, sec. 5.1 (ALP and "The Wisdom of Crowds")], the later [163, sec. 4 (Diversity)] and perhaps also [147][149, sec. 7]) re using a weighted mixture of theories - rather than a single theory - for prediction. With other section headings (like) "Putting it all together", "The Guiding Probability Distribution" (GPD) and "Training Sequences" (mentioning Conceptual Jump Size [CJS], and see also [163, sec. 6 (Training Sequences)]), the paper could be summarised as telling of using universal Levin search (Lsearch) [162, Appendix A] with a GPD to help construct training sequences.

The first words and the last words (both in quotations, and separated) of the conclusions in this paper from [162, sec. "In Conclusion"] are:

"We have a method for designing training sequences. We have a method for updating the guiding probability distribution. We have a method for detecting/measuring "learning" in the system.

These three techniques are adequate for designing a true AGI." and "... enabling the system to significantly improve itself." [162, sec. "In Conclusion"].

And, finally, [162, Appendix B] (like [161, sec. 3]) seems to be a variant of the elusive model paradox and "red herring sequence" [32, footnote 211][33, p455][34, sec. 7.5][110][83].

Apart from the later co-authored [166], Ray Solomonoff's last paper was the posthumously published Solomonoff (2011) [163], which is appropriately a survey summary with an eye to the future, initially mentioning [163, sec. 1 (Discovery)] the use of "... unidirectional input and output tapes, and an infinite bidirectional work tape.". The point is also made (as it is in [187, sec. 2.2.5]) that "general purpose programming languages such as Fortran, LISP, C, C++, Basic, APL, Maple, Mathematica, ..." are also universal. In [163, sec. 2 (Completeness and Incomputability)], he highlights: "It is notable that completeness and incomputability are complementary properties: It is easy to prove that any *complete* prediction method must be incomputable. Moreover, any computable prediction method can not be *complete* - there will always be a large space of regularities for which its predictions are catastrophically poor."

The reader is referred to sec. 3.1 and [139][140, p426, col. 1, Theorem 3 (17)][148][161] variously for (re-)statements of the fundamental convergence result [140, p426, col. 1, Theorem 3 (17)] and for statements about completeness and incomputability (and the reader is also referred to the relevant places in this current paper where these papers [139][140, p426, col. 1, Theorem 3 (17)][148][161, secs. 3 and 11] are cited and there is accompanying discussion of MML's statistical consistency and [what I see as its] completeness - together with its [consequent] incomputability [191][187, chap. 2]). Statisticians and econometricians should take particular note of this, even if some might contend that it is retrospectively trivial. In short, if there is a (Turing computable) language from which the data is being generated but which the inference method is not able to express, the inference method will not be able to find the regularity.

Let us make this point immediately above more concrete (as many current statisticians, econometricians and data miners have less than little training in algorithmic information theory and computability). Consider the construction from [32, footnote 211][34, sec. 7.5] but instead modify it to have some computable inference method, C (whether this is Akaike's AIC [2, 1, 3], Schwarz's

BIC [109] or whatever). Let $C(x_1, ..., x_i, ..., x_n)$ be the predicted continuation of the sequence $(x_1, ..., x_i, ..., x_n)$ to x_{n+1}. In the spirit of [32, footnote 211], let $A(x_{n+1}) = C(x_1, ..., x_i, ..., x_n) + 1$. In the spirit of [33, p455][34, sec. 7.5] (with the function C restricted to take values of 0 or 1), let $B(x_{n+1}) = 1 - C(x_1, ..., x_i, ..., x_n)$. The functions A and B are clearly computable (and, indeed, inferrable), but the computability of C prevents it from being able to learn the likes of A and B. This all said, being sufficiently expressive does not on its own guarantee statistical consistency - as (e.g.) with Maximum Likelihood. Similarly, being sufficiently expressive and incomputable does likewise not guarantee statistical consistency - see, e.g., [32, footnote 130].

The issue of Bayesianism and subjectivity (from [128, sec. 1.3][128, sec. 2.5 and Appendix I][139, Introduction and sec. 1][149, sec. 2, p4], sec. 3.3 and [153, sec. 1][155, sec. 4][161, sec. 4 (Subjectivity)][162, Subjectivity]) is raised again in [163, sec. 3 (Subjectivity)], with another comment for statisticians, econometricians and others on the non-Bayesian approach advocated by Sir Ronald A. Fisher (1890 - 1962), regarded by many as the father[30] of modern statistics: "The great statistician, R. A. Fisher, ... wanted to make statistics a "true science" free of the subjectivity that had been so much a part of its history.

I feel that Fisher was seriously wrong in this matter, and this his work in this area has profoundly damaged the understanding of statistics in the scientific community - damage from which it is recovering all too slowly." [163, sec. 3]. (A seemingly similar sentiment is given by I. J. Good in [55, sec. 7, p112].)

To presume to quote from elsewhere: "Note the fact that the statistical consistency is coming from the information-theoretic properties of MML and the" statistical "invariance is actually coming from the Bayesian prior." [32, sec. 0.2.5, p540]. Perhaps digressing, we note that both the Solomonoff posterior-weighted predictive distribution and the single best (or MML) inference (both of which, from sec. 4.2, are Bayesian) are statistically invariant under re-parameterisation.

Next is [163, sec. 4 (Diversity)], which follows on from earlier notes - such as, e.g., sec. 1.2, text near footnote 28, [156, sec. 1 (ALP and "The Wisdom of Crowds")][161, sec. 5 (Diversity and Understanding)][161, sec. 5.1 (ALP and "The Wisdom of Crowds")][162, sec. Diversity] and perhaps also [147][149, sec. 7]. Like at least (many or) most of these, [163, sec. 4 (Diversity)] concerns using a weighted mixture of theories - rather than a single theory - for prediction.

The completeness and statistical consistency (and other merits) of approaches to inference and prediction based on algorithmic information theory have been discussed here a few times, but "There is, however another aspect of algorithmic probability that people find disturbing - it would seem to take too much time and memory to find a good prediction. ... There is a technique for implementing ALP that seems to take as little time as possible to find regularities in data" [163, sec. 2], and this is then discussed in [163, sec. 5 (Computation Costs)], which gives an example advocating a universal Levin search.

---

[30] Perhaps after the Rev. Thomas Bayes (circa 1701 - 1761) and Carl F. Gauss (1777 - 1855).

Next, [163, sec. 6 (Training Sequences)] returns to one of those issues in artificial intelligence special to Ray - that of training sequences, also addressed earlier (as far back as the 1960s) in sec. 1.3 and [131][135, sec. II, p1689 col. 2][136, sec. 7][141, 145, 146][94, sec. 4][148, sec. 4.3][151][162, sec. "In Conclusion"]. The discussion of training sequences is understandably accompanied by a related early concept (also from the 1960s, as per [128, page 1][141, abstract][146, sec. 4][148, secs. 4.2 and 4.3][162, sec. "Training sequences"]), namely T_i/P_i from [163, sec. 6, equation (4)], accompanied with (its name) "I call this upper bound the "conceptual jump size" (CJS)" [163, sec. 6 (Training Sequences)]. For those of us interested in education, we note the last paragraph of this section: "Learning to train very intelligent machines should give very useful insights on how to train human students as well".

Ray's last sole-authored paper finishes with [163, sec. 7 (Where Are We Now?)], and refers - among other places - to the "open problems" from [146, sec. 8 (Present State of Development of the System? Near Term Goals, More Distant Goals Time Scales for These Goals)].

Just as we read and re-read [173] and Turing's thoughts re the future, it seems appropriate to (re-)read [146, sec. 8], [161, sec. 11 (The future of ALP - some open problems)] and [163, sec. 7 (Where Are We Now?)], accompanied (of course) by [114].

4   Further Notes (And Perhaps Some Afterthoughts)

Here are some further notes regarding Ray Solomonoff's work and, perhaps particularly, (algorithmic) information theory.

4.1   Uniqueness of Logarithm-Loss Information-Theoretic Cost

The log(arithm)-loss scoring system, which sees probabilistic predictions p_i made for various events (e_i) and gives a score of $-\log p_j$ if event e_j (of probability p_j) occurs, was advocated for the binomial distribution [55] (and presumably also the multinomial distribution [55, p112]) by I. J. Good. It is very much in the spirit of Shannon's information theory [111], where code length equals negative logarithm of probability. This log-loss scoring system can be applied more generally to multinomial [55, p112][43, p4, Table 3], Gaussian [36][34, sec. 3.4] and other distributions [60, footnote 5].

But, unlike the popular "right"/"wrong" scoring system used widely in areas including machine learning, data mining and information retrieval, the information-theoretic log-loss scoring system is unique (plus or minus an additive or multiplicative constant) in being invariant to re-framing of questions (see [32, footnote 175][33, pp437-438][34, sec. 3] for details).

In similar vein, the Kullback-Leibler divergence (from true to inferred distribution) [and its reverse, from the inferred to the true distribution] is likewise unique in being invariant to re-framing [33, p438][34, sec. 3.6].

We make three further comments here before summarising. First, an information-theoretic compression-based competition has been running using the abovementioned log-loss scoring system since 1995 [44][32, sec. 0.2.5, p541, col. 2] for Australian AFL football (with a Gaussian competition based on the margin starting in 1996 [36][34, sec. 3.5]). Second, one can introduce a Bayesian prior for the log-loss scoring system, as originally tried somewhat unsuccessfully (with ratios of logarithms) in [65]. The correction (stated verbally in 2002) from [171, sec. 4.2][32, footnote 176][34, sec. 3.4] takes logarithms of ratios of probabilities (equivalent to differences in logarithms of probabilities when at least one of these is finite). This is appropriate when, e.g., in quiz shows [34, sec. 3.3], some questions might be deemed a priori easier/harder than others. Third, log-loss scoring can be used on Bayesian networks (or directed graphical models) [25, sec. 9], where it has previously been used as a numerical approximation to the Kullback-Leibler divergence between two Bayesian nets [25, sec. 9][34, sec. 3.6][60, footnote 5].

In summary, as in this section and elsewhere, information theory has much to recommend it (including uniqueness). Universal Turing Machines (UTMs) are (as the name suggests) universal, and Solomonoff's approach of combining UTMs and information theory might be argued by many to be (retrospectively) self-evident.

4.2   Prediction, Inference, Induction, Explanation

The issue of inductive inference (or induction) to a single theory was considered by Ray Solomonoff [120, perhaps especially early sections][124, sec. 2.6 (especially top of page 10)] before (as above) he later settled into prediction using a weighted mixture of theories. Other places to see this distinction between prediction (using a Solomonoff weighted mixture of theories) and inductive inference (using a single theory, as with Minimum Message Length [MML]) discussed include [187, sec. 10.1][59, p1514][34, sec. 4.1]. See also secs. 1.2 and 3.3 (and perhaps elsewhere).

A related issue is prediction not by a weighted mixture of models, but rather by the best single predictive model within the class of models being considered - a notion which has been referred to as the minimum expected Kullback-Leibler distance estimator (often abbreviated to minEKL or MEKLD) [35][187, sec. 4.7][37][34, sec. 4.1]. See also [27].

One of the many reasons for appreciating these distinctions is Wallace's resolution of entropy's (supposedly, but) not being the arrow of time by observing that we infer the past but predict the future [187, chap. 8].

Let us now turn to "approximations" and approximations.

In abovementioned writings, Ray would refer to Minimum Message Length (MML) [188, 189, 195, 191, 187] (designed to be inference to the best - or most probable - explanation) and (the later) Minimum Description Length (MDL) [100] as "approximations", even if their developers might not have thought or think of them in precisely those terms [187, chap. 10]. Re the MML "approximation", its purest from is Strict MML [189][187, chap. 3][34, sec. 6], but approximations to this exist in turn, including those from [195][187, chap. 4-5] and (e.g.) MMLD (or I_{1D}) [32, sec. 0.2.2][51][187, secs. 4.10 and 4.12.2 and chap. 8, p360][34, sec. 6.3]. The modification to MMLD presented by L. J. Fitzgibbon in [51, eq (7)] was later modified by D. F. Schmidt [106][32, footnotes 64-65]. The MML approach - of the single best explanation - can be used for hypothesis testing [32, sec. 0.2.5, p539, col. 1], to fortify claims supporting Occam's razor [91][32, footnote 18], and to address the modelling choice of generative vs discriminative [32, sec. 0.2.5].

A discussion is made in [33, pp451-452] of the appearance of lattice constants (κ_d) in the Wallace-Freeman (1987) approximation [195] and the appearance over a decade later of hexagonal-like regions for Strict MML for the trinomial distribution (with $d = 2$, for which the hexagon is the optimally tesselating Voronoi region) [187, p166, fig. 3.1]. I am grateful to Emanuele Viterbo for explaining to me that this is due to approximately quadratic behaviour of the logarithm (or other) function(s) within the relevant region(s). And one indeed expects a similar result re SMML and optimally tesselating Voronoi regions for higher d.

Penultimately, let us now use a decision tree example to compare the (single model) MML framework with a version of the (weight across several models) predictive framework. The case we take is in the spirit of [197, sec. 4], where some data can be modelled either as having no split and simply being $[150, 50]$ (denoting 150 in class 1 and 50 in class 2) or (alternatively) as having a split on attribute 1 (Att_1) with $[90, 10]$ in the left (yes) path and $[60, 40]$ in the right (no) path. Describing the tree topology will be more expensive if there is a split, with an additional cost being the logarithm of the number of attributes to describe which attribute is being split on [197, sec. 4][187, sec. 7.2]. We assume this additional cost not to be very large. On the other hand, the purification of the data as $[90, 10]$ and $[60, 40]$ will result in it being far cheaper to describe the contents of these two leaves than to describe the unsplit $[150, 50]$. In terms of "right"/"wrong" predictive accuracy, the split offers nothing, as both the unsplit and the split version will always predict the left class (class 1) - and there are probably still some in the machine learning and presumably data mining communities who would advocate not doing the split. But, whether for marketing (campaign success vs cost), medical or other matters (see, e.g., [55, sec. 7 (vi)][161, sec. 1]), we often need to estimate probabilities, as the uniqueness results from sec. 4.1 also tell us. The information-theoretic MML approach tells us this, and it is perhaps no great surprise that the Solomonoff predictive approach will put far greater weight on the models with the split than the models without the split (even if the leaf probability estimates are slightly different in the two approaches, with the predictive approach advocating the MEKLD [equivalently posterior mean] estimator). Both the MML approach and the Solomonoff predictive approach will have similar predictive probabilities [35] and (in similar vein) similar code-lengths for compressing the data. I note almost parenthetically that extensions to Naive Bayes such as AODE and AnDE [198] could probably be enhanced by this more principled way of combining and weighting probabilities - and possibly with relatively little additional computational cost.

Papers in this collection using one or more of these MML-based approximations or some variations include [107, 88, 87]. Papers in this collection using some MDL-based approximations include [169, 67].

4.3   How to Choose a Bayesian Prior?

As discussed in many places throughout this paper, these techniques (as summarised in sec. 4.2) are Bayesian, but just *how* might we (*"objectively"*) choose the prior? There are discussions in [187, sec. 2.3.12][31] of how to choose a *simplest* UTM. Another possibility would be to choose the simplest UTM, U, such that $U = V$ in [6, corollary 3.5].

On a much restricted class of problems where the statistical likelihood is not universal but rather is twice differentiable, some advocate the use of the (so-called) Jeffreys "prior" [72], although this often does not normalise. One attempt to salvage the Jeffreys "prior" (to the degree that this can be done) is given in [34, sec. 7.1].

4.4   Information Theory, (Artificial) Intelligence and Recognising It

Following so much of Ray Solomonoff's abovementioned work(s), in 1982, Greg Chaitin (author of [22, 21, 23]) suggested [24, sec. 6 (Directions for Future Research)] "f. Develop formal definitions of intelligence and measures of its various components; apply information theory and complexity theory to AI.". As per sec. 2, independent work in the 1990s [38, 39, 64, 40, 58, 86] and [104] advocated the use of (algorithmic) information theory (and compression) to give (static) universal tests of intelligence [34, sec. 7.3].

Legg and Hutter [79] later suggested having a universal Solomonoff distribution over environments, and suggested that intelligence could be quantified as a doubly infinite sum (with some incomputabilities). This was intended as a definition (or measure) rather than a test, partly (but not only) because it did not incorporate time. A test was developed following similar principles in [59] and humans were compared to machines on a supposedly equal footing in such a test (even if with somewhat unclear results) in [69, 70], with a similar theme followed slightly later in [80].

The measure (or definition) in [79] could be made more general (or "more universal") by first noting the following observations:

– Ayumu the chimpanzee in Kyoto, Japan, can remember the locations of the digits 1 to 9 randomly placed on a screen in a time-frame in which many humans would struggle to recall the location of any one of these. In similar vein, many half-fluent speakers of a language will be able to recall and process a sentence if it is spoken to them slowly, but will simply become lost if the sentence is spoken at full speed. These comments concern the speed of the environment's output and (correspondingly) the agent's input - and they remain true no matter how much extra thinking time the agent has after the (all too fast) input has finished.

- regarding the issue of the speed of the agent's output, the prominent physicist, Stephen W. Hawking, often requires relatively long periods of time to communicate what would otherwise be far faster from him. The problem is not his internal neural processing ability but rather the speed of his output (devices or) communication. A similar comment applies to people with locked-in syndrome.
- redundant TMs [32, sec. 0.2.7, p544, col. 2][59, p1514, footnote 6] are TMs with redundant input and output which (for this reason) can not be universal (in the sense of a UTM) but, with the correct pre-processing (create redundancies) and post-processing (remove redundancies), can mimic UTMs[31]. A giraffe and a whale are both bigger than a human, who is in turn bigger than an ant - and (whether or not it incorporates redundant [U]TMs) appropriate spatial resolution needs to be given for these agents.
- at least partly relevant is the case of Canadian Scott Routley, who can communicate - albeit, like Stephen Hawking, slowly - via the use of an additional communication channel, namely, an fMRI scanner.
- possibly also see [136, sec. 7 (Dolphin Talk)] from sec. 3.

The Legg-Hutter definition [79] might be "more universal" if it allowed varying input and output durations (possibly with a universal distribution over these speeds, bearing in mind that some agents might have similar speeds of operation in processing input but vastly different in output or vice versa), and possibly optimising over spatial resolution. The issue of recognising life and intelligence (from the greater machine kingdom [63]) from elsewhere [32, sec. 0.2.5, p542] should be facilitated by a willingness to be "more universal" and allow different spatio-temporal resolutions (and speeds). Some of these criticisms possibly also apply to at least parts of the test(s) in [59]. There is also the observation that, like us predominantly earth-bound humans, it is reasonable to put large weight on environments in which agents have a reasonable chance of survival [62].

The Monte Carlo AIXI (MC-AIXI) work [175] is most impressive. As has been stated elsewhere (and as per [42] and sec. 4.2), it would be good to re-visit this using MML. Regarding the comparison of the predictive and MML approaches for the decision tree example in sec. 4.2, it seems that some of the MC-AIXI calculations [175] might need re-visiting.

4.5   A Music Note

We are often taught that the major chord in music of a note, 4 semitones above the note and then 3 semitones above that (7 semitones above the original note) sounds harmonic and/or melodic because the frequencies are in the ratio 4:5:6. And, yet, they are not. Rather, with 12 semitones in an octave and each semitone step having a frequency ratio of $1:2^{1/12}$, the notes' frequencies are in the ratio $4:(4 \times 2^{1/3}):(4 \times 2^{7/12})$ [or $(5 \times 2^{-1/3}):5:(5 \times 2^{1/4})$], or approximately 4.0000:5.0397:5.9932 [or approximately 3.9685:5.0000:5.9460]. In short, I guess that the approximation (to 4:5:6) works well enough.

---

[31] Possibly see the loosely related footnote 29.

It has been said of the American composer and music theorist, Harry Partch, that (rather than 12 equal tones) he advocated the division of the octave into 43 unequal tones (and I have heard the number 37 mentioned). To some degree, this is a problem of creating simple ratios (the octave is 1:2) and near (or approximately) simple ratios - perhaps balanced with relatively few divisions per octave. (Possibly see also [130, sec. VII].)

4.6 Originality, Creativity, Humour, Illusion

Perhaps following sec. 4.4, the originality of something is presumably measured by how different it is to things which preceded it. This could be quantified by (e.g.) (i) such an idea's having a large Hamming distance from existing ideas, and/or (ii) it requiring a large amount of information to describe/encode it in terms of (a suitable encoding of) existing ideas, and/or (iii) the underlying model's having a large Kullback-Leibler distance from the other models.

Something is presumably creative if it can repeatedly demonstrate originality. Humour [32, sec. 0.2.7, p545][34, sec. 7.7, p967] (especially puns), illusions and (cryptic) crossword clues often require finding connections (simple and concise, of relatively little information content) between things not previously recognised to be related.

I think that the above suggestions re something's being "creative" are consistent with Ray Solomonoff's notions from [131, 145] and secs. 1.3 and 3.2.

4.7 Some Further Work

Open problems and exercises to be worked on have been given in (e.g.) [146, sec. 8][151, sec. 8][161, sec. 11][163, sec. 7][32, sec. 0.2.7][34, sec. 7.7].

Other problems include (whether, as per sec. 4.2, by prediction, induction or whatever) using the discussed approaches of (algorithmic) information theory to address (e.g.) the following:

- k-nearest neighbours (k-NN) and recommender systems,
- building upon MML Bayesian networks with continuous and discrete attributes [25, 26], MML Bayesian nets with latent factors [177], Wallace's earlier work on MML Bayesian nets [187, sec. 7.4][32, sec. 0.2.2, p526, col. 1] and MML time series [52, 107] to re-visit or generalise the dynamic Bayesian network (DBN) scheme from [97],
- extending MML time series [52, 107] to re-visit (econometric) GARCH (or introduce moving averages [MA] to extend it to GARCHMA),
- fleshing out the ideas from [28] (extending [190, 194]),
- re-visiting the lovely story of early ideas re information retrieval (IR) [114, sec. 5] to (re-)address the mixture modelling approaches of (e.g.) [199],
- replacing Maximum Likelihood in Approximate Bayesian Computation (ABC),
- addressing (so-called) non-parametrics (in statistics and econometrics) with some appropriate Turing machine (prior),

- re-visiting K. Zuse and S. Wolfram on the universe as a cellular automaton - perhaps as per [133, sec. 3.2],
- Inference@Home (similarly parallel to SETI@Home and Folding@Home),
- exploring the notion of LNPPP [32, sec. 0.2.7][34, sec. 5.3], where the (universal) distribution of statistical environments was and is intended to be generated using a (universal) Turing machine,
- in physics, entropy is often defined as $\sum_i -p_i \log p_i$, where a multinomial distribution is assumed, the Maximum Likelihood estimates are used (or presumed), and the entropy is then said to be the negative log-likelihood divided by (N) the number of particles. Whether or not we divide by N, are we not interested in the information content [12]? Can this be applied to other likelihood functions rather than just the multinomial - and, more specifically, can this be re-framed in terms of a universal distribution?
- footnotes 26 and 28 (or the text next to them) and the Peter principle [34, sec. 7.7, p969] draw our attention to political and other problems (e.g., [workplace] psychopaths, bullies, convincing liars, etc.) that many of us have known in (e.g.) the workplace. Could the methods of inductive inference and prediction mentioned here be used (perhaps with some notions from graph theory) to analyse (possibly experimental) data to create one or more better (and more robust) hierarchies of information flow, obtaining of opinions and views (and evidence) and decision making? (Possibly see [55, sec. 7 (vi)].)

4.8   From Here

2012 was the centenary of the birth of Alan M. Turing, on whose Universal Turing Machines and (the) quest for machine intelligence so much of Ray Solomonoff's work has been built. 2013 is appropriately The International Year of Statistics (Statistics2013, www.statistics2013.org), an area in which Ray's work will continue to grow. 2013 is also the International Year of Mathematics of Planet Earth (http://mpe2013.org , http://mathsofplanetearth.org.au). Among other things, I think of Ray's "never ending source of joy in discovery!" [153, sec. 3] and his questioning the confidence in (current) extreme value theory (from sec. 3.2) [145, sec. 1]. I also think of his warning from [136, sec. 1] in 1967 which I expand upon from secs. 1.1 and 3: "... the dangers posed are very serious and the problems very difficult. It would be well if a large number of intelligent humans devote a lot of thought to these problems before they arise. It is my feeling that the realization of artificial intelligence will be a sudden occurrence. ..."

Acknowledgements. Thank you (again) to all those thanked at the front of this volume. Thank you to the sponsors, the Program Committee, the referees (at least one of whom wished not to be named), Grace Solomonoff (who has contributed the wonderful [114]), the other invited speakers, Alex Solomonoff, the other authors, their co-authors, the presenters, and the other conference delegates. Thank you to the late Ray Solomonoff for a wonderful body of work, for a life well lived and for bringing us together. Thank you also to Joy Reynolds, Genevieve Oreski, Dr Rebecca Robinson, RJD and (with apologies) anyone who I might have forgotten.

P.S.: As well as the earlier picture of Ray and the cover figure, perhaps also see a figure by RJD at www.csse.monash.edu.au/~dld/RaySolomonoffsVision.html

References

1. Akaike, H.: Statistical prediction information. Ann. Inst. Statist. Math. 22, 203–217 (1970)
2. Akaike, H.: Information theory and an extension of the maximum likelihood principle. In: Petrov, B.N., Csaki, F. (eds.) Proceedings of the 2nd International Symposium on Information Theory, pp. 267–281 (1973)
3. Akaike, H.: Factor Analysis and AIC. Psychometrika 52(3), 317–332 (1987)
4. Amir, A., Amin, A.H.M., Khan, A.: Developing machine intelligence within P2P networks using a distributed associative memory. In: Dowe, D.L. (ed.) Solomonoff Festschrift. LNCS (LNAI), vol. 7070, pp. 439–443. Springer, Heidelberg (2013)
5. Balduzzi, D.: Falsification and future performance. In: Dowe, D.L. (ed.) Solomonoff Festschrift. LNCS (LNAI), vol. 7070, pp. 65–78. Springer, Heidelberg (2013)
6. Barmpalias, G., Dowe, D.L.: Universality probability of a prefix-free machine. Philosophical Transactions of the Royal Society A [Mathematical, Physical & Engineering Sciences] (Phil Trans. A) 370, 3488–3511 (2012)
7. Barron, A.R., Cover, T.M.: Minimum complexity density estimation. IEEE Transactions on Information Theory 37, 1034–1054 (1991)
8. Baxter, R.A., Oliver, J.J.: MDL and MML: Similarities and differences. Technical report TR 94/207, Dept. of Computer Science, Monash University, Clayton, Victoria 3168, Australia (1995)
9. Bergen, M.S., Bishop, W.B., Buchanan, B.L., Dilworth, R.P., Ackerlind, E., Solomonoff, R.J., et al.: Part n-circuit theory; information theory. In: IEEE International Convention Record, p. 293. Institute of Electrical and Electronics Engineers, U.S.A. (1957)
10. Boulton, D.M.: Numerical classification based on an information measure. Master's thesis, M.Sc. thesis, Basser Computing Dept., University of Sydney, Sydney, Australia (1970)
11. Boulton, D.M.: The Information Measure Criterion for Intrinsic Classification. PhD thesis, Dept. Computer Science, Monash University, Clayton, Australia (August 1975)
12. Boulton, D.M., Wallace, C.S.: The information content of a multistate distribution. J. Theor. Biol. 23, 269–278 (1969)
13. Boulton, D.M., Wallace, C.S.: A program for numerical classification. Computer Journal 13(1), 63–69 (February 1970)
14. Boulton, D.M., Wallace, C.S.: A comparison between information measure classification. In: Proc. of the Australian & New Zealand Association for the Advancement of Science (ANZAAS) Congress (August 1973) (abstract)
15. Boulton, D.M., Wallace, C.S.: An information measure for hierarchic classification. Computer Journal 16(3), 254–261 (1973)
16. Boulton, D.M., Wallace, C.S.: Occupancy of a rectangular array. Computer Journal 16(1), 57–63 (1973)
17. Boulton, D.M., Wallace, C.S.: An information measure for single link classification. Computer Journal 18(3), 236–238 (1975)

18. Brennan, M.H.: Data processing in the early cosmic ray experiments in Sydney. Computer Journal 51(5), 561–565 (2008); Christopher Stewart WALLACE (1933-2004) memorial special issue

19. Brennan, M.H., Millar, D.D., Wallace, C.S.: Air showers of size greater than 10^5 particles - (1) core location and shower size determination. Nature 182, 905–911 (October 4, 1958)

20. Campbell, D.: The Semimeasure Property of Algorithmic Probability - "Feature" or "Bug"? In: Dowe, D.L. (ed.) Solomonoff Festschrift. LNCS (LNAI), vol. 7070, pp. 79–90. Springer, Heidelberg (2013)

21. Chaitin, G.J.: On the length of programs for computing finite sequences. Journal of the Association for Computing Machinery 13, 547–569 (1966)

22. Chaitin, G.J.: On the simplicity and speed of programs for computing infinite sets of natural numbers. Journal of the Association for Computing Machinery 16(3), 407–422 (1969)

23. Chaitin, G.J.: Randomness and Mathematical Proof. Scientific American 232(5), 47–52 (May 1975)

24. Chaitin, G.J.: Godel's theorem and information. International J. of Theoretical Physics 21(12), 941–954 (1982)

25. Comley, J.W., Dowe, D.L.: General Bayesian networks and asymmetric languages. In: Proc. Hawaii International Conference on Statistics and Related Fields, June 5-8 (2003)

26. Comley, J.W., Dowe, D.L.: Minimum message length and generalized Bayesian nets with asymmetric languages. In: Grünwald, P., Pitt, M.A., Myung, I.J. (eds.) Advances in Minimum Description Length: Theory and Applications (MDL Handbook), ch. 11, pp. 265–294. M.I.T. Press (April 2005) ISBN 0-262-07262-9; Final camera-ready copy submitted in October 2003. [Originally submitted with title: "Minimum Message Length, MDL and Generalised Bayesian Networks with Asymmetric Languages".]

27. Balduzzi, D.: Falsification and future performance. In: Dowe, D.L. (ed.) Solomonoff Festschrift. LNCS (LNAI), vol. 7070, pp. 65–78. Springer, Heidelberg (2013)

28. Dale, P.E.R., Dale, M.B., Dowe, D.L., Knight, J.M., Lemckert, C.J., Low Choy, D.C., Sheaves, M.J., Sporne, I.: A conceptual model for integrating physical geography research and coastal wetland management, with an Australian example. Progress in Physical Geography 34(5), 605–624 (October 2010)

29. Dean, Thomas, Boddy: An analysis of time-dependent planning. In: Proc. 7th National Conference on Artificial Intelligence, pp. 49–54 (1998)

30. Dessalles, J.-L.: Algorithmic simplicity and relevance. In: Dowe, D.L. (ed.) Solomonoff Festschrift. LNCS (LNAI), vol. 7070, pp. 119–130. Springer, Heidelberg (2013)

31. Dowe, D.L.: Discussion following "Hedging predictions in machine learning, A. Gammerman and V. Vovk". Computer Journal 2(50), 167–168 (2007)

32. Dowe, D.L.: Foreword re C. S. Wallace. Computer Journal 51(5), 523–560 (2008); Christopher Stewart WALLACE (1933-2004) memorial special issue

33. Dowe, D.L.: Minimum Message Length and statistically consistent invariant (objective?) Bayesian probabilistic inference - from (medical) "evidence". Social Epistemology 22(4), 433–460 (2008)

34. Dowe, D.L.: MML, hybrid Bayesian network graphical models, statistical consistency, invariance and uniqueness. In: Bandyopadhyay, P.S., Forster, M.R. (eds.) Handbook of the Philosophy of Science. Philosophy of Statistics, vol. 7, pp. 901–982. Elsevier (2011)

35. Dowe, D.L., Baxter, R.A., Oliver, J.J., Wallace, C.S.: Point estimation using the Kullback-Leibler loss function and MML. In: Wu, X., Kotagiri, R., Korb, K. (eds.) PAKDD 1998. LNCS (LNAI), vol. 1394, pp. 87–95. Springer, Heidelberg (1998)

36. Dowe, D.L., Farr, G.E., Hurst, A.J., Lentin, K.L.: Information-theoretic football tipping. Technical report TR 96/297, Dept. of Computer Science, Monash University, Clayton, Victoria 3168, Australia (1996)

37. Dowe, D.L., Gardner, S., Oppy, G.R.: Bayes not bust! Why simplicity is no problem for Bayesians. British Journal for the Philosophy of Science 58(4), 709–754 (2007)

38. Dowe, D.L., Hajek, A.R.: A computational extension to the Turing test. In: Proceedings of the 4th Conference of the Australasian Cognitive Science Society, Newcastle, NSW, Australia (September 1997)

39. Dowe, D.L., Hajek, A.R.: A computational extension to the Turing test. Technical Report 97/322, Dept. Computer Science, Monash University, Australia 3168 (October 1997)

40. Dowe, D.L., Hajek, A.R.: A non-behavioural, computational extension to the Turing test. In: Proceedings of the International Conference on Computational Intelligence & Multimedia Applications (ICCIMA 1998), Gippsland, Australia, pp. 101–106 (February 1998)

41. Dowe, D.L., Hernández-Orallo, J.: I.Q. tests are not for machines, yet. Intelligence 40(2), 77–81 (March 2012)

42. Dowe, D.L., Hernández-Orallo, J., Das, P.K.: Compression and intelligence: Social environments and communication. In: Schmidhuber, J., Thórisson, K.R., Looks, M. (eds.) AGI 2011. LNCS, vol. 6830, pp. 204–211. Springer, Heidelberg (2011)

43. Dowe, D.L., Krusel, N.: A decision tree model of bushfire activity. Technical report TR 93/190, Dept. of Computer Science, Monash University, Clayton, Vic. 3800, Australia (September 1993)

44. Dowe, D.L., Lentin, K.L.: Information-theoretic footy-tipping competition - Monash. Computer Science Association Newsletter (Australia), 55–57 (December 1995)

45. Edgoose, T., Allison, L.: MML Markov classification of sequential data. Stats. and Comp. 9(4), 269–278 (1999)

46. Edwards, R.T., Dowe, D.L.: Single factor analysis in MML mixture modelling. In: Wu, X., Kotagiri, R., Korb, K.B. (eds.) PAKDD 1998. LNCS, vol. 1394, pp. 96–109. Springer, Heidelberg (April 1998)

47. Ellison, T.M.: Categorisation as topographic mapping between uncorrelated spaces. In: Dowe, D.L. (ed.) Solomonoff Festschrift. LNCS (LNAI), vol. 7070, pp. 131–141. Springer, Heidelberg (2013)

48. Evans, T.: A heuristic program of solving geometric analogy problems. PhD thesis, Mass. Inst. Tech., Cambridge, Mass., U.S.A. (1963) Also available from AF Cambridge Research Lab, Hanscom AFB, Bedford, Mass., U.S.A.: Data Sciences Lab., Phys. and Math. Sci. Res. Paper 64, Project 4641 (1963)

49. Evans, T.: A heuristic program to solve geometric-analogy problems. In: Proc. SJCC, vol. 25, pp. 327–339 (1965)

50. Da Silva Filho, R.I., da Rocha, R.L.A., Guiraldelli, R.H.G.: Learning in the limit: A mutational and adaptive approach. In: Dowe, D.L. (ed.) Solomonoff Festschrift. LNCS (LNAI), vol. 7070, pp. 106–118. Springer, Heidelberg (2013)

51. Fitzgibbon, L.J., Dowe, D.L., Allison, L.: Univariate polynomial inference by Monte Carlo message length approximation. In: Proceedings of the 19th International Conference on Machine Learning (ICML 2002), pp. 147–154. Morgan Kaufmann (2002)

52. Fitzgibbon, L.J., Dowe, D.L., Vahid, F.: Minimum message length autoregressive model order selection. In: Proc. Int. Conf. on Intelligent Sensors and Information Processing, Chennai, India, pp. 439–444 (January 2004)

53. Freivalds, R.: Algorithmic information theory and computational complexity. In: Dowe, D.L. (ed.) Solomonoff Festschrift. LNCS (LNAI), vol. 7070, pp. 142–154. Springer, Heidelberg (2013)

54. Fresco, N.: A critical survey of some competing accounts of concrete digital computation. In: Dowe, D.L. (ed.) Solomonoff Festschrift. LNCS (LNAI), vol. 7070, pp. 155–173. Springer, Heidelberg (2013)

55. Good, I.J.: Rational decisions. J. Roy. Statist. Soc. (B) 14(1), 107–114 (1952)

56. Good, I.J.: Speculations concerning the first ultraintelligent machine. Advances in Computers 6, 31–88 (1965)

57. Hall, J.S.: Further reflections on the timescale of AI. In: Dowe, D.L. (ed.) Solomonoff Festschrift. LNCS (LNAI), vol. 7070, pp. 174–183. Springer, Heidelberg (2013)

58. Hernández-Orallo, J.: Beyond the Turing test. Journal of Logic, Language and Information 9(4), 447–466 (2000)

59. Hernández-Orallo, J., Dowe, D.L.: Measuring universal intelligence: Towards an anytime intelligence test. Artificial Intelligence Journal 174(18), 1508–1539 (2010)

60. Hernández-Orallo, J., Dowe, D.L.: Potential Properties of Turing Machines. Technical report 2012/271, Clayton School of I.T., Monash University, Clayton, Vic. 3168, Australia, 22 pp. (August 3, 2012)

61. Hernández-Orallo, J., Dowe, D.L.: On Potential Cognitive Abilities in the Machine Kingdom. Minds and Machines 23, 179–210 (2013),
http://dx.doi.org/10.1007/s11023-012-9299-6

62. Hernández-Orallo, J., Dowe, D.L., España-Cubillo, S., Hernández-Lloreda, M.V., Insa-Cabrera, J.: On more realistic environment distributions for defining, evaluating and developing intelligence. In: Schmidhuber, J., Thórisson, K.R., Looks, M. (eds.) AGI 2011. LNCS, vol. 6830, pp. 82–91. Springer, Heidelberg (2011)

63. Hernández-Orallo, J., Dowe, D.L., Hernández-Lloreda, M.V.: Universal Psychometrics: Measuring Cognitive Abilities in the Machine Kingdom. Accepted to Cognitive Systems Research (See also Technical report 2012/267, Clayton School of I.T., Monash University)

64. Hernandez-Orallo, J., Minaya-Collado, N.: A formal definition of intelligence based on an intensional variant of Kolmogorov complexity. In: Proceedings of the International Symposium of Engineering of Intelligent Systems, pp. 146–163. ICSC Press (1998)

65. Hope, L.R., Korb, K.: Bayesian information reward. In: McKay, B., Slaney, J.K. (eds.) AI 2002. LNCS (LNAI), vol. 2557, pp. 272–283. Springer, Heidelberg (2002)

66. Horning, J.: A procedure for grammatical inference. In: Proc. IFIP Congress, Amsterdam, North Holland, vol. 71, Amsterdam, North Holland

67. Hu, B., Rakthanmanon, T., Hao, Y., Evans, S., Lonardi, S., Keogh, E.: Towards discovering the intrinsic cardinality and dimensionality of time series using MDL. In: Dowe, D.L. (ed.) Solomonoff Festschrift. LNCS (LNAI), vol. 7070, pp. 184–197. Springer, Heidelberg (2013)

68. Hutter, M.: New Error Bounds for Solomonoff Prediction. J. Comput. Syst. Sci. 62(4), 653–667 (2001)

69. Insa-Cabrera, J., Dowe, D.L., España-Cubillo, S., Hernández-Lloreda, M.V., Hernández-Orallo, J.: Comparing humans and AI agents. In: Schmidhuber, J., Thórisson, K.R., Looks, M. (eds.) AGI 2011. LNCS, vol. 6830, pp. 122–132. Springer, Heidelberg (2011)

70. Insa-Cabrera, J., Dowe, D.L., Hernández-Orallo, J.: Evaluating a reinforcement learning algorithm with a general intelligence test. In: Lozano, J.A., Gámez, J.A., Moreno, J.A. (eds.) CAEPIA 2011. LNCS, vol. 7023, pp. 1–11. Springer, Heidelberg (2011)

71. Jankowski, N.: Complexity measures for meta-learning and their optimality. In: Dowe, D.L. (ed.) Solomonoff Festschrift. LNCS (LNAI), vol. 7070, pp. 198–210. Springer, Heidelberg (2013)

72. Jeffreys, H.: An invariant form for the prior probability in estimation problems. Proc. of the Royal Soc. of London A 186, 453–454 (1946)

73. Langdon Jr., G.G.: An introduction to arithmetic coding. IBM Journal of Research and Development 28(2), 135–149 (1984)

74. Langdon Jr., G.G., Rissanen, J.J.: A simple general binary source code. IEEE Transactions on Information Theory 28(5), 800–803 (1982)

75. King, P.A.: Design of a conscious machine. In: Dowe, D.L. (ed.) Solomonoff Festschrift. LNCS (LNAI), vol. 7070, pp. 211–222. Springer, Heidelberg (2013)

76. Kolmogorov, A.N.: Three approaches to the quantitative definition of information. Problems of Information Transmission 1, 4–7 (1965)

77. Kolmogorov, A.N.: Logical basis for information theory and probability theory. IEEE Transactions on Information Theory 14, 662–664 (1968)

78. Lattimore, T., Hutter, M.: No free lunch versus occam's razor in supervised learning. In: Dowe, D.L. (ed.) Solomonoff Festschrift. LNCS (LNAI), vol. 7070, pp. 223–235. Springer, Heidelberg (2013)

79. Legg, S., Hutter, M.: Universal intelligence: A definition of machine intelligence. Minds and Machines 17(4), 391–444 (November 2007)

80. Legg, S., Veness, J.: An approximation of the universal intelligence measure. In: Dowe, D.L. (ed.) Solomonoff Festschrift. LNCS (LNAI), vol. 7070, pp. 236–249. Springer, Heidelberg (2013)

81. Levin, L.A.: Universal sequential search problems. Problems of Information Transmission 9(3), 265–266 (1973)

82. Levin, L.A.: Universal heuristics: How do humans solve "Unsolvable" problems? In: Dowe, D.L. (ed.) Solomonoff Festschrift. LNCS (LNAI), vol. 7070, pp. 53–54. Springer, Heidelberg (2013)

83. Lewis, D.K., Shelby-Richardson, J.: Scriven on human unpredictability. Philosophical Studies: An International Journal for Philosophy in the Analytic Tradition 17(5), 69–74 (1966)

84. Li, M.: Partial match distance. In: Dowe, D.L. (ed.) Solomonoff Festschrift. LNCS (LNAI), vol. 7070, pp. 55–64. Springer, Heidelberg (2013)

85. Li, M., Vitányi, P.M.B.: An Introduction to Kolmogorov Complexity and its applications. Springer (1997)

86. Mahoney, M.: Text compression as a test for artificial intelligence. In: Proc. National Conf. on Artificial Intelligence, U.S.A., p. 970. AAAI / John Wiley & Sons (1999)

87. Makalic, E., Allison, L.: MMLD inference of multilayer perceptrons. In: Dowe, D.L. (ed.) Solomonoff Festschrift. LNCS (LNAI), vol. 7070, pp. 261–272. Springer, Heidelberg (2013)

88. Makalic, E., Schmidt, D.F.: Minimum message length analysis of the behrens–fisher problem. In: Dowe, D.L. (ed.) Solomonoff Festschrift. LNCS (LNAI), vol. 7070, pp. 250–260. Springer, Heidelberg (2013)

89. Miyabe, K.: An optimal superfarthingale and its convergence over a computable topological space. In: Dowe, D.L. (ed.) Solomonoff Festschrift. LNCS (LNAI), vol. 7070, pp. 273–284. Springer, Heidelberg (2013)

90. Molloy, S.B., Albrecht, D.W., Dowe, D.L., Ting, K.M.: Model-Based Clustering of Sequential Data. In: Proceedings of the 5th Annual Hawaii International Conference on Statistics, Mathematics and Related Fields (January 2006)

91. Needham, S.L., Dowe, D.L.: Message length as an effective Ockham's razor in decision tree induction. In: Proc. 8th Int. Workshop on Artif. Intelligence and Statistics (AI+STATS 2001), pp. 253–260 (January 2001)

92. Özkural, E.: Diverse consequences of algorithmic probability. In: Dowe, D.L. (ed.) Solomonoff Festschrift. LNCS (LNAI), vol. 7070, pp. 285–298. Springer, Heidelberg (2013)

93. van Heerden, P.J.: A general theory of prediction. Technical report, Polaroid Corp., Cambridge 39, Massachusetts, U.S.A., Privately circulated report (1963)

94. Paul, W.J., Solomonoff, R.J.: Autonomous theory building systems. Neural Networks and Adaptive Learning, Schloss Reisenberg, Knowledge Processing and its Applications Series (1990)

95. Paul, W.J., Solomonoff, R.J.: Autonomous theory building systems. Annals of Operations Research 55(1), 179–193 (1995)

96. Pelckmans, K.: An adaptive compression algorithm in a deterministic world. In: Dowe, D.L. (ed.) Solomonoff Festschrift. LNCS (LNAI), vol. 7070, pp. 299–305. Springer, Heidelberg (2013)

97. Pérez-Ariza, C.B., Nicholson, A.E., Korb, K.B., Mascaro, S., Hu, C.H.: Causal discovery of dynamic Bayesian networks. In: Thielscher, M., Zhang, D. (eds.) AI 2012. LNCS, vol. 7691, pp. 902–913. Springer, Heidelberg (2012)

98. Petersen, S.: Toward an algorithmic metaphysics. In: Dowe, D.L. (ed.) Solomonoff Festschrift. LNCS (LNAI), vol. 7070, pp. 306–317. Springer, Heidelberg (2013)

99. Rissanen, J.J.: Generalized Kraft inequality and arithmetic coding. IBM J. Res. Develop. 20(3), 198–203 (1976)

100. Rissanen, J.J.: Modeling by shortest data description. Automatica 14, 465–471 (1978)

101. Rissanen, J.J.: Information and Complexity in Statistical Modeling. Information Science and Statistics. Springer (2007)

102. Rissanen, J.J., Langdon Jr., G.G.: Arithmetic coding. IBM Journal of Research and Development 23(2), 149–162 (1979)

103. Rzepka, R., Muramoto, K., Araki, K.: Limiting context by using the web to minimize conceptual jump size. In: Dowe, D.L. (ed.) Solomonoff Festschrift. LNCS (LNAI), vol. 7070, pp. 318–326. Springer, Heidelberg (2013)

104. Sanghi, P., Dowe, D.L.: A computer program capable of passing I.Q. tests. In: 4th International Conference on Cognitive Science (and 7th Australasian Society for Cognitive Science Conference), Univ. of NSW, Sydney, Australia, vol. 2, pp. 570–575 (July 2003)

105. Schmidhuber, J.: Optimal ordered problem solver. Technical report TR IDSIA-12-02, IDSIA, Lugano, Switzerland, (July 31, 2002), http://www.idsia.ch/~juergen/oops.html

106. Schmidt, D.F.: Minimum Message Length Inference of Autoregressive Moving Average Models. PhD thesis, Faculty of Information Technology, Monash University (2008)

107. Schmidt, D.F.: Minimum message length order selection and parameter estimation of moving average models. In: Dowe, D.L. (ed.) Solomonoff Festschrift. LNCS (LNAI), vol. 7070, pp. 327–338. Springer, Heidelberg (2013)

108. Schwartz, J., Solomonoff, R.J.: Photoelectric chopper for guided missiles. Electronics (November 1954)

109. Schwarz, G.: Estimating dimension of a model. Ann. Stat. 6, 461–464 (1978)
110. Scriven, M.: An essential unpredictability in human behavior. In: Wolman, B.B., Nagel, E. (eds.) Scientific Psychology: Principles and Approaches, pp. 411–425. Basic Books (Perseus Books) (1965)
111. Shannon, C.E.: A mathematical theory of communication. The Bell System Technical Journal 27, 379–423 (July 1948), 623–656 (October 1948)
112. Silvescu, A., Honavar, V.: Abstraction super-structuring normal forms: Towards a theory of structural induction. In: Dowe, D.L. (ed.) Solomonoff Festschrift. LNCS (LNAI), vol. 7070, pp. 339–350. Springer, Heidelberg (2013)
113. Solomonoff, A.: Locating a discontinuity in a piecewise-smooth periodic function using bayes estimation. In: Dowe, D.L. (ed.) Solomonoff Festschrift. LNCS (LNAI), vol. 7070, pp. 351–365. Springer, Heidelberg (2013)
114. Solomonoff, G.: Ray solomonoff and the new probability. In: Dowe, D.L. (ed.) Solomonoff Festschrift. LNCS (LNAI), vol. 7070, pp. 37–52. Springer, Heidelberg (2013)
115. Solomonoff, R.J.: An exact method for the computation of the connectivity of random nets. Bulletin of Mathematical Biophysics 14(2), 153–157 (1952)
116. Solomonoff, R.J.: An optically driven airborne chopper. In: Proceedings of the 3rd Typhoon Symposium, p. 205 (1953)
117. Solomonoff, R.J.: Effects of Heisenberg's principle on channel capacity. Proceedings of the I.R.E. 43, 484 (April 1955)
118. Solomonoff, R.J.: An inductive inference machine. Dartmouth Summer Research Project on Artificial Intelligence, A privately circulated report (August 1956)
119. Solomonoff, R.J.: An inductive inference machine. In: IRE Convention Record, Section on Information Theory, Part 2, pp. 56–62 (1957)
120. Solomonoff, R.J.: The mechanization of linguistic learning. In: Proceedings of the Second International Congress on Cybernetics, Namur, Belgium, pp. 180–193 (May 1958)
121. Solomonoff, R.J.: Utility evaluation. Publication VI23 30, Zator Co. and Air Force Office of Scientific Research, U.S.A. (April 1958)
122. Solomonoff, R.J.: A new method for discovering the grammars of phrase structure languages. In: Proceedings of the International Conference on Information Processing. UNESCO, Paris, France (1959)
123. Solomonoff, R.J.: A progress report on machines to learn to translate languages and retrieve information. In: Advances in Documentation and Library Science, Vol. III, Part 2 (Reprint from Proceedings of International Conference for Standards on a Common Language for Machine Searching and Translation 1959), vol. III, pp. 941–953. Interscience Publishers (September/October 1959)
124. Solomonoff, R.J.: Progress report: Research on inductive inference for the year ending 31 March 1959. Technical Report ZTB-130, Zator Co. and Air Force Office of Scientific Research, U.S.A. (May 1959)
125. Solomonoff, R.J.: A preliminary report on a general theory of inductive inference. Technical Report V-131, Zator Co. and Air Force Office of Scientific Research, Cambridge, Mass., U.S.A. (February 1960)
126. Solomonoff, R.J.: A preliminary report on a general theory of inductive inference (revision of Report V-131). Technical Report ZTB-138, Zator Co. and Air Force Office of Scientific Research, Cambridge, Mass., U.S.A. (November 1960)
127. Solomonoff, R.J.: A coding method for inductive inference. Technical Report ZTB-140, Zator Co. [and perhaps Rockford Research Co.] (Prepared for Air Force Office of Scientific Research, Air Research and Development Command, U.S. Air Force), Cambridge, Mass., U.S.A. (April 1961)

128. Solomonoff, R.J.: Progress report: Research in inductive inference for the period 1 April 1959 to 30 November 1960. Technical Report ZTB 139, Rockford Research Co. and Air Force Office of Scientific Research, U.S.A. (January 1961)

129. Solomonoff, R.J.: Comments on Dr. S. Watanabe's paper. Synthese 14(2), 97–100 (September 1962)

130. Solomonoff, R.J.: An inductive inference code employing definitions. Technical Report ZTB-141, Zator Co. [and perhaps Rockford Research Co.] (Prepared for Air Force Office of Scientific Research, Air Research and Development Command, U.S. Air Force), Cambridge, Mass., U.S.A. (April 1962)

131. Solomonoff, R.J.: Training sequences for mechanized induction. In: Yovits, M., Jacobi, Goldstein (eds.) Self-Organizing Systems, pp. 425–434. Spartan Books (1962)

132. Solomonoff, R.J.: A formal theory of inductive inference. Information and Control 7, 1–22, 224–254 (1964)

133. Solomonoff, R.J.: A formal theory of inductive inference: Part I. Information and Control 7(1), 1–22 (March 1964)

134. Solomonoff, R.J.: A formal theory of inductive inference: Part II. Information and Control 7(2), 224–254 (June 1964)

135. Solomonoff, R.J.: Some recent work in artificial intelligence. Proceedings of the IEEE 54(12), 1687–1697 (December 1966)

136. Solomonoff, R.J.: Inductive inference research status, spring, 1967. Technical Report RTB 154, Rockford Research Co. and Air Force Office of Scientific Research, 140 1/2 Mt, Auburn St., Cambridge, Mass., U.S.A. (July 1967)

137. Solomonoff, R.J.: The search for artificial intelligence. Electronics and Power 14(1), 8–11 (January 1968)

138. Solomonoff, R.J.: The adequacy of complexity models of induction. In: Logic, Methodology and Philosophy of Science: Proceedings of the Fifth International Congress, London, Ontario, Canada, pp. 19–20 (September 1975) (Section VI)

139. Solomonoff, R.J.: Inductive inference theory - a unified approach to problems in pattern recognition and artificial intelligence. In: Proceedings of the Fourth International Joint Conference on Artificial Intelligence, Tbilisi, Georgia, U.S.S.R, vol. 1, pp. 274–280 (September 1975), http://world.std.com/~rjs/pubs.html, http://world.std.com/~rjs/tblisi75.pdf

140. Solomonoff, R.J.: Complexity-based induction systems: Comparisons and convergence theorems. IEEE Transaction on Information Theory, IT-24(4), 422–432 (1978)

141. Solomonoff, R.J.: Perfect training sequences and the costs of corruption — a progress report on inductive inference research. Technical report, Oxbridge Research, Cambridge, MA, U.S.A. (August 1982)

142. Solomonoff, R.J.: Optimum sequential search. Technical report, Oxbridge Research, Cambridge, Mass., U.S.A. (June 1984)

143. Solomonoff, R.J.: The time scale of artificial intelligence; reflections on social effects. Human Systems Management 5, 149–153 (1985)

144. Solomonoff, R.J.: Two kinds of complexity. Technical report, Oxbridge Research, Cambridge, Mass., U.S.A. (1985)

145. Solomonoff, R.J.: The application of algorithmic probability to problems in artificial intelligence. In: Kanal, L.N., Lemmer, J.F. (eds.) Uncertainty in Artificial Intelligence, pp. 473–491. Elsevier Science Publishers B.V. (1986); Also in: Kochen, M., Hastings, H.M.: Advances in Cognitive Science. AAAS Selected Symposia Series, pp. 210–227. AAAS, Washington, D.C. (1988)

146. Solomonoff, R.J.: A system for incremental learning based on algorithmic probability. In: Proceedings of the Sixth Israeli Conference on Artificial Intelligence, Computer Vision and Pattern Recognition, Tel Aviv, Israel, pp. 515–527 (December 1989)

147. Solomonoff, R.J.: Does algorithmic probability solve the problem of induction? In: Dowe, D.L., Korb, K.B., Oliver, J.J. (eds.) Proceedings of the Information, Statistics and Induction in Science (ISIS) Conference, Melbourne, Australia, pp. 7–8. World Scientific (August 1996) ISBN 981-02-2824-4

148. Solomonoff, R.J.: The discovery of algorithmic probability. Journal of Computer and System Sciences 55(1), 73–88 (1997)

149. Solomonoff, R.J.: Does algorithmic probability solve the problem of induction? Report, Oxbridge Research, P.O.B. 400404, Cambridge, Mass. 02140, U.S.A. (1997), http://world.std.com/~rjs/isis96.pdf

150. Solomonoff, R.J.: Two kinds of probabilistic induction. Computer Journal 42(4), 256–259 (1999); Special Issue on Kolmogorov Complexity

151. Solomonoff, R.J.: Progress in incremental machine learning. In: NIPS Workshop on Universal Learning Algorithms and Optimal Search, Whistler, BC, Canada. NIPS (2002)

152. Solomonoff, R.J.: Progress in incremental machine learning (Preliminary report for NIPS 2002 workshop on universal learners and optimal search). Technical report, Technical Report IDSIA-16-03, IDSIA, Lugano, Switzerland (2003); Given at NIPS Conference, Whistler, B.C., Canada (December 14, 2002)

153. Solomonoff, R.J.: The universal distribution and machine learning. The Computer Journal 46(6), 598–601 (2003); Inaugural Kolmogorov Lecture, CLRC, Royal Holloway, University of London, England, U.K. (February 27, 2003)

154. Solomonoff, R.J.: Algorithmic probability, AI and NKS (given at Midwest NKS Conference, U.S.A.) (October 2005), http://world.std.com/~rjs/lects.html; also www.cs.indiana.edu/~dgerman/2005midwestNKSconference/keynotes/ray-j-solomonoff.ram

155. Solomonoff, R.J.: Lecture 1: Algorithmic probability (given at M.I.T., Cambridge, Ma., U.S.A.) (2005), http://world.std.com/~rjs/lects.html

156. Solomonoff, R.J.: Lecture 2: Applications of algorithmic probability. (given at M.I.T., Cambridge, Ma., U.S.A.) (2005), http://world.std.com/~rjs/lects.html

157. Solomonoff, R.J.: Machine learning - past and future, Dartmouth, N.H., U.S.A., (July 13-15, 2006); Lecture given in 2006 at AI@50, The Dartmouth A. I. Conference: The Next Fifty Years. (Revision August 11, 2009)

158. Solomonoff, R.J.: Incomputability in games, wars and economics — inductive inference in hostile environments. Logic, Computability and Randomness, page 19 (2007)

159. Solomonoff, R.J.: The probability of "undefined" (non-converging) output in generating the universal probability distribution. Information Processing Letters 106(6), 238–240 (2007)

160. Solomonoff, R.J.: Three kinds of probabilistic induction: Universal distributions and convergence theorems. Computer Journal 51(5), 566–570 (2008); Christopher Stewart WALLACE (1933-2004) Memorial Special Issue

161. Solomonoff, R.J.: Algorithmic probability: Theory and applications. In: Dehmer, M., Emmert-Streib, F. (eds.) Information Theory and Statistical Learning. Springer Science and Business Media, pp. 1–23. Springer, N.Y., U.S.A. (2009)

162. Solomonoff, R.J.: Algorithmic probability, heuristic programming and AGI. In: Proceedings of the Third Conference on Artificial General Intelligence, AGI 2010, Lugano, Switzerland, pp. 251–257. IDSIA (March 2010)

163. Solomonoff, R.J.: Algorithmic Probability – Its Discovery – Its Properties and Application to Strong AI, pp. 149–157. World Scientific Publishing Company (2011)

164. Solomonoff, R.J., Rapoport, A.: Structure of random nets. In: Proc. Int. Cong. Mathematicians, Providence, R.I., U.S.A., pp. 674–675. American Mathematical Society (1950)

165. Solomonoff, R.J., Rapoport, A.: Connectivity of random nets. Bulletin of Mathematical Biophysics 13(2), 107–117 (1951)

166. Solomonoff, R.J., Saleeby, E.G.: On the application of algorithmic probability to autoregressive models. In: Dowe, D.L. (ed.) Solomonoff Festschrift. LNCS (LNAI), vol. 7070, pp. 366–385. Springer, Heidelberg (2013)

167. Strannegard, C., Amirghasemi, M., Ulfsbacker, S.: An anthropomorphic method for number sequence problems. In: Cognitive Systems Research (in press, 2013), doi:10.1016/j.cogsys.2012.05.003

168. Sunehag, P., Hutter, M.: Principles of solomonoff induction and AIXI. In: Dowe, D.L. (ed.) Solomonoff Festschrift. LNCS (LNAI), vol. 7070, pp. 386–398. Springer, Heidelberg (2013)

169. Suzuki, J.: MDL/Bayesian criteria based on universal coding/Measure. In: Dowe, D.L. (ed.) Solomonoff Festschrift. LNCS (LNAI), vol. 7070, pp. 399–410. Springer, Heidelberg (2013)

170. Takahashi, H.: Algorithmic analogies to Kamae-Weiss theorem on normal numbers. In: Proceedings of Solomonoff 85th Memorial Conference. Springer (2013)

171. Tan, P.J., Dowe, D.L.: Decision forests with oblique decision trees. In: Gelbukh, A., Reyes-Garcia, C.A. (eds.) MICAI 2006. LNCS (LNAI), vol. 4293, pp. 593–603. Springer, Heidelberg (2006)

172. Turing, A.M.: On computable numbers, with an application to the Entscheidungsproblem. Proc. London Math. Soc. 2 42, 230–265 (1936)

173. Turing, A.M.: Computing machinery and intelligence. Mind 59, 433–460 (1950)

174. Ulam, S.: Tribute to John von Neumann. Bull. American Mathematical Soc. 64(3), 1–49 (1958)

175. Veness, J., Ng, K.S., Hutter, M., Uther, W., Silver, D.: A Monte-Carlo AIXI Approximation. J. Artificial Intelligence Research 40, 95–142 (2011)

176. Vinge, V.: Technological singularity. In: VISION-21 Symposium Sponsored by NASA Lewis Research Center and the Ohio Aerospace Institute, vol. 30, p. 31 (March 1993)

177. Visser, G., Dale, P.E.R., Dowe, D.L., Ndoen, E., Dale, M.B., Sipe, N.: A novel approach for modeling malaria incidence using complex categorical household data: The minimum message length (MML) method applied to Indonesian data. Computational Ecology and Software 2(3), 140–159 (2012)

178. Visser, G., Dowe, D.L.: Minimum message length clustering of spatially-correlated data with varying inter-class penalties. In: Proc. 6th IEEE International Conf. on Computer and Information Science (ICIS) 2007, pp. 17–22 (July 2007)

179. Visser, G., Dowe, D.L., Uotila, J.P.: Enhancing MML clustering using context data with climate applications. In: Nicholson, A., Li, X. (eds.) AI 2009. LNCS, vol. 5866, pp. 350–359. Springer, Heidelberg (2009)

180. Wallace, C.S.: Digital computers. In: Butler, S.T., Messel, H. (eds.) Atoms to Andromeda, pp. 215–245. Shakespeare-Head, Sydney (1966)

181. Wallace, C.S.: An improved program for classification. In: Proc. of the 9th Australian Computer Science Conference (ACSC-9), pp. 357–366 (February 1986); Published as Proc. of ACSC-9, vol. 8(1)

182. Wallace, C.S.: Classification by minimum-message-length encoding. In: Akl, S.G., Fiala, F., Koczkodaj, W.W. (eds.) Advances in Computing and Information - ICCI 1990. LNCS, vol. 468, pp. 72–81. Springer, Heidelberg (1990)

183. Wallace, C.S.: Classification by minimum-message-length inference. In: Working Notes AAAI Spring Symposium Series, Stanford Uni., Calif., U.S.A., pp. 65–69 (1990)

184. Wallace, C.S.: False oracles and SMML estimators. In: Dowe, D.L., Korb, K.B., Oliver, J.J. (eds.) Proceedings of the Information, Statistics and Induction in Science (ISIS) Conference, Melbourne, Australia, pp. 304–316. World Scientific (August 1996) ISBN 981-02-2824-4; Was previously Tech. Rept. 89/128, Dept. Comp. Sci., Monash Univ., Australia (June 1989)

185. Wallace, C.S.: Intrinsic classification of spatially correlated data. Computer Journal 41(8), 602–611 (1998)

186. Wallace, C.S.: The MIT Encyclopedia of the Cognitive Sciences (MITECS), chapter Minimum description length (major review), pp. 550–551. The MIT Press, London (1999) ISBN: 0-262-73124-X

187. Wallace, C.S.: Statistical and Inductive Inference by Minimum Message Length. Springer (May 2005)

188. Wallace, C.S., Boulton, D.M.: An information measure for classification. Computer J. 11(2), 185–194 (1968)

189. Wallace, C.S., Boulton, D.M.: An invariant Bayes method for point estimation. Classification Society Bulletin 3(3), 11–34 (1975)

190. Wallace, C.S., Dowe, D.L.: Intrinsic classification by MML - the Snob program. In: Proc. 7th Australian Joint Conf. on Artificial Intelligence, pp. 37–44. World Scientific (November 1994)

191. Wallace, C.S., Dowe, D.L.: Minimum message length and Kolmogorov complexity. Computer J. 42(4), 270–283 (1999)

192. Wallace, C.S., Dowe, D.L.: Refinements of MDL and MML coding. Computer Journal 42(4), 330–337 (1999)

193. Wallace, C.S., Dowe, D.L.: Rejoinder. Computer Journal 42(4), 345–347 (1999)

194. Wallace, C.S., Dowe, D.L.: MML clustering of multi-state, Poisson, von Mises circular and Gaussian distributions. Statistics and Computing 10, 73–83 (January 2000)

195. Wallace, C.S., Freeman, P.R.: Estimation and inference by compact coding. Journal of the Royal Statistical Society Series B 49(3), 240–252 (1987); See also Discussion on pp. 252-265

196. Wallace, C.S., Georgeff, M.P.: A general objective for inductive inference. Technical Report #83/32, Department of Computer Science, Monash University, Clayton, Australia, Reissued in June 1984 as TR No. 44 (March 1983)

197. Wallace, C.S., Patrick, J.D.: Coding decision trees. Machine Learning 11, 7–22 (1993)

198. Webb, G.I., Boughton, J., Zheng, F., Ting, K.M., Salem, H.: Learning by extrapolation from marginal to full-multivariate probability distributions: Decreasingly naive Bayesian classification. Machine Learning 86(2), 233–272 (2012)

199. Wei Xing, Croft, W.B.: LDA-based document models for ad-hoc retrieval. In: Proc. 29th ACM SIGIR Conference on Research and Development in Information Retrieval, SIGIR 2006, New York, NY, USA, pp. 178–185 (2006)

200. Wood, I., Sunehag, P., Hutter, M. (Non-)Equivalence of universal priors. In: Dowe, D.L. (ed.) Solomonoff Festschrift. LNCS (LNAI), vol. 7070, pp. 417–425. Springer, Heidelberg (2013)

201. Woodward, J., Swan, J.: A syntactic approach to prediction. In: Dowe, D.L. (ed.) Solomonoff Festschrift. LNCS (LNAI), vol. 7070, pp. 426–438. Springer, Heidelberg (2013)

Ray Solomonoff and the New Probability

Grace Solomonoff*

Oxbridge Research
Cambridge, Mass. 02140
trovaxo@yahoo.com
http://world.std.com/~rjs

Abstract. This is the story of Ray Solomonoff's Life and Times. He was there at Dartmouth in 1956 when Artificial Intelligence was first given its name, and took part in the major events during this unique era right up to his death in 2009. His invention in 1960 of Algorithmic Probability, with its multiple descriptions of data, led to better ways of handling data and prediction for machine learning. The theorems that are part of his discovery lie at the heart of Algorithmic Information Theory. Ray championed probability in AI during the decades it was unpopular and lived to see a renaissance in systems that learn and reason using probability. The story of his life is the story of a great adventure.

Keywords: Solomonoff, Artificial Intelligence, Algorithmic Probability, Algorithmic Information Theory, Inductive Inference, Kolmogorov Complexity.

1 Introduction

This is the story of Ray Solomonoff's life, beginning with the immigration of his parents from Russia to the U.S. in the early 1900's and Ray's birth in 1926. There was a cheerful dedication in Ray's life: from his childhood enthusiasm for math and science, to his contribution in 1956 to the birth of Artificial Intelligence, his invention of a new probability and his participation in major events during this unique era right up to his death in 2009. His greatest achievement was the invention of Algorithmic Probability. His vision of probability and machines that think will be part of our future.

2 Early Years

Ray's mother, Sarah Mashman, was born in Sevastopol, a port city in Ukraine, located on the Black Sea coast of the Crimea peninsula. She graduated from high school in 1911.

---

* Thanks to Donald Rosenthal and Julie Sussman for their invaluable help. Some of this report appeared in (open sources) Algorithms, 3(3), 2010, and Oxbridge Research. Thanks to Oxbridge Research (open source), Marcus Hutter, Henry Tirri, Juergen Schmidhuber, Alex Solomonoff for permission to reprint pictures.

D.L. Dowe (Ed.): Solomonoff Festschrift, LNAI 7070, pp. 37–52, 2013.

Before the Russian Revolution of 1917 there was a part of Russia called the Pale of Settlement: It included present-day Poland, Lithuania, the Crimea and the Ukraine. Jewish people were restricted to that area.

During around 1890-1910, the Czarist government was coming apart and blaming it on the Jews, and anti-Jewish persecution was particularly intense at this time. About 1/3 or 1/2 of all the Jews in Russia emigrated, mostly to the U.S. Ray's parents were part of this wave.

Sevastopol, a wealthy city, was exempt from the Ukrainian Pale. Only the fact that Sarah's father was the local blacksmith, with specialized knowledge, enabled his family to live there. Sarah immigrated to New York about three years after high school. She got a job as a nurse's aide, and on the side began an amateur career of acting.

Rays father, Phillip Julius Solomonoff, would never tell where he was from, but Vilna (in Lithuania) is on his passport. He got inspired with revolutionary fervor and in 1917 when the Russian revolution started, he and cousin Esoc went to "visit revolution." They returned soon after discovering that the shooting was with real bullets.

Julius joined a Polish ship, and made his way to the U.S., where he jumped ship and ended up in New York. Julius was an illegal alien all his life. But he studied at Cooper Union in New York City to be a plumber and was first in his class. He met Sarah, and they lived in New York, where in 1922 their first son George was born. In 1924 they moved to Cleveland, Ohio, a Midwest city, called the largest small town in the U.S.

And Ray was born July 25, 1926.

Pictures: 1. Ray and his father. 2. Ray with his brother George. Ray is on the left, already with his penetrating gaze. 3. The obligatory picture of Ray on a horsie.

Ray grew up during the depression. His father was a mechanic but his work never paid enough to cover the rent. His parents had to move frequently, which was a trauma to them; but Ray and George thought it was great — they got to meet new kids, have new adventures.

When they finally settled down. Ray built a lab in his parents' cellar. To vent the smoke from his experiments, he drilled a hole through the wall behind some bushes. His parents never found it, and it remained unseen when the house was sold and was there until the day the place was torn down, around 1998. But his parents were really tolerant anyway. Sarah once described sweeping the rug and hearing a multitude of tiny explosions from some grains of something scattered about from a experiment gone awry.

In later life Ray made quite a few inventions, for friends or home use. For example he made a Hurry clock for Marvin Minsky — a clock that was labeled "Hurry"; he removed a gear so it ran very fast — I guess you'd know you were always late.

But his greatest pleasure was in theories and discovery

He wrote "I first experienced the pure joy of mathematical discovery when I was very young — learning algebra. I didn't really see why one of the axioms was 'obvious', so I tried reversing it and exploring the resultant system. For a few hours I was in this wonderful never-never land that I myself had created! The joy of exploring it only lasted until it became clear that my new axiom wouldn't work, but the motivation of the joy of discovery continued for the rest of my life."

"The motivation for the discovery of Algorithmic Probability was somewhat different. It was the result of 'motivated discovery' — like the discovery of the double helix in biology, but with fewer people involved and relatively little political skullduggery. The goal I set grew out of my early interest in science and mathematics. I found that while the discoveries of the past were interesting to me, I was even more interested in how people discovered things. Was there a general technique to solve all mathematical problems? Was there a general method by which scientists could discover all scientific truths?" [18]

And so by 1942, around the age of 16, Ray became captivated by the idea of finding a general technique to solve all problems. He felt already that scientists used probability in induction when they invented theories to account for data. This was when he first began to study induction. Even at this age, probability was part of his thinking.

He organized notebooks using key letters: TM meant Thinking Machine. His later notes all use key letters such as ALP for Algorithmic Probability, TS for Training Sequences, even HR for horse racing.

He went to Glenville High School, noted for its famous graduates. After graduation there was a hiatus in his studies, for World War II intervened. The draft began in 1940, and in November 1944 Ray joined the Navy to train in and then teach radio and was stationed in Gulfport, Mississippi.

After the war, in 1946 he went to the University of Chicago on the GI bill. The University was at its height: Enrico Fermi, Rudolf Carnap, Nicolas Rashevsky, Anatole Rapoport were among Ray's teachers.

3   From the University to the Birth of AI

In 1950 in a letter Ray writes "for the last 4 or 5 years cybernetics has been my chief scientific interest" ... "about a month and a half ago I worked out a method of devising a machine that would 'think'." But "the bubble broke. One found that the machine wouldn't work as well as expected" ... "But it was all a very wonderful adventure — somewhat disturbing at times, but nonetheless wonderful." At that time he also tried to get together a group of scientists interested in thinking machines, but did not succeed. By then Ray was convinced that thinking machines were feasible (the name Artificial Intelligence did not yet exist).

Claude Shannon's paper in 1948, and subsequent developments in information theory over the next few years, greatly influenced Ray during college. Shannon thought that information was something that could be quantified and that the quantity of information was related to its probability.

Rudolf Carnap was Ray's professor of Philosophy and Probability. Carnap was a "logical positivist." He felt that logical syntax should provide a system of concepts, a language, by the help of which the results of logical analysis would be exactly formulable. Problems, such as what language to use, presented too many difficulties to be successful, but the idea of combining language, information and probability was part of what led to Ray's discovery.

Ray studied mathematical biology with Rapoport and Rashevsky. His first published reports were three papers on neural nets, two with Anatole Rapoport in 1950-52, that are regarded as the earliest statistical analysis of networks.

Here are some of the items Ray was reading during college:

"Foundations of the Theory of Probability" (Kolmogorov); "Experience and Prediction" (Reichenbach); "Journal of Applied Physics"; "The Impact of Science on Society" (Russell)...

Here are some more of the items Ray was reading during college:

"Astounding Science Fiction"; "Thrilling Wonder Stories"; "Operation Fantast"; "Flash Gordon"...

Actually he was quite influenced by science fiction. His favorite movie was 'The Shape of Things to Come', that tells of a visionary people who would save a dying world through technology.

In the 40's and 50's Science Fiction also represented something that was happening in the U.S., and in Europe also, a view that amazing things were possible through technology. The government began sponsoring projects that used information technology.

Meanwhile, the computer was rapidly becoming important. In 1941 the electronic computer had been introduced to the public. Ray was fascinated by them. Later, in the early 1970's Ray even built a computer, hand-wired it — sort of tapestry-like.

These were some of the early inventions and ideas that influenced Ray.

Pictures: 1. A family portrait when Ray was in high school (Ray on the left). 2. Ray in the Navy. 3. The computer that Ray made.

4   The Beginnings of AI

After college, Ray got a job in New York, working at Technical Research Group. He met Marvin Minsky at a conference. Minsky and Ray became lifelong close friends, and Ray often visited Cambridge, Massachusetts, where Minsky lived.

This was when Minsky and John McCarthy introduced him to another great idea: The Turing machine. It was a revelation.

The Turing machine was a concept of Alan Turing's, a British mathematician who lived 1912-1954. In 1936 Turing described a "universal computing machine" that could theoretically be programmed to solve any problem capable of solution by a specially designed machine. The "Turing machine" foreshadowed the digital computer.

Consider a computer as a finite state machine operating on a finite symbol set. A program tape on which a binary program is written feeds from left to right into the machine. The machine looks at the tape, changes its state according to the program, writes some output, and then gets the next part of the tape. A special Turing machine, the universal Turing machine, has an infinite memory, an input tape that goes only one way, and a work tape — this machine could mimic any other computer.

Ray wrote "It gave me a quick intuitive grasp of many ideas that I had before found incomprehensible. It is not unusual for the translation of a problem into a new language to have this wonderful effect." [18]

In Cambridge, Ray had frequent discussions with Marvin Minsky and John McCarthy and others about thinking, mathematics and machines. Then in 1956 John McCarthy organized a little group to brainstorm on machine intelligence. They picked Dartmouth, New Hampshire for their venue. The principal participants would include John, Ray, Marvin, Tenchard More, Alan Newell, Herb Simon, and 4 other researchers.

McCarthy decided to give this new science a name: And so in the summer of 1956, the science named Artificial Intelligence was born.

The idea was that the 10 participants would brainstorm during 2 months at Dartmouth, and then in 10 months would come up together with some Great AI Idea. Oh sure! You have 10 mad scientists with 10 totally different orientations toward AI. What do you get? (10 totally different Great AI Ideas.)

From most of these ideas came logic-based, deterministic programs. Ray presented a paper on how machines could be made to improve themselves, by using unsupervised learning from examples. This paper was not probabilistic, but was new in that it replaced semantic with symbolic representation.

In 2010 Marvin wrote me: "In the early 1950's I developed many theories about ways to make neural networks learn — but none of these seemed likely to lead to high-level kinds of idea. But once Ray showed me his early ideas about symbolic 'inductive inference scheme', these completely replaced my older approach. So Ray's ideas provided the start of many, later, steps toward Artificial Intelligence."

The first question in Ray's outline for work in Thinking Machines at the Dartmouth Summer was "What is Probability?" Ray advocated a probabilistic approach to machine intelligence at this first meeting on AI in 1956, and continued to push on this dream for decades when such a view was controversial.

The Dartmouth Summer had difficulties; the Ford Foundation gave less funding than McCarthy hoped for, and some of the attendees spent little time there.

Of the programs from that summer, the most well known is Newell and Simon's Logical Theorist, and soon after that, their General Problem Solver. Their focus, as was that of McCarthy, was logic based and highly specialized. This led to "expert system" programs — for example, aids to medical diagnosis, or minerals prospecting. Really at this point there came a schism between the specialized, deterministic and the more generalized kinds of programs. The more rigidly logical projects were immediately applicable, and so AI became known by these programs. Probabilistic based programs were largely ignored. They were not well integrated into the world of computing, while logic based programs were ideal for "if-then" and "do loops".

5   The Discovery of Algorithmic Probability

Calvin Mooers was an attendee at the MIT Information Theory Symposium in September 1956. Ray's paper from the Dartmouth Summer Project, "An Inductive Inference Machine," was circulated there. Calvin liked Ray's ideas and invited him to come work with him in information retrieval. He got the perfect government contract for Ray to work with him. In creating his proposal he wrote Ray: "There seems to be developing a good possibility that would permit me to put you to work on doing long-range thinking on 'inductive inference machines' and whatever else they may touch upon. This would be a program of purely speculative thinking, and I would set up the support so *that* is understood. While the money would come from an interest in information retrieval, I would want the thinking untrammeled, and my thesis is that what you are doing, and what I am doing in information retrieval, have a common meeting ground that will develop in due time." And he got the grant! Don't you wish you got a grant like that!

Ray received government funding during the next few years. He never would again.

So Ray moved up to Cambridge, to work full time on his ideas about induction and machine intelligence.

Here he is at Marvin's house — and here — his thinking is pretty untrammeled...

Over the next few years Ray worked on machine intelligence, programming computers, use of the Turing machine, and coding methods. He still didn't have a really good way of combining them.

Ray had met Noam Chomsky in the mid 50's and read Chomsky's works on context-free language. Ray realized this language could be a basis for solving Carnap's problem. Working at Calvin's Zator Company, Ray expanded this language into a stochastic form for all types of patterns: it was a probabilistic language. Normally one thinks of a language where either something is a sentence or is not a sentence. In a probabilistic language something has a probability of being a sentence. This provided the breakthrough he needed.

Using the Universal Turing Machine as the operator, Ray established that the generator of these patterns could be put in a binary, probabilistic form; the grammar of this language was somewhat like descriptions where simple descriptions were more likely than complex ones. He called this Algorithmic Probability, and he used it in a General Theory of Inductive Inference. In this discovery, in 1960, Ray became a founder of Algorithmic Information Theory.[21]

Prior to this discovery, the usual method of calculating probability was based on frequency: take the ratio of favorable results to the total number of trials. Ray seriously revised this definition of probability. Algorithmic Probability is based on the length of random programs (algorithms) input into a universal Turing machine that produce a given sequence of symbols as output — the shorter programs being most likely.

His paper, "A Preliminary Report on a General Theory of Inductive Inference" is his first known publication of Algorithmic Probability and was published by Calvin's company in February 1960,[10] with a revision in November 1960.

[11] He published a more complete exposition in two 1964 papers for the Journal of Information and Control.[12],[13]

In a letter in 2011, Marcus Hutter wrote: "Ray Solomonoff's universal probability distribution M(x) is defined as the probability that the output of a universal monotone Turing machine U starts with string x when provided with fair coin flips on the input tape. Despite this simple definition, it has truly remarkable properties, and constitutes a universal solution of the induction problem." (See also [7])

Algorithmic Probability combines several major ideas; of these, two might be considered more philosophical and two more mathematical.

The first is related to the idea of Occam's Razor: the simplest theory is the best. Ray's 1960 paper states "We shall consider a sequence of symbols to be 'simple' and have high a priori probability if there exists a very brief description of this sequence — using of course some stipulated description method. More exactly, if we use only the symbols 0 or 1 to express our description, we will assign the probability of 2^{-N} to a sequence of symbols, if its shortest possible binary description contains N digits." [11][10]

The second idea is similar to that of Epicurus: it is an expansion on the shortest code theory; if more than one theory explains the data, keep all of the theories. Ray writes "Equation 1 uses only the 'minimal binary description' of the sequence it analyzes. It would seem that if there are several different methods of describing a sequence, each of these methods should be given *some* weight in determining the probability of that sequence." [11][10]

$$P(x)_M = \sum_{i=1}^{\infty} 2^{-|s_i(x)|}$$

This is the formula he developed to give each possible explanation the right weight. (The probability of sequence x with respect to Turing Machine M is the total sum of 2 to the minus length of each string s that produces an output that begins with x.)

Closely related is the third idea of its use in a Bayesian framework. The universal prior is taken over the class of all computable measures; no hypothesis will have a zero probability. Using program lengths of all programs that could produce a particular start of the string, x, Ray gets the prior distribution for x, used in Bayes rule for accurate probabilities to predict what is most likely to come next as the start is extrapolated. The Universal Probability Distribution functions by its sum to define the probability of a sequence, and by using the weight of individual programs to give a figure of merit to each program that could produce the sequence. [11][12]

The fourth idea shows that the choice of machine, while it could add a constant factor, would not change the probability ratios very much. These probabilities are machine independent; this is the invariance theorem that is considered a foundation of Algorithmic Information Theory.[11][13]

Here is another beautiful picture of this formula in a little different format: The photoshopped picture is by Marcus Hutter, using a photo by Jürgen Schmidhuber.

In 1965 the great Russian mathematician Andrey Kolmogorov published the first idea (simplicity) and fourth idea (machine independence) in the journal Problems of Information Transmission.[4] Kolmogorov had also been working with Turing machines, and had been giving lectures at Moscow University on the subject of complexity. Like Ray, he revised the frequentist view of probability. He wrote "The basic discovery, which I have accomplished independently from and simultaneously with R. Solomonoff, lies in the fact that the theory of algorithms enables us to eliminate this arbitrariness by the determination of a 'complexity' which is almost invariant (the replacement of one method by another leads only to the supplement of the bounded term)."[21]

Paul Vitányi writes that Kolmogorov's introduction of complexity "was motivated by information theory and problems of randomness. Solomonoff introduced algorithmic complexity independently and earlier and for a different reason: inductive reasoning. Universal a priori probability, in the sense of a single prior probability that can be substituted for each actual prior probability in Bayes's rule was invented by Solomonoff with Kolmogorov complexity as a side product, several years before anybody else did."[21]

Vitányi notes: "we will associate Solomonoff's name with the universal distribution, and Kolmogorov's name with the descriptional complexity."[6] Kolmogorov was interested in the information content of a string, while Ray was interested in the predictive power of a string.

With respect to thinking machines: If a machine is working on a set of problems, the algorithm it uses may only work for some problems. If you can use probability in the best possible way to estimate how likely each one in a whole set of algorithms is, then if one program (algorithm) doesn't work, you have a good method, a probabilistic way, to search for another.

Ray's ideas were ahead of his time, especially here in America. He gave some lectures at local universities. Often students didn't know what he was talking about (he wasn't too good at explaining this stuff anyway!). Students would fall asleep or quietly escape out the side door.

Never mind; meanwhile he bought some land in New Hampshire and built a house. Since he didn't know anything about building a house, he got a book. He built the house as a cube, since that was easiest. He had real sloping roof, to let the snow off.

He didn't know about heating, but he knew about electric light bulbs, and in those days a light bulb was 80% heat and only 20% light, so he heated the house with light bulbs. His friend Al Jenks told me recently that Al would bring his friends over, ostensibly to meet Ray, but actually to show them that Ray really did heat his house entirely with light bulbs — two long rows along the ceiling from wall to wall.

Pictures: 1. the house. 2: house decor. 3. A later picture by Alex Solomonoff of Ray working on the house.

It had no windows, but you could pull out long sections of the wall from floor to roof and put in screens during the summer.

And it was shortly after he finished the house that he met...ME.

Pictures: 1. My baby picture. 2. A few years after meeting Ray. 3. Ray, a few years before meeting me.

In 1969, I met Ray at a party at a friend's house. We often went to the house Ray built in New Hampshire.

I wrote poetry and saw that good poems often have good metaphors. A metaphor is an alternate description of something; it helps you see in a different way. The goal is to make the subject of the poem meaningful or beautiful. When Ray told me what he was doing, just like those students, I didn't know what he was talking about, but his multiple theories and multiple descriptions seemed like a mathematical analogue to poetry. It felt like we were on some kind of similar adventure. But even if our goals had been different, we shared interests and feelings — our life has been this way forever.

We had an apartment in Harvard Square, Cambridge, which we kept through the 90's. Harvard Square was where you met everybody as you wandered around with your backpack. We were there during the Vietnam War protests. From the building roof we watched the Weathermen break bank windows. We were there during the days of the flower children. Ray was a friend of the poet Allen Ginsberg. Whenever we were at Ginsberg's poetry readings he would hand Ray his watch to monitor the time.

Our apartment had a lot of stuff: electronics and computer "toys" and building materials; but mainly our apartment had books — stacks and stacks of papers and books. All the walls had bookshelves, even the ceiling had bookshelves hanging from it across the hallway.

Ray read voraciously about all kinds of things, but was focused on his prediction theory, talking to others, often at the AI Lab at MIT. It was a very exciting time.

In 1970 since the military had stopped funding civilian science, Ray formed his own one-man company, "Oxbridge Research," an extremely eclectic organization.

On the right, a portrait of Ray in 1984. On the left, a portrait of Ray in Oxbridge Research's Chemical Experimentation Lab, making our most important invention: the liquid helium zonk. The zonks are a whole class of drinks. One example: take a banana, two kinds of rum, lemon and honey and blend them in a blender, then freeze into a subzero mush. Other inventions were the pickled herring cocktail and studies of the brightness of various drinks with mixes that fluoresced in ultraviolet light.

In 1975 Chaitin, who had developed a version of descriptional (Kolmogorov) complexity later in the 1960's, wrote about complexity in the Scientific American. In 1978 Leonid Levin and Peter Gács came to America and were very supportive and interested in Ray's probability theory.

6   The Guerrilla Workshop

However — the dominant researchers used deductive, logic-based methods; deterministic expert systems were the popular products of AI. Many scientists felt uncertainty just wouldn't work in this field. The turning point, at least in the U.S.— was in 1985.

The first workshop on Uncertainty in AI (UAI) was in 1985. How did it happen? The program note was sort of like the Declaration of Independence.

It says: "This workshop came about as a result of a panel discussion at the AAAI conference at Austin, Texas, U.S., in 1984. This panel was on the problem of the representation of uncertainty in Artificial intelligence." ... "Some speakers implied that more than one number was necessary to represent uncertainty, while others stated that numbers should not be used at all! Except for a valiant rearguard defense by Judea Pearl, everyone on the panel agreed that probability as a representation of uncertainty either was misguided or inadequate for the task. Several of us who have been using probability within AI, as well as engineers and physicists, know this conclusion to be false, and our outrage at this denigrating of probability was the spur that triggered this workshop."

This workshop has continued ever since, and was a starting point that led to a revolution in mainstream AI. It is now the annual Conference in Uncertainty in AI (UAI), hosted by AAAI. For this workshop Ray gave a paper on how to apply the universal distribution to problems in AI: the best order of searching for solutions is $T1/P1$, where $T1$ is the time needed to test the trial and $P1$ the probability of success of that trial — the shorter codes getting the higher probability. This is based on the search technique invented by Leonid Levin,[5] so Ray called it Lsearch.

I remember that first meeting: Ray called it a guerrilla workshop. But it marked an acceptance of many aspects of probability by mainstream AI. There still is conflict in AI circles over the use of probability. But the logic and probabilistic reasoning are moving closer. For example, I believe John McCarthy shifted his focus from deductive logic in his development of what he calls 'circumscription', which is more probabilistic. Things like fuzzy logic and Bayesian work lie in the probabilistic area.

Ray inspired many people, especially young people. Our nephew Alex would visit from Cleveland. He says "There was nothing like this for me in Cleveland. Ray talked about mathematics in a way that made it exciting." Ray influenced him to get his Ph.D. in mathematics, and we have remained close to Alex ever since.

Pictures: 1. Alex's Ph.D. graduation, May 1992. 2. Ray, me, our niece Nickie, and Alex in 2007.

7   Later Work

Ray spent the rest of his life discovering, proving aspects, refining and enlarging his General Theory of Inductive Inference, with the goal of having machines that could solve hard problems. He stressed that machine intelligence did not need to emulate human intelligence, and probably that it would not.

He wrote about the problem of incomputability. His quotable quote: "Incomputability — it's not a bug, it's a feature!" Systems that are computable will not be complete. The incomputability is because some algorithms can never be evaluated because it would take too long. But these programs will at least be recognized as possible solutions. On the other hand, any computable system is incomplete. There will always be descriptions outside that system's search space which will never be acknowledged or considered, even in an infinite amount of time. Computable predictions models hide this fact by ignoring such algorithms. Minimum Description Length, for example, first cuts out some space and then chooses the shortest program. Minimum Message Length of Chris Wallace does acknowledge incomputability; it is closer to Algorithmic Probability.[22][23] It chooses only the shortest code to work with, however, while Algorithmic Probability uses as many as there is time for.

In other papers Ray wrote about how best to limit search by limits on time or computation cost. He developed methods for working with other types of data, not just sequences. He categorized problems into various types such as "inversion problems" and "time-limited optimization problems" and developed ways of dealing with the different types.

Throughout his career Ray was concerned with the potential benefits and dangers of AI, discussing it in many of his published reports. In 1985 he analyzed a likely evolution of AI, giving a formula predicting when it would reach the "Infinity Point." This Infinity Point is an early version of the "Singularity" later made popular by Ray Kurzweil.[16]

During most of his life, Ray worked independently, developing his theories without any academic or industrial support. Paul Vitányi notes "it is unusual to find a productive major scientist that is not regularly employed at all."

However, he would meet frequently with Minsky, Shannon, and others at MIT, and with other researchers throughout the world. We went to many countries and conferences meeting amazing and dedicated people. There was Saarland University in Saarbrücken, Germany, where Wolfgang Paul invited Ray to do research in 1990-1991. There was the ISIS conference in Australia in 1996; after it the indefatigable David Dowe drove us for miles along the Great Ocean Road and we explored the ancient and beautiful rain forest there. Later we stayed with Paul Vitányi, who traveled with us by bus and car, and then we visited other areas. When Ray was a little boy, he thought about being a naturalist; Dr. Doolittle was one of his favorite books. How could he not be entranced by seeing Cassowaries? There was his visiting professorship at the Dalle Molle Institute for Artificial Intelligence in Lugano, Switzerland, run by Jürgen Schmidhuber. The researchers at that Institute were so cohesive. We had community meals — memorable spaghetti dinners with coffee from their super espresso machine. There was our visit, in 1998, to the dynamic Computer Research Learning Center, at Royal Holloway, University of London, which Alex Gammerman had just founded. Later Ray gave the first Kolmogorov lecture there, receiving the Kolmogorov Award. Ray was a visiting professor there until his death.

Here are some pictures from over the years:

Pictures: 1. Ming Li, his wife Jessie Zou, Ray and me, maybe in the 1990's. 2. and 3. Pictures by Jürgen Schmidhuber and Henry Tirri. at NIPS Workshop on Universal Learning Algorithms and Optimal Search, 2002.

Ray was happy when the AGI08 conference occurred; this was first of the AGI conferences focused on Artificial General Intelligence, moving as far away as possible from narrowly focused and highly specialized programs.

Eric Horvitz, for many years the President of AAAI, notes Ray "advocated the probabilistic approach to machine intelligence at the first meeting on AI in 1956, continued to push on this dream for decades when such a view was controversial, and lived to see a renaissance in systems that learn and reason under uncertainty, relying on representations of probability — a perspective that is now at the foundation of modern AI research."

But of all his productive life, his greatest invention is Algorithmic Probability and his General Theory of Inductive Inference.

Leonid Levin wrote that Ray "had a very powerful and general approach. In the future, his ideas will have more influence."

And his whole life Ray did what he loved doing. Vitányi notes "But from all the elder people (not only scientists) I know, Ray Solomonoff was the happiest, the most inquisitive, and the most satisfied. He continued publishing papers right up to his death at 83."[3]

Ray enjoyed life up to the end, organizing a gorgeous costume for Halloween at the end of October; and also continued with his serious side, his work on Algorithmic Probability and prediction, completing a paper for AGI 10, in late November 2009, just before he died.

In his last paper, for AGI10, Ray discussed what he called "The Guiding Probability Distribution" — a nice updating method, and a name that seems to me like something that was guiding him too. So he had a long happy life, which is something to celebrate. And even more than that, he had a shining vision he followed for his whole life, and it guided him right to the very end.

References

1. Carnap, R.: Logical Foundations of Probability (1950)
2. Chomsky, A.N.: Three models for the description of language. IRE Transactions on Information Theory, IT-2(3), 113–124 (1956)
3. Gács, P., Vitányi, P.: Raymond J. Solomonoff 1926 – 2009. IEEE Information Theory Society Newsletter 61(11) (March 2011)
4. Kolmogorov, A.N.: Three approaches to the quantitative definition of information. Problems of Information Transmission 1(1), 1–7 (1965)
5. Levin, L.A.: Universal search problems. Problemy Peredaci Informacii (9), 115–116 (1973); Translated in Problems of Information Transmission 9, 265–266
6. Li, M., Vitányi, P.: An Introduction to Kolmogorov Complexity and Its Applications, 3rd edn. Springer, N.Y. (2008)
7. Rathmanner, S., Hutter, M.: A philosophical treatise of universal induction. Entropy (13), 1076–1136 (2011)

8. Shannon, C.E.: The mathematical theory of communication. Bell System Technical Journal (27), 379–423, 623–656 (1948)

9. Solomonoff, R.J.: An inductive inference machine. Dartmouth Summer Research Project on Artificial Intelligence (August 1956); A privately circulated report

10. Solomonoff, R.J.: A preliminary report on a general theory of inductive inference. Technical Report V-131, Zator Co. and Air Force Office of Scientific Research, Cambridge, Mass. (February 1960)

11. Solomonoff, R.J.: A preliminary report on a general theory of inductive inference (revision of Report V-131). Technical Report ZTB-138, Zator Co. and Air Force Office of Scientific Research, Cambridge, Mass. (November 1960)

12. Solomonoff, R.J.: A formal theory of inductive inference: Part I. Information and Control 7(1), 1–22 (1964)

13. Solomonoff, R.J.: A formal theory of inductive inference: Part II. Information and Control 7(2), 224–254 (1964)

14. Solomonoff, R.J.: Inductive inference theory - a unified approach to problems in pattern recognition and artificial intelligence. In: Proceedings of the Fourth International Joint Conference on Artificial Intelligence, Tbilisi, Georgia, U.S.S.R., vol. 1, pp. 274–280 (September 1975)

15. Solomonoff, R.J.: Complexity-based induction systems: Comparisons and convergence theorems. IEEE Transactions on Information Theory, IT-24(4), 422–432 (1978)

16. Solomonoff, R.J.: The time scale of artificial intelligence; reflections on social effects. Human Systems Management 5, 149–153 (1985)

17. Solomonoff, R.J.: The application of algorithmic probability to problems in artificial intelligence. In: Kanal, L.N., Lemmer, J.F. (eds.) Uncertainty in Artificial Intelligence, pp. 473–491. Elsevier Science Publishers, B.V., B.V (1986); Kochen, M., Hastings, H.M. (eds.) Advances in Cognitive Science. AAAS Selected Symposia Series, pp. 210–227. AAAS, Washington, D.C (1988)

18. Solomonoff, R.J.: The discovery of algorithmic probability. Journal of Computer and System Sciences 55(1), 73–88 (1997)

19. Solomonoff, R.J.: Three kinds of probabilistic induction: Universal distributions and convergence theorems. The Computer Journal 51(5), 566–570 (2008); Christopher Stewart Wallace (1933-2004) Memorial Special issue

20. Turing, A.M.: On computable numbers, with an application to the entsheidungsproblem. Proc. London Math. Soc. 42, 230–265 (1937)

21. Vitányi, P.: Obituary: Ray Solomonoff, founding father of algorithmic information theory. CWI, Amsterdam (2009)

22. Wallace, C.S., Boulton, D.M.: An information measure for classification. The Computer Journal 11, 185–194 (1968)

23. Wallace, C.S., Dowe, D.L.: Minimum message length and Kolmogorov complexity. Computer Journal 42(4), 270–283 (1999); Special Issue on Kolmogorov Complexity

Universal Heuristics: How Do Humans Solve "Unsolvable" Problems?

Leonid A. Levin[*]

Computer Science Department, Boston University, 111 Cummington St.,
Boston, MA 02215, USA

Abstract. Lots of crucial problems defeat current computer arts but yield to our brains.

A great many of them can be put in the form of inverting easily computable functions. Still other problems, such as extrapolation, are related to this form. We have no idea which difficulties are intrinsic to these problems and which just reflect our ignorance. We will remain puzzled pending major foundational advances such as, e.g., on P=?NP.

And yet, traveling salesmen do get to their destinations, mathematicians do find proofs of their theorems, and physicists do find patterns in transformations of their elementary particles! How is this done, and how could computers emulate their success?

Brains of insects solve problems of such complexity and with such efficiency, as we cannot dream of. Yet, few of us would be flattered with a comparison to the brain of an insect :-). What advantage do we, humans, have? One is the ability to solve new problems, those on which evolution did not train generations of our ancestors. We must have some pretty universal methods, not restricted to the specifics of focused problems. Of course, it is hard to tell how, say, the mathematicians search for their proofs. Yet, the diversity and dynamism of math achievements suggest that some pretty universal methods must be at work.

In fact, whatever the difficulty of inverting functions $x=f(y)$ is, we know a "theoretically" optimal algorithm for all such problems, one that cannot be sped-up[1] by more than a constant factor, even on a subset of instances x. It searches for solutions y, but in order of increasing complexity $\mathbf{Kt}$, not increasing length: short solutions may be much harder to find than long ones. $\mathbf{Kt}(y|x)$ can be defined as the minimal sum of (1) the bit-length of a prefixless program p transforming x into y and (2) the log of the running time of p.[2]

Extrapolations could be done by double-use of this concept. The likelihood of a given extrapolation consistent with known data decreases exponentially

---

[*] Supported by NSF grant CCF-1049505.
[1] The speed is defined to include the time for running f on the solution y to check it.
[2] Realistically, p runs on data which specify the instance, but also encompass other available relevant information, possibly including access to a huge database, such as a library, or even the Internet.

D.L. Dowe (Ed.): Solomonoff Festschrift, LNAI 7070, pp. 53–54, 2013.

with the length of its shortest description. This principle, known as Occam's Razor, was clarified in papers by Ray Solomonoff and his followers (see also http://arxiv.org/abs/1107.1458v5 and its references).

Decoding short descriptions should not take more time than the complexity of the process that generated the data. The major hurdle in implementing Occam's Razor is finding short descriptions: it may be exponentially hard. Yet, this is an inversion problem, and the above optimal search applies. Such approaches contrast with the methods employed currently by CS - universal algorithms are used heavily, but mostly for negative results.

The point of this note is to emphasize the following problem:
The above methods are optimal only up to constant factors. Nothing is known about these factors, and simplistic attempts make them completely unreasonable. Current theory cannot even answer straight questions, such as, e.g., is it true that some such optimal algorithm cannot be sped-up 10-fold on infinitely many instances? Yet humans do seem to use such generic methods successfully, raising hopes for a reasonable approach to these factors.

Partial Match Distance
In Memoriam Ray Solomonoff 1926-2009

Ming Li

School of Computer Science, University of Waterloo,
Waterloo, Ont. N2L 3G1, Canada
mli@uwaterloo.ca
http://www.cs.uwaterloo.ca/~mli

Abstract. In this expository article, we discuss a complementary notion of information distance for partial matches. Information Distance $D_{\max}(x,y) = \max\{K(x|y), K(y|x)\}$ measures the distance between two objects by the minimum number of bits that are needed to convert them to each other. However, in many applications, often some objects contain too much irrelevant information which overwhelms the relevant information we are interested in. Information distance based on partial information also should not satisfy the triangle inequality. To deal with such problems, we have introduced an information distance for partial matching. It turns out the new notion is precisely $D_{\min}(x,y) = \min\{K(x|y), K(y|x)\}$, complementary to the $D_{\max}$ distance. I will give some recent applications of the $D_{\min}$ distance.

1 Introduction

We are here to celebrate the 85th birthday of our dear friend Ray Solomonoff, poshumously. The photo in Figure 1 was taken over 10 years ago in front of Ray and Grace's home, in Summerville, Massachusetts. Two people in the picture have already left us: Grace's husband Ray and my wife Jessie. During that visit, my wife was very impressed with Ray's adventurous spirit of experimenting things. This photo reminds me of the quick process of randomization of a human life and thus we should only do research that matters. Ray did just that.

In the 1960s, Solomonoff [31, 32], Kolmogorov [14], and Chaitin [4] independently introduced what we call today Kolmogorov complexity. Ray's work was several years before the other two inventors. The fact that the field was named after Kolmogorov is perhaps unfair to Ray, but he has never really complained to us [21]. A relevant theory of message length was introduced by Boulton and Wallace in 1968; see [37]. If Kolmogorov complexity may be seen as about information in one string, then in the 1990s, we [2] have defined Information Distance to measure the amount of information needed to convert between two strings. The Information Distance between strings x and y is

$$D_{\max} = \max\{K(x|y), K(y|x)\},$$

D.L. Dowe (Ed.): Solomonoff Festschrift, LNAI 7070, pp. 55–64, 2013.

Fig. 1. Right: Grace, Ray. Left: Jessie and Ming

where $K(x|y)$ is the Kolmogorov complexity of x condition on y. This work has motivated active theoretical investigations in [6, 22, 23, 30, 35, 36]. Started in [3, 18], this notion has also been applied to many applications in [1, 5, 7–10, 12, 13, 15–17, 19, 24–29, 33]. A more complete list of practical applications and theoretical investigations of Information Distance can be found in the 3rd edition our our book [21].

Despite of its wonderful theoretical properties such as universality and the abovementioned applications, Information Distance cannot deal with applications with overwhelming irrelevant information. This article intends to discuss an extension of the $D_{\max}$ distance to solve the partial matching problem and describe some practical applications, as reported in [38–40]. This is an informal expository article, instead of an original research publication. Especially, the work of [38] is underway and it will be reported in full elsewhere.

2 Partial Matching

The theoretical universality of $D_{\max}$ did not imply that it can be universally applied in practical applications. The reason mainly comes from partial matching where the triangle inequality does not hold. Fagin and Stockmeyer gave one such example [11]. As Veltkamp puts it [34]: under partial matching, the distance between a man and a horse is larger than the sum of the distances between a man and a centaur, Figure 2, and between a centaur and a horse.

Fig. 2. A centaur

Perhaps this is because we pay more attention to things that are similar, as they cannot happen by coincidence, and we ignore the differences.

When you met a stranger, and discovered that you were from the same high school, didn't you suddenly feel you were much closer to the stranger? When you went to the first date, didn't you try to come up with some topic that would bring the two of you closer? In the academic world, this phenomenon is reflected by the "Erdös number". We all feel closely related via a third person Paul Erdös. All these are cases of partial matching in our daily lives. Next we give three examples of partial matching in our research.

When we studied whole genome phylogeny in the early 1990's, we thought about using $D_{\max}$ to measure distances between two genomes. However, sister species like E. coli and H. influenzae have very different genome lengths. E. coli's genome contains about 4.8 million basepairs while H. influenzae's genome 1.8 million basedpairs. Thus, the Information Distance $D_{\max}$ between H. influenzae genome any genome of similar length would be closer than that of H. influenzae and E. coli. In genome evolution, deletion is easy, especially when a species is under environmental pressure. Information Distance $D_{\max}$ does not model this situation well. We have tried to use normalized information distance to alleviate this problem in [18] and later in [19]. Especially, we have defined in [19] the normalized information distance

$$d_{\max}(x, y) = \frac{\max\{K(x|y), K(y|x)\}}{\max\{K(x), K(y)\}}.$$

Later when we design our question answering (QA) system QUANTA, we met three problems caused by partial matching [39]. The first problem is how to remove the impact of irrelevant information. Consider the question: "Which city is Lake Washington by?" There are several cities around Lake Washington: Seattle, Kirkland, and Bellevue, which are all good answers. The most popular answer Seattle contains overwhelmingly irrelevant information, not related to the lake. The $d_{\max}$ measure chooses a city with higher complexity (lower probability) such as Bellevue. Thus the most obvious answer Seattle is excluded. The second problem is: should an "information distance" really satisfy the triangle inequality? Consider a QA problem: The concept of "Marilyn Monroe" is pretty far from the concept "president". However, Marilyn Monroe is very close to "JFK" and "JFK" is very close to the concept of "president". An information distance must reflect what "we think" to be similar. What "we think" to be similar apparently does not really satisfy triangle inequality. The third problem is the neighborhood density issue. Some objects are popular, such as Seattle mentioned above, and they are close to many other concepts. To model this phenomenon properly is our third problem. We need to relax the neighborhood constraints of Eq. 1 below

$$\sum_y 2^{-D(x,y)} \le 1. \tag{1}$$

to allow some selected (very few) elements to have much denser neighborhoods. In fact, for the $D_{\text{sum}}(x,y) = K(x|y) + K(y|x)$ distance defined in [2], we have already observed similar phenomenon many years ago, and proved a theorem about "tough guys having fewer neighbors", [21], Theorem 8.3.8. Note that this third problem is closely related to the first problem: only when we allow a few popular objects to have very dense neighborhoods, it is then possible that they are selected more often.

Recently we have been working on a QA system with voice input. Voice recognition technologies are not yet ready for practical usage due to noisy environment and speaker diversity. We solve this question by collecting a set Q of over 30 million human asked questions from the internet. When the voice recognition system generates several candidates q_i, $i = 1, 2, 3$, from a human asked question, we wish to compute a question q such that q is "supported" by Q and q is close to q_i, $i = 1, 2, 3$. The information distance between q and Q cannot be measured by D_{max}, as obviously Q contains an overwhelming amount of irrelevant information.

3   The D_{min} Distance

Recall the original motivation of information distance, in Eq (2),

$$D_{\text{max}}(x,y) =_{\text{definition}} E(x,y) = \min\{|p| : U(x,p) = y, \ U(y,p) = x\} \tag{2}$$

we asked for the smallest number of bits that must be used to convert between x and y. While keeping this original motivation in mind, we notice some information in x or y are not relevant to this conversion, they can be kept aside in this conversion process. We thus define [20]: with respect to a universal Turing machine U, the cost of conversion between x and y is:

$$E_{\text{min}}(x,y) = \min\{|p| : U(x,p,r) = y, \ U(y,p,q) = x,$$
$$|p| + |q| + |r| \le E(x,y)\}, \tag{3}$$

To interpret, the above definition separates r as the information for x and q as the information for y. Define $D_{\text{min}}(x,y) = E_{\text{min}}(x,y)$. We have only informally proved following theorem in the past [20]. Here we give the complete proof.

Theorem 1. *Modulo an additive* $O(\log(|x| + |y|))$ *factor,*

$$D_{\text{min}}(x,y) = \min\{K(x|y), K(y|x)\}.$$

Proof. Without loss of generality, assume that $K(y|x) \geq K(x|y)$. In the original proof of $E(x, y) = \max\{K(x|y), K(y|x)\}$, in [2, 21], it is known that there exists a program p of length $K(x|y)$ and q of length $K(y|x) - K(x|y)$, such that

$$U(xq, p) = y; \quad U(y, p) = xq.$$

Thus p is a program that, on input x and q, outputs y, and, on input y, outputs x. Since $|p| = K(x|y)$, we know

$$D_{\min}(x, y) \leq \min\{K(x|y), K(y|x)\}.$$

We also need to show that q contains no information about x by proving $K(x|q) = K(x)$. By the Symmetry of Information theorem (Theorem 2.8.2 in [21], page 182), we have

$$K(xq) = K(x|q) + K(q) = K(q|x) + K(x).$$

Note that p is always the shortest length program, but q may not be. Thus if $K(x|q) < K(x)$, then we must have $K(q|x) < K(q)$. Thus we can construct y via x, p, plus $K(q|x)$ bits. That is: $K(y|x) < K(q) + |p| = K(y|x)$, contradiction.

Now we show

$$D_{\min}(x, y) \geq \min\{K(x|y), K(y|x)\}.$$

Assume this is not true, i.e. assume that $p \leq K(x|y)$. Then let $\sigma = K(x|y) - |p|$. Then $K(y|x) \leq |p| + |q|$ where q is the shortest description of information needed to compute y from x, p, and q. However in this case $r \geq \sigma$ as this is the minimum amount of information needed to compute x from y and p. Thus

$$|p| + |q| + r|$$
$$\geq K(y|x) + |r|$$
$$\geq K(y|x) + \sigma$$
$$> E(x, y) = \max\{K(x|y), K(y|x)\},$$

violating the condition in 3. Thus we have shown $D_{\min}(x, y) \geq \min\{K(x|y), K(y|x)\}$. This finishes the proof of the theorem. $\square$

Observe the following interesting phenomena:

- The extra information q in the proof of Theorem 1 contains no information about x, it is the irrelevant information in y, in a minimal sense.
- On the other hand, $r = \epsilon$, for extra information of x. Essentially, this because we need $K(x|y) + |q|$ bits to specify y, and need no extra information to specify x.
- While $D_{\min}(x, y)$ is symmetric and positive, it does not satisfy the triangle inequality. To see this, let x and y be independent long Kolmogorov random strings, and $z = \epsilon$ the empty string. Then $D_{\min}(x, y) > D_{\min}(x, z) + D_{\min}(z, y) = O(1)$.
- $D_{\min}(x, y)$ satisfies Eq. 1 only for random x's. This is perhaps not a surprise as $D_{\text{sum}}(x, y) = D_{\min}(x, y) + D_{\max}(x, y)$. In the new metric $D_{\min}$, "good guys" (Kolmogorov simple objects) have even more neighbors than D_{sum}.

We can also normalize $D_{\min}$ similar to that of $D_{\max}$:

$$d_{\min}(x, y) = \frac{\min\{K(x|y), K(y|x)\}}{\min\{K(x), K(y)\}}. \tag{4}$$

$d_{\min}(x, y)$ is symmetric and positive, but it does not satisfy triangle inequality. To see this, let $K(X) \geq |X| = n$ for a large n. Partition $X = x_1 x_2 x_3$, with $|x_i| = n/3$. Let $z = x_1$, $x = x_1 x_2$, $y = x_1 x_3$. Then

$$d_{\min}(x, y) \approx 1/2$$

which is much bigger than

$$d_{\min}(x, z) + d_{\min}(z, y) = O(1/n).$$

While it is clear that $D_{\min}(x, y) \leq D_{\max}(x, y)$, it is not clear if such a relationship would hold for $d_{\min}$ vs $d_{\max}$. The following theorem shows that this holds after all.

Theorem 2. *For all x, y, $d_{\min}(x, y) \leq d_{\max}(x, y)$.*

Proof. Given a pair of x and y, without loss of generality, assume that $K(x|y) \leq K(y|x)$. By the Symmetry of Information Theorem (Theorem 2.8.2 in [21], page 182), we know that up to an additive logarithmic factor,

$$K(xy) = K(x|y) + K(y) = K(y|x) + K(x).$$

Thus, from $K(x|y) \leq K(y|x)$, we derive $K(x) \leq K(y)$. Hence $d_{\min}(x, y) = K(x|y)/K(x)$, and $d_{\max}(x, y) = K(y|x)/K(y)$. Since $K(x|y) \leq K(x)$, we have

$$d_{\min}(x, y) = \frac{K(x|y)}{K(x)} \leq \frac{K(x|y) + \Delta}{K(x) + \Delta},$$

for any $\Delta \geq 0$. Setting $\Delta = K(y) - K(x)$, and using the Symmetry of Information Theorem again on the top, the righthand side becomes $d_{\max} = K(y|x)/K(y)$, and the theorem hence follows. $\square$

4   Question Answering

We have been working on a Question Answering (QA) system. In [39, 40], we have used $d_{\min}(x, y)$ to compute the distance between a question x and an answer y. The $d_{\min}$ prefers more popular answers such at Seattle over less popular answers such as Bellevue. The Kolmogorov complexity terms in the $d_{\min}$ expression was approximated using the Shannon-Fano encoding of the internet frequencies, [8]. This system will be combined with the vioce input system to become a QA-via-voice system. Part of this project was supported by the Canadian IDRC for building a cross language QA system for the users in the third world countries. The ability of using the voice input allows the illiterate or visually impaired users in the third world countries to also search the web via our cross language QA engine. In the developed countries, such an application will allow drivers to talk to their GPS's, children to talk to their Talking Toms and R2-D2s, and mothers, or fathers, to tell their smart phones to tell a bed time story for their kids, as I am already doing.

5   Voice Recognition Correction

We now discuss an on-going project that uses our new information distance theory. Mobile devices have given QA systems a very promising application platform. A QA system can be of practical usage on a smart phone if the questions can be input via voice. However the current voice recognition technologies, the best of which by Google, Dragon, Microsoft, are some steps away from being practical. This is due to noisy environment and speaker diversity. We [38] have decided to overcome this problem by using the internet information. We have downloaded over 30 million questions asked by the users from the internet. Let Q be this set of 30 million questions. Let q_1, q_2, q_3 be three candidates generated by the speech recognition software from the user speech input. Informally, we wish to compute a quesion q such that q is close to (in some sense) Q, and close to q_1, q_2, q_3, as shown below

$$\{q_1, q_2, q_3\} \longleftrightarrow q \longleftrightarrow Q$$

and hopefully q is what the user had in mind. By q being "close" in some sense to Q, we mean that there some sort of patterns one can extract from Q, for example "who is the mayor of CITY". We have done one experiment using a Microsoft QA set of 300 questions, and found 99% of these questions have reasonable corresponding "patterns" in Q. Apparently, for each q, we are only interested in some small number of questions in Q not most other questions in Q. This is clearly a matter of partial matching and we are interested in the shortest way of using Q to encode q. Thus we can formalize our problem as: find q that minimizes

$$\delta D_{\min}(Q, q) + D_{\max}(\{q_1, q_2, q_3\}, q)$$

where $\delta > 1$ is a constant. The rest of the story is encoding which we will ignore in this article. This was implemented on as part of a QA-by-voice system on the Iphones.

Testing such a system is tricky, as it heavily depends on individual speakers and questions. However in one particular test of 164 questions by a mixture of non-native and native English speakers, Google voice recognition system recognized 110 questions correctly, our system corrected 39 google results that were previously erroneous and but wrongly changed 5 correct results to wrong questions. Thus in total, our system had 144 correct answers out of 164 total, or 88%, whereas the Google original voice recognition output had 66% correct. Here are some examples where we have corrected Google voice recognition outputs. I asked "what do frogs eat?" The Google voice recognition returned: "What is front seat", "what is frogs eat", and "what does the front seat". Our server returned "What does frogs eat". Another example: I asked "How many Indian groups are in New Hampshire". Google voice recognition returned 3 candidates: "How many indian groups are you new hampshire", "How many indian groups are the new hampshire", "albany indian groups are you new hampshire", our server returned: "How many Indian groups are in New Hampshire". Another example: I asked "who won the world series in 1997". Google voice recognition returned 3 candidates: "holanda series in 1997", "hole on the world series in 1997", "hol on the world series in 1997". Our system returned: "who won the world series in 1997".

Sometimes even if the voice recognition software is perfect, the speakers might not speak correctly. Our system corrects those errors too. The following is one such example (from my own speech; I forgot to say "get"). The Google voice reconition recognized my speech perfectly and output three candidates with the first one having the highest probability: Why do people addicted to the games (my original speech); Why do people addicted to the names; Why do people addicted to the canes; Our system returned: Why do people get addicted to the games.

Acknowledgements. This work was supported in part by NSERC Grant OGP0046506, Canada Research Chair program and a CFI infrastructure grant, an NSERC Collaborative Grant, Premier's Discovery Award, Killam Prize, and an IDRC grant.

References

1. Ané, C., Sanderson, M.J.: Missing the Forest for the Trees: Phylogenetic Compression and Its Implications for Inferring Complex Evolutionary Histories. Systematic Biology 54(1), 146–157 (2005)
2. Bennett, C.H., Gacs, P., Li, M., Vitanyi, P., Zurek, W.: Information Distance. IEEE Trans. Inform. Theory 44(4), 1407–1423 (1998) (STOC 1993)
3. Bennett, C.H., Li, M., Ma, B.: Chain letters and evolutionary histories. Scientific American 288(6), 76–81 (2003) (feature article)
4. Chaitin, G.J.: On the Simplicity and Speed of Programs for Computing Infinite Sets of Natural Numbers. Journal of the ACM 16(3), 407
5. Chen, X., Francia, B., Li, M., Mckinnon, B., Seker, A.: Shared information and program plagiarism detection. IEEE Trans. Information Theory 50(7), 1545–1550 (2004)
6. Chernov, A.V., Muchnik, A.A., Romashchenko, A.E., Shen, A.K., Vereshchagin, N.K.: Upper semi-lattice of binary strings with the relation "x is simple conditional to y". Theoret. Comput. Sci. 271, 69–95 (2002)
7. Cilibrasi, R., Vitányi, P.M.B., de Wolf Algorithmic, R.: clustring of music based on string compression. Comput. Music J. 28(4), 49–67 (2004)
8. Cilibrasi, R., Vitányi, P.M.B.: The Google similarity distance. IEEE Trans. Knowledge and Data Engineering 19(3), 370–383 (2007)
9. Cilibrasi, R., Vitányi, P.M.B.: Clustering by compression. IEEE Trans. Inform. Theory 51(4), 1523–1545 (2005)
10. Cuturi, M., Vert, J.P.: The context-tree kernel for strings. Neural Networks 18(4), 1111–1123 (2005)
11. Fagin, R., Stockmeyer, L.: Relaxing the triangle inequality in pattern matching. Int'l J. Comput. Vision 28(3), 219–231 (1998)
12. Keogh, E., Lonardi, S., Ratanamahatana, C.A.: Towards parameter-free data mining. In: KDD 2004, pp. 206–215 (2004)
13. Kirk, S.R., Jenkins, S.: Information theory-baed software metrics and obfuscation. J. Systems and Software 72, 179–186 (2004)

14. Kolmogorov, A.N.: Three Approaches to the Quantitative Definition of Information. Problems Inform. Transmission 1(1), 1–7 (1965)
15. Kraskov, A., Stögbauer, H., Andrzejak, R.G., Grassberger, P.: Hierarchical clustering using mutual information. Europhys. Lett. 70(2), 278–284 (2005)
16. Kocsor, A., Kertesz-Farkas, A., Kajan, L., Pongor, S.: Application of compression-based distance measures to protein sequence classification: a methodology study. Bioinformatics 22(4), 407–412 (2006)
17. Krasnogor, N., Pelta, D.A.: Measuring the similarity of protein structures by means of the universal similarity metric. Bioinformatics 20(7), 1015–1021 (2004)
18. Li, M., Badger, J., Chen, X., Kwong, S., Kearney, P., Zhang, H.: An information-based sequence distance and its application to whole mitochondrial genome phylogeny. Bioinformatics 17(2), 149–154 (2001)
19. Li, M., Chen, X., Li, X., Ma, B., Vitanyi, P.M.B.: The similarity metric. IEEE Trans. Information Theory 50(12), 3250–3264 (2004)
20. Li, M.: Information distance and its applications. Int'l J. Found. Comput. Sci. 18(4), 669–681 (2007)
21. Li, M., Vitanyi, P.: An introduction to Kolmogorov complexity and its applications, 3rd edn. Springer (2008)
22. Muchnik, A.A.: Conditional comlexity and codes. Theoretical Computer Science 271(1), 97–109 (2002)
23. Muchnik, A.A., Vereshchagin, N.K.: Logical operations and Kolmogorov complexity II. In: Proc. 16th Conf. Comput. Complexity, pp. 256–265 (2001)
24. Nykter, M., Price, N.D., Larjo, A., Aho, T., Kauffman, S.A., Yli-Harja, O., Shmulevich, I.: Critical networks exhibit maximal information diversity in structure-dynamics relationships. Phy. Rev. Lett. 100, 058702(4) (2008)
25. Nykter, M., Price, N.D., Aldana, M., Ramsey, S.A., Kauffman, S.A., Hood, L.E., Yli-Harja, O., Shmulevich, I.: Gene expression dynamics in the macrophage exhibit criticality. Proc. Nat. Acad. Sci. USA 105(6), 1897–1900 (2008)
26. Otu, H.H., Sayood, K.: Bioinformatics 19(6), 2122–2130 (2003); A new sequence distance measure for phylogenetic tree construction
27. Pao, H.K., Case, J.: Computing entropy for ortholog detection. In: Int'l Conf. Comput. Intell., Istanbul, Turkey, December 17-19 (2004)
28. Parry, D.: Use of Kolmogorov distance identification of web page authorship, topic and domain. In: Workshop on Open Source Web Inf. Retrieval (2005), http://www.emse.fr/OSWIRO5
29. Costa Santos, C., Bernardes, J., Vitányi, P.M.B., Antunes, L.: Clustering fetal heart rate tracings by compression. In: Proc. 19th IEEE Intn'l Symp. Computer-Based Medical Systems, Salt Lake City, Utah, June 22-23 (2006)
30. Shen, A.K., Vereshchagin, N.K.: Logical operations and Kolmogorov complexity. Theoret. Comput. Sci. 271, 125–129 (2002)
31. Solomonoff, R.: A Formal Theory of Inductive Inference, Part I. d Information and Control 7(1), 1–22 (1964)
32. Solomonoff, R.: A Formal Theory of Inductive Inference, Part II. Information and Control 7(2), 224–254 (1964)
33. Varre, J.S., Delahaye, J.P., Rivals, E.: Transformation distances: a family of dissimilarity measures based on movements of segments. Bioinformatics 15(3), 194–202 (1999)
34. Veltkamp, R.C.: Shape Matching: Similarity Measures and Algorithms, invited talk. In: Proc. Int'l Conf. Shape Modeling Applications 2001, Italy, pp. 188–197 (2001)

35. Vereshchagin, N.K., V'yugin, M.V.: Independent minimum length programs to translate between given strings. Theoret. Comput. Sci. 271, 131–143 (2002)
36. V'yugin, M.V.: Information distance and conditional complexities. Theoret. Comput. Sci. 271, 145–150 (2002)
37. Wallace, C.S., Dowe, D.L.: Minimum Message Length and Kolmogorov Complexity. Computer Journal 42(4) (1999)
38. Yang, T., Wang, D., Zhu, X., Li, M.: Information distance between what I said and what it heard. Manuscript in preparation (August. 2011)
39. Zhang, X., Hao, Y., Zhu, X., Li, M.: Information distance from a question to an answer. In: Proc. 13th ACM SIGKDD, August 12-15, pp. 874–883 (2007)
40. Zhang, X., Hao, Y., Zhu, X., Li, M.: New information measure and its application in question answering system. J. Comput. Sci. Tech. 23(4), 557–572 (2008)

Falsification and Future Performance

David Balduzzi

MPI for Intelligent Systems, Tuebingen, Germany
`david.balduzzi@tuebingen.mpg.de`

Abstract. We information-theoretically reformulate two measures of capacity from statistical learning theory: empirical VC-entropy and empirical Rademacher complexity. We show these capacity measures count the number of hypotheses about a dataset that a learning algorithm *falsifies* when it finds the classifier in its repertoire minimizing empirical risk. It then follows from that the future performance of predictors on *unseen* data is controlled in part by how many hypotheses the learner falsifies. As a corollary we show that empirical VC-entropy quantifies the message length of the true hypothesis in the optimal code of a particular probability distribution, the so-called actual repertoire.

1 Introduction

This note relates the number of hypotheses falsified by a learning algorithm to the expected future performance of the predictor it outputs. It does so by reformulating two basic results from statistical learning theory information-theoretically.

Suppose we wish to predict an unknown physical process $\sigma^* : \mathcal{X} \to \mathcal{Y}$ occurring in nature after observing its outputs $(y_1, \ldots, y_l)$ on sample $\mathcal{D} = (x_1, \ldots, x_l)$ of its inputs, where inputs arise according to unknown distribution P. One method is to take a repertoire $\mathcal{F}$ of functions from $\mathcal{X} \to \mathcal{Y}$ and choose the predictor $\hat{f} \in \mathcal{F}$ that best approximates σ^* on the observed data. How confident can we be in $\hat{f}$'s future performance on unseen data?

Statistical learning theory provides bounds on $\hat{f}$'s expected future performance by quantifying a tradeoff implicit in the choice of repertoire $\mathcal{F}$. At first glance, the bigger the repertoire the better since the best approximation to σ^* in $\mathcal{F}$ can only improve as more more functions are added to $\mathcal{F}$. However, increasing $\mathcal{F}$, and improving the approximation on observed data, can *reduce* future performance due to overfitting. As a result, the bounds depend on both the accuracy with which $\hat{f}$ approximates σ^* on the observed data and the capacity of repertoire $\mathcal{F}$, see Theorems 9 and 10.

We wish to connect statistical learning theory with Popper's ideas about falsification. Popper argued that no amount of positive evidence confirms a theory [11]. Rather, theories should be judged on the basis of how many hypotheses they falsify. A theory is *falsifiable* if there are possible hypotheses about the world (i.e. data) that are not consistent with the theory. A bold theory falsifies (disagrees with) many potential hypotheses about observed data. Testing a bold theory, by checking that the hypotheses it disagrees with are in fact false,

D.L. Dowe (Ed.): Solomonoff Festschrift, LNAI 7070, pp. 65–78, 2013.

provides corroborating evidence. If a theory has been thoroughly tested then (perhaps) we can have confidence in its predictions. Popper's criticism of positive confirmation was devastating. However, and hence the "perhaps", he failed to provide a rationale for trusting the predictions of severely tested theories.

To understand how falsifying hypotheses affects future performance we reformulate learning as a kind of *measurement*. Before doing so, we need to describe precisely what we mean by measurement.

Given physical system X with state space $S(X)$, a classical measurement is a function $f : S(X) \to \mathbb{R}$. For example a thermometer f maps configurations (positions and momenta) of particles in the atmosphere to real numbers. When the thermometer outputs $15°C$ it generates information by specifying that atmospheric particles were in a configuration in $f^{-1}(15) \subset S(X)$. The information generated by the thermometer is a brute physical fact depending on how the thermometer is built and its output. We quantify the information, see §2, by comparing the size of the total configuration space $S(X)$ with the size of the pre-image $f^{-1}(15)$. The smaller the pre-image, the more informative the measurement, see §2 for details.

More generally, any (classical) physical process $f : \mathcal{X} \to \mathcal{Y}$ can be thought of as performing measurements by taking inputs in $\mathcal{X}$ to outputs in $\mathcal{Y}$. Section §4 introduces an important example, the *min-risk* $\mathbf{R}_{\mathcal{F},\mathcal{D}} : \Sigma(\mathcal{X}, \mathcal{Y}) \to \mathbb{R}$, which outputs the minimum value of the empirical risk over repertoire $\mathcal{F}$ on a hypothesis space $\Sigma(\mathcal{X}, \mathcal{Y})$. Finding the min-risk is a necessary step in finding the best approximation $\hat{f}$ to σ^* in $\mathcal{F}$. Since computing the min-risk requires actually implementing it as a physical process somehow or other, the measurements it performs and the effective information it generates are brute physical facts, no different in kind than the information generated by a thermometer.

It turns out that the min-risk categorizes hypotheses in Σ according to how well they are approximated by predictors in repertoire $\mathcal{F}$. Proposition 12 shows that the effective information generated by the min-risk is (essentially) the empirical VC-entropy. Moreover, the effective information generated by the min-risk "counts" the number of hypotheses about $\mathcal{D}$ that $\mathcal{F}$ falsifies, see Eq. (13). As a consequence, Corollary 13, we obtain that the future performance of predictor $\hat{f}$ is controlled by (i) how well $\hat{f}$ fits the observed data; (ii) how many hypotheses about the data the min-risk rules out and (iii) a confidence term.

It follows that, assuming the assumptions of the theorems below hold, bounds on future performance are brute physical facts resulting from the act of minimizing empirical risk, and so falsifying potential hypotheses, on observed data.

A consequence of our results, Corollary 15, is that empirical VC-entropy is essentially the minimal length of the true hypothesis under the optimal code for the actual repertoire (a distribution depending on the min-risk). This suggests there may be interesting connections between VC-theory and the minimum message length (MML) approach to induction proposed by Wallace and Boulton [15, 16].

Finally, section §4.2 reformulates empirical Rademacher complexity via falsification. Here we build on Solomonoff's probability distribution introduced in [12]. In short, we take Solomonoff's definition and substitute the *min-risk* in place of the universal Turing machine, thereby obtaining what we refer to as the Rademacher distribution – a *non-universal* analog of Solomonoff's distribution. Rademacher complexity is then computed using the expectation of the min-risk over the Rademacher distribution, see Proposition 17.

The min-risk thus provides a bridge that not only connects VC-theory to a computable analog of Solomonoff's seminal distribution, but also sheds light on how falsification provides guarantees on future performance.

Related Work. The connection between Popper's ideas on falsifiability and statistical learning theory was pointed out in [5,7,14]. However, these works focus on VC-dimension, which does not relate to falsification as directly as VC-entropy and Rademacher complexity which we consider here. Further, VC-entropy is a more fundamental concept in statistical learning theory than VC-dimension since VC-dimension is defined in terms of the limit behavior of the growth function, which is an upper bound on VC-entropy [14]. For more details on the link between MML and algorithmic probability, see [17].

2   Measurement

We consider a toy universe containing probabilistic mechanisms (input/output devices) of the following form

Definition 1. *Given finite sets $\mathcal{X}$ and $\mathcal{Y}$, a **mechanism** is a Markov matrix $\mathfrak{m}$ defined by conditional probability distribution $p_{\mathfrak{m}}(y|x)$.*

Mechanisms generate information about their inputs by assigning them to outputs [1,2].

Definition 2. *The **actual repertoire** (or **measurement**) specified by $\mathfrak{m}$ outputting y is the probability distribution*

$$p_{\mathfrak{m}}(x|y) := \frac{p_{\mathfrak{m}}(y|x)}{p(y)} \cdot p_{unif}(x),$$

*where $p_{unif}(x) = \frac{1}{|\mathcal{X}|}$ is the uniform distribution. The **effective information** generated by the measurement is*

$$ei(\mathfrak{m}, y) := H\left[p_{\mathfrak{m}}(X|y)\middle\|p_{unif}(X)\right],$$

where $H[p\|q] = \sum_i p_i \log_2 \frac{p_i}{q_i}$ is Kullback-Leibler divergence.

The Kullback-Leibler divergence $H[p\|q]$ can be interpreted informally as the number of Y/N questions needed to get from distribution q to distribution p. However, as pointed out in [6], Kullback-Leibler divergence is invariant with respect to the "framing of the problem" – the ordering and structure of the questions – suggesting it is a suitable measure of information-theoretic "effort".

The definition of measurement is motivated by the special case where p_m assigns probabilities that are either 0 or 1; in other words, when it corresponds to a set-valued function $f : \mathcal{X} \to \mathcal{Y}$. The measurement performed by f is

$$p_f(x|y) = \begin{cases} \frac{1}{|f^{-1}(y)|} & \text{if } f(x) = y \\ 0 & \text{else,} \end{cases}$$

where $|\cdot|$ denotes cardinality. The support of $p_f(X|y)$ is the preimage $f^{-1}(y) \subset \mathcal{X}$. All elements of the support are assigned equal probability – they are treated as an undifferentiated list. The measurement $p_m(X|y)$ therefore generalizes the notion of preimage to the probabilistic setting.

The effective information generated by f outputting y is $ei(f, y) = \log_2 \frac{|\mathcal{X}|}{|f^{-1}(y)|}$:

$$\begin{aligned} ei(f, y) &= & \log_2 |\mathcal{X}| & - & \log_2 |f^{-1}(y)| \\ &= & \Big(\text{no. potential inputs}\Big) & - & \Big(\text{no. inputs in pre-image}\Big) \\ &= & \Big(\text{no. inputs ruled out}\Big), \end{aligned} \tag{1}$$

where inputs are counted in bits (after logarithming). Effective information is maximal ($\log_2 |\mathcal{X}|$ bits) when a single input leads to y, and is minimal (0 bits) when *all* inputs lead to y. In the first case, observing f output y tells us exactly what the input was, and in the latter case, it tells us nothing at all.

2.1   Semantics

Next we consider two approaches to characterizing the meaning of measurements. The first relates to possible world semantics [9]. Here, the meaning of a sentence is given by the set of possible worlds in which it is true. Meaning is thus determined by considering all counterfactuals. For example, the meaning of "That car is 10 years old" is the set of possible worlds where the speaker is pointing to a car manufactured 10 years previously. Since the set of contains cars of many different colors, we see that color is irrelevant to the meaning of the sentence.

More precisely, the meaning of sentence S is a map from possible worlds W to truth values $v_S : W \to \{0, 1\}$. Equivalently, the meaning of a sentence is

$$\begin{aligned} W & \supset & v_S^{-1}(1) \\ \Big(\text{possible worlds}\Big) & \supset & \Big(\text{worlds where } S \text{ is true}\Big). \end{aligned} \tag{2}$$

Inspired by possible world semantics, we propose

Definition 3. *The **meaning** of output y by mechanism $\mathfrak{m}$ is*

$$\begin{aligned} p_{unif}(X) & \to & p_{\mathfrak{m}}(X|y) \\ \Big(\text{possible inputs}\Big) & \to & \Big(\text{inputs that cause } y\Big). \end{aligned} \tag{3}$$

For a deterministic function this reduces to $\mathcal{X} \supset f^{-1}(y)$.

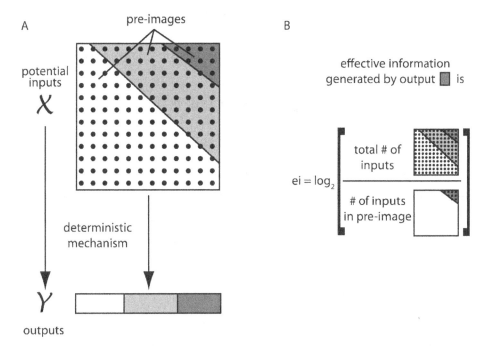

Fig. 1. The effective information generated by measurements. (A) A deterministic device can receive 144 inputs and produce 3 outputs. (B): Each input is implicitly assigned to a category (shaded areas). The information generated by the dark gray output is $\log_2 144 - \log_2 9 = 4$ bits.

Grounding meanings in mechanisms yields four advantages over the possible worlds approach. First, it replaces the difficult to define notion of a possible world with the concrete set of inputs the mechanism is physically capable of receiving. Second, in possible world semantics the work of determining whether or not a sentence is true is performed somewhat mysteriously offstage, whereas the meaning of a measurement is determined via Bayes' rule. Third, the approach generalizes to probabilistic mechanisms. Finally, we can compute the effective information generated by a measurement, whereas there is no way to quantify the information content of a sentence in possible world semantics.

2.2 Risk

The second, pragmatic notion of meaning characterizes usefulness. We consider a special case, well studied in statistical learning theory, where usefulness relates to predictions [14].

Let $\Sigma(\mathcal{X}, \mathcal{Y}) = \{\sigma : \mathcal{X} \to \mathcal{Y}\}$ be the set of all functions (deterministic mechanisms) mapping $\mathcal{X}$ to $\mathcal{Y} = \{-1, +1\}$. We will often write Σ for short. Suppose there is a random variable X taking values in $\mathcal{X}$ with unknown distribution

P and an unknown mechanism $\sigma^* \in \Sigma$, the *supervisor*, who assigns labels to elements of $\mathcal{X}$.

Definition 4. *The **risk** quantifies how well mechanism f approximates an unknown or partially known mechanism σ^*:*

$$\mathbf{R}(f) = \sum_{x \in \mathcal{X}} \mathbb{I}\big[f(x) \neq \sigma^*(x)\big] \cdot p(x). \tag{4}$$

It is the probability that f and σ^* disagree on elements of $\mathcal{X}$.

Unfortunately, the risk cannot be computed since P and σ^* are unknown.

Definition 5. *Given a finite sample $\mathcal{D} = (x_1, \ldots, x_l) \in \mathcal{X}^l$ with labels $\mathcal{L} = \sigma^* \mathcal{D} = (y_1, \ldots, y_l) \in \mathcal{Y}^l$, the **empirical risk** of $f : \mathcal{X} \to \mathcal{Y}$*

$$\mathbf{R}(f, \mathcal{D}, \mathcal{L}) = \frac{1}{l} \sum_{i=1}^{l} \mathbb{I}\big[f(x_i) \neq y_i\big] \tag{5}$$

is the fraction of the data $\mathcal{D}$ on which f and σ^* disagree.

The empirical risk provides a computable approximation to the (true) risk.

Remark 6. *Note that in this paper, sets $\mathcal{X}$ and $\mathcal{Y}$ are both finite. Similarly, the training data $\mathcal{D} \in \mathcal{X}^l$ and labels $\mathcal{L} \in \mathcal{Y}^l$ also live in finite sets.*

3   Statistical Learning Theory

Suppose we wish to predict the unknown supervisor σ^* based on its behavior on labeled data $(\mathcal{D}, \mathcal{L})$. A simple way to find a mechanism in repertoire $\mathcal{F} \subset \Sigma(\mathcal{X}, \mathcal{Y})$ that approximates σ^* well is to minimize the empirical risk.

Definition 7. *Given repertoire $\mathcal{F} \subset \Sigma$ and unlabeled data $\mathcal{D} \in \mathcal{X}^l$, define **learning algorithm***

$$\mathcal{A}_{\mathcal{F}, \mathcal{D}} : \Sigma \to \mathcal{F} : \sigma \mapsto \arg\min_{f \in \mathcal{F}} \mathbf{R}(f, \mathcal{D}, \sigma\mathcal{D}) \tag{6}$$

which finds the mechanism in $\mathcal{F}$ that minimizes empirical risk.

Learning algorithm $\mathcal{A}_{\mathcal{F}, \mathcal{D}}$ finds the mechanism in $\mathcal{F}$ that appears, based on the empirical risk, to best approximate σ^*. Empirical risk stays constant or decreases as $\mathcal{F}$ is enlarged, suggesting that the larger the repertoire the better.

This is not true in general since minimizing risk – and *not* empirical risk – is the goal. There is a tradeoff: increasing the size of $\mathcal{F}$ leads to overfitting the data which can increase risk even as empirical risk is reduced.

The tendency of a repertoire to overfit data depends on its size or capacity. We recall two measures of capacity that are used to bound risk: empirical VC-entropy [13] and empirical Rademacher complexity [8].

Definition 8. *Given unlabeled data $\mathcal{D} \in \mathcal{X}^l$ and repertoire $\mathcal{F} \subset \Sigma$ let*

$$q_{\mathcal{D}} : \mathcal{F} \to \mathbb{R}^l : f \mapsto \Big(f(x_1), \dots, f(x_l) \Big). \tag{7}$$

*The empirical **VC-entropy**[1] of $\mathcal{F}$ on $\mathcal{D}$ is $\mathcal{V}(\mathcal{F}, \mathcal{D}) := \log_2 |q_{\mathcal{D}}(\mathcal{F})|$, where $|q_{\mathcal{D}}(\mathcal{F})|$ is the number of distinct points in the image of $q_{\mathcal{D}}$.*
*The empirical **Rademacher complexity** of $\mathcal{F}$ on $\mathcal{D}$ is*

$$\mathcal{R}(\mathcal{F}, \mathcal{D}) = \frac{1}{|\Sigma|} \sum_{\sigma \in \Sigma} \left[\sup_{f \in \mathcal{F}} \frac{1}{l} \sum_{i=1}^{l} \sigma(x_i) \cdot f(x_i) \right]. \tag{8}$$

VC-entropy "counts" how many labelings of $\mathcal{D}$ the classifiers in $\mathcal{F}$ fit perfectly. Rademacher complexity is a weighted count of how many labelings of $\mathcal{D}$ functions in $\mathcal{F}$ fit well.
   The following theorems are shown in [3] and [4] respectively:

Theorem 9 (empirical VC-entropy bound)
With probability $1 - \delta$, the expected risk is bounded by

$$\mathbf{R}(f) \le \mathbf{R}(f, \mathcal{D}, \mathcal{L}) + c_1 \sqrt{\frac{\mathcal{V}(\mathcal{F}, \mathcal{D})}{l}} + c_2 \sqrt{\frac{1 - \log_2 \delta}{l}} \tag{9}$$

for all $f \in \mathcal{F}$, where the constants are $c_1 = \sqrt{\frac{6}{\log_2 e}}$ and $c_2 = \sqrt{\frac{1}{\log_2 e}}$.

Theorem 10 (empirical Rademacher bound)
For all $\delta > 0$, with probability at least $1 - \delta$,

$$\mathbf{R}(f) \le \mathbf{R}(f, \mathcal{D}, \mathcal{L}) + \mathcal{R}(\mathcal{F}, \mathcal{D}) + c_3 \sqrt{\frac{1 - \log_2 \delta}{l}}, \tag{10}$$

for all $f \in \mathcal{F}$, where $c_3 = \sqrt{\frac{2}{\log_2 e}}$.

The tradeoff between empirical risk and capacity is visible in the first two terms on the right-hand sides of the bounds.
   The left-hand sides of Eqs (9) and (10) cannot be computed since P and σ^* are unknown. Remarkably, the right-hand sides depend only on mechanism f chosen from repertoire $\mathcal{F}$, labeled data $(\mathcal{D}, \mathcal{L})$ and desired confidence δ. The theorems assume data is drawn *i.i.d.* according to P and labeled according to σ^*; it make no assumptions about the distribution P on $\mathcal{X}$ or supervisor σ^*, except that they are *fixed*.

---

[1] VC-entropy is the *expectation* of empirical VC-entropy [14]. Also, note the standard definition of VC-entropy uses $\log_e$ rather than $\log_2$.

4   Falsification

This section reformulates the results from statistical learning theory to show how the past falsifications performed by a learning algorithm control future performance. We show that the empirical VC-entropies and Rademacher complexities admit interpretations as "counting" (in senses made precise below) the number of hypotheses falsified by a particular measurement performed when learning.

We start by introducing a special mechanism, the min-risk, which is used implicitly in learning algorithm $\mathcal{A}_{\mathcal{F},\mathcal{D}}$. As we will see, the structure of the measurements performed by the min-risk determine the capacity of the learning algorithm.

Definition 11. *Given repertoire $\mathcal{F} \subset \Sigma$ and unlabeled data $\mathcal{D} \in \mathcal{X}^l$, define the* **min-risk** *as the minimum of the empirical risk on $\mathcal{F}$:*

$$\mathbf{R}_{\mathcal{F},\mathcal{D}} : \Sigma \to \mathbb{R} : \sigma \mapsto \min_{f \in \mathcal{F}} \mathbf{R}(f, \mathcal{D}, \sigma\mathcal{D}). \tag{11}$$

The min-risk is a mechanism mapping supervisors σ in Σ to the empirical risk of their best approximations $\mathcal{A}_{\mathcal{F},\mathcal{D}}(\sigma)$ in $\mathcal{F}$, see Fig. 2. Note that inputs to the min-risk are themselves mechanisms.

We suggestively interpret the setup as follows. Suppose a scientist studies a universe where inputs in $\mathcal{X}$ appear according to distribution P, and are assigned labels in $\mathcal{Y}$ by unknown physical process σ^*. The *hypothesis space* is $\Sigma(\mathcal{X}, \mathcal{Y})$, the set of all possible (deterministic) physical processes that take $\mathcal{X}$ to $\mathcal{Y}$.

The scientist's goal is to learn to predict physical process σ^*, on the basis of a small sample of labeled data $(\mathcal{D}, \mathcal{L})$. She has a *theory*, repertoire $\mathcal{F}$, and a method, $\mathcal{A}_{\mathcal{F},\mathcal{D}}$, which she uses to fit some particular $\hat{f} \in \mathcal{F}$ given $\mathcal{L}$.

The most important question for the scientist is: How reliable are predictions made by $\hat{f}$ on *new* data? We will show that $\hat{f}$'s reliability depends on the measurements performed by the min-risk – i.e. on the work done by the scientist when she applies method $\mathcal{A}_{\mathcal{F},\mathcal{D}}$ to find $\hat{f}$.

4.1   Empirical VC Entropy

Empirical VC-entropy is, essentially, the effective information generated by the min-risk when it outputs a perfect fit:

Proposition 12 (VC-entropy via effective information)
Empirical VC entropy is

$$\mathcal{V}(\mathcal{F}, \mathcal{D}) = l - ei\left(\mathbf{R}_{\mathcal{F},\mathcal{D}}, 0\right). \tag{12}$$

Proof: Let $\mathcal{X} = \mathcal{D} \cup \mathcal{D}^c$ and $|\mathcal{X}| = m$. Then $\Sigma = \{\sigma : \mathcal{D} \to \mathcal{Y}\} \times \{\sigma : \mathcal{D}^c \to \mathcal{Y}\}$. By definition

$$ei\left(\mathbf{R}_{\mathcal{F},\mathcal{D}}, 0\right) = \log_2 |\Sigma| - \log_2 |\mathbf{R}_{\mathcal{F},\mathcal{D}}^{-1}(0)|,$$

with $\log_2 |\Sigma| = m$. It remains to show that $|\mathbf{R}_{\mathcal{F},\mathcal{D}}^{-1}(0)| = 2^{m-l} \cdot |q_{\mathcal{D}}(\mathcal{F})|$. Points in the image of $q_{\mathcal{D}}$ correspond to labelings σ of the data by functions in $\mathcal{F}$.

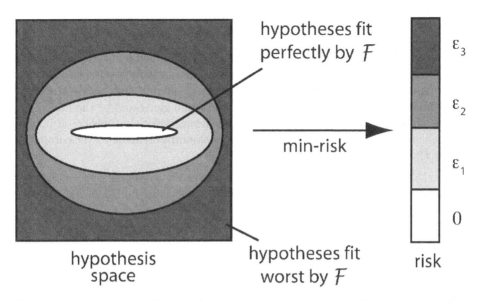

Fig. 2. The structure of the measurement performed by the min-risk. The min-risk categorizes potential hypothesis in Σ according to how well they are fit by mechanisms in theory $\mathcal{F}$.

Thus, $|q_{\mathcal{D}}(\mathcal{F})|$ counts distinct labelings of $\mathcal{D}$ that $\mathcal{F}$ fits perfectly. These occur with multiplicity 2^{m-l} in the pre-image by the product decomposition of Σ above. ∎

We interpret the result as follows. Suppose the scientist applies theory $\mathcal{F}$ to explain her labeled data and perfectly fits function $\hat{f} = \mathcal{A}_{\mathcal{F},\mathcal{D}}(\sigma^*)$ with risk $\epsilon = 0$.

By Definition 3, the meaning of her work is $\Sigma \supset \mathbf{R}_{\mathcal{F},\mathcal{D}}^{-1}(0)$: the set of mechanisms that her theory $\mathcal{F}$ fits perfectly. The effective information generated by her work is

$$
\begin{aligned}
ei(\mathbf{R}_{\mathcal{F},\mathcal{D}},0) = \qquad \log_2|\Sigma| \qquad &- \qquad \log_2|\mathbf{R}_{\mathcal{F},\mathcal{D}}^{-1}(0)| \\
= \Big(\text{total no. of hypotheses}\Big) &- \Big(\text{no. that theory fits}\Big) \qquad (13)\\
= \Big(\text{no. of hypotheses falsified}\Big),
\end{aligned}
$$

where hypotheses are counted in bits (after logarithming). A theory is informative if it rules out many potential hypotheses [11].

The number of hypotheses the scientist falsifies when using theory $\mathcal{F}$ to fit $\hat{f}$ has implications for its future performance:

Corollary 13 (information-theoretic empirical VC bound)
With probability $1 - \delta$, the risk of predictor $\hat{f} = \mathcal{A}_{\mathcal{F},\mathcal{D}}(\sigma^*)$ outputted by learning algorithm $\mathcal{A}_{\mathcal{F}}$ is bounded by

$$
\mathbf{R}(f) \le \mathbf{R}(f,\mathcal{D},\mathcal{L}) + c_1\sqrt{1 - \frac{ei(\mathbf{R}_{\mathcal{F},\mathcal{D}},0)}{l}} + c_2\sqrt{\frac{1 - \log_2\delta}{l}}. \qquad (14)
$$

Proof: By Theorem 9 and Proposition 12.   ∎

The corollary states that minimizing empirical risk embeds expectations about the future into predictors. So long as the corollary's assumptions hold, future performance by $\hat{f}$ is controlled by: (i) the output of the min-risk, i.e. the fraction ϵ of the data that $\hat{f}$ fits; (ii) the effective information generated by the min-risk, i.e. the number (in bits) of hypotheses the learning algorithm falsifies if it fits perfectly; and (iii) a confidence term. The only assumption made by the corollary is that P and σ^* are *fixed*.

Remark 14. *The theorem provides no guarantees on the future performance of a theory that "explains everything", i.e. $\mathcal{F} = \Sigma$, no matter how well it fits the data. This follows since effective information is zero when $\mathcal{F} = \Sigma$, and so the second term on the right-hand side of Eq. (14) is $c_1 \approx 2$.*

Reformulating the above result in terms of code lengths suggests a connection between VC-theory and minimum message length (MML), see [16] and §6.6 of [6]. Recall that, given probability distribution $p(X)$, the message length of event x in an optimal binary code is $\mathrm{len}(x) := -\log_2 p(x)$.

Corollary 15 (VC-entropy controls code length of true hypothesis)
Denote the min-risk by $\mathfrak{m} = \mathbf{R}_{\mathcal{F},\mathcal{D}}$. The length of the true hypothesis $\hat{\sigma}$ in the optimal code for the actual repertoire specified by the min-risk, $p_{\mathfrak{m}}(\Sigma|\epsilon = 0)$, is

$$\mathrm{len}(\hat{\sigma}) = \mathcal{V}(\mathcal{F}, \mathcal{D}) + \big(|\mathcal{X}| - |\mathcal{D}|\big).$$

Proof: By Proposition 12 we have $-\log_2 p_{\mathfrak{m}}(\hat{\sigma}|\epsilon = 0) = \log_2 |\mathbf{R}_{\mathcal{F},\mathcal{D}}^{-1}(0)|$.   ∎

The length of the message describing the true hypothesis in the actual repertoire's optimal code is the empirical VC-entropy plus a term, $(|\mathcal{X}|-|\mathcal{D}|) = (m-l)$, that decreases as the amount of training data increases. The shorter the message, the better the predictor's expected performance (for fixed empirical risk).

4.2   Empirical Rademacher Complexity

VC-entropy only considers hypotheses that theory $\mathcal{F}$ fits perfectly. Rademacher complexity is an alternate capacity measure that considers the distribution of risk across the entire hypothesis space. This section explains Rademacher complexity via an analogy with Solomonoff probability [12,17].

We first recall Solomonoff's definition. Given universal Turing machine T, define (unnormalized) **Solomonoff probability**

$$p_T(s) := \sum_{\{i|T(i)=s\bullet\}} 2^{-\mathrm{len}(i)}, \tag{15}$$

where the sum is over strings[2] i that cause T to output s as a prefix, and $\mathrm{len}(i)$ is the length of i. We adapt Eq. (15) by replacing Turing machine T with min-risk $\mathbf{R}_{\mathcal{F},\mathcal{D}} : \Sigma \to \mathbb{R}$.

---

[2] A technical point is that no proper prefix of i should output s.

Definition 16. *Equipping hypothesis space with the uniform distribution p_{unif} (Σ), all hypotheses have length $len(\sigma) = |\mathcal{X}| = \log_2 |\Sigma|$ in the optimal code. Set the **Rademacher distribution** for the min-risk $\mathfrak{m} = \mathbf{R}_{\mathcal{F},\mathcal{D}}$ as*

$$p_{\mathfrak{m}}(\epsilon) := \sum_{\{\sigma | R_{\mathcal{F},\mathcal{D}}(\sigma) = \epsilon\}} 2^{-len(\sigma)} = \begin{cases} \frac{\left|\mathbf{R}_{\mathcal{F},\mathcal{D}}^{-1}(\epsilon)\right|}{|\Sigma|} & \text{if } \epsilon \in \mathbf{R}_{\mathcal{F},\mathcal{D}}(\Sigma) \\ 0 & \text{else.} \end{cases} \tag{16}$$

The Rademacher distribution is constructed following Solomonoff's approach after substituting the min-risk as a "special-purpose Turing machine" that only accepts hypotheses in finite set Σ as inputs. It tracks the fraction of hypotheses in Σ that yield risk ϵ.

The Rademacher distribution arises naturally as the denominator when using Bayes' rule to compute the actual repertoire $p_{\mathfrak{m}}(\Sigma|\epsilon)$:

$$p_{\mathfrak{m}}(\sigma|\epsilon) = \frac{p_{\mathfrak{m}}(\epsilon|\sigma)}{p_{\mathfrak{m}}(\epsilon)} \cdot p_{unif}(\sigma), \quad \text{where } p_{\mathfrak{m}}(\epsilon|\sigma) = \begin{cases} 1 & \text{if } \mathbf{R}_{\mathcal{F},\mathcal{D}}(\sigma) = \epsilon \\ 0 & \text{else.} \end{cases}$$

Proposition 17 (Rademacher complexity via min-risk)

$$\mathcal{R}(\mathcal{F}, \mathcal{D}) = 1 - 2 \cdot \mathbb{E}\big[\epsilon \,\big|\, p_{\mathfrak{m}}(\epsilon)\big]. \tag{17}$$

Proof: We refer to $\mathbb{E}\big[\epsilon \,\big|\, p_{\mathfrak{m}}(\epsilon)\big]$ as the expected min-risk. From Eq. (8),

$$\mathcal{R}(\mathcal{F}, \mathcal{D}) = \frac{1}{|\Sigma|} \sum_{\sigma \in \Sigma} \left[\sup_{f \in \mathcal{F}} \frac{1}{l} \sum_{i=1}^{l} \sigma(x_i) \cdot f(x_i) \right].$$

Observe that $\frac{1}{l}\sum_{i=1}^{l} \sigma(x_i) \cdot f(x_i) = 1 - 2\mathbf{R}(f, \mathcal{D}, \sigma)$. It follows that $\sup_{f \in \mathcal{F}} \frac{1}{l}\sum_{i=1}^{l} \sigma(x_i) \cdot f(x_i) = 1 - 2\mathbf{R}_{\mathcal{F},\mathcal{D}}(\sigma)$, which implies

$$\mathcal{R}(\mathcal{F}, \mathcal{D}) = 1 - 2\sum_{\sigma \in \Sigma} \frac{\mathbf{R}_{\mathcal{F},\mathcal{D}}(\sigma)}{|\Sigma|} = 1 - 2\sum_{\epsilon} \epsilon \cdot \frac{\left|\mathbf{R}_{\mathcal{F},\mathcal{D}}^{-1}(\epsilon)\right|}{|\Sigma|}. \qquad \blacksquare$$

Rademacher complexity is low if the expected min-risk is high. The expected min-risk admits an interesting interpretation. For any hypothesis $\sigma \in \mathbf{R}_{\mathcal{F},\mathcal{D}}^{-1}(\epsilon)$ the classifier $\hat{f}_\sigma := \mathcal{A}_{\mathcal{F},\mathcal{D}}(\sigma) \in \mathcal{F}$ outputted by the learning algorithm yields incorrect answers on fraction $\epsilon = \frac{1}{l}\sum_{i=1}^{l} \mathbb{I}[\hat{f}_\sigma(x_i) \neq \sigma(x_i)]$ of the data. It follows that

$$\sum_{\epsilon} p_{\mathfrak{m}}(\epsilon) \cdot \epsilon = \sum_{\epsilon} \frac{\left|\mathbf{R}_{\mathcal{F},\mathcal{D}}^{-1}(\epsilon)\right|}{|\Sigma|} \cdot \frac{1}{l}\sum_{l} \mathbb{I}[\hat{f}_\sigma(x_i) \neq \sigma(x_i)]$$

$$= \sum_{\epsilon} \Big(\text{fraction of hypotheses falsified}\Big) \cdot \Big(\text{on fraction } \epsilon \text{ of the data}\Big).$$

A bold theory $\mathcal{F}$ is one for which $\mathbb{E}[\epsilon|p_{\mathbf{m}}(\epsilon)]$ is high, meaning that its predictors (the classifiers it tries to fit to data) are sufficiently narrow that it would falsify most hypotheses on most of the data.

When a bold theory happens to fit labeled data well, it is guaranteed to perform well in future:

Corollary 18 (information-theoretic empirical Rademacher bound)
With probability $1 - \delta$, the risk of predictor $\hat{f} = \mathcal{A}_{\mathcal{F}}(\mathcal{D}, \mathcal{L})$ outputted by learning machine $\mathcal{A}_{\mathcal{F}}$ is bounded by

$$\mathbf{R}(f) \leq \mathbf{R}(f, \mathcal{D}, \mathcal{L}) + \left[1 - 2 \sum_{\epsilon} \epsilon \cdot 2^{-ei(\mathbf{R}_{\mathcal{F},\mathcal{D},\epsilon})} \right] + c_3 \sqrt{\frac{1 - \log_2 \delta}{l}} \qquad (18)$$

Proof: By Proposition 17 and definition of effective information we have

$$\mathcal{R}(\mathcal{F}, \mathcal{D}) = 1 - 2 \sum_{\epsilon} \epsilon \cdot \frac{|\mathbf{R}_{\mathcal{F},\mathcal{D}}^{-1}(\epsilon)|}{|\Sigma|} = 1 - 2 \sum_{\epsilon} \frac{\epsilon}{2^{ei(\mathbf{R}_{\mathcal{F},\mathcal{D},\epsilon})}}.$$

The result follows by Theorem 10.   ■

Rademacher complexity is low if the min-risk's sharp measurements (high ei) are accurate (low ϵ), and conversely. Analogously to Corollary 13, the Rademacher bound implies the future performance of a classifier depends on: (i) the fraction ϵ of the data that $\hat{f}$ fits; (ii) the weighted (by the fraction ϵ of data that falsifies them) sum of the fraction of hypotheses falsified; and (iii) a confidence term. Once again, the only assumption is that P and σ^* are *fixed*.

5   Discussion

Learning according to algorithm $\mathcal{A}_{\mathcal{F},\mathcal{D}}$ entails computing the min-risk, which classifies hypotheses about $\mathcal{D}$ according to how well they are approximated by predictors in repertoire $\mathcal{F}$. Repertoires that rule out many hypotheses when they fit labeled data $(\mathcal{D}, \mathcal{L})$ generate more effective information than repertoires that "approximate everything". As a consequence, when and if an informative repertoire fits labeled data well, Corollary 13 implies we can be confident in future predictions on unseen data.

A pleasing consequence of reformulating empirical VC-entropy and empirical Rademacher complexity in terms of falsifying hypotheses is that it directly connects Popper's intuition about falsifiable theories to statistical learning theory, thereby providing a rigorous justification for the former.

Our motivation for reformulating learning theory information-theoretically arises from a desire to better understand the role of information in biology. Although Shannon information has been heavily and successfully applied to biological questions, it has been argued that it does not fully capture what biologists mean by information since it is not semantic. For example, Maynard Smith states that "In biology, the statement that A carries information about B implies that A has the form it does because it carries that information" [10]. Shannon information was invented to study communication across prespecified channels, and lacks any semantic content. Maynard Smith therefore argues that a different notion of information is needed to understand in what sense evolution and development embed information into an organism.

It may be fruitful to apply statistical learning theory to models of development. One possible approach is to consider analogs of repertoire $\mathcal{F}$. For example, $\mathcal{F}$ may correspond to the repertoire of possible adult forms a zygote could develop into. The particular adult form chosen, $\hat{f} \in \mathcal{F}$, depends on the historical interactions $(\mathcal{D}, \mathcal{L})$ between the organism and its environment, assuming these can be suitably formalized. The information generated by the organism's development would then have implications for its future interactions with its environment. More speculatively, a similar tactic could be applied to quantify the information embedded in populations by inheritance and natural selection.

Acknowledgements. I thank David Dowe and Samory Kpotufe for useful comments on an earlier version of this paper.

References

1. Balduzzi, D., Tononi, G.: Integrated Information in Discrete Dynamical Systems: Motivation and Theoretical Framework. PLoS Comput. Biol. 4(6), e1000091 (2008)
2. Balduzzi, D., Tononi, G.: Qualia: the geometry of integrated information. PLoS Comput. Biol. 5(8), e1000462 (2009)
3. Boucheron, S., Lugosi, G., Massart, P.: A Sharp Concentration Inequality with Applications. Random Structures and Algorithms 16(3), 277–292 (2000)
4. Bousquet, O., Boucheron, S., Lugosi, G.: Introduction to Statistical Learning Theory. In: Bousquet, O., von Luxburg, U., Rätsch, G. (eds.) Machine Learning 2003. LNCS (LNAI), vol. 3176, pp. 169–207. Springer, Heidelberg (2004)
5. Corfield, D., Schölkopf, B., Vapnik, V.: Falsification and Statistical Learning Theory: Comparing the Popper and Vapnik-Chervonenkis Dimensions. Journal for General Philosophy of Science 40(1), 51–58 (2009)
6. Dowe, D.L.: MML, hybrid Bayesian network graphical models, statistical consistency, invariance and uniqueness. In: Handbook of the Philosophy of Science. Philosophy of Statistics, vol. 7, pp. 901–982. Elsevier (2011)
7. Harman, G., Kulkarni, S.: Reliable Reasoning: Induction and Learning Theory. MIT Press (2007)
8. Koltchinskii, V.: Rademacher penalties and structural risk minimization. IEEE Trans. Inf. Theory 47, 1902–1914 (2001)
9. Lewis, D.: On the Plurality of Worlds. Basil Blackwell, Oxford (1986)
10. Maynard Smith, J.: The Concept of Information in Biology. Philosophy of Science 67, 177–194 (2000)
11. Popper, K.: The Logic of Scientific Discovery. Hutchinson (1959)

12. Solomonoff, R.J.: A formal theory of inductive inference I, II. Inform. Control 7, 1–22, 224-254 (1964)
13. Vapnik, V.: Estimation of Dependencies Based on Empirical Data. Springer (1982)
14. Vapnik, V.: Statistical Learning Theory. John Wiley & Sons (1998)
15. Wallace, C.S.: Statistical and Inductive Inference by Minimum Message Length. Springer (2005)
16. Wallace, C.S., Boulton, D.M.: An information measure for classification. The Computer Journal 11, 185–194 (1968)
17. Wallace, C.S., Dowe, D.L.: Minimum Message Length and Kolmogorov Complexity. The Computer Journal 42(4), 270–283 (1999)

The Semimeasure Property of Algorithmic Probability – "Feature" or "Bug"?

Douglas Campbell

Philosophy Programme, University of Canterbury, Christchurch 8041, New Zealand
douglas.campbell@canterbury.ac.nz

Abstract. An unknown process is generating a sequence of symbols, drawn from an alphabet, $\mathcal{A}$. Given an initial segment of the sequence, how can one predict the next symbol? Ray Solomonoff's theory of inductive reasoning rests on the idea that a useful estimate of a sequence's true probability of being outputted by the unknown process is provided by its *algorithmic probability* (its probability of being outputted by a species of probabilistic Turing machine). However algorithmic probability is a "semimeasure": i.e., the sum, over all $x \in \mathcal{A}$, of the conditional algorithmic probabilities of the next symbol being x, may be less than 1. Solomonoff thought that algorithmic probability must be normalized, to eradicate this semimeasure property, before it can yield acceptable probability estimates. This paper argues, to the contrary, that the semimeasure property contributes substantially, in its own right, to the power of an algorithmic-probability-based theory of induction, and that normalization is unnecessary.

Keywords: Algorithmic probability, sequence prediction, inductive reasoning, Solomonoff induction, Solomonoff normalization, semimeasure, convergence theorem.

1 Introduction

This paper is about whether a certain property of algorithmic probability (ALP) – namely, its so-called "semimeasure" property – should be regarded as a "bug" (i.e., as a source of theoretical weakness, that must be worked around and corrected for) or as a "feature" (i.e., as serving a useful or necessary function) within the context of an ALP-based theory of inductive reasoning. I will begin by describing ALP and its application to inductive inference. Next I will describe the semimeasure property of ALP, and explain why it is commonly considered to be a bug that must be eradicated and patched over with an *ad hoc* normalization procedure. Finally I will contend that this negative assessment of the semimeasure property's worth is incorrect. I will argue that the semimeasure property is properly seen as being a valuable and important feature of ALP, which makes a major contribution to the power, scope and elegance of an ALP-based theory of inductive reasoning. I will demonstrate that to normalize ALP is to pay a high price, in terms of lost theoretical elegance, in order to attain a result – the

D.L. Dowe (Ed.): Solomonoff Festschrift, LNAI 7070, pp. 79–90, 2013.

elimination of the semimeasure property – that is wholly undesirable in the first place. It is to "cut off the nose of ALP to spite its face", so to speak.

2   Notation

The symbol, $\wedge$, denotes the empty string, "". $|x|$ denotes the length, in symbols, of the string, x. E.g., $|\wedge| = 0$ and $|ABC| = 3$. xy denotes the concatenation of strings x and y. $\wedge x = x = x\wedge$, and $|xy| = |x| + |y|$. The *prefixes* of a string include all initial segments of the string. Every string is a prefix of itself, $\wedge$ is a prefix of every string, and x is a prefix of xy.

3   Algorithmic Probability (ALP)

The concept of ALP involves a type of computing device that I shall here call a *Solomonoff machine*. Such a machine is a finite state automaton equipped with an indefinitely expandable internal working memory, which accepts a sequence of randomly generated binary digits as input, and which emits another sequence of binary digits as output. At each step, the machine either might or might not accept a randomly generated digit of input, and might or might not emit a digit of output. Over the full course of its operation it might accept either a finite, or an infinite, number of input digits, and it might emit either a finite, or an infinite, number of output digits. It has no capacity to retract or modify its output, so each digit of output is "set in stone" the moment it is produced. The indeterministic process that generates its input is "fair", 0s and 1s being equiprobable.

A Solomonoff machine can be concretely realized as a probabilistic "monotonic" Turing machine with three tapes, these being: (i) a two-way, read-only, initially blank work tape; (ii) a one-way, read-only input tape pre-inscribed with an ongoing randomly generated binary sequence; and (iii) a one-way, write-only, unidirectionally accessible, initially blank output tape with the alphabet, $\{0, 1\}$.

Let Sx denote a particular Solomonoff machine (having some particular state-transition table).

The string, y, *encodes* the string, z, on Sx, iff any input to Sx prefixed by y will result in Sx's output being prefixed by z. (So, for example, if Sa's output must start with 11 provided its input starts with 010, then 010 encodes 11 on Sa.)[1]

Let Fx be the function computed by Sx. $Fx(y) = z$ iff z is the longest string encoded by y on Sx. (So, for example, if 010 encodes 11 on Sa, but if it encodes neither 110 or 111 on Sa, then $Fa(010) = 11$.)

A given Solomonoff machine will usually produce any one of a variety of different outputs with different probabilities, its output depending on which particular random input it is fed with. Let Px denote the probability distribution, over binary output strings, associated with Sx. $Px(z) = q$ just in case the probability

---

[1] This is similar to the notion of Educated Turing Machine in [1, sec. 4][2, sec. 2.3].

of Sx's output being prefixed by the binary string, z, is q. $Px(w|z)$ denotes the *conditional probability* of Sx's next symbols of output constituting the binary string w, given that Sx's output to date is z. $Px(w|z) = Px(zw)/Px(z)$.

The string, p, is a *program* that causes Sx to *simulate* Sy, iff, for any string z, $Fx(pz) = Fy(z)$. In other words, the effect of Sx receiving an input prefixed by a program that causes Sx to simulate Sy is to cause Sx to "change personalities" (so to speak), by thereafter exhibiting input-output behavior indistinguishable from that of Sy. ($\wedge$ is a program that causes every Solomonoff machine to simulate itself.)

A *universal Solomonoff machine* is a Solomonoff machine that can be programmed to simulate any Solomonoff machine. That is, if Su is universal, then for any Solomonoff machine, Sx, there is a program that causes Su to simulate Sx.

Let the *reference machine*, Sm, be some particular universal Solomonoff machine that has been selected, by us, to serve as our benchmark for measuring the ALP of strings. The ALP of any string, x, is simply $Pm(x)$. That is, a string's ALP is the probability of our reference machine's output being prefixed by the string. ALP is obviously *machine-dependent*, in the sense that the ALP of a string will tend to vary depending on which particular universal Solomonoff machine we choose to be our reference machine.

4   The Semimeasure Property of ALP

A probability distribution, ρ, over binary sequences is a *measure* if and only if $\rho(x) = \rho(x0) + \rho(x1)$ for any string, x. In other words, it is a measure if the conditional probabilities it assigns to the next symbol after x being a 0 and to the next symbol after x being a 1 must always, for any x, sum to unity. On the other hand, ρ is a *semimeasure* if and only if there is some string, x, such that $\rho(x) > \rho(x0) + \rho(x1)$. For example, suppose that $\rho(010) = 0.6$, while $\rho(0100) = 0.3$ and $\rho(0101) = 0.1$. This being so, not all the probability assigned by ρ to the sequence "010" is split between and inherited by the two, longer strings "0100" and "0101". Some of the shorter string's probability (0.2 of the 0.6) instead "goes missing", so to speak. This makes ρ a semimeasure.

Recall that $Pm(x)$ is the probability of Sm's output being prefixed by x. Having outputted x, Sm must next do one of three different things: (i) it might output another 0; (ii) it might output another 1; or (iii) it might stop outputting 0s and 1s once and for all as a result of either having halted or having gone into an infinite, unproductive loop. Sm always, for any x, has a non-zero probability of doing the last of these things (there being a non-zero probability that Sm's random input will start with a program that causes it to simulate a second Solomonoff machine that will always, regardless of its input, output x and then halt). It follows that $Pm(x) > Pm(x0) + Pm(x1)$, which makes Pm a semimeasure, not a measure.

5   ALP's Application to Induction, and the Semimeasure Problem

ALP was discovered by Ray Solomonoff, who used it as the central ingredient of a theory of inductive reasoning [3, 4]. The theory concerns a method for accomplishing a certain type of sequence prediction task. By way of illustrating the task, let's imagine that a black box has fallen to Earth from a place unknown. Attached to the black box's exterior is a symbol-stamping mechanism, through which is threaded an initially blank tape. Casual inspection of the mechanism reveals that it is capable of stamping only two types of symbols onto the tape – 0s and 1s – and that each symbol will be stamped on the tape to the immediate right of its predecessor. Both the ordering of these symbols, and the timing of each symbol's delivery, are under the control of a process hidden within the black box. We have little or no idea what this process might be, but the gradually accumulating sequence of symbols it produces is exposed to our view. The black box receives no input. Let the *black box task* be the task of making a probabilistic prediction about the black box's next symbol of output, based on its observed output-to-date.

Two types of method for accomplishing the black box task may be distinguished. A *three-way method* is a method which accepts any given binary string of the black box's output-to-date, and then assigns conditional probabilities to each of three distinct possibilities, these being: (i) the next symbol will be a 0; (ii) the next symbol will be a 1; and (iii) the black box will never output another 0 or 1 again, and so the next symbol on the black box's output tape (together with all subsequent symbols) will default to _ (where _ represents a blank). A *two-way method*, on the other hand, assigns conditional probabilities to only two possibilities: (i) the next symbol will be a 0; and (ii) the next symbol will be a 1. A two-way method should obviously be used only if the possibility of the black box's output terminating can be dismissed out of hand. Such might be the case because one knows from the outset that the process operating in the box will keep producing binary digits forever (e.g., perhaps one has been told as much by a trustworthy source who has looked into the box).

Let $\mu(x)$ denote the true, objective probability of the black box's output being prefixed by the binary string, x, and let $\mu(y|x)$ denote the conditional probability of the black box's next symbols of output comprising the string, y, given that its output-to-date is x. $\mu(y|x) = \mu(xy)/\mu(x)$. If the process in the black box is somehow guaranteed by facts about its constitution to keep producing 0s and 1s forever, then μ will be a measure. Otherwise, if there is a non-zero objective probability of the black box's output terminating at some point, then μ will be a semimeasure. If the process in the black box is deterministic then, for any string x, either $\mu(x) = 0$ or $\mu(x) = 1$. If it is indeterministic then there will be some strings x such that $0 < \mu(x) < 1$.

The essential idea behind Solomonoff's theory of induction is that we should predict the output of the black box (or equivalent symbol source) by assuming it has the same output producing dispositions as our reference machine. In its simplest form, the idea is that we should use $Pm(x)$ as an estimate of $\mu(x)$ (or, equivalently, $Pm(y|x)$ as an estimate of $\mu(y|x)$). So, for instance, if the reference machine would, if its output-to-date were "0011", have a probability of 0.3 of next outputting a 0, and if the black box's output-to-date is "0011", then, so the idea goes, we should assign a probability of 0.3 to the black box's next symbol of output being a 0.[2]

Solomonoff focused specifically on using ALP to develop a two-way method for predicting the extension of a binary string. He seems not to have considered using it to construct a three-way method. Hence, at least as far as Solomonoff was concerned, μ must be a measure, and there are only two things that the black box might legitimately do next – output a 0, or output a 1. (Indeed, Li and Vitanyi report that Solomonoff, "viewed the notion of measure as sacrosanct" [12, p. 280].) But, as we have seen, Pm is a semimeasure, and there are, at any point in time, *three* things the reference machine might do next – output a 0, output a 1, or stop producing binary output. Hence a problem arises (the "semimeasure problem", as I will call it). Since a two-way method must divide conditional probability only between the possibilities of the next symbol being a 0 or of it being a 1, the conditional probabilities it assigns to these two possibilities should sum to unity. However, because the reference machine divides probability between *three* future possibilities, not just two, the conditional probabilities it apportions to 0 and to 1 may (and in fact, always will) sum to a value less than unity.

Solomonoff addressed this problem by describing a normalization operation that converts the semimeasure, Pm, into a corresponding measure, Pm' [4, 13]. This operation works by, in effect, taking the probability of the reference machine receiving a random input that will cause it to terminate its output after outputting the binary string, x, and then redistributing this probability back over all random inputs to the reference machine that will cause it to output at least one more 0 or 1 after x. This is done recursively, for progressively longer strings, x. That is:

$$Pm'(\wedge) = 1$$

$$Pm'(x0) = Pm'(x)\frac{Pm(x0)}{Pm(x0) + Pm(x1)}$$

$$Pm'(x1) = Pm'(x)\frac{Pm(x1)}{Pm(x0) + Pm(x1)}$$

---

[2] Solomonoff's theory of induction is to be contrasted with the closely related *Minimum Message Length* (MML) approach of Wallace and Boulton [5–10]. For a comparison of the two approaches, see [1] and [2, p. 404]. Some proponents of MML argue that Solomonoff's theory isn't really a theory of "induction" at all (see, for instance, [2, p. 405–407] and [11, p. 930–931]), with one of the thoughts being that, whereas genuine induction involves reasoning from a body of observations to a general hypothesis, Solomonoff's procedure yields no such general hypothesis, and instead yields only predictions about future observations (of upcoming 0s and 1s). I contend that Solomonoff's procedure is genuinely inductive, in at least the sense that it yields predictions about the future behaviour of the black box *that are not deductively implied* by anything that is known about the black box or its output to date. However pursuing this issue would take me far from the topic of this paper.

Solomonoff's considered proposal was that we should predict the black box's output by using the measure, Pm', rather than the un-normalized semimeasure, Pm, as an estimate of μ [4].

6   "Bug" or "Feature"?

Solomonoff himself made mention of a distinction between the "features" and "bugs" of ALP while defending his theory of induction from a pair of criticisms [14]. The first criticism concerns the fact that the values of $Pm(x)$ and $Pm'(x)$ are uncomputable, and hence largely unknowable in practice. The second concerns the fact that these values are also radically dependent on our particular choice of reference machine, and to this extent arbitrary and subjective. Solomonoff responded to these criticisms by maintaining that both the uncomputability and the machine-dependence of ALP are to be properly seen as playing useful, and indeed indispensible, roles in his theory of induction, rather than as being sources of theoretical weakness. Specifically, he held that uncomputability is simply a necessary flipside of completeness: that ALP is uncomputable precisely because it can be used to detect and extrapolate *any* computable regularity or pattern in a sequence of data [15]. In a similar vein, he held that machine dependence is vital in enabling us to factor in whatever prior information we might possess about the symbol source. Our prior knowledge about the symbol source should, Solomonoff maintained, be directly reflected in our particular choice of reference machine [16]. He summed up the situation by saying that both ALP's uncomputability and its machine-dependence count as "necessary features" of his theory, not as "bugs" [14].

Following Solomonoff's lead, let's count among the "features" of ALP any of its properties that should be celebrated by a proponent of an ALP-based theory of induction for the valuable role they play in the theory, and let's count among its "bugs" those of its properties (if any) that are to be regretted for the problems and weaknesses they introduce. When Solomonoff held that uncomputability and machine-dependence are features, not bugs, of ALP, he was charging critics of his theory of induction with overlooking ways in which these properties can be turned to the theory's advantage, by being made to serve useful or necessary functions within it. It is clear that Solomonoff himself regarded the semimeasure property as a genuine "bug" in the idea that we should use ALP to predict the output of the symbol source, for – as just explained – he used a normalization procedure to eradicate it, and did not attempt to show that it can be exploited to play a useful role in the theory. I will now try to show that it is instead properly regarded as being a very valuable "feature".

7   Another Way of Tackling the Semimeasure Problem

We've seen that the semimeasure problem arises because, whereas the black box must do one of only *two* things next – output a 0, or output a 1 – the reference machine can instead do either one of *three* things next – output a 0, output a 1, or terminate its output. However this disparity between the ranges of behaviours the two devices can exhibit arises only when it is stipulated from the outset that the black box's output can't terminate. When a three-way method is used to predict the black box's output, no such stipulation is in force. Hence, provided we use ALP to construct a three-way method, rather than a two-way method, then each and every possible behaviour of the reference machine corresponds directly to a possible behaviour of the black box, and *vice versa*.

The following proposal for resolving the semimeasure problem therefore suggests itself: whereas Solomonoff used ALP to construct a two-way method for predicting the extension of a binary sequence, we will instead use it to construct a three-way method. In other words, we will include the possibility of the black box's output terminating among the set of alternative outcomes to which a probability must be assigned. The probability we assign to the black box's output terminating after it has outputted the string, x, will be identical to the probability of the reference machine's output terminating after it has outputted x. Under this proposal, ALP's semimeasure property doesn't merely cease to be a "bug" in an ALP-based theory of induction, but instead acquires the status of being a useful and necessary "feature", for in order for a three-way method to assign a certain quantity of probability to the possibility that the sequence has terminated, it must leave the selfsame quantity of probability unassigned either to the possibility that the next symbol will be a 0 or to the possibility that it will be a 1. Hence the probability distribution that such a method is based on must be a semimeasure, and cannot be a measure.

We now have two proposals on the table, which I will call *Solomonoff's proposal* (it being the proposal that Solomonoff championed) and the *new proposal* respectively. According to Solomonoff's proposal, the proper goal of an ALP-based theory of induction is to construct a maximally reliable two-way method for predicting the continuation of a binary series, and the normalized measure, $Pm'(x)$, should be used as an estimate of $\mu(x)$. According to the new proposal, on the other hand, ALP is best used to construct a three-way method for making such predictions, and the unnormalized semimeasure, $Pm(x)$, should be used as an estimate of $\mu(x)$. Both proposals circumvent the semimeasure problem, and are on an equal footing in this respect, but I will now offer reasons to believe that the new proposal is nevertheless superior to Solomonoff's.

The first and most important reason concerns Solomonoff's own grounds for thinking that ALP-based predictions about the black box's output are likely to be any good. I will argue that these grounds offer stronger support to the new proposal than they do to Solomonoff's own proposal.

The following concepts and notation will be useful. Let a *padded string* be a binary string with a _ appended to its rightmost end. (E.g., "0110_" is a padded string.) Let $\rho(x_-)$ denote the probability assigned by ρ to the possibility that the binary string, x, won't be followed by any more 0s or 1s. That is, $\rho(x_-) = \rho(x) - \rho(x0) - \rho(x1)$. Notice that if ρ assigns a non-zero probability to any padded string, then ρ is a semimeasure. Let's say that the distribution, ρ *dominates* the distribution, ν, iff there is some non-zero probability, p, such that, for any binary or padded string x, $\rho(x) \geq p\nu(x)$. So, for example, if, for any binary or padded x, the probability assigned by ρ to x never undershoots the probability assigned by ν to x by more than a multiplicative factor of, say, 0.3, then ρ dominates ν (to within a factor of 0.3).

Now, let's suppose that we use a distribution, ρ as an estimate of μ. It can be shown [4] that, on assumption that ρ dominates μ, then, as time goes by and as the black box's output-to-date grows in length, the conditional probabilities that we assign to the next symbol by using ρ will rapidly converge to match the true, objective probabilities that are assigned to this symbol by μ. That is, if $o_{1...n}$ denotes the black box's first n symbols of output and o_n denotes its nth symbol of output, then $\lim_{n\to\infty}[\rho(o_n|o_{1...n-1}) - \mu(o_n|o_{1...n-1})] = 0$.

This is encouraging, for it means that our estimate of μ will yield good predictions in the long run provided that it dominates μ. But how can we arrange for our estimate of μ to dominate μ when – ignorant as we are about what is in the black box – we know little or nothing about the nature of μ itself? Solomonoff's answer is that we can maximize our chances of "catching" μ within the set of distributions that are dominated by our estimate simply by casting our net very widely indeed. A probability distribution, ρ is *computable* iff there is a classical Turing machine that will, when given a binary string, x, as input, output an encoding of $\rho(x)$. Solomonoff showed that Pm' is "universal" in the sense that it dominates *every computable measure* [4]. Hence Pm' will dominate μ if μ is a computable measure.

That's the good news. The bad news is that if μ is a semimeasure – which is to say, if the process in the black box has the capacity to produce a terminating output – then Solomonoff's convergence result doesn't provide us with any assurance that Pm' will yield accurate probabilistic predictions in the long run. This limitation of Pm' is unsurprising, for, after all, Pm' was designed by Solomonoff to provide us with a two-way method for making predictions, and as such it is to be used only when it is known that the black box's output *won't terminate*. But it is still a very serious limitation, for, after all, it is perfectly possible that the process in the black box will stop outputting 0s and 1s at some point.[3] Ideally, we would like our estimate of μ to yield accurate predictions irrespective of what is in the black box, and irrespective of the nature of μ. The more distributions that are dominated by our estimate of μ, the smaller the risk of μ escaping domination by it, and so the greater the chances that the estimate will lead us to the true probabilities [17, p. 28]. In order for the estimate to be able to lead us to the true probabilities even if the black box can produce

---

[3] For example, C.S. Wallace [2, p. 407] imagines a process that examines all the stable isotopes of the chemical elements, one by one, in order of their atomic weight, outputting extensive data about their physical, chemical and spectroscopic properties as it goes. After examining lead-208 the process will stop, lead-208 being the last stable isotope, and so the sequence of data it is producing will terminate at this point. A predictor who has observed a sufficiently long initial segment of this data sequence should ideally be able to predict both that the sequence will eventually terminate, and the point at which it will do so.

a terminating output, we need it to dominate, not just distributions that are measures, but also distributions that are semimeasures.

Is there a distribution we might use as our estimate of μ, which dominates, not just all computable measures, but also all computable semimeasures? Indeed, there is, and it is none other than the original, unnormalized version of ALP, Pm. As a first step to understanding why Pm dominates such a large class of distributions, it will help to introduce the notion of a *Solomonoff distribution*, this simply being a distribution that is associated with some particular (universal or non-universal) Solomonoff machine. That is, ρ is a Solomonoff distribution iff there is some Solomonoff machine, Sy, such that, for all binary strings x, $\rho(x) = Py(x)$. Some Solomonoff distributions are measures, while others are semimeasures. The Solomonoff distribution, Px, is a measure iff, regardless of which randomly generated input the corresponding Solomonoff machine, Sx, is supplied with, its binary output will never stop. On the other hand, if there is at least one possible input to Sx that will result in its output terminating at some point, then Px is a semimeasure.

It is easily shown that Pm dominates all Solomonoff distributions, including all those that are measures and all those that are semimeasures. To see this, suppose ρ is some Solomonoff distribution. This being so, there will be some Solomonoff machine, St, whose probability of producing an output prefixed by x is $\rho(x)$. Since our reference machine, Sm, is universal, there will be some program, g, that will cause it to simulate St. The probability of g occurring as a prefix of Sm's randomly generated input is simply $1/2^{|g|}$. If g does occur as a prefix of Sm's input, then, when Sm has read in g, it will begin simulating St, and from this point forward it will exhibit output-producing propensities indistinguishable from those of St. Thus Sm has a probability of at least $1/2^{|g|}$ of simulating St, and if it does simulate St then it will, like St, have a probability of $\rho(x)$ of producing an output prefixed by x. This means that Sm's own probability of producing an output prefixed by x must be at least $1/2^{|g|}\rho(x)$, from which it follows that Pm dominates ρ (to within a factor of $1/2^{|g|}$). As for ρ, so for any Solomonoff distribution, whether it be a measure or a semimeasure.

Every computable distribution – whether it be a measure or a semimeasure – is a Solomonoff distribution. In order to see this, recall that if ρ is computable then there is a classical Turing machine that, when given a binary string x as input, will produce an encoding of $\rho(x)$ as output. Given this classical Turing machine, we can easily engineer a Solomonoff machine, Sh, that simulates the classical Turing machine in order to determine, for any binary string x, the value of $\rho(x)$, and which then outputs a sequence prefixed by x with a probability of $\rho(x)$, while using the randomly generated sequence of 0s and 1s on its own input tape as a source of indeterminism. Since Sh's design ensures that $Sh(x) = \rho(x)$ for all binary x, ρ is a Solomonoff distribution.

Since Pm dominates all Solomonoff distributions, and since all computable distributions are Solomonoff distributions, Pm dominates all computable distributions, including not just all the computable measures that are dominated by Pm', but also all computable semimeasures. This being so, a three-way inductive reasoning method based on Pm is inherently less risky than a two-way method based on Pm'. The conditions that μ must satisfy in order for the former method to be guaranteed to yield accurate probabilistic predictions in the long run are considerably weaker and less demanding than those it must satisfy in order for the latter method to yield the same guarantee. The point might be put by saying that Pm is "more universal" than Pm', in the sense that Pm dominates a much larger class of computable distributions than Pm' does.

The second reason for preferring the new proposal to Solomonoff's proposal is pragmatic, and concerns the practical utility of the inductive methods they prescribe. We can safely use Solomonoff's two-way method only when we can be certain, ahead of time, that the process we are predicting will keep outputting symbols forever. It is, however, surely impossible to find any real-life example of a process that satisfies this condition. Science teaches us that the universe we inhabit is governed by the second law of thermodynamics, and that it is fated, if not to a Big Crunch, then to heat-death. Hence, far from it being the case that we can ever be *perfectly certain* that a symbol source we are dealing with will keep producing output for eternity, the smart money will always be on its output eventually terminating. Our background knowledge about our world may provide us with but little information about the likely symbol-producing propensities of the black box, but it does at least tell us that terminations of output are probably in the offing. This being so, we must, when we are doing induction in the real world, use a method that will yield acceptable results if μ is a semimeasure. A three-way method based on Pm satisfies this requirement, while a two-way method based on Pm' does not.

The third reason has to do with the comparative simplicity and elegance of the two proposals. The fundamental idea behind an ALP-based theory of induction is that an hypothesis that attributes certain output-producing dispositions to a symbol source can be represented by a program that causes the reference machine to itself manifest these selfsame output-producing dispositions. Some programs, of course, cause the reference machine to have a non-zero probability of producing a terminating output. Solomonoff thought that such terminating programs "do not result in useful output" [13, p. 567]. But if we take to its natural conclusion the idea that programs represent hypotheses about the output-producing dispositions of the symbol source, then why should we not hold instead that such a program, which causes the reference machine to have a certain chance of producing an output that ends, represents a hypothesis that says the symbol source has this same chance of producing an output that ends? Why not indeed! There is no principled reason not to, and if we do then the resulting theory of induction is both more elegant, in view of the fact that it doesn't arbitrarily treat terminations of output differently than 0s and 1s, and more predictively powerful, since it yields a three-way method that can cope with terminations of output, rather than a two-way method that can't. On the other hand, if, like Solomonoff, we treat the reference machine's terminating outputs as being predictively meaningless, then we are left to confront the semimeasure problem, and must wheel in a normalization operation to surmount it. The inclusion of a normalization operation further complicates the theory and detracts from its elegance.

The final reason I offer for thinking that the new proposal should be preferred over Solomonoff's proposal concerns certain technical objections to the normalization operation that the new proposal avoids by simply dispensing with normalization altogether. These include, for instance, the objection that there are several rival methods of normalizing, each yielding measures with different properties, and no very compelling reason to choose one over another [12, p. 281]; the objection (due to Robert M. Solovay) that every choice of normalization operation has an unboundedly large impact on the relative probabilities assigned to some particular sequence [12, p. 301] (but c.f. [18]); and the objection that, while Pm is at least lower semicomputable, Pm' is not even computable in this restricted sense.

To conclude, it is my contention that ALP's property of being a semimeasure appears to be a "bug" in an ALP-based theory of induction only if one insists on trying to whack the round peg of ALP into the square hole of a two-way method for predicting a black box's output. The semimeasure problem evaporates entirely if one accepts terminations of output as being events worthy of prediction, and therefore uses ALP to construct a three-way method for making predictions.

References

1. Wallace, C., Dowe, D.: Minimum message length and Kolmogorov complexity. Computer Journal 42, 270–283 (1999)
2. Wallace, C.: Statistical and Inductive Inference by Minimum Message Length. Information Science and Statistics. Springer (2005)
3. Solomonoff, R.: A formal theory of inductive inference: Parts 1 and 2. Information and Control 7, 1–22, 224–254 (1964)
4. Solomonoff, R.: Complexity-based induction systems: Comparisons and convergence theorems. IEEE Trans. Infor. Theory IT-24, 422–432 (1978)
5. Wallace, C., Boulton, D.: An information measure for classification. Computer Journal 11(2), 185–194 (1968)
6. Boulton, D., Wallace, C.: The information content of a multistate distribution. J. Theoret. Biol. 23, 269–278 (1969)
7. Boulton, D., Wallace, C.: A program for numerical classification. The Computer Journal 13(1), 63–69 (1970)
8. Boulton, D., Wallace, C.: An information measure for hierarchic classification. The Computer Journal 16(3), 254–261 (1973)
9. Wallace, C., Boulton, D.: An invariant Bayes method for point estimation. Classification Society Bull. 3(3), 11–34 (1975)
10. Boulton, D., Wallace, C.: An information measure for single-link classification. The Computer Journal 18(3), 236–238 (1975)
11. Dowe, D.L.: MML, hybrid Bayesian network graphical models, statistical consistency, invariance and uniqueness. In: Bandyopadhyay, P., Forster, M. (eds.) Philosophy of Statistics. Handbook of the Philosophy of Science, vol. 7, Elsevier (2011)
12. Li, M., Vitányi, P.: An introduction to Kolmogorov complexity and its applications, 2nd edn. Springer (1997)

13. Solomonoff, R.: Three kinds of probabilistic induction: universal distributions and convergence theorems. The Computer Journal: Christopher Stewart Wallace (1933-2004); Memorial Special Issue 51, 566–570 (2008)
14. Solomonoff, R.: The Kolmogorov lecture: The universal distribution and machine learning. Computer Journal 46, 598–601 (2003)
15. Solomonoff, R.: The discovery of algorithmic probability. Journal of Computer and System Sciences 55, 73–88 (1997)
16. Solomonoff, R.: Does algorithmic probability solve the problem of induction? Technical Report (1997)
17. Hutter, M.: On generalized computable universal priors and their convergence, IDSIA-05-05 (2005)
18. Solomonoff, R.: The probability of "undefined" (non-converging) output in generating the universal probability distribution. Inf. Process. Lett. 106, 238–240 (2008)

Inductive Inference and Partition Exchangeability in Classification

Jukka Corander[1,3], Yaqiong Cui[1], and Timo Koski[2]

[1] Department of Mathematics and Statistics, University of Helsinki,
FI-00014, Finland
{jukka.corander,yaqiong.cui}@helsinki.fi
[2] Department of Mathematics, Royal Institute of Technology,
S-100 44 Stockholm, Sweden
tjtkoski@kth.se
[3] Department of Mathematics, Åbo Akademi University, FI-20500 Turku, Finland

Abstract. Inductive inference has been a subject of intensive research efforts over several decades. In particular, for classification problems substantial advances have been made and the field has matured into a wide range of powerful approaches to inductive inference. However, a considerable challenge arises when deriving principles for an inductive supervised classifier in the presence of unpredictable or unanticipated events corresponding to unknown alphabets of observable features. Bayesian inductive theories based on de Finetti type exchangeability which have become popular in supervised classification do not apply to such problems. Here we derive an inductive supervised classifier based on partition exchangeability due to John Kingman. It is proven that, in contrast to classifiers based on de Finetti type exchangeability which can optimally handle test items independently of each other in the presence of infinite amounts of training data, a classifier based on partition exchangeability still continues to benefit from a joint prediction of labels for the whole population of test items. Some remarks about the relation of this work to generic convergence results in predictive inference are also given.

Keywords: Bayesian learning, classification, exchangeability, inductive inference.

1 Introduction

Ever since Ray Solomonoff introduced his pioneering views on inductive inference [1], machine learning community has witnessed a steadily growing interest at the quest of unravelling the foundations of this field. This, of course, is an extremely bold enterprise given the universal relevance of the questions related to induction, and therefore, one could argue that the most concrete leaps forward have been achievable by narrowing down the focus to particular problems of inductive inference. Indeed, when considering the realm of classification, we have witnessed a tremendous development of both the theory and applications since the early inductive approaches [2-4]. At the conceptual level, most intensive developments

D.L. Dowe (Ed.): Solomonoff Festschrift, LNAI 7070, pp. 91–105, 2013.

of inductive classifiers have taken place in the context of tree- and network-like constructs that are used to map conditional probabilities of both observable features of items, their labels and other latent random variables involved in the models. Broad overviews of various methods based on trees, forests and networks can be found in [5-7]. As some of these constructs are too flexible to be pursuable in the presence of sparse training data, simpler generative classifiers such as naive Bayes, have continued to thrive despite of the more advanced alternatives [8].

Over the past century, numerous arguments have been put forward to support the view that in a world where uncertainty and noisy observations reign, inductive inference should be Bayesian. In particular, de Finetti's work on exchangeability has played a central role in these developments [9],[10]. However, the Bayesian perspective is far from universally accepted and many other approaches to inductive reasoning have had a peaceful coexistence with it over several decades [11-13].

In the context of classification, a particularly intriguing challenge arises when we attempt to build principles of classification out of observed discrete-valued features possessing unknown alphabets. de Finetti type arguments do not apply to such data, and consequently it is less intuitive how a coherent Bayesian inductive classifier could look like when unpredictable events can occur. One feasible answer to our quest lies in the theory of exchangeable random partitions developed by Sir John Kingman [14-17], see also the elegant discussion of its appearances within several fields of study and its inductive implications by Sandy Zabell [10]. Here we harness the particular form of partition exchangeability to arrive at an inductive supervised classifier as a generalization of more standard classifiers arising under de Finetti type exchangeability.

It is worth noting that in other fields of machine learning, such as in compression, prediction and unsupervised modeling of text data, problems of inference related to unknown alphabets have gained more attention and several solutions have been proposed [18-20]. Interestingly, the line of work on data compression with unknown alphabets presented in [19] is very closely related to that of Kingman and his predecessors, but it appears to have been derived completely independently. The Bayesian hierarchical Dirichlet prior introduced in [18] is combined with a multinomial likelihood for prediction of a single test item feature using a training set that may be very sparse in relation to the size of the underlying alphabet over which predictions are made. An example of unsupervised text analysis in such large discrete domains is represented by the discrete hierarchical Dirichlet process model in [20]. The main difference between these works and the current problem is that we consider simultaneous prediction of labels for a population of test items when feature distributions are inductively learned from training data.

We demonstrate that classifiers based on partition exchangeability behave differently from classifiers derived under de Finetti type exchangeability in [21],[22], where it was shown that marginal and simultaneous predictive classifiers of test data become congruent almost surely when the amount of training data tends to infinity. Under partition exchangeability a positive probability always remains for the event that marginal and simultaneous predictive classifiers do not coincide, such that the population of test data items will play a clear role when assessing how surprising any particular observed event is. The gain in classification accuracy achieved by a joint labeling of the population of test items in the presence of sparse training data was also demonstrated in practice in [21] and the optimality of such a predictive approach has also been considered in [23],[24].

The article is structured as follows. In Section 2 we consider the behavior of supervised predictive classifiers in relation to generic convergence results in predictive inference. Classifiers under partition exchangeability are introduced and their properties are examined in Section 3. The last section provides some concluding comments and remarks.

2   Supervised Predictive Classification under Partition Exchangeability

Seymour Geisser pioneered the idea that generative supervised classification of multiple test items should be performed jointly, instead of predicting the labels independently (marginally) for each test item [25],[26]. Recently, this idea was made explicitly operational through introduction of random urn models for the simultaneous classification and also developed further using a marginalization operation over joint labels based on decision-theoretic arguments [21],[22].

Denote the set of m available training items by M and correspondingly the set of n test items by N. For each item we observe a finite vector of d features, such that the element for the feature j takes values in an alphabet $\mathcal{X}_j, j = 1, ..., d$. In particular, these alphabets are not assumed known or fixed a priori, or even after observing the training items, such that the test items may harbor feature values not previously seen. This poses a challenge for the inductive inference, as an assumption of a fixed alphabet for a feature would necessitate a retrospective change of the predictive probabilities for all previous items whenever a new test item with a previously unobserved feature value appears. Examples of features where such a characteristic is an intrinsic property of the observation process are genes with novel alleles, corpuses extended with new words, etc.

A solution to the problem with induction in this setting arises by an application of the theory of partition exchangeability [14], which acknowledges the presence of previously unanticipated phenomena when predictive probabilities are formed from data. Partition exchangeability has been used in the context of unsupervised classification of genetic data [27],[28], however, we are not aware of any earlier attempts to define generative supervised classification models based on this theory.

For notational simplicity, we will consider each feature alphabet as the set $\mathcal{X}_j = \{1, \ldots, r_j\}$, where r_j is a positive, non-fixed integer remaining implicit in our analysis for all $j = 1, \ldots, d$. A training item $i \in M$ is then characterized by a feature vector $\mathbf{z}_i$, with the elements $z_{ij} \in \mathcal{X}_j, j = 1, ..., d$. Similarly, we have for a test item $i \in N$ the feature vector $\mathbf{x}_i$, with elements $x_{ij} \in \mathcal{X}_j$. Collections of the training and test data vectors are denoted by $\mathbf{z}^{(M)}$ and $\mathbf{x}^{(N)}$, respectively.

Let the training data represent k classes, such that T is a joint labeling of all the training items. In simultaneous supervised classification we will assign labels to all the items in N in a joint fashion. A joint labeling $S = (s_1, \ldots, s_k), s_c \subseteq N, c = 1, \ldots, k$, is an ordered partition of N such that the classes are identified by those present in T. Since any particular subset of classes present in T must be allowed to lack test items, some classes can remain empty in S, in which case the actual number of classes in S is $1 \leq k' \leq k$. A structure S implies a partition of the feature vectors, such that $\mathbf{x}^{(s_c)}, s_c \subseteq N$, represents the collection of data for the items in class $c = 1, \ldots, k$. Let $\mathcal{S}$ denote the space of eligible simultaneous classification structures for a given N.

Using a stochastic urn model for supervised classification [21], a prior probability $p(S|T)$ of a classification structure S is obtained conditionally on the known fixed classification T of the training data. Here we simply assume that the prior $p(S|T)$ is the uniform distribution over $\mathcal{S}$ as constructed in [21]. Given a prior and the collections of training and test data, a simultaneous classifier is based on the posterior distribution over $\mathcal{S}$, which is defined as

$$p(S|\mathbf{x}^{(N)}, \mathbf{z}^{(M)}, T) = \frac{p(\mathbf{x}^{(N)}|\mathbf{z}^{(M)}, S, T)p(S|T)}{\sum_{S \in \mathcal{S}} p(\mathbf{x}^{(N)}|\mathbf{z}^{(M)}, S, T)p(S|T)}, \tag{1}$$

where $p(\mathbf{x}^{(N)}|\mathbf{z}^{(M)}, S, T)$ is the conditional predictive probability for the entire observed population of test data. In contrast, a marginal classifier specifies the predictive probabilities independently for each test item, such that the joint distribution becomes

$$p(\mathbf{x}^{(N)}|\mathbf{z}^{(M)}, \mathring{S}, T) = \prod_{c=1}^{k} \prod_{i \in \mathring{s}_c} p(\mathbf{x}_i|\mathbf{z}^{(c)}, \mathring{S}, T), \tag{2}$$

where $\mathring{S}, \mathring{s}_c$ indicate the overall labeling implied by the individual assignment of the labels to the items in N and $\mathbf{z}^{(c)}$ is the training data for class c.

The predictive inferences under a simultaneous and a marginal classifier can be related to certain generic results about learnability and merging of predictive measures. Consider a sequence of stochastic variables $\{X_i\}_{i=1}^{\infty}$ in finite state spaces with corresponding σ-fields. Given any $\{X_i\}_{i=1}^{n}$, one may assess the probability of any event for a finite horizon prediction $\{X_i\}_{i \geq n+1}^{n+l}$. As in [29], one can define a *merging* between two measures $P^m(A) = P(A|\{X_i\}_{i=1}^{m}), Q^m(A) = Q(A|\{X_i\}_{i=1}^{m})$ such that

$$\max_{n \geq m, A \in \sigma(\{X_i\}_{i \geq n+1}^{n+l})} | P^m(A) - Q^m(A) | < \epsilon, \tag{3}$$

with Q-probability one. Consider that Q is the 'true' generating measure and P is our model. Then the finite horizon event predictions at arbitrary times in the future will approach the true forecasts provided by Q. In [30] Solomonoff shows that the subjective posterior one step prediction merges in mean square with the 'the true computable measure'. Under a stronger version of merging, it follows as in [31] that if P and Q are two measures for a sequence of discrete random variables $\{X_n\}_{n\geq1}$ and $Q << P$, then P merges with Q. Here $Q << P$ means that Q is dominated by P, and thus $Q(A) > 0$ implies that $P(A) > 0$, i.e., we cannot be surprised by an event that actually happens.

If P is chosen such that it corresponds to the predictive probability mass distribution

$$p(\mathbf{x}^{(N)}|S) = \int_\Theta p(\mathbf{x}^{(N)} \mid \theta,S)dF(\theta|S), \tag{4}$$

and correspondingly, if Q corresponds to the predictive probability mass distribution

$$q(\mathbf{x}^{(N)}|S) = \int_\Theta p(\mathbf{x}^{(N)} \mid \theta,S)dQ(\theta|S), \tag{5}$$

with appropriately defined parameter space Θ, then if also $dQ|S << dF|S$ on Θ, we have that $Q << P$. Assume that

$$P^m \leftrightarrow p(\mathbf{x}^{(N)}|S,T,\mathbf{z}^{(M)}) = \int_\Theta p(\mathbf{x}^{(N)} \mid \theta,S)dP(\theta|T,\mathbf{z}^{(M)}), \tag{6}$$

$$Q^m \leftrightarrow q(\mathbf{x}^{(N)}|S,T,\mathbf{z}^{(M)}) = \int_\Theta p(\mathbf{x}^{(N)} \mid \theta,S)dQ(\theta|T,\mathbf{z}^{(M)}), \tag{7}$$

then we have

$$\max_{n\geq m, A\in\sigma(\{X_i\}_{i\geq n+1}^{n+l})} | P^m (A) - Q^m (A) | < \epsilon. \tag{8}$$

The interpretation of this is that the finite horizon event predictions at arbitrary times in the future will approach the true forecasts provided by Q, where predictions based on P are conditioned on $S,T,\mathbf{z}^{(M)}$. This property of P can be termed as a 'sufficient for prediction' in supervised classification using simultaneous predictive probabilities.

Another form of learnability related to Q^m given by

$$q(\mathbf{x}^{(N)}|S,T,\mathbf{z}^{(M)}) = \int_\Theta p(\mathbf{x}^{(N)} \mid \theta,S)dQ(\theta|T,\mathbf{z}^{(M)}), \tag{9}$$

is obtained using exchangeability, since by de Finetti, Q merges with the measure Q_θ given by any $p(\mathbf{x}^{(N)}|\theta, S)$ chosen from $Q(\theta|S)$. From the inductive perspective it is essential that for prediction and supervised classification we actually need not estimate the (randomly chosen) 'true' Q_θ, which can as well be regarded as a tool for making infinite horizon event predictions. Finally, since $\mathcal{S}$ is finite, under the de Finetti type assumptions with *a priori given alphabets* yielding merging and learnability, it is shown in [21] that the difference

$$| \max_{S\in\mathcal{S}} p(\mathbf{x}^{(N)}|S,T,\mathbf{z}^{(M)}) - \max_{S\in\mathcal{S}} q(\mathbf{x}^{(N)}|S,T,\mathbf{z}^{(M)})| \tag{10}$$

becomes arbitrarily small for large m. Moreover, it is also shown that the same convergence behavior is obtained even if $p(\mathbf{x}^{(N)}|S,T,\mathbf{z}^{(M)})$ is replaced by $p(\mathbf{x}^{(N)}|\mathbf{z}^{(M)}, \overset{\circ}{S},T)$, i.e. the marginal classifier can accurately approximate the predictions under the true model in the presence of a very large amount of training data. The result can be intuitively understood in terms of consistent predictive learning, as the predictive generating measures of classes are infinite mixtures in Bayesian learning, which tend to fixed measures as the amount of training data increases. Consequently, the dependence of labels arising from the uncertainty about these measures gradually vanishes towards the limit. Here we will explore how the simultaneous and marginal forms of inductive inference will relate to each other under the circumstances where alphabets of discrete-valued features are not fixed *a priori*.

For the purpose of later examination of predictive probabilities, we will consider separately the process of establishing sufficient statistics from the data $\mathbf{x}^{(N)}$ alone and jointly from $\mathbf{z}^{(M)}$ and $\mathbf{x}^{(N)}$, conditional on S and T. Given a structure S, sufficient statistics arise under *partition exchangeability* for each subset of data $\mathbf{x}^{(s_c)}$. More specifically, we assume an unrestricted form of exchangeability [21],[28] which implies a product predictive measure over the d features. The operative interpretation of this form of exchangeability is that the features are modeled as conditionally independent given S.

Given a structure S with k classes, a predictive model is obtained by assuming exchangeable equivalence relations for each feature in each class [28],[32]. For counting purposes, we assign indices to items in s_c using an arbitrary permutation of integers $1, ..., |s_c|$. To simplify the notation we use $n_c = |s_c|$ to denote the cardinality of a class in the sequel. Let $I(\cdot)$ be an indicator function and l index a value in the alphabet $\mathcal{X}_j$. Define $n_{cjl} = \sum_{i \in s_c} I(x_{ij} = l)$ as the frequency of items in class c that carried the value l for the feature j. Then, the information in $\mathbf{x}^{(s_c)}$ can be compressed for each feature in terms of the count

$$\rho_{cjt} = \sum_{l=1}^{\infty} I(n_{cjl} = t), \tag{11}$$

which defines the frequency of distinct feature values that have been observed exactly t times for feature j in class c. Further, let $\rho_{cj} = (\rho_{cjt})_{t=1}^{n_c}$ denote a partition of the integer n_c into a vector of such counts. In a series of works by John Kingman, e.g. [17], an explicit predictive model for observed values of single feature of the above type was established using the following definition.

Definition 1. Partition exchangeability. *A random partition ρ_{cj} is said to be exchangeable, if any two partitions of n_c having the same partition vector, have the same predictive probability $p(\rho_{cj})$.*

Kingman [17] discussed the relationship between the de Finetti type exchangeability and the above alternative form of exchangeability. A more general discussion of these exchangeabilities in the context of inductive inference is found in [10]. Kingman's representation theorem establishes that the predictive distribution of the observations for a single feature equals under the partition exchangeability a Poisson-Dirichlet(ψ) distribution with parameter ψ

$$p(\rho_{cj}) = \frac{n_c!}{\psi(\psi+1)\cdots(\psi+n_c-1)} \prod_{t=1}^{n_c} \left\{ \left(\frac{\psi}{t}\right)^{\rho_{cjt}} \frac{1}{\rho_{cjt}!} \right\}. \tag{12}$$

This particular probability result is also known as the Ewens sampling formula and it arises as an infinite mixture of probability measures over an infinite-dimensional simplex. By assuming that the partitions for distinct classes and features are unrestrictedly exchangeable given S, we obtain the following product predictive measure for the entire collection of test data:

$$
p(\mathbf{x}^{(N)}|S) = \prod_{c=1}^{k} \prod_{j=1}^{d} \frac{n_c!}{\psi(\psi+1)\cdots(\psi+n_c-1)} \prod_{t=1}^{n_c} \left\{ (\frac{\psi}{t})^{\rho_{cjt}} \frac{1}{\rho_{cjt}!} \right\}. \tag{13}
$$

We now turn our attention to the inductive inference process where predictions about $\mathbf{x}^{(N)}$ are also conditioned on the training data $\mathbf{z}^{(M)}$ and their *a priori* given labeling T. Given that m_c and m_{cjl} are defined analogously to n_c and n_{cjl}, respectively, we obtain the partition vector $\tilde{\boldsymbol{\rho}}_{cj} = (\rho_{cjt})_{t=1}^{n_c+m_c}$ with elements given by

$$
\tilde{\rho}_{cjt} = \sum_{l=1}^{\infty} I(n_{cjl} + m_{cjl} = t). \tag{14}
$$

Using Bayes' theorem and the above result based on the Kingman's representation theorem, the predictive probability of the test data supervised by the training data and the two joint labelings S, T can be written as

$$
p(\mathbf{x}^{(N)}|\mathbf{z}^{(M)}, S, T) = \frac{p(\mathbf{x}^{(N)}, \mathbf{z}^{(M)}|S, T)}{p(\mathbf{z}^{(M)}|T)}
$$

$$
= \frac{\prod_{c=1}^{k} \prod_{j=1}^{d} \frac{(m_c+n_c)!}{\psi(\psi+1)\cdots(\psi+m_c+n_c-1)} \prod_{t=1}^{m_c+n_c} \left\{ (\frac{\psi}{t})^{\tilde{\rho}_{cjt}} \frac{1}{\tilde{\rho}_{cjt}!} \right\}}{\prod_{c=1}^{k} \prod_{j=1}^{d} \frac{m_c!}{\psi(\psi+1)\cdots(\psi+m_c-1)} \prod_{t=1}^{m_c} \left\{ (\frac{\psi}{t})^{\rho_{cjt}} \frac{1}{\rho_{cjt}!} \right\}}
$$

$$
= \prod_{c=1}^{k} \prod_{j=1}^{d} \frac{\frac{(m_c+n_c)!}{m_c!}}{(\psi+m_c)(\psi+m_c+1)\cdots(\psi+m_c+n_c-1)} \frac{\prod_{t=1}^{m_c+n_c} \left\{ (\frac{\psi}{t})^{\tilde{\rho}_{cjt}} \frac{1}{\tilde{\rho}_{cjt}!} \right\}}{\prod_{t=1}^{m_c} \left\{ (\frac{\psi}{t})^{\rho_{cjt}} \frac{1}{\rho_{cjt}!} \right\}}. \tag{15}
$$

3 Asymptotic Properties of Supervised Classifiers under Partition Exchangeability

We will now examine how the predictive probabilities for simultaneous and marginal supervised classifiers introduced in the previous section relate to each other in the presence of increasing amounts of training data. As discussed earlier, these two predictive probabilities need not in general be equal, even if the test data were generated *i.i.d.* from the same underlying distribution as the training data. The asymptotic equality of simultaneous and marginal classifiers with respect to an increasing amount of available training data was established in [21],[22] for two families of distributions under de Finetti type of exchangeability. Here we show that this property does not hold under the classification model arising from the partition exchangeability. An intuitive implication of this result is that the simultaneous classifier enjoys the advantage of jointly modeling the entire population of labels of test items, such that it can better assess the level of surprise in any particular observed event in relation to other events. Moreover, this effect does not wear out almost surely even if the amount of training data tends to infinity.

First, we need to introduce some additional notation for the marginal classifier. Let $\tilde{\rho}_{cjt}^{(i)}$ denote the updated sufficient statistic (see eq. (14)) when data $\mathbf{x}_i$ from only a single test item is taken into account, defined as $\tilde{\rho}_{cjt}^{(i)} = \sum_{l=1}^{\infty} I(m_{cjl} + n_{i;cjl} = t), t = 1, \ldots, m_c + 1$, where $n_{i;cjl}$ is the observed frequency of category l for feature j in item i. Thus, there is only a single value $l_j^{(i)}$, such that $n_{i;cjl_j^{(i)}} = 1$, and $n_{i;cjl_j^{(i)}} = 0$, otherwise. Consequently, we can rewrite $\tilde{\rho}_{cjt}^{(i)}$ as

$$\tilde{\rho}_{cjt}^{(i)} = \sum_{l=1}^{\infty} I(m_{cjl} + n_{i;cjl} = t) = \rho_{cjt} - I(m_{cjl_j^{(i)}} = t) + I(m_{cjl_j^{(i)}} = t - 1). \quad (16)$$

It further follows that, if $m_{cjl^{(i)}} > 0$, there is always a single frequency $t_j^{(i)}$, such that $m_{cjl^{(i)}} = t_j^{(i)}$ and $\tilde{\rho}_{cjt}^{(i)} = \rho_{cjt}$ for all $t \neq t_j^{(i)}$ and $t \neq t_j^{(i)} + 1$. In cases where $m_{cjl^{(i)}} = 0$, item i carries a unique value for feature j and the updating of sufficient statistics behaves slightly differently in the following two cases. If no other unique values are present in class c for this feature, then $\tilde{\rho}_{cjt}^{(i)} = \rho_{cjt}$ for all $t > 1$ and $\tilde{\rho}_{cj1}^{(i)} = 1$. If there are multiple unique values present in class c for this feature, then $\tilde{\rho}_{cjt}^{(i)} = \rho_{cjt}$ for all $t > 1$ and $\tilde{\rho}_{cj1}^{(i)} = \rho_{cj1} + 1$. In order to avoid burdening the notation excessively, we will not explicitly consider this distinction in the lemma below. Note that the above definition of $\tilde{\rho}_{cjt}^{(i)}$ still holds in all these different cases.

To compare the predictive probabilities of simultaneous and marginal classifiers, we now consider the case with $S = \mathring{S}$. The following lemma shows how the two probabilities are related to each other when the amount of training data increases.

Lemma 1. *Asymptotic behavior of the difference of log predictive probabilities for simultaneous and marginal classifiers under partition exchangeability. Let m_c be very large for all $c = 1, \ldots, k$. Then*

$$\log p(\mathbf{x}^{(N)}|\mathbf{z}^{(M)}, S, T) - \log p(\mathbf{x}^{(N)}|\mathbf{z}^{(M)}, \mathring{S}, T)$$

$$\approx \sum_{c=1}^{k} \sum_{j=1}^{d} \left\{ \sum_{t=1}^{m_c+n_c} \tilde{\rho}_{cjt} \log(\frac{\psi}{t}) - \sum_{t=1}^{m_c} \rho_{cjt} \log(\frac{\psi}{t}) + \sum_{i \in s_c} \log(\frac{t_j^{(i)} + 1}{t_j^{(i)}}) \right.$$

$$\left. - \sum_{t=1}^{m_c+n_c} \log(\tilde{\rho}_{cjt}!) + \sum_{t=1}^{m_c} \log(\rho_{cjt}!) - \sum_{i \in s_c} \log(\rho_{cjt_j^{(i)}}) + \sum_{i \in s_c} \log(\rho_{cj(t_j^{(i)}+1)}) \right\}.$$

Proof. The logarithm $\log p(\mathbf{x}^{(N)}|\mathbf{z}^{(M)}, S, T)$ of the predictive probability equals

$$\sum_{c=1}^{k}\sum_{j=1}^{d}\{\log[(m_c + n_c)!] - \log(m_c!) - \log[(\psi + m_c)(\psi + m_c + 1)\cdots(\psi + m_c + n_c - 1)]$$

$$+ \sum_{t=1}^{m_c+n_c}\tilde{\rho}_{cjt}\log(\frac{\psi}{t}) - \sum_{t=1}^{m_c}\rho_{cjt}\log(\frac{\psi}{t}) - \sum_{t=1}^{m_c+n_c}\log(\tilde{\rho}_{cjt}!) + \sum_{t=1}^{m_c}\log(\rho_{cjt}!)\}.$$

Correspondingly, the logarithm for the marginal classifier is

$$\log p(\mathbf{x}^{(N)}|\mathbf{z}^{(M)}, \mathring{S}, T) = \sum_{c=1}^{k}\sum_{i\in s_c}\sum_{j=1}^{d}\{\log[(m_c + 1)!] - \log(m_c!) - \log(\psi + m_c)$$

$$+ \sum_{t=1}^{m_c+1}\tilde{\rho}_{cjt}^{(i)}\log(\frac{\psi}{t}) - \sum_{t=1}^{m_c}\rho_{cjt}\log(\frac{\psi}{t}) - \sum_{t=1}^{m_c+1}\log(\tilde{\rho}_{cjt}^{(i)}!) + \sum_{t=1}^{m_c}\log(\rho_{cjt}!)\}.$$

To arrive at the stated result, we will first show that the differences of the foremost terms in the two expressions of the log probabilities tend to 0 as m_c increases. To start, recall the Ramanujan equation for log factorial, which is given by

$$\log(a!) = a\log a - a + \frac{1}{6}\log\{a + 4a^2 + 8a^3 + \epsilon(a)/30\} + \frac{1}{2}\log\pi,$$

where the error term $\epsilon(a)$ is bounded as $3/10 < \epsilon(a) < 1$ and $\epsilon(a) \to 1$ when $a \to \infty$. It then follows that

$$\log[(m_c + n_c)!] - \log(m_c)! - \sum_{i\in s_c}\log[(m_c + 1)!] + \sum_{i\in s_c}\log(m_c!)$$

$$\approx (m_c + n_c)\log(m_c + n_c) - (m_c + n_c) + \frac{1}{6}\log[(m_c + n_c) + 4(m_c + n_c)^2 + 8(m_c + n_c)^3]$$

$$- m_c\log(m_c) + m_c - \frac{1}{6}\log(m_c + 4m_c^2 + 8m_c^3) + n_c m_c\log(m_c) - n_c m_c + \frac{n_c}{6}\log(m_c + 4m_c^2 + 8m_c^3)$$

$$- n_c(m_c + 1)\log(m_c + 1) + n_c(m_c + 1) - \frac{n_c}{6}\log[(m_c + 1) + 4(m_c + 1)^2 + 8(m_c + 1)^3]$$

$$= m_c\log(1 + \frac{n_c}{m_c}) - m_c n_c\log(1 + \frac{1}{m_c}) + n_c\log(1 + \frac{n_c - 1}{m_c + 1})$$

$$+ \frac{1}{6}\log[\frac{(m_c + n_c) + 4(m_c + n_c)^2 + 8(m_c + n_c)^3}{m_c + 4m_c + 8m_c}] - \frac{n_c}{6}\log[\frac{(m_c + 1) + 4(m_c + 1)^2 + 8(m_c + 1)^3}{m_c + 4m_c^2 + 8m_c^3}].$$

Using the standard series expansion $\log(1 + y) = y - \frac{1}{2}y^2 + \frac{1}{3}y^3 - \cdots$, the result above can be further simplified to the expression

$$\log[(m_c + n_c)!] - \log(m_c!) - \sum_{i\in s_c}\log[(m_c + 1)!] + \sum_{i\in s_c}\log(m_c!)$$

$$= m_c[\frac{n_c}{m_c} - \frac{1}{2}(\frac{n_c}{m_c})^2 + \cdots] - m_c n_c[\frac{1}{m_c} - \frac{1}{2}(\frac{1}{m_c})^2 + \cdots] + n_c[\frac{n_c - 1}{m_c + 1} - \frac{1}{2}(\frac{n_c - 1}{m_c + 1})^2 + \cdots]$$

$$+ \frac{1}{6}\log\{\frac{(m_c + n_c) + 4(m_c + n_c)^2 + 8(m_c + n_c)^3}{m_c + 4m_c^2 + 8m_c^3}\}$$

$$- \frac{n_c}{6}\log\{\frac{(m_c + 1) + 4(m_c + 1)^2 + 8(m_c + 1)^3}{m_c + 4m_c^2 + 8m_c^3}\},$$

which tends to 0 when m_c increases. For the difference of the intermediate terms in the log predictive probabilities a similar convergence result holds such that

$$-\log[(\psi + m_c)(\psi + m_c + 1) \cdots (\psi_{cj} + m_c + n_c - 1)] + \sum_{i \in s_c} \log(\psi + m_c)$$

$$= \log \frac{(\psi + m_c)^{n_c}}{(\psi + m_c)(\psi + m_c + 1) \cdots (\psi + m_c + n_c - 1)} \xrightarrow[m_c \to \infty]{} 0.$$

Note that the order of the error terms is not explicitly included in the above derivations to avoid too extensive and tedious expressions. To establish the remaining parts of the lemma, note first that $\tilde{\rho}_{cjt_j^{(i)}}^{(i)} = \rho_{cjt_j^{(i)}} - 1$ and $\tilde{\rho}_{cj(t_j^{(i)}+1)}^{(i)} = \rho_{cj(t_j^{(i)}+1)} + 1$. Then, we obtain that $\sum_{t=1}^{m_c+1} \tilde{\rho}_{cjt}^{(i)} \log(\frac{\psi}{t})$ equals

$$\sum_{t=1}^{m_c} \rho_{cjt} \log(\frac{\psi}{t}) - \rho_{cjt_j^{(i)}} \log(\frac{\psi}{t_j^{(i)}}) - \rho_{cj(t_j^{(i)}+1)} \log(\frac{\psi}{t_j^{(i)}+1})$$

$$+\tilde{\rho}_{cjt_j^{(i)}}^{(i)} \log(\frac{\psi}{t_j^{(i)}}) + \tilde{\rho}_{cj(t_j^{(i)}+1)}^{(i)} \log(\frac{\psi}{t_j^{(i)}+1})$$

$$= \sum_{t=1}^{m_c} \rho_{cjt} \log(\frac{\psi}{t}) - \log(\frac{\psi}{t_j^{(i)}}) + \log(\frac{\psi}{t_j^{(i)}+1}) = \sum_{t=1}^{m_c} \rho_{cjt} \log(\frac{\psi}{t}) - \log(\frac{t_j^{(i)}+1}{t_j^{(i)}}).$$

By using the same relationships between the original and updated sufficient statistics, we have that $\sum_{t=1}^{m_c+1} \log(\tilde{\rho}_{cjt}^{(i)}!)$ equals

$$\sum_{t=1}^{m_c} \log(\rho_{cjt}!) - \log(\rho_{cjt_j^{(i)}}!) - \log(\rho_{cj(t_j^{(i)}+1)}!) + \log(\tilde{\rho}_{cjt_j^{(i)}}^{(i)}!) + \log(\tilde{\rho}_{cj(t_j^{(i)}+1)}^{(i)}!)$$

$$= \sum_{t=1}^{m_c} \log(\rho_{cjt}!) - \log(\rho_{cjt_j^{(i)}}) + \log(\rho_{cj(t_j^{(i)}+1)} + 1).$$

Using these two results, the stated lemma follows after some tedious rearrangements of the terms. ∎

The result in the above lemma highlights the difference between the simultaneous and marginal classifiers in terms of inductive reasoning. In the simultaneous classifier the log predictive probabilities contrast the changes of sufficient statistics between the training data and the entire population of test items as a whole. Instead, the marginal classifier sums the changes induced by each test item separately and therefore, it by definition never pays attention to how surprising any observed event is in relation to the events observed for the remaining population of test items. The following theorem shows explicitly that this difference can persist even in the presence of increasing amounts of training data.

Theorem 1. *Convergence of log predictive probabilities for simultaneous and marginal classifiers under partition exchangeability. For any $m \in \mathbb{Z}^+$, and any $m_c \geq m, c = 1, ..., k$, there exists $\epsilon > 0$ such that*

$$P[|\log p(\mathbf{x}^{(N)}|\mathbf{z}^{(M)}, S, T) - \log p(\mathbf{x}^{(N)}|\mathbf{z}^{(M)}, \overset{\circ}{S}, T)| > \epsilon] > 0.$$

Proof. To arrive at the stated result, it is necessary to show that a positive probability remains for the event that the two classifiers disagree, despite of the amount of training data present. To demonstrate this, we will consider log ratios of the predictive probabilities under two particular classification structures and show that their difference need not converge to zero. Let $S = \overset{\circ}{S}$ be a labeling of n test items and S' the labeling derived from S by re-assigning a single item i from class c_1 to class c_2. Let $n'_{c_1} = n_{c_1} - 1$, $n'_{c_2} = n_{c_2} + 1$, and let $\tilde{\rho}'_{c_1jt}, \tilde{\rho}'_{c_2jt}$ denote the updated sufficient statistics under S'. Since the two labelings S, S' are identical apart from the classes c_1, c_2, log ratio of the predictive probabilities $\log p(\mathbf{x}^{(N)}|\mathbf{z}^{(M)}, S, T) - \log p(\mathbf{x}^{(N)}|\mathbf{z}^{(M)}, S', T)$ under the simultaneous classifier can be written as

$$\log p(\mathbf{x}^{(s_{c_1})}, \mathbf{z}^{(M)}|S,T) + \log p(\mathbf{x}^{(s_{c_2})}, \mathbf{z}^{(M)}|S,T) - \log p(\mathbf{x}^{(s_{c_1})}, \mathbf{z}^{(M)}|S',T) - \log p(\mathbf{x}^{(s_{c_2})}, \mathbf{z}^{(M)}|S',T)$$

$$= \sum_{j=1}^{d} \left\{ \left[\log \frac{(m_{c_1}+n_{c_1})!}{\psi(\psi+1)\cdots(\psi+m_{c_1}+n_{c_1}-1)} + \sum_{t=1}^{m_{c_1}+n_{c_1}} \tilde{\rho}_{c_1jt}\log(\frac{\psi}{t}) + \sum_{t=1}^{m_{c_1}+n_{c_1}} \log\frac{1}{\tilde{\rho}_{c_1jt}!} \right] \right.$$

$$+ \left[\log \frac{(m_{c_2}+n_{c_2})!}{\psi(\psi+1)\cdots(\psi+m_{c_2}+n_{c_2}-1)} + \sum_{t=1}^{m_{c_2}+n_{c_2}} \tilde{\rho}_{c_2jt}\log(\frac{\psi}{t}) + \sum_{t=1}^{m_{c_2}+n_{c_2}} \log\frac{1}{\tilde{\rho}_{c_2jt}!} \right]$$

$$- \left[\log \frac{(m_{c_1}+n'_{c_1})!}{\psi(\psi+1)\cdots(\psi+m_{c_1}+n'_{c_1}-1)} + \sum_{t=1}^{m_{c_1}+n'_{c_1}} \tilde{\rho}'_{c_1jt}\log(\frac{\psi}{t}) + \sum_{t=1}^{m_{c_1}+n'_{c_1}} \log\frac{1}{\tilde{\rho}'_{c_1jt}!} \right]$$

$$- \left. \left[\log \frac{(m_{c_2}+n'_{c_2})!}{\psi(\psi+1)\cdots(\psi+m_{c_2}+n'_{c_2}-1)} + \sum_{t=1}^{m_{c_2}+n'_{c_2}} \tilde{\rho}'_{c_2jt}\log(\frac{\psi}{t}) + \sum_{t=1}^{m_{c_2}+n'_{c_2}} \log\frac{1}{\tilde{\rho}'_{c_2jt}!} \right] \right\}.$$

Given the simple relationships between the sufficient statistics, the above expression can be further simplified to

$$\sum_{j=1}^{d} \left\{ \log(m_{c_1}+n_{c_1}) - \log(m_{c_2}+n_{c_2}+1) - \log(\psi+m_{c_1}+n_{c_1}-1) + \log(\psi+m_{c_2}+n_{c_2}) \right.$$

$$+ \left[\sum_{t=1}^{m_{c_1}+n_{c_1}} \tilde{\rho}_{c_1jt}\log(\frac{\psi}{t}) - \sum_{t=1}^{m_{c_1}+n'_{c_1}} \tilde{\rho}'_{c_1jt}\log(\frac{\psi}{t}) \right] + \left[\sum_{t=1}^{m_{c_2}+n_{c_2}} \tilde{\rho}_{c_2jt}\log(\frac{\psi}{t}) - \sum_{t=1}^{m_{c_2}+n'_{c_2}} \tilde{\rho}'_{c_2jt}\log(\frac{\psi}{t}) \right]$$

$$- \left. \left[\sum_{t=1}^{m_{c_1}+n_{c_1}} \log(\tilde{\rho}_{c_1jt}!) - \sum_{t=1}^{m_{c_1}+n'_{c_1}} \log(\tilde{\rho}'_{c_1jt}!) \right] - \left[\sum_{t=1}^{m_{c_2}+n_{c_2}} \log(\tilde{\rho}_{c_2jt}!) - \sum_{t=1}^{m_{c_2}+n'_{c_2}} \log(\tilde{\rho}'_{c_2jt}!) \right] \right\}.$$

Assume now that item i carries a unique value for feature j and no other unique values are present in classes c_1, c_2 for this feature. This event has a strictly positive probability [10]. Then, the vectors of sufficient statistics $\tilde{\rho}_{c_1jt}, \tilde{\rho}'_{c_1jt}$ are identical apart from the first element, such that $\tilde{\rho}_{c_1j1} = 1, \tilde{\rho}'_{c_1j1} = 0$. Consequently, the difference in the first square bracket equals $\log(\psi)$. Similarly, we obtain for the second square bracket: $\tilde{\rho}_{c_2j1} = 0, \tilde{\rho}'_{c_2j1} = 1$, and thus, the difference equals $-\log(\psi)$. Using a similar argument, differences in both remaining two square brackets equal zero. Finally, with an increasing m_c the log ratio of predictive probabilities then converges to zero under the simultaneous classifier.

This can be interpreted as an intuitive result, since the surprising event observed for item i is equally surprising in both populations represented by s_{c_1}, s_{c_2} and the corresponding training data sets.

Consider now the log ratio of predictive probabilities under the marginal classifier. Since the predictive probabilities of all items apart from i are identical, the log ratio simplifies to $\log p(\mathbf{x}_i, \mathbf{z}^{(M)}|i \in s_{c_1}, T) - \log p(\mathbf{x}_i, \mathbf{z}^{(M)}|i \in s_{c_2}, T)$ which equals

$$\sum_{j=1}^{d} \left\{ \left[\log \frac{(m_{c_1}+1)!}{\psi(\psi+1)\cdots(\psi+m_{c_1}+1-1)} + \sum_{t=1}^{m_{c_1}+1} \tilde{\rho}_{c_1 jt}{}^{(i)} \log(\frac{\psi}{t}) - \sum_{t=1}^{m_{c_1}+1} \log(\tilde{\rho}_{c_1 jt}{}^{(i)}!) \right] \right.$$
$$\left. - \left[\log \frac{(m_{c_2}+1)!}{\psi(\psi+1)\cdots(\psi+m_{c_2}+1-1)} + \sum_{t=1}^{m_{c_2}+1} \tilde{\rho}_{c_2 jt}{}^{(i)} \log(\frac{\psi}{t}) - \sum_{t=1}^{m_{c_2}+1} \log(\tilde{\rho}_{c_2 jt}{}^{(i)}!) \right] \right\}.$$

As for the simultaneous classifier, difference of the foremost terms not involving the sufficient statistics converges to zero when m_c increases. However, here the difference of the latter terms can be arbitrarily large, as it depends basically on the difference between the sufficient statistics derived from the training data for the two classes. Thus, there is a positive probability for the event that the two classifiers disagree, even if the difference of log ratios would converge to zero for the remaining $d-1$ features.   ■

4   Discussion

How should a classifier reason when an unpredictable event is observed, and more importantly, how could a classifier be built when one does not know what can be anticipated in the future? Standard Bayesian inductive inference does not easily provide the tools necessary for coherently updating the conditional probabilities of events when we see values that were not previously seen or even anticipated. Retrospectively changing an alphabet upon arrival of new observations can of course be done, but this is an *ad hoc* approach not based on a probabilistic framework which inductively updates its predictions about the future in an autonomous manner. A truly inductive approach to prediction of a single future feature value using a hierarchical Dirichlet prior was introduced in [18], however, in a context different from classification.

We have demonstrated that an inductive supervised classification principle in the presence of unpredictable or unanticipated events corresponding to unknown alphabets of observable features arises under the assumption of partition exchangeability for data from a categorical feature. Moreover, joint modeling of the labels of a population of test items appears as a natural approach, since it is capable of assessing the degree of surprise of an observed event for a test item in relation to both the other test items and the training data.

The basic rationale behind the use of joint classification models under de Finetti type exchangeability stems from the fact that item labels perceived as random quantities remain dependent even under an *i.i.d.* sampling model, as long as the generating probability measures for the classes are not exactly known. In contrast to a *marginal* classifier which predicts the label for each item separately based on an *i.i.d.* assumption, i.e. conditionally independent feature data given a fixed generating measure learned from the training items, a *joint*, or *simultaneous* classifier exploits the dependence which may have a considerable effect in the presence of sparse training data. A *marginalized* predictive classifier takes an additional step further for any single item by treating the labels of remaining items as nuisance parameters and deriving the predictive distribution of a label through its marginal posterior from the joint distribution of all the labels.

A concrete application of a classifier based on exchangeable partitions arises for instance when categories of features cannot be directly observed, but only their frequencies within a pool of items, which represents either training or test data. An example of such a problem is classification of documents with identical or partially identical content which are encrypted with different keys. In fact, some central elements of the probability calculus related to the frequency distributions of words identified as sufficient statistics were already recognized by Alan Turing and Irving Good as a part of the decryption activities at Bletchley Park during World War II as noted in [10].

As mentioned earlier, gains in classification accuracy are accessible through joint modeling of multiple test items and the optimality of such an approach has been considered by multiple authors [21-24] in different classification contexts. An interesting issue for future work would be to consider instead a log loss scoring as suggested in [33],[34]. Another line of future development would be to examine how the models in [18],[20] would behave asymptotically for a simultaneous prediction of a population of test items when supervised by an infinite amount of training data. It is currently an open question whether their asymptotic predictions would show similar characteristics as the predictions derived here under partition exchangeability, or if they would be reducible to a set of marginal predictions as under de Finetti type exchangeability.

References

1. Solomonoff, R.J.: A formal theory of inductive inference. Part I. Inf. Control 7, 1–22 (1964)
2. Hunt, E.B., Marin, J., Stone, P.J.: Experiments in induction. Academic Press, New York (1966)
3. Chow, C.K., Liu, C.N.: Approximating discrete probability distributions with dependence trees. IEEE Trans. Inf. Theory 14, 462–467 (1968)
4. Bailey, N.T.J.: Probability methods of diagnosis based on small samples. In: Mathematics and Computer Science in Biology and Medicine. H.M. Stationery Office, London (1965)
5. Jain, A.K., Duin, R.P.W., Mao, J.: Statistical pattern recognition: A review. IEEE Trans. Patt. Anal. Mach. Intell. 22, 4–37 (2000)
6. Duda, R.O., Hart, P.E., Stork, D.G.: Pattern classification, 2nd edn. Wiley, New York (2000)

7. Bishop, C.M.: Pattern recognition and machine learning. Springer, New York (2007)
8. Hand, D.J., Yu, K.: Idiot's Bayes: not so stupid after all. Int. Stat. Rev. 69, 385–398 (2001)
9. Jeffrey, R.: Probabilism and induction. Topoi 5, 51–58 (1986)
10. Zabell, S.L.: Predicting the unpredictable. Synthese 90, 205–232 (1992)
11. Angluin, D., Smith, C.H.: Inductive inference: Theory and methods. ACM Comput. Surv. 15, 237–268 (1983)
12. Michalski, R.S.: A theory and methodology of inductive learning. Artif. Intell. 20, 111–161 (1983)
13. Solomonoff, R.J.: Three kinds of probabilistic induction: universal distributions and convergence theorems. Christopher Stewart WALLACE (1933-2004); Memorial Special Issue. Comput. J. 51, 566–570 (2008)
14. Kingman, J.F.C.: The population structure associated with the Ewens sampling formula. Theor. Pop. Biol. 11, 274–283 (1977)
15. Kingman, J.F.C.: The representation of partition structures. J. London Math. Soc. 18, 374–380 (1978)
16. Kingman, J.F.C.: Random partitions in population genetics. Proc. Roy. Soc. A 361, 1–20 (1978)
17. Kingman, J.F.C.: Uses of exchangeability. Ann. Probab. 6, 183–197 (1978)
18. Friedman, N., Singer, Y.: Efficient Bayesian parameter estimation in large discrete domains. In: Kearns, M.J., Solla, S.A., Cohn, D.A. (eds.) Advances in Neural Information Processing Systems, vol. 11, pp. 417–423 (1998)
19. Orlitsky, A., Santhanam, N.P., Zhang, J.: Universal compression of memoryless sources over unknown alphabets. IEEE Trans. Inf. Theory 50, 1469–1481 (2004)
20. Wang, C., Blei, D.M.: Decoupling sparsity and smoothness in the discrete hierarchical Dirichlet process. In: Bengio, Y., Schuurmans, D., Lafferty, J., Williams, C.K.I., Culotta, A. (eds.) Advances in Neural Information Processing Systems, vol. 22, pp. 1982–1989 (2009)
21. Corander, J., Cui, Y., Koski, T., Sirén, J.: Have I seen you before? Principles of predictive classification revisited. Stat. Comput. 23, 59–73 (2013)
22. Cui, Y., Corander, J., Koski, T., Sirén, J.: Predictive Gaussian classifiers. Submitted to Bayesian Analysis (2013)
23. Ripley, B.D.: Pattern Recognition and Neural Networks. Cambridge University Press, Cambridge (1996)
24. Nádas, A.: Optimal solution of a training problem in speech recognition. IEEE Transactions on Acoustics, Speech, and Signal Processing 33, 326–329 (1985)
25. Geisser, S.: Predictive discrimination. In: Krishnajah, P.R. (ed.) Multivariate analysis, pp. 149–163. Academic Press, New York (1966)
26. Geisser, S.: Predictive Inference: An introduction. Chapman & Hall, London (1993)
27. Dawson, K.J., Belkhir, K.: A Bayesian approach to the identification of panmictic populations and the assignment of individuals. Genet. Res. 78, 59–77 (2001)
28. Corander, J., Gyllenberg, M., Koski, T.: Random partition models and exchangeability for Bayesian identification of population structure. Bull. Math. Biol. 69, 797–815 (2007)
29. Jackson, M.O., Kalai, E., Smorodinsky, R.: Bayesian representation of stochastic processes under learning: de Finetti revisited. Econometrics 67, 875–893 (1999)
30. Solomonoff, R.J.: Complexity-based induction systems: comparisons and convergence theorems. IEEE Trans. Inf. Theory 24, 422–432 (1978)

31. Blackwell, D., Dubins, L.: Merging of opinions with increasing information. Ann. Math. Stat. 33, 882–886 (1962)
32. Joyce, P.: Partition Structures and sufficient statistics J. Appl. Prob. 35, 622–632 (1998)
33. Dowe, D.L.: Foreword re C. S. Wallace. Christopher Stewart WALLACE (1933-2004); Memorial Special Issue. Comput. J. 51, 523–560 (2008)
34. Dowe, D.L.: MML, hybrid Bayesian network graphical models, statistical consistency, invariance and uniqueness. In: Bandyopadhyay, P.S., Forster, M.R. (eds.) Handbook of the Philosophy of Science - Philosophy of Statistics, pp. 901–982. Elsevier, Oxford (2011)

Learning in the Limit:
A Mutational and Adaptive Approach

Reginaldo Inojosa da Silva Filho, Ricardo Luis de Azevedo da Rocha,
and Ricardo Henrique Gracini Guiraldelli

Computing Engineering Department
Engineering School of the University of São Paulo,
Av. Luciano Gualberto s/n Trav 3, n.158 São Paulo - SP, Brazil
`reginaldo.uspoli@gmail.com`, `{rlarocha,rguira}@usp.br`

Abstract. The purpose of this work is to show the strong connection between learning in the limit and the second-order adaptive automaton. The connection is established using the mutating programs approach, in which any hypothesis can be used to start a learning process, and produces a correct final model following a step-by-step transformation of that hypothesis by a second-order adaptive automaton. Second-order adaptive automaton learner will be proved to acts as a learning in the limit one[1].

Keywords: Inductive Inference, Learning Model, Code Mutation, Adaptive Devices, Automata Theory.

1 Introduction

Ray Solomonoff was the father of the general theory of inductive inference [11], a fruitful area of study that generated many developments in artificial intelligence [5,13]. In short, the goal of inductive inference is to identify the unknown object by picking out one of a (typically infinite) set of hypothesis for this object [1]. The hypothesis is a finite representation of the object and may be consistent with the given incrementally growing segments of object example inputs. It is possible to define many ways to the hypothesis choice and each one, in practice, determines a whole new learning model; the main ones are the probabilistic approach [5,13] and the enumerations strategies [4]. But, as pointed out by Wallace, Dowe and Solomonoff himself, the so-called "Solomonoff Induction" is actually prediction [13,2,12], rather than induction. Therefore, the approach used in this work is closely related to Wallace's Minimum Message Length (MML) approach, but was inspired by Solomonoff's paper [11].

Thus, consider the following constraint: what if the only way to generate a new hypothesis was by "recycling" a former one? What would the behavior of the learner be if the generation of a new hypothesis implies the transformation of an older one? What kind of transformation would be necessary?

---

[1] The work reported here received support through FAPESP grant 2010/09586-0.

D.L. Dowe (Ed.): Solomonoff Festschrift, LNAI 7070, pp. 106–118, 2013.

This kind of hypothesis needs to be a "changeable" one to be reused, that is, it would have a "plasticity" feature to adapt to new inputs for which it is not prepared; therefore, the changes must happen in the representation structure used to describe the hypothesis. Using a biological metaphor, the hypothesis must have the mutational property, with the learner having the responsibility to apply transformations in the hypothesis. The use of this kind of metaphor, nonetheless, is not new: Solomonoff was also interested in the study of mutating programs [6]. Now, this work proposes a mutational computational model, called second-order adaptive automaton, aimed at the problem of inductive inference and in which this "changeable" behavior is an essential property of the model itself.

A successful mutation means that the learner has adapted to the new inputs. The fact that learning can be represented by an adaptive process is the fundamental premise of this work. The last two decades presented the development and emergence of new computational models that deviate from a basis on mechanical machines structures and become similar to evolutive, collaborative and biologically inspired models; among these, self-modifying devices [8,10] are prominent ones, which have been developed under a formalism based on automata theory and is one of the basis to represent the adaptive behavior of the model defined here.

The description of the inductive inference under an adaptive aspect will be made using the Emil Mark Gold learning in the limit model [3], also called identification in the limit. Responsible for branch of inductive inference, Gold studied the learning problem for recursive functions and formal languages. In his model, the inductive inference is an infinite process; a learner identifies a language if the generation of hypotheses converges to one and no other changes occur, although new inputs of the language are presented to the learner indefinitely.

The text is organized as follows: section 2 describes the notation and technical preliminaries concerning automata theory and first-order adaptive automata, basis for the second-order adaptive automata; section 3 presents the the second-order adaptive automata. Section 4 shows the relationship between second-order adaptive automata and learning in the limit. Finally, section 5 presents the conclusion and further works to be developed.

2   The First-Order Adaptive Automaton

Adaptive automaton belongs to the category of self-modifying devices. It is a computational model equivalent to Turing Machine [7] and has the non-deterministic finite state automaton as formulation basis. Its major characteristic is the ability to decide how to modify its own structure in response to some external input, without the interference of any external agent. The first appearance of the adaptive automata has some inconsistencies in its description, but this fact was corrected later in a complete formalization, performed using the automata transformations concept [10]. This formalization, developed in the present section, is known as **first-order adaptive automata** (FOAA). However, some introductory concepts are presented before for unequivocal understanding of the FOAA definition.

2.1 Notations and Technical Preliminaries

The main concepts used in this work, mostly concerning automata theory, as well the pertinent notation, are summarized in table 1.

Table 1. Notation for technical preliminaries related to the automata theory

$\mathbb{N} = \{0, 1, 2, \dots\}$	The set of natural numbers
$I = \{i_0, i_1, \dots, i_m\}$	Finite arbitrary indexed set
$rem(I, x) = \{I - \{x\} : x \in I\}$ with $(x \notin I)$	Removal function
$ins(I, x) = \{i_0, i_1, \dots, i_{m+1}\}$ with $i_{m+1} = x$	Insertion function
Σ	An alphabet of symbols
$\alpha \in \Sigma$	A symbol of the alphabet
$L \subseteq \Sigma^*$	A language over Σ
$t \in L$	A string of L
ε	An empty string
$\theta = (t_0, t_1, \dots)$, with $t_k \in L$ for $k \in \mathbb{N}$	A text of L
$\theta[n] = (t_1, t_2, \dots t_n)$, with $t_k \in L$ for $0 \leq k \leq n$	the n-initial segment of θ
$seq(\theta)$	the family of all segments
$M^0 = (Q, q_0, E, \Sigma, \partial)$	A non-deterministic automaton
$Q = \{q_1, \dots, q_n\}$	The set of states of M^0
$q_0 \in Q$	The initial state of M^0
$E \subseteq Q$	The accepting states set of M^0
$\partial \subseteq Q \times \{\Sigma \cup \{\varepsilon\}\} \times Q$	The state transition relation
$\partial = \{\delta_1, \delta_2, \dots, \delta_i\}$	The transitions set of M^0
$\delta = (q', \alpha, q'')$ with $\{q', q''\} \subseteq Q$ and $\alpha \in \Sigma$	A transition of M^0
$(q', t) \in Q \times \Sigma^*$ with $q' \in Q$	A configuration of M^0
(q_0, t)	The initial configuration of M^0

A **scalar hierarchical structure**[9] is indicated by $\langle a_n \langle a_{n-1} \dots \langle a_1 \langle a_0 \rangle \rangle \rangle \rangle$, and is interpreted as follows: if a_{i+1} is a formal system defined by an ordered n-tuple, then a_i is a n-tuple element, for $0 \leq i \leq (n-1)$.

2.2 Automata Transformations

Given the non-numerical set $\mathcal{M}^0$ of all non-deterministic finite state automaton under an alphabet Σ, for any element $M^0 \in \mathcal{M}^0$ and the state transition relation ∂ of M^0, a **proper transition** is defined as:

$$\delta_{pro} = \delta : \delta \in \partial \tag{1}$$

Otherwise, a **foreign transition** is defined as:

$$\delta_{for} = \delta : \delta \notin \partial \tag{2}$$

A sequence of proper transitions belong to M^0 and represented by

$$\lambda_{pro} = (\delta_{pro_1}, \ldots, \delta_{pro_m}) \tag{3}$$

is called a **positive sequence**. In turn, a transitions sequence

$$\lambda_{for} = (\delta_{for_1}, \ldots, \delta_{for_n}) \tag{4}$$

of foreign transition for M^0 is called a **negative sequence**.

Given a negative and a positive sequence for an automaton M^0, the sequence:

$$\phi = (\lambda_{for}, \lambda_{pro}) \tag{5}$$

is defined as a **first-order transformation pair**.

Employing the proper and foreign transition concepts, as well the definition of removal and insertion functions, it is possible to define transformation functions for all members of $\mathscr{M}^0$. Thus, the δ-**removal operation** and δ-**insertion operation** are defined, respectively, by:

$$f_k^- M^0 = f^-(\delta_{pro_k}, M^0) = (Q, q_0, E, \Sigma, \mathbf{rem}(\partial, \delta_{pro_k})) \tag{6}$$
$$f_k^+ M^0 = f^+(\delta_{for_k}, M^0) = (\mathbf{ins}(\mathbf{ins}(Q, q'), q''), q_0, E, \Sigma, \mathbf{ins}(\partial, \delta_{for_k})) \tag{7}$$

with $\delta_{pro_k} \in \lambda_{pro}$ and $\delta_{for_k} \in \lambda_{for}$.

Now, using this two operators, it is possible to introduce the concept of **first-order adaptive function**:

$$\mathbb{F}_\phi M^0 \triangleq \mathbb{F}(\phi, M^0) = F_{\lambda_{pro}}^- F_{\lambda_{for}}^+ M^0 \tag{8}$$

in which

$$F_{\lambda_{pro}}^- M^0 \triangleq F^-(\lambda_{pro}, M^0) = (f_m^- \circ f_{m-1}^- \circ \ldots \circ f_2^- \circ f_1^-) M^0 \tag{9}$$

$$F_{\lambda_{for}}^+ M^0 \triangleq F^+(\lambda_{for}, M^0) = (f_n^+ \circ f_{n-1}^+ \circ \ldots \circ f_2^+ \circ f_1^+) M^0 \tag{10}$$

are the **first-order removal transformation** and **first-order insertion transformation**.

Definition 1 (First-order Adaptive Automata). *A First-Order Adaptive Automata (FOAA) is the quadruple $M^1 = (M^0, \Phi, \phi^0, \partial^1)$, in which $M^0 \in \mathscr{M}^0$ is called **first-order subjacent device**. Set Φ of the first-order transformation pairs is called **adaptive behavior set**. The element $\phi^0 \in \Phi$ is a void transformation pair called **null behavior**. Set ∂^1 is the **first-order adaptive transition relation**. Each element of ∂^1 takes the form $\delta_{i,k}^1 = (\delta_i, \langle M^1 \langle \mathbb{F}_{\phi_k} M^0 \rangle \rangle)$, for*

$\phi_k \in \Phi$ and $\delta_i \in \partial$ in which ∂ is the first-order subjacent device state-transition relation.

Any extension of the automaton concept implies a new expression for it. Hence, the traditional elements of the automata theory (step function, etc.) were brought into the FOAA model.

The **one step function** shows how the FOAA changes from one configuration to another:

$$(q', t) \vdash_{[\mathbb{F}_{\phi_k} M^0]} (q'', w) \Leftrightarrow \exists \alpha \in \Sigma : \alpha w = t \tag{11}$$

in which q'' is a state of $\mathbb{F}_{\phi_k} M^0$ and $((q', \alpha, q''), \langle M^1 \langle \mathbb{F}_{\phi_k}(M^0) \rangle \rangle) \in \partial^1$ for $\phi_k \in \Phi$. The **closure of the one step function** for a FOAA is defined as:

$$(q', t) \vdash^*_{[\mathbb{F}_{\phi_{k_j}} ... \mathbb{F}_{\phi_{k_2}} \mathbb{F}_{\phi_{k_1}} M^0]} (q'', w) \tag{12}$$

iff $(q' = q'')$ and $(w = t)$ or rules 1, 2 and 3 are all satisfied as defined below:

1. $t = a_0 a_1 \ldots a_j w$ with $a_i \in \Sigma$ for $0 \le i \le j$
2. $\exists (\phi_{k_1}, \phi_{k_2}, \ldots \phi_{k_{j+1}})$ with $\phi_{k_i} \in \Phi$ for $1 \le i \le j$
3. $\exists\ p_1, p_2 \ldots p_j \in Q$ in which Q belongs to first-order subjacent device, such that,
   for $j \in \mathbb{N}$:

$$(q', t) \vdash_{[\mathbb{F}_{\phi_{k_1}} M^0]} (p_1, a_1 a_2 a_3 \ldots a_j w)$$
$$\vdash_{[\mathbb{F}_{\phi_{k_2}} \mathbb{F}_{\phi_{k_1}} M^0]} (p_2, a_2 a_3 \ldots a_j w) \vdash_{[\mathbb{F}_{\phi_{k_3}} \mathbb{F}_{\phi_{k_2}} \mathbb{F}_{\phi_{k_1}} M^0]} \cdots$$
$$\vdash_{[\mathbb{F}_{\phi_{k_j}} ... \mathbb{F}_{\phi_{k_2}} \mathbb{F}_{\phi_{k_1}} M^0]} (p_j, a_j w)$$
$$\vdash_{[\mathbb{F}_{\phi_{k_{j+1}}} \mathbb{F}_{\phi_{k_j}} ... \mathbb{F}_{\phi_{k_2}} \mathbb{F}_{\phi_{k_1}} M^0]} (q'', w)$$

The **language recognized by the FOAA** is

$$L(M^1) = \{t : (q_0, t) \vdash^*_{[\mathbb{F}_{\phi_{k_j}} ... \mathbb{F}_{\phi_{k_2}} \mathbb{F}_{\phi_{k_1}} M^0]} (q_f, \varepsilon)\} \tag{13}$$

Special case in which the behavior set is $\Phi = \{\phi^\emptyset\}$, the necessary condition for a string to be accepted by a FOAA assuming the form:

$$(q_0, t) \vdash^*_{[\mathbb{F}_{\phi^\emptyset} ... \mathbb{F}_{\phi^\emptyset} \mathbb{F}_{\phi^\emptyset} M^0]} (q_f, \varepsilon) = (q_0, w) \vdash^*_{M^0} (q_f, \varepsilon)$$

3   The Second-Order Adaptive Automaton

Now, taking the set $\mathscr{M}^1$ of all first-order adaptive automata $M^1 = (M^0, \Phi, \phi^\emptyset, \partial^1)$ for a fixed Σ and applying the same method used for the set $\mathscr{M}^0$ (the definition of basic insertion and removal operations for FOAAs transitions), analogous to what occurred in the previous section, it is possible to obtain similar concepts,

Table 2. Set of operations that structures the SOAA

$\delta_{pro}^1 = \delta^1 : \delta^1 \in \partial^1$	δ^1-**proper transition**
$\delta_{for}^1 = \delta^1 : \delta^1 \notin \partial^1$	δ^1-**foreign transition**
$\lambda_{pro}^1 = (\delta_{pro_1}^1, \dots, \delta_{pro_m}^1)$	δ^1-**positive sequence**
$\lambda_{for}^1 = (\delta_{for_1}^1, \dots, \delta_{for_m}^1)$	δ^1-**negative sequence**
$\psi \triangleq (\lambda_{for}^1, \lambda_{pro}^1)$	δ^1-**transformation pair**
$g_k^- M^1 = g^-(\delta_{pro_k}^1, M^1) = (M^0, \Phi, \phi^0, \mathbf{rem}(\partial^1, \delta^1))$	δ^1-**removal operation**
$g_k^+ M^1 = g^+(\delta_{for_k}^1, M^1) = (M^0, \mathbf{ins}(\Phi, \phi), \phi^0, \mathbf{ins}(\partial^1, \delta^1))$	δ^1-**insertion operation**

now to study the first-order adaptive automata set features under a set of operators. Therefore, the table below summarizes these concepts and their definitions:

The **second-order adaptive function** is the operator

$$\mathbb{G}_\psi \triangleq \mathbb{G}(\psi, M^1) = G_{\lambda_{pro}^1}^- G_{\lambda_{for}^1}^+ M^1 \tag{14}$$

in which

$$G_{\lambda_{pro}^1}^- M^1 \triangleq G^-(\lambda_{pro}^1, M^1) = (g_m^- \circ g_{m-1}^- \circ \dots \circ g_2^- \circ g_1^-)M^1 \tag{15}$$

$$G_{\lambda_{for}^1}^+ M^1 \triangleq G^+(\lambda_{for}^1, M^1) = (g_n^+ \circ g_{n-1}^+ \circ \dots \circ g_2^+ \circ g_1^+)M^1 \tag{16}$$

are the **second-order removal transformation** and **second-order insertion transformation**, respectively. Similar with the first-order case, the pair ψ^0 is called of **void** second-order characteristic pair. Thus, for an empty second-order characteristic pair, $\mathbb{G}_{\psi^0} M^1$, it is equal to M^1.

Definition 2 (Second-Order Adaptive Automata). *A Second-Order Adaptive Automata (SOAA) is the quadruple* $M^2 = (M^1, \Psi, \psi_0, \partial^2)$, *in which* $M^1 \in \mathscr{M}^1$ *is called* **second-order subjacent device***. The set* $\Psi = \{\psi_0, \psi_1, \dots, \psi_n\}$ *of second-order transformation pairs is called* **second-order adaptive behavior set***. The element* ψ_0 *is a void transformation pair called* **null behavior***. In the* **second-order adaptive transition relation** ∂^2, *each element take the form* $\delta_{i,k,j}^2 = (\delta_{i,k}^1, \langle M^2 \langle \mathbb{G}_{\psi_j} M^1 \rangle \rangle)$, *for* $\psi_j \in \Psi$ *and* $\delta_{i,k}^1 \in \partial^1$, *in which* ∂^1 *is the second-order subjacent device state-transition relation.*

The **one step function** shows how the SOAA changes from one configuration to another and is defined below:

$$(q', t) \vdash_{[\langle \mathbb{G}_{\psi_j} M^1 \langle \mathbb{F}_{\phi_k} M^0 \rangle \rangle]} (q'', w) \Leftrightarrow \exists \alpha \in \Sigma : \alpha w = t \tag{17}$$

in which q'' is a state of $\mathbb{F}_{\phi_k} M^0$ for $\delta_{i,k,j} = (\delta_{i,k}, \langle M^2 \langle \mathbb{G}_{\psi_j} M^1 \rangle \rangle) \in \partial^2$, $\delta_{i,k} = (\delta_i, \langle M^1 \langle \mathbb{F}_{\phi_k} M^0 \rangle \rangle) \in \partial^1$ and $\delta_i = (q', \alpha, q'') \in \partial$ with $\phi_k \in \Phi$ and $\psi_j \in \Psi$.

For any $s \in \mathbb{N}$, the **closure of the one step function for a SOAA** is defined as:

$$(q', t) \vdash_{[\langle \mathbb{G}_{\psi_{j_s}} \dots \mathbb{G}_{\psi_{j_2}} \mathbb{G}_{\psi_{j_1}} M^1 \langle \mathbb{F}_{\phi_{k_s}} \dots \mathbb{F}_{\phi_{k_2}} \mathbb{F}_{\phi_{k_1}} M^0 \rangle \rangle]}^* (q'', w) \tag{18}$$

iff $(q' = q'')$ and $(w = t)$ or rules 1 to 4 are all satisfied as defined below:

1. $t = a_0 a_1 \ldots a_s w$ with $a_z \in \Sigma$ for $0 \leq z \leq s$
2. $\exists (\phi_{k_1}, \phi_{k_2}, \ldots \phi_{k_{s+1}})$ with $\phi_{k_z} \in \Phi$ for $1 \leq z \leq s$
3. $\exists (\psi_{j_1}, \psi_{j_2}, \ldots \psi_{j_{s+1}})$ with $\psi_{j_z} \in \Psi$ for $1 \leq z \leq s$
4. $\exists\ p_1, p_2 \ldots p_s \in Q$ with Q belongs to First-order subjacent device such that:

$$(q', t) \vdash_{[\langle \mathbb{G}_{\psi_{j_1}} M^1 \langle \mathbb{F}_{\phi_{k_1}} M^0 \rangle \rangle]} (p_1, a_1 a_2 a_3 \ldots a_s w)$$
$$\vdash_{[\langle \mathbb{G}_{\psi_{j_2}} \mathbb{G}_{\psi_{j_1}} M^1 \langle \mathbb{F}_{\phi_{k_2}} \mathbb{F}_{\phi_{k_1}} M^0 \rangle]} (p_2, a_2 a_3 \ldots a_s w)$$
$$\vdash_{[\langle \mathbb{G}_{\psi_{j_3}} \mathbb{G}_{\psi_{j_2}} \mathbb{G}_{\psi_{j_1}} \langle \mathbb{F}_{\phi_{k_3}} \mathbb{F}_{\phi_{k_2}} \mathbb{F}_{\phi_{k_1}} M^0 \rangle \rangle]} \ldots$$
$$\vdash_{[\langle \mathbb{G}_{\psi_{j_s}} \ldots \mathbb{G}_{\psi_{j_2}} \mathbb{G}_{\psi_{j_1}} M^1 \langle \mathbb{F}_{\phi_{k_s}} \ldots \mathbb{F}_{\phi_{k_2}} \mathbb{F}_{\phi_{k_1}} M^0 \rangle \rangle]} (p_s, a_s w)$$
$$\vdash_{[\langle \mathbb{G}_{\psi_{j_{s+1}}} \mathbb{G}_{\psi_{j_s}} \ldots \mathbb{G}_{\psi_{j_2}} \mathbb{G}_{\psi_{j_1}} M^1 \langle \mathbb{F}_{\phi_{k_{s+1}}} \mathbb{F}_{\phi_{k_s}} \ldots \mathbb{F}_{\phi_{k_2}} \mathbb{F}_{\phi_{k_1}} M^0 \rangle \rangle]} (q'', w)$$

The language recognized by the SOAA is:

$$L(M^2) = \{ t : (q_0, t) \vdash^*_{[\langle \mathbb{G}_{\psi_{j_s}} \ldots \mathbb{G}_{\psi_{j_2}} \mathbb{G}_{\psi_{j_1}} M^1 \langle \mathbb{F}_{\phi_{k_j}} \ldots \mathbb{F}_{\phi_{k_2}} \mathbb{F}_{\phi_{k_1}} M^0 \rangle \rangle]} (q_f, \varepsilon) \} \tag{19}$$

In the special case in which the second-order behavior set is $\Psi = \{\psi^0\}$, the necessary condition for a string to be accepted by a SOAA assumes the form:

$$(q_0, t) \vdash^*_{[\langle \mathbb{G}_{\psi^0} \ldots \mathbb{G}_{\psi^0} \mathbb{G}_{\psi^0} M^1 \langle \mathbb{F}_{\phi_{k_j}} \ldots \mathbb{F}_{\phi_{k_2}} \mathbb{F}_{\phi_{k_1}} M^0 \rangle \rangle]} (q_f, \varepsilon) =$$
$$(q_0, t) \vdash^*_{[\mathbb{F}_{\phi_{k_j}} \ldots \mathbb{F}_{\phi_{k_2}} \mathbb{F}_{\phi_{k_1}} M^0]} (q_f, \varepsilon)$$

In this case, the recognition of string t is made by the initial second-order subjacent device. The SOAA assumes the behavior of the FOAA, which is equivalent to the Turing Machine.

4   Second-Order Adaptive Automata and Learning in the Limit

This section will show the advantage of using the SOAA as an identification in the limit Inductive Inference Machine for formal languages. By definition, SOAA transforms FOAAs by applying on them second-order adaptive actions. Now, it is necessary to demonstrate how this behavior can be used to "recycle" the former hypothesis created in a learning in the limit process, as stated in the Introduction, and what kind of formal languages a SOAA can learn in the limit. Firstly, the main definitions related to the Gold identification in the limit are presented. Then, an illustrating example of learning in the limit using a SOAA is presented in subsection 4.1.

Definition 3 (Inductive Inference Machine)

Let a target formal language indexable class $\mathcal{L}$ and a hypothesis set $\mathcal{H}$ composed by an useful enumerable formal model class (grammars, Turing machines, recursive functions, etc) to represent the members of the target languages class. Given the family $seq(\theta)$ for $\theta \in text(L)$, in which L belongs to $\mathcal{L}$, an inductive inference machine (IIM in short) is defined as an effective procedure in which it computes any partial or total mapping $IIM \subseteq seq(\theta) \times \mathcal{H}$.

The IIM **changes its mind** if two consecutives output hypotheses are different, i.e., $IIM(\theta[m]) \neq IIM(\theta[m+1])$ for $m \geq 0$.

The expression

$$IIM(\theta) \downarrow = h \Leftrightarrow \exists(n \in \mathbb{N})\exists(h \in \mathcal{H})(\forall m \geq n)[IIM(\theta[m])] = h \qquad (20)$$

means that the inductive inference machine **converges**, i.e., the potential infinite sequence $[IIM(\theta[m])]_{m \in \mathbb{N}}$ of outputs converges on θ to $h \in \mathcal{H}$.

Definition 4 (Identification in the Limit). *Let $\mathcal{L}$ be an indexed family of languages, given a convenient hypothesis space $\mathcal{H}$. IIM **Lim-identifies** $\mathcal{L} \Leftrightarrow \forall(L \in \mathcal{L})\exists(h \in \mathcal{H} : L(h) = L)[IIM(\theta) \downarrow = h].$*

The second-order adaptive function concept allows deriving definitions of language classes based only on the SOAA characteristics. One of these classes is shown below.

Definition 5 (Confined Adaptive Problem). *Given a FOAA M^1 and a language L in which $L \neq L(M^1)$, let $C_\propto = (\mathbb{G}_{\psi_i}, \ldots, \mathbb{G}_{\psi_j}, \ldots, \mathbb{G}_{\psi_k})$ be a sequence of second-order adaptive functions. If the language L can be expressed in terms of M^1 and $C_\propto$ as follows in equation 21:*

$$L = L((\mathbb{G}_{\psi_i} \ldots (\mathbb{G}_{\psi_j} \ldots (\mathbb{G}_{\psi_k}(M^1))\ldots)\ldots)) \qquad (21)$$

*then L is called a **confined adaptive problem**, sequence $C_\propto$ is called **metamorphosis sequence** and M^1 is a **seed** for L.*

Definition 6 (Linear Confined Adaptive Problem Class)

*Given a finite second-order adaptive functions set $\mathcal{G}$, let the indexable class $\mathcal{L}_\mathcal{G} = \{L_n\}_{n \in \mathbb{N}}$ of confined adaptive problems, all based on the same seed L_0, in which the metamorphosis of L_i is a subsequence of the L_{i+1} metamorphosis. For all languages $L_i \in \mathcal{L}_\mathcal{G}$, if all elements of the sequence $C_{\propto_i}$, belongs to L_i, are elements of $C_\mathcal{G}$, then $\mathcal{L}_\mathcal{G}$ is called a **Linear Confined Adaptive Problem Class** and set $\mathcal{G}$ is called a **mutation set**.*

Theorem 1. *Given a Confined Adaptive Problem L and any text θ of L, there is a SOAA M^2 and a Natural number $n > 0$, for which:*

$$\begin{cases} L \neq L(M^2) & for \ \theta[n] \\ L = L(M^2) & for \ \theta[n+1] \end{cases}$$

Proof (by construction). Take a SOAA in which its subjacent device M^1 is a seed for a Confined Adaptive Problem L. Let Ψ be a behavior set in which all elements of $C_\propto$ are elements of Ψ, too. With the valid seed M^1 for L, it is possible to define a second-order adaptive transition relation in which the computation of text θ assumes the form:

$(q_0, t_1) \vdash^*_{[\langle \mathbb{G}_{\psi_{j_s}} \ldots \mathbb{G}_{\psi_{j_2}} \mathbb{G}_{\psi_{j_1}} M^1 \rangle]} (q', w')$

$(q_0, t_2) \vdash^*_{[\langle \mathbb{G}_{\psi_{j_t}} \ldots \mathbb{G}_{\psi_{j_2}} \mathbb{G}_{\psi_{j_1}} (M^1)' \rangle]} (q'', w'')$

$\ldots$

$(q_0, t_{n-1}) \vdash^*_{[\langle \mathbb{G}_{\psi_{j_u}} \ldots \mathbb{G}_{\psi_{j_2}} \mathbb{G}_{\psi_{j_1}} (M^1)^{(n-2)} \rangle]} (q^{n-1}, w^{n-1})$

$(q_0, t_n) \vdash^*_{[\langle \mathbb{G}_{\psi_{j_w}} \ldots \mathbb{G}_{\psi_{j_2}} \mathbb{G}_{\psi_{j_1}} (M^1)^{(n-1)} \rangle]} (q^n, w^n)$

$(q_0, t_{n+1}) \vdash^*_{[\langle \mathbb{G}_{\psi_{j_p}} \ldots \mathbb{G}_{\psi_{j_2}} \mathbb{G}_{\psi_{j_1}} (M^1)^n \rangle]} (q_f, \epsilon)$

$(q_0, t_{n+2}) \vdash^*_{[\langle \mathbb{G}_{\psi_{j_v}} \ldots \mathbb{G}_{\psi_{j_2}} \mathbb{G}_{\psi_{j_1}} (M^1)^{(n+1)} \rangle]} (q_f, \epsilon)$

$\ldots$

$(q_0, t_{n+k}) \vdash^*_{[\langle \mathbb{G}_{\psi_{j_l}} \ldots \mathbb{G}_{\psi_{j_2}} \mathbb{G}_{\psi_{j_1}} (M^1)^{(n+(k-1))} \rangle]} (q_f, \epsilon)$

for $q', q'', \ldots, q^{n-1}, q^n$ different from q_f; $w', w'', \ldots, w^{n-1}, w^n$ different from ϵ and

$(M^1)' = \mathbb{G}_{\psi_{j_s}} \ldots \mathbb{G}_{\psi_{j_2}} \mathbb{G}_{\psi_{j_1}} M^1$

$(M^1)'' = \mathbb{G}_{\psi_{j_t}} \ldots \mathbb{G}_{\psi_{j_2}} \mathbb{G}_{\psi_{j_1}} (M^1)'$

$\ldots$

$(M^1)^{n-1} = \mathbb{G}_{\psi_{j_u}} \ldots \mathbb{G}_{\psi_{j_2}} \mathbb{G}_{\psi_{j_1}} (M^1)^{n-2}$

$(M^1)^n = \mathbb{G}_{\psi_{j_w}} \ldots \mathbb{G}_{\psi_{j_2}} \mathbb{G}_{\psi_{j_1}} (M^1)^{n-1}$

$(M^1)^{n+1} = \mathbb{G}_{\psi_{j_p}} \ldots \mathbb{G}_{\psi_{j_2}} \mathbb{G}_{\psi_{j_1}} (M^1)^n$

$\ldots$

such that the execution of adaptive transitions generates the sequence of the adaptive transformations below

$$L = L(\mathbb{G}_{\psi_{j_p}} \ldots \mathbb{G}_{\psi_{j_w}} \ldots \mathbb{G}_{\psi_{j_u}} \ldots \mathbb{G}_{\psi_{j_t}} \ldots \mathbb{G}_{\psi_{j_s}} \ldots \mathbb{G}_{\psi_{j_2}} \mathbb{G}_{\psi_{j_1}} M^1)$$

and, for any t_{n+k} in which $k > 1$, the following expression holds

$$(M^1)^{(n+(k-1))} = (M^1)^{(n+1)}$$

Thus, for $n > 0$, there is a SOAA for the Confined Adaptive Problem such that

$$\begin{cases} L \neq L(M^2) & for \ (t_1, t_2, \ldots, t_n) \\ L = L(M^2) & for \ (t_{n+1}, \ldots) \end{cases} \qquad \square$$

Theorem 2. *For $m \in \mathbb{N}$, and given a function $P(M^2, \theta[m]) = M^1$ that returns M^1, which is the subjacent device FOAA of the second-order M^2, then after processing the segment text $\theta[m]$, there is a SOAA M^2 in which the function $P(M^2, .)$ is an IIM and P **Lim-identifies** any language L_i of $\mathcal{L}_{C_\infty}$, for any text θ belonging to L_i.*

Proof. As seen in theorem 1, for any Confined Adaptive Problem L, it is possible to construct a SOAA M^2 such that:

$$\begin{cases} L \neq L(M^2) & for\ \theta[n] \\ L = L(M^2) & for\ \theta[n+1] \end{cases}$$

Thus, it is possible to claim that

$$\exists(n \in \mathbb{N})\exists(M^1 \in \mathcal{M}^1 : L(M^1) = L)(\forall m \geq n)[P(M^2, \theta[m]) = M^1]$$

in other words,

$$\exists(M^1 \in \mathcal{M}^1 : L(M^1) = L)[P(M^2, \theta[m]) \downarrow = M^1]$$

meaning that the function $P(M^2, .)$ **Lim-identifies** L.

According to definition 6, the metamorphosis sequence of any L_i (with $i \geq 0$) of $\mathcal{L}_{C_\infty}$ is a subsequence of the metamorphosis sequence of L_z, with $z \geq i$. Thus, using theorem 2, the following assertions holds:

for L_0 $\exists(P(M_0^2, .)) : P(M_0^2, .)$ **Lim-identifies** (L_0)
for L_1 $\exists(P(M_1^2, .)) : P(M_1^2, .)$ **Lim-identifies** (L_0, L_1)
for L_2 $\exists(P(M_2^2, .)) : P(M_2^2, .)$ **Lim-identifies** (L_0, L_1, L_2)
...

for L_i $\exists(P(M_i^2, .)) : P(M_i^2, .)$ **Lim-identifies** $(L_0, L_1, L_2, \ldots, L_i)$
...

for L_n $\exists(P(M_n^2, .)) : P(M_n^2, .)$ **Lim-identifies** $\mathcal{L}_{C_\infty}$ □

An important consequence of Theorem 2 has an immediate impact on the choice relation over the hypotheses space.

Corollary 1. *Set $\mathcal{M}^1$ is an admissible hypotheses space.*

4.1 Illustrating Example

Let $\Sigma = \{a, b, c\}$ be an alphabet, and $t = abc$ a string over Σ^*. Based on the string t, it is possible to define the class of formal languages below:

$$I = \{L_0 = a^n b^n c, L_1 = a^n b c^n, L_2 = ab^n c^n\}$$

Now, consider the following situation: there is a text θ that belongs to an unknown language X. The only information about language X is the fact that it belongs to class I. The question is: would it be possible to obtain a SOAA that identifies the language X represented by sequence θ? If I is a Confined Adaptive Problem Class, then the response is yes. Thus, to answer the question, it is necessary to verify whether I is a Confined Adaptive Problem Class or not.

Proof (I is a Confined Adaptive Problem Class).
The proof that I is a Confined Adaptive Problem Class is lengthy. For space limitation reasons, only the proof sketch will be given here. All elements of I can surely be represented by FOAAs. Let M_0^1 represents the FOAA for the language

L_0 of I. One possible adaptive function $\mathbb{F}_0$ for this FOAA is "for a number n of symbols 'a' recognized, transform the M^0 to accept the same number of symbols 'b' in the string".

The next step is to verify that all language members of I are Confined Adaptive Problems. Thus, it is necessary to verify if there are metamorphosis sequences for L_1 and L_2. If there are such metamorphosis sequences, then the first sequence is

$$C_{\propto_2} = (\mathbb{G}_2, \mathbb{G}_1)$$

and it performs the transformation sequence below:

$$L_2 = L((\mathbb{G}_2(\mathbb{G}_1(M_0^1))))$$

in which the two second-order adaptive functions $\mathbb{G}_2$ and $\mathbb{G}_2$ must have the following characteristics:

- $\mathbb{G}_1$: Replace the second symbol of $\mathbb{F}_0$ with the symbol 'c' and transform $\mathbb{F}_0$ in $\mathbb{F}_1$.
- $\mathbb{G}_2$: Replace the first symbol of $\mathbb{F}_1$ with the symbol 'b' and transform $\mathbb{F}_1$ in $\mathbb{F}_2$.

And the second sequence is

$$C_{\propto_1} = (\mathbb{G}_1)$$

that performs the transformation sequence below:

$$L_1 = L(\mathbb{G}_1(M_0^1))$$

But sequence $C_{\propto_1}$ is a subsequence of $C_{\propto_2}$ and generates the language L_1. Considering that the second-order adaptive functions set used to create the transformation sequences is finite, then it is a mutation set. Thus, I is a Confined Adaptive Problem.   □

5 Conclusion

As stated in the Introduction it is possible to define many ways to the hypothesis choice and each one, in practice, determines a whole new learning model; the main ones are the probabilistic approach and the enumerations strategies. The approach used in this work is closely related to Wallace's Minimum Message Length (MML) approach, but was inspired by Solomonoff's paper [11].

A strong connection between learning in the limit and the SOAA was shown by Theorems 1 and 2. The connection is established using Solomonoff's approach to mutating programs. The purpose is to represent a learning process using the SOAA, and this learner acts as a learning in the limit one. Thus, from this point of view, any hypothesis can be used to start a learning process, and, following a step-by-step transformation of that hypothesis by a SOAA, produces a correct final model, when computational learning can be effective.

Hence, inductive inference can be envisioned in a new and different way using this kind of learner. The SOAA can be used as a learner for formal languages, as illustrated by the example in section 4.1. There are many applications for the learning process defined in this paper; one clearly comes from on-line learning. Since it is a non-stop process, it is suitable for continuous learning, and as the previous hypothesis can be used to produce new ones, the second-order adaptive automaton seems to be an appropriate choice for diverse environments.

5.1 Future Work

As a future work, some of the applications mentioned here will be implemented, to run them in order to generate a benchmark comparing the second-order adaptive approach to some others. A lot of work need to be done before a product ready to be used can be generated, but the path to be followed has been established.

It is necessary to define all the limitations of the computational model and then define the learning limitations of this adaptive learning process. Some constraints and limits of the adaptive automata hierarchy have to be formally defined. For the purposes of this work, the second-order was sufficient. Another task to be carried out is investigate the necessity of third or higher order.

References

1. Chater, N., Vitányi, P.: "Ideal learning" of natural language: positive results about learning from positive evidence. Journal of Mathematical Psychology 51(3), 135–163 (2007)
2. Dowe, D.L.: MML, hybrid Bayesian network graphical models, statistical consistency, invariance and uniqueness. In: Handbook of the Philosophy of Science (HPS). Philosophy of Statistics, vol. 7, pp. 901–982. Elsevier (2011)
3. Gold, E.: Language identification in the limit. Information and Control 10(5), 447–474 (1967)
4. Li, M., Vitányi, P.: Computational Machine Learning in Theory and Praxis. In: van Leeuwen, J. (ed.) Computer Science Today. LNCS, vol. 1000, pp. 518–535. Springer, Heidelberg (1995)
5. Li, M., Vitányi, P.: An introduction to Kolmogorov complexity and its applications, 3rd edn. Springer Publishing Company, Incorporated (2008)
6. Paul, W.J., Solomonoff, R.J.: Autonomous theory building systems. Technical Report D 6600, Computer Science Department, University of Saarbruecken, Germany (1990)
7. de Azevedo da Rocha, R. L., Neto, J.J.: Adaptive automaton, limits and complexity compared to the Turing machine - in Portuguese Autômato Adaptativo, Limites e Complexidade em Comparação com Máquina de Turing. In: Proceedings of the I Congress of Logic Applied to Technology, LAPTEC 2000, São Paulo, Faculdade SENAC de Ciências Exatas e Tecnologia, pp. 33–48 (2000)

8. Rubinstein, R.S., Shutt, J.N.: Self-modifying finite automata. In: Pehrson, B., Simon, I. (eds.) Proceedings of the 13th IFIP World Computer Congress, Amsterdam. Technology and Foundations: Information Processing 1994, vol. I, pp. 493–498. North-Holland (1994)

9. Salthe, S., Matsuno, K.: Self-organization in hierarchical systems. Journal of Social and Evolutionary Systems 18(4), 327–338 (1995)

10. Silva Filho, R.I., de Azevedo da Rocha, R.L.: Adaptive Finite Automaton: a New Algebraic Approach. In: Dobnikar, A., Lotrič, U., Šter, B. (eds.) ICANNGA 2011, Part II. LNCS, vol. 6594, pp. 275–284. Springer, Heidelberg (2011)

11. Solomonoff, R.J.: A formal theory of inductive inference. parts I and II. Information and Control 7(2), 224–254 (1964)

12. Solomonoff, R.J.: Does algorithmic probability solve the problem of induction? In D. L. Dowe, K. B. Korb, and J. J Oliver, editors. In: Dowe, D.L., Korb, K.B.,, J. (eds.) Proceedings of the Information, Statistics and Induction in Science (ISIS) Conference, Melbourne, Australia, pp. 7–8. World Scientific (August 1996)

13. Wallace, C.S.: Statistical and Inductive Inference by Mininum Message Length. Springer (2005)

Algorithmic Simplicity and Relevance

Jean-Louis Dessalles

Telecom ParisTech, 46 rue Barrault, F-75013 Paris, France
dessalles@Telecom-ParisTech.fr, www.dessalles.fr

Abstract. The human mind is known to be sensitive to complexity. For instance, the visual system reconstructs hidden parts of objects following a principle of maximum simplicity. We suggest here that higher cognitive processes, such as the selection of relevant situations, are sensitive to *variations* of complexity. Situations are *relevant* to human beings when they appear *simpler to describe than to generate*. This definition offers a predictive (*i.e.* falsifiable) model for the selection of situations worth reporting (interestingness) and for what individuals consider an appropriate move in conversation.

Keywords: Simplicity, relevance, interestingness, unexpectedness.

1   Complexity, Simplicity and the Human Mind

Almost half a century ago, Ray Solomonoff suggested that inductive learning is guided by simplicity [1]. In 1999, Nick Chater drew attention to the fact that several other human cognitive processes are guided by a principle of minimum complexity [2-3]. Figure 1 illustrates the fact that our visual system reconstructs hidden parts of shapes by preferring simplest patterns.

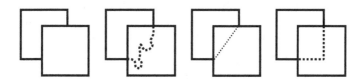

Fig. 1. Hidden shapes are as the least complex ones (after [2])

Surprisingly, the same principle seems to be at work also in higher cognitive processes. Simplicity explains the sensitivity to coincidences [4-5]. It accounts for cognitive biases such as representativeness [6]. It makes predictions about how news elicit emotion, depending on parameters such as proximity, rarity or prominence [7]. Simplicity, defined as the discrepancy between universal probability distribution and uniform distribution, has been used to measure subjective improbability [8]. Complexity has also been related to the feeling of beauty and its variations has been claimed to define interestingness [9]. Complexity is also claimed to be involved in several human traits such as supernatural beliefs, creativity, humor and fiction ([9]; [10] p. 545; [11] p. 967).

D.L. Dowe (Ed.): Solomonoff Festschrift, LNAI 7070, pp. 119–130, 2013.

Our own work on interestingness led us to develop *simplicity theory* (ST) [7], [12]. The central claim of ST is that subjective probability depends on the difference between generation complexity and description complexity. In these previous developments of ST, interestingness (which is a form of relevance) was merely equated with unexpectedness. The present paper is an attempt to bring the notion of *relevance* closer to an operational definition, based on algorithmic theory, by defining feature relevance and by distinguishing first-order from second-order relevance. In what follows, I will first mention some previous attempts to define relevance, and remind that it is a crucial issue. Then I will briefly outline the central notions of Simplicity Theory, and show how ST can provide a formal definition of relevance. I will then illustrate through examples the explanatory power of the definition. In the conclusion, I will consider the current limits of the theory by mentioning recent work on the impact of emotion on relevance.

2   Relevance

Relevance is an empirical phenomenon. Human conversation is a risky game in which speakers dare not misjudge what is worth telling, lest they be punished by being considered socially inept [13]. Being relevant is an essential part of what constitutes human intelligence, as opposed to what we share with other animals. Historically, the main contribution to a theory of relevance was offered by Dan Sperber and Deirdre Wilson [14]. These authors introduce two new notions: cognitive effect and cognitive cost. They define a linguistic utterance as relevant if it maximizes the former and minimizes the latter.

The main merit of this definition is to place the problem on the cognitive ground. Relevance is no longer a question of social convention [15], nor a mere statistical observation about what is generally said and not said in specific contexts. Relevant utterances are supposed to result from genuine computations. Unfortunately, Sperber and Wilson do not provide details about how these computations are performed.

In previous studies, we distinguished two forms of relevance in language, depending on the conversational mode [7]. *Narrative relevance* corresponds to interestingness. A good model of narrative relevance should explain how speakers select events worth reporting in conversational narratives. *Argumentative relevance*, on the other hand, controls the appropriateness of conversational moves during a discussion. Together, conversational narratives and discussions represent more than 90% of conversational time [7].

Algorithmic simplicity may offer a predictive model of narrative relevance [7]. The present paper proposes a few formal definitions about what makes an event relevant. It will also explore how far the same model can be extended to argumentative relevance.

3   Simplicity Theory

Simplicity Theory (ST) defines simplicity, not in absolute terms, but as the difference in complexity between expectations and observation. To do so, it distinguishes the standard notion of *description* complexity from *generation* complexity.

The *description complexity* $C(s)$ of a situation s is the length of the shortest description of s that the observer may achieve. This notion coincides with Kolmogorov complexity, but the choice of the machine is not free. The description machine is bound to be the observer, with her previous knowledge and computing abilities.

Generation complexity $C_w(s)$ measures expectations about s, in complexity terms. It is defined as the length of the minimal program that must be given to the "world" for it to generate s. Again, this corresponds to the standard definition of Kolmogorov complexity, except that the machine is bound to function according to what the observer knows about the world's constraints (note that the "world" has no objective character here). In particular, s is supposed to be generated according to some causal process. This constraint affects $C_w(s)$, which may therefore depart from $C(s)$.

The restriction to particular machines, together with a limited time constraint as in [9], makes $C(s)$ and $C_w(s)$ computable. Both computations, however, differ significantly. The description complexity $C(s)$ of a situation that the observer already encountered may be given by its address in memory. If the observer's memory is organized as a binary tree, then $C(s)$ depends on the location of s on that tree. In the computation of $C(s)$ and $C_w(s)$, each bit counts. It is therefore crucial that addresses in memory be minimal in length. A minimal (maximally compact) code is easy to design for lists, using a positional code. Table 1 offers an example of positional code for a list. Note that the code is not self-delimited: this is the price to pay for having a compact code; as a consequence, one must allow the use of a punctuation symbol, or equivalently suppose that code segmentation is performed at a preprocessing stage.

When the observer's memory structure is unavailable, it is sometimes possible to assess the relative complexity of items (objects, people, places…) by comparing their relative ranks on the Web using the number of hits given by a search engine. It is for instance easy to compute the complexity of US presidents, as shown in table 1 (note that G.H. Bush is downgraded, as many pages about him do not mention the middle initial). The code used to compute complexity is designed to be maximally compact (more compact that a prefix-free code). With this code, once the list of US-president is available, its first item, B. Obama, is meant by default and its complexity is zero.

Generation complexity $C_w(s)$ is computed in a different way. The most basic generation machine is a uniform lottery among N objects, in which case $C_w(s) = \log(N)$. When several independent lotteries are used, the complexities add up to give $C_w(s)$. In contrast to the observation machine, the generation machine can be considered to be memory-less. If the same number n comes out twice in a row in a Lottery game, the generation complexity of the double event is $2 \times C_w(n)$, whereas its description complexity is only $C(n)$.

Table 1. Web-complexity of the 10 last US presidents, using a non self-delimited code

President	Number of hits	Code	Complexity
Barak Obama	263000000		0
George W. Bush	63300000	0	1
John Kennedy	57500000	1	1
Bill Clinton	46200000	00	2
Ronald Reagan	32200000	01	2
Jimmy Carter	18200000	10	2
Richard Nixon	14200000	11	2
Lyndon Johnson	13200000	000	3
Gerald Ford	9900000	001	3
George H. Bush	6260000	010	3

The central notion of ST is *unexpectedness* $U(s)$. It is defined as:

$$U(s) = C_w(s) - C(s) \qquad (1)$$

In a Lottery game, all draws are supposed to have the same generation complexity $C_w(s) \approx 6 \times \log(49)$ (supposing that 6 numbers are drawn between 1 and 49). When a remarkable combination such as 1–2–3–4–5–6 comes out, description complexity $C(s)$ is much smaller, and $U(s)$ reaches significant value.

Figure 2 illustrates the difference between generation and description. The black ball has to go trough five binary choices before reaching a leaf s of the tree. Therefore, $C_w(s) = 5$. If s is indistinguishable from other leaves, then $C(s) = \log(32) = 5$ and $U(s) = 0$. If s happens to be the only white leaf, then in this case $C(s) = 0$ (as 'being white' is the only apparent feature among leaves) and $U(s) = 5$.

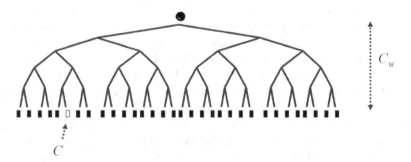

Fig. 2. Generation complexity *vs.* description complexity

More generally, generation complexity is given by the complexity of the simplest causal scenario or theory that may have produced the actual situation (about causality and complexity, see [11], section 7.4). Dowe proposes a computation in which theories are ranked by their complexity ([10] p. 545, note 206): a special list of theories, called 'miracles', is located somewhere in the theory hierarchy; for some observers, for whom miracles are not stored too deep in the complexity-based hierarchy, invoking miracles might be a parsimonious way to account for the generation of a given state of affairs. This illustrates the fact that $C_w(s)$ is observer-dependent, as well as description complexity $C(s)$. Whenever these computations are available, relevance can be quantitatively defined.

4   Relevance from an Algorithmic Perspective

We must distinguish two cases. A situation, or a property of a situation, may be relevant because it contributes to making a topic interesting. We call this quality *first-order relevance*. A situation or a property may also be relevant because it makes a previous (relevant) topic *less* relevant. We call this quality *second-order relevance*, or *2-relevance*. We define these two notions in turn.

4.1   First-Order Relevance

Relevance cannot be equated with failure to anticipate [16]: white noise is 'boring', although it impossible to predict and is thus always 'surprising', even for an optimal learner. Our definition of unexpectedness, given by (1), correctly declares white noise uninteresting, as its value s at a given time is hard to describe but also equally hard to generate (since a white noise amounts to a uniform lottery), and therefore $U(s) = 0$.

Following definition (1), some situations can be 'more than expected'. For instance, if s is about the death last week of a 40-year old woman who lived in a far place hardly known to the observer, then $U(s)$ is likely to be negative, as the minimal description of the woman will exceed in length the minimal parameter settings that the world requires to generate her death. If death is compared with a uniform lottery, then $C_w(s)$ is the number of bits required to 'choose' the week of her death: $C_w(s) \approx \log_2(52 \times 40) = 11$ bits. If we must discriminate the woman among all currently living humans, we need $C(s) = \log_2(7 \times 10^9) = 33$ bits, and $U(s) = 11 - 33 = -22$ is negative. *Relevant* situations are unexpected situations.

$$s \text{ is relevant if } U(s) = C_w(s) - C(s) > 0 \tag{2}$$

Relevant situations are thus simpler to describe than to generate. In our previous example, this would happen if the dying woman lives in the vicinity, or is an acquaintance, or is a celebrity. Relevance is detected either because the world generates a situation that turns out to be simple for the observer, or because the situation that is observed was thought by the observer to be 'impossible' (*i.e.* hard to generate).

In other contexts, some authors have noticed the relation between *interestingness* and unexpectedness [9, 16], or suggested that the *originality* of an idea could be measured by the complexity of its description using previous knowledge ([10], p. 545). All these definitions compare the complexity of the actual situation s to some reference, which represents the observer's expectations. For instance, the notion of *randomness deficiency* ([8], ch. 4 p. 280) compares actual situation to the output of a uniform lottery. The present proposal differs by making the notion of expectation (here: generation) explicit, and by contrasting its complexity $C_w(s)$ with description complexity $C(s)$.

Situations correspond to states of the world. As such, they cannot be grasped in every detail. This is not a problem, however, as we can focus on specific aspects of a given situation. Relevant aspects constitute the essential part of narratives. Consider a feature f that is present in situation s. For instance, the fact that a given individual, Ryan, is eating a hot-dog. Considering f as a logical predicate, this means that $f(s)$ is regarded as true. We may write, on the generation side:

$$C_w(s) \le C_w(f(s)) + C_w(s \mid f(s)) \tag{3}$$

If Ryan could choose freely among 16 possible sandwiches, the first term $C_w(f(s))$ amounts to $C_w(f(s)) = \log(16) = 4$ bits. However, if we know that Ryan is Muslim, $C_w(f(s))$ can reach significant values as, by default, non-eating pork is a low *mutable* property (see section 5.2) for Muslims. On the description side, we have:

$$C(s) \le C(f) + C(s \mid f(s)) \tag{4}$$

In contrast with (3), $f(s)$ needs only to be described through a description of f and not to be generated as a fact. The term $C(f)$ measures the conceptual complexity of f for the observer in the current context. In the example of Ryan's meal, the conceptual complexity of 'hot-dog' can be estimated by the logarithm of the rank of this type of food in a list of typical meals or in short-term memory.

Features are relevant with respect to a given situation if they contribute to unexpectedness.

$$f \text{ is relevant w.r.t. } s \text{ if } \quad U(f(s)) = C_w(f(s)) - C(f) > 0 \tag{5}$$

Definitions (2) and (5) control what is worth telling when reporting or signaling an event in conversation. Note that if f is the conjunction of several sub-properties, those sub-properties need not be relevant separately. The art of telling narratives is to assemble elements that, together, produce unexpectedness. A conjecture is that every descriptive element, in spontaneous narratives, is intended to make relevance eventually maximal.

4.2   Second-Order Relevance

An admissible reaction to relevant topics consists in attempting to diminish their unexpectedness. The following definition concerns a piece of information t that may alter unexpectedness.

$$\text{if } U(s \mid t) < U(s), \text{ then } t \text{ is 2-relevant w.r.t. } s$$

In the previous example, t may be the fact that Ryan lost faith. More generally, any move that diminishes $U(s)$ is 2-relevant w.r.t. s. This definition covers not only the phenomenon of trivialization [7] ("The same happened to me…"), but also any attempt to diminish $C_w(s)$ by simplifying the generation scenario (*i.e.* by providing an explanation).

5   Examples

5.1   The 'Nude Model' Story

The story in figure 3 is adapted from a spontaneous conversation analyzed by Neal Norrick [17]. The story is about a fortuitous encounter with a model who was previously seen posing in the nude. Elements indicated in bold face are commented on below.

> B: It was just about **two weeks ago**. And then we did some figure drawing. Everyone was kind of like, "oh my God, we can't believe it." We- y'know, **Midwest College**, y'know,
> [...]
> B: like a ... **nude models** and stuff. And it was really weird, because then, like, **just last week**, we went downtown one night to see a movie, and we were sitting in [a restaurant], like downtown, waiting for our movie, and **we saw her** in the [restaurant], and it was like, "that's our model" (laughing) **in clothes**
> A: (laughs) Oh my God.
> B: we were like "oh wow." It was really weird. **But it was her**. (laughs)
> A: Oh no. Weird.
> B: I mean, that's weird when you run into somebody **in Chicago**.
> A: yeah.

Fig. 3. The Nude Model story (after [17])

The mention "just last week" is not here by chance. Recent events are simple to describe, what makes them more likely to appear unexpected. Intuitively, the story is better so, than if the time reference had been "one year ago". Formula (1) explains why. If a is the typical duration of this kind of episode, then the complexity of locating the event at time location T in the past amounts to $\log_2(T/a)$ bits. Formula (1) predicts logarithmic recency effects: unexpectedness varies as $-\log_2(T)$. If B had not made temporal location explicit, she would have implicitly meant "at some point in my life". The mention "just last week" is thus relevant according to (5).

When B locates the initial episode by mentioning "two weeks ago", she also makes a relevant move. This story is about a coincidence. It depicts two situations in which B has encountered the model. When two independently generated situations s_1 and s_2 bear some resemblance, the joint event is unexpected. It has been observed that Kolmogorov complexity is the right tool to quantify the intensity of coincidences ([11] p. 967). Coincidences can indeed be shown to be unexpected, according to definition (1). Let us first observe that generation complexity captures the idea that the coinciding situations are independent:

$$s_1 \text{ and } s_2 \text{ are } \textit{independent} \text{ if } \quad C_w(s_1 \wedge s_2) = C_w(s_1) + C_w(s_2) \tag{6}$$

We get:

$$U(s_1 \wedge s_2) \geq C_w(s_1) + C_w(s_2) - C(s_1) - C(s_2 \mid s_1) \tag{7}$$

We see from (7) that the resemblance between s_1 and s_2 is crucial for producing unexpectedness, as it makes $C(s_2 \mid s_1)$ smaller than $C(s_2)$. In particular, the temporal location of s_1 may be used to locate s_2. If Δ is the temporal distance between s_1 and s_2, then s_2 can be located from s_1 using only $\log_2(\Delta/a)$ bits. The economy in the description generates unexpectedness. The mention "two weeks ago" is thus essential.

The model's nudity is essential to the story. With a dressed model, the story would be much poorer indeed. This simple property, having been seen naked, makes the model simple to B's eyes, in two ways. The model belongs to the restricted set of the n people who were naked in B's company. Her complexity is at most $C(model|naked) \leq \log_2(n)$. But nudity makes the model simple in another way. She was that (unique) person who was seen posing in the nude in a Midwest College.

The mention "Midwest College" indeed contributes to the story's unexpectedness. B makes it explicit that figure drawing with a nude model is a truly exceptional situation in such an institution. Interest would lessen if B had been attending an art school with regular life drawing. This time, unexpectedness is due to the difficulty of generating the situation. Nude models do not belong to Midwest colleges. Generating a situation that contradicts this statement is as complex as the statement's mutability is low (see section 5.2).

The obvious mention "in clothes" contributes to the complexity contrast: the minimal scenario that allowed B to see the same person in public twice, once naked, once in clothes, cannot be simple.

The actual presence of the model in the restaurant ("But it was her") is crucial. The description complexity of the dressed person would have been significantly larger if she just looked like the nude one. The mention "we saw her" is relevant in a similar way. B reports the event as a first-hand story. The same anecdote would appear less interesting if it had happened to one of B's friend C. The complexity of C would have been subtracted from $U(s)$.

B feels the necessity of mentioning a fact which is also obvious to her interlocutor, when she specifies "in Chicago". The size of the city, measured for instance by the number N of its buildings, matters here. If the second encounter is supposed to be generated through a lottery, then generating the presence of the model in a specified place amount to $\log_2(N)$. So the relevance increases as $\log_2(N)$ (note that if there were k people in that place, then a term $-\log_2(k)$ comes from the description side, due to the indeterminacy).

We observe that by equating relevance with simplicity (complexity drop) and with unexpectedness, we are able to account for the various parameters that control interest in this story. This is a non-trivial and falsifiable result, which is in line with the importance of algorithmic complexity in cognitive computations.

5.2   The 'Rally' Discussion

Let's consider now relevance within a discussion. The discussion in figure 4 occurred between French students. F will graduate in a few months and will no longer be a student next year. When F claims he wants to participate in the rally next year,

F- This rally, wonderful! I'm ready to come back from Toulouse next year to participate.

G- Yes, but it is only for students, isn't it?

T- No, no, it's open to everyone.

F- There were people from Arcade!

G- Yes, but they were sponsors!

Fig. 4. The Rally discussion (translated from French)

G points to an inconsistency. The reminder of the discussion is about whether the contradiction is real or not.

In the discussion of figure 4, G draws attention to a logical clash between three propositions: $\neg f_1$ = 'not being a student', f_2 = 'participate in the rally' and f_3 = 'the rally is only for students' ($\neg$ refers to negation). As we will see, the effect of G's first utterance is to increase the generation complexity of f_2, and so to make the situation unexpected. This is what makes G's move relevant.

Several links exist between logic and generation complexity. Some are listed below ($\supset$ refers to implication):

$$C_w(a \vee b) = \min(C_w(a), C_w(b)) \tag{8}$$

$$C_w(a \wedge b) \leq C_w(a) + C_w(b) \tag{9}$$

$$\text{If } (a \supset b), \text{ then } C_w(a) \geq C_w(b) \tag{10}$$

In our example, the incompatibility between $\neg f_1$, f_2 and f_3 can be rewritten: $f_2 \supset (f_1 \vee \neg f_3)$. We get:

$$C_w(f_2) \geq C_w(f_1 \vee \neg f_3)$$

and thus:

$$C_w(f_2) \geq \min(C_w(f_1), C_w(\neg f_3)) \tag{11}$$

G's point is that both f_1 (F will still be a student next year) and $\neg f_3$ (the rally is open to anyone) are hard to generate, and so is f_2 (F's participation). Due to the large value of $C_w(f_2)$, f_2 appears unexpected and G's point is relevant.

Generation complexity can be linked to the notion of *mutability* [18]. Facts about the world are memorized with 'necessity' values that are due to beliefs. I believe that my bank account balance is positive and I believe that the capital city of France is Paris, but the former belief is more mutable than the latter. To measure mutability, we have to consider the least complex combination of circumstances that can change the observer's belief toward a proposition f. For my bank account to be in the red right now, I must imagine an abnormal expense that I would have forgotten, or some computer error, or that my salary has been seized by some unknown court decision. Let's call $H(f)$ the least complex scenario that can produce f. We may write:

$$C_w(f) = C_w(H(f)) \tag{12}$$

The mutability $M(f)$ of f can be defined as:

$$M(f) = - C_w(H(\neg f)) = - C_w(\neg f) \tag{13}$$

(note that mutability is always negative). When $H(\neg f)$ is complex, $\neg f$ is complex to generate and the fact f is not mutable ($M(f) \ll -1$). $M(f)$ might be retrieved from memory, or directly computed by finding out the most convincing (or least unconvincing) scenario $H(\neg f)$. It can be also inherited through (10) which can be rewritten $C_w(\neg b) \geq C_w(\neg a)$:

$$\text{If } (a \supset b), \text{ then } M(a) \geq M(b) \tag{14}$$

The conversation of figure 4 offers an example of 2-relevance. F's second utterance: "There were people from Arcade", is meant to refute f_3. Those people work in a company and are not students, and yet they were among participants. So $(\neg f_1 \wedge f_2)$ is easy to generate. Since $f_3 \supset \neg (\neg f_1 \wedge f_2)$, we get from (14) that $M(f_3) \geq -C_w((\neg f_1 \wedge f_2))$. f_3 is therefore highly mutable. Relation (11) no longer constrains $C_w(f_2)$ to be large. F's second utterance is thus 2-relevant.

More generally, any attempt to solve a problematic fact f will be 2-relevant. The solution may be a belief revision or a new and simpler scenario $H(f)$. In any case, it leads to a diminution of $C_w(f)$, which may be named 'compression', as in Gregory Chaitin's aphorism "comprehension is compression" [19] (see [11], section 7.3 for a review of ideas about compression and explanation).

6   Discussion

What precedes is an attempt to account for the phenomenon of relevance in terms of complexity. The principal departure from standard algorithmic theory is that we distinguish between generation complexity and description complexity, and that all computations are performed on specific 'machines'. This approach offers numerous advantages. For instance, it predicts that the relevance of an event occurring at distance d from the observer varies like $2 \times \log_2(d)$ [12]. It also predicts that for an object s randomly taken from a class r to be relevant, both the class and the reason f that makes s unique must be simple:

$$C(s) \leq C(r) + C(f \mid r) + C(s \mid r \wedge f)$$

If there are N objects in the class, then $C_w(s) = \log(N)$. If we assume uniqueness of s knowing r and f, $C(s \mid r \wedge f) = 0$ and:

$$U(s) \geq \log_2(N) - C(r) - C(f \mid r) \tag{15}$$

Relation (15) may be tested by its predictions of relevance in a collection of records such as the Guinness Book. It also open the way to automated news selection.

Another advantage of the algorithmic approach to relevance is that it is closer to the possibility of implementation than alternative definitions, such as [14]. As illustrated in table 1, description complexity values can be assessed through various practical means. Generation complexity values can be computed using (6), (8), (10) to combine the parameter settings of simple machines such as lotteries.

One limitation of the above definition of relevance is that it does not take emotion into account. The emotional scale $E(s)$ on which an event or discussion topic s is placed is an essential ingredient of relevance. It is not equivalent to speak about the loss of people's life or the loss of ten Euros. Relevance $I(s)$ is a function of the emotional scale and of unexpectedness:

$$I(s) = F(E(s), U(s)) \tag{16}$$

Relation (16) means that once the emotional scale is determined, emotional intensity (and thus relevance) is entirely controlled by unexpectedness. F is an increasing function of its two arguments. Determining the nature of F remains a problem and is a topic of future investigations.

We are aware of the fact that the notions developed in this paper may benefit from a formal description of the generation machine and of the observation machine. This research program is motivated by the assumption that the human brain is sensitive to algorithmic complexity [2], even at higher cognitive levels where relevance is processed. The results already obtained are encouraging. They show that algorithmic complexity is not bound to deal with theoretical computer science and prove mathematical theorems, but can also be used to model particular machines such as the human mind. We expect that other important aspects of cognitive processes will be analyzed using an algorithmic complexity approach, and that these new insights will lead to implementations.

References

1. Solomonoff, R.J.: A Formal Theory of Inductive Inference. Information and Control 7(1), 1–22 (1964), http://world.std.com/~rjs/1964pt1.pdf
2. Chater, N.: The search for simplicity: A fundamental cognitive principle? The Quaterly J. of Exp. Psychol. 52 (A), 273–302 (1999)
3. Chater, N., Vitányi, P.: Simplicity: a unifying principle in cognitive science? Trends in cogn. Sc. 7(1), 19–22 (2003)
4. Feldman, J.: How surprising is a simple pattern? Quantifying 'Eureka!'. Cognition 93, 199–224 (2004)
5. Dessalles, J.-L.: Coincidences and the encounter problem: A formal account. In: Love, B.C., McRae, K., Sloutsky, V.M. (eds.) Pr. of the 30th Annual Conf. of the Cognitive Science Society, pp. 2134–2139. Cognitive Science Society, Austin (2008), http://www.dessalles.fr/papiers/pap.conv/Dessalles_08020201.pdf
6. Kahneman, D., Tversky, A.: Subjective probability: A judgement of representativeness. Cogn. Psychol. 3, 430–454 (1972)

7. Dessalles, J.-L. (2008), La pertinence et ses origines cognitives - Nouvelles théories. Hermes-Science Publications, Paris, http://pertinence.dessalles.fr
8. Li, M., Vitányi, P.: An introduction to Kolmogorov complexity and its applications, 3rd edn. Springer, New York (1997)
9. Schmidhuber, J.: Simple Algorithmic Theory of Subjective Beauty, Novelty, Surprise, Interestingness, Attention, Curiosity, Creativity, Art, Science, Music, Jokes. Journal of SICE 48(1), 21–32 (2009), http://www.idsia.ch/~juergen/sice2009.pdf
10. Dowe, D.L.: Foreword re C. S. Wallace. The Computer Journal 51(5), 523–560 (2008)
11. Dowe, D.L.: MML, hybrid Bayesian network graphical models, statistical consistency, invariance and uniqueness. In: Bandyopadhyay, P.S., Forster, M.R. (eds.) Handbook of the Philosophy of Science. Philosophy of Statistics, vol. 7, pp. 901–982. Elsevier, Amsterdam (2011)
12. http://www.simplicitytheory.org
13. Polanyi, L.: So What's the point? Semiotica 25(3), 207–241 (1979)
14. Sperber, D., Wilson, D.: Relevance: Communication and cognition. Blackwell, ed., Oxford (1986,1995)
15. Grice, H.P.: Logic and conversation. In: Cole, P., Morgan, J.L. (eds.) Syntax and Semantics. Speech acts, vol. III, pp. 41–58. Academic Press, New York (1975)
16. Schmidhuber, J.: What's interesting? Lugano, CH: Technical Report IDSIA-35-97 (1997), ftp://ftp.idsia.ch/pub/juergen/interest.ps.gz
17. Norrick, N.R.: Conversational narrative: storytelling in everyday talk. J. Benjamins Publ. Comp., Amsterdam (2000)
18. Kahneman, D., Miller, D.T.: Norm theory: Comparing reality to its alternatives. Psychol. Rev. 93(2), 136–153 (1986)
19. Chaitin, G.J.: On the intelligibility of the universe and the notions of simplicity, complexity and irreducibility. In: Hogrebe, Bromand (eds.) Grenzen und Grenzüberschreitungen, vol. XIX, pp. 517–534. Akademie Verlag, Berlin (2004)

Categorisation as Topographic Mapping between Uncorrelated Spaces

T. Mark Ellison

IO Institute of Linguistics, Australia
mark@iolinguistics.com

Abstract. In this paper, I propose a neurophysiologically plausible account for the evolution of arbitrary, categorical mental relationships. Topographic, or structure-preserving, mappings are widespread within animal brains. If they can be shown to generate behaviours in simulation, it is plausible that they are responsible for them in vivo. One behaviour has puzzled philosophers, psychologists and linguists alike: the categorical nature of language and its arbitrary associations between categories of form and meaning. I show here that arbitrary categorical relationships can arise when a topographic mapping is developed between continuous, but uncorrelated activation spaces. This is shown first by simulation, then identified in humans with synaesthesia. The independence of form and meaning as sensory or conceptual spaces automatically results in a categorial structure being imposed on each, as our brains attempt to link the spaces with topographic maps. This result suggests a neurophysiologically plausible explanation of categorisation in language.

1 Introduction

Solomonoff's 1964 paper *A Formal Theory of Inductive Inference* [29] was a landmark in the study of learning. It brought together the philosophical problem of induction, probability theory, information theory, computability and formal language theory. It related shortness of coding length with goodness of fit, presaging the well-known induction methods of MML/MDL [35,24]. Of particular interest to cognitive science and natural language processing was his exploration of grammar induction, an analogue of which occurs in the development of every speaker of every natural language. In the current paper, I explore an aspect of language learning which complements the grammar induction task addressed by Solomonoff, asking: how do our brains construct categorial symbols out of the continous inputs they receive? Where the universal Turing machine was the abstract computational notion at the basis of Solomonoff's exploration of learning, the topographic mapping is the basis of the current paper.

Topographic mappings are relations between two spaces which preserve similarity: similar points in one space are related to similar points in the other. As the name suggests, this is an ideal property for maps of territory: nearby geographic locations should be nearby on the map, places far from each other should appear distant on the map.

D.L. Dowe (Ed.): Solomonoff Festschrift, LNAI 7070, pp. 131–141, 2013.

Topographic maps in the brain were first noticed as a result of the work of Penfield and Boldrey [20,26]. Directly stimulating the brains of locally anaesthetised epilepsy patients allowed them to explore the qualia associated with particular points on the brain. For the most part, they found that sensations attributed to nearby points on the human surface or entrails resulted from stimulating nearby parts of the brain.

Since this initial work, researchers have both found new topographic structures in the brain [28], and identified previously known structures as resulting from constructing maximally topographic connections from complex inputs [7]. Section 2 discusses these natural topographic mappings in more detail, supporting the premiss that such mappings are widespread and a plausible neurophysiological explanation for cognitive phenomena.

It is possible to define formally what constitutes a topographic map [8], and to construct them algorithmically. Section 3 considers some general definitions and implementations. The crux of the paper comes in section 3.5. When a topographic map is constructed between two spaces on the basis of uncorrelated pairs of inputs and outputs, it is found to exhibit a remarkable form. It shows sectioning of the input into contiguous chunks that map onto a single value or a small connected range of values.

This result is important, because it suggests a neurophysiological explanation for categorisation in language. Language is inherently categorical. The word *cat* consists of the same sequence of phonemes whether said by a small child with a lisp, or sung by an operatic contralto. These variations do not matter for the identity of the word, but there is a limit. Pronounced like *cute*, and the word *cat* is no longer there at all, even though the sounds are similar.

Likewise the meanings of words are categorical. The class refered to by *cat* does not blend, even in response to variations in pronunciation, into *kite* or *coat*. Why is this the case? It is logically possible to imagine a language which was directly iconic: a language of drawn pictures, or as Bickerton imagined, dolphins refering to objects by mimicking their sonar profile [3].

In section 4, I discuss linguistic and cognitive categories and argue that these can be driven by forcing topographic mappings between uncorrelated spaces, one of which consequently becomes the space of representation, and the other, the space of meaning. For example, the well-studied colour categories could arise by mappings from the sensory colour space (along with other sensory and conceptual spaces) onto a space of phonetic expressions.

In fact, we can find direct evidence for this type of categorisation in the experience of synaesthetes. Section 5 relates the categorical nature of synaesthetic associations to a likely neurophysiological explanation: a topographic mapping between cortical areas dealing with the associated qualia.

The final section 6 draws the argument together to support a neurophysiologically plausible account of the development of linguistic and other categorical cognitive processes: topographic mappings created between spaces receiving uncorrelated inputs.

2   Topographic Mappings in the Brain

Topographic mappings relate similar or nearby inputs to similar or nearby outputs. These kinds of mappings are found between the senses and the cortex, between different parts of the cortex (and other parts of the brain), and between the cortex and the motor system. They seem to be a ubiquitous part of neural processing [32].

2.1   Easy to See Mappings

In animal sensory systems, the inputs are primary sensors arranged over a sense field as retinas in the case of sight, the skin in the case of touch, the organs of Corti in the case of hearing, and so on. The outputs are areas of the cortex devoted to sythesising information from these inputs, such as the primary visual cortex. The mapping of the sense of touch onto the cortex is relatively simple.

Penfield and Boldrey [20,26] sought to express only the area of cortex assigned to particular somatosensory organs in their first homunculus. Consequently, the mapping onto the cortical slice was not shown, but it was implied. If an area of cortex could be mapped onto the hand, so that its appropriate size could be determined, this implied that points within the hand were within a single region in the cortex, and stimuli from outside the hand were processed further away. A more direct mapping between body part and cortex is seen in the homunculus of Penfield and Rasmussen [21]. The topographic nature is clearly visible, for example, a point in the arm is mapped closer to nearer points on the same appendage than to further points. (See [26] for a history of the homunculus.)

Recent fine-grained studies such as [11] have used techniques such as magnetic resonance imaging to create fine-grained maps of the motor and somatosensory cortices. These studies show that while there some overlap of cortical areas responding to the actions of individual fingers, there are orderly somatotopies.

Topographic mappings are also found repeatedly in the visual cortex. The next section deals with the relation between topographic mappings and ocular dominance stripes. Suffice it to say for the moment that the primary visual cortex maps inputs from the visual field according to their position in retina. Recently, specialised topographic mappings of visual inputs that also integrate infromation from other senses have been found [28,25,30]. In fact, some [9] assume retinotopicity to determine boundaries for optical representations in the cortex.

These kinds of mapping also occur with auditory stimuli. [15] finds topographic mappings of modulation density by frequency in the cortex.

2.2   Continuous and Discrete - Ocular Dominance Stripes

Some topographic mappings into cortical structure are easy to see. A two-dimensional sensory field is mapped into a two-dimensional cortical area, with geometry preserved. Other kinds of topographic mapping are not so transparent, as they appear to display rampant discontinuity.

Ocular dominance stripes (or *columns*) were first named such by Hubel and Wiesel [13], although they had noted the phenomenon earlier [12]. They identified columns of cells in the cortex which responded to input from one eye only. These columns were arranged into contiguous striping patterns over the visual cortex.

In work for which they were awarded the Nobel prize, they showed that these stripes were developmentally conditioned and affected by environmental stimuli. When young kittens lost stimuli from one eye, the other took over the cortical areas normally used for signals from the occluded eye. Similar effects have been shown in primates [16].

Ocular dominance stripes have been found in non-mammals such as owls [22] and (in extraordinary circumstances) frogs [14].

Despite our considerable understanding of forces that can cause or disrupt the development of ocular dominance columns, there is no consensus as to their function [1]. There is a model of their development, however, that sees them as a natural (but not necessarily inevitable) consequence of constructing a topographic mapping from two positively correlated planar sources of information onto the cortex.

Goodhill [7] introduced a model for the mapping from eye to brain which is capable of developing both the topographic structure of the mapping as well as the ocular dominance striping. The striping occurs because the inputs to the two eyes are positively correlated in binocular vision. The model predicts that increasing correlation leads to narrower stripes. More to the point, it suggests that when correlations of this kind are present we should not be surprised to find dominance striping along with it.

This prediction seems to have been born out in two results in different species. In one study of frogs [14], the authors implanted a node which developed into a third eye in the growing frog, on the same side as one of the existing eyes, creating binocular vision on that side. The two eyes developed, with some of the visual input from one eye sharing cortical projection with the other. In the shared cortex, ocular dominance stripes resulted.

The two eyes on this side had highly correlated inputs, having overlapping visual fields. The fact that striping occurred in just this case supports Goodhill's analysis of striping as a side-effect of constructing a topographic map from multiple correlated inputs.

Further evidence for this analysis comes from studies of platypus bill sensing reported by Pettigrew [22]. The platypus has electrosensors and mechanosensors intermingled in its bill, and despite these sensors having separate pathways to the brain, they map cortically with striping similar to ocular dominance striping. This is no surprise to the topographic explanation: if the animal is integrating information from two highly correlated topographic arrays (two eyes looking in the same direction or electro- and mechano-sensors spread out on the same surface), then dominance striping is a likely way to bring relevant information together in the brain.

So ocular dominance stripes despite, or even because of, their discontinuities can be regarded as optimal topographic mappings from one space, made up of two disjointed but correlated parts, to contiguous space. As we shall see in section 3.5, this is not the only way to get chunking and discontinuities from topographic mappings.

In summary then, topographic mappings arise frequently in the brain; the more we look for them, the more we find them. They integrate knowledge from different receptive fields, and even different sense types. Furthermore, they can give rise to complex discontinuous structures.

3   The Topographic Extrapolation

This section presents a measure of topographicity, and extends it to finding the most topographic extensions of given data, in a manner similar to that described by Ellison [6].

3.1   Measuring Topographicity

Goodhill and Sejnowski [8] offered the general evaluation measure for the topographicity of functions shown in (1) (symbols have been changed to avoid confusion).

$$C(f) = \sum_{i \in I} \sum_{j \in I} s_I(i,j) s_O(f(i), f(j)) \tag{1}$$

Here s_I and s_O are similarity measures on the input and output spaces respectively. $C(f)$ is the measure of how topographic the space is, with larger values for more topographic mappings. Both the s_I and s_O are assumed to be everywhere non-zero. Consequently $C(f)$ (if finite) is maximised for f which match small values of s_I with small values of s_O and large with large. See Goodhill and Sejnowski's discussion for more details.

The definition can be extended to apply to any finite collection D of input-output data points (2).

$$C(D) = \sum_{(i,o) \in D} \sum_{(j,p) \in D} s_I(i,j) s_O(o,p) \tag{2}$$

3.2   Extrapolation

Solomonoff [29], following Carnap [5], couched learning problems as sequence extrapolation coding problems. He started by defining a cost for a sequence as the length of the shortest program for a given universal Turing machine which would generate that sequence. From this was constructed an answer to the extrapolation problem: the best extrapolation of a sequence is the one which gives the smallest increment in the cost function.

The same approach can determine the most topographic extrapolation from a given set of input-output pairs D. Since s_I and s_O are similarity measures, rather than cost functions or distances, larger $C(D)$ is better. Consequently, we seek to maximise the change in $C(D)$ resulting from the addition of the new pair (x, y), as expressed in (3).

$$C(D \cup \{(x,y)\}) - C(D) = 2 * \sum_{(i,o) \in D} s_I(i,x)s_O(o,y) + s_I(x,x)s_O(y,y) \quad (3)$$

We assume that the self-similarity of each point in the input space and the output space are constant: $s_I(x, x)$ does not depend on x, nor $s_O(y, y)$ on y. This means that the whole equation is maximised when the summation is maximised, allowing us the concise form shown in (4) for the best extrapolation.

In what follows, we will write $S(x, y|D)$ for the term $\sum_{(i,o) \in D} s_I(i, x)s_O(o, y)$.

$$E(D) = (x, y)|x \in I, y \in O \text{ that minimise } S(x, y|D) \quad (4)$$

The extrapolation can be limited to selecting the best output for a given input x. If this is done for all values of $x \in I$, we exrapolate a most topographic function fitting the data (5).

$$F(D) = \{(x, y)|x \in I, y \in O \text{ where } y \text{ uniquely minimises } S(x, y|D)\} \quad (5)$$

Frequently, $F(D)$ is only a partial function. If there are multiple maxima for $S(x, y)$ for some x, then no y uniquely minimises this function. For these values of x, the function remains undefined.

3.3   A Normal Similarity Measure

In the simulations which follow, I use a probability-based similarity measure. This measure parallels the notion of confusion probabilities as discussed by the author in an earlier paper on induction [6]. It is defined, for an arbitrary space in equation (6). One parameter to the measure is scale constant σ assumed constant over the whole space.

$$s(x, y) = N(x - y; \sigma) \quad (6)$$

The measure has not been normalised over either x or y to retain its commutativity, so will not act here as a probability distribution. It can be proven that given this similarity measure, for any finite data set D, the extrapolated function $F(D)$ is continuous wherever it is defined.

3.4   Extrapolation from Highly Topographic Functions

At this point, it is worth looking at the extrapolation from data which is highly topographic. For simplicity, take the one-dimensional unit interval $[0, 1]$ as both input and output space.

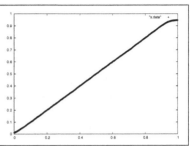

A program, dubbed OPTOPO, was developed in PYTHON to extrapolate pointwise the most topographic function matching a given input data set, based on the optimisation derived in section 3.2.

Data was generated by mapping each of 20 points equally spaced along the unit interval to itself. These were then used to extrapolate values covering the same interval at 0.001 spacing. A graph of the resulting extrapolations appears in figure 1. The similarity measures are normal density functions

Fig. 1. Topographic extrapolation from 20 points of $io = i$ on the unit interval to the 1000 points

as described in section 3.3, with scale constants σ set for input and output spaces to 0.04.

In general, we can expect strongly topographic data, in the sense of equation (2), to give rise to extrapolations matching those functions.

3.5   Independently Varying Spaces

In the last example, a thousand points were extrapolated from 20 belonging to the already topographic identity function. This function was recovered, apart from small curvature at the extremes ends of the interval. Now we explore the other extreme: what happens when the training data is random and uncorrelated?

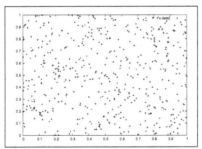

Training data was generated, consisting of 500 points with random input and output values drawn from a flat distribution over the unit interval. A scatter plot of this data is shown in figure 2.

Applied to this training data, OPTOPO returned the function shown in figure 3 as the most topographic that could be deduced from the data. The most remarkable feature of this graph is that it shows a largely smooth, continuous function with only a handful of discontinuities.

Fig. 2. Input data to the topographic mapping between uncorrelated spaces: 500 points in $[0, 1] \times [0, 1]$

Between the discontinuities, we have continuous maps from input to output. Although the mapping output is usually fairly level, there is sometimes variation. In these cases the variation is smooth. An input point between two close neighbours maps onto an output point between the projections of those neighbours.

The explanation of this combination of smooth mapping plus discontinuity lies in the fact that we are looking for the most topographic output value o for each input i. The smooth similarity measures turn the scattered host of input data points into a continuously contoured scalar field over the input-output plane. Constructing the most topographic extrapolation function is a process of maximising the evaluation for each input value. The scalar field over the plane has ridges of higher values, and these are what we see defining the contiguous categories in the input. Transitions from one ridge to another happen when a falling ridge of values is overtaken by a rising ridge, as the focus moves along input values.

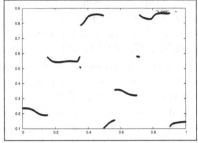

Fig. 3. The most topographic (i.e. the most probable) function accounting for the uncorrelated input data

This transitional discontinuity is of the kind made famous in the *Catastrophe Theory* of Rene Thom [33].

Functions with this kind of discontinuity define a categorisation of the input. Inputs within a connected region belong to one category. Inputs from regions separated by discontinuities come from different categories. Topographic mappings offer an easy route from continous spaces to categorisation, and this suggests elegant new explanations for the origin and nature of language.

4   Explaining the Categorical Nature of Language

Language is both symbolic and categorical. It is symbolic because there is no intrinsic, or to use Peirce's [19] terms, no indexical and no iconic, relation between the space of meanings, and the space of linguistic representations. No in-

Fig. 4. Iconic representation of fire

dexical relationship means that there is no physical association of our units of meanings with what they represent: our word *fire* does not share the same relationship with actual fire that actual smoke does. No iconic relationship means that there is no structure-preserving mapping which relates the word *fire* to what it represents. In contrast, the sign for fire shown in figure 4, is an iconic representation: while this image has no physical connection to fire, the qualia of looking at the image share structural similarities to a view of a fire. But not being iconic or indexical does not account for the categorical nature of natural language symbols.

So language is a connection between uncorrelated spaces of meaning and representation. Could language be a topographic mapping between these spaces? If so, it would explain the categorical nature of both meanings (eg. colour classes, genders, emotions, etc.) and forms in language (eg. the phonological forms of words). If this were the case, we would expect two features of language: arbitrary categorisation, with categories varying from language to language, and a globally non-topographic function from form to meaning.

Language categories are arbitrary, and they certainly vary from language to language, although there may be functional pressures which limit variation.

Variation in the number and phonetic realisation of phonemes is one example. Language-specificity is more hotly debated, however, with regard to semantic categories. Nevertheless researchers report tracking shifts in categorisation as children adapt to the language they are acquiring [4,17,18].

Vocabulary also shows no strong large scale topographic relation between meaning and form. Shillcock et al [27] and Tamariz [31] looked for large-scale systematicity in the meanings of monomorphemic words in English and Spanish respectively. Effects were found, but primarily for localised domains such as pause fillers, and for limited phonetic features.

So the evidence agrees with a model in which word forms are related to their meanings by a topographic mapping linking uncorrelated spaces.

5   Synaesthesia

Synaesthesia is the leakage of qualia from one sensory input to another. For example, someone might see – in their mind's eye – the colour *red* when they hear the word *hurry*, or smell olives when seeing square objects. For an overview of synaesthesia, see [10].

De Thornley Head [34] finds that pitch-colour synaesthetes have reliable mappings from pitches onto colours (unlike non-synaesthetes), and takes this as evidence that synaesthesia is a perceptual phenomenon apart from memory, metaphor or imagery. He interprets the mapping itself in the following way. Pitches and colours are broken into regions by some unclear mechanism. These regions are then associated in an arbitrary fashion. There can be smooth topographic mappings within the regions so associated, but no such connections hold when region boundaries are crossed.

These findings agree with a model in which synaesthesia is the result of additional connectivity, a topographic map, linking an auditory representation with a representation of colour. That synaesthesia results from structural brain differences is supported experimentally [2,23]. For the most part, auditory and colour stimulus arrive from the senses uncorrelated. Consequently, the topographic map developed has the form of figure 3: discontinuous regions of input mapped smoothly onto arbitrary and disconnected regions of output.

6   Conclusion

The purpose of this paper was to propose a neurophysiologically plausible explanation for the formation of arbitrary categorisations. The core of this explanation is that, as seen in section 2, topographic mappings are commonplace in the brain, turning up even when their nature is less than obvious, as in the case of ocular dominance striping. To make the explanation concrete, a formal description of topographic mappings was presented in section 3. This section finished with the core result of this paper: the most topographic linkage between two uncorrelated spaces can be a categorical mapping with, at most, in-category smooth mapping. Section 4 and section 5 explored some of the phenomena which might be explained using this result. Monomorphemic vocabulary shows little large-scale correlation of similarity of phonetic form and similarity of meaning, instead linking somewhat arbitrary categories of meaning to arbitrary (though systematic) categories of form. Similarly, pitch-colour synaesthetics show only local smoothness in their mapping of one modality to the other; the mapping consists of connections between somewhat arbitrary chunks of the pitch and colour spaces. Topographic mappings between uncorrelated spaces explain both these phenomena.

References

1. Adams, D.L., Horton, J.C.: Ocular dominance columns: Enigmas and challenges. The Neuroscientist 15(1), 62–77 (2009)
2. Bargary, G., Mitchell, K.J.: Synaesthesia and cortical connectivity. Trends in Neurosciences 31(7), 335–342 (2008)
3. Bickerton, D.: King of the sea, 1st edn. Random House (1979)
4. Borovsky, A., Elman, J.: Language input and semantic categories: A relation between cognition and early word learning. Journal of Child Language 33(04), 759–790 (2006)
5. Carnap, R.: Logical Foundations of Probability. University of Chicago Press, Chicago (1950)
6. Ellison, T.M.: Induction and inherent similarity. In: Similarity and Categorization, pp. 29–50. Oxford University Press (2001)
7. Goodhill, G.J.: Topography and ocular dominance: a model exploring positive correlations. Biological Cybernetics 69(2), 109–118 (1993); PMID: 8373882
8. Goodhill, G.J., Sejnowski, T.J.: A unifying objective function for topographic mappings. Neural Computation 9(6), 1291–1303 (1997)
9. Greenlee, M.W.: Human cortical areas underlying the perception of optic flow: brain imaging studies. International Review of Neurobiology 44, 269–292 (2000)
10. Harrison, J.E., Baron-Cohen, S.: Synaesthesia: Classic and Contemporary Readings. Wiley-Blackwell (January 1997)
11. Hlutk, P., Solodkin, A., Gullapalli, R.P., Noll, D.C., Small, S.L.: Somatotopy in human primary motor and somatosensory hand representations revisited. Cerebral Cortex 11(4), 312–321 (2001)
12. Hubel, D.H., Wiesel, T.N.: Receptive fields, binocular interaction and functional architecture in the cat's visual cortex. The Journal of Physiology 160(1), 106–154 (1962) PMID: 14449617 PMCID: 1359523
13. Hubel, D.H., Wiesel, T.N.: Receptive fields and functional architecture of monkey striate cortex. The Journal of Physiology 195(1), 215–243 (1968)
14. Ide, C., Fraser, S., Meyer, R.: Eye dominance columns from an isogenic double-nasal frog eye. Science 221(4607), 293–295 (1983)
15. Langers, D.R.M., Backes, W.H., van Dijk, P.: Spectrotemporal features of the auditory cortex: the activation in response to dynamic ripples. NeuroImage 20(1), 265–275 (2003) PMID: 14527587
16. Le Vay, S., Wiesel, T.N., Hubel, D.H.: The development of ocular dominance columns in normal and visually deprived monkeys. The Journal of Comparative Neurology 191(1), 1–51 (1980)
17. Majid, A., Boster, J.S., Bowerman, M.: The cross-linguistic categorization of everyday events: A study of cutting and breaking. Cognition 109(2), 235–250 (2008)

18. Majid, A., Gullberg, M., van Staden, M., Bowerman, M.: How similar are semantic categories in closely related languages? a comparison of cutting and breaking in four germanic languages. Cognitive Linguistics 18(2), 179–194 (2007)

19. Peirce, C.S., Hartshorne, C., Weiss, P., Burks, A.W.: Collected Papers of Charles Sanders Peirce. Harvard University Press (1931, 1958), http://books.google.com/books?id=G7IzSoUFx1YC

20. Penfield, W., Boldrey, E.: Somatic motor and sensory representation in the cerebral cortex of man as studied by electrical stimulation. Brain 60(4), 389–443 (1937)

21. Penfield, W., Rasmussen, T.: The Cerebral Cortex of Man. Macmillian (1950)

22. Pettigrew, J.D.: Bi-sensory, striped representations: comparative insights from owl and platypus. Journal of Physiology-Paris 98(1-3), 113–124 (2004)

23. Ramachandran, V., Hubbard, E.: Synaesthesia – a window into perception, thought and language. Journal of Consciousness Studies 8(12), 3–34 (2001)

24. Rissanen, J.: Modeling by shortest data description. Automatica 14, 465–471 (1978)

25. Schluppeck, D., Glimcher, P., Heeger, D.J.: Topographic organization for delayed saccades in human posterior parietal cortex. Journal of Neurophysiology 94(2), 1372–1384 (2005) PMID: 15817644

26. Schott, G.D.: Penfield's homunculus: a note on cerebral cartography. Journal of Neurology, Neurosurgery, and Psychiatry 56(4), 329–333 (1993) PMID: 8482950 PMCID: 1014945

27. Shillcock, R., Kirby, S., McDonald, S., Brew, C.: Filled pauses and their status in the mental lexicon (2001)

28. Silver, M.A., Kastner, S.: Topographic maps in human frontal and parietal cortex. Trends in Cognitive Sciences 13(11), 488–495 (2009)

29. Solomonoff, R.J.: A formal theory of inductive inference. Information and Control, 1–22, 224–254 (1964)

30. Swisher, J.D., Halko, M.A., Merabet, L.B., McMains, S.A., Somers, D.C.: Visual topography of human intraparietal sulcus. The Journal of Neuroscience 27(20), 5326–5337 (2007)

31. Tamariz, M.: Exploring systematicity between phonological and context-cooccurrence representations of the mental lexicon. The Mental Lexicon 3, 259–278 (2008)

32. Thivierge, J., Marcus, G.F.: The topographic brain: from neural connectivity to cognition. Trends in Neurosciences 30(6), 251–259 (2007)

33. Thom, R.: Structural stability and morphogenesis. Addison Wesley Publishing Company (1989)

34. de Thornley Head, P.: Synaesthesia: Pitch-Colour isomorphism in RGB-Space? Cortex 42(2), 164–174 (2006)

35. Wallace, C.S., Boulton, D.M.: An information measure for classification. Computer Journal 11(2), 195–209 (1968)

Algorithmic Information Theory
and Computational Complexity

Rūsiņš Freivalds*

Institute of Mathematics and Computer Science, University of Latvia, Raiņa bulvāris
29, Riga, LV-1459, Latvia

Abstract. We present examples where theorems on complexity of computation are proved using methods in algorithmic information theory. The first example is a non-effective construction of a language for which the size of any deterministic finite automaton exceeds the size of a probabilistic finite automaton with a bounded error exponentially. The second example refers to frequency computation. Frequency computation was introduced by Rose and McNaughton in early sixties and developed by Trakhtenbrot, Kinber, Degtev, Wechsung, Hinrichs and others. A transducer is a finite-state automaton with an input and an output. We consider the possibilities of probabilistic and frequency transducers and prove several theorems establishing an infinite hierarchy of relations. We consider only relations where for each input value there is exactly one allowed output value. Relations computable by weak finite-state transducers with frequency $\frac{km}{kn}$ but not with frequency $\frac{m}{n}$ are presented in a non-constructive way using methods of algorithmic information theory.

1 Introduction

Physicists are well aware that physical indeterminism is a complicated phenomenon and probabilistical models are merely reasonably good approximations of reality. The problem "What is randomness?" has always been interesting not only for philosophers and physicists but also for computer scientists. The term "nondeterministic algorithm" has been deliberately coined to differ from "indeterminism" [24].

Probabilistic (randomized) algorithms form one of central notions in Theory of Computation [23,9,6,7]. However, since long ago computer scientists have attempted to develop notions and technical implementations of these notions that would be similar to but not equal to randomization.

The notion of frequency computation was introduced by G. Rose [25] as an attempt to have an absolutely deterministic mechanism with properties similar to probabilistic algorithms. The definition was as follows. A function $f: w \to w$

---

* The research was supported by Agreement with the European Regional Development Fund (ERDF) 2010/0206/2DP/2.1.1.2.0/10/APIA/VIAA/011 and by Project 271/2012 from the Latvian Council of Science.

D.L. Dowe (Ed.): Solomonoff Festschrift, LNAI 7070, pp. 142–154, 2013.

is (m,n)-computable, where $1 \le m \le n$, iff there exists a recursive function R: $w^n \to w^n$ such that, for all n-tuples $(x_1, \cdots, x_n)$ of distinct natural numbers,

$$card\{i : (R(x_1, \cdots, x_n))_i = f(x_i)\} \ge m.$$

Frequency computations became increasingly popular when relation between frequency computation and computation with a small number of queries was discovered [3,4,20]. Many papers have been written to distinguish properties of frequency algorithms from the properties of probabilistic algorithms [27,28,18,19,1,6,8,9,17].

We consider problems similar to those in the classical papers [27,18,2,12] for finite-state transducers. We found that the situation is very much different. We do not attempt to present a full theory of frequency finite-state transducers. Quite the opposite. We prove only one technical theorem which is not yet published anywhere but this theorem has an important feature. Theorem 5 proves the existence of certain relations and their complexity but these relations are not shown explicitly. Their existence is proved using methods of algorithmic information theory originated by R. Solomonoff [26].

2   Tools from Algorithmic Information Theory

Definition 1. *We say that the numbering* $\Psi = \{\Psi_0(x), \Psi_1(x), \Psi_2(x), \ldots\}$ *of 1-argument partial recursive functions is* **computable** *if the 2-argument function* $U(n,x) = \Psi_n(x)$ *is partial recursive.*

Definition 2. *We say that a numbering* Ψ *is reducible to the numbering* η *if there exists a total recursive function* $f(n)$ *such that, for all* n *and* x, $\Psi_n(x) = \eta_{f(n)}(x)$.

Definition 3. *We say that a computable numbering* φ *of all 1-argument partial recursive functions is a* **Gödel numbering** *if every computable numbering (of any class of 1-argument partial recursive functions) is reducible to* φ.

Definition 4. *We say that a Gödel numbering* ϑ *is a* **Kolmogorov numbering** *if for arbitrary computable numbering* Ψ *(of any class of 1-argument partial recursive functions) there exist constants* $c > 0, d > 0$, *and a total recursive function* $f(n)$ *such that:*

1. for all n *and* x, $\Psi_n(x) = \vartheta_{f(n)}(x)$,
2. for all n, $f(n) \le c \cdot n + d$.

Kolmogorov Theorem. [21] There exists a Kolmogorov numbering.

3   Mirage Codes Using Algorithmic Information Theory

Linear codes form the simplest class of codes. The alphabet used is a fixed choice of a finite field $GF(q) = F_q$ with q elements. For most of this paper we consider a special case of $GF(2) = F_2$. These codes are binary codes.

A generating matrix G for a linear $[n, k]$ code over F_q is a k-by-n matrix with entries in the finite field F_q, whose rows are linearly independent. The linear code corresponding to the matrix G consists of all the q^k possible linear combinations of rows of G. The requirement of linear independence is equivalent to saying that all the q^k linear combinations are distinct. The linear combinations of the rows in G are called codewords. However we are interested in something more. We need to have the codewords not merely distinct but also as far as possible in terms of Hamming distance. Hamming distance between two vectors $v = (v_1, \ldots, v_n)$ and $w = (w_1, \ldots, w_n)$ in F_{q^k} is the number of indices i such that $v_i \neq w_i$.

The textbook [13] contains

Theorem A. For any integer $n \geq 4$ there is a $[2n, n]$ binary code with a minimum distance between the codewords at least $n/10$.

However the proof of the theorem in [13] has a serious defect. It is non-constructive. It means that we cannot find these codes or describe them in a useful manner. This is why P.Garret calls them mirage codes. Algorithmic information theory was used in the paper [11] to describe this non-constructivity in terms of algorithms and Kolmogorov complexity. A useful additional property was also obtained which made these codes to be "nearly cyclic".

We would wish to prove a reasonable counterpart of Theorem A for cyclic mirage codes, but this attempt fails. Instead we consider binary generating matrices of a bit different kind. Let p be an odd prime number, and x be a binary word of length p. The generating matrix $G(p, x)$ has p rows and $2p$ columns. Let $x = x_1 x_2 x_3 \ldots x_p$. (In the crucial application of these matrices the word $x = x_1 x_2 x_3 \ldots x_p$ will be of maximal Kolmogorov complexity, i.e. there will be no possibility to compress this word in such a way that the word can be restored uniquely.) The first p columns (and all p rows) make a unit matrix with elements 1 on the main diagonal and 0 in all the other positions. The last p columns (and all p rows) make a cyclic matrix with $x = x_1 x_2 x_3 \ldots x_p$ as the first row, $x = x_p x_1 x_2 x_3 \ldots x_{p-1}$ as the second row, and so on.

Lemma 1. *For arbitrary* x, *if the word* $h_1 h_2 h_3 \ldots h_p h_{p+1} h_{p+2} h_{p+3} \ldots h_{2p}$ *is a codeword in the linear code corresponding to* $G(p, x)$, *then the word* $h_p h_1 h_2 \ldots h_{p-1} h_{2p} h_{p+1} h_{p+2} \ldots h_{2p-1}$ *is also a codeword.*

Above we introduced a special type generating matrices $G(p, x)$ where p is an odd prime and x is a binary word of length p. Now we introduce two technical auxiliary functions. If z is a binary word of length $2p$, then $d(z)$ is the subword of z containing the first p symbols, and $e(z)$ is subword of z containing the last p symbols. Then $z = d(z)e(z)$.

There exist many distinct Kolmogorov numberings. We now fix one of them and denote it by η. Since Kolmogorov numberings give indices for all partial recursive functions, for arbitrary x and p, there is an i such that $\eta_i(p) = x$. Let $i(x, p)$ be the minimal i such that $\eta_i(p) = x$. It is easy to see that if $x_1 \neq x_2$, then $i(x_1, p) \neq i(x_2, p)$. We consider all binary words x of length p and denote by $x(p)$ the word x such $i(x, p)$ exceed $i(y, p)$ for all binary words y of length p different from x. It is obvious that $i \geq 2^p - 1$.

We introduce a partial recursive function $\mu(z, \epsilon, p)$ defined as follows. To define $\mu(z, \epsilon, p)$ we consider all 2^p binary words x of the length p. If z is not a binary word of length $2p$, then $\mu(z, \epsilon, p)$ is not defined. If ϵ is not in $\{0, 1\}$, then $\mu(z, \epsilon, p)$ is not defined. If z is a binary word of length $2p$ and $\epsilon \in \{0, 1\}$, then we consider all $x \in \{0, 1\}^p$ such that the first p symbols of the codeword generated by $G(p, x)$ equal the last p symbols of the same codeword.

If there are no such x, then $\mu(z, \epsilon, p)$ is not defined. If there is only one such x, then $\mu(z, \epsilon, p) = x$. If there are two such x, then

$$\mu(z, \epsilon, p) = \begin{cases} \text{the first such } x \text{ in the lexicographical order, for } \epsilon = 1 \\ \text{the second such } x \text{ in the lexicographical order, for } \epsilon = 0 \end{cases}$$

If there are more than two such x, then $\mu(z, \epsilon, p)$ is not defined.

Now we introduce a computable numbering of some partial recursive functions. This numbering is independent of p.

For each p (independently from other values of p) we order the set of all the 2^{2p} binary words z of length $2p$: $z_0, z_1, z_2, \ldots, z_{2^{2p}-1}$. We define z_0 as the word $000\ldots0$. We strictly follow a rule "if the word z_i contains less symbols 1 than the word z_j, then $i < j$". Words with equal number of the symbol 1 are ordered lexicographically. Hence $z_{2^{2p}-1} = 111\ldots1$.

For each p, we define

$$\Psi_0(p) = \mu(z_0, 0, p)$$
$$\Psi_1(p) = \mu(z_0, 1, p)$$
$$\Psi_2(p) = \mu(z_1, 0, p)$$
$$\Psi_3(p) = \mu(z_1, 1, p)$$
$$\Psi_4(p) = \mu(z_2, 0, p)$$
$$\Psi_5(p) = \mu(z_2, 1, p)$$
$$\ldots$$
$$\Psi_{2^{2p+1}-2}(p) = \mu(z_{2^{2p}-1}, 0, p)$$
$$\Psi_{2^{2p+1}-1}(p) = \mu(z_{2^{2p}-1}, 1, p)$$

For $j \geq 2^{2p+1}$, $\Psi_j(p)$ is undefined.

We have fixed a Kolmogorov numbering η and we have just constructed a computable numbering Ψ of some partial recursive functions.

Lemma 2. *There exist constants $c > 0$ and $d > 0$ (independent of p) such that for arbitrary i there is a j such that*

1. $\Psi_i(t) = \eta_j(t)$ for all t, and
2. $j \leq ci + d$.

Proof. Immediately from Kolmogorov Theorem.

Until now we considered generating matrices $G(p, x)$ for independently chosen p and x. From now on we consider only special primes p and special words x. Namely, we consider only odd primes p such that 2 is a primitive root modulo p, and we consider only words x of length p such that $i(x, p)$ exceed $i(y, p)$ for all binary words y of length p different from x. It is obvious that $i \geq 2^p - 1$. We denote such an x by $x(p)$.

We wish to prove that the matrices $G(p, x(p))$ have an important property: if p is sufficiently large, then Hamming distances between arbitrary two codewords in this linear code is at least $\frac{4p}{19}$.

We consider generating matrices $G(p, x(p))$ for linear codes where p is an odd prime such that 2 is a primitive root modulo p, and, as defined above, $x(p)$ is a binary word of length p such that $\eta_i(p) = x(p)$ implies $i \geq 2^p - 1$. We denote the corresponding linear code by $LC_2(p)$.

Several technical lemmas are proved in [10,11]. They imply that, if p is sufficiently large and the Hamming distance between arbitrary two codewords is less than $\frac{4p}{19}$ then the word x used in the definition of the generating matrix of the linear code can be compressed. Since we choose x to be incompressible (i.e. having maximum Kolmogorov complexity) there is a contradiction. Hence for such linear codes Hamming distances between arbitrary two codewords are no less than $\frac{4p}{19}$.

4   Probabilistic Automata

We say that a language L is recognized with bounded error with an interval (p_1, p_2) if $p_1 < p_2$ where $p_1 = sup\{prob_x | x \notin L\}$ and $p_2 = inf\{prob_x | x \in L\}$.

We say that a language L is recognized with a probability $p > \frac{1}{2}$ if the language is recognized with interval $(1 - p, p)$.

In the preceding section we constructed a binary generating matrix $G(p, p(x))$ for a linear code. Now we use this matrix to construct a probabilistic reversible automaton $R(p)$.

The matrix $G(p, x(p))$ has $2p$ columns and p rows. The automaton $R(p)$ has $4p + 1$ states, $2p$ of them being accepting and $2p + 1$ being rejecting. The input alphabet consists of 2 letters.

The (rejecting) state q_0 is special in the sense that the probability to enter this state and the probability to exit from this state during the computation equals 0. This state always has the probability $\frac{17}{36}$. The states $q_1, q_2, \ldots, q_{4p}$ are related to the columns of $G(p, x(p))$ and should be considered as $2p$ pairs $(q_1, q_2), (q_3, q_4), \ldots, \ldots (q_{4p-1}, q_{4p})$ corresponding to the $2p$ columns of $G(p, x(p))$. The states $q_1, q_3, q_5, q_7, \ldots, q_{4p-1}$ are accepting and the states $q_2, q_4, q_6, q_8, \ldots, q_{4p}$ are rejecting. The initial probability distribution is as follows:

$$\begin{cases} \frac{17}{36}, \text{ for } q_0, \\ \frac{19}{72p}, \text{ for each of } q_1, q_3, \ldots, q_{4p-1}, \\ 0, \text{ for each of } q_2, q_4, \ldots, q_{4p}. \end{cases}$$

The processing of the input symbols a, b is deterministic. Under the input symbol a the states are permuted as follows:

$$
\begin{array}{llll}
q_1 \to q_3 & q_2 \to q_4 & q_{2p+1} \to q_{2p+3} & q_{2p+2} \to q_{2p+4} \\
q_3 \to q_5 & q_4 \to q_6 & q_{2p+3} \to q_{2p+5} & q_{2p+4} \to q_{2p+6} \\
q_5 \to q_7 & q_6 \to q_8 & q_{2p+5} \to q_{2p+7} & q_{2p+6} \to q_{2p+8} \\
\cdots & \cdots & \cdots & \cdots \\
\\
q_{2p-3} \to q_{2p-1} & q_{2p-2} \to q_{2p} & q_{4p-3} \to q_{4p-1} & q_{4p-2} \to q_{4p} \\
q_{2p-1} \to q_1 & q_{2p} \to q_2 & q_{4p-1} \to q_{2p+1} & q_{4p} \to q_{2p+2}
\end{array}
$$

The permutation of the states under the input symbol b depends on $G(p, x(p))$. Let the entries of $G(p, x(p))$ be given by

$$
G(p, x(p)) = \begin{pmatrix}
g_{11} & g_{12} & \cdots & g_{1\,2p} \\
g_{21} & g_{22} & \cdots & g_{2\,2p} \\
\cdots & \cdots & \cdots & \cdots \\
g_{p1} & g_{p2} & \cdots & g_{p\,2p}
\end{pmatrix}.
$$

For arbitrary $i \in \{1, 2, \ldots, p\}$,

$$
\begin{cases}
q_{2i-1} \to q_{2i-1} & \text{, if } g_{1i} = 0 \\
q_{2i} \to q_{2i} & \text{, if } g_{1i} = 0 \\
q_{2i-1} \to q_{2i} & \text{, if } g_{1i} = 1 \\
q_{2i} \to q_{2i-1} & \text{, if } g_{1i} = 1.
\end{cases}
$$

Theorem 1. *If 2 is a primitive root for infinitely many distinct primes then there exists an infinite sequence of regular languages $L_1, L_2, L_3, \ldots$ in a 2-letter alphabet and a sequence of positive integers $p(1), p(2), p(3), \ldots$ such that for arbitrary j:*

1. *any deterministic finite automaton recognizing L_j has at least $2^{p(j)}$ states,*
2. *there is a probabilistic reversible automaton with $(4p(j)+1)$ states recognizing L_j with the probability $\frac{19}{36}$.*

Corollary 1. *Assume Generalized Riemann Hypothesis. Then conclusions of Theorem 1 hold.*

5 Definitions of Transducers

A finite state transducer is a finite state machine with two tapes: an input tape and an output tape. These tapes are one-way, i.e. the automaton never returns to the symbols once read or written. Transducers compute relations between the input words and output words. A deterministic transducer produces exactly one output word for every input word processed.

In this paper we consider strengths and weaknesses of deterministic and frequency transducers. Of course, if a relation is such that several output words are possible for the same input word, then the relation cannot be computed by a deterministic transducer. Hence for such relations there is no way to expect a similar determinization theorem. Hence we restrict ourselves to consider in this paper only relations producing exactly one output word for every input word processed.

Definition 5. *We say that a relation $R(x, y)$ is* left-total, *if for arbitrary x there is exactly one y satisfying $R(x, y)$.*

We use standard definitions of deterministic, nondeterministic and probabilistic transducers, which are well-established in theoretical computer science literature [14].

We consider all our transducers as machines working infinitely long. At every moment, let x be the word having been read from the input tape up to this moment, and let y be the word written on the output tape up to this moment. Then we say that the pair (x, y) belongs to the relation computed by the transducer.

Definition 6. *A frequency transducer with parameters (m, n) is a transducer with n input tapes and n output tapes. Every state of the transducer is defined as $(a_1, a_2, \cdots, a_n)$-accepting where each $a_i \in \{$ accepting , nonaccepting $\}$. We say that a left-total relation R is (m, n)-computed by the transducer if for arbitrary n-tuple of pairwise distinct input words $(x_1, x_2, \cdots, x_n)$ there exist at least m distinct values of x_i such that the i-th output y_i satisfies $(x_i, y_i) \in R$.*

We consider frequency transducers like all other transducers as machines working infinitely long. At every moment, let x be the word having been read from the input tape up to this moment, and let y be the word written (and accepted) on the output tape up to this moment. Then we say that the pair (x, y) belongs to the relation computed by the transducer. However, in the case when the input words are too short, there is a problem how to define (m, n)-computation correctly. We have concentrated on so-called weak frequency computation when the transducer forces the input words to be of different length.

Definition 7. *We say that a frequency transducer is performing a* weak (m, n)-*computation with parameters $(b_1, b_2, \cdots b_n)$, where $b_1, b_2, \cdots b_n$ are distinct integers, if the transducer is constructed in such a way that in the beginning of the work the transducer reads the first b_1 symbols from the input word x_1, the first b_2 symbols from the input word x_2, $\cdots$, the first b_n symbols from the input word x_n and at all subsequent moments reads exactly 1 new symbol from every input tape. This ensures that at all moments the input words $(x_1, x_2, \cdots, x_n)$ are distinct. There is no requirement of the correctness of the results when the length of input words is $(b_1, b_2, \cdots b_n)$ but at all moments afterwards there exist at least m distinct values of x_i such that the i-th output y_i satisfies $(x_i, y_i) \in R$.*

6   Frequency Transducers

First of all, it should be noted that a frequency transducer does not specify uniquely the relation computed by it. For instance, a transducer with 3 input tapes and 3 output tapes $(2, 3)$-computing the relation

$$R(x, y) = \begin{cases} \text{true, if } x = y \text{ and } x \neq 258714, \\ \text{true, if } y = 0 \text{ and } x = 258714, \\ \text{false, if} \qquad \qquad \text{otherwise.} \end{cases}$$

can output $y = x$ for all possible inputs and, nonetheless, the result is always correct for at least 2 out of 3 inputs since the inputs always distinct. Please notice that the program of the frequency transducer does not contain the "magical" number 258714. Hence the number of states for an equivalent deterministic transducer can be enormously larger.

Theorem 2. *There exists a left-total relation R $(2, 3)$-computed by a weak finite-state frequency transducer and not computed by any deterministic finite-state transducer.*

Proof. We consider the relation

$$R(x, y) = \begin{cases} \text{true, if } y = 1^{|x|} & \text{and } |x| \equiv 0 (mod3), \\ \text{true, if } y = 1^{|x|} & \text{and } |x| \equiv 1 (mod3) \\ \text{true, if } y = 1^{|x|-1} & \text{and } |x| \equiv 2 (mod3) \\ \text{false, if} & \text{otherwise.} \end{cases}$$

The weak finite-state frequency $(2, 3)$-transducer starts with reading 1 symbol from the first input tape, 2 symbols from the second input tape and 3 symbols from the third input tape and reads exactly 1 symbol from each input tape at any subsequent moment. Hence at any moment the transducer has no more than one input word x_i with $|x_i| \equiv 2 (mod3)$. To have a correct result for the other two input words, it suffices to keep the length of the output being equal the length of the corresponding input. In case if the length of the input is $|x_i| \equiv 2 (mod3)$, the state becomes nonaccepting.

The relation cannot be computed by a deterministic transducer because the length of the output y decreases when the length of of the input increases from $3k + 1$ to $3k + 2$. □

This proof can easily be extended to prove the following Theorem 3.

Theorem 3. *If $m < n$ then there exists a left-total relation R (m, n)-computed by a weak finite-state frequency transducer and not computed by any deterministic finite-state transducer.*

Theorem 4. *There exists a left-total relation R $(2, 4)$-computed by a weak finite-state frequency transducer and not computed by any finite-state $(1, 2)$-frequency transducer.*

Proof. We consider the relation

$$R(x, y) = \begin{cases} \text{true, if } y = 1^{|x|} \text{ and } |x| \equiv 2 (mod7), \\ \text{true, if } y = 1^{|x|} \text{ and } |x| \equiv 4 (mod7), \\ \text{true, if } y = 1^{|x|} \text{ and } |x| \equiv 5 (mod7), \\ \text{true, if } y = 1^{|x|} \text{ and } |x| \equiv 6 (mod7), \\ \text{true, if } y = 0 \quad \text{and } |x| \equiv 0 (mod7), \\ \text{true, if } y = 0 \quad \text{and } |x| \equiv 1 (mod7), \\ \text{true, if } y = 0 \quad \text{and } |x| \equiv 3 (mod7), \\ \text{false, if} \quad \text{otherwise.} \end{cases}$$

(1) The weak finite-state frequency $(2, 4)$-transducer starts with reading 1 symbol from the first input tape, 2 symbols from the second input tape and 3 symbols from the third input tape, 4 symbols from fourth input tape and reads exactly 1 symbol from each input tape at any moment. The transducer always outputs $y_i = 1^{|x_i|}$ on the i-th output tape. Since the transducer can count the length of the input modulo 7, the false outputs (in cases $|x_i|$ congruent to 0,1 or 3 (mod 7)) are not accepted.

At every moment the lengths of the input words are $k, k + 1, k + 2, k + 3$ for some natural k. At least two of them are congruent to 2,4,5 or 6 (mod 7).

(2) Assume that the relation is $(1, 2)$-computed by a transducer performing a *weak* $(1, 2)$-computation with parameters (b_1, b_2). Whatever the difference $d = b_2 - b_1$, there exists a value of s such that both $s + b_1$ and $s + b_2$ are congruent to 2,4,5 or 6 (mod 7). Hence the transducer produces two wrong results on the pair $1^{s+b_1}, 1^{s+b_2}$ in contradiction with the $(1, 2)$-computability.   □

Unfortunately, it is not clear how to generalize the explicit construction of the relation $R(x, y)$ in Theorem 4 to prove distinction between (m, n)-computability and (km, kn)-computability for weak finite-state frequency transducers. Luckily, there is a non-constructive method to do so. This method is based on usage of algorithmic information theory.

Definition 8. *We define a transformation I which takes words $x \in \{0,1\}^*$ into $I(x) \in \{0,1\}^*$ by the following rule. Every symbol 0 is replaced by 1100110100 and every symbol 1 is replaced by 1011001010.*

Definition 9. *We define a transformation J which takes words $x \in \{0,1\}^*$ into $J(x) \in \{0,1\}^*$ by the following rule. Every symbol 0 is replaced by 0100110100 and every symbol 1 is replaced by 0011001010.*

Lemma 3. *For arbitrary $x \in \{0,1\}^*$ the result of the transformation I is a word $I(x)$ such that $| I(x) |= 10 | x |$, and $I(x)$ contains equal number of zeros and ones.*

Lemma 4. *For arbitrary $x \in \{0,1\}^*$ the result of the transformation J is a word $J(x)$ such that $| J(x) |= 10 | x |$, and every subword y of $J(x)$ such that $| J(x) |= 10$ contains no more than 5 symbols 1.*

Definition 10. *We define a transformation K which takes words $x \in \{0,1\}^*$ into a 2-dimensional array*

$$K(x) = \begin{pmatrix} K_{11} & K_{12} & \cdots & K_{1n} \\ K_{21} & K_{22} & \cdots & K_{2n} \\ \cdots & \cdots & \cdots & \cdots \\ K_{n1} & K_{n2} & \cdots & K_{nn} \end{pmatrix}$$

of size $10 | x | \times 10 | x |$ by the following rule. The first row $\left(K_{11} \ K_{12} \cdots K_{1n} \right)$ copies $I(x)$. Every next row is a cyclic copy of the preceding one:

$$\left(K_{s1} \ K_{s2} \cdots K_{sn} \right) = \left(K_{(s-1)2} \ K_{(s-1)3} \cdots K_{(s-1)1} \right).$$

Definition 11. *We define a transformation L which takes words $x \in \{0,1\}^*$ into a 2-dimensional array*

$$L(x) = \begin{pmatrix} L_{11} & L_{12} & \cdots & L_{1n} \\ L_{21} & L_{22} & \cdots & L_{2n} \\ \cdots & \cdots & \cdots & \cdots \\ L_{n1} & L_{n2} & \cdots & L_{nn} \end{pmatrix}$$

of size $10 \mid x \mid \times 10 \mid x \mid$ by the following rule. The first row $\left(L_{11}\ L_{12} \cdots L_{1n} \right)$ copies $J(x)$. Every next row is a cyclic copy of the preceding one:

$$\left(L_{s1}\ L_{s2} \cdots L_{sn} \right) = \left(L_{(s-1)2}\ L_{(s-1)3} \cdots L_{(s-1)1} \right).$$

There is a dichotomy: 1) either there exist 4 rows (say, with numbers b_1, b_2, b_3, b_4) in $K(x)$ such that in every column Z such that among the values $K_{(b_1)z}$, $K_{(b_2)z}$, $K_{(b_3)z}, K_{(b_4)z}$ there are exactly 2 zeros and 2 ones, or 2) for arbitrary 4 rows (with numbers b_1, b_2, b_3, b_4 in $K(x)$) there is a column z such that among the values $K_{(b_1)z}, K_{(b_2)z}, K_{(b_3)z}, K_{(b_4)z}$ there are at least 3 values equal to 1. (Please remember that by Lemma 4 the total number of zeros and ones in every row is the same.) We will prove that if the Kolmogorov complexity of x is maximal and the length of x is sufficiently large then the possibility 1) does not exist.

Lemma 5. *If n is sufficiently large and x is a Kolmogorov-maximal word of length n then for arbitrary 4 rows (with numbers b_1, b_2, b_3, b_4 in $K(x)$) there is a column z such that among the values $K_{(b_1)z}, K_{(b_2)z}, K_{(b_3)z}, K_{(b_4)z}$ there are at least 3 values equal to 1.*

Proof. Assume from the contrary that there exist 4 rows (say, with numbers b_1, b_2, b_3, b_4) in $K(x)$ such that in every column z such that among the values $K_{(b_1)z}, K_{(b_2)z}, K_{(b_3)z}, K_{(b_4)z}$ there are exactly 2 zeros and 2 ones. By definition of K, $K_{(b_i)z} = K_{1(z+b_i-1)}$. Hence every assertion "among the values $K_{(b_1)z}, K_{(b_2)z}, K_{(b_3)z}, K_{(b_4)z}$ there are exactly 2 zeros and 2 ones" can be written as "among the values $K_{1(c_1)}, K_{1(c_2)}, K_{1(c_3)}, K_{1(c_4)}$ there are exactly 2 zeros and 2 ones" which is equivalent to "among the values $I(d_1), I(d_2), I(d_3), I(d_4)$ there are exactly 2 zeros and 2 ones".

Every value $I(d)$ was obtained from a single letter in the word x. Namely, the letters $I(10j + 1), I(10j + 2), \cdots, I(10j + 10)$ were obtained from the j-th letter $x(j)$ of x. $I(10j + 1) = 1$ both for $x(j)$ being a or b. $I(10j + 2) = 1$ if $x(j)$ equals a but not b. $I(10j + 3) = 1$ if $x(j)$ equals b but not a. Hence we introduce a functional

$$h(x(j)) = \begin{cases} 1 & \text{, if } d \equiv 0 \pmod{10} \\ \overline{x(j)} & \text{, if } d \equiv 1 \text{ or } 4 \text{ or } 5 \text{ or } 7 \pmod{10} \\ x(j) & \text{, if } d \equiv 2 \text{ or } 3 \text{ or } 6 \text{ or } 8 \pmod{10} \\ 0 & \text{, if } d \equiv 9 \pmod{10} \end{cases}$$

Using this functional we transform every assertion of "among the values $I(d_1), I(d_2), I(d_3), I(d_4)$ there are exactly 2 zeros and 2 ones" type into a Boolean formula "among the values $h(x_{j_1}), h(x_{j_2}), h(x_{j_3}), h(x_{j_4})$ there are exactly 2 zeros and 2 ones".

Let a set S of such Boolean formulas be given. We say that another formula F is independent from the set S if F cannot be proved using formulas from the set S. For instance, if F contains a variable not present in any formula of S then F is independent from S.

Take a large integer n and consider the set T of all binary words from $\{a, b\}^{2n}$. There are 2^{2n} words in T. Let T_1 be the subset of T containing all words with equal number of a's and b's. Cardinality of T_1 equals $2^{2n-o(n)}$. The set S contains $2n$ formulas but not all of them are independent. However, since each formula contains only 4 variables, there are at least $\frac{2n}{4}$ independent formulas in S. Apply one-by-one these independent formulas and removes from T_1 all the words where some formula fails. Notice that application of a new formula independent from the preceding ones remove at least half of the words. Hence after all removals no more than $2^{\frac{3n}{2}-o(n)}$ words remain. Effective enumeration of all the remaining words and usage of Kolmogorov numbering as in Section 4 gives a method to compress each x to a length not exceeding $\frac{3n}{2} - o(n)$. This contradicts non-compressibility of Kolmogorov-maximal words.   □

Since independence of formulas in our argument was based only on the used variables the same argument proves the following lemma.

Lemma 6. *If n is sufficiently large and x is a Kolmogorov-maximal word of length n then for arbitrary 4 rows (with numbers b_1, b_2, b_3, b_4 in $L(x)$) there is a column z such that among the values $L_{(b_1)z}, L_{(b_2)z}, L_{(b_3)z}, L_{(b_4)z}$ there are at least 3 values equal to 1.*

We are ready to prove the main theorem of this paper.

Theorem 5. *There exists a left-total relation R $(3,6)$-computed by a weak finite-state frequency transducer and not computed by any finite-state $(2,4)$-frequency transducer.*

Proof. Consider the relation

$$R(x, y) = \begin{cases} \text{true, if } y = 1^{|x|} \text{ and } \mid x \mid \equiv j (mod\,n) \text{ and } L_{1j} = 0 \\ \text{true, if } y = 0 \quad \text{and } \mid x \mid \equiv j (mod\,n) \text{ and } L_{1j} = 1 \\ \text{false, if} \qquad\qquad \text{otherwise.} \end{cases}$$

where $L(x)$ is as described above.   □

References

1. Ablayev, F.M., Freivalds, R.: Why sometimes probabilistic algorithms can be more effective. In: Wiedermann, J., Gruska, J., Rovan, B. (eds.) MFCS 1986. LNCS, vol. 233, pp. 1–14. Springer, Heidelberg (1986)
2. Austinat, H., Diekert, V., Hertrampf, U., Petersen, H.: Regular frequency computations. Theoretical Computer Science 330(1), 15–20 (2005)

3. Beigel, R., Gasarch, W.I., Kinber, E.B.: Frequency computation and bounded queries. Theoretical Computer Science 163(1/2), 177–192 (1996)
4. Case, J., Kaufmann, S., Kinber, E.B., Kummer, M.: Learning recursive functions from approximations. Journal of Computer and System Sciences 55(1), 183–196 (1997)
5. Degtev, A.N.: On (m,n)-computable sets. In: Moldavanskij, I., Gos, I. (eds.) Algebraic Systems, pp. 88–99. Universitet (1981)
6. Freivalds, R., Karpinski, M.: Lower Space Bounds for Randomized Computation. In: Shamir, E., Abiteboul, S. (eds.) ICALP 1994. LNCS, vol. 820, pp. 580–592. Springer, Heidelberg (1994)
7. Freivalds, R., Karpinski, M.: Lower Time Bounds for Randomized Computation. In: Fülöp, Z. (ed.) ICALP 1995. LNCS, vol. 944, pp. 183–195. Springer, Heidelberg (1995)
8. Freivalds, R.: Complexity of probabilistic versus deterministic automata. In: Barzdins, J., Bjorner, D. (eds.) Baltic Computer Science. LNCS, vol. 502, pp. 565–613. Springer, Heidelberg (1991)
9. Freivalds, R.: Models of computation, Riemann Hypothesis and classical mathematics. In: Rovan, B. (ed.) SOFSEM 1998. LNCS, vol. 1521, pp. 89–106. Springer, Heidelberg (1998)
10. Freivalds, R.: Non-constructive methods for finite probabilistic automata. International Journal of Foundations of Computer Science 19(3), 565–580 (2008)
11. Freivalds, R.: Amount of nonconstructivity in finite automata. Theoretical Computer Science 411(38-39), 3436–3443 (2010)
12. Freivalds, R., Zeugmann, T., Pogosyan, G.R.: On the Size Complexity of Deterministic Frequency Automata. In: Dediu, A.-H., Martín-Vide, C., Truthe, B. (eds.) LATA 2013. LNCS, vol. 7810, pp. 287–298. Springer, Heidelberg (2013)
13. Garret, P.: The Mathematics of Coding Theory. Pearson Prentice Hall, Upper Saddle River (2004)
14. Gurari, E.: An Introduction to the Theory of Computation, ch. 2.2. Computer Science Press, an imprint of E. H. Freeman (1989)
15. Harizanova, V., Kummer, M., Owings, J.: Frequency computations and the cardinality theorem. The Journal of Symbolic Logic 57(2), 682–687 (1992)
16. Hinrichs, M., Wechsung, G.: Time bounded frequency computations. Information and Computation 139, 234–257 (1997)
17. Kaņeps, J., Freivalds, R.: Minimal Nontrivial Space Complexity of Probabilistic One-Way Turing Machines. In: Rovan, B. (ed.) MFCS 1990. LNCS, vol. 452, pp. 355–361. Springer, Heidelberg (1990)
18. Kinber, E.B.: Frequency calculations of general recursive predicates and frequency enumeration of sets. Soviet Mathematics Doklady 13, 873–876 (1972)
19. Kinber, E.B.: Frequency computations in finite automata. Kibernetika (2), 7–15 (1976), Russian; English translation in Cybernetics 12, 179–187 (1976)
20. Kinber, E.B., Gasarch, W.I., Zeugmann, T., Pleszkoch, M.G., Smith, C.H.: Learning Via Queries With Teams and Anomalies. In: Proceedings of COLT 1990, pp. 327–337 (1990)
21. Kolmogorov, A.N.: Three approaches to the quantitative definition of information. Problems in Information Transmission 1, 1–7 (1965)
22. McNaughton, R.: The Theory of Automata, a Survey. Advances in Computers 2, 379–421 (1961)
23. Rabin, M.O.: Probabilistic automata. Information and Control 6(3), 230–245 (1963)

24. Michael, O.: Rabin and Dana Scott. Finite automata and their decision problems. IBM Journal of Research and Development 3(2), 115–125 (1959)
25. Rose, G.F.: An extended notion of computability. In: Abstracts of International Congress for Logic, Methodology and Philosophy of Science, p. 14 (1960)
26. Solomonoff, R.: A Formal Theory of Inductive Inference, Part II. Information and Control 7(2), 224–254 (1964)
27. Trakhtenbrot, B.A.: On the frequency computation of functions. Algebra i Logika 2, 25–32 (1964) (Russian)
28. Trakhtenbrot, B.A.: Frequency Algorithms and Computations. In: Becvar, J. (ed.) MFCS 1975. LNCS, vol. 32, pp. 148–161. Springer, Heidelberg (1975)

A Critical Survey of Some Competing Accounts of Concrete Digital Computation

Nir Fresco

School of History and Philosophy, The University of New South Wales, Sydney, Australia
Fresco.Nir@Gmail.com

Abstract. This paper deals with the question: what are the key requirements for a physical system to perform digital computation? Oftentimes, cognitive scientists are quick to employ the notion of computation *simpliciter* when asserting basically that cognitive activities are computational. They employ this notion as if there is a consensus on just what it takes for a physical system to compute. Some cognitive scientists in referring to digital computation simply adhere to Turing computability. But if cognition is indeed computational, then it is *concrete* computation that is required for explaining cognition as an embodied phenomenon. Three accounts of computation are examined here: 1. *Formal Symbol Manipulation.* 2. *Physical Symbol Systems* and 3. *The Mechanistic account.* I argue that the differing requirements implied by these accounts justify the demand that one commits to a particular account when employing the notion of digital computation in regard to physical systems, rather than use these accounts interchangeably.

Keywords: Concrete computation, Computability, Symbols, Semantics, Information Processing, Cognitive Systems, Turing Machines.

1 Introduction

All too often, cognitive scientists are quick to employ the notion of computation *simpliciter* when asserting basically that cognitive activities are computational. Unfortunately, it seems that a clearer understanding of computation is distorted by philosophical concerns about cognition. Some researchers in referring to *digital* computation simply adhere to Alan Turing's notion of *computability* when attempting to explain cognitive behaviour. Still, classical computability theory studies what functions on the natural numbers are computable, and not the spatiotemporal constraints that are inherent to cognitive phenomena.

Any analysis of cognitive phenomena that is based solely on mathematical formalisms of computability, is at best incomplete. It has been proven that Emil Post's machines, Stephen Kleene's formal systems model, Kurt Gödel's recursive functions model, Alonzo Church's lambda calculus, and Turing Machines (TMs) – are all extensionally equivalent. They all identify the same class of functions, in terms of the sets of arguments and values that they determine, as computable (Kleene 2002: pp. 232-233).

D.L. Dowe (Ed.): Solomonoff Festschrift, LNAI 7070, pp. 155–173, 2013.

However, *concrete digital computation* as it is actualised in physical systems seems to be a more appropriate candidate for the job of explaining cognitive phenomena.[1] It is not in vain that the reigning trends in contemporary cognitive science (whether it be connectionism or dynamicism) emphasise the embeddedness and embodiment of cognitive agents. This is one motivation for examining extant accounts of concrete computation, before we can make any sense of talk about 'cognitive computation', 'neural computation' or 'biological computation'.

There are many extant accounts of digital computation in physical systems on offer. Only three accounts are examined in this paper for lack of space.[2]

1. According to the *Formal Symbol Manipulation (FSM) account*, a physical system performs digital computation when it processes semantically interpreted (not just interpretable) symbols (Pylyshyn 1984: pp. 62, 72).
2. According to the *Physical Symbol Systems (PSS) account*, a physical system performs digital computation when it consists of symbols and processes operating on these symbols that designate other entities (Newell 1980: p. 157).
3. According to the *Mechanistic account*, a physical system performs digital computation if it manipulates input strings of digits, depending on the digits' type and their location on the string, in accordance with a rule defined over the strings (and possibly the system's internal states) (Piccinini and Scarantino 2011: p. 8).

No novel account of computation is offered here. The goal of this paper is to examine the conflict among well-known accounts and argue that they imply sufficiently distinct requirements for a physical system to compute to justify the demand that one commits to a particular account when employing the notion of concrete digital computation. Whilst the main driver here is cognitive science, this demand is unbiased. It applies just as well to biology, astronomy and any other science in which 'computation' is employed as explanans for some physical phenomenon. In the following three sections, I survey the FSM, PSS and Mechanistic accounts respectively. In the fifth section, I defend my argument for the non-equivalence of extant accounts of concrete computation.

2   The Formal Symbol Manipulation Account

According to this account digital computing systems are formal symbol manipulators. They manipulate symbol tokens which themselves are representations of the subject matter the computation is about, in accordance with some purely formal principles

---

[1] For the purposes of this paper, I shall remain neutral on whether cognition can indeed be *fully* explained computationally. Arguably, cognition involves the processing of information, and it is not entirely clear that information processing is equivalent to digital computation. This question can remain unanswered for now.

[2] These particular three accounts nicely demonstrate that extant accounts of computation are not only intensionally different, but also extensionally different, irrespective of their representational character. For a detailed analysis of Turing's account, Hilary Putnam & John Searle's trivialisation of computation, a reconstruction of Brian C. Smith's participatory account and the Algorithm Execution account see Fresco (2011).

(Scheutz 2002: p. 13). Although these manipulated symbols have both semantic and syntactic properties, only the latter are causally efficacious. Chief proponents of this account are Jerry Fodor (1975), Zenon Pylyshyn (1984; 1989) and John Haugeland (1985). Fodor asserts that "computations just are processes in which representations have their causal consequences in virtue of their form" (Fodor 1980: p. 68). Haugeland's well-known formalist's motto stated that "if you take care of the syntax, the semantics will take care of itself" (Haugeland 1985: p. 106). A computing system as an interpreted automatic formal system takes care of the syntax.

Furthermore, such systems are organised in three distinct levels: the semantic level, the symbolic level and the physical level (Pylyshyn 1989: pp. 58-59). This explanation framework of complex systems has some similarity to David Marr's tripartite model of complex systems: the computational level, the algorithmic level and the physical level (Marr 1982: p. 22). At the *semantic* level, symbolic expressions are transformed in the computing system in a way that coherently preserve their meaning and ensures that they continue to "make sense" when semantically interpreted. Marr's computational level, however, is a *function-theoretic* characterisation of the system in terms of the function it computes (i.e., its computational capacity). This computation may contingently involve the assignment of semantic contents. At the *symbolic* level the system operates in terms of *representations* and their transformations. Computing systems can operate at the semantic level only because of this middle level. Marr's algorithmic level also need not be aligned with the symbolic level, for his analysis is not necessarily committed to symbol-manipulation computation. At the physical level, the state transitions of the computing system correspond to some symbolic expressions and are connected by physical laws (Pylyshyn 1984: p. 58). This particular level is indeed analogous to Marr's physical level.

The FSM account identifies six key requirements for a physical system to perform digital computation.[3] The first requirement is that the system *be programmable to allow maximal plasticity of function*. In order to exclude such systems as mere calculators and interpreted automatic systems that are not formal (e.g., analogue computers), the class of computing systems is restricted to those that are programmable (Haugeland 1985: pp. 258-259). It is one of the foundational principles of computer science that the operations of digital computing systems be fully programmable (ibid: p. 126). Despite the rigidity of the physical structure of digital computing systems and the interconnections of their components, these systems are capable of maximal plasticity of function. This plasticity is enabled by their operation

---

[3] Pylyshyn argues that there is a missing requirement specifying what makes it the case that a symbol X represents, say, a particular daisy, rather than something else. The *computational theory of mind* has always been missing that part (Pylyshyn, personal communication). Specifically, he argues that the minimum function needed for this representation relation to obtain is that there be some causal or nomologically supported dependency between the daisy and X (Pylyshyn 2007: p. 82). However, it is not clear that conventional digital computing systems require that a similar causal relation obtain between a symbol and an external represented object for them to compute (a representation *internal* to the computing system, e.g., an instruction in memory, is not problematic).

being programmable to behave in accordance with any finitely specifiable function (Pylyshyn 1984: p. 53). It is also the basis for Turing's vision that a computer can (in principle) be made to exhibit intelligent activity to an arbitrary degree (thereby passing the Turing's test).

The second requirement is that the system operate using *internally represented rule-governed transformations of interpretable symbolic expressions*. As a formal system, by following the formal rules of transformation operating on symbolic expressions the semantic interpretation must make sense of those expressions. The computing system operates as a black box that automatically manipulates the symbolic tokens according to formal rules and when interpreted they make "sense in the contexts in which they're made" (Haugeland 1985: p. 106). The regularities of computing systems are rule-governed, rather than law-like. So any explanation of a computational process must make reference to what is represented by the (semantically interpreted) computational states and rules, rather than just to causal state transitions (Pylyshyn 1984: p. 57).

Moreover, it is a key property of computing systems that semantic interpretations of computational states must be consistent. Since computations follow a particular set of semantically interpreted rules, semantic interpretations of computational states cannot be given capriciously (ibid: p. 58), still these interpretations need not be unique. This is analogous to the rules of existential generalisations, universal instantiations etc. that apply to formulas in virtue of their syntactic form, but their salient property is semantical in that they are truth preserving (Fodor & Pylyshyn 1988: p. 29).

The third requirement is that the *computational states of the system must correspond to equivalence classes of physical states* such that their members are indistinguishable from the point of view of their function (Pylyshyn 1984: p. 56). There exists a primitive mapping from atomic symbols to relatively elementary physical states, and a mapping specification of the structure of complex expressions onto the structure of relatively complex physical states. The structure-preserving mapping is typically given recursively. This ensures that the relation between atomic symbols (e.g., 'A' and 'B'), and composite expressions (e.g., 'A&B'), is encoded in terms of a physical relation between constituent states that is functionally equivalent to the physical relation used to encode the relation between more complex expressions (e.g., 'A&B' and 'C') and their composite expression (e.g., '(A&B)&C'). Furthermore, the physical counterparts of the symbolic expressions and their structural properties cause the behaviour of the computing system. If you change the symbols, the system will behave differently (Fodor & Pylyshyn 1988: pp. 14, 17).

The fourth requirement is that the system *support an arbitrarily large number of representations* (Pylyshyn 1984: p. 62). Conventional computing systems' architecture requires that there be distinct symbolic expressions for each object, event or state of affairs it can represent (Fodor & Pylyshyn 1988: p. 57). This raises the question how so many semantically interpreted operations are possible if the number of expressions is arbitrary large. For a fixed number of expressions some sort of a lookup table could be implemented. However, this is not possible for an arbitrarily large number of representations (Pylyshyn 1984: pp. 61-62). Instead, this capability is achieved by the fifth requirement.

The fifth requirement is that the system *be capable of capitalising on the compositional nature of expressions as determined by the constituent expressions and the rules used to combine them.* By supporting simple rules that operate on simple individual symbols the system is capable of an arbitrary large number of symbolic expressions. Complex expressions are realised and transformed by means of instantiating constituent expressions of representations (ibid). The semantics of composite symbolic expression is determined in a consistent way by the semantics of its constituents (Fodor & Pylyshyn 1988: p. 16). For instance, the semantics of 'the daisies in the vase on the table by the door' is determined by 'the daisies in the vase on the table', which is determined by 'the daisies in the vase'. Most of the symbolic expressions in computing systems as interpreted automatic formal systems are complexes, whose semantics is determined by their systematic composition Haugeland 1985: p. 96).

Finally, implicitly, the sixth requirement is that the system's *functional architecture include an accessible memory.* As in the idealised TM, a computing system must have a memory that allows writing of symbolic expressions and then reading them. This memory may consist of a running tape, a set of registers or any other storage media (Pylyshyn 1989: p. 56). The memory's capacity, its organisation and means of accessing it are properties of the specific functional architecture of the system. Most modern architectures are register-based, in which symbols and symbolic expressions are stored and later retrieved by their numeric or symbolic address (ibid: pp. 72-73). Although the set of computable functions does not depend on the particular system implementation of the memory, the time complexity of computation does vary (retrieving a particular string from a table could be, under certain conditions, be made independent of the number of strings stored and the size of the table) (Pylyshyn 1984: p. 97-99).

3   The Physical Symbol Systems Account

According to this account, championed by Allen Newell and Herbert Simon, digital computing systems are physical symbol systems.[4] They consist of sets of symbols, which are physical patterns that can occur as components of symbol structures or expressions (Newell and Simon 1976: p. 116). Computing systems also include a collection of processes that operate on these expressions to create, modify or destroy other expressions. Further, a physical symbol system is situated in a world of objects that is wider than just these symbolic expressions. The PSS account is indeed similar to the FSM account (as will be shown below), but there are also some differences that cannot be easily dismissed.

---

[4] The PSS hypothesis deals primarily with the intelligence of symbol systems and relates to minds and artificial intelligence. I will mostly limit my discussion to the PSS account of computation.

Newell and Simon (1976: p. 117) maintained that a physical symbol system is an instance of a Universal Turing machine (UTM). They discovered that UTMs always contain within them a particular notion of symbol and symbolic behaviour. Tautologically, physical symbol systems are universal (Newell 1980: p. 155). Their capacity to solve problems is accomplished by producing and progressively modifying symbol structures until they produce a solution structure, particularly by means of a heuristic search[5] (Newell and Simon 1976: p. 120). There are two basic aspects to each search, namely its object (i.e., what is being searched) and its scope (i.e., the set of objects within which the search is conducted). In computing systems each aspect must be made explicit in terms of specific structures and processes, since a system cannot search for an object that it cannot recognise (Haugeland 1985: p. 177). Computing systems (as all UTMs) solve problems mostly by using heuristic search, for they have limited processing resources.

The PSS account identifies seven key requirements for a physical system to perform digital computation. The first requirement is that the system *consist of a set of symbols and a set of processes that operate on them and produce through time an evolving collection of symbolic expressions*. At any given time, the system contains a collection of symbolic structures and processes operating on expressions to produce other expressions. Such processes are the creation, modification, reproduction and destruction of symbolic expressions through time (ibid: p. 116). These processes operate on and transform *internal* symbolic structures, or in other words the system executes computer programs that operate on data structures (Bickhard and Terveen 1995: p. 92).

The second requirement is that the system either *affect a designated object or behave in ways that are dependent on that object*. An entity (i.e., a symbol) X designates (i.e., is about or stands for) an entity (e.g., an object or a symbol) Y relative to a process P, if when X is P's input, P's behaviour depends on Y. Designation is grounded in the physical behaviour of P when its action could be at a distance if X (the input to P) stands for a distal object. This 'action at a distance' is accomplished by a mechanism of access (that is realised in physical computing systems) to three types of entities: symbol structures, operators[6] and roles in symbol structures. The set of processes includes programs, whose input could also be symbolic expressions. If an expression can be created at T_i that is dependent on an entity in some way, processes can exist in the system that at T_{i+1}, take that expression as input and behave in a way dependent on that entity. Thus, these expressions designate that entity (Newell 1980: pp. 156-157).

The third requirement is that the system *be capable of interpreting an expression, if it designates some process and given that expression the system can execute that process*. Interpretation is defined as the act of accepting an expression that designates a process as input and then executing that process (ibid: pp. 158-159). This is similar

---

[5] It is not clear that artificial digital computing systems (e.g., physical instantiations of UTMs) must use heuristic search as the only means for solving computational problems. Clearly, many algorithms are not based on any search mechanism, but rather a finite sequence of instructions to solve a particular problem.

[6] Operators are symbols that have an external semantics built into them (Newell 1980: p. 159).

to the process of indirectly executing computer programs by an interpreter program. The interpreter reads an expression E as input and if it is recognised as a program (or a procedure), rather than a data structure, it is then executed. This capability is necessary to allow the flexibility of UTMs to create expressions for their own behaviour and then produce that very behaviour. The total processes in the computing system can be decomposed to the basic structure of (control + (operators + data)) that is paradigmatic in all programming languages. The control continuously brings together operators and data to yield the desired behaviour.

The fourth requirement is *the existence of expressions that designate every process of which the machine is capable* (Newell and Simon 1976: p. 116). This requirement is self-explanatory and is necessary to support the full plasticity of behaviour of UTMs.

The fifth requirement is that the system be capable of distinguishing between some expressions as data and others as programs (Newell 1980: p. 166). This is a property of all UTMs that must be able to recognise some expressions as data when creating or modifying them at time T_i and then interpret them as programs at time T_j. The concept of universality, which is one of Turing's seminal contributions, unifies data and programs by way of the UTM taking programs of other (simulated) machines as data (as well as the inputs inscribed on the tapes of those simulated machines).

The sixth requirement is that the system have *a stable memory to ensure that once expressions are created they continue to exist until they are explicitly modified or deleted* (Newell and Simon 1976: p. 116). This requirement stems from the coupling of read/write operations in computing systems. Each of these operations requires its counterpart to be productive in affecting the system's behaviour. A read operation only retrieves expressions that were written to memory (and persisted). Conversely, a write operation of expressions, which are never subsequently read, is redundant (Newell 1980: p. 163).

Lastly, the seventh requirement is that the system *be capable of handling an unbounded number of expressions and realising the absolute maximal class of input/output functions using these expressions*. This requirement is weaker than the requirement for unbounded memory. The structural requirements for universality are not dependent on unbounded memory. Rather they are dependent on the system's capability to handle an unbounded number of expressions (Newell and Simon 1976: p. 116) and realise the absolute maximal class of input/output functions using these expressions (Newell 1980: p. 178).

4   The Mechanistic Account of Computation

According to the Mechanistic account, proposed by Gualtiero Piccinini (2007), digital computing systems are digit-processing mechanisms. They are mechanisms, which can be ascribed the function of generating output strings from input strings in accordance with a general rule (or map) that applies to all strings and depends on the input strings and (possibly) internal states for its application (ibid: p. 516). This account relies essentially on three conceptual elements: *I.* Medium independence of the vehicles (digits) processed. They could be implemented in a variety of ways (such as mechanical components, electronic components, optical components etc.); *II*. The function of the system is to process those vehicles irrespective of their particular physical implementation; *III*. The operation of the system is performed in accordance with rules, which need not necessarily be algorithms or programs (as in the case of special purpose TMs or finite state automata, hereafter FSA).

Moreover, the mathematical notion of computation (i.e., computability) only applies directly to abstract systems, such as TMs or FSA, but not to physical systems. Computability is typically defined over strings of letters (often called symbols) from a finite alphabet (ibid: pp. 509-510). But not every process that is defined over strings of letters counts as computation (e.g., the generation of a random string of letters). To overcome this gap, Piccinini (2007: pp. 510-512) introduces the notion of a *digit* as the concrete counterpart to the formal notion of a *letter*. A digit is a stable state of a component that is processed by the mechanism.[7] Strings of digits (i.e., sequences of digits) can be either data or rules, so they are essentially the same kind of thing and differ only in the functional role they play during processing by the computing system (Piccinini and Scarantino 2011: pp. 7-8). Digits are permutable. Components that process digits of one type are functionally capable of processing digits of any other type.

The mechanistic account identifies four key requirements for a physical system to perform digital computation. The first requirement is that the system *process tokens of the same digit type in the same way and tokens of different digit types in different ways*. Under normal conditions, digits of the same type in a computing system affect primitive components of the system in sufficiently similar ways, thereby their dissimilarities make no difference to the output produced. For instance, two inputs to a XOR gate that are sufficiently close to a certain voltage (labelled type '1') yield an output of a voltage sufficiently close to a different specific value (labelled type '0'). However, that does not imply that for any two input types, a primitive component *always* yields outputs of different types. Two different inputs can yield the same computational output, such in the case of a NOR gate. Input types '1,1', '0,1' and '1,0' give rise to outputs of type '0'. Still, it is essential that the NOR gate yield different responses to tokens of different types, thus responding to input types '0,0' differently from other input types. Differences between digit types must suffice for the component to differentiate between them, so as to yield the correct outputs.

The second requirement is that the system *process all digits belonging to a string (of digits) during the same functionally relevant time interval and in a way that respects the ordering of the digits within that string*. When a computing system is sufficiently large and complex, there has to be some way to ensure synchronisation among all digits belonging to a particular string. The components of a computing system interact over time, and given their physical characteristics, there is only a

---

[7] In ordinary electronic computers digits are states of physical components of the machine (e.g., memory cells). In other cases, such as old punched card computers, strings of digits were implemented as sequences of holes (or lack thereof) on cards (Piccinini, personal communication).

limited amount of time during which their interaction can produce the correct result, which is consistent with the ordering of digits within strings. In primitive computing components and simple circuits it is mostly the temporal ordering of digits that is responsible for producing the correct result. So if, for example, digits, which are supposed to be summed together, enter an adder mechanism at times that are too far apart, they will not be added correctly (ibid: p. 513). In more complex components, processing of all digits belonging to a string must proceed in a way that also respects the spatial ordering of the digits within the string. Each digit in the sequence must be processed until we reach the last digit in the string. In some atypical cases the ordering of digits makes no difference to a computation (e.g., summing up all the numbers in an array or calculating the length of a sequence of symbols).

The third requirement is that *all the system's components that process digits stabilise only on states that count as digits*. Components can be in one of several stable states. In a binary computing system memory cells, for instance, can be in either of two stable states, each of which constitutes a digit. Upon receiving some physical stimulus (e.g., the pressing of a key), a memory cell enters a state on which it must stabilise. Memory cells stabilise on states corresponding to either of two digit types, typically labeled '0' and '1', that are processed by the computing system. If memory cells did not have the capacity to stabilise on one of these digit types, the memory would cease to function as such and the computer would cease to operate normally (ibid: p. 511).

The fourth requirement is that the *components of the system be functionally organised and synchronised so that external inputs, together with the digits stored in memory, be processed by the relevant components in accordance with a set of instructions*.[8] During each time interval, the processing components transform external input (if such exists) and previous memory states in a manner that corresponds to the transition of each computational state to its successor. The external input combined with the initial memory state constitute the initial string of a particular computation. Intermediate memory states constitute the relevant intermediate strings. Similarly, the output produced by the system (together with the final memory state) constitutes the final string. As long as the components of the system are functionally organised and synchronised so that their processing respects the well-defined ordering of the manipulated digits, the operation of the system can be described as a series of snapshots. The computational rule specifies the relationship that obtains between inputs and their respective outputs produced by modifying snapshots according to a set of instructions (ibid: pp. 509, 515).

5   Discussion

The literature contains many attempts to clarify the notions of computation *simpliciter* and digital computation, in particular. Matthias Scheutz, for example, has argued that

---

[8] Strictly, this requirement applies to systems that Piccinini dubs "fully digital" computing systems (Piccinini, personal communication). Other systems, which he dubs "input-output" digital computing systems, take digital inputs and produce digital outputs in accordance with a rule, but do not execute a step-by-step program (e.g., some connectionist networks).

there is no satisfactory account of implementation to answer questions critical for computational cognitive science (1999: p. 162). He does not offer a new account of concrete computation. Instead he suggests approaching the implementational issue by starting with physical digital systems progressively abstracting away from some of their physical properties until a (mathematical) description remains of the function realised. In a similar vein, David Chalmers (2011) also focuses on the implementational issue, only to offer a new mathematical formalism of computability that is based on combinatorial state automata (supplanting the traditional finite state automata). He too argues that a theory of implementation is crucial for (digital) computation to establish its foundational role in cognitive science. The motivation behind both Scheutz and Chalmers' efforts to clarify the notion of implementation is to block attempts by Putnam and Searle (and others) to trivialise computation (and undermine computationalism).

Other notable discussions of computation in cognitive science include David Israel (2002), Oron Shagrir (2006), Piccinini (2006, Piccinini & Scarantino 2011), Smith (2002, 2010) and the (long) list continues. Israel (2002) claims that often it seems that a better understanding of computation is hampered by philosophical concerns about mind or cognition. Yet "[o]ne would, alas, have been surprised at how quick and superficial such a regard [to computation] has been" (ibid: p. 181). Shagrir (2006) examines a variety of individuating conditions of computation showing that most of them are inadequate for being either too narrow or too wide. Although he does not provide a definitive answer as to what concrete computation is, he points out that neither connectionism nor neural computation nor computational neuroscience is compatible with the widespread assumption that digital computation is executed over representations with combinatorial structure.

Importantly, two uncommon examples of genuine attempts to explicate the notion of computation are Piccinini's and Smith's. Piccinini (2006) demonstrates how on various readings of computation, some have argued that computational explanation is applicable to psychology, but not, for instance, to neuroscience. Still, neuroscientists routinely appeal to computations in their research. Elsewhere, Piccinini examines the implications of different types of digital computation (as well as their extensions' relations of class inclusion) for computational theses of cognition (Piccinini and Scarantino 2011).

But as far as I am aware, nobody else in the literature has ever undertaken a more ambitious project than Smith to systematically examine the extant accounts of computation and their role in both computer science and cognitive science. In his 2002 "The foundations of computing", Smith lists the following six construals of computation: FSM, Effective Computability, Algorithm Execution, Digital State Machines, Information Processing and PSS. [9] His *Age of Significance* project (which is now long coming) aims to shed some light on the murky notion of computation, putting each one of these construals under careful scrutiny (Smith 2010). Surprisingly enough, Smith concludes that there is *no* adequate account of computation and *never*

---

[9] In an unpublished chapter from the Age of Significance, Smith adds the following construals: Calculation of a Function, Interactive Agents, Dynamics and Complex Adaptive Systems.

will be one. For computers per se are not "a genuine subject matter: they are not sufficiently special" (ibid: p. 38). Pace Smith, I do not believe that there is a compelling reason to reject *all* accounts of computation as inadequate, let alone to preclude the possibility of ever coming up with an adequate account. Still, I strongly agree that the accounts are different and many of them are indeed inadequate for explaining concrete computation.

My main argument here proceeds as follows:

- (P1) There are many accounts of digital computation at our disposal.
- (P2) These accounts establish different (but not all irreducibly different) requirements for a physical system to perform digital computation.
- (P3) Therefore, extant accounts of computation are non-equivalent.
- (P4) Cognitive capacities are sometimes explained by invoking digital computation terminology.
- (P5) When employing an equivocal interpretation, one needs to commit to an explicit interpretation (or account).
- Therefore, one needs to commit to an explicit account of computation when explaining cognitive capacities by invoking digital computation terminology. Specifically, any computational thesis of cognition is unintelligible without a commitment to a specific account of computation.

The truth of the first premise is evident in the philosophical literature (cf. Piccinini 2007; Shagrir 1999; and Smith 2002, 2010). In addition to the FSM, PSS and Mechanistic accounts examined here, there are also the Algorithm Execution account, the Gandy-Sieg account, the Information Processing account as well as others.

Similarly, premise four (at least) seems self-evident. Computationalists take premise four for granted (Fodor 1975, Pylyshyn 1984, Newell & Simon 1976, Marr 1982, van Rooij 2008) and so do some connectionists. *Radical* dynamicists do not subscribe to the computational theory of mind (Van Gelder & Port 1995, Thelen & Smith 1994), yet they reject it without committing to any particular account of computation proper. For they presuppose that digital computation is inherently representational. *Other* dynamicists do not deny that *some* aspects of cognition may be representational and be subject to a computational explanation.

Yet, this presupposition is unjustified. Digital computation (but not computationalism) could be explained without invoking any representational properties (barring internal representations) by appealing to causal or functional properties instead (see Fresco 2010 and Piccinini 2008a). As van Rooij (2008: p. 964) rightly points out, computation and computationalism have become associated with the symbolic tradition, but only sometimes with specific models in this tradition. Some accounts of concrete digital computation are indeed representational (cf. the reconstruction of Smith's participatory account in Fresco (2011) as well as the FSM and PSS accounts discussed above), but others need not be (cf. Copeland 1996, Chalmers 1994, the Mechanistic account discussed above). This simply reinforces the need to commit to a particular account of computation.

Moreover, premise five simply calls for disambiguation when there is an equivocation in terms. When some phenomenon is open to two interpretations or more, we should commit to one interpretation to avoid ambiguity. For instance, the concept depression has at least two typical meanings. In the sentence, "The great depression started in most countries in 1929 and lasted for a long time", it is clear that 'depression' means a long-term downturn in economic activity. On the other hand, in the sentence, "Long depression leads to making irrational decisions", 'depression' means something different. Similarly, when one asserts that hierarchical planning or linguistic tasks, for example, are computational, one ought to commit to a particular account of computation.[10] Is it in virtue of executing an algorithm, formally manipulating symbols, or implementing a TM that cognitive agents engage in hierarchical planning?

Furthermore, the commitment to a particular interpretation should be consistent to avoid further ambiguity. From the two sentences above it follows that irrational decisions were made in the countries that suffered the Great Depression in 1929. This conclusion would only validly follow from its premises, if 'depression' had the *same* interpretation in both premises. Otherwise, whilst this conclusion may be *plausible*, it does not follow. This is also known as the fallacy of equivocation. Similarly, if one explains a particular cognitive capacity in virtue of an explicit account of concrete digital computation, one has to consistently adhere to that account. An explanation of a linguistic task in virtue of formal symbol manipulation and then in virtue of algorithm execution ceases to be a coherent story, since they are not equivalent.

Importantly, not only are the extant accounts of concrete digital computation *intensionally* different, they are also *extensionally* different. These accounts offer different perspectives on what a physical computing system does. But rather than having the same *extension*, these accounts end up denoting different classes of computing systems. For example, the second requirement of the FSM account excludes computing systems that are neither program-controlled nor programmable[11]. For such systems do not follow semantically represented rules, instead the "rules" are hardwired. A physical symbol system is explicitly classified by Newell and Simon as an instance of a UTM (1976: p. 117). This classification is also derivable from the conjunction of the fourth and fifth requirements of the PSS account. Also, the FSM and PSS accounts exclude computing systems such as Gandy machines[12] and discrete neural networks, for they violate Turing's locality condition and do not necessarily operate on explicit symbolic expressions. The Mechanistic account, on the other hand,

---

[10] To be clear, *digital computation* is not ambiguous in the same sense that *depression* is. The aforementioned accounts offer specific proposals for how 'digital computation' should be understood, but they are still related by a more general sense of 'digital computation'. The example above is simply meant to emphasise the need for disambiguation.

[11] A special purpose TM is an example of a program-controlled system that is not programmable.

[12] A Gandy machine (introduced by Turing's student, Robin Gandy in 1980) can be conceptualised as multiple TMs working in parallel, sharing the same tape and possibly writing on overlapping regions of it.

is far less restrictive in terms of the systems it classifies as digital computing systems, including UTMs, and special purpose TMs, but also FSAs, discrete neural networks, primitive logic gates and even hypercomputers (see figure 1).

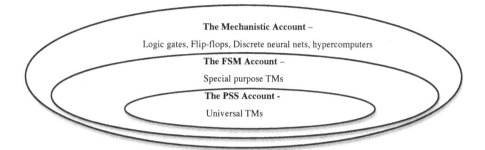

Fig. 1. With the exception of hypercomputers, UTMs are the most powerful and flexible computing systems in the class above (e.g., they can simulate any discrete neural net). Still, UTMs (and physical approximations thereof) do not exhaust all types of digital computing systems. The Mechanistic account is the broadest of the three accounts examined.

Prima facie, it might seem that premise two is self-defeating, but this is not the case. A possible consequence of *all* the requirements not being irreducibly different is some overlap between requirements of various accounts. Thus, the requirements that are implied by one account *could be* reduced to some of the other requirements.[13] And if all the requirements could be reduced to a coherent minimal set of key requirements, then this would constitute a *single* account of computation. Premise three would then no longer follow from the preceding premises. However, premise two suggests that although *some* of the requirements may overlap, not *all* of them do. For instance, the fourth key requirement of the Mechanistic account presupposes in some cases the existence of memory (whose cells stabilise on certain digits). Similarly, the sixth requirement of the PSS account and the sixth requirement of the FSM account both demand memory for storing and retrieving symbolic expressions. Still, some requirements of one account, such as spatiotemporal synchronisation of processing digits belonging to the same string (i.e., the Mechanistic account second requirement), cannot be reduced to any of the requirements of the competing accounts.

Possible challenges to my conclusion might be that some of the key requirements implied by different accounts could be synthesised or that one could simultaneously subscribe to two accounts or more. The first challenge may result in sidestepping the demand to commit to an explicit account. But even if that were the case, such a synthesis would simply yield a new (possibly adequate!) account of computation. The second challenge needs unpacking. It can be interpreted in one of two ways. Firstly, it could be interpreted as subscribing to more than one account simultaneously for

---

[13] An overlap among requirements clearly does not imply a reduction from one requirement to another. My intent here is to address a possible criticism to the effect that premise three would no longer follow as an intermediate conclusion from its preceding premises.

explaining different cognitive capacities respectively. I do not see that as a problem. There is still a need to commit to a particular account for each relevant cognitive capacity. But this could have some other consequences, such as explaining cognitive behaviour in a non-unified manner by resorting to a plethora of computational models. It will require a compelling account of how the different computational (cognitive) subsystems interrelate.

Secondly, the challenge could be interpreted as subscribing to several accounts simultaneously, since cognitive explanations by nature span multiple levels. This is consistent with Marr's (1982) tripartite analysis. For instance, we could hold that (1) cognitive computations are inherently representational. At the same time, we could also hold without being inconsistent that (2) these computations are constrained in terms of any one of the formalisms of computability, and lastly that (3) they occur in the brain, which is embodied and situated in the real world. This is all well and good. Still, as I have argued above, concrete computation (but perhaps not cognitive computation) could be explained without necessarily invoking any representational properties (e.g., by the Mechanistic account above or the Algorithm Execution account in Copeland 1996). If one wishes to commit to a representational account of digital computation, since *cognition* is representational, one should firstly justify *why* computation proper *is* representational. Also, subscribing to an account of concrete computation and to a formalism of computability simultaneously does not introduce any conflict.

Although some of the key requirements of the three accounts overlap, others do not, suggesting that there is sufficient dissimilarity between these accounts. For example, the conjunction of the fourth[14] and fifth requirements of the PSS account can be reduced to the FSM account's first requirement. The PSS account's fourth and fifth requirements amount to the universality property of soft-programmable computing systems that is achieved by means of symbolic expressions used either as data or as programs ensuring maximal plasticity of function. In addition, both the FSM account's fourth requirement and the first part of the PSS account's seventh requirement demand the capacity to handle an unbounded number of representations[15] (or symbolic expressions designating some entities).

Another seemingly important similarity between the FSM and PSS accounts (but not the Mechanistic account) is that computing systems engage in information processing at the *symbolic* level. For instance, Fodor and Pylyshyn (1988: p. 52) claim that "conventional computers typically operate in a 'linguistic mode', inasmuch

---

[14] The PSS account's fourth requirement demands the existence of expressions that represent every process of which the machine is capable to support the full plasticity of behaviour of the computing system. But it is not clear why it is necessary that *every* such expression exist. There could be a mismatch between the set of all functions and the set of all expressions representing them. For instance, some functions could be the serial invocation of several expressions (themselves representing other functions).

[15] Only the FSM account explicitly states that the unbounded number of representations is produced by means of compositionality.

as they process information by operating on syntactically structured expressions". As well, Newell and Simon's (1972: p. 870) fundamental working assumption is that "the programmed computer and human problem solver are both species belonging to the genus IPS" (that is information processing systems). The Mechanistic account, on the other hand, does not equate information processing and digital computation.[16] Still, it is not clear in what sense the information-processing characterisation of computing systems adds anything operative to the classification of certain physical systems as performing digital computation. This is stipulating that processing of information amounts to the production, modification and deletion of information.

A well-known non-semantic reading of information is based on Claude Shannon's concept of information (1948), but it is not clear what processing of Shannon Information amounts to. His theory dealt with information syntactically: whether and how much information is conveyed. Its basic idea is coding messages into a binary system at the bare minimum of bits we need to send to get our message across while abstracting from the physical media of communication. The amount of information conveyed is defined as the uncertainty (or entropy) associated with particular messages. The deletion and modification of information is only possible in the presence of noise. Noisy channels may displace information, but this is not the same as a deliberate deletion of information in computing systems, say to free up memory resources or reduce the size of a database. Although error detection and correction methods modify information to offset noise, symbolic expressions could be modified for many purposes other than error correction. The production of new information is more problematic, for the only source of new information, according to Shannon (1948: p. 12), is *uncertainty*.

Another possible non-semantic reading of information is based on *Algorithmic Information*, which was introduced by Ray Solomonoff and Andrei Kolmogorov. But even on this reading, it is not immediately clear what information processing amounts to in the context of concrete computation. The algorithmic information of a string X is defined as the length of the shortest program on a UTM that generates X as its output. Algorithmic information seems a more suitable candidate as the basis of an information processing characterisation of computation. For it is defined over algorithms, rather than over randomness of messages. Yet, the problem of processing algorithmic information remains, as it is invariant to the process of computation itself.

Importantly, as stated by Solomonoff, the actual value of Kolmogorov complexity of a string is incomputable, it can only be approximated (2009: pp. 6-7). This limitation prevents us from actually having a full description of all the possible optimal algorithms (that are also enumerable) to solve a specific problem (Calude 2009: p. 82, Calude et al, 2011). Still, a variation on algorithmic information theory, which is not based on UTMs but rather on Finite State Transducers, does allow us to compute the complexity of strings. This variation, however, comes at the cost of

---

[16] Instead, according to the Mechanistic account, information processing entails *generic* computation (the superclass of both digital computation and analogue computation) (Piccinini and Scarantino 2011: pp. 33-34). For information is a medium-independent concept. However, *digital* computation does not entail information processing, because although digits *could* carry information, they *need not* do so essentially.

Turing universality that does not apply to finite state transducers, since there is no universal transducer (Calude et al, 2011). Yet, algorithmic information theory will have a limited capacity to explain cases in which information is deleted and/or modified whilst the overall information complexity of the computing system does not decrease.

Other possible candidates for the *information processing* characterisation of computing systems alluded to by the FSM and PSS accounts are based on a semantic reading of information. Two main types of semantic information are *factual* information and *instructional* information. The former type is objective propositional information representing some facts or states of affairs, and arguably only qualifies as information if it is true (yet, this is a contentious claim). The latter type is not *about* facts or state of affairs, so it is not qualified alethically (Floridi 2009: pp. 35-36). Instructional information is conveyed either unconditionally (e.g., step 1: do this, step 2: do that) or conditionally (e.g., if X do this, otherwise do that). The subtleties of semantic information are not discussed further here for lack of space. However, since algorithms are finite sets of instructions, instructional information seems a plausible candidate as the basis of characterising digital computation as information processing.

Moreover, the Mechanistic account is grounded in *physical mechanisms* that perform computations, whereas both the FSM and PSS accounts are grounded in *symbolic* computation and *semantics*. Digits in the Mechanistic account are *not* symbols, but rather states of components (and are as physical as it gets). So, they have no representational character and their processing is independent of any (external) semantics. The second requirement of the FSM account, in contrast, emphasises that symbolic expressions are manipulated according to *formal* rules and must always be semantically interpretable even following numerous manipulations. The second requirement of the PSS account emphasises that symbols are manipulated in virtue of their semantics.

Incidentally, the semantics of symbols and their manipulation is a key difference between the PSS and FSM accounts. Although both accounts are based on the manipulation of symbols at the heart of the computational process, they diverge on how semantics enters this process. According to the FSM account's second requirement, symbols are formally manipulated *in virtue of* their syntax, but they are always semantically interpretable. It is a property of automatic formal systems that symbolic expressions continue to "make sense" when manipulated by truth-preserving rules. On this view, the formal manipulation of symbols based on their syntax is sufficient for the operation of the computing system. And the semantics of the manipulated symbolic expressions is epiphenomenal on their syntax.

However, the second requirement of the PSS account reveals that processes in computing systems are *causally* affected by the semantics of symbols. The behaviour of a process P (with X as its input) depends on a potentially distal entity Y, which is designated by X. The designation requirement is vague, for it leaves the ways in which a process depends on some entity unspecified. It might be the case that Newell and Simon took it for granted that symbols *symbolise* by definition and so they have not explicated where their external semantics comes from. If indeed *external* semantics is required for computation, then this gap is too big to be left unexplicated.

Internal access to symbols and expressions in a conventional digital computer is an assignment operation of, say, a symbol to some other internal entity and it is a primitive in its architecture (e.g., for memory retrieval). But there is no similar primitive for the external environment (Bickhard and Terveen 1995: pp. 93-94).

Additionally, the Mechanistic account emphasises the importance of synchronisation of processing digits belonging to the same string, whereas both the PSS and FSM accounts ignore temporal constraints of concrete computation. According to the second requirement of the Mechanistic account, with the growth in complexity of the computing system it becomes more crucial that digits belonging to the same string be processed in the same functionally relevant time interval. The other two accounts, while recognising the temporal aspects of concrete computation, do not explicitly mandate any temporal constraints on computing systems.

In sum, the above differences discussed as well as others clearly confirm that the extant accounts of concrete digital computation are not equivalent. The key motivation behind both the FSM and PSS accounts is advancing a substantive empirical hypothesis about how human cognition works, namely, that cognition is essentially a computational system of the specified sort. The Mechanistic account, on the other hand, has a different and less ambitious motivation. Rather than advancing an empirical hypothesis about cognition. Piccinini's goal in formulating his account is to provide a general characterisation of digital computing systems. He attempts to exclude as many paradigmatic cases of non-computing systems (such as planetary systems, digestive systems, mouse traps, etc.) as possible. At the same time, his account classifies many (but not too many) systems as performing digital computation. The FSM account is more restrictive and excludes any systems that are neither programmable nor program-controlled from the class of computing systems. The PSS account is even more restrictive, as it includes only UTMs (and physical approximations thereof) as genuinely computational.[17] Regardless of the (doubtful) representational character of computation presumed by the FSM and PSS accounts, they are simply too restrictive as accounts of concrete computation proper.

6   Conclusion

There is no question whether mathematical formalisms of computability are adequate analyses of *abstract* computation, but they are of the wrong kind to explain *concrete* computation. Any particular formalism does not specify the relationship between abstract and concrete computation. It is at the physical level that the algorithm (or more precisely, program) is specified and constrained by the implementing physical medium. So, stipulating that any complete account of a physical phenomenon must *also* consider its physical implementation, an explicit account of concrete computation has to be specified for a complete account of concrete computing systems.

---

[17] PSS yields a very restrictive class of computing systems that makes sense when considering cognitive systems. Since cognition exhibits substantial flexibility, it is unreasonable to assume that it is an instance of, say, a special purpose TM.

My main argument was that well-known accounts of concrete computation entail sufficiently distinct requirements for a physical system to compute, justifying the demand that one commits to a particular account when employing the notion of concrete computation. But despite the apparent straightforwardness of this argument, all too often its implied moral is surprisingly ignored by philosophers and cognitive scientists alike. The notions of computation *simpliciter* and digital computation, in particular, are employed without much awareness of what they mean exactly. At times, extant accounts are even used interchangeably as though they were equivalent (when they are not even extensionally equivalent). If we take cognition to be a physical phenomenon that can be explained computationally, we should state explicitly what we mean by (digital) computation. Otherwise, a computational thesis of cognition remains unintelligible.

Acknowledgments. Thanks are due to Eli Dresner, Gualtiero Piccinini and Frances Egan for providing helpful comments on a recent draft of this paper. I would also like to thank two anonymous referees for the Solomonoff 85th memorial conference for useful comments. I am grateful to Phillip Staines for detailed comments on various drafts of this paper. All these comments contributed to this final version, which, I trust, is much improved.

References

1. Bickhard, M.H., Terveen, L.: Foundational issues in artificial intelligence and cognitive science: Impasse and solution. Elsevier Scientific, Amsterdam (1995)
2. Calude, C.S.: Information: The algorithmic paradigm. In: Sommaruga, G. (ed.) Formal Theories of Information. LNCS, vol. 5363, pp. 79–94. Springer, Heidelberg (2009)
3. Calude, C.S., Salomaa, K., Roblot, T.K.: Finite state complexity. Theoretical Computer Science 412(41), 5668–5677 (2011), doi:10.1016/j.tcs.2011.06.021
4. Chalmers, D.: On implementing a computation. Minds and Machines 4, 391–402 (1994)
5. Chalmers, D.J.: A computational foundation for the study of cognition. Journal of Cognitive Science 12(4), 323–357 (2011)
6. Copeland, B.J.: What is computation? Synthese 108, 335–359 (1996)
7. Floridi, L.: Philosophical conceptions of information. In: Sommaruga, G. (ed.) Formal Theories of Information. LNCS, vol. 5363, pp. 13–53. Springer, Heidelberg (2009)
8. Fodor, J.A.: The language of thought. Harvard University Press, Cambridge (1975)
9. Fodor, J.A.: Methodological solipsism considered as a research strategy in cognitive science. Behavioral and Brain Sciences 3, 63–73 (1980)
10. Fodor, J.A., Pylyshyn, Z.W.: Connectionism and cognitive architecture: a critical analysis. Cognition 28, 3–71 (1988)
11. Fresco, N.: Explaining computation without semantics: keeping it simple. Minds and Machines 20, 165–181 (2010)
12. Fresco, N.: Concrete Digital Computation: What Does it Take for a Physical System to Compute? Journal of Logic, Language and Information 20(4), 513–537 (2011), doi:10.1007/s10849-011-9147-8
13. Gandy, R.: Church's thesis and principles for mechanisms. In: Barwise, J., Keisler, H.J., Kunen, K. (eds.) The Kleene Symposium, pp. 123–148. North-Holland, Amsterdam (1980)

14. Haugeland, J.: AI: the very idea. The MIT Press, Cambridge (1985)
15. Israel, D.: Reflections on Gödel's and Gandy's reflections on Turing's thesis. Minds and Machines 12, 181–201 (2002)
16. Kleene, S.C.: Mathematical logic. Dover, New York (2002)
17. Marr, D.: Vision: a computational investigation into the human representation and processing visual information. Freeman & Company, New York (1982)
18. Newell, A., Simon, H.A.: Human problem solving. Prentice-Hall, Englewood (1972)
19. Newell, A., Simon, H.A.: Computer science as an empirical enquiry: symbols and search. Communications of the ACM 19, 113–126 (1976)
20. Newell, A.: Physical symbol systems. Cognitive Science 4, 135–183 (1980)
21. Piccinini, G.: Computational explanation in neuroscience. Synthese 153, 343–353 (2006)
22. Piccinini, G.: Computing mechanisms. Philosophy of Science 74, 501–526 (2007)
23. Piccinini, G.: Computation without representation. Philosophical Studies 137, 205–241 (2008a)
24. Piccinini, G.: Computers. Pacific Philosophical Quarterly 89, 32–73 (2008b)
25. Piccinini, G., Scarantino, A.: Information processing, computation, and cognition. Journal of Biological Physics 37, 1–38 (2011)
26. Pylyshyn, Z.W.: Computation and cognition. The MIT Press, Cambridge (1984)
27. Pylyshyn, Z.W.: Computing in cognitive science. In: Posner, M.I. (ed.) Foundations of Cognitive Science, pp. 51–91. The MIT Press, Cambridge (1989)
28. Pylyshyn, Z.W.: Things and places: how the mind connects with the world (Jean Nicod Lectures). The MIT Press, Cambridge (2007)
29. Scheutz, M.: When physical systems realize functions. Minds and Machines 9, 161–196 (1999)
30. Scheutz, M.: Computationalism – the next generation. In: Scheutz, M. (ed.) Computationalism: New Directions, pp. 1–22. The MIT Press, Cambridge (2002)
31. Shagrir, O.: What is computer science about? The Monist 82, 131–149 (1999)
32. Shagrir, O.: Why we view the brain as a computer. Synthese 153, 393–416 (2006)
33. Shannon, C.E.: A mathematical theory of communication. Mobile Computing and Communications Review 5, 1–55 (1948)
34. Smith, B.C.: The foundations of computing. In: Scheutz, M. (ed.) Computationalism: New Directions, pp. 23–58. The MIT Press, Cambridge (2002)
35. Smith, B.C.: Age of significance: Introduction (2010), http://www.ageofsignificance.org (retrieved May 3, 2010)
36. Solomonoff, R.J.: Algorithmic probability - theory and applications. In: Emmert-Streib, F., Dehmer, M. (eds.) Information Theory and Statistical Learning, pp. 1–23. Springer Science+Business Media, NY (2009)
37. Thelen, E., Smith, L.B.: A dynamical systems approach to the development of cognition and action. The MIT press, Cambridge (1994)
38. van Gelder, T., Port, R.F.: It's about time: an overview of the dynamical approach to cognition. In: van Gelder, T., Port, R.F. (eds.) Mind as Motion. The MIT Press, Cambridge (1995)
39. van Rooij, I.: The tractable cognition thesis. Cognitive Science 32, 939–984 (2008)

Further Reflections on the Timescale of AI

J. Storrs Hall

Institute for Molecular Manufacturing, Palo Alto, CA 94301 USA

Abstract. Solomonoff [9] explored the possibilities of the future course of AI development, including social effects of the development of intelligent machines which can be produced with exponentially decreasing costs. He introduced arguably the first formal mathematical model of what has since come to be known as the technological Singularity. Since that time a veritable plethora of such models has appeared [8]. We examine the milestones and model in light of 25 years more experience, and offer a revised version.

Milestones for AI

Ray Solomonoff, in [9], proposes a list of milestones for a discussion of the further course of AI. Briefly, they are:

A. Dartmouth, 1956: AI began as a distinct enterprise. This is the only milestone which was considered to have been accomplished at the time of the paper.
B. A general theory of problem solving is achieved: it would cover such capabilities associated with intelligence as learning, concept formation, and knowledge representation.
C. A self-improving machine (or program) is created.
D. Computers are able to learn by reading existing natural language text.
E. An AI has a problem solving capacity equivalent to a human.
F. An AI has a problem solving capacity near that of computer science community.
G. An AI has a problem solving capacity many times that of CS community.

In the intervening 25 years, much has happened, but milestone A is still the only one which has actually occured. However, at least something has been learned, so we can say more about the milestones as they might happen in the future.

Milestone B, a general theory, was presumably to be the sort of crowning formalization to AI that the science of thermodynamics was to the engineering of steam engines. In some sense, Solomonoff's own work and the succeeding efforts by such researchers as Levin and Hutter remain the best attempts we have in that direction. Furthermore, there is a substantial subfield of machine learning theory, and outside of AI there has grown up a substantial field of optimal control theory and estimation. We might well look for the ultimate origins of an AI theory in the unification of these fields.

Even so, it should be remembered that engineers had been building steam engines for a century before Carnot conceived the basic principles of thermodynamics. What current best theories of AI lack is the ability to analyze a given

D.L. Dowe (Ed.): Solomonoff Festschrift, LNAI 7070, pp. 174–183, 2013.

learning or problem-solving design and predict its performance, the way we can analyze any given steam engine using thermodynamics. Historical precedent tells us that we will probably have working AIs, built heuristically and improved by experimentation, before we have a proper theory. Thus we should expect Milestone B to be one of the later, rather than one of the earlier, ones to occur.

It is not clear that Milestones C and D are distinct, especially as AI has developed since 1985. Consider how a human learns: the vast majority (for many people, the entirety) of what we learn is not original discoveries but the takeup of culturally accumulated knowledge from peers, parents, teachers, and books. A completely competent AI might operate exactly the same way; it would not be a Newton or an Einstein (nor indeed a Solomonoff!), but it would be human-level as measured against the average representative of *homo sapiens.*

This is not to say that such a machine would not need endogenous learning capability. It is clear that human learning is not simply storing symbolic representations, but the construction of mental programs for prediction and control. Contrast, for example, the verbal instruction with the internal control-system formation attendant on learning to ride a bicycle. Solomonoff writes:

> ... many of the more interesting human activities are mainly performed by the unconscious mind. If the unconscious mind works very much like the conscious mind (but we are merely less aware of its workings), then there is no difficulty here. However, if as is widely suspected, the unconscious mind is significantly different from the conscious, then the present expansion of expert systems will have serious limitations.

And so it proved. Today's more competent AI and robotic systems have, in addition to the logical superstructure of the 80s' expert systems, a substantial semantics of their domains of expertise comprised of predictive simulation codes, control systems, statistical models derived from vast corpuses of relevant data, and so forth. An AI that learned from reading (or other symbolic instruction) would presumably use the symbolic input to form a scaffolding that would greatly accelerate, but not eliminate, the subsequent (perhaps search-based) program-construction effort.

Thus at least one reasonable view of the ultimate shape of learning machines implies that milestones C and D are complementary, rather than separable, achievements.

If the capabilities of a C-D AI are integrated into an appropriate cognitive architecture, one would be fairly close to milestone E, human equivalence. Solomonoff [10] discusses the qualities desirable in a human-equivalent (or better) machine:

> I would like it to give a better understanding of the relation of quantum mechanics to general relativity. I would like it to discover cures for cancer and AIDS. I would like it to find some very good high temperature superconductors. I would not be disappointed if it were unable to pass itself off as a rock star.

It seems reasonable to imagine that if such a machine had a human brain's equivalent of processing power, it might make discoveries at the rate of a human. (We discuss this in more detail below.) If so, milestones E, F, and G are primarily a function of available processing power. When we have a working version of a human-equivalent AI, we can readily duplicate it into one or more research communities, corporations, or similar enterprises. It might or might not be possible to integrate minds, enhance communication, or the like, by redesigning various mental processes and/or applying more processing power or memory to a given individual AI than the human brain affords. However, for the sake of this (or Solomonoff's original) argument, that would be merely an optimization and not necessary to the main point.

Singularity

[9] contains arguably the first formal model of an increase in processing power leading to a mathematical singularity of intellectual capacity.[1] This predicted an asymptotic rise at a date that depended on various model parameters, and very likely was influential in the adoption of the name "Singularity" for the concept.

The intuition for such a hyperbolic growth curve is straightforward. Suppose that technological progress can be parceled into a series of fixed-size problems, the solution of each of which can be done with some fixed number x of machine operations. Current progress, with roughly a fixed number of human minds (and thus a linear rate of problems solved), appears capable of inducing an exponential improvement rate in computing hardware (measured in operations per dollar). The rate is usually measured in time, but in the model, could just as well be measured in (the linearly related) total number of problems solved.

Once we can obtain, for an affordable outlay, problem-solving capability in AI form of a size comparable to the current technical community, the dynamic changes. If we double the brains available, we halve the time to solve the next problem in our list. Since we're measuring computational improvement in problems solved, the next generation of computers is available in half the time, and (again for a fixed cost) we can redouble our problem-solving ability. Thus the next set of problems is solved in one quarter the original time, and the next in one eighth, and so forth, providing us the solution of an infinite series of problems in a finite time.

As Solomonoff hastens to point out,

> Usually, when infinities like this one occur in science, they indicate a breakdown of the validity of the equations as we approach the infinity point.

He proceeds to speculate that the breakdown in this case would be the end of the Moore's Law computational improvement. In practice, it could be any of a vast number of things. Computational speedup is only one of the many

---

[1] Von Neumann and Good had earlier advanced informal models, and Asimov predicted "an Intellectual Revolution" by analogy to the Industrial Revolution.

feedback loops in the improvement of technology as a whole. Most of these have to go through various physical processes (starting with building the capital equipment which fabricates microchips, but including such mundane necessities as the transportation of raw materials and finished machines). Any one of these would form a bottleneck if the rest were significantly accelerated.

There is a second, perhaps more subtle problem with a hyperbolic model. As the problem-solving intervals decrease exponentially in duration, causing an asymptotic increase in problems solved, they also cause an asymptotic increase in the fixed-per-interval expenditure for machinery. In other words, the model consumes an infinite amount of physical resources in finite time, as well.

We can form a more realistic model of the self-improvement process by considering a sector where Moore's Law is strongly active already, namely the semiconductor industry.

Moore's Law

Consider the (US) semiconductor industry over the past 15 or so years, where a measurable Moore's Law has been operating. Notably, in this period, design automation has contributed enormously to the ability of mere human beings to design the staggeringly complex microprocessors and other components that make up current-day computers. This ranges from architecture to electronic phenomena to geometric design of chip masks to allow for refraction effects of the UV light used to expose the chips under construction.

Thus feedback from increasing processing power and software sophistication in semiconductor manufacture is an excellent proxy for the kind of increased smarts to be expected in an AI takeoff, and in a sector with nicely measurable results. Furthermore, for the past 15 years, the industry (in the US[2]) has been remarkably stable: it can be considered statistically to have a constant annual output value of $75 billion, spending $15 billion on raw material, $8.25 billion on capital equipment, and $12.75 billion on research and development.[3] The number of production workers has been more or less even over the period at about 85 thousand, but the number of non-production workers has shrunk from 93 thousand in 1997 to 62 thousand in 2007.

Meanwhile the performance of the product has been increasing at a faster-than-exponential rate:

The equation for the quadratic fit is $f(t) = 0.000723t^2 - 2.69t + 2496$, i.e. ops/sec/$1000 is predicted to be $Q(t) = 10^{f(t)}$ for t the year number.[4] This is

---

[2] The semiconductor industry in other regions, notably Asia/Pacific, has expanded considerably over the period.

[3] US Bureau of the Census, Economic census numbers for semiconductor manufacturing sector (NIACS code 334413), economic census for 1992, 1997, 2002, and 2007. *cf.* http://factfinder.census.gov/home/saff/main.html?_lang=en. After correcting for correlation with the overall US economy, a null hypothesis of the steady state given cannot be rejected at a 95% confidence level.

[4] Figures before 2000 from Kurzweil 2005, figures from 2004 and 2011 from machines constructed by the author.

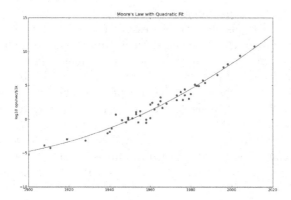

Fig. 1. Moore's Law with a quadratic growth-rate fit, from Kurzweil's and the author's data

the form of the integral of the product of a linear term and an exponential, which suggests a model with a linear network effect as well as capital re-investment.

Given that the raw material input to the industry is essentially constant and the dollar value is constant, $Q(t)$ can be taken to represent the intelligence with which the atoms of raw materials are rearranged into products; a relatively pure measure of innovation. Thus the semiconductor industry as a whole manages a $Q(t)$ improvement from a fixed 28% reinvestment rate.

According to the curve, cost of computation has dropped by a factor of 152,000 since 1985. The net present value of a human engineer of the sort participating in the semiconductor industry is about $1 million. The amount of computation necessary to host an AI at a human level, given reasonably optimal algorithms, can be estimated at (very roughly) 100 teraops, or 1e14 ops/sec. On the curve, this will be available for $1 million in 2013, and for $1000 in 2026.

A Series of Growth Modes

Hanson [3] analyzes the economic history of the human race as a series of distinct changes in the growth rate. At least two major accelerations can be identified. The growth rate for humanity's gross output jumped by about a factor of 250 with agriculture, and by a factor of 60 with the Industrial Revolution.

The fact that the Moore's Law growth rate is changing lends credence to a proposition that it might be in the process of shifting from one mode to another.

Hanson speculates that the next jump in the series, assuming the pattern holds, might well occur within the coming century: the industrial economy has seen roughly as many doubling times as the agrarian period did.

We find the analysis of historical growth as a series of growth modes with intervening phase changes to be compelling, but the endogenous model in which phase changes are precipitated simply by the number of doubling times from a previous one to be little short of numerology. We will advance an alternative theory below.

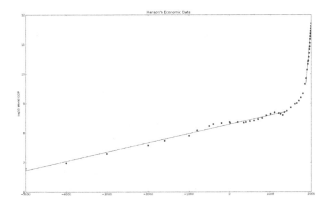

Fig. 2. Hanson's data for agrarian and industrial growth modes, with the Renaissance / Industrial Revolution knee between

What Technology Wants

Von Neumann [6] hypothesized what he called the "complexity barrier:"

> There is thus this completely decisive property of complexity, that there exists a critical size below which the process of synthesis is degererative, but above which the phenomenon of synthesis, if properly arranged, can become explosive, in other words, where syntheses of automata can proceed in such a manner that each automaton will produce other automata which are more complex and of higher potentialities than itself.

Three recent studies of the phenomenon of technological progress in human communities [5,4,7], give credence to von Neumann's concept of the complexity barrier. Technological progress in human societies depends on the complexity – size and network effects – of the economic and intellectual community within which economic and intellectual intercourse are possible. Isolated societies, even though composed of people just as industrious and intelligent as the larger ones, tend to regress and lose technologies instead of progressing and inventing new ones. Aboriginal Tasmania is a classic example of this phenomenon. There seems to be some point of complexity above which a society is self-improving, and below which it is not.

We hypothesize that the complexity barrier is closer to milestone F (CS community) than to E (single human) – and possibly past it.

Kelly's work in particular is strongly based on the notion that at any particular state of knowledge, there is a certain set of inventions available to be discovered as the next step. Thus in some sense, technological creativity is analogous to explorers in a landscape following valleys and mountain passes; the directions they take are determined by the landscape rather than their internal compasses. Visionary geniuses who are ahead of their time – da Vinci, Babbage, and Drexler spring to mind – find their ideas impossible to implement. Ideas on the frontier of the technium, to use Kelly's term for the corpus of technical knowledge at a given time, tends to be independently and simultaneously reinvented. Substantial empirical evidence is given for this position.

An Exogenous Model of Technological Growth

On this view, Hanson's model of growth-rate phase changes can be reinterpreted. Instead of some internal dynamic in the technium producing a phase change after some number of doubling times, the roughly regular progression of phase shifts can be better explained as a result of the terrain in the idea-space through which the technium is expanding. A fractal distribution of "fertile valleys" – of volumes of idea-space affording rapid growth and high productivity – would account for the overall shape of the series of growth phase changes. The timing and other parameters, however, would depend on particulars of the terrain and could not be predicted in detail from the preceding series. Valleys would occur at random with a frequency inversely proportional to their sizes.

On this view, the technium is an expanding volume in an idea space of high dimensionality. When it contacts a valley, expansion into the valley proceeds at a higher-than-normal rate, producing the super-exponential growth characteristic of a phase shift. Once the valley is saturated, growth reverts to the simple exponential but at a higher rate due to the increased size and dimensionality of the frontier.

For example, a very early technium consisting of fire, clothing, crude shelter, and chipped flint tools – the "Mousterian toolkit" – vastly expanded the inventory of geographical locations in which humans could live. This afforded a higher population growth rate than a steady-state existence in clement climes. In this case the entropy increase in the accessible space was very literally determined by the actual physical terrain.

While it is perilous to generalize, it is possible to discern a pattern to the phase changes, which we hope tells us something about the typical forms of the terrain. Arguably, each phase change in physical capability is accompanied by (and somewhat preceded by) a corresponding increase in informational capability:

Informational development	physical development
Manual dexterity	Mousterian toolkit
Language	Agriculture
Writing	Civilization
Printing press, science	Industrial Revolution
Internet, AI	?

One striking aspect of the list is that each stage involved mastery of some self-replicating phenomenon: fire, crops, ideas, machine tools, and, we presume, ultimately programs.

It is difficult to attribute growth rates to many of these phenomena, but the penultimate pair has a compelling symmetry: with the introduction of the printing press and the acceptance of the scientific method, scientific publication shifted from a growth mode esentially the same as the existing overall economic one of about 0.1% to about 5%. Within a few centuries – very quickly on the timescales under discussion – physical economic output shifted into a 5% growth-rate mode.

The speculation that suggests itself is that the core of an idea-space valley affording a given growth mode is surrounded by a halo, which the frontier of the technium reaches first, of techniques by which information can be handled in the growth mode. The obvious inference is that current Moore's Law information technology growth will be completed by a revolution in physical capability that brings the rest of the economy up to a Moore's Law-like growth rate. We cannot say where this will stabilize; our $Q(t)$ fit indicates a growth rate of 100%, doubling time one year, around 2069.

A (Very Vague) Prognostication

Here is a revised list of milestones, with speculation on when they might occur:

1. Solomonoff's C and D, a program able to learn from the corpus of human-readable information, might well happen in the coming decade, although it would not be too surprising if it happened in the 2020s instead.
2. Convincing evidence of the economic productivity of 1. causes capital to flow into AI in a manner similar to the build-up of the internet in the 1990s.
3. Within a decade, programs have been constructed and educated to the point of being productive scientists, engineers, doctors, lawyers, accountants, etc. Investment in these is in proportion for the demand for them in the overall economy.
4. A Moore's Law-like trend in physical manufacturing, already visible today in technologies like rapid prototyping, produces by 2030 or so a capability for Moore's Law-like growth rates in physical capital formation.
5. AI inventors and designers are necessary – and sufficient – to find something useful to do with the capacity in 4.
6. The confluence of design and manufacturing capability in 5., and neither factor by itself, will make it possible for the economy as a whole to move into a 70% to 100% annual growth mode.

The key to natural language understanding has been known since Winograd's work [11] in the 1970s. With a deep semantic model – programs able to simulate, predict, and perform what is being talked about – just about any parsing method will work, albeit some more efficiently than others. The "road not taken" in AI was to combine this insight with machine learning and automatic programming into a system which could use linguistic context to formulate learning problems at the frontier of its knowledge, e.g. picking up the meaning of new words from context, that were small enough to be tractable to the machine learning and automatic programming techniques.

Since that time, machine learning has acquired a substantial theoretical basis and an arsenal of powerful methods. Automatic programming has received less attention but computing power is now such that relatively primitive approaches such as genetic programming have achieved substantive results, e.g. patentable designs.

Meanwhile, interest in inferring information from text has burgeoned, along with the amount of text available on the Internet. The rapidly increasing amount of video available means that the primary human venue for learning new words – examples of their use in reference to objects and phenomena than can be independently seen and heard – is now a viable pathway to language acquisition. Progress in the field is such that an estimate of success within a decade is mildly optimistic but not outrageously so.

The single most important determiner of the economic growth rate is the productivity of capital: how long it takes a given unit of capital to produce an equivalent unit of product. Currently this is about 15 years, for a growth rate of 5%.

Moore's original observation had to do with shrinking transistors, making them not only more numerous and cheaper but faster as well. The same phenomenon holds for physical devices: physical production machinery with parts the size of current VLSI transistors (22 nm) could operate at megahertz mechanical frequencies [1], making them thousands of times faster than current machines at capital-replication tasks.

To sum up: the "Singularity" can best be thought of as the second half of the information technology revolution, extending it to most physical and intellectual work. Overall economic growth rates will shift from their current levels of roughly 5% to Moore's Law-like rates of 70% to 100%. The shift will probably take on the order of a decade (paralleling the growth of the internet), and probably fall somewhere in the 30s or 40s.

Reflections on Social Effects

If we built a system of 1000 AIs, all running 1000 times faster than biological humans and connected by appropriate communications networks, it would be difficult to avoid the impression that a hyperhuman intellect had been created. But it wouldn't, in principle, be able to understand anything that those humans couldn't have understood given enough centuries. In some sense, the point is moot: No individual can understand all that the scientific community knows, in any event. What happens in the future will become more and more fantastic, and understandable only in broad, vague generalities by current-day humans, whether done by AIs or flesh-and-blood humans. With AIs it may happen faster, but it will follow the same track. Given a graph of knowledge and capabilities as they would have increased in a purely human future, the one with AIs is the same, following the same valleys in idea space, but with the dates moved up.

The scientific community in some sense isn't composed of people, but of ideas. Human brains are a substrate, and AIs can be, if we are reasonably careful how we build them, a similar substrate. This is particularly obvious in the case of AIs which learn primarily from uptake of the cultural corpus. AIs will be composed entirely of human ideas, and everything they ever think of will be traceable back to us in direct line of memetic descent.

There is one proviso: a future in which we understand AI could well be different from one in which we don't understand it [2]. It seems possible that the knowledge of how to build a formal, mechanical system that nevertheless exhibits learning, adaptability, and common sense, could revolutionize the effectiveness of our corporate and political structures — whether we built physical robots or not.

We can only end by agreeing with Solomonoff's closing sentiment:

> What seems most certain is that the future of man – both scientfiic and social – will be far more exciting than the wildest eras of the past.

References

1. Drexler, K.E.: Nanosystems: Molecular Machinery, Manufacturing, and Computation. Wiley Interscience, New York (1992)
2. Hall, J.S.: Beyond AI: Creating the Conscience of the Machine. Prometheus, Amherst (2007)
3. Hanson, R.: Long-term growth as a sequence of exponential modes. Tech. rep., George Mason University (2000), http://hanson.gmu.edu/longgrow.pdf
4. Johnson, S.: Where Ideas Come From. Penguin/Riverhead, New York (2010)
5. Kelly, K.: What Technology Wants. Viking, New York (2010)
6. von Neumann, J.: Theory of Self-Reproducing Automata. University of Michigan (1966)
7. Ridley, M.: The Rational Optimist. Harper, New York (2010)
8. Sandberg, A.: An overview of models of technological singularity. In: AGI10 workshop on Roadmaps to AGI and the Future of AGI (2010)
9. Solomonoff, R.J.: The time scale of artificial intelligence: Reflections on social effects. Human Systems Management 5, 149–153 (1985)
10. Solomonoff, R.J.: Machine learning - past and future. In: AI@50, The Dartmouth Artificial Intelligence Conference (2006)
11. Winograd, T.: Understanding Natural Language. Academic Press (1972)

Towards Discovering the Intrinsic Cardinality and Dimensionality of Time Series Using MDL

Bing Hu[1], Thanawin Rakthanmanon[1], Yuan Hao[1], Scott Evans[2],
Stefano Lonardi[1], and Eamonn Keogh[1]

[1] Department of Computer Science & Engineering, University of California,
Riverside, CA 92502, USA
[2] GE Global Research
{bhu002,rakthant,yhao002}@ucr.edu, evans@ge.com,
{stelo,eamonn}@cs.ucr.edu

Abstract. Most algorithms for mining or indexing time series data do not operate directly on the original data, but instead they consider alternative representations that include transforms, quantization, approximation, and multi-resolution abstractions. Choosing the best representation and abstraction level for a given task/dataset is arguably the most critical step in time series data mining. In this paper, we investigate techniques that discover the natural *intrinsic* representation model, dimensionality and alphabet cardinality of a time series. The ability to discover these intrinsic features has implications beyond selecting the best parameters for particular algorithms, as characterizing data in such a manner is useful in its own right and an important sub-routine in algorithms for classification, clustering and outlier discovery. We will frame the discovery of these intrinsic features in the Minimal Description Length (MDL) framework. Extensive empirical tests show that our method is simpler, more general and significantly more accurate than previous methods, and has the important advantage of being essentially parameter-free.

Keywords: Time Series, MDL, Dimensionality Reduction.

1 Introduction

Most algorithms for indexing or mining time series data operate on higher-level representations of the data, which include transforms, quantization, approximations and multi-resolution approaches. For instance, Discrete Fourier Transform (DFT), Discrete Wavelet Transform (DWT), Adaptive Piecewise Constant Approximation (APCA) and Piecewise Linear Approximation (PLA) are models that all have their advocates for various data mining tasks and each has been used extensively [3]. However the question of choosing the best abstraction level and/or representation of the data for a given task/dataset still remains open. In this work, we investigate this problem by discovering the natural intrinsic model, dimensionality and (alphabet) cardinality of a time series. We will frame the discovery of these intrinsic features in the Minimal Description Length (MDL) framework [11] [21] [28]. MDL is the

D.L. Dowe (Ed.): Solomonoff Festschrift, LNAI 7070, pp. 184–197, 2013.
© Springer-Verlag Berlin Heidelberg 2013

cornerstone of many bioinformatics algorithms [7][20], but it is arguably underutilized in data mining [9].

The ability to discover the intrinsic dimensionality and cardinality of time series has implications beyond setting the best parameters for data mining algorithms, as characterizing data in such a manner is useful in its own right to understand/describe the data and an important sub-routine in algorithms for classification, clustering and outlier discovery. To illustrate this, consider the three unrelated datasets in **Fig.1**.

Fig. 1. Three unrelated industrial time series with low intrinsic cardinality. I) Evaporator (channel one). II) Winding (channel five). III) Dryer (channel one).

The number of unique values in each time series is, from left to right, 14, 500 and 62. However, we might reasonably claim, that the *intrinsic* alphabet cardinality is instead 2, 2, and 12 respectively. As it happens, an understanding of the processes that produced these data would perhaps support this claim [10]. In these datasets, and indeed in many real-world datasets, there is a big difference between the *actual* and *intrinsic* cardinality. Similar remarks apply to dimensionality.

Before we define more precisely what we mean by *actual* versus *intrinsic* cardinality, we should elaborate on the motivations behind our considerations. Our objective is generally not simply to save memory: if we are wastefully using eight bytes per time point instead of using the mere three bytes made necessary by the intrinsic cardinality, the memory space saved is significant, but memory is getting cheaper every day, which is rarely a bottleneck in data mining tasks. There are instead many other reasons why we may wish to find the true intrinsic model, cardinality and dimensionality of the data:

- There is an increasing interest in using specialized hardware for data mining [24]. However, the complexity of implementing data mining algorithms in hardware typically grows super linearly with the cardinality of the alphabet. For example, FPGAs usually cannot handle cardinalities greater than 256[24].
- Some data mining algorithms benefit from having the data represented in the lowest *meaningful* cardinality. As a trivial example, in the stream: ..0, 0, 1, 0, 0, 1, 0, 0, 1, we can easily find the rule that a '1' follows two appearances of '0'. However, notice that this rule is *not* apparent in this string: ..0, 0, 1.0001, 0.0001, 0, 1, 0.000001, 0, 1 even though it is essentially the same time series.
- Most time series indexing algorithms critically depend on the ability to reduce the dimensionality [3]or the cardinality [16]of the time series (or both[1][2]) and searching over the compacted representation in main memory. However, setting the best level of representation remains a black art.
- In resource-limited devices, it may be helpful to remove the spurious precision induced by a cardinality/dimensionally that is too high (see example below).
- Knowing the intrinsic model, cardinality and dimensionality of a dataset allows us to create very simple outlier detection models. We simply look for data where

the parameters discovered in new data differ from our expectations learned on training data. This is a simple idea, but as we show, it can be very effective.

To enhance our appreciation of the potential utility of knowing the intrinsic cardinality and dimensionality of the data, we briefly consider an application in classification. Suppose we wish to build a time series classifier into a device with a limited memory footprint such as a cell phone, pacemaker, or autonomous robotic drone. Let us suppose we have only 20kB available for the classifier, and that (as is the case with the benchmark dataset, *TwoPat*) each time series exemplar has a dimensionality of 128 and takes 4 bytes per value [10].

One could choose decision trees or Bayesian classifiers because they are space efficient, however it is well known that nearest neighbor classifiers are *very* difficult to beat for time series problems [3]. If we had simply stored forty random samples in the memory for our nearest neighbor classifier, the average error rate over fifty runs would be a respectable 58.7% for a four-class problem. However, we could also down-sample the *dimensionality* by a factor of two, either by skipping every second point, or by averaging pairs of points (as in SAX [16]) and place eighty reduced quality samples in memory. Or perhaps we could instead reduce the *alphabet cardinality*, by reducing the precision of the original four bytes to just one byte, thus allowing 160 reduced-fidelity objects to be placed in memory. Many other combinations of dimensionality and cardinality reduction could be tested, which would trade reduced fidelity to the original data for more exemplars stored in memory. In this case, a dimensionality of 32 and a cardinality of 6 allow us to place 852 objects in memory and achieve an error rate of about 90.75%, a remarkable accuracy improvement given the limited resources.

In general, testing all the combinations of parameters is computationally infeasible. Furthermore, while in this case we have class labels to guide us through the search of parameter space, this would not be the case for other unsupervised data mining algorithms, such as clustering, motif discovery [15], outlier discovery etc.

As we shall show, our MDL framework allows us to automatically discover the parameters that reflect the intrinsic model/cardinality/dimensionally of the data without requiring external information or expensive cross validation search.

2   Definitions and Notation

We begin with the definition of a time series:

Definition 1: A *time series* T is an ordered list of numbers. $T=t_1,t_2,....,t_m$. Each value t_i is a finite precision number and m is the length of time series T.

Before continuing we must justify the decision of (slightly) quantizing the time series. MDL is only defined for discrete values[1], but most time series are real-valued.

---

[1] The closely related technique of MML (see Minimum Message Length footnote 61 footnotes 137-138 in 4, footnote 88 and sec. 6.5 in 5 and 26) *does* allow for continuous real-valued data. However, here we stick the more familiar MDL formulation.

The obvious solution is to reduce the original number of possible values to a manageable amount. However the reader may object that such a drastic reduction in precision must surely lose some significant information. However this is *not* the case. To illustrate this point, we performed a simple experiment. From each of the twenty diverse datasets in the UCR archive [10] we randomly extracted one hundred pairs of time series. For each pair of time series we measured their Euclidean distance in the original high dimensional space, and then in the quantized 256-cardinality space, and used these pair of distances to plot a point in a scatter plot.

Fig.2 shows the results. The figure illustrates that all the points fall close to the diagonal, thus the quantization makes no *perceptible* difference. Beyond this subjective visual test, we also reproduced the heavily cited UCR time series classification benchmark experiments [10], replacing the original data with the 256-cardinality version. In no case did it make more than one tenth of one percent difference to classification accuracy. Given this, we simply reduce all the time series data to its 256 cardinality version in this work, by using a *discretization* function :

Definition 2: *Discretization* is a function that is used to normalize a real-valued time series T into b-bit discrete values in the range $[-2^{b-1}, 2^{b-1}-1]$. It is defined as following:

$$Discretization_b(T) = round\left(\frac{T - min}{max - min}\right) * (2^b - 1) - 2^{b-1}$$

where *min* and *max* are the minimum and maximum value in T, respectively

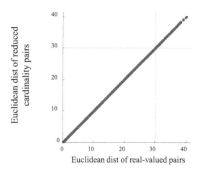

Fig. 2. Each point on this plot corresponds to a pair of time series: the x-axis corresponds to their Euclidean distance, while the y-axis corresponds to the Euclidean distance between the 8-bit quantized representations of the same pair

For any time series T, we are interested in determining how many bits it takes to represent it. We can thus define the description length of a time series. Note that in our experiments all real values are discretized to 8-bit discrete values.

Definition 3: A *description length DL* of a time series T is the total number of bits required to represent it. When Huffman coding is used to compress the time series T, the description length of time series T is defined by:

$$DL(T) = |HuffmanCoding(T)|$$

In the current literature, the number of bits required to store the time series depends on the idiosyncrasies of the data format or hardware device, not on any intrinsic properties of the data or domain. However we are really interested in knowing the minimum number of bits to exactly represent the data, the *intrinsic* amount of information in the time series. Unfortunately, in the general case this is not calculable, as it is the Kolmogorov complexity of the time series [14]. However, we can approximate the Kolmogorov complexity by compressing the data, using say Huffman coding[28][29]. The (lossless) compressed file size is clearly an upper bound to the *DL* of the time series [30].

One of the key steps in finding the intrinsic cardinality and/or dimensionality is converting a given time series to other representation or model, e.g., by using DFT or DWT. We call that representation, a *hypothesis*:

Definition 4: A *hypothesis* H is a representation of a discrete time series T after applying a transformation M.

In general, there are many possible transforms. Examples include the Discrete Wavelet Transform (DWT), the Discrete Fourier transform (DFT), the Adaptive Piecewise Linear Approximation (APCA), the Piecewise Linear Approximation (PLA), etc[3]. **Fig.3.** show three illustrative examples, DFT, APCA, and PLA. In this paper, we demonstrate our ideas using one these commonly used representations (relegating the other two to our expanded technical report [31]). However our ideas apply to all time series models (see [3]for a survey of representations).We use the term *model* interchangeably with the term *hypothesis* in this work.

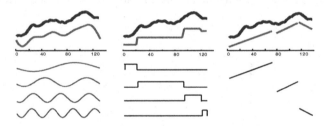

Fig. 3. *"Consider a very long sequence of symbols ...We shall consider such a sequence of symbols to be simple if there exists a very brief description of this sequence - using, some sort of **stipulated description method**".* Ray Solomonoff [25]. A time series T shown in bold/blue and three different models of it shown in fine/red: from left to right: DFT, APCA, and PLA. In each case the coefficients of DFT, APCA, or PLA can be considered the ***stipulated description method***.

Definition 5: A *reduced description length* of a time series T given hypothesis H is the number of bits used for encoding time series T, exploiting information in the hypothesis H, i.e., $DL(T|H)$, and the number of bits used for encoding H, i.e., $DL(H)$. Thus, the reduced description length is defined as: $DL(T, H) = DL(H) + DL(T|H)$

The first term, $DL(H)$, called the *model cost*, is the number of bits required to store the hypothesis H. We will give concrete examples later, but in brief, the model cost for say the piecewise linear approximation would include the bits need to encode the mean, slope and length of each linear segment. The second term, $DL(T|H)$, called the *correction cost* (in some works it is called the *description cost* or *error term*) is the number of bits required to rebuild whole time series T from the *given* hypothesis H. There are many possible ways to encode T by H. However, if we just simply store the differences between T and H, we can easily re-generate a whole time series T from the information we have. Thus, in this paper we simply use $DL\ (T\,|\,H) = DL\ (T\text{-}H)$.

3   MDL Modeling of Time Series

For concreteness, we will consider a simple worked example comparing two possible dimensionalities of data. Note that here we are assuming a cardinality of 16, and a model of APCA. However, more generally we do not need to make such assumptions. Let us consider a sample time series T of length 24:

$$T = 1\ 1\ 1\ 2\ 3\ 4\ 5\ 6\ 7\ 8\ 9\ 10\ 11\ 11\ 12\ 12\ 12\ 12\ 11\ 11\ 10\ 10\ 9\ 7$$

In **Fig.4**. *left*, we show a plot of this data.

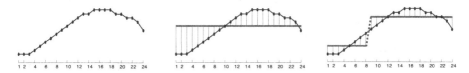

Fig. 4. *left)*A sample time series T. *middle)*Time series T (blue/fine), approximated by a one-dimensional APCA approximation H_1 (red/bold). The error for this model is represented by the vertical lines. *right)* Time series T (blue/fine), approximated by a two-dimensional APCA approximation H_2 (red/bold). Vertical lines represent the error for this model.

We can attempt to model this data with a single constant line, a special case of APCA. We begin by finding the mean of *all* the data, which (rounding in our integer space) is eight. We can create a hypothesis H_1 to model this data, which as shown in **Fig.4**.*middle*. It is simply a constant line with a mean of eight. There are 16 possible values this model *could* have had. Thus $DL\ (H_1) = 4$ bits. This model H_1 has a significant amount of error[2] modeling T, and we must account for this. The errors e_1, represented by the length of the vertical lines in **Fig.4**.*middle* are:

$$e_1 = 7\ \ 7\ \ 7\ \ 6\ \ 5\ \ 4\ \ 3\ \ 2\ \ 1\ \ 0\ \ \text{-1 -2 -3 -3 -4 -4 -4 -4 -3 -3 -2 -2 -1}\ \ 1$$

As noted in Definition 5, the cost to represent these errors is the correction cost or the number of bits encoding e_1 using Huffman coding, which is 82 bits. Thus the overall cost to represent T with a one-dimensional model or its reduced description length is:

$$DL\ (T, H_1) = DL\ (T|H_1) + DL\ (H_1)$$
$$DL\ (T, H_1) = 82 + 4 = 86\ \text{bits}$$

Now we can test to see if hypothesis H_2, which models the data with *two* constant lines could reduce the description length. **Fig.4**.*right* shows the two segment approximation lines created by APCA.As we expect, the error e_2 shown as the vertical lines in **Fig.4**. *right* is smaller than the error e_1. In particular, the error e_2 is:

$$e_2 = 2\ \ 2\ \ 2\ \ 1\ \ 0\ \text{-1 -2 -3}\ \ 3\ \ 2\ \ 1\ \ 0\ \text{-1 -1 -2 -2 -2 -2 -1 -1}\ \ 0\ \ 0\ \ 1\ \ 3$$

---

[2] The word *error* has a pejorative meaning not intended here, some authors prefer to use *correction cost*.

The number of bits encoding e_2 using Huffman coding or the correction cost to generate the time series T given the hypothesis H_2, DL $(T \mid H_2)$, is 65 bits. Although the correction cost is smaller than one-dimensional APCA, the model cost is larger. In order to store two constant lines, two constant numbers corresponding to the height of each line and a pointer indicating the end position of the first line are required. Thus, the reduced description length of model H_2 is:

$$DL\ (T,\ H_2) = DL\ (T|H_2) + DL\ (H_2)$$
$$DL\ (T,\ H_2) = 65 + 2*\log_2(16) + [\log_2(24)] = 78\text{bits}$$

Because we have $DL\ (T,\ H_2) < DL\ (T,\ H_1)$, we prefer H_2 as a proper number of segments for our data. Clearly we are not done yet, we should also test H_3, H_4, etc., corresponding to 3, 4, etc. piecewise constant segments. Moreover, we can also test alterative models corresponding to different levels of DFT or PLA representation. In addition, we can also test different cardinalities, because it is possible that the 16-value cardinality was unnecessary for this domain. For example, suppose we had been given T_2 instead:

$$T_2 = 0\ 0\ 0\ 0\ 4\ 4\ 4\ 4\ 4\ 0\ 0\ 0\ 0\ 8\ 8\ 8\ 8\ 8\ 8\ 12\ 12\ 12\ 12\ 12$$

Here, if we tested multiple hypotheses as to the cardinality of this data, we would hope to find that the hypothesis H_4^C that attempts to encode the data with a cardinality of just 4 would result in the smallest model.

We have shown a detailed example for APCA. However essentially all the time series representations can be encoded in a similar way. As shown with three representative examples in **Fig.3**, essentially all the time series models consist of a set of basic functions that are linearly combined to produce an approximation of the data.

As we apply our ideas to each representation, we must be careful to correctly "charge" each model for its approximation level. For example, each APCA segment requires two numbers, to encode its mean value and its length. However, PLA segments require three numbers, mean value, segment length and slope. Each DFT coefficient requires two numbers to encode the amplitude and phase of each sine wave, however, because of the complex conjugate property, we get a "free" coefficient for each one we record[2][3]. In previous comparisons of the indexing performance of various time series representations, many authors (including one of the current authors [13]) have given an advantage to one representation by the counting cost to represent an approximation incorrectly. The ideas in this work do explicitly assume a fair comparison. Fortunately, the community seems more aware of this problem in recent years[2][9].

3.1   Generic MDL for Time Series Algorithm

In the last section, we use a toy example for demonstrating how to compute the reduced description length of a time series with competing hypothesis. In this section, we will show a detailed generic version of our algorithm, and then explain our algorithm in detail for the three most commonly used time series representations.

Our algorithm can not only discover the intrinsic cardinality and dimensionality of an input time series, but also be used to find the right model or data representation for the given time series. The following pseudo code shows a high-level view of our algorithm for discovering the best model, cardinality, and dimensionality which will minimize the total number of bits required to store the input time series.

Because MDL is at the heart of our algorithm, the first step in our algorithm is to quantize a real-valued time series into a discrete-value (but fine-grained) time series, T (line 1). Next, we consider each model, cardinality, and dimensionality one by one (line 3-5). Then a hypothesis H is created based on the selected model and parameters (line 6). For example, a hypothesis H shown in **Fig.4**.*middle* is created when the model M=APCA, cardinality c=16, and dimensionality d=1.

The reduced description length defined in Definition 5 is then calculated (line 7), and our algorithm returns the model and parameters which can minimize the reduced description length for encoding T (line 8-13).

```
Algorithm: Generic MDL Algorithm
Input: TS: time series
Output:    best_model:  best model
best_card :  best cardinality
best_dim  :  best dimensionality
   1.   T = Discretization (TS)
   2.   Bsf = ∞
 3.   for all M in {APCA, PLA, DFT}
 4.       for all cardinality c
 5.           for all dimensionality d
 6.               H = ModelRespresentation(T,M,c,d)
 7.               total_cost = DL(H) + DL(T|H)
 8.               if ( bsf>total_cost)
 9.                   bsf = total_cost
 10.                      best_model = M
 11.                      best_card = c
 12.                      best_dim = d
 13.                  end if
 14.              end for
 15.          end for
 16.  end for
```

For concreteness we will now consider one specific version of our generic algorithm, for Adaptive Piecewise Constant Approximation. In an extended technical report version of this paper we consider Piecewise Linear Approximation and Discrete Fourier Transformation to the same level of detail [31].

3.2   Adaptive Piecewise Constant Approximation

As we have seen in previous section, APCA model is simple; it only contains constant lines. The following pseudo code for APCA is very similar to the generic algorithm. First of all, we do quantization on the input time series (line 1). Then, we evaluate all cardinalities from 2 to 256 and dimensionalities from 2 to the maximum possible number, which is a half of the length of input time series TS (line 3-4). Note that if the dimensionality was more than $m/2$, some segments will contain only one point.

```
Algorithm: IntrinsicDiscovery for APCA
    1.  T = Discretization (TS)
    2.  bsf = ∞
3.  for c = 2 to 256
4.        for d = 2 to m/2
5.                H = APCA(T, c, d)
6.                model_cost = d*log₂(c)+(d-1)*log₂(m)
7.                total_cost = model_cost + DL(T-H)
8.                if ( bsf>total_cost)
9.                    bsf = total_cost
10.                   best_card = c
11.                   best_dim = d
12.               end if
13.      end for
    14. end for
```

Then, a hypothesis H is created using the values of cardinality c and dimensionality d, as shown in **Fig.4**. *Right* when c=16and d=2. The model contains d constant segments so the model cost is the number of bits required for storing d constant numbers, and d-1 pointers to indicate the offset of the end of each segment (line 6). The difference between T and H is also required to rebuild T. The correction cost (Definition 5) is computed; then the reduced description length is the combination of the model cost and the correction cost (line 7). Finally, the hypothesis which minimized this value is returned as an output of the algorithm (line 8-13).

4   Experimental Evaluation

We begin with a simple sanity check on the classic problem specifying the correct time series model, cardinality and dimensionality, given an observation of a corrupted version of it. While this problem has received significant attention in the literature [6][22][23], our MDL method has two significant advantages over existing works; It is parameter-free, whereas most other methods require several parameters to be set, and MDL can specify the model, cardinality and dimensionality, whereas other methods typically only consider model and/or dimensionality. To eliminate the possibility of data bias [12]we consider a ten year-old instantiation [23]of a classic benchmark problem[6]. In **Fig.5**we show the classic Donoho-Johnstone block benchmark. The underlying model used to produce it is a twelve piecewise constant sections with Gaussian noise added.

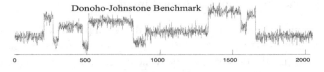

Fig. 5. A version of the Donoho-Johnstone block benchmark created ten years ago and downloaded from [23]

The task is challenging because some of the piecewise constant sections are very short and thus easily dismissed during a model search. There have been dozens of algorithms that applied to this problem (indeed, to this *exact* instance of data) in the last decade, which should we compare to? Most of these algorithms have several parameters, in some cases as many as six [8].We argue that comparisons to such methods are pointless, since our *explicit* aim is to introduce a parameter-free method. The most cited *parameter-free* method to address this problem is the L-Method of [22].In essence, the L-Method is a "knee-finding" algorithm. It attempts to explain the residual error vs. size-of-model curve using all possible pairs of two regression lines. **Fig.6**.*top* shows one such pairs of lines, from one to ten and from eleven to the end. The location that produces the minimum sum of the residual errors of these two curves **R**, is offered as the optimal model, as we can see in **Fig.6**.*bottom* this occurs at location ten, a good estimate of the true value of twelve.

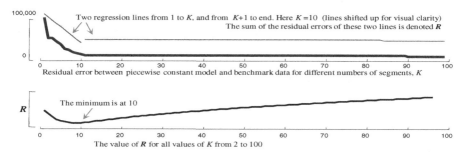

Fig. 6. The knee finding L-Method *top*) A residual error vs. size-of-model curve (bold/blue) is modeled by all possible pairs of regression lines (light/red). Here just one possibility is shown. *bottom*) The location that minimizes the summed residual error of the two regression lines is given as the optimal "knee".

We also tested several other methods, including [27]. However no other parameter-free or parameter-lite method we found produced intuitive (much less correct) results.

We can now attempt to solve this problem with our MDL approach. **Fig.7**shows that of the 64 different piecewise constant models it evaluated, MDL chose the twelve-segment model, the *correct* answer. The left part in **Fig.7**uses a cardinality of 256, but the same answer is retuned for(at least) every cardinality from 8 to 256.

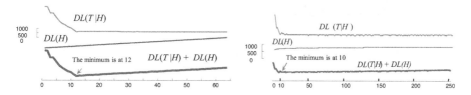

Fig. 7. *left)* The description length of the Donoho-Johnstone block benchmark time series is minimized at a <u>dimensionality</u> corresponding to twelve piecewise constant segments, which is the correct answer [23]. *right)* The description length of the Donoho-Johnstone block benchmark time series is minimized with a <u>cardinality</u> of ten, which is the true cardinality [23].

Beyond outperforming other techniques at the task of finding the correct *dimensionality* of a model, MDL can also find the intrinsic *cardinality* of a dataset, something that methods[22][27]are not even defined for. In the right part of **Fig.7**we have repeated the previous experiment, but this time fixing the dimensionality to twelve as suggested above, and testing all possible cardinality values from 2 to 256.

Here MDL indicates a cardinality of ten, which is the *correct answer* [23]. We also re-implemented the most referenced *recent* paper on time series discretization [18]. The algorithm is stochastic, and requires the setting of five parameters. In one hundred runs over multiple parameters we found it consistently underestimated the cardinality of the data (the mean cardinality was 7.2).

Before leaving this example, we show one further significant advantage of MDL over existing techniques. Both [22][27]try to find the optimal dimensionality, *assuming* the underlying model is known. However in many circumstances we may not know the underlying model. As we show in **Fig.8**, with MDL we can relax even this assumption. If our MDL scoring scheme is allowed to choose over the cross product of model = {APCA, PLA, DFT}, dimensionality = {1 to 512} and cardinality = {2 to 256}, it correctly chooses the right model, dimensionality *and* cardinality.

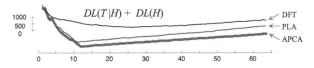

Fig. 8. The description length of the Donoho-Johnstone block benchmark time series is minimized with a piecewise constant model (APCA), not a piecewise linear model (PLA) or Fourier representation (DFT)

4.1 An Example Application in Physiology

The *Muscle* dataset studied by Mörchen and Ultsch[17]describes the muscle activation of a professional inline speed skater. The authors calculated the muscle activation from the original EMG (Electromyography) measurements by taking the logarithm of the energy derived from a wavelet analysis. **Fig.9**.*Left.top* shows an excerpt. At first glance it seems to have two states, which corresponds to our (perhaps) naive intuitions about skating and muscle physiology.

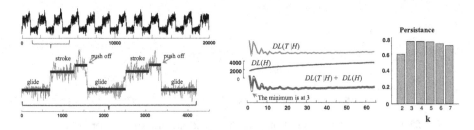

Fig. 9. Left .*top*) An excerpt from the Muscle dataset. *Left.bottom*) A zoomed-in section of the Muscle dataset which had its model, dimensionality and cardinality set by MDL. *Right.left*) The description length of the muscle activation time series is minimized with a cardinality of three, which is the correct answer. *Right. right*) The Persist algorithm predicts a value of four.

We can test this binary assumption by using MDL to find the model, dimensionality and cardinality. The results for model and dimensionality are objectively correct, as we might have expected given the results in the previous section, but the results for cardinality, shown in **Fig.9**.*Right. left* in are worth examining.

Our MDL method suggests a cardinality of three. Glancing back at **Fig.9** shows why. At the end of the *stroke* there is an additional level corresponding to an additional *push-off* by the athlete. This feature was noted by physiologists that worked with Mörchen and Ultsch [17]. However, their algorithm weakly predicts a value of four[3]. Here once again we find the MDL can beat rival approaches, even though the rival approach attempted the most favorable parameter tuning.

5   Discussion of Time and Space Complexity and Conclusions

The space complexly of our algorithm is linear in the size of the original data. The time complexity of the algorithms in pseudo code in section 3.2 and 3.3 are optimized for simplicity, and appear quadratic in the time series length. However, we can do the DFT/PLA/APCA decomposition *once* at the finest granularity, and cache the results, leaving only a loop that performs efficient calculations on integers. After this optimization, the time taken for our algorithms becomes an inconsequential fraction of the time it takes to do PLA or APCA *once*, and only slightly slower than the time it takes to do DFT *once*. We therefore omit timing experiments.

We have shown that a simple methodology based on MDL can robustly specify the intrinsic model, cardinality and dimensionality of time series data from a wide variety of domains. While we have followed the more familiar MDL notation of Rissanen [20][21] and Grünwald [28], the basic idea we are leveraging off harkens back to the ideas of Solomonoff [25]and Wallace [26]. These ideas seem underexploited and underappreciated in the data mining community (to which the current authors most closely identify), and we hope our empirical research efforts will partly redress this.

Our method significant advantages over revival methods in that it is more general and is essentially parameter-free. We have further shown applications of our ideas to resource-limited classification and anomaly detection.

Acknowledgments and Notes. This project was supported by the Department of the United States Air Force, Air Force Research Laboratory under Contract FA8750-10-C-0160, and by NSF grants 0803410/ 0808770. The first two authors contributed equally and did the bulk of the work, and should be consider *joint* first authors.

References

1. Assent, I., Krieger, R., Afschari, F., Seidl, T.: The TS-Tree: Efficient Time Series Search and Retrieval. In: EDBT (2008)
2. Camerra, A., Palpanas, T., Shieh, J., Keogh, E.: iSAX 2.0: Indexing and Mining One Billion Time Series. In: International Conference on Data Mining (2010)

---

[3] The values for $k = 3$, 4 or 5 do not differ by more than 1%.

3. Ding, H., Trajcevski, G., Scheuermann, P., Wang, X., Keogh, E.: Querying and mining of time series data: experimental comparison of representations and distance measures. PVLDB 1(2), 1542–1552 (2008)
4. Dowe, D.L.: Foreword re C. S. Wallace. Computer Journal 51(5), 523–560 (2008)
5. Dowe, D.L.: MML, hybrid Bayesian network graphical models, statistical consistency, invariance and uniqueness. In: Handbook of the Philosophy of Science Philosophy of Statistics, pp. 901–982. Elsevier (2011)
6. Donoho, D.L., Johnstone, I.M.: Ideal spatial adaptation via wavelet shrinkage. Journal of Biometrika 81(3), 425–455 (1994)
7. Evans, S.C., et al.: MicroRNA target detection and analysis for genes related to breast cancer using MDL compress. EURASIP J. Bioinform. Syst. Biol., 1–16 (2007)
8. García-López, D.-A., Acosta-Mesa, H.-G.: Discretization of Time Series Dataset with a Genetic Search. In: Aguirre, A.H., Borja, R.M., Garciá, C.A.R. (eds.) MICAI 2009. LNCS, vol. 5845, pp. 201–212. Springer, Heidelberg (2009)
9. Jonyer, I., Holder, L.B., Cook, D.J.: Attribute-Value Selection Based on Minimum Description Length. In: International Conference on Artificial Intelligence (2004)
10. Keogh, E., Xi, X., Wei, L., Ratanamahatana, C.A.: The UCR Time Series Classification/Clustering Homepage (2006), http://www.cs.ucr.edu/~eamonn/time_series_data/
11. Kontkanen, Pand Myllym, P.: MDL histogram density estimation. In: Proceedings of the Eleventh International Workshop on Artificial Intelligence and Statistics (2007)
12. Keogh, E., Kasetty, S.: On the Need for Time Series Data Mining Benchmarks: A Survey and Empirical Demonstration. Journal of Data Mining and Knowledge Discovery 7(4), 349–371 (2003)
13. Keogh, E.J., Pazzani, M.J.: A Simple Dimensionality Reduction Technique for Fast Similarity Search in Large Time Series Databases. In: Terano, T., Liu, H., Chen, A.L.P. (eds.) PAKDD 2000. LNCS, vol. 1805, pp. 122–133. Springer, Heidelberg (2000)
14. Li, M., Vitanyi, P.: An Introduction to Kolmogorov Complexity and Its Applications, 2nd edn. Springer (1997)
15. Lin, J., Keogh, E., Lonardi, S., Patel, P.: Finding motifs in time series. In: Proc. of 2nd Workshop on Temporal Data Mining (2002)
16. Lin, J., Keogh, E., Wei, L., Lonardi, S.: Experiencing SAX: a novel symbolic representation of time series. Journal of Data Mining and Knowledge Discovery 15(2), 107–144 (2007)
17. Mörchen, F., Ultsch, A.: Optimizing time series discretization for knowledge discovery. In: KDD, pp. 660–665 (2005)
18. Pednault, E.P.D.: Some Experiments in Applying Inductive Inference Principles to Surface Reconstruction. In: IJCAI, pp. 1603–1609 (1989)
19. Palpanas, T., Vlachos, M., Keogh, E.J., Gunopulos, D.: Streaming Time Series Summarization Using User-Defined Amnesic Functions. IEEE Trans. Knowl. Data Eng. 20(7), 992–1006 (2008)
20. Rissanen, J.: Stochastic Complexity in Statistical Inquiry. World Scientific, Singapore (1989)
21. Rissanen, J., Speed, T., Yu, B.: Density estimation by stochastic complexity. IEEE Trans. On Information Theory 38, 315–323 (1992)
22. Salvador, S., Chan, P.: Determining the Number of Clusters/Segments in Hierarchical Clustering/Segmentation Algorithms. In: ICTAI, pp. 576–584 (2004)
23. Sarle, W.S.: Donoho-Johnstone Benchmarks: Neural Net Results (1999), ftp://ftp.sas.com/pub/neural/dojo/dojo.html

24. Sart, D., Mueen, A., Najjar, W., Niennattrakul, V., Keogh, E.: Accelerating Dynamic Time Warping Subsequence Search with GPUs and FPGAs. In: IEEE International Conference on Data Mining (2010)
25. Solomonoff. R. J.: A Preliminary Report on a General Theory of Inductive Inference, Contract AF 49(639)-376. Report ZTB-138, Zator Co., Cambridge, Mass. (November 1960)
26. Wallace, C.S., Boulton, D.M.: An information measure for classification. Computer Journal 11(2), 185–194 (1968)
27. Zhao, Q., Hautamaki, V., Fränti, P.: Knee point detection in BIC for detecting the number of clusters. In: Blanc-Talon, J., Bourennane, S., Philips, W., Popescu, D., Scheunders, P. (eds.) ACIVS 2008. LNCS, vol. 5259, pp. 664–673. Springer, Heidelberg (2008)
28. Grünwald, P. (ed.): Advances in Minimum Description Length: Theory and Applications. MIT Press (2005)
29. Vereshchagin, N., Vitanyi, P.: Rate distortion and denoising of individual data using Kolmogorov complexity. IEEE Trans. Information Theory 56(7), 3438–3454 (2010)
30. De Rooij, S., Vitányi, P.: Approximating Rate-Distortion Graphs of Individual Data: Experiments in Lossy Compression and Denoising. IEEE Transactions on Computers (2011)
31. URL: Expanded Technical Report version of this paper, http://www.cs.ucr.edu/~bhu002/LNCS

Complexity Measures for Meta-learning
and Their Optimality

Norbert Jankowski

Department of Informatics, Nicolaus Copernicus University, Toruń, Poland

Abstract. Meta-learning can be seen as alternating the construction of configuration of learning machines for validation, scheduling of such tasks and the meta-knowledge collection.
   This article presents a few modifications of complexity measures and their application in advising to scheduling test tasks—validation tasks of learning machines in meta-learning process. Additionally some comments about their optimality in context of meta-learning are presented.

1 Introduction

To talk about complexity and its connections with meta-learning we need to define the learning problem and the learning machine first. The *learning problem* $\mathcal{P}$ is represented by the pair of data $D \in \mathcal{D}$ and model space $\mathcal{M}$. Finding the best solution for $\mathcal{P}$ is usually an NP-hard problem and we must be satisfied with suboptimal solutions found by learning machines defined as processes

$$L \ : \ \mathcal{K}_L \times \mathcal{D} \to \mathcal{M} \tag{1}$$

where $\mathcal{K}_L$ is the space of configuration parameters of L.
   The task of finding the best possible model for fixed data D, can be replaced by the task of finding the best possible learning machine L.
   Note that learning machines may be simple or complex. In case of complex machines a learning machine is composed of several other learning machines:

$$L = L_1 \circ L_2 \circ \ldots \circ L_k. \tag{2}$$

For example, a composition of a data transformation machine and a classifier machine or classifiers committee which is composed of several machines. Additionally it is not necessary to distinguish between learning and non-learning machines. Test procedures estimating some measures of learning machines accuracies, adaptation etc. can also be seen as another machines. And then the time and space complexity may touch more sophisticated structure which consists of learning machines and some testing procedures as well.
   Meta-learning algorithm (MLA) is just another type of learning algorithm (with another data and model spaces). The most characteristic feature of meta-learning is that it learns how to learn. Typically meta-learning uses conclusions of other learning tasks formulated and evaluated (during the run of meta-learning). This is why meta-learning algorithms realize followings actions in a loop: formulation and starting of the test tasks, collection of results and meta-knowledge. For a review of different meta-learning approaches, see [1].

D.L. Dowe (Ed.): Solomonoff Festschrift, LNAI 7070, pp. 198–210, 2013.

The goal of meta-learning may be defined by: *maximization of the probability of finding best possible solution of given problem $\mathcal{P}$ within given search space in as short time as possible.*

In consequence the meta-learning algorithms should carefully order testing tasks during the progress of the search, basing on information about complexity (as it will be seen) and build meta-knowledge based on the experience from passed tests. It is highly necessary to avoid test tasks that could accumulate too large amount of time, since it would decrease the probability of finding the most interesting solutions.

This is why the *complexity approach* is presented in further part of the text.

2   Complexity Measures for Learning Machines

The above definition of a learning problem describes what data analysts usually do, but it neglects the fact that the time that can be spent on solving the problem is always limited. We never have an infinite amount of time for finding satisfactory solutions, even in the case of scientific research. This is why the meta-learning should work with respect to time limits, but indeed it should based on reformulated definition of learning problem.

The *restricted learning problem* is a learning problem $\mathcal{P}$ with defined time limit for providing the solution.

Such definition of the problem of learning from data is much more realistic in comparison to the original one (whenever it is used to research purpose or commercial purpose). It should be preferred also for research purposes. In a natural way, it reflects the reality of data analysis challenges, where deadlines are crucial, but it is also more adequate for real business applications, where solutions must be found in appropriate time and any other applications with explicit or implicit time constraints.

Meta-learning algorithms should favor simple solutions and start the machines that provide them before the more complex ones. It means that MLAs should start with maximally plain learning machines. But what does (should) plain mean? In that case plain or not plain is not equivalent with single or complex learning machine (when looking at the structure of machine). The complexity measure should be used to reflect the space and time needs of given algorithm (also for learning machines of complex structure). What's more, sometimes a composition of a transformation and a classifier may be indeed of smaller complexity than the classifier without transformation. It is true because when using a transformation, the data passed to the learning process of the classifier may be of smaller complexity and, as a consequence, classifier's learning is simpler and the difference between the classifier learning complexities, with and without transformation may be bigger than the cost of the transformation. This proves that real complexity is not reflected directly by structure of a learning machine.

Complexity measures by Solomonoff, Kolmogorov and Levin. To obtain the right order in the searching queue of learning machines, a complexity measure should be used. Solomonoff [2,3,4] and Kolmogorov [5] (see [6] too) defined complexity by:

$$C_K(P) = \min_p \{l_p \; : \text{if program } p \text{ prints } P \text{ and halts}\}, \tag{3}$$

where l_p is the length of program p. Unfortunately, this definition is inadequate from the practical side, because it is not computable. Levin's definition [6] introduced a term responsible for time consumption:

$$C_L(P) = \min_p \{c_L(p) \; : \text{if program } p \text{ prints } P \text{ and then halts within time } t_p\} \tag{4}$$

where

$$c_L(p) = l_p + \log t_p. \tag{5}$$

In the case of Levin's definition (Eq. 4) it is possible to realize [7] the Levin Universal Search (LUS) [8,6] but the problem is that this algorithm is NP-hard. This means that, in practice, it is impossible to find an exact solution to the optimization problem.

Generators flow defines search space. The strategy of meta-learning is different than the one of LUS. The LUS searches in an infinite space between all possible programs. Meta-learning uses the functional definition of the search space, which is not infinite. This means that the search space is, indeed, strongly limited. The *generators flow* is assumed to generate machine configurations which are "rational" from the point of view of given problem $\mathcal{P}$.

Generators flow is a directed graph of *machine generators*. Thanks to the graph connection the definition of appropriate graph is natural. However, a deep description of this topic will, most certainly, exceed the page limit. The generators flow is defined *individually* for each learning problem $\mathcal{P}$. However similar configurations of the generator flow may be shared by classifiers (for example). Generators flow should reflect all accessible knowledge about problem $\mathcal{P}$ and provide several configurations of machines which performance should be tested—it increases the probability of finding a better solution. Thanks to such definition of generators flow, the searching space is finite, however it may consist of many configurations, usually so many as to make it impossible to validate all of them. To validate appropriate configurations the complexity measure will be used to order the test task basing on machine configurations.

Complexity in the context of machines. The complexity can not be computed from the learning machines themselves, but from configurations of learning machines and descriptions of their inputs. Because meta-learning for organizing the order has to know the complexity before the machine is ready for use. In most cases, there is no direct analytical way of computing the machine complexity on the basis of its configuration. The halting problem directly implies impossibility of calculation of time and memory usage of a learning process in general. Therefore the approximators of complexity have to be contracted.

Modifications of complexity measures and their optimality. Each meta-learning algorithm may be seen in the following way: it postulates some learning machines and provides appropriate tests to estimate the quality of each learning machine. But in case of time-restricted learning there is a time limit t. In such case, testing all postulated learning machines may be impossible because summed testing times of all the candidates may exceed the time limit t.

Assume that we have restricted the learning problem $\mathcal{P}$ with a time limit t and a meta-learning algorithm postulates learning machines $m_1, m_2, \ldots, m_q$, with testing times of $t_1, t_2, \ldots, t_q$ respectively. When not all of the tests can be done within the time limit $(\sum_i t_i > t)$ and if we assume that each test is equally promising, then to maximize the expected value of the best test result obtained within the time, we need to run as many tests as possible. Therefore, an **optimal order** of the tests is an order $i_1, i_2, \ldots, i_m$ of nondecreasing testing times:

$$t_{i_1} \leq t_{i_2} \leq \ldots \leq t_{i_m}, \tag{6}$$

and the choice of first m shortest tests such that

$$m = \arg \max_{1 \leq k \leq q} \left[\sum_{l=1,\ldots,k} t_{i_l} \leq t \right], \tag{7}$$

is an **optimal choice** of respective learning machines. The proof of this property is trivial. Thanks to the sorted permutation in Eq. 6 the m from above equation is highest. And this directly maximizes the probability of finding best solution on above assumptions.

This implies that meta-learning in complexity definition have to use time in calculation of complexity:

$$c_t(p) = t_p. \tag{8}$$

This property is very important because it clearly answers the main problem of MLA about the choice and order of learning machine tests.

Even if we do not assume that learning machines are not equally promising, the complexity measure may be adjusted to maximize the expected value of test results (see Eq. 11).

The property of optimal ordering the test tasks means that in case of ordering programs (machines) only on the basis of their length (as it was defined in Eq. 3) is not rational in the context of learning machines (and non-learning machines too). The problem of using Levin's additional term of time Eq. 5, in real applications, is that it is not rigorous enough in respecting time. For example, a program running 1024 times longer than another one may have just a little bigger complexity (just $+10$). Note that in case of Levin's complexity (Eq. 5) one unit more of space was equivalent to double time. This in not acceptable in practice of computational intelligence.

On the other hand, total rejection of the length l_p is also not recommended because machines always have to *fit* in the memory, which is limited too.

In learning machines, typically the time complexity exceeds significantly the memory complexity. This is why measure of complexity should combine time and memory together:

$$c_a(p) = l_p + t_p/\log t_p. \tag{9}$$

Although the time part may seem to be respected less than the memory part, it is not really so, because, as mentioned above, almost always time complexity exceeds significantly memory complexity. Thus, in fact, memory part dominates anyway, so the order of performing tests is very sensitive to time requirements. What's more, the order of machines based on the time t_p and based on $t_p/\log t_p$ are equivalent. The length component l_p just "keeps in mind" the limited resources of memory and the whole c_a defines some balance between the two complexities.

Complexity measure and quarantine. The approximation of the complexity of a machine is used. Because of this approximation and because of the halting problem (we never know whether given test task will finish or not) an additional penalty term is added to the above definition:

$$c_b(p) = [l_p + t_p/\log t_p]/q(p), \tag{10}$$

where $q(p)$ is a function term responsible for reflecting reliability of $c_a(p)$ estimate and is used to correct the approximation in case it was wrong. In other case it is equal to 1.

At start of the test task p the MLAs use $q(p) = 1$ (generally $q(p) \leq 1$) for the estimations, but in the case when the estimated time (as a part of the complexity) is not enough to finish task test p, the test task p is aborted and the reliability is decreased. The aborted test task is moved to a *quarantine* according to the new value of complexity reflecting the change of the reliability term and another task is started according to the order. This mechanism prevents from running test tasks for unpredictably long time of execution or even infinite time. Otherwise the MLA would be very brittle and susceptible to running tasks consuming unlimited CPU resources. This is extremely useful in the framework of restricted learning problem.

Corrections of complexity for unequally promising machines. Another extension of the complexity measure is possible thanks to the fact that MLAs are able to collect meta-knowledge during learning or for a priori knowledge. Such knowledge may influence the order of waiting test tasks. The optimal way of doing this, is adding a new term to the $c_b(p)$ to shift the start time of given test in appropriate direction:

$$c_m(p) = [l_p + t_p/\log t_p]/[q(p) \cdot a(p)]. \tag{11}$$

$a(p)$ reflects the attractiveness of the test task p.

While $c_a(p)$ was a measure aimed at such order of the tasks that maximizes the expected value of results, the factor $1/a(p)$ is a correction to the initial assumption of equal a priori probabilities in optimal ordering of different programs (or machines). This means that the assumption that machines are equally promising may be corrected by additional term in complexity.

What machines are we interested in the complexity of? The generators flow provides machine configurations which subsequently one by one are nested inside separate copies of test template. The test template is used to define the goal of the problem $\mathcal{P}$. It may be defined in different ways depending on the problem $\mathcal{P}$, for example it may calculate average error. However the common divisor of all testing procedures is that it consists of learning of the given machine and testing of this machine.

A good definition of the testing procedure should naturally reflect the usage of tested machine. And by the same complexity of such test procedure with nested tested machine reflects the complete behaviour of the machine really well: a part of the complexity formula reflects the complexity of learning of the given machine and the rest reflects the complexity of computing the test (for example, classification or approximation test). The costs of learning are very important because without learning there is no model. The complexity of the testing part is also very important, because it reflects the simplicity of further use of the model. Some machines learn quickly and require more effort to make use of their outputs (like kNN classifiers), while others learn for a long time and after that may be very efficiently exploited (like many neural networks). Therefore, the test procedure should be as similar to the whole life cycle of a machine as possible (and of course as trustful as possible).

Approximation of complexity basing on configuration and input description. To understand the needs of complexity computing we need to go back to the task of learning. To provide a learning machine, regardless whether it is a simple one or a complex machine or a machine constructed to help in the process of analysis of other machines, its configuration and inputs must be specified. Complexity computation must reflect the information from configuration and inputs. The recursive nature of configurations, together with input–output connections, may compose quite complex information flow. Sometimes, the inputs of submachines become known just before they are started, i.e. after the learning of other machines[1] is finished. This is one of the most important reasons why determination of complexity, on the contrary to actual learning processes, must base on *meta-inputs*, not on exact inputs (which remain unknown). Meta-inputs are counterparts of inputs in the "meta-world". Meta-inputs contain descriptions (as *informative* as possible) of inputs which "explain" or "comment" every useful aspect of each input that could be helpful in determination of the complexity.

To facilitate recurrent determination of complexity—which is obligatory because of basing on a recurrent definition of machine configuration and recurrent structure of real machines—the functions, which compute complexity, must also provide meta-outputs, because such meta-outputs will play a crucial role in computation of complexities of machines which read the outputs through their inputs. In conclusion, a function computing the complexity for machine $\mathcal{L}$ should be a transformation

$$\mathcal{D}_{\mathcal{L}} \; : \; \mathcal{K}_{\mathcal{L}} \times \mathcal{M}_{+} \to R^2 \times \mathcal{M}_{+}, \tag{12}$$

---

[1] Machines which provide necessary outputs.

where the domain is composed by the configurations space $\mathcal{K}_{\mathcal{L}}$ and the space of meta-inputs $\mathcal{M}_+$, and the results are the time complexity, the memory complexity and appropriate meta-outputs.

The problem is not as easy as the form of the function in Eq. 12. Finding the right function for the given learning machine $\mathcal{L}$ may be impossible. This is caused by unpredictable influence of some configuration elements and of some inputs (meta-inputs) a on the machine complexity. Configuration elements are not always as simple as scalar values. In some cases configuration elements are represented by functions or by subconfigurations. Similar problem concerns meta-inputs. In many cases, meta-inputs can not be represented by a simple chain of scalar values. Often, meta-inputs need their own complexity determination tool to reflect their functional form. For example, a committee of machines, which plays a role of a classifier, will use other classifiers (inputs) as "slave" machines. It means that the committee will use classifiers' outputs, and the complexity of using the outputs depends on the outputs, not on the committee itself. This shows that sometimes, the behaviour of meta-inputs/outputs is not trivial and proper complexity determination requires another encapsulation.

Meta Evaluators. To enable such high level of generality, the concept of *meta-evaluators* has been introduced. The general *goal of meta-evaluator* is

- to evaluate and exhibit *appropriate aspects* of complexity representation basing on some meta-descriptions like meta-inputs or configuration[2].
- to exhibit a functional description of complexity aspects (comments) useful for further reuse by other meta evaluators[3].

To enable complexity computation, every learning machine gets its own meta evaluator.

Because of recurrent nature of machines (and machine configuration) and because of nontriviality of inputs (its role, which sometimes have complex functional form), meta evaluators are constructed not only for machines, but also for outputs and other elements with "nontrivial influence" on machine complexity.

Learning Evaluators. The approximation framework is defined in very general way and enables building evaluators using approximators for different elements like learning time, size of the model, etc. Additionally, every evaluator that uses the approximation framework, may define special functions for estimation of complexity. This is useful for example to estimate time of instance classification etc.

The complexity control in meta-learning does not require very accurate information about tasks complexities. It is enough to know, whether a task needs a few times more of time or memory than another task. Moreover, although for some algorithms the approximation of complexity is not so accurate, the quarantine prevents from capturing too much resources.

---

[2] In case of a machine to exhibit complexity of time and memory.

[3] In case of a machine the meta-outputs are exhibited to provide source of complexity information for readers of machine inputs.

The approximation framework enables to construct series of *approximators* for single evaluators. The *approximators* are functions approximating a real value on the basis of a vector of real values. They are learned from examples, so before the learning process, the learning data has to be collected for each approximator.

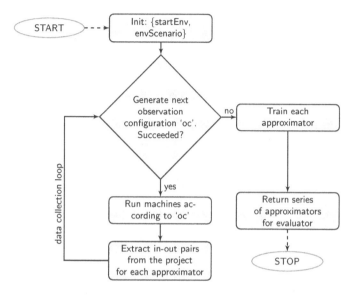

Fig. 1. Process of building approximators for single evaluator

Figure 1 presents the general idea of creating the approximators for an evaluator. To collect the learning data, proper information is extracted from observations of "machine behavior". To do this an "environment" for machine monitoring must be defined. The environment configuration is sequentially adjusted, realized and observed (compare the data collection loop in the figure). Observations bring the subsequent instances of the training data (corresponding to current state of the environment and expected approximation values). Changes of the environment facilitate observing the machine in different circumstances and gathering diverse data describing machine behaviour in different contexts.

The environment changes are determined by initial representation of the environment (the input variable startEnv) and specialized *scenario*, which defines how to modify the environment to get a sequence of machine observation configurations i.e. configurations of the machine being examined which is nested in a more complex machine structure. Generated machine observation configurations should be as realistic as possible—the information flow similar to expected applications of the machine, allows better approximation desired complexity functions. Each time, a next configuration 'oc' is constructed, machines are created and run according to 'oc', and when the whole project is ready, the learning data is collected. Full control of data acquisition is possible thanks to proper methods implemented by the evaluators.

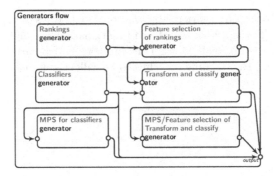

Fig. 2. Generators flow used in tests

After the data are collected appropriate approximators are learned and meta-evaluator becomes ready to approximate the complexity or even other quantities.

3   Example of an Application

The generators flow used in my experiments is presented in Fig. 2. Without going into the details (because of the page limit) of meaning of the presented generators flow, assume it generates machines presented in Table 1.

Machine configuration notation. To present complex machine configurations in a compact way, I introduce a special notation that enables us to sketch complex configurations of machines inline as a single term. For example, the following text:

[[[RankingCC], FeatureSelection], [kNN (Euclidean)], TransformAndClassify]

denotes a complex machine, where a feature selection submachine (FeatureSelection) selects features from the top of a correlation coefficient based ranking (RankingCC), and next, the dataset composed of the feature selection is an input for a kNN with Euclidean metric—the combination of feature selection and kNN classifier is controlled by a TransformAndClassify machine. The following notation represents an MPS (ParamSearch) machine which optimizes parameters of a kNN machine:

ParamSearch [kNN (Euclidean)]

Benchmarks. Because complexity analysis is not the main thread of this article, I have presented examples on two datasets selected from the UCI machine learning repository [9]: vowel and splice.

Diagram description. The results obtained for the benchmarks are presented in the form of diagrams: Fig. 3 and Fig. 4. The diagrams present information about times of starting, stopping and breaking of each task, about complexities (global, time and memory) of each test task, about the order of the test tasks

Table 1. Machine configurations produced by the generators flow of Fig. 2 and the enumerated sets of classifiers and rankings

1	kNN (Euclidean)
2	kNN [MetricMachine (EuclideanOUO)]
3	kNN [MetricMachine (Mahalanobis)]
4	NBC
5	SVMClassifier [KernelProvider]
6	LinearSVMClassifier [LinearKernelProvider]
7	[ExpectedClass, kNN [MetricMachine (EuclideanOUO)]]
8	[LVQ, kNN (Euclidean)]
9	Boosting (10x) [NBC]
10	[[[RankingCC], FeatureSelection], [kNN (Euclidean)], TransformAndClassify]
11	[[[RankingCC], FeatureSelection], [kNN [MetricMachine (EuclideanOUO)]], TransformAndClassify]
12	[[[RankingCC], FeatureSelection], [kNN [MetricMachine (Mahalanobis)]], TransformAndClassify]
13	[[[RankingCC], FeatureSelection], [NBC], TransformAndClassify]
14	[[[RankingCC], FeatureSelection], [SVMClassifier [KernelProvider]], TransformAndClassify]
15	[[[RankingCC], FeatureSelection], [LinearSVMClassifier [LinearKernelProvider]], TransformAndClassify]
16	[[[RankingCC], FeatureSelection], [ExpectedClass, kNN [MetricMachine (EuclideanOUO)]], TransformAndClassify]
17	[[[RankingCC], FeatureSelection], [LVQ, kNN (Euclidean)], TransformAndClassify]
18	[[[RankingCC], FeatureSelection], [Boosting (10x) [NBC]], TransformAndClassify]
19	[[[RankingFScore], FeatureSelection], [kNN (Euclidean)], TransformAndClassify]
20	[[[RankingFScore], FeatureSelection], [kNN [MetricMachine (EuclideanOUO)]], TransformAndClassify]
21	[[[RankingFScore], FeatureSelection], [kNN [MetricMachine (Mahalanobis)]], TransformAndClassify]
22	[[[RankingFScore], FeatureSelection], [NBC], TransformAndClassify]
23	[[[RankingFScore], FeatureSelection], [SVMClassifier [KernelProvider]], TransformAndClassify]
24	[[[RankingFScore], FeatureSelection], [LinearSVMClassifier [LinearKernelProvider]], TransformAndClassify]
25	[[[RankingFScore], FeatureSelection], [ExpectedClass, kNN [MetricMachine (EuclideanOUO)]], TransformAndClassify]
26	[[[RankingFScore], FeatureSelection], [LVQ, kNN (Euclidean)], TransformAndClassify]
27	[[[RankingFScore], FeatureSelection], [Boosting (10x) [NBC]], TransformAndClassify]
28	ParamSearch [kNN (Euclidean)]
29	ParamSearch [kNN [MetricMachine (EuclideanOUO)]]
30	ParamSearch [kNN [MetricMachine (Mahalanobis)]]
31	ParamSearch [NBC]
32	ParamSearch [SVMClassifier [KernelProvider]]
33	ParamSearch [LinearSVMClassifier [LinearKernelProvider]]
34	ParamSearch [ExpectedClass, kNN [MetricMachine (EuclideanOUO)]]
35	ParamSearch [LVQ, kNN (Euclidean)]
36	ParamSearch [Boosting (10x) [NBC]]
37	ParamSearch [[[RankingCC], FeatureSelection], [kNN (Euclidean)], TransformAndClassify]
38	ParamSearch [[[RankingCC], FeatureSelection], [kNN [MetricMachine (EuclideanOUO)]], TransformAndClassify]
39	ParamSearch [[[RankingCC], FeatureSelection], [kNN [MetricMachine (Mahalanobis)]], TransformAndClassify]
40	ParamSearch [[[RankingCC], FeatureSelection], [NBC], TransformAndClassify]
41	ParamSearch [[[RankingCC], FeatureSelection], [SVMClassifier [KernelProvider]], TransformAndClassify]
42	ParamSearch [[[RankingCC], FeatureSelection], [LinearSVMClassifier [LinearKernelProvider]], TransformAndClassify]
43	ParamSearch [[[RankingCC], FeatureSelection], [ExpectedClass, kNN [MetricMachine (EuclideanOUO)]], TransformAndClassify]
44	ParamSearch [[[RankingCC], FeatureSelection], [LVQ, kNN (Euclidean)], TransformAndClassify]
45	ParamSearch [[[RankingCC], FeatureSelection], [Boosting (10x) [NBC]], TransformAndClassify]
46	ParamSearch [[[RankingFScore], FeatureSelection], [kNN (Euclidean)], TransformAndClassify]
47	ParamSearch [[[RankingFScore], FeatureSelection], [kNN [MetricMachine (EuclideanOUO)]], TransformAndClassify]
48	ParamSearch [[[RankingFScore], FeatureSelection], [kNN [MetricMachine (Mahalanobis)]], TransformAndClassify]
49	ParamSearch [[[RankingFScore], FeatureSelection], [NBC], TransformAndClassify]
50	ParamSearch [[[RankingFScore], FeatureSelection], [SVMClassifier [KernelProvider]], TransformAndClassify]
51	ParamSearch [[[RankingFScore], FeatureSelection], [LinearSVMClassifier [LinearKernelProvider]], TransformAndClassify]
52	ParamSearch [[[RankingFScore], FeatureSelection], [ExpectedClass, kNN [MetricMachine (EuclideanOUO)]], TransformAndClassify]
53	ParamSearch [[[RankingFScore], FeatureSelection], [LVQ, kNN (Euclidean)], TransformAndClassify]
54	ParamSearch [[[RankingFScore], FeatureSelection], [Boosting (10x) [NBC]], TransformAndClassify]

(according to their complexities, compare Table 1) and about accuracy of each tested machine.

In the middle of the diagram—see the first diagram in Fig. 3—there is a column with task ids (the same ids as in table 1). But the order of rows in the diagram reflects complexities of test tasks. It means that the most complex tasks are placed at the top and the task of the smallest complexities is visualized at the bottom. For example, in Fig. 3, at the bottom, I can see task ids 4 and 31 which correspond to the Naive Bayes Classifier and the ParamSearch [NBC] classifier. At the top, I can see task ids 54 and 45, as the most complex ParamSearch test tasks of this benchmark. Task order in the second example (Fig. 4) is completely different.

On the right side of the *Task id* column, there is a plot presenting starting, stopping and breaking times of each test task. For an example of restarted task please look at Fig. 3, at the topmost task-id 54—there are two horizontal bars corresponding to the two periods of the task run. The break means that the task was started, broken because of exceeded allocated time and restarted when the tasks of larger complexities got their turn. The breaks occur for the tasks, for which the complexity prediction was too optimistic. Two different diagrams (in Fig. 3 and 4) easily bring the conclusion that the amount of inaccurately predicted time complexity is quite small (there are very few broken bars). Note that, when a task is broken, its subtasks, that have already been computed are not recalculated during the test-task restart (due to the machine unification mechanism and machine cache [10]). At the bottom, the *Time line* axis can be seen. The scope of the time is $[0, 1]$ interval to show the times relative to the start and the end of the whole MLA computations.

On the left side of the *Task-id* column, the accuracies of classification test tasks and their approximated complexities are presented. At the bottom, there is the *Accuracy* axis with interval from 0 (on the right) to 1 (on the left side). Each test task has its own gray bar starting at 0 and finished exactly at the point corresponding to the accuracy. So the accuracies of all the tasks are easily visible and comparable. Longer bars show higher accuracies.

The leftmost column of the diagram presents ranks of the test tasks (the ranking of the accuracies).

Between the columns with the task ids and the accuracy-ranks, on top of the gray bars corresponding to the accuracies, some thin solid lines can be seen. The lines start at the right side (just like the accuracy bars) and go to the right according to proper magnitudes. For each task, the three lines correspond to total complexity (the upper line), memory complexity (the middle line) and time complexity (the lower line)[4]. All three complexities are the approximated complexities (see Eq. 10 and 11). Approximated complexities presented on the left side of the diagram can be easily compared visually to the time-schedule obtained in the real time on the right side of the diagram. Longer lines mean higher complexities. The longest line is spread to maximum width. The others are proportionally shorter. So the complexity lines at the top of the diagram

---

[4] In the case of time complexity, $t/\log t$ is plotted, not the time t itself.

are long while the lines at the bottom are almost invisible. It can be seen that sometimes the time complexity of a task is smaller while the total complexity is larger and vice versa. For example, see tasks 42 and 48 again in Fig. 3 (table 1 describes tasks numbers).

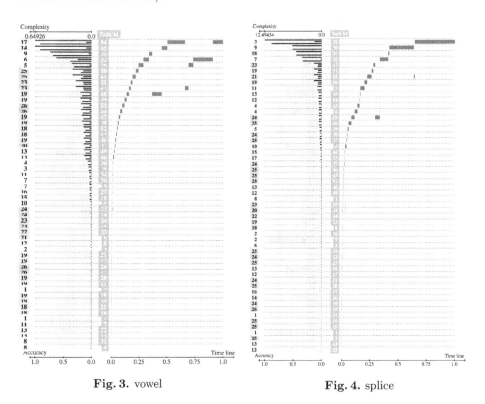

Fig. 3. vowel   **Fig. 4.** splice

If you like to see more results or in better resolution please download the document at http://www.is.umk.pl/~norbert/publications/11-njCmplxEval-Figs.pdf.

4   Summary

Modified measures of the complexity in context of meta-learning are really an efficient tool, especially for restricted learning problems.

The most important feature of the presented MLA is that thanks to complexity measures it facilitates finding accurate solutions in the order of increasing complexity. Simple solutions are started before the complex ones, to support finding simple and accurate solutions as soon as possible. Presented illustrations (diagrams) clearly show that approximation of complexity can be used to control the order of testing tasks to maximize the probability that right solution will be find.

What's more with the help of collected meta-knowledge the complexity measure adjusts the order of test tasks online to favor more promising learning machines.

References

1. Brazdil, P., Giraud-Carrier, C., Soares, C., Vilalta, R.: Metalearning: Applications to Data Mining. Springer (2009)
2. Solomonoff, R.: A preliminary report on a general theory of inductive inference. Technical Report V-131, Cambridge, Ma.: Zator Co. (1960)
3. Solomonoff, R.: A formal theory of inductive inference part i. Information and Control 7(1), 1–22 (1964)
4. Solomonoff, R.: A formal theory of inductive inference part ii. Information and Control 7(2), 224–254 (1964)
5. Kolmogorov, A.N.: Three approaches to the quantitative definition of information. Prob. Inf. Trans. 1, 1–7 (1965)
6. Li, M., Vitányi, P.: An Introduction to Kolmogorov Complexity and Its Applications. Text and Monographs in Computer Science. Springer (1993)
7. Jankowski, N.: Applications of Levin's universal optimal search algorithm. In: Kącki, E. (ed.) System Modeling Control 1995, vol. 3, pp. 34–40. Polish Society of Medical Informatics, Łódź (May 1995)
8. Levin, L.A.: Universal sequential search problems. Problems of Information Transmission 9 (1973), translated from Problemy Peredachi Informatsii (Russian)
9. Merz, C.J., Murphy, P.M.: UCI repository of machine learning databases (1998), http://www.ics.uci.edu/~mlearn/MLRepository.html
10. Grąbczewski, K., Jankowski, N.: Saving time and memory in computational intelligence system with machine unification and task spooling. Knowledge-Based Systems 24(5), 570–588 (2011)

Design of a Conscious Machine

P. Allen King

30 Gibson St, Needham Mass, USA, 02492
allen@a-king.us

Abstract. We define here the primary concepts needed to make a hardware machine with intelligence capabilities similar to animals and humans, a machine that innately imitates, unconsciously initiates attention shifts, wonders what if, learns why, and improves from mistakes. We will specify the functional requirements for a few particularly important parts, as connectionist schemas. This poses several problems for established disciplines of AI, to produce computational algorithms of the kinds required here. These notes will guide the next phase, where the schemas described here will be turned into code intended to learn to play the Super Mario Brothers video game.

Keywords: connectionism, semantic networks, world model, brain state, reenactment, simulation, consciousness, cognition, prediction error, evolutionary computing, machine learning.

1 Introduction

What is the essence of the functions that the mechanisms of our nerves and brains perform as we live our lives and learn to do better? We seek functions that soak up the ways of the world like sponges, and allow the being they control to prosper. How might these be implemented by cortical minicolumns as atoms of the cortex? As a starting point, we explore some massively parallel algorithms, algorithms that might underlie these human-like effects. Our architecture is constructed of a synergetic combination of mechanisms, each of which embodies an aspect of cognition, and together synergize important elements. How we came up with the architecture is of less importance than how well the pieces actually perform together.

Neurology is useful to our work here mostly because it attempts to understand the best existence proof of intelligence we have, the brain. We must constantly study the brain, especially when charting key architectural decisions. We get glimpses of a simpler set of organizing principles for animal intelligence through the study of different kinds of animals, as well as the embryonic development. To keep combined explanations understandably simple, some very simple individual models have been used. They explain essential operation just enough to achieve the desired system's synergies, but avoid any undue complexity to mimic human behavior. Two examples: the simple model that "evolution learns" something is a welcomed simplification from the precise form. We also resurrect Kornski's concept of the Grandmother Cell [1], to be used as a simplistic short-hand for the distributed data representation of the cortex, nicely hiding the complexity full distributed data representations.

D.L. Dowe (Ed.): Solomonoff Festschrift, LNAI 7070, pp. 211–222, 2013.
© Springer-Verlag Berlin Heidelberg 2013

Engineering is useful in our work here too. This is the start of an engineering plan, to build a computational medium containing the hard parts of cognition, into which experience will naturally grow un-aided. I have been involved in a half dozen large engineering projects, like the world's largest shared memory multi-processor and the world's largest scalable router. Every one of those projects involved dozens of people and had an architectural document at its core which started by describing a set of mathematical, almost cartoon-like operations upon which the rest was built. This document hopes to at least start such a plan for an AI. There are many ties to existing work given throughout, in areas such as Evolutionary Computing, Machine Learning, and Connectionism. This theory poses interesting questions for each, to come up with implementations for the various parts of the straw man pieces we propose. Once an operational prototype is constructed, the work of psychology and other fields will be able to directly contribute muscle to our straw man.

Section 2 describes how the being's worldly knowledge is held in elements, and how they work. Section 3 follows the operation of system so constructed. It ends with a list of things not in the model, lest they be forgotten. Finally, in Section 4, some critical implementation choices and details are discussed.

2   Functional Requirements

Here we define requirements that a lower level implementation must satisfy to implement factals as we imagine them, so factals work as advertised. Currently it is easier to express this functionality as the operation of groups. The operation of individual factals should be derived from that.

2.1   Worldly Facts

The computing elements we will define are called Factals. Each factal maintains a particular one-bit predicate fact[1] about the world state [2]. As an example, one such fact might be "I am standing", which is at this moment either true or false (or characterized by a probability). All information the being has about the current conditions of the world is held in the active state of its factals; All information about models of the world are held in their interconnection patterns. Having this one form provides a major simplification to our understanding of the cortex, since the inner workings of all factals are similar. These functions include, we believe, a) constantly instantiating new factals to record newly explored parts of the enormous state space. Perhaps thousands must be born per second. We believe factals in a garden have the ability to learning at birth the fact that establishes their identity, thus each claiming its unique informational territory in a hierarchy of sophistication, where facts there range from very simple (e.g. "it is red") to very highly sophisticated (e.g. "He will succeed"). b) A factal continually makes an estimation of the current truth of its fact in the being's perceived environment. Finally, c) a factal polls the desires of neighbors, and, acting through other factals makes the fact become true in the world if it can. (E.g. That I desire that 'my body is I standing' factal should be true causes

---

[1] This definition could be expanded to an analog bimodal probability if needed.

[2] We presume the simple case that all observers agree on the facts.

me to stand.) The architecture proposed here provides the being with many special abilities to support its learning of the world – it provides a computational environment that automatically embodies most of the capabilities required for consciousness.[3] The use of binary predicates preclude world models from having scalar world computations such as x = 3.72 + v*t supported. This decision simplifies the core, but requires multi-factal solutions, using fuzzy coding methods [2].

There are several ways of encoding the estimate that a factal makes. It might be a) the probability of truth, a value between 0 and 1.0 representing occurrence frequency statistically. This probability is updated when new information arrives, using Bayesian-like rules where new information is combined with existing a-priori information to produce an a-posteriori prediction (which is then compared to the actual for learning). b) This may extend as far as the belief networks of Pearl [3]. Another promising scheme is to c) encode the raw importance of this truth as its estimate. If two estimates compete, the more important one wins. d) Still other encoding strategies involve changing and averaging, needed for global convergence of the backbone of a simulation network.

2.2   Smaller Factal Groups

A **Worldly Variable** (or variable for short) encodes information which is best expressed as an enumerated range of possible values (e.g. `color={red, green,white}`). It is implemented as a finite array of factals, one for each potential value. The range of a world variable may take on may change after learning[4]. Although a world variable may take on arbitrary estimates for its values, it is said to be "well behaved" if statistically it has at most one significantly active value at a time (and nil data is coded with all 0 values). We use algorithms which work best if this is the case, such as those in [4].

Related Aspects are a groups of related variables in the data plane that are known to all refer to the same underlying physical object. **Plants** are groups of connected factals with a common purpose and reward structure. (Section 4 describe two plants: trees and coincidence records.) **Gardens** are Evolutionary Computing environments which support the growth of plants.

2.3   Cognitive Functions

A factal has a physical manifestation which manages the operation of a fact in the cognitive mechanism being constructed. We also assume all mechanisms of a factal are collocated (possibly accounting for the neurological form of the minicolumn[5]). The functionality we believe is required to animate a factal is three-fold: a) situational reactions, b) reenactment simulation, and c) long term digital storage. To explain of their function, we resort to a metaphor called the **Forest Castle Journal**, as shown in Figure 1 below. (Although the description is metaphoric, precise algorithms are implied.)

---

[3] We do not define consciousness, although we identify some of its functional correlates.

[4] This may require lower level support, involving neural or tubulin fascillation.

[5] Thus we might predict that older 3-layer archio cortex has no Reenactment simulator and/or Semantic Network.

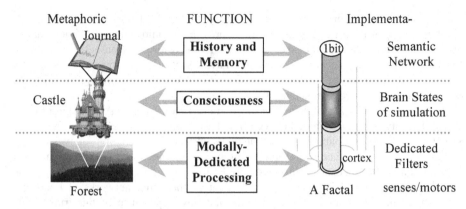

Fig. 1. Shows the Forest-Castle-Journal, with their attributes, and packaging as Factal

There is an "Enchanted Forest" and in the forest there is a "Magical Castle" and in the castle there is the "Journal of All". The castle (enlivened by the actions of its inhabitants) controls and manages the forest for the castle's purpose (e.g. to quarry granite or collect honey). Things in the forest will continue on as they were without the castle's attention. All the history of the forest, including how castle has interacted with it, is kept in the Journal. It also contains a complete set of models of what happens in the forest. Castle inhabitants read the journal, and go into the forest and improve it. The journal is also indexed so that, at any moment of time, it is poised to have the castle predict the future of the forest. The Journal is thought of as software, while the castle and forest hardware. The forest is thought of as analog while the castle and journal digital. The forest part of each factal is where the unconscious real time data flow processing of the data plane occurs, that determines the being's situation and its instant reaction to it [5]. The castle part selects a particular forest area (but usually just one at a time[6]) to supervise its learning. (An interesting example is given in Section 4.3.) A forest area can get the castle's attention in dire circumstances like fire. The mechanisms of the castle are strong functional correlates of consciousness.

2.4   Macro Structures of the Whole Cortex (Brodmann)

The **Data Plane** operates real-time, as the forest. It contains selected factals of the brain which represents the experiences in various ways in different places. It can be thought of as a billion-bit computer word of factals, with specific sparse operations [6]. There is much internal structure to this word, since most of a factal's connections are local, thus they are grouped into various kinds, modalities, and specialties of information, called information domains. These are probably the origin of Brodmann areas. The protocol binding the areas together into a single data plane is formed in layers, as are factals themselves, with a well defined interface for each: a) it maintains

---

[6] This is just to keep things simple initially. Later, all kinds of synergies may be found by splitting the data plane into independent sections.

consistent representations across the cortex of the current brain state, using data flow machine built from these related aspects, and processes associations as well. [7] With the ability to extract causality and representations, factals organize to (simplistically) detect lines in V1, 2d objects in V2, V3 … V4 motion, color, etc. We here believe that there are many further bidirectional filter layers above that, embodying the upper levels of our understanding. There are filters formed by all of our knowledge to the most sophisticated explanations we have of the world, passing through many cognitive areas such as the "what/where" paths and "the remembered present" [Edelman] All of the nuances we understand are held in this data plane.

3   Processing in an Information Domain

Figure 2 shows the processing of a domain in more detail.

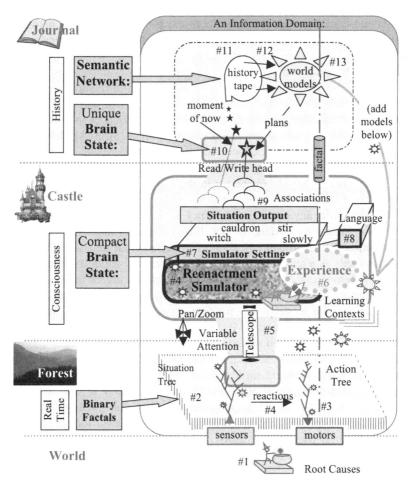

Fig. 2. Shows a given information domain, with its four interacting areas: the world, a real-time area, an attentional area, a semantic network

The "Information Domain" a machine can construct is limited by the information at its inputs. Restricting the number of factals inputs to domain is an effective way to limit the number of factals required to implement it. The same processing applies whether the information domain is very small (e.g. finite state machine sized), or very large (e.g. a whole brain). (There is much of interest in between as well.) The being in the figure is experiencing a scene from Macbeth, as shown in a cartoon (#1). A single factal (of many) is show in red. The various languages used for descriptions are shown arrayed vertically: factals, two kinds of brain states, and semantic networks. Remember throughout. All information flow in the brain is bidirectional, it is possible to recall a particular brain state from a history tape and move it down through layers into the simulator. There it is re-enacted it in simulation, and re-experience. (To try this out now: think of your first kiss. Hopefully, you just recalled a brain state from memory and re-experienced it.)

A **dedicated real-time area** in the bottom contains a Situation Tree (#2), Action trees (#3) and containing known behaviors, and low level reactions between them (e.g. stranger → don't trust) (#4). Situation dynamically marks the being's cognitive information space, as cairns mark trails above the tree-line. Where we are (amongst the cairns) can be evaluated at any time (presuming each estimates how close we are to it), and we can desire to be at a different cairn. Information for situation is determined at each level of the sophistication hierarchy, in one of three ways: a) **Sensation:** involves detecting causes based on the coincidences in lower level more sensory factals. This is sometimes called spatial pooling [8]. b) **Modeling** involves detecting causes based on coincidences between past and present, to form a forward predictive model. This temporal pooling also helps recover hidden state. c) **Expecting** comes from higher (more global) places in the hierarchy and bias the local choices. They focus attention and set learning contexts. Information from each of these may or may not be present at any one moment. They are combined by Bayesian methods in the data plane. Presence of redundant modalities fosters learning.

An **attentional mechanism** can connect to various real-time areas of the forest. This is shows this as a telescope (#5), which can pan and zoom to various things we call zombies. Zombies are areas of the forest which do not currently have the attention of consciousness. The attentional mechanism feeds the **Reenactment Simulator**, a generative or forward model which predicts sensory information by mapping from causes to sensory consequences. It provides an internal model of the causal dependencies amongst states of the external world.

We believe that to experience some phenomenon (#6) one must first simulate it inside the brain[7]. The Reenactment Simulator provides a single detailed analysis for a wide variety of patterns presented it. Descartes describes a similar element of consciousness, which Daniel Dennett names the Cartesian Theater [9]. (Descartes falsely claims it was localized in one spot.) Many others, including Helmholtz explored the central role of simulators in cognition. All this happened before our minds knew computers and could build simulators.

---

[7] We do not speculate here on why this might be so, but believe that once this part of the design is working, answers to such questions will be clearer.

The **simulation parameters** (#7) (bidirectional) are the highest level of the Reenactment Simulator, and become part of the Situation Output. The typology of the sub-simulator configuration can be serialized by language (#8) and then de-serialized in the brain of another[8], effectively transferring a meme. The **Situation Output** is the final output of situation, which is very much like a generalized form of place cells [10]. Limiting its values is important. Its elements are the basis for expressing every experience. The situation output is not well behaved, and must be fed into a schema of **Coincidence Records** (#9) to form a **Unique Brain State** (#10), a single-factal representation for every experienced pattern of the simulation output. It is built as a series of trees with shared leaves. These trees may also include internal analysis, attitudes, and actions associated with an experience. May additional factals may have to be added to encode each new experience, especially if it is novel.

The **Semantic Network** has nodes which are Unique Brain States and links which indicate related states. The Reenactment Simulator can act as a write head, creating a tape as links recording past experiences. A list of these past now's form a history tape, a perfect linear **history tape** of the past (#11). An organic network **editing process**es "condenses meaning" (#12) and morphs the linear tapes into individual, separately usable **models** (#13), which are then inserted into the operation of the Reenactment Simulator, and the Situation and Action trees. The factals of the Semantic Network also have links that are read by the Reenactment Simulator, to guide it in the prediction of the future. Links have two ends to connect factals. (Links also have additional pointers to type and strength.) Some link types carry truth estimates during Situation, to create the estimate of a factal from its neighbors. Other types connect factals of the Semantic Network, adding meanings by their presence.

3.1 Caveats

We have described the simple model of cognition, but there are still many critical details which must be added for this design to be used in scalable systems the size of the brain. What is missing includes adding: continuous time, organic (not toy) encodings, decentralizing data, noisy data, world variables that are not well behaved, inaccuracy of efficient optimizations, seamless module boundaries, non-ideal situations, managing combinatorial explosions, detecting equivalent forms, limited fact instantiation rates, and distribution of centralized functions.

4   Implementation Notes

Implementations may take multiple incidents to learn (e.g. to actually get the factals into a network). Implementations may use lossy information compression if it attempts to preserve meaning as much as possible. We believe that much of the robust nature of human thought is a synergetic byproduct of such mechanisms. Implementations may contain statistics on the number of occurrences akin to those of N-Arm Bandit processes [11]e to aid growth and culling.

---

[8] This is easiest to understand when the a-priori informational structures in the two beings are identical. When they aren't it's harder.

4.1   The Modeling Strategy

The brain knows it has good models of the world, if they are able to predict the future properly. We uses many small models, rather than one big model for two reasons: a) model building algorithms generally scale supra-linearly with the number of inputs (making big models is harder), and b) smaller models can be wired together differently in different situations, giving greater cognitive power to the simulation. A small model is shown in Figure 3 below. In it, the function $G(Z_i)$, the predicted value

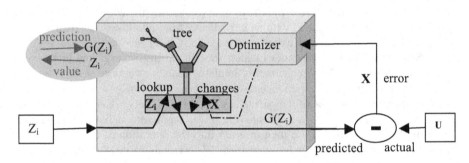

Fig. 3. An modeling element, in modeling mode

of a World Variable U, is computed using a tree. The tree acts as a dynamic decoder [12], switching experiences to the leaf that best characterizes the current Z_i, and growing new leaves as new experiences enter. The estimate $G(Z_i)$ is retrieved from selected leaf; the answer returns back the same path to the trunk. When the result inaccurately predicts U, an error signal X is generated and the tree updated to accept blame. This might involve adjusting Stoller split thresholds [13], but commonly involves adding new branches at the culpable part of the tree, to distinguish the new condition. New branches are usually chosen to be switched by the most active unused dimension in the elements of Z_i. The conditions that caused the error are active in the path and this makes updating easier. For delayed reinforcement, a mechanism to save and recall those conditions, as they were at the time the estimate was made, is required.

4.2   Coincidence Records

Coincidence Records are used to record that a particular set of things (those connected to the inputs) have ever occurred together. It is instantiated as quickly as possible after the first occurrence. Coincidence Records are composable – it is possible to make a new Coincidence Record from the outputs of several more detailed ones. (Thus the lower levels of coincidence trees tend to live scattered (but contained within) specific Brodmann areas, and they are integrated in other areas of the data plane.) A schema of Coincidence Records is defined to generating a very large variable called the Unique Situation, which is well-defined and has a single-factal representations of all patterns encountered in the Situation Output.

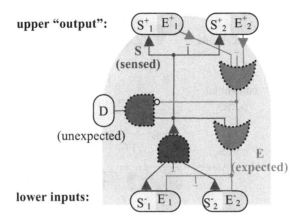

Fig. 4. A Coincidence Recorder, formed as a Bidirectional AND

Bidirectional Coincidence Record elements are used. Figure 4 above shows one with two inputs and two users, but they can have many more (up to some implementation limit). The elements inside this bidirectional unit are unidirectional. In it, activating all the lower "sensory inputs" in the pattern activates the upper "output". (The names "input" and "output" are with respect to these sensory signals, shown here in red going up the hierarchy.) Companion expectation signals shown in green, flow down the hierarchy. Activating the expectation of an upper "output" causes an expectation of the pattern to appear on the lower "inputs". Coincidence Records also have an output D, that indicates that its association is TRUE but not expected. Other mechanisms monitor these unexpected signals during learning, and construct minimal trees to contain them. A generalized form performs a weighted sum and threshold, instead of the AND. By adjusting the threshold, it can perform fuzzy matches by using mid-threshold values, and a bidirectional OR. The OR is useful in declaring that all of its inputs are equivalent, hence decreases combinatorial explosions.

4.3   Hippocampal Routing

Evolution seems to have an insatiable desire for more associations, beyond what we have shown with coincidence records. We propose the hippocampus performs a vital role in determining associations at the macroscopic level, where it acts like a "castle" in a central role closely akin to short term memory. Figure 5 below shows the system operation, as follows: Absent pre-filters and sharing, the current situation is fed directly to the hippocampus, which determines new associations. The hippocampus can learn new associations quickly, but can hold only a limited number of them. Once an association has been learned, the hippocampus also has the ability to transfer it to a much less expensive and more effective form, as a cortical pre-filter build from new axons and synapses. With the pre-filter in place, the hippocampus no longer has indication of the association, freeing space for new associations to be learned. One can think of the hippocampus as a CPU cache, writing its data back to memory, the cortex.

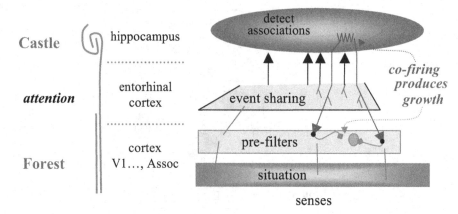

Fig. 5. Shows the brain of a being, where the associations located in the hippocampus are used to grow filters

Learned associations are moved to the cortex as Pre-filters using a process I call Hebbian Arborization. In it, axons are attracted to dendrite sites with which they co-fire. It operates using axonal growth cones which are hyper-sensitive to the direction of signals that are coincident in time with their firing. This forms a Hebbian network which is much denser than classical Hebbian networks, and operates by growth rather than adjustment. The hippocampus repeatedly co-fires the coincident ports in a form of rehearsal, which dramatically accelerates the speed of Hebbian Arborization. (It can proceed continually when the brain is idle.) In our metaphor, this is the castle teaching the forest. The brain might have evolved this way if the computation for learning associations grows supra-linearly but can be shared amongst groups of factals.

Event Sharing is yet another way to significantly increase the number of potential inputs signals, by organizing them into mutually exclusive groups in advance. We imagine a concentration multiplexor in the entorhinal cortex (EC) which selects which group is active.

In summary, we have described a simple model with significantly human characteristics. In Algorithms to seeks out causes have been postulated. Much more background is available at http://brain-gears.blogspot.com.

References

1. Gross, C.: Genealogy of the "Grandmother Cell". History of Neurosci. (2002)
2. Stoica, A., Wingate, M., McLaughlin, P.: Fuzzy modelling and simulation for a fencing robot. In: 2nd Int. Conf. on Modelling and Simulation MS 1993, July 12-15 (1993)
3. Halpern, J., Pearl, J.: Causes and Explanations: A Structural-Model Approach. In: Proceedings of the Seventeenth Conference on Uncertainly in AI (2001)
4. Hawkins, J: On intelligence. Times Books (2003)
5. Gladwell, M.: Blink: the power of thinking without thinking. Little Brown & Co.
6. Kanerva, P.: Sparse Distributed Memory. MIT Press (1988)

7. Rumelhart. D.: Parallel Distributed Processing (1986)
8. George, D., Hawkins, J.: Hierarchical Temporal Memory Concepts, Theory, and Terminology. Numenta Inc.
9. Dennett, D.: Consciousness Explained (1991)
10. Moser, E., Kropff, E., Britt-Moser, M.: Place Cells, Grid Cells, and the Brain's Spatial Representation System. Annual Review of Neuroscience (2008)
11. Gittins, J.C.: Bandit Processes and Dynamic Allocation Indices. J. R. Statist. Soc. B 41(2), 148–177 (1979)
12. Weidemann, H., Stear, E.: Entropy Analysis of Parameter Estimation. Information and Control 14 (1969)
13. de Sá, J.P.M., Gama, J., Sebastião, R., Alexandre, L.A.: Decision trees using the minimum entropy-of-error principle. In: Jiang, X., Petkov, N. (eds.) CAIP 2009. LNCS, vol. 5702, pp. 799–807. Springer, Heidelberg (2009)

In Dedication to Ray Solomonoff

I worked at the MIT AI Lab at the same time as Ray did in the '60's although never directly with him. After leaving MIT and making a good living in the 128 electronics belt, I got to know Ray as a regular in Arthur Shurcliff's "Science Discussion Group", which met monthly in a Chinese restaurant in back of MIT. It was formed by people who enjoyed of discussing Science. Ray was an old timer when I joined mid '80's. He always exhibited the ability to take a set of concepts into some level of advanced mathematical understanding. He would listen for a while, and then offer some pretty mathematical understanding that would make me smile. When I pushed on him, he seemed to have an impressive weight to his understanding, but unfortunately we did not pursue it with him. I remember once driving him home, when he excitedly shared how if "he could get X to do Y, than it was probable that Z". I never quite understood what X was, but I knew he'd be up late that night figuring it out.

My wife asked me how Ray's work affected mine, and I had to answer that in fact, I did not really know. Perhaps it supplies others such as myself a measurement tool. If you know, tell me. I do know that both of us came from the same place and have a strong desire to describe some part of human cognition, and thus make the task of understanding the human mind easier. And so I dedicate this work to Ray Solomonoff's always-curious spirit, which has often inspired mine.

Circa 2005, on the left with Murry Denolsky, in the middle facing Arthur Shurcliff, discussing world oil models, if I remember right. To Ray's left at the table are Fred Happgood, Eric Anderson, unknown, Bill Skocpol, Arthur Shurcliff and Hugh Field. On the right, Rays wife Grace, Steve Wintham, …

No Free Lunch versus Occam's Razor
in Supervised Learning

Tor Lattimore[1] and Marcus Hutter[1,2,3]

[1] Australian National University, Canberra, Australia
[2] ETH Zürich, Switzerland
[3] NICTA
{tor.lattimore,marcus.hutter}@anu.edu.au

Abstract. The No Free Lunch theorems are often used to argue that domain specific knowledge is required to design successful algorithms. We use algorithmic information theory to argue the case for a universal bias allowing an algorithm to succeed in all interesting problem domains. Additionally, we give a new algorithm for off-line classification, inspired by Solomonoff induction, with good performance on all structured (compressible) problems under reasonable assumptions. This includes a proof of the efficacy of the well-known heuristic of randomly selecting training data in the hope of reducing the misclassification rate.

Keywords: Supervised learning, Kolmogorov complexity, no free lunch, Occam's razor.

1 Introduction

The No Free Lunch (NFL) theorems, stated and proven in various settings and domains [16,26,27], show that no algorithm performs better than any other when their performance is averaged uniformly over all possible problems of a particular type.[1] These are often cited to argue that algorithms must be designed for a particular domain or style of problem, and that there is no such thing as a general purpose algorithm.

On the other hand, Solomonoff induction [18,19] and the more general AIXI model [9] appear to universally solve the sequence prediction and reinforcement learning problems respectively. The key to the apparent contradiction is that Solomonoff induction and AIXI do not assume that each problem is equally likely. Instead they apply a bias towards more structured problems. This bias is universal in the sense that no class of structured problems is favored over another. This approach is philosophically well justified by Occam's razor.

The two classic domains for NFL theorems are optimisation and classification. In this paper we will examine classification and only remark that the case for optimisation is more complex. This difference is due to the active nature of optimisation where actions affect future observations.

---

[1] Such results have been less formally discussed long before by Watanabe in 1969 [25].

D.L. Dowe (Ed.): Solomonoff Festschrift, LNAI 7070, pp. 223–235, 2013.

Previously, some authors have argued that the NFL theorems do not disprove the existence of universal algorithms for two reasons.

1. That taking a uniform average is not philosophically the right thing to do, as argued informally in [7].
2. Carroll and Seppi in [1] note that the NFL theorem measures performance as misclassification rate, where as in practise, the utility of a misclassification in one direction may be more costly than another.

We restrict our consideration to the task of minimising the misclassification rate while arguing more formally for a non-uniform prior inspired by Occam's razor and formalised by Kolmogorov complexity. We also show that there exist algorithms (unfortunately only computable in the limit) with very good properties on all structured classification problems.

The paper is structured as follows. First, the required notation is introduced (Section 2). We then state the original NFL theorem, give a brief introduction to Kolmogorov complexity, and show that if a non-uniform prior inspired by Occam's razor is used, then there exists a free lunch (Section 3). Finally, we give a new algorithm inspired by Solomonoff induction with very attractive properties in the classification problem (Section 4).

2   Preliminaries

Here we introduce the required notation and define the problem setup for the No Free Lunch theorems.

Strings. A finite string x over alphabet X is a finite sequence $x_1 x_2 x_3 \cdots x_{n-1} x_n$ with $x_i \in X$. An infinite string x over alphabet X is an infinite sequence $x_1 x_2 x_3 \cdots$. Alphabets are usually countable or finite, while in this paper they will almost always be binary. For finite strings we have a length function defined by $\ell(x) := n$ for $x = x_1 x_2 \cdots x_n$. The empty string of length 0 is denoted by ϵ. The set X^n is the set of all strings of length n. The set X^* is the set of all finite strings. The set X^∞ is the set of all infinite strings. Let x be a string (finite or infinite) then substrings are denoted $x_{s:t} := x_s x_{s+1} \cdots x_{t-1} x_t$ where $s \leq t$. A useful shorthand is $x_{<t} := x_{1:t-1}$. Let $x, y \in X^*$ and $z \in X^\infty$ with $\ell(x) = n$ and $\ell(y) = m$ then

$$xy := x_1 x_2, \cdots x_{n-1} x_n y_1 y_2 \cdots y_{m-1} y_m$$
$$xz := x_1 x_2, \cdots x_{n-1} x_n z_1 z_2 z_3 \cdots$$

As expected, xy is finite and has length $\ell(xy) = n + m$ while xz is infinite. For binary strings, we write $\#1(x)$ and $\#0(x)$ to mean the number of 0's and number of 1's in x respectively.

Classification. Informally, a classification problem is the task of matching features to class labels. For example, recognizing handwriting where the features are images and the class labels are letters. In supervised learning, it is (usually) unreasonable to expect this to be possible without any examples of correct classifications. This can be solved by providing a list of feature/class label pairs representing the true classification of each feature. It is hoped that these examples can be used to generalize and correctly classify other features.

The following definitions formalize classification problems, algorithms capable of solving them, as well as the loss incurred by an algorithm when applied to a problem, or set of problems. The setting is that of transductive learning as in [3].

Definition 1 (Classification Problem). *Let X and Y be finite sets representing the feature space and class labels respectively. A classification problem over X, Y is defined by a function $f : X \to Y$ where $f(x)$ is the true class label of feature x.*

In the handwriting example, X might be the set of all images of a particular size and Y would be the set of letters/numbers as well as a special symbol for images that correspond to no letter/number.

Definition 2 (Classification Algorithm). *Let f be a classification problem and $X_m \subseteq X$ be the training features on which f will be known. We write f_{X_m} to represent the function $f_{X_m} : X_m \to Y$ with $f_{X_m}(x) := f(x)$ for all $x \in X_m$. A classification algorithm is a function, A, where $A(f_{X_m}, x)$ is its guess for the class label of feature $x \in X_u := X - X_m$ when given training data f_{X_m}. Note we implicitly assume that X and Y are known to the algorithm.*

Definition 3 (Loss function). *The loss of algorithm A, when applied to classification problem f, with training data X_m is measured by counting the proportion of misclassifications in the testing data, X_u.*

$$L_A(f, X_m) := \frac{1}{|X_u|} \sum_{x \in X_u} [\![A(f_{X_m}, x) \neq f(x)]\!]$$

where $[\![\ ]\!]$ is the indicator function defined by, $[\![expr]\!] = 1$ if expr is true and 0 otherwise.

We are interested in the expected loss of an algorithm on the set of all problems where expectation is taken with respect to some distribution P.

Definition 4 (Expected loss). *Let $\mathcal{M}$ be the set of all functions from X to Y and P be a probability distribution on $\mathcal{M}$. If X_m is the training data then the expected loss of algorithm A is*

$$L_A(P, X_m) := \sum_{f \in \mathcal{M}} P(f) L_A(f, X_m)$$

3   No Free Lunch Theorem

We now use the above notation to give a version of the No Free Lunch Theorem of which Wolpert's is a generalization.

Theorem 1 (No Free Lunch). *Let P be the uniform distribution on $\mathcal{M}$. Then the following holds for any algorithm A and training data $X_m \subseteq X$.*

$$L_A(P, X_m) = |Y - 1|/|Y| \tag{1}$$

The key to the proof is the following observation. Let $x \in X_u$, then for all $y \in Y$, $P(f(x) = y|f|_{X_m}) = P(f(x) = y) = 1/|Y|$. This means no information can be inferred from the training data, which suggests no algorithm can be better than random.

Occam's razor/Kolmogorov Complexity. The theorem above is often used to argue that no general purpose algorithm exists and that focus should be placed on learning in specific domains.

The problem with the result is the underlying assumption that P is uniform, which implies that training data provides no evidence about the true class labels of the test data. For example, if we have classified the sky as blue for the last 1,000 years then a uniform assumption on the possible sky colours over time would indicate that it is just as likely to be green tomorrow as blue, a result that goes against all our intuition.

How then, do we choose a more reasonable prior? Fortunately, this question has already been answered heuristically by experimental scientists who must endlessly choose between one of a number of competing hypotheses. Given any experiment, it is easy to construct a hypothesis that fits the data by using a lookup table. However such hypotheses tend to have poor predictive power compared to a simple alternative that also matches the data. This is known as the principle of parsimony, or Occam's razor, and suggests that simple hypotheses should be given a greater weight than more complex ones.

Until recently, Occam's razor was only an informal heuristic. This changed when Solomonoff, Kolmogorov and Chaitin independently developed the field of algorithmic information theory that allows for a formal definition of Occam's razor. We give a brief overview here, while a more detailed introduction can be found in [13]. An in depth study of the philosophy behind Occam's razor and its formalisation by Kolmogorov complexity can be found in [12,15]. While we believe Kolmogorov complexity is the most foundational formalisation of Occam's razor, there have been other approaches such as MML [23] and MDL [8]. These other techniques have the advantage of being computable (given a computable prior) and so lend themselves to good practical applications.

The idea of Kolmogorov complexity is to assign to each binary string an integer valued *complexity* that represents the length of its shortest description. Those strings with short descriptions are considered simple, while strings with long descriptions are complex. For example, the string consisting of 1,000,000 1's can easily be described as "one million ones". On the other hand, to describe a string generated by tossing a coin 1,000,000 times would likely require a description about 1,000,000 bits long. The key to formalising this intuition is to choose a universal Turing machine as the language of descriptions.

Definition 5 (Kolmogorov Complexity). *Let U be a universal Turing machine and $x \in \mathcal{B}^*$ be a finite binary string. Then define the plain Kolmogorov* *complexity $C(x)$ to be the length of the shortest program (description) p such that $U(p) = x$.*

$$C(x) := \min_{p \in \mathcal{B}^*} \{\ell(p) : U(p) = x\}$$

It is easy to show that C depends on choice of universal Turing machine U only up to a constant independent of x and so it is standard to choose an arbitrary *reference* universal Turing machine.

For technical reasons it is difficult to use C as a prior, so Solomonoff introduced monotone machines to construct the Solomonoff prior, $\mathbf{M}$. A monotone Turing machine has one read-only input tape which may only be read from left to right and one write-only output tape that may only be written to from left to right. It has any number of working tapes. Let T be such a machine and write $T(p) = x$ to mean that after reading p, x is on the output tape. The machines are called monotone because if p is a prefix of q then $T(p)$ is a prefix of $T(q)$. It is possible to show there exists a universal monotone Turing machine U and this is used to define monotone complexity Km and Solomonoff's prior, $\mathbf{M}$.

Definition 6 (Monotone Complexity). *Let U be the reference universal monotone Turing machine then define Km, $\mathbf{M}$ and KM as follows,*

$$Km(x) := \min \{\ell(p) : U(p) = x*\}$$
$$\mathbf{M}(x) := \sum_{U(p)=x*} 2^{-\ell(p)}$$
$$KM(x) := -\log \mathbf{M}(x)$$

where $U(p) = x*$ means that when given input p, U outputs x possibly followed by more bits.

Some facts/notes follow.

1. For any n, $\sum_{x \in \mathcal{B}^n} \mathbf{M}(x) \leq 1$.
2. Km, $\mathbf{M}$ and KM are incomputable.
3. $0 < KM(x) \approx Km(x) \approx C(x) < \ell(x) + O(1)^2$

To illustrate why $\mathbf{M}$ gives greater weight to simple x, suppose x is simple then there exists a relatively short monotone Turing machine p, computing it. Therefore $Km(x)$ is small and so $2^{-Km(x)} \approx \mathbf{M}(x)$ is relatively large.

Since $\mathbf{M}$ is a semi-measure rather than a proper measure, it is not appropriate to use it in place of P when computing expected loss. However it can be normalized to a proper measure, $\mathbf{M}_{norm}$ defined inductively by

$$\mathbf{M}_{norm}(\epsilon) := 1 \qquad \mathbf{M}_{norm}(xb) := \mathbf{M}_{norm}(x)\frac{\mathbf{M}(xb)}{\mathbf{M}(x0) + \mathbf{M}(x1)}$$

---

[2] The approximation $C(x) \approx Km(x)$ is only accurate to $\log \ell(x)$, while $KM \approx Km$ is almost always very close [5,6]. This is a little surprising since the sum in the definition of $\mathbf{M}$ contains 2^{-Km}. It shows that there are only comparitively few short programs for any x.

Note that this normalisation is not unique, but is philosophically and technically the most attractive and was used and defended by Solomonoff. For a discussion of normalisation, see [13, p.303]. The normalised version satisfies $\sum_{x \in \mathcal{B}^n} \mathbf{M}_{norm}(x) = 1$.

We will also need to define $\mathbf{M}/KM$ with side information, $\mathbf{M}(y; x) := \mathbf{M}(y)$ where $x*$ is provided on a spare tape of the universal Turing machine. Now define $KM(y; x) := -\log \mathbf{M}(y; x)$. This allows us to define the complexity of a function in terms of its output relative to its input.

Definition 7 (Complexity of a function). *Let $X = \{x_1, \cdots, x_n\} \subseteq \mathcal{B}^k$ and $f : X \to \mathcal{B}$ then define the complexity of f, $KM(f; X)$ by*

$$KM(f; X) := KM(f(x_1)f(x_2) \cdots f(x_n); x_1, x_2, \cdots, x_n)$$

An example is useful to illustrate why this is a good measure of the complexity of f.

Example 1. Let $X \subseteq \mathcal{B}^n$ for some n, and $Y = \mathcal{B}$ and $f : X \to Y$ be defined by $f(x) = [\![x_n = 1]\!]$. Now for a complex X, the string $f(x_1)f(x_2) \cdots$ might be difficult to describe, but there is a very short program that can output $f(x_1)f(x_2) \cdots$ when given $x_1 x_2 \cdots$ as input. This gives the expected result that $KM(f; X)$ is very small.

Free Lunch Using Solomonoff Prior. We are now ready to use $\mathbf{M}_{norm}$ as a prior on a problem family. The following proposition shows that when problems are chosen according to the Solomonoff prior that there is a (possibly small) free lunch.

Before the proposition, we remark on problems with maximal complexity, $KM(f; X) = O(|X|)$. In this case f exhibits no structure allowing it to be compressed, which turns out to be equivalent to being random in every intuitive sense [14]. We do not believe such problems are any more interesting than trying to predict random coin flips. Further, the NFL theorems can be used to show that no algorithm can learn the class of random problems by noting that almost all problems are random. Thus a bias towards random problems is not much of a bias (from uniform) at all, and so at most leads to a decreasingly small free lunch as the number of problems increases.

Proposition 1 (Free lunch under Solomonoff prior). *Let $Y = \mathcal{B}$ and fix a $k \in \mathbb{N}$. Now let $X = \mathcal{B}^n$ and $X_m \subset X$ such that $|X_m| = 2^n - k$. For sufficiently large n there exists an algorithm A such that*

$$L_A(\mathbf{M}_{norm}, X_m) < 1/2$$

The proof is omitted due to space limitations, but the idea is very simple. Consider the algorithm such that $A(f|_{X_m}, x) = 1$ if $f(x) = 1$ for all $x \in X_m$ and $A(f|_{X_m}, x)$ is random otherwise. Then show that if the amount of training data is extremely large relative to the testing data then the Solomonoff prior assigns greater weight to the function $f_1(x) := 1$ for all x than the set of functions satisfying $f(x) = 1$ for all $x \in X_m$ but $f(x) \neq 1$ for some $x \in X_u$.

The proposition is unfortunately extremely weak. It is more interesting to know exactly what conditions are required to do much better than random. In the next section we present an algorithm with good performance on all well structured problems when given "good" training data. Without good training data, even assuming a Solomonoff prior, we believe it is unlikely that the best algorithm will perform well.

Note that while it appears intuitively likely that any non-uniform distribution such as $\mathbf{M}_{norm}$ might offer a free lunch, this is in fact not true. It is shown in [17] that there exist non-uniform distributions where the loss over a problem family is independent of algorithm. These distributions satisfy certain symmetry conditions not satisfied by $\mathbf{M}_{norm}$, which allows Proposition 1 to hold.

4   Complexity-Based Classification

Solomonoff induction is well known to solve the online prediction problem where the true value of each classification is known after each guess. In our setup, the true classification is only known for the training data, after which the algorithm no longer receives feedback. While Solomonoff induction can be used to bound the number of total errors while predicting deterministic sequences, it gives no indication of when these errors may occur. For this reason we present a complexity-inspired algorithm with better properties for the offline classification problem.

Before the algorithm we present a little more notation. As usual, let $X = \{x_1, x_2, \cdots, x_n\} \subseteq \mathcal{B}^k$, $Y = \mathcal{B}$ and let $X_m \subseteq X$ be the training data. Now define an indicator function χ by $\chi_i := [\![x_i \in X_m]\!]$.

Definition 8. *Let $f \in Y^X$ be a classification problem. The algorithm A^* is defined in two steps.*

$$\tilde{f} := \arg\min_{\tilde{f} \in Y^X} \left\{ KM(\tilde{f}; X) : \chi_i = 1 \implies \tilde{f}(x_i) = f(x_i) \right\}$$

$$A^*(f_{X_m}, x_i) := \tilde{f}(x_i)$$

Essentially A^* chooses for its model the simplest $\tilde{f}$ consistent with the training data and uses this for classifying unseen data. Note that the definition above only uses the value $y_i = f(x_i)$ where $\chi_i = 1$, and so it does not depend on unseen labels.

If $KM(f; X)$ is "small" then the function we wish to learn is simple so we should expect to be able to perform good classification, even given a relatively small amount of training data. This turns out to be true, but only with a good choice of training data. It is well known that training data should be "broad enough", and this is backed up by the example below and by Theorem 2, which give an excellent justification for random training data based on good theoretical

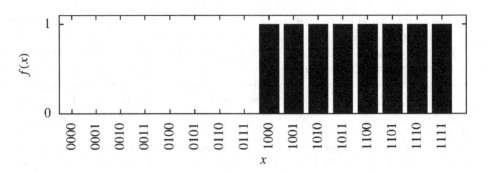

Fig. 1. A simple problem

(Theorem 2) and philosophical (AIT) underpinnings. The following example demonstrates the effect of bad training data on the performance of A^*.

Example 2. Let $X = \{0000, 0001, 0010, 0011, \cdots, 1101, 1110, 1111\}$ and $f(x)$ be defined to be the first bit of x as in Figure 1. Now suppose $\chi = 1^8 0^8$ (So the algorithm is only allowed to see the true class labels of x_1 through x_8). In this case, the simplest $\tilde{f}$ consistent with the first 16 data points, all of which are zeros, is likely to be $\tilde{f}(x) = 0$ for all $x \in X$ and so A^* will fail on every piece of testing data!

On the other hand, if $\chi = 001010011101101$, which was generated by tossing a coin 16 times, then $\tilde{f}$ will very likely be equal to f and so A^* will make no errors. Even if χ is zero about the critical point in the middle ($\chi_8 = \chi_9 = 0$) then $\tilde{f}$ should still match f mostly around the left and right and will only be unsure near the middle.

Note, the above is not precisely true since for small strings the dependence of KM on the universal monotone Turing machine can be fairly large. However if we increase the size of the example so that $|X| > 1000$ then these quirks disappear for natural reference universal Turing machines.

Definition 9 (Entropy). Let $\theta \in [0, 1]$

$$H(\theta) := \begin{cases} -[\theta \log \theta + (1 - \theta) \log(1 - \theta)] & \textit{if } \theta \neq 0 \textit{ and } \theta \neq 1 \\ 0 & \textit{otherwise} \end{cases}$$

Theorem 2. *Let $\theta \in (0, 1)$ be the proportion of data to be given for training then:*

1. *There exists a $\chi \in \mathcal{B}^\infty$ (training set) such that for all $n \in \mathbb{N}$, $\theta n - c_1 < \#1(\chi_{1:n}) < \theta n + c_1$ and $nH(\theta) - c_2 < KM(\chi_{1:n})$ for some $c_1, c_2 \in \mathbb{R}^+$.*
2. *For $n = |X|$, the loss of algorithm A^* when using training data determined by χ is bounded by*

$$L_{A^*}(f, X_m) < \frac{2KM(f; X) + KM(X) + c_2 + c_3}{n(1 - \theta - c_1/n) \log(1 - \theta + c_1/n)^{-1}}$$

where c_3 is some constant independent of all inputs.

This theorem shows that A^* will do well on all problems satisfying $KM(f; X) = o(n)$ when given good (but not necessarily a lot) of training data. Before the proof, some remarks.

1. The bound is a little messy, but for small θ, large n and simple X we get $L_{A^*}(f, X_m) \stackrel{\approx}{<} 2KM(f; X)/(n\theta)$.
2. The loss bound is extremely bad for large θ. We consider this unimportant since we only really care if θ is small. Also, note that if θ is large then the number of points we have to classify is small and so we still make only a few mistakes.
3. The constants c_1, c_2 and c_3 are relatively small (around 100-500). They represent the length of the shortest programs computing simple transformations or encodings. This *is* dependent on the universal Turing machine used to define the Solomonoff distribution, but for a *natural* universal Turing machine we expect it to be fairly small [9, sec.2.2.2].
4. The "special" χ is not actually that special at all. In fact, it can be generated easily with probability 1 by tossing a coin with bias θ infinitely often. More formally, it is a μ Martin-Löf random string where $\mu(1|x) = \theta$ for all x. Such strings form a μ-measure 1 set in $\mathcal{B}^\infty$.

Proof (Theorem 2). The first is a basic result in algorithmic information theory [13, p.318]. Essentially choosing χ to be Martin-Löf random with respect to a Bernoulli process parameterized by θ. From now on, let $\bar{\theta} = \#1(\chi)/n$. For simplicity we write $x := x_1 x_2 \cdots x_n$, $y := f(x_1)f(x_2)\cdots f(x_n)$, and $\tilde{y} := \tilde{f}(x_1)\tilde{f}(x_2)\cdots\tilde{f}(x_n)$. Define indicator ψ by $\psi_i := [\![\chi_i = 0 \wedge y_i = \tilde{y}_i]\!]$. Now note that there exists $c_3 \in \mathbb{R}$ such that

$$KM(\chi_{1:n}) < KM(\psi_{1:n}; y, \tilde{y}) + KM(y; x) + KM(\tilde{y}; x) + KM(x) + c_3 \quad (2)$$

This follows since we can easily use y, $\tilde{y}$ and $\psi_{1:n}$ to recover $\chi_{1:n}$ by $\chi_i = 1$ if and only if $y_i = \tilde{y}_i$ and $\psi_i \neq 1$. The constant c_3 is the length of the reconstruction program. Now $KM(\tilde{y}; x) \leq KM(y; x)$ follows directly from the definition of $\tilde{f}$. We now compute an upper bound on $KM(\psi)$. Let $\alpha := L_{A^*}(f, X_m)$ be the proportion of the testing data on which A^* makes an error. The following is easy to verify:

1. $\#1(\psi) = (1 - \alpha)(1 - \bar{\theta})n$
2. $\#0(\psi) = (1 - (1 - \alpha)(1 - \bar{\theta}))n$
3. $y_i \neq \tilde{y}_i \implies \psi_i = 0$
4. $\#1(y \oplus \tilde{y}) = \alpha(1 - \bar{\theta})n$ where $\oplus$ is the exclusive or function.

We can use point 3 above to trivially encode ψ_i when $\tilde{y}_i \neq y_i$. Aside from these, there are exactly $\bar{\theta}n$ 0's and $(1 - \alpha)(1 - \bar{\theta})n$ 1's. Coding this subsequence using frequency estimation gives a code for $\psi_{1:n}$ given y and $\tilde{y}$, which we substitute into (2).

$$nH(\bar{\theta}) - c_2 \leq KM(\chi_{1:n}) \leq KM(\psi_{1:n}; y, \tilde{y}) + KM(y; x) + KM(\tilde{y}; x)$$
$$+ KM(x) + c_3 \quad (3)$$
$$\leq 2KM(y; x) + KM(x) + nJ(\bar{\theta}, \alpha) + c_3$$

where $J(\bar{\theta}, \alpha) := \left[\bar{\theta} + (1 - \bar{\theta})(1 - \alpha)\right] H\left(\bar{\theta} / \left[\bar{\theta} + (1 - \bar{\theta})(1 - \alpha)\right]\right)$. An easy technical result (Lemma 1 in the appendix) shows that for $\bar{\theta} \in (0, 1)$

$$0 \leq \alpha(1 - \bar{\theta}) \log \frac{1}{1 - \bar{\theta}} \leq H(\bar{\theta}) - J(\bar{\theta}, \alpha)$$

Therefore $n\alpha(1 - \bar{\theta}) \log \frac{1}{1-\bar{\theta}} \leq 2KM(y; x) + KM(x) + c_2 + c_3$. The result follows by rearranging and using part 1 of the theorem.   □

Since the features are known, it is unexpected for the bound to depend on their complexity, $KM(X)$. Therefore it is not surprising that this dependence can be removed at a small cost, and with a little extra effort.

Theorem 3. *Under the same conditions as Theorem 2, the loss of A^* is bounded by*

$$L_{A^*}(f, X_m) < \frac{2KM(f; X) + 2\left[\log |X| + \log\log |X|\right] + c}{n(1 - \theta - c_1/n) \log(1 - \theta + c_1/n)^{-1}}$$

where c is some constant independent of inputs.

This version will be preferred to Theorem 2 in cases where $KM(X) > 2$ $[\log |X| + \log\log |X|]$. The proof of Theorem 3 is almost identical to that of Theorem 2.

Proof sketch: The idea is to replace equation (2) by

$$KM(\chi_{1:n}, x) < KM(\psi_{1:n}; y, \tilde{y}) + KM(y; x) + KM(\tilde{y}; x) + KM(x) + c_3 \quad (4)$$

Then use the following identities $K(\chi_{1:n}; x, K(x)) + K(x) < K(\chi_{1:n}, x) - K(\ell(x)) < KM(\chi_{1:n}, x)$ where the inequalities are true up to constants independent of x and χ. Next a counting argument in combination with Stirling's approximation can be used to show that for most χ satisfying the conditions in Theorem 2 have $KM(\chi_{1:n}) < K(\chi_{1:n}) < K(\chi_{1:n}; x, K(x)) + \log \ell(x) + r$ for some constant $r > 0$ independent of x and χ. Finally use $KM(x) < K(x)$ for all x and $K(\ell(x)) < \log \ell(x) + 2\log\log \ell(x) + r$ for some constant $r > 0$ independent of x to rearrange (4) into

$$KM(\chi_{1:n}) < KM(\psi_{1:n}; y, \tilde{y}) + KM(y; x) + KM(\tilde{y}; x) + 2\log \ell(x)$$
$$+ 2\log\log \ell(x) + c$$

for some constant $c > 0$ independent of χ, ψ, x and y. Finally use the techniques in the proof of Theorem 2 to complete the proof.   □

5   Discussion

Summary. Proposition 1 shows that if problems are distributed according to their complexity, as Occam's razor suggests they should, then a (possibly small) free lunch exists. While the assumption of simplicity still represents a bias towards certain problems, it is a universal one in the sense that no style of structured problem is more favoured than another.

In Section 4 we gave a complexity-based classification algorithm and proved the following properties:

1. It performs well on problems that exhibit some compressible structure, $KM(f;X) = o(n)$.
2. Increasing the amount of training data decreases the error.
3. It performs better when given a good (broad/randomized) selection of training data.

Theorem 2 is reminiscent of the transductive learning bounds of Vapnik and others [3,20,21], but holds for *all* Martin-Löf random training data, rather than with high probability. This is different to the predictive result in Solomonoff induction where results hold with probability 1 rather than for all Martin-Löf random sequences [11]. If we assume the training set is sampled randomly, then our bounds are comparable to those in [3].

Unfortunately, the algorithm of Section 4 is incomputable. However Kolmogorov complexity can be approximated via standard compression algorithms, which may allow for a computable approximation of the classifier of Section 4. Such approximations have had some success in other areas of AI, including general reinforcement learning [22] and unsupervised clustering [2].

Occam's razor is often thought of as the principle of choosing the simplest hypothesis matching your data. Our definition of simplest is the hypothesis that minimises $KM(f;X)$ (maximises $M(f;X)$). This is perhaps not entirely natural from the informal statement of Occam's razor, since $M(x)$ contains contributions from all programs computing x, not just the shortest. We justify this by combining Occam's razor with Epicurus principle of multiple explanations that argues for all consistent hypotheses to be considered. In some ways this is the most natural interpretation as no scientist would entirely rule out a hypothesis just because it is slightly more complex than the simplest. A more general discussion of this issue can be found in [4, sec.4]. Additionally, we can argue mathematically that since $KM \approx Km$, the simplest hypothesis is very close to the mixture.[3] Therefore the debate is more philosophical than practical in this setting.

An alternative approach to formalising Occam's razor has been considered in MML [23]. However, in the deterministic setting the probability of the data given the hypothesis satisfies $P(D|H) = 1$. This means the two part code reduces to the code-length of the prior, $\log(1/P(H))$. This means the hypothesis with minimum message length depends only on the choice of prior, not the complexity of coding the data. The question then is how to choose the prior, on which MML gives no general guidance. Some discussion of Occam's razor from a Kolmogorov complexity viewpoint can be found in [10,12,15], while the relation between MML and Kolmogorov complexity is explored in [24].

Assumptions. We assumed finite X, Y, and deterministic f, which is the standard transductive learning setting. Generalisations to countable spaces may still be possible using complexity approaches, but non-computable real numbers prove more difficult. One can either argue by the strong Church-Turing thesis

---

[3] The bounds of Section 4 would depend on the choice of complexity at most logarithmically in $|X|$ with KM providing the uniformly better bound.

that non-computable reals do not exist, or approximate them arbitrarily well. Stochastic f are interesting and we believe a complexity-based approach will still be effective, although the theorems and proofs may turn out to be somewhat different.

Acknowledgements. We thank Wen Shao and reviewers for valuable feedback on earlier drafts and the Australian Research Council for support under grant DP0988049.

References

1. Carroll, J., Seppi, K.: No-free-lunch and Bayesian optimality. In: IJCNN Workshop on Meta-Learning (2007)
2. Cilibrasi, R., Vitanyi, P.: Clustering by compression. IEEE Transactions on Information Theory 51(4), 1523–1545 (2005)
3. Derbeko, P., El-yaniv, R., Meir, R.: Error bounds for transductive learning via compression and clustering. In: NIPS, vol. 16 (2004)
4. Dowe, D.: MML, hybrid Bayesian network graphical models, statistical consistency, invariance and uniqueness. In: Handbook of Philosophy of Statistics, vol. 7, pp. 901–982. Elsevier (2011)
5. Gács, P.: On the relation between descriptional complexity and algorithmic probability. Theoretical Computer Science 22(1-2), 71–93 (1983)
6. Gács, P.: Expanded and improved proof of the relation between description complexity and algorithmic probability (2008) (unpublished)
7. Giraud-Carrier, C., Provost, F.: Toward a justification of meta-learning: Is the no free lunch theorem a show-stopper. In: ICML Workshop on Meta-Learning, pp. 9–16 (2005)
8. Grünwald, P.: The Minimum Description Length Principle. MIT Press Books, vol. 1. The MIT Press (2007)
9. Hutter, M.: Universal Artificial Intelligence: Sequential Decisions based on Algorithmic Probability. Springer, Berlin (2004)
10. Hutter, M.: A complete theory of everything (will be subjective). Algorithms 3(4), 329–350 (2010)
11. Hutter, M., Muchnik, A.: On semimeasures predicting Martin-Löf random sequences. Theoretical Computer Science 382(3), 247–261 (2007)
12. Kirchherr, W., Li, M., Vitanyi, P.: The miraculous universal distribution. The Mathematical Intelligencer 19(4), 7–15 (1997)
13. Li, M., Vitanyi, P.: An Introduction to Kolmogorov Complexity and Its Applications, 3rd edn. Springer (2008)
14. Martin-Löf, P.: The definition of random sequences. Information and Control 9(6), 602–619 (1966)
15. Rathmanner, S., Hutter, M.: A philosophical treatise of universal induction. Entropy 13(6), 1076–1136 (2011)
16. Schaffer, C.: A conservation law for generalization performance. In: Proceedings of the Eleventh International Conference on Machine Learning, pp. 259–265. Morgan Kaufmann (1994)
17. Schumacher, C., Vose, M., Whitley, L.: The no free lunch and problem description length. In: Spector, L., Goodman, E.D. (eds.) GECCO 2001: Proc. of the Genetic and Evolutionary Computation Conf., pp. 565–570. Morgan Kaufmann, San Francisco (2001)

18. Solomonoff, R.: A formal theory of inductive inference, Part I. Information and Control 7(1), 1–22 (1964)
19. Solomonoff, R.: A formal theory of inductive inference, Part II. Information and Control 7(2), 224–254 (1964)
20. Vapnik, V.: Estimation of Dependences Based on Empirical Data. Springer, New York (1982)
21. Vapnik, V.: The Nature of Statistical Learning Theory, 2nd edn. Springer, Berlin (2000)
22. Veness, J., Ng, K.S., Hutter, M., Uther, W., Silver, D.: A Monte Carlo AIXI approximation. Journal of Artificial Intelligence Research 40, 95–142 (2011)
23. Wallace, C., Boulton, D.: An information measure for classification. The Computer Journal 11(2), 185–194 (1968)
24. Wallace, C., Dowe, D.: Minimum message length and Kolmogorov complexity. The Computer Journal 42(4), 270–283 (1999)
25. Watanabe, S., Donovan, S.: Knowing and guessing; a quantitative study of inference and information. Wiley, New York (1969)
26. Wolpert, D.: The supervised learning no-free-lunch theorems. In: Proc. 6th Online World Conference on Soft Computing in Industrial Applications, pp. 25–42 (2001)
27. Wolpert, D., Macready, W.: No free lunch theorems for optimization. IEEE Transactions on Evolutionary Computation 1(1), 67–82 (1997)

A   Technical Proofs

Lemma 1 (Entropy inequality).

$$0 \le \alpha(1 - \theta) \log \frac{1}{1 - \theta} \tag{5}$$

$$\le H(\theta) - [\theta + (1 - \theta)(1 - \alpha)] \, H\left(\frac{\theta}{\theta + (1 - \theta)(1 - \alpha)}\right) \tag{6}$$

With equality only if $\theta \in \{0, 1\}$ or $\alpha = 0$

Proof. First, (5) is trivial. To prove (6), note that for $\alpha = 0$ or $\theta \in \{0, 1\}$, equality is obvious. Now, fixing $\theta \in (0, 1)$ and computing.

$$\frac{\partial}{\partial \alpha} \left[H(\theta) - [\theta + (1 - \theta)(1 - \alpha)] \, H\left(\frac{\theta}{\theta + (1 - \theta)(1 - \alpha)}\right) \right]$$
$$= (1 - \theta) \log \frac{1 - \alpha(1 - \theta)}{(1 - \alpha)(1 - \theta)}$$
$$\ge (1 - \theta) \log(1 - \theta)^{-1}$$

Therefore integrating both sides over α gives,

$$\alpha(1 - \theta) \log(1 - \theta)^{-1} \le H(\theta) - [\theta + (1 - \theta)(1 - \alpha)] \, H\left(\frac{\theta}{\theta + (1 - \theta)(1 - \alpha)}\right)$$

as required.   □

An Approximation of the Universal Intelligence Measure

Shane Legg[1] and Joel Veness[2]

[1] DeepMind Technologies Ltd
shane@deepmind.com
[2] University of Alberta, Edmonton, AB, Canada
veness@cs.ualberta.ca

Abstract. The *Universal Intelligence Measure* is a recently proposed formal definition of intelligence. It is mathematically specified, extremely general, and captures the essence of many informal definitions of intelligence. It is based on Hutter's Universal Artificial Intelligence theory, an extension of Ray Solomonoff's pioneering work on universal induction. Since the Universal Intelligence Measure is only asymptotically computable, building a practical intelligence test from it is not straightforward. This paper studies the practical issues involved in developing a real-world UIM-based performance metric. Based on our investigation, we develop a prototype implementation which we use to evaluate a number of different artificial agents.

1 Introduction

A fundamental problem in *strong* artificial intelligence is the lack of a clear and precise definition of intelligence itself. This makes it difficult to study the theoretical or empirical aspects of broadly intelligent machines. Of course there is the well-known Turing Test [20], however this paradoxically seems to be more about dodging the difficult problem of explicitly defining intelligence than addressing the real issue. We believe that until we have a more precise definition of intelligence, the quest for generally intelligent machines will lack reliable techniques for measuring progress.

One recent attempt at an explicit definition of intelligence is the *Universal Intelligence Measure* [13]. This is a mathematical, non-anthropocentric definition of intelligence that draws on a range of proposed informal definitions of intelligence, algorithmic information theory [14], Solomonoff's model of universal inductive inference [17,18], and Hutter's AIXI theory of universal artificial intelligence [8,9]. This paper conducts a preliminary investigation into the potential for this particular measure of intelligence to serve as a practical metric for evaluating real-world agent implementations.

D.L. Dowe (Ed.): Solomonoff Festschrift, LNAI 7070, pp. 236–249, 2013.

2   Background

We now briefly describe the recently introduced notion of a Universal Intelligence Test, the Universal Intelligence Measure and the practical issues that arise when attempting to evaluate the performance of broadly intelligent agents.

2.1   Universal Intelligence Tests

[4] introduce the notion of a *Universal Intelligence Test*, a test designed to be able to quantitatively assess the performance of artificial, robotic, terrestrial or even extra-terrestrial life, without introducing an anthropocentric bias. Related discussion on the motivation behind such tests is given by [1,3,16]. With respect to our goal of wanting to build more powerful artificial agents, we strongly support the introduction of such general purpose tests. Having a suite of such tests, with each emphasizing different, measurable aspects of intelligence, would clearly help the community build more powerful and robust general agents. This paper introduces our own such test, which works by approximating the Universal Intelligence Measure.

2.2   Universal Intelligence Measure

After surveying some 70 informal definitions of intelligence proposed by various psychologists and artificial intelligence researchers, Legg and Hutter [13] argue that the informal definition:

> *"intelligence measures an agent's ability to achieve goals in a wide range of environments"*,

broadly captures many important properties associated with intelligence. To formalise this intuition, they used *reinforcement learning* [19], a general framework for goal achieving agents in unknown environments. In this setting, cycles of interaction occur between the agent and the environment. At each cycle, the agent sends an action to the environment, that then responds with an observation and (scalar) reward. The agent's goal is to choose its actions, based on its previous observations and rewards, so as to maximise the rewards it receives over time. With a little imagination, it is not hard to see that practically *any* problem can be expressed in this framework, from playing a game of chess to writing an award-winning novel.

In their setup, both the agent and environment are expressed as conditional probability measures over interaction sequences. To formalise a 'wide range of environments', the set of all Turing computable environments is used, with the technical constraint that the sum of returned rewards is finitely bounded. Finally, the agent's performance over different environments is then aggregated into a single result. To encourage agents to apply Occam's Razor, as advocated by [13], each environment is weighted according to its complexity, with simpler environments being weighted more heavily. This is elegantly achieved by using the algorithmic prior distribution [14]. The universal intelligence of an agent π can then be defined as,

$$\Upsilon(\pi) := \sum_{\mu \in E} 2^{-K(\mu)} V_\mu^\pi \tag{1}$$

where μ is an environment from the set E of all computable reward bounded environments, $K(\cdot)$ is the Kolmogorov complexity, and $V_\mu^\pi := \mathbb{E}(\sum_{i=1}^\infty R_i)$ is the expected sum of future rewards when agent π interacts with environment μ.

This theoretical measure of intelligence has a range of desirable properties. For example, the most intelligent agent under this measure is Hutter's AIXI, a universal agent that converges to optimal performance in any environment where this is possible for a general agent [9]. At the other end of the scale, it can be shown that the Universal Intelligence Measure sensibly orders the performance of simple adaptive agents. Thus, the measure spans an extremely wide range of capabilities, from the simplest reactive agents up to universally optimal agents. Unlike the pass or fail Turing test, universal intelligence is a continuous measure of performance and so it is more informative of incremental progress. Furthermore, the measure is non-anthropocentric as it is based on the fundamentals of mathematics and computation rather than human imitation.

The major downside is that the Universal Intelligence Measure is only a theoretical definition, and is not suitable for evaluating real-world agents directly.

3   Algorithmic Intelligence Quotient

The aim of the Universal Intelligence Measure was to define intelligence in the most general, precise and succinct way possible. While these goals were achieved, this came at the price of asymptotic computability. In this section we will show how a practical measure of machine intelligence can be defined via approximating this notion. While we will endeavor to retain the spirit of the Universal Intelligence Measure, the emphasis of this section will be on practicality rather than theoretical purity. We will call our metric the *Algorithmic Intelligence Quotient* or AIQ[1] for short.

3.1   Environment Sampling

One way to define an Occam's Razor prior is to use the Universal Distribution [17]. The universal prior probability, with respect to a reference machine $\mathcal{U}$, of a sequence beginning with a finite string of bits x is defined as

$$M_\mathcal{U}(x) := \sum_{p:\mathcal{U}(p)=x*} 2^{-\ell(p)},$$

---

[1] IQ was originally a quotient, but is now normalised to a Gaussian. AIQ is also not a quotient, however we use the name since "IQ" is well understood to be a measure of intelligence.

where $\mathcal{U}(p) = x*$ means that the universal Turing machine $\mathcal{U}$ computes an output sequence that begins with x when it runs program p, and $\ell(p)$ is the length of p in bits. As the Kolmogorov complexity of $x*$ is the length of the shortest program for $x*$, by definition, it follows that the largest term in M is given by $2^{-K(x*)}$. Thus, the set of all sequences that begin with a low complexity string will have a high prior probability under M, in accordance with Occam's Razor. The difference now is that the lengths of all programs that generate strings beginning with x are used to define the prior, not just the shortest program.

The advantage of switching to this related distribution is that it is much easier to sample from. As the probability of sampling a program p by uniformly sampling consecutive bits is $2^{-\ell(p)}$, to sample a sequence from M we just randomly sample a program p and run it on $\mathcal{U}$. This method of sampling has been used to create the test data sequences that make up the Generic Compression Benchmark [15]. Here we will use this technique to sample environments for the Universal Intelligence Measure. More precisely, having defined a prefix-free universal Turing machine $\mathcal{U}$, we generate a finite sample of N programs $S := p_1, p_2, \ldots, p_N$ by uniformly generating bits until we reach the end of each program. This is not a set as the same program can be sampled many times. The estimate of agent π's universal intelligence is then,

$$\hat{\Upsilon}(\pi) := \frac{1}{N} \sum_{i=1}^{N} \hat{V}_{p_i}^{\pi},$$

where we have replaced the expectation V_μ^π with $\hat{V}_{p_i}^\pi$ which is defined to be the empirical total reward returned from a single trial of environment $\mathcal{U}(p_i)$ interacting with agent π. Since we are sampling the space of *programs* that define environments, rather than the space of environments directly, multiple programs can define the same environment. Notice that the weighting by $2^{-\ell(p_i)}$ is no longer needed as the probability of a program being sampled decreases by $\frac{1}{2}$ for every additional bit. The natural idea of performing a Monte Carlo sample over environments is also used by [4] and [16] in their related work.

3.2   Environment Simulation

We need to be able to run each sampled program on our reference machine $\mathcal{U}$. A technical problem we face is that some programs will not halt, and due to the infamous halting problem, we know there is no process that can always determine when this is the case. The extent of this problem can be reduced by choosing a reference machine where non-halting programs are relatively unlikely, or one which aids the detection of many non-halting programs. Even so, we would still have non-halting problems to deal with.

From a practical perspective there is not much difference between a program that does not halt and one that simply runs for too long: in both cases the program needs to be discarded. To determine if this is the case, we first run the program on the reference machine. If the program exceeds our computation limit in any cycle, the program is discarded. In the future, more powerful hardware will allow us to increase this limit to obtain more accurate AIQ estimates.

3.3   Temporal Preference

In the Universal Intelligence Measure, the total reward that an environment can return is upper bounded by one. Because all computable environments that respect this constraint are considered, in effect the Universal Intelligence Measure considers all computable distributions of rewards. Theoretically this is elegant, but practically we have no way of knowing if a program will respect the bound.

A more practical alternative is *geometric discounting* [19] where we allow the environment to generate any reward in any cycle so long as the reward belongs to a fixed bounded interval. Rewards are then scaled by a factor that decreases geometrically with each interaction cycle. Under such a scheme the reward sum is bounded and thus we can bound the remaining reward left in a trial. For example, we can terminate each trial once the possible remaining reward drops below a certain value.

While this is elegant, it is not very computationally efficient when we are interested in learning over longer time frames. This is since the later cycles, where the agent has most likely learnt the most, are the most heavily discounted. Thus, we will focus here on undiscounted, bounded rewards over fixed length trials.

3.4   Reference Machine Selection

When looking at converting the Universal Intelligence Measure into a concrete test of intelligence, a major issue is the choice of a suitable reference machine. Unfortunately, there is no such thing as a canonical universal Turing machine, and the choice that we make can have a significant impact on the test results. Very powerful agents such as AIXI will achieve high universal intelligence no matter what reference machine we choose, assuming we allow agents to train from samples prior to taking the test, as suggested in [13]. For more limited agents however, the choice of reference machine is important. Indeed, in the worst case it can cause serious problems [7]. When used with typical modern reinforcement learning algorithms and a fairly natural reference machine, we expect the performance of the test to lie between these two extremes. That is, we expect that the reference machine will be important, but perhaps not so important that we will be unable to construct a useful test of machine intelligence. Providing some empirical insight into this is one of the main aims of this paper.

Before choosing a reference machine, it is worth considering, in broad terms, the effect that different reference machines will have on the intelligence measure. For example, if the reference machine is like the Lisp programming language, environments that can be compactly described using lists will be more probable. This would more heavily weight these environments in the measure, and thus if we were trying to increase the universal intelligence of an agent with respect to this particular reference machine, we would progress most rapidly if we focused our effort on our agent's ability to deal with this class of environments.

Table 1. Standard BF program symbols along with their C equivalents

BF		C
>	move pointer right	p++;
<	move pointer left	p--;
+	increment cell	*p++;
-	decrement cell	*p--;
.	write output	putchar(*p);
,	read input	*p = getchar();
[	if cell is non-zero, start loop	while(*p) {
]	return to start of loop	}

On the other hand, with a more Prolog like reference machine, environments with a logical rule structure would be more important. More generally, with a simple reference machine, learning to deal with small mathematical, abstract and logical problems would be emphasised as these environments would be the ones computed by small programs. These tests would be more like the sequence prediction and logical puzzle problems that appear in some IQ tests.

What about very complex reference machines? This would permit all kinds of strange machines, potentially causing the most likely environments to have bizarre structures. As we would like our agents to be effective in dealing with problems in the real world, if we do use a complex reference machine, it seems the best choice would be to use a machine that closely resembles the structure of the real world. Thus, the Universal Intelligence Measure would become a simulated version of reality, where the probability of encountering any given challenge would reflect its real world likelihood. Between these extremes, a moderately complex reference machine might include three dimensional space and elementary physics. While complex reference machines allow the intelligence measure to be better calibrated to the real world, they are far more difficult to develop. Thus, at least for our first set of tests, we focus on using a very simple reference machine.

3.5   BF Reference Machine

One important property of a reference machine is that it should be easy to sample from. The easiest languages are ones where all programs are syntactically valid and there is a unique end of program symbol. One language with this feature is Urban Müller's BF language. It has just 8 symbols, listed in Table 1 along with their C equivalents, where we have used C **stdin** and **stdout** at the input and output tapes, and **p** is a pointer to the work tape.

To convert BF for use as a reference machine the agent's action information is placed on input tape cells, then the program is run, and the reward and observation information is collected from the output tape. Reward is the first symbol on the output tape and is normalised to the range -100 to +100. The following symbol is the observation. All symbols on the input, output and work tapes are integers, with a modulo applied to deal with under/over flow conditions. As discussed in Section 3.2, we set a time limit for the environment's computation in each interaction cycle, here 1000 computation steps. To encourage programs to terminate, we interpret any attempt to write excess reward and observation cells as a signal to halt computation for that interaction cycle. As a result about 90% of programs do not exceed the computation limit and halt with output for each cycle.

As we do not wish our environments to always be deterministic, we have added to BF the instruction % which writes a random symbol to the current work tape cell. Furthermore, we also place a history of previous agent actions on the input tape. This solves the problem of what to do when a program reads too many input symbols, and it also makes it easier for the environment to compute functions of the agent's past actions. Finally, after randomly sampling a program we remove any pointless code, such as "+-", "><" and "[]". This produces faster and more compact programs, and discards the most common type of pointless infinite loop. We also discard programs that do not contain any instructions to either read from the input or write to the output.

Finally, the first bit of the program indicates whether the reward values are negated or not. By randomly setting this bit, randomly acting agents have an AIQ of zero, a natural baseline suggested by [4].

3.6   Variance Reduction Techniques for AIQ Estimation

Obtaining an accurate estimate of an agent's AIQ using simple Monte-Carlo sampling can be time consuming. This is due to the relatively slow rate at which the standard error decays as the number of samples increases, along with the fact that for many agents, simulating even a single episode is quite demanding. To help our implementation provide statistically significant results within reasonable time constraints, we applied a number of techniques that significantly reduced the variance of our AIQ estimates.

The first technique was to simply exploit the parallel nature of Monte Carlo sampling so that the test could be run on multiple cores. On present day hardware, this can easily lead to a 10x performance improvement over a single core implementation.

The second technique was to use *stratified sampling*. It works as follows: first, the sample space Ω is partitioned into k mutually exclusive sets $\Omega_1, \Omega_2, \ldots, \Omega_k$ such that $\bigcup_{i=1}^{k} \Omega_i = \Omega$. Each Ω_i is called a *stratum*. The total probability mass $\Pr[X \in \Omega_i]$ associated with each of the k strata needs to be known in advance. Given a sample $(X_1, X_2, \ldots, X_n)$, the stratified estimate $\hat{X}_{ss}$ is given by,

$$\hat{X}_{ss} := \sum_{i=1}^{k} \Pr[X \in \Omega_i] \left(\frac{1}{n_i} \sum_{j=1}^{n} X_j \mathbb{I}[X_j \in \Omega_i] \right)$$

where $n_k := \sum_{i=1}^{n} \mathbb{I}[X_i \in \Omega_k]$. It can be interpreted as a convex combination of k simple Monte Carlo estimates, and is easily shown to be unbiased. For a fixed sample size, the optimal way to allocate samples is in proportion to the standard deviation of each stratum, weighted by the stratum's probability mass. More precisely, if $f_X(x)$ is the density function of X and $f_k(x) \propto \mathbb{I}[x \in \Omega_k] f_X(x)$ is the density function associated with the random variable Y_k associated with stratum k, the optimal allocation ratio is achieved when $n_k \propto \sqrt{\mathrm{Var}[Y_k]} \Pr[X \in \Omega_k]$. To do this we must estimate $\mathrm{Var}[Y_k]$ during sampling and adapt which strata we are drawing samples from accordingly. Intuitively, the algorithm is identifying those parts of the sample space which have the most variance and are of the most significance to the final result, and concentrating the sampling effort in these regions. There are various algorithms for adaptive stratified sampling, however we have chosen the method developed by [2] as they have derived the confidence intervals for the estimate of the mean, a feature we will use when reporting our results. In AIQ, we stratified on a combination of simple properties of each environment program, including the length and the presence of particular patterns of BF symbols. This particular technique gave roughly a 4x performance increase.

Another variance reduction technique we used was *common random numbers*. Rather than estimating the AIQ of two agents π and π' from independent samples from the environment distribution, we instead estimate the difference,

$$\hat{\Delta}(\pi, \pi') := \hat{\Upsilon}(\pi') - \hat{\Upsilon}(\pi)$$

using a single set of program samples. This technique is particularly important when an agent designer is deciding whether or not to accept a new version of the agent. Intuitively, common random numbers reduces the chance of one agent performing better due to being evaluated on an easier sample. More precisely,

$$\mathrm{Var}[\hat{\Delta}(\pi, \pi')] = \mathrm{Var}[\hat{\Upsilon}(\pi')] + \mathrm{Var}[\hat{\Upsilon}(\pi)] - 2\mathrm{Cov}[\hat{\Upsilon}(\pi'), \hat{\Upsilon}(\pi)].$$

If independent samples were used for $\hat{\Upsilon}(\pi')$ and $\hat{\Upsilon}(\pi)$ the covariance would vanish. However, since we are using a single sample and have assumed that the AIQs of π and π' are positively correlated (which makes sense if π' is an incremental improvement over π), $\mathrm{Cov}[\hat{\Upsilon}(\pi'), \hat{\Upsilon}(\pi)]$ is positive and thus $\mathrm{Var}[\hat{\Delta}(\pi, \pi')]$ is reduced.

The final variance reduction technique we used was *antithetic variates*. The intuition is quite straightforward: instead of using one sample, use two samples in such a way that the resultant estimators for the first and second sample are negatively correlated. These can then be combined to balance each other out, thus reducing the total variance. More formally, if $\hat{Y}_1$ and $\hat{Y}_2$ are two unbiased estimates of a quantity of interest, then $\hat{X} = \frac{1}{2}[\hat{Y}_1 + \hat{Y}_2]$ is also an unbiased estimator, with

$$\mathrm{Var}(\hat{X}) = \frac{1}{4}\left[\mathrm{Var}(\hat{Y}_1) + \mathrm{Var}(\hat{Y}_2) + 2\mathrm{Cov}(\hat{Y}_1, \hat{Y}_2)\right].$$

Thus if the two estimates are negatively correlated, $\mathrm{Var}(\hat{X})$ is reduced. A common way to achieve this is to sample in pairs, with each element of the pair

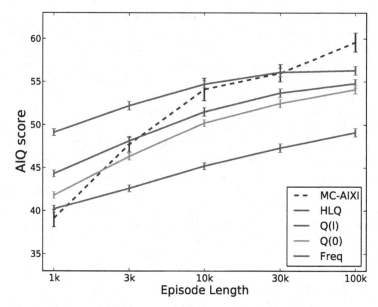

Fig. 1. Estimated AIQ scores of agents as a function of episode length

directly opposing the other in some sense. In our AIQ implementation, since the first bit of each program specifies whether or not to negate the rewards, applying antithetic variates was trivial: we simply ran each program twice, once with the first bit off, once with the first bit on. This lead to a performance improvement that varied based on the agent being tested. With the exception of the Random agent (where there was a massive negative correlation), the performance improvements were typically smaller than a factor of 1.5x.

4   Empirical Results

We implemented AIQ with the variance reduction techniques previously described, along with the extended BF reference machine. Our code is open source and available for download at www.vetta.org/aiq. It should run on any platform containing Python and the Scipy library. We have also implemented a number of reinforcement learning agents to test AIQ with. The simplest agent is called Random, which makes uniformly random actions. A slightly more complex agent is Freq, that computes the average reward associated with each action, ignoring observation information. It chooses the best action in each cycle except for a fixed fraction of the time when it tries a random action. We have implemented the $Q(\lambda)$ algorithm [23], which subsumes the simpler $Q(0)$ algorithm as a special case, and also $HLQ(\lambda)$ which is similar except that it automatically adapts its learning rate [10]. Finally, we have created a wrapper for MC-AIXI [21,22], a more advanced reinforcement learning agent that can be viewed as an approximation to Hutter's AIXI.

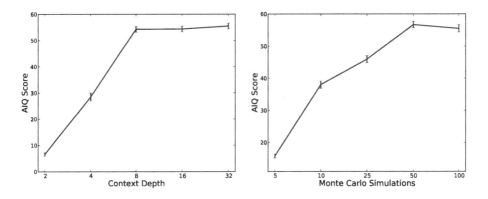

Fig. 2. Estimated AIQ of MC-AIXI as the context depth and search effort is varied

4.1 Comparison of Artificial Agents

For our first set of tests we took the BF reference machine and set the number of symbols on the tape to 5. We then tested all our agents without discounting on a range of different episode lengths. With the exception of MC-AIXI, which is significantly more computationally expensive, we performed 10,000 samples in each test. As expected, the AIQ of the Random agent was zero. For the other agents we ran parameter sweeps to find the best performing settings. These results appear in Figure 1, with the error bars representing approximate 95% confidence intervals.

For 100k length episodes the agents' AIQ scores appear in the order that we would expect: Random (not shown), Freq, $Q(0)$, $Q(\lambda)$, $HLQ(\lambda)$ and MC-AIXI. As the episode lengths decrease, the agent's have less learning time in each trial and thus their scores decline. Except for MC-AIXI, the relative ranking of the agents remained the same. It seems MC-AIXI's complex world model is relatively slow to learn but ultimately the most powerful. Our initial attempts at modifying MC-AIXI to be similarly high scoring on shorter runs failed. Longer tests may be needed in order to determine whether some of the more complicated agents have reached their maximal AIQ.

Similar tests to the above were performed with 2, 10 and 20 symbol tapes. The results were qualitatively the same, but with larger action and observation spaces the learning times increased for all agents. We also increased the number of cells used to represent the observations, usually set to 1, which had the same effect. We then tried reversing the order of the observation and the reward on the tape, which lead to results that were qualitatively the same. We experimented with discounting, and the results were consistent with the undiscounted results using shorter episodes lengths. We also increased the computation limit per cycle and did not see any measurable effect. Thus our initial findings were that the results seemed relatively robust to minor modifications of the reference machine.

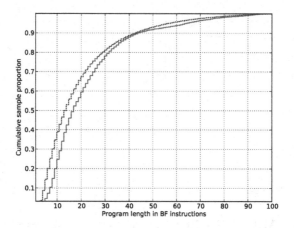

Fig. 3. A comparison of the BF program lengths in the environment distribution compared to the environments chosen by the adaptive sampler. The dashed blue line shows the cumulative proportion of BF environments satisfying a given maximum program length. The solid green line shows the cumulative proportion of BF environments sampled by our variance reduction enhanced adaptive sampling procedure.

4.2   Measuring Agent Scalability

The MC-AIXI agent has a parameter that sets the context depth of its prediction algorithm, in effect controlling the maximal size of the world model that it can learn. It also has a parameter that specifies the number of Monte Carlo simulations it generates, in effect controlling the amount of effort that it puts into planning for each interaction cycle. These two parameters allow us to vary the power of the MC-AIXI agent along two fundamentally different dimensions. We did this with a 5 symbol BF reference machine, as before, and with 50k length episodes. The results of these tests appear in Figure 2. While increasing the agent's search effort consistently increased its AIQ score, the results for the context depth appear to have plateaued at a depth of 8, though with the present error bars it is impossible to tell for sure. This warrants future investigation. For example, it may be the case that larger context depths help only if the episode length is longer than 50,000.

4.3   Environment Distribution

We next ran some tests to help characterise our environment sampling procedure.

Our first test involved generating 2×10^5 legal BF environment programs satisfying the criteria listed in Section 3.5. For example, programs that ran too long or didn't have both a read and a write instruction were discarded. The dashed blue line in Figure 3 shows the resultant empirical cumulative distribution of program lengths across the space of BF environments. Although the number of programs at any given length decays exponentially, this result shows that a significant amount of the total probability mass is still allocated to relatively complex environments with description lengths of 20 symbols or more.

Our next test involved inspecting the distribution of programs sampled by our adaptive sampler when evaluating the HLQ agent. This is shown by the green line on Figure 3. This shows that the adaptive sampler reduces the proportion of programs of length 10 or less from almost 40% to 20%. On the other hand, from length 20 to 40 the green line climbs more quickly then the blue one. Thus we see that the adaptive sampler has moved the sampling effort away from programs shorter than 20 symbols, and focused its effort on the 20 to 40 symbol range.

We also visually inspected a variety of generated environments. While it is true that extremely short programs, for example those of less than 5 symbols, do not generate very interesting environments, we found that by the time we got to programs of length 30, many environments (at least to our eyes) seemed quite incomprehensible.

5   Related Work and Discussion

[5] developed a related test, called the C-test, that is also based on a very simple reference machine. Like BF it uses a symbolic alphabet with an end wrap around. Unlike BF, which is a tape based machine, the C-test uses a register machine with just three symbol registers. This means that the state space for programs is much smaller than in BF. Another key difference is that the C-test considers generated sequences of symbols, rather than fully interactive environments. In our view, this makes it not a complete test of intelligence. For example, the important problem of exploration does not feature in a non-interactive setting. Extending the C-test reference machine to be interactive would likely be straightforward: simply add instructions to read and write to input and output tapes, the same way BF does. It would be interesting to see how AIQ behaves when using such a reference machine.

A different approach is used in [12] and [11]. Here an interactive reinforcement learning setting is considered, however the space of environments is no longer sampled from a Turing complete reference machine. Instead a small MDP is used (3, 6 and 9 states) with uniformly random transitions. Which state is punishing or rewarding follows a fixed random path through this state space. To measure the complexity of environments, the gzip compression algorithm is applied to a description of the environment. While this makes the test tractable, in our view it does so in a way that deviates significantly from the Universal Intelligence Measure that we are attempting to approximate with AIQ. Interestingly, in their setting human performance was not better than the simple tabular Q-learning algorithm. We suspect that this is because their environments have a simple random pattern structure, something that algorithms are well suited for compared to humans.

Another important difference in our work is that we have directly sampled from program space. This is analogous to the conventional construction of the Solomonoff prior, which samples random bit sequences and treats them as programs. With this approach all programs that compute some environment count towards the environment's effective complexity, not just the shortest, though the shortest clearly has the largest impact. This makes AIQ very efficient in practice since we can just run sampled programs directly, avoiding the need to have to compute complexity values through techniques such as brute force program search. For example, to compute the complexity of a 15 symbol program, the C-test required the execution of over 2 trillion programs. For longer programs, such as many that we have used in our experiments, this would be completely intractable. One disadvantage of our approach, however, is that we never know the complexity of any given environment; instead we know just the length of one particular program that computes it.

6 Conclusion

We have taken the theoretical model of Universal Intelligence set out in [13] and converted it into a practical test for machine intelligence. To do this we have randomly sampled programs from a simple universal Turing machine, drawing inspiration at points from [4], and the related work in [6]. In all of our tests the AIQ scores behaved sensibly, with agents expected to be more intelligent having higher AIQ. Naturally, no empirical test can confirm that a test of intelligence is indeed "correct", rather it can only confirm that the theoretical model behaves as expected when suitably approximated, and that no insurmountable difficulties arise when attempting this. We believe that our present efforts have been successful in this regard, but more work is clearly required.

Perhaps the most worrying potential problem with the Universal Intelligence Measure is its dependence on the choice of reference machine, as highlighted by [7]. While we accept that problematic reference machines exist, it was our belief that if we chose a fairly simple and natural reference machine, the resulting intelligence test would behave sensibly. While we have only provided one data point to support this claim here, the fact that it was the first and only reference machine that we tried gives us hope that it is not overly special. Furthermore, we found that the results were qualitatively the same for a range of minor modifications to the BF reference machine. Obviously, further reference machines will need to be implemented and tested to gain a greater understanding of these issues.

Acknowledgements. This research was supported by Swiss National Science Foundation grant number PBTIP2-133701.

References

1. Dowe, D.L., Hajek, A.R.: A non-behavioural, computational extension to the Turing Test. In: Intl. Conf. on Computational Intelligence & Multimedia Applications (ICCIMA 1998), Gippsland, Australia, pp. 101–106 (February 1998)
2. Étoré, P., Jourdain, B.: Adaptive optimal allocation in stratified sampling methods. Methodology and Computing in Applied Probability 12(3), 335–360 (2010)
3. Hernández-Orallo, J.: Beyond the Turing Test. J. Logic, Language & Information 9(4), 447–466 (2000)

4. Hernández-Orallo, J., Dowe, D.L.: Measuring universal intelligence: Towards an anytime intelligence test. Artificial Intelligence 174(18), 1508–1539 (2010)
5. Hernández-Orallo, J., Minaya-Collado, N.: A formal definition of intelligence based on an intensional variant of Kolmogorov complexity. In: Proc. Intl. Symposium of Engineering of Intelligent Systems (EIS 1998), pp. 146–163. ICSC Press (1998)
6. Hernández-Orallo, J.: A (hopefully) Non-biased Universal Environment Class for Measuring Intelligence of Biological and Artificial Systems. In: Baum, E., Hutter, M., Kitzelmann, E. (eds.) 3rd Intl. Conf. on Artificial General Intelligence, pp. 182–183. Atlantis Press (2010)
7. Hibbard, B.: Bias and no free lunch in formal measures of intelligence. Journal of Artificial General Intelligence 1(1), 54–61 (2009)
8. Hutter, M.: Towards a universal theory of artificial intelligence based on algorithmic probability and sequential decisions. In: Flach, P.A., De Raedt, L. (eds.) ECML 2001. LNCS (LNAI), vol. 2167, pp. 226–238. Springer, Heidelberg (2001)
9. Hutter, M.: Universal Artificial Intelligence: Sequential Decisions based on Algorithmic Probability, 300 pages. Springer, Berlin (2005),
   http://www.hutter1.net/ai/uaibook.htm
10. Hutter, M., Legg, S.: Temporal difference updating without a learning rate. In: Advances in Neural Information Processing Systems, vol. 20, pp. 705–712. MIT Press, Cambridge (2008)
11. Insa-Cabrera, J., Dowe, D.L., España-Cubillo, S., Hernández-Lloreda, M.V., Hernández-Orallo, J.: Comparing Humans and AI Agents. In: Schmidhuber, J., Thórisson, K.R., Looks, M. (eds.) AGI 2011. LNCS (LNAI), vol. 6830, pp. 122–132. Springer, Heidelberg (2011)
12. Insa-Cabrera, J., Dowe, D.L., Hernández-Orallo, J.: Evaluating a reinforcement learning algorithm with a general intelligence test. In: Lozano, J.A., Gámez, J.A., Moreno, J.A. (eds.) CAEPIA 2011. LNCS, vol. 7023, pp. 1–11. Springer, Heidelberg (2011)
13. Legg, S., Hutter, M.: Universal intelligence: A definition of machine intelligence. Minds and Machines 17(4), 391–444 (2007)
14. Li, M., Vitányi, P.M.B.: An introduction to Kolmogorov complexity and its applications, 3rd edn. Springer (2008)
15. Mahoney, M.: Generic compression benchmark (2008),
   http://www.mattmahoney.net/dc/uiq
16. Schaul, T., Togelius, J., Schmidhuber, J.: Measuring Intelligence through Games. ArXiv e-prints (September 6, 2011), http://arxiv.org/abs/1109.1314v1
17. Solomonoff, R.J.: A formal theory of inductive inference: Part 1 and 2. Inform. Control 7(1-22), 224–254 (1964)
18. Solomonoff, R.J.: Complexity-based induction systems: comparisons and convergence theorems. IEEE Trans. Information Theory IT-24, 422–432 (1978)
19. Sutton, R., Barto, A.: Reinforcement learning: An introduction. MIT Press, Cambridge (1998)
20. Turing, A.M.: Computing Machinery and Intelligence. Mind 59, 433–460 (1950)
21. Veness, J., Ng, K.S., Hutter, M., Silver, D.: Reinforcement learning via AIXI approximation. In: Proc. 24th AAAI Conference on Artificial Intelligence, pp. 605–611. AAAI Press, Atlanta (2010)
22. Veness, J., Ng, K.S., Hutter, M., Uther, W., Silver, D.: A Monte-Carlo AIXI Approximation. Journal of Artificial Intelligence Research (JAIR) 40(1), 95–142 (2011)
23. Watkins, C.J.C.H.: Learning from Delayed Rewards. PhD thesis, King's College, Oxford (1989)

Minimum Message Length Analysis of the Behrens–Fisher Problem

Enes Makalic and Daniel F. Schmidt

The University of Melbourne
Centre for MEGA Epidemiology
Carlton VIC 3053, Australia
{emakalic,dschmidt}@unimelb.edu.au

Abstract. Given two sequences of Gaussian data, the Behrens–Fisher problem is to infer whether there exists a difference between the two corresponding population means if the population variances are unknown. This paper examines the Behrens–Fisher-type problem within the minimum message length framework of inductive inference. Using a special bounding on a uniform prior over the population means, a simple Bayesian hypothesis test is derived that does not require computationally expensive numerical integration of the posterior distribution. The minimum message length procedure is then compared against well-known methods on the Behrens–Fisher hypothesis testing problem and the estimation of the common mean problem showing excellent performance in both cases. Extensions to the generalised Behrens–Fisher problem and the multivariate Behrens–Fisher problem are also discussed.

1 Introduction

Consider two mutually independent sequences of i.i.d. data denoted by $\mathbf{y}_1 = (y_{11}, \ldots, y_{1n_1})'$ and $\mathbf{y}_2 = (y_{21}, \ldots, y_{1n_2})'$ and generated by the following Gaussian model:

$$y_{ij} \sim N(\mu_i, \tau_i), \tag{1}$$

where $(i = 1, 2; j = 1, \ldots, n_i)$ and $\boldsymbol{\mu} = (\mu_1, \mu_2)'$ and $\boldsymbol{\tau} = (\tau_1, \tau_2)'$ are the unknown sequence means and variances respectively. The Behrens–Fisher problem is to infer whether there exists a difference between the two population means; that is, whether $\mu_1 = \mu_2$. This paper examines the Behrens–Fisher problem using the minimum message length (MML) principle of inductive inference. The minimum message length approach provides a Bayesian solution that does not require computationally expensive numerical integration of the posterior probability density. The corresponding solution is easily extendable to testing for equality of variances and the generalised Behrens–Fisher problem where the data comprises more than two sequences (that is, $i > 2$).

When the population variances $\boldsymbol{\tau}$ are assumed to be known, or their ratio $\rho = \tau_1/\tau_2$ is specified, a common frequentist solution to the Behrens–Fisher

D.L. Dowe (Ed.): Solomonoff Festschrift, LNAI 7070, pp. 250–260, 2013.

problem is a hypothesis test based on a Student t pivot. There does not exist a non-randomised frequentist procedure independent of the data for obtaining exact confidence intervals if the population variances are unknown [1]. A common practical solution in this case is to use the Student t pivot with Satterthwaite's approximation for the number of degrees of freedom [2]. An alternative solution is to use a fiducial probability distribution [3,4] or a fully Bayesian approach. An excellent review of the fiducial and Bayesian solutions to the Behrens–Fisher problem is given in [5].

2   Minimum Message Length (MML)

The minimum message length (MML) principle [6,7,8] offers a Bayesian framework for inference that is rooted in information theory and is a practical implementation of the theory of inductive inference proposed initially by Solomonoff [9], Kolmogorov [10] and Chaitin [11]. The underlying idea is to view the problem of estimation and model selection as one of data compression. Such an approach naturally leads to criteria that balance a trade-off between the model fit and the model complexity. The model fit is measured by the amount of information, $I(\mathbf{y}|\boldsymbol{\theta})$, required to encode the data using a given model; $I(\mathbf{y}|\boldsymbol{\theta})$ commonly includes the negative log-likelihood function. The model complexity denotes the amount of information, $I(\boldsymbol{\theta})$, needed to encode the selected model relative to some chosen prior beliefs. In this two part decomposition the statement of the chosen model is generally named the *assertion* and the statement of the data using this model is named the *detail*. The model that minimises the sum

$$I(\mathbf{y}, \boldsymbol{\theta}) = I(\boldsymbol{\theta}) + I(\mathbf{y}|\boldsymbol{\theta})$$

of the assertion and the detail is accepted as the most *a posteriori* likely explanation of the data in light of the chosen prior beliefs. While the quantity $I(\mathbf{y}, \boldsymbol{\theta})$ can be exactly calculated using the strict MML prescription of [12], this is generally computationally intractable and approximations are used instead. The most commonly used approximation is the MML87 formula of [8], which under suitable regularity conditions gives the joint codelength of model $\boldsymbol{\theta} \in \boldsymbol{\Theta} \subset \mathbb{R}^k$ and data $\mathbf{y}$ as

$$I_{87}(\mathbf{y}, \boldsymbol{\theta}) = \underbrace{-\log \pi(\boldsymbol{\theta}) + \frac{1}{2} \log |\mathbf{J}(\boldsymbol{\theta})| + \frac{k}{2} \log \kappa_k}_{I_{87}(\boldsymbol{\theta})} + \underbrace{\frac{k}{2} - \log p(\mathbf{y}|\boldsymbol{\theta})}_{I_{87}(\mathbf{y}|\boldsymbol{\theta})}, \qquad (2)$$

where k is the number of free parameters, $p(\mathbf{y}|\boldsymbol{\theta})$ is the likelihood function, $\pi(\cdot)$ denotes a prior distribution over the parameter space $\boldsymbol{\Theta}$, $\mathbf{J}(\boldsymbol{\theta})$ is the Fisher information matrix, and κ_k is the normalised second moment of an optimal quantising lattice in k-dimensions. For many dimensions κ_k is not known, and it is common to use the approximation ([6], p. 237)

$$c(k) = \frac{k}{2} \log \kappa_k + \frac{k}{2} \approx -\frac{k}{2} \log(2\pi) + \frac{1}{2} \log(k\pi) + \psi(1),$$

where $\psi(\cdot)$ is the digamma function. In this paper, all codelengths are measured in *nits* (nats), or base-e digits, and as such "log" denotes the natural logarithm. The Wallace–Freeman approximation states that the model $\hat{\theta}_{87}(\mathbf{y})$ that minimises (2) is the most *a posteriori* likely explanation of the data in the light of the chosen priors. Note that the model space Θ may be enlarged to include models of many different classes if the parameter vector is suitably partitioned into continuous parameters and discrete, structural parameters and these are handled accordingly. In this way, MML treats both parameter estimation and model class selection on the same footing. The Wallace–Freeman approximation provides codelengths (and therefore estimates) that are invariant under smooth, one-to-one reparameterisations of the parameters and has shown to be consistent in difficult inference problems; for example, the Neyman–Scott problem [13].

3   MML and the Behrens–Fisher Problem

Consider the Behrens–Fisher problem from (1) and let $\mathbf{y} = (\mathbf{y}_1', \mathbf{y}_2')'$ denote the vector comprising two sequences of data with $n = (n_1 + n_2)$ total data points. The solution to the Behrens–Fisher problem within the message length framework requires: (1) the codelength of the data under the assumption that the population means are equal (that is, $\mu_1 = \mu_2$), and (2) the codelength of the data assuming there exist two population means (that is, $\mu_1 \neq \mu_2$). The model resulting in the shortest codelength is then deemed to be *a posteriori* most likely to have generated the data.

3.1   Shared Population Mean

The model with a single population mean for two data sequences is examined first. The model parameters $\boldsymbol{\theta} = (\mu, \boldsymbol{\tau}')' \in \mathbb{R}^3$ and $\boldsymbol{\tau} = (\tau_1, \tau_2)'$ are considered unknown and must be inferred from the data. Application of the Wallace–Freeman codelength (2) requires a likelihood function, a corresponding Fisher information and prior densities for all parameters. The negative log-likelihood function is

$$-\log p(\mathbf{y}|\boldsymbol{\theta}) = \frac{n}{2}\log 2\pi + \frac{1}{2}\sum_{i=1}^{2}\left(n_i \log \tau_i + \frac{1}{\tau_i}\sum_{j=1}^{n_i}(y_{ij}-\mu)^2\right). \qquad (3)$$

The determinant of the Fisher information matrix, $\mathbf{J}(\boldsymbol{\theta})$, is

$$|\mathbf{J}(\boldsymbol{\theta})| = \left(\prod_{i=1}^{2}\frac{n_i}{2\tau_i^2}\right)\left(\frac{n_1}{\tau_1}+\frac{n_2}{\tau_2}\right). \qquad (4)$$

It remains to specify the prior densities over the parameters $\boldsymbol{\theta}$. The population variances are considered independent of the mean and given conjugate, scale invariant, prior densities over some compact set Ξ; for example, let $\Xi =$

$(a, b) \times (a, b)$ where $0 < a < b < \infty$. This prior is reasonable as it indicates no preference for any particular measurement scale of the data. Since the two variance parameters are common to both models under consideration, the choice of a prior density and the support Ξ (that is, the choice of a and b) for the variances has no effect on the model selection procedure. Following the procedure in [14], the population mean is given a uniform prior over a special compact support in order to avoid the Jeffreys–Lindley paradox. The chosen support for this prior density can obtained by the following argument. First note that the observed data $\mathbf{y}$ is generated from the model

$$\mathbf{y} = \mathbf{y}_* + \boldsymbol{\varepsilon},$$

where $\boldsymbol{\varepsilon} \sim N_n(\mathbf{0}, \boldsymbol{\Sigma}_n)$ and $\mathbf{y}_*$ is the noise-free data (the "signal"). It is clear that

$$E(\mathbf{y}'\mathbf{y}) = \mathbf{y}_*'\mathbf{y}_* + \mathrm{tr}\,(\boldsymbol{\Sigma}_n). \tag{5}$$

where $E(\cdot)$ denotes the expectation operator. For any value of the population mean μ, one can construct an estimate of $\mathbf{y}_*$, say $(\mathbf{1}_n \hat\mu)$, and since $\mathrm{tr}\,(\boldsymbol{\Sigma}_n)$ is unknown and strictly positive, by (5), this estimate should satisfy

$$\mathbf{y}'\mathbf{y} \geq (\mathbf{1}_n\hat\mu)' \, (\mathbf{1}_n\hat\mu) = n\hat\mu^2, \tag{6}$$

where $\mathbf{1}_n$ is a $(n \times 1)$ vector of ones. From (6), the feasible parameter set $\Lambda_1 \subset \mathbb{R}$ is

$$\Lambda_1 = \{\mu : n\mu^2 \leq \mathbf{y}'\mathbf{y}\}.$$

A suitable prior for the population mean is then a uniform density defined over the support Λ_1. Within the context of MML, this prior is perfectly acceptable as the data component of the prior (that is, $\mathbf{y}'\mathbf{y}/n$) can be encoded, with codelength $O(\log n)$, prior to encoding the parameters, and the data given the parameters (see below). Further arguments for this choice of prior density are given in Appendix A. The complete prior density for all parameters is

$$\pi(\boldsymbol{\theta}) = \pi_\mu(\mu)\pi_{\boldsymbol{\tau}}(\boldsymbol{\tau}), \tag{7}$$

$$\pi(\mu) = \frac{1}{\mathrm{vol}(\Lambda_1)} = \left(\frac{n}{4\mathbf{y}'\mathbf{y}}\right)^{1/2}, \quad \mu \in \Lambda_1, \tag{8}$$

$$\pi_{\boldsymbol{\tau}}(\boldsymbol{\tau}) = (\Omega\tau_1\tau_2)^{-1}, \quad \tau_1, \tau_2 \in \Xi, \tag{9}$$

where $\Omega > 0$ is a suitable normalisation constant. Substituting (3), (4) and (7) into (2) yields the total codelength $I_{87}(\mathbf{y}, \mu, \boldsymbol{\tau})$

$$\frac{n}{2}\log 2\pi + \frac{1}{2}\sum_{i=1}^{2}\left(n_i \log \tau_i + \frac{1}{\tau_i}\sum_{j=1}^{n_i}(y_{ij} - \mu)^2\right) + \frac{1}{2}\log\left(\frac{n_1}{\tau_1} + \frac{n_2}{\tau_2}\right)$$

$$+ \frac{1}{2}\log\left(\frac{\Omega^2(\mathbf{y}'\mathbf{y})}{n}\prod_{i=1}^{2}n_i\right) + c(3), \quad (10)$$

where $c(3) = -2 \cdot 32$. Minimising (10) numerically yields the Wallace–Freeman parameter estimates

$$(\hat{\mu}, \hat{\tau}) = \arg\min_{\mu, \tau} \{I_{87}(\mathbf{y}, \mu, \tau)\}. \tag{11}$$

The Wallace–Freeman estimate of μ is equal to the maximum likelihood estimate only when the variances are known. The optimal Wallace–Freeman model under the assumption the data shares a common mean has codelength $I_{87}(\mathbf{y}, \hat{\mu}, \hat{\tau})$.

In its current form, the total codelength (10) is not strictly valid as the prior density for the population mean is a function of the observed data $\mathbf{y}'\mathbf{y}$. This is easily rectified if one assumes existence of a suitable preamble code stating the data constant (that is, $\mathbf{y}'\mathbf{y}/n$) prior to transmitting the data itself. The length of this code can be shown to be approximately $\log(n)/2$ nits. As the preamble code is now common to both models under consideration (that is, both codelengths are extended by $\log(n)/2$ nits) it has no effect on the choice of model made by MML and is omitted from further discussion.

3.2   Different Population Means

Consider now the model where the population mean differs between the two data sequences. The model parameters $\boldsymbol{\theta} = (\boldsymbol{\mu}', \boldsymbol{\tau}')' \in \mathbb{R}^4$, where $\boldsymbol{\mu} = (\mu_1, \mu_2)'$, are again considered unknown and must be inferred from the data. Following the same argument as in Section 3.1 the feasible parameter set for the population means is now the ellipsoid

$$\Lambda_2 = \left\{ (\mu_1, \mu_2) : \sum_{i=1}^{2} n_i \mu_i^2 \leq \mathbf{y}'\mathbf{y} \right\}$$

with volume $\mathrm{vol}(\Lambda_2) = \pi \mathbf{y}'\mathbf{y}/\sqrt{n_1 n_2}$. The prior densities for the population variances are taken to be equivalent to (9). The determinant of the Fisher information matrix is

$$|\mathbf{J}(\boldsymbol{\theta})| = \prod_{i=1}^{2} \left(\frac{n_i^2}{2\tau_i^3} \right).$$

Following the procedure in Section 3.1, the total Wallace–Freeman codelength $I_{87}(\mathbf{y}, \hat{\mu}, \hat{\tau})$ is

$$\frac{n}{2} \log 2\pi + \frac{1}{2} \left(\sum_{i=1}^{2} (n_i - 1) \log \hat{\tau}_i \right) + \frac{n-2}{2} + \log \left(\mathbf{y}'\mathbf{y}\sqrt{n_1 n_2} \, \Omega\pi/2 \right) + c(4), \tag{12}$$

where

$$\hat{\mu}_i = \frac{1}{n_i} \sum_{j=1}^{n_i} y_{ij}, \quad \hat{\tau}_i = \frac{1}{n_i - 1} \sum_{j=1}^{n_i} (y_{ij} - \hat{\mu}_i)^2, \quad (i = 1, 2) \tag{13}$$

are the Wallace–Freeman parameter estimates $\hat{\boldsymbol{\theta}}_{87}(\mathbf{y})$, and $c(4) = -3 \cdot 14$. In this case, the Wallace–Freeman parameter estimates are the same as the regular unbiased estimates.

3.3 MML Hypothesis Testing

Let $\delta = (I_{87}(\mathbf{y}, \hat{\mu}, \hat{\boldsymbol{\tau}}) - I_{87}(\mathbf{y}, \hat{\boldsymbol{\mu}}, \hat{\boldsymbol{\tau}}))$ denote the difference in Wallace–Freeman codelengths between the model with a shared population mean (10) and a model with two population means (12). Within the minimum message length framework, the optimal hypothesis is the one resulting in the briefest encoding. Thus, if $\delta < 0$, the hypothesis of a single population mean for the Behrens–Fisher problem is deemed optimal, and vice versa. The term $\exp(-\delta)$ can be directly interpreted as the posterior odds in favour of the model with a common population mean. Large values of $\exp(-\delta)$, perhaps ten or greater, indicate strong preference to the simpler model with a single population mean.

4 Simulation and Discussion

The minimum message length procedure was compared against well-known methods on the Behrens–Fisher hypothesis testing problem (see Examples 1 and 2) and the estimation of the common mean problem (see Example 3).

Example 1. Hypothesis testing. The minimum message length solution to the Behrens–Fisher problem was compared against two alternative approaches: (1) a popular frequentist method, and (2) a Bayesian approach [15]. For the frequentist procedure, the null distribution of $\Delta = (\mu_2 - \mu_1)$ was approximated by a Student t density with Satterthwaite's approximation for the relevant degrees of freedom. In the Bayesian procedure, the prior density for the parameters was taken to be the vague reference prior distribution $\pi(\boldsymbol{\theta}) \propto (\tau_1 \tau_2)^{-1}$ for $\boldsymbol{\mu}$ and $\log \boldsymbol{\tau}$ and the Cochran and Cox method was used to approximate the posterior density of Δ (see equation (33) in [5]). Interestingly, a Bayesian procedure with these prior distributions is numerically equivalent to Fisher's fiducial inference procedure for the Behrens–Fisher problem [5].

The testing setup was as follows: (1) randomly choose the true hypothesis $(\mu_1 = \mu_2)$ or $(\mu_1 \neq \mu_2)$ with equal probability, (2) sample all parameters from their respective prior densities, and (3) sample data $\mathbf{y}$ from the resulting model with $(n_1, n_2) \in \{5, 10, 25, 50, 100, 500\}^2$. The population variances were sampled from the compact set $\tau_i \in \Xi = [0 \cdot 01, 20]$ for $(i = 1, 2)$; the normalisation constant is then $\Omega \approx 57 \cdot 77$. The population mean(s) were uniformly sampled from $(-5 \leq \mu_i \leq 5)$. For each data set, the Wallace–Freeman, frequentist and Bayesian procedures were asked to nominate which of the two possible hypotheses was used to generate the data. To aid in comparison, the minimum message length tests were completed first and the resultant empirical type I error rate was chosen as the significance level for the frequentist and Bayesian procedures. This is necessary as the MML principle has no in-built notion of type I and type II error rates. By controlling the type I error rate, the performance of the three methods can be compared solely on the number of type II errors. The number of times each criterion selected the generating hypothesis was then recorded (see Table 1). The entire procedure was repeated for 10^4 iterations. As an alternative, the probability of choosing the hypothesis $(\mu_1 = \mu_2)$ was set to the observed type

I error rate of the MML procedure, and the experiments repeated as before. This did not result in any significant changes to results and their interpretation.

The MML criterion obtained superior scores when there was an imbalance in the generated data; for example, $(n_1, n_2) = (5, 500)$. When the sample size was small, $(n_1, n_2 < 25)$, the MML criterion obtained a higher proportion of correct classifications compared to both the frequentist and the Bayesian approaches. These differences in performance may potentially be attributed to the accuracies of the various approximations used in the three procedures as well as the choice of prior density over the population means. As expected, all tested criteria performed well for moderate and large samples sizes.

Table 1. Proportion of times each criterion correctly selected the data generating hypothesis

Criterion	n_1				n_2		
		5	10	25	50	100	500
	5	82·9	84·8	86·4	86·6	86·4	85·9
	10	85·0	86·9	87·8	89·4	89·8	90·0
MML	25	85·9	89·2	90·7	92·3	92·5	93·2
	50	86·9	89·3	91·8	93·4	93·6	94·8
	100	86·8	90·2	92·5	93·8	95·0	96·1
	500	86·5	89·8	93·7	95·1	96·0	97·3
	5	81·4	83·2	84·7	84·3	83·7	82·6
	10	83·5	86·3	87·4	88·7	88·9	89·3
Student t	25	84·1	88·3	90·5	91·5	92·1	92·6
	50	84·9	88·3	91·6	93·1	93·3	94·5
	100	83·9	88·7	92·1	93·7	95·0	95·9
	500	82·7	88·0	93·2	94·8	96·1	97·2
	5	81·3	83·2	84·7	84·2	83·6	82·4
	10	83·2	86·4	87·4	88·7	88·9	89·2
Bayesian	25	83·9	88·3	90·5	91·5	92·2	92·6
	50	84·8	88·4	91·6	93·1	93·3	94·5
	100	83·6	88·7	92·0	93·7	95·0	95·9
	500	82·5	88·0	93·2	94·8	96·1	97·2

Example 2. Driving time data ([16], p. 83; [5]). The driving times along two different routes from a person's house to work were measured; there were $n_1 = 5$ trips for the first route and $n_2 = 11$ trips for the second route. The complete data set is given below

$$\mathbf{y}_1 = (6·5, 6·8, 7·1, 7·3, 10·2),$$
$$\mathbf{y}_2 = (5·8, 5·8, 5·9, 6·0, 6·0, 6·0, 6·3, 6·3, 6·4, 6·5, 6·5).$$

The task is to determine whether there is a difference in the average travel times for the two routes. For this problem, both the frequentist and Bayesian procedures find that the difference between the two means is not significant at a significance level of $\alpha = 0·05$. The Wallace–Freeman codelengths for the model with a common population mean and the model with two different population means were 19·30 nits and 20·14 nits respectively. Thus, the MML approach prefers the model with one population mean with a posterior odds of 2·3.

Example 3. Parameter estimation. The performance of the Wallace–Freeman estimator (11) is now compared against the maximum likelihood (ML) estimator on the problem of inferring the common mean of two normal populations with unknown variances; that is, the true hypothesis is assumed to be $(\mu_1 = \mu_2)$ and the MML and ML methods are compared solely on their parameter estimation performance. The testing setup was as follows: (1) sample all parameters $\theta = (\mu, \tau_1, \tau_2)' \in \mathbb{R}^3$ from their respective prior densities, (2) sample data $\mathbf{y}$ from the resulting model with $(n_1, n_2) \in \{5, 10, 25, 50, 100, 500\}^2$. The population variances were sampled from the compact set $\tau_i \in \Xi = [0 \cdot 1, 5]$ for $(i = 1, 2)$; the normalisation constant is then $\Omega \approx 15 \cdot 30$. The common population mean was uniformly sampled from $(-5 \leq \mu \leq 5)$. For each data set, the Wallace–Freeman (11) estimator and the maximum likelihood estimator were used to infer the parameters θ. The entire procedure was repeated for 10^5 iterations. Following each iteration, the Kullback–Leibler (KL) divergence [17] of the two estimators from the data generating distribution was computed. The results expressed in terms of the median KL divergence are presented in Table 2. The Wallace–Freeman estimator is clearly superior to the maximum likelihood estimator for small samples sizes $(n_1, n_2 \leq 25)$. The two criteria performed similarly when there was a large imbalance in the sample sizes which agrees with the results presented in [18]. Both the Wallace–Freeman and ML estimators performed identically for all samples sizes $(n_1, n_2 \geq 50)$.

Table 2. The median Kullback–Leibler divergence computed over 10^5 iterations between the data generating distribution and the MML and ML estimators

Estimator n_1				n_2			
		5	10	25	50	100	500
	5	0·329	0·208	0·126	0·094	0·074	0·055
	10	0·207	0·137	0·082	0·059	0·045	0·029
MML	25	0·127	0·082	0·050	0·035	0·025	0·014
	50	0·095	0·060	0·035	0·024	0·017	0·009
	100	0·074	0·045	0·025	0·017	0·012	0·006
	500	0·055	0·029	0·014	0·009	0·006	0·002
	5	0·416	0·239	0·136	0·098	0·077	0·055
	10	0·237	0·149	0·086	0·061	0·046	0·029
ML	25	0·137	0·086	0·051	0·036	0·025	0·014
	50	0·099	0·062	0·036	0·025	0·017	0·009
	100	0·077	0·046	0·026	0·017	0·012	0·006
	500	0·056	0·029	0·014	0·009	0·006	0·002

5   Extensions

It is relatively straightforward to extend the Wallace–Freeman codelength formulae from Section 3 to the generalised Behrens–Fisher problem. The data now comprises $(d > 2)$ mutually independent samples of i.i.d. sequences generated by the following Gaussian model:

$$y_{ij} \sim N(\mu_i, \tau_i), \tag{14}$$

where $(i = 1, \ldots, d; j = 1, \ldots, n_i)$ and $\boldsymbol{\mu} = (\mu_1, \ldots, \mu_d)'$ and $\boldsymbol{\tau} = (\tau_1, \ldots, \tau_d)'$ are the unknown sequence means and variances respectively. The complete data set is denoted by $\mathbf{y} = (\mathbf{y}_1', \ldots, \mathbf{y}_d')'$ and comprises $n = (n_1 + \cdots + n_d)$ samples. The generalised Behrens–Fisher problem is testing whether or not there exists a difference between the population means; that is, whether $(\mu_1 = \mu_2 = \cdots = \mu_d)$.

Consider first the Wallace–Freeman codelength under the assumption that there exists a common population mean across the d data sequences. The parameter vector is $\boldsymbol{\theta} = (\mu, \boldsymbol{\tau}')' \in \mathbb{R}^{d+1}$, and assuming the uniform prior density for the population mean (8) and conjugate scale invariant prior densities for the population variances $\pi_\tau(\boldsymbol{\tau}) = (\Omega_d \tau_1 \tau_2 \ldots \tau_d)^{-1}$, the total Wallace–Freeman codelength is

$$\frac{n}{2} \log 2\pi + \frac{1}{2} \sum_{i=1}^{d} \left(n_i \log \tau_i + \frac{1}{\tau_i} \sum_{j=1}^{n_i} (y_{ij} - \mu)^2 \right) + \frac{1}{2} \log \left(\sum_{i=1}^{d} \frac{n_i}{\tau_i} \right)$$
$$+ \frac{1}{2} \log \left(\frac{\Omega_d^2(\mathbf{y}'\mathbf{y})}{n} \prod_{i=1}^{d} n_i \right) + c(d+1),$$

where Ω_d is a suitable normalisation constant. As in Section 3, the total codelength must be numerically minimised for $(\mu, \boldsymbol{\tau}')'$.

The Wallace–Freeman codelength for the model in which $(\mu_1, \ldots, \mu_d)$ are free parameters is easily derived from (12). The feasible parameter set for the d population means is now a hyper-ellipsoid

$$\Lambda_d = \left\{ (\mu_1, \mu_2, \ldots, \mu_d) : \sum_{i=1}^{d} n_i \mu_i^2 \leq \mathbf{y}'\mathbf{y} \right\},$$

resulting in the uniform prior density

$$\pi_\mu(\boldsymbol{\mu}) = \frac{1}{\text{vol}(\Lambda_d)} = \frac{\Gamma(d/2+1)}{(\pi \mathbf{y}'\mathbf{y})^{(d/2)}} \left(\prod_{i=1}^{d} n_i \right)^{(1/2)}, \quad \boldsymbol{\mu} \in \Lambda_d.$$

where $\Gamma(\cdot)$ is the gamma function. Invariant conjugate scale prior densities are again used for the population variances. The total Wallace–Freeman codelength for the model with d population means is then

$$\frac{n}{2} \log 2\pi + \frac{1}{2} \left(\sum_{i=1}^{d} (n_i - 1) \log \hat{\tau}_i \right) + \frac{n-d}{2} + \frac{d}{2} \log (\pi \mathbf{y}'\mathbf{y}) + \frac{1}{2} \sum_{i=1}^{d} \log \left(\frac{n_i}{2} \right)$$
$$- \log \Gamma(d/2 + 1) + \log \Omega_d + c(2d)$$

where the Wallace–Freeman estimates of $\boldsymbol{\tau}$ are equivalent to those in (13).

Testing the hypothesis of the existence of a common mean across the d data sequences follows the same procedure as per Section 3.3. This process can also be extended to other hypothesis tests, such as testing for a common population variance. Furthermore, an analysis of the multivariate Behrens–Fisher problem under the minimum message length framework is possible given Wallace–Freeman codelengths for a multivariate normal distribution ([6], pp. 261–264).

A   Prior Distribution over the Population Means

Consider the standard linear regression model for data $\mathbf{y} \in \mathbb{R}^n$

$$\mathbf{y} = \mathbf{X}\boldsymbol{\beta} + \boldsymbol{\varepsilon}$$

where $\mathbf{X}$ is a $(n \times p)$ design matrix, $\boldsymbol{\beta} \in \mathbb{R}^p$ denotes the coefficient vector and $\boldsymbol{\varepsilon} \in \mathbb{R}^n$ are zero mean i.i.d. Gaussian variates with covariance matrix $\boldsymbol{\Sigma}$. The Behrens–Fisher problem is then a special case of the linear regression model for a suitable choice of design matrix $\mathbf{X}$ and noise covariance matrix $\boldsymbol{\Sigma}$. The aim here is to derive a prior density $\pi(\cdot)$ for the coefficients $\boldsymbol{\beta}$ which can be used in the absence of any subjective knowledge.

Ideally, the prior density should give each combination of regression coefficients the same probability. A possible choice is to use an independent uniform prior for each coefficient, however this requires arbitrary bounding of the parameter space and the resulting model selection criteria would be highly dependent on the chosen support. An alternative approach is to exploit the fact that the observed data $\mathbf{y}$ are generated by the model

$$\mathbf{y} = \mathbf{y}_* + \boldsymbol{\varepsilon},$$

where $\mathbf{y}_*$ denotes the "true" signal. Note that

$$\mathrm{E}\left[\mathbf{y}'\mathbf{y}\right] = \mathbf{y}_*'\mathbf{y}_* + \mathrm{tr}\left(\boldsymbol{\Sigma}\right).$$

where $\mathrm{E}[\cdot]$ denotes the expectation operator. Having observed $\mathbf{y}$, one can form an estimate, say $\hat{\mathbf{y}} = \mathbf{X}\hat{\boldsymbol{\beta}}$, of the true signal. Since the covariance matrix $\boldsymbol{\Sigma}$ is strictly positive definite, it is expected that the estimate, $\hat{\mathbf{y}}'\hat{\mathbf{y}}$, should satisfy

$$\mathbf{y}'\mathbf{y} \geq \hat{\mathbf{y}}'\hat{\mathbf{y}} = \hat{\boldsymbol{\beta}}'\left(\mathbf{X}'\mathbf{X}\right)\hat{\boldsymbol{\beta}}. \tag{15}$$

The least-squares estimates, the James-Stein shrunken least squares estimates [19], and other estimates that obtain minimax squared error risk satisfy restriction (15), which offers strong support for this choice of prior. Hence, the feasible parameter space for the regression coefficients is given by the hyper-ellipsoid

$$\Lambda = \{\boldsymbol{\beta} : \boldsymbol{\beta}'\left(\mathbf{X}'\mathbf{X}\right)\boldsymbol{\beta} \leq \mathbf{y}'\mathbf{y}\}.$$

A suitable joint prior density for the regression coefficients is then

$$\pi(\boldsymbol{\beta}) = \frac{1}{\mathrm{vol}(\Lambda)} = \frac{\Gamma(p/2+1)\sqrt{|\mathbf{X}'\mathbf{X}|}}{(\pi\mathbf{y}'\mathbf{y})^{p/2}}, \quad \boldsymbol{\beta} \in \Lambda \tag{16}$$

where $\Gamma(\cdot)$ is the gamma function. This is a uniform prior over the volume of the feasible set Λ and is equivalent to assigning the same probability mass to each possible combination of regressors. The prior density (16) has been used to derive an MML model selection criterion for linear regression models that has the desirable property of being invariant under full-rank affine transformations of the design matrix [14].

References

1. Scheffé, H.: On solutions of the Behrens-Fisher problem, based on the t-distribution. The Annals of Mathematical Statistics 14(1), 35–44 (1943)
2. Satterthwaite, F.E.: An approximate distribution of estimates of variance components. Biometrics Bulletin 2(6), 110–114 (1946)
3. Fisher, R.A.: Inverse probability. Proceedings of the Cambridge Philosophical Society 26, 528–535 (1930)
4. Fisher, R.A.: The fiducial argument in statistical inference. Annals of Eugenics 6, 391–398 (1935)
5. Kim, S.H., Cohen, A.S.: On the Behrens–Fisher problem: A review. Journal of Educational and Behavioral Statistics 23(4), 356–377 (1998)
6. Wallace, C.S.: Statistical and Inductive Inference by Minimum Message Length, 1st edn. Information Science and Statistics. Springer (2005)
7. Wallace, C.S., Boulton, D.M.: An information measure for classification. Computer Journal 11(2), 185–194 (1968)
8. Wallace, C.S., Freeman, P.R.: Estimation and inference by compact coding. Journal of the Royal Statistical Society (Series B) 49(3), 240–252 (1987)
9. Solomonoff, R.J.: A formal theory of inductive inference. Information and Control 7(2), 1–22, 224–254 (1964)
10. Kolmogorov, A.N.: Three approaches to the quantitative definition of information. Problems of Information Transmission 1(1), 1–7 (1965)
11. Chaitin, G.J.: A theory of program size formally identical to information theory. Journal of the Association for Computing Machinery 22(3), 329–340 (1975)
12. Wallace, C., Boulton, D.: An invariant Bayes method for point estimation. Classification Society Bulletin 3(3), 11–34 (1975)
13. Dowe, D.L., Wallace, C.S.: Resolving the Neyman-Scott problem by minimum message length. In: Proc. 28th Symposium on the Interface, Sydney, Australia. Computing Science and Statistics, vol. 28, pp. 614–618 (1997)
14. Schmidt, D.F., Makalic, E.: MML invariant linear regression. In: Nicholson, A., Li, X. (eds.) AI 2009. LNCS, vol. 5866, pp. 312–321. Springer, Heidelberg (2009)
15. Jeffreys, H.: Note on the Behrens–Fisher formula. Annals of Eugenics 10, 48–51 (1940)
16. Lehmann, E.L.: Nonparametrics: Statistical methods based on ranks. Mcgraw–Hill (1974)
17. Kullback, S., Leibler, R.A.: On information and sufficiency. The Annals of Mathematical Statistics 22(1), 79–86 (1951)
18. Pal, N., Lin, J.J., Chang, C.H., Kumar, S.: A revisit to the common mean problem: Comparing the maximum likelihood estimator with the Graybill-Deal estimator. Computational Statistics & Data Analysis 51(12), 5673–5681 (2007)
19. Sclove, S.L.: Improved estimators for coefficients in linear regression. Journal of the American Statistical Association 63(322), 596–606 (1968)

MMLD Inference of Multilayer Perceptrons

Enes Makalic[1] and Lloyd Allison[2]

[1] Centre for MEGA Epidemiology, The University of Melbourne
Carlton, VIC 3053, Australia
emakalic@unimelb.edu.au
[2] Faculty of Information Technology, Monash University
Clayton, VIC 3800, Australia
lloyd.allison@monash.edu.au

Abstract. A multilayer perceptron comprising a single hidden layer of neurons with sigmoidal transfer functions can approximate any computable function to arbitrary accuracy. The size of the hidden layer dictates the approximation capability of the multilayer perceptron and automatically determining a suitable network size for a given data set is an interesting question. This paper considers the problem of inferring the size of multilayer perceptron networks with the MMLD model selection criterion which is based on the minimum message length principle. The two main contributions of the paper are: (1) a new model selection criterion for inference of fully-connected multilayer perceptrons in regression problems, and (2) an efficient algorithm for computing MMLD-type codelengths in mathematically challenging model classes. Empirical performance of the new algorithm is demonstrated on artificially generated and real data sets.

1 Introduction

Artificial neural networks are commonly used in nonlinear modelling and have become an important tool in the modern machine learning repertoire. Perhaps the most commonly used neural network architecture in practice is the multilayer perceptron. A multilayer perceptron (MLP) with a single hidden layer of sigmoidal neurons can approximate any computable function to arbitrary accuracy provided enough neurons are present in the hidden layer [1]. Applications of MLPs exist in many different areas including bond rating [2], pattern recognition [3] and medicine [4], among others.

Formally, let $\mathcal{M}_{k_h}$ correspond to a single hidden layer MLP comprising k_h hidden neurons. Given a k_d-dimensional ($k_d > 0$) input vector $\mathbf{x} \in \mathbb{R}^{k_d}$ and a target datum $y \in \mathbb{R}$, an MLP model $\mathcal{M}_{k_h}$ for explaining the pair $(\mathbf{x}, y)$ is

$$y = f(v_0, \mathbf{v}, \mathbf{w_0}, \mathbf{w}; \mathbf{x}) + \epsilon = v_0 + \sum_{j=1}^{k_h} v_j \phi(\mathbf{w}_j' \mathbf{x} + w_{j0}) + \epsilon \qquad (1)$$

where $\epsilon \sim \mathrm{N}(0, \tau)$ is a zero-mean Gaussian random variable with variance $\tau > 0$, the nonlinear transfer function is a sigmoidal function $\phi(\cdot) = \tanh(\cdot)$, and the

D.L. Dowe (Ed.): Solomonoff Festschrift, LNAI 7070, pp. 261–272, 2013.

network parameters $v_0 \in \mathbb{R}$, $\mathbf{v} = (v_1, \ldots, v_{k_h})' \in \mathbb{R}^{k_h}$, $\mathbf{w_0} = (w_{01}, \ldots, w_{0k_h})' \in \mathbb{R}^{k_h}$ and $\mathbf{w} = (\mathbf{w}_1', \ldots, \mathbf{w}_{k_h}')' \in \mathbb{R}^{k_d \times k_h}$ denote the output bias, the output weights, the hidden biases and the hidden weights, respectively. The neural network weights and biases may be stacked into a single parameter vector $\boldsymbol{\theta} = (v_0, \mathbf{v}', \mathbf{w_0}', \mathbf{w}')' \in \mathbb{R}^k$, where $k = k_h(k_d + 2) + 1$ is the total number of network parameters, not including the noise variance. The parameters $(\boldsymbol{\theta}, \tau)$ and the number of hidden neurons ($k_h > 0$) are considered unknown and must be inferred from a data set

$$\mathcal{D} = \{(\mathbf{x}_1, y_1), \ldots, (\mathbf{x}_n, y_n)\}, \qquad \mathbf{x}_i \in \mathbb{R}^{k_d}, y_i \in \mathbb{R}, (i = 1, \ldots, n) \qquad (2)$$

comprising n input-output pairs. Increasing the number of hidden neurons k_h results in a more complex model with more free parameters. The task then is to determine the smallest k_h such that the resultant neural network fits the observed data well without overfitting.

This paper examines the problem of inferring fully connected, single hidden layer MLP networks within the minimum message length framework. The two main contributions of the paper are: (1) a new model selection criterion for inference of MLPs that is based on the MMLD codelength approximation [5–7], and (2) an efficient algorithm for computing MMLD-type codelengths in mathematically challenging model classes.

2　Minimum Message Length (MML)

The minimum message length (MML) [8, 9, 7] principle of inductive inference states that the model that yields the briefest encoding, or the best compression, of data in a hypothetical message is optimal. MML can be thought of as a practical implementation of the theory of inductive inference proposed initially by Solomonoff [10], Kolmogorov [11] and Chaitin [12]. Here, the hypothetical message consists of two parts: (1) a statement, commonly called the *assertion*, describing a particular model $\boldsymbol{\theta} \in \Theta \subset \mathbb{R}^k$, and (2) encoding of the data $\mathbf{y}$ using the assertion model $\boldsymbol{\theta}$ (referred to as the *detail*). Let $I(\boldsymbol{\theta})$ and $I(\mathbf{y}|\boldsymbol{\theta})$ denote the length of the assertion and the detail respectively; the length is measured in some convenient unit such as a binary digit (bit) or a base-e digit (nit). The total length of the two-part message, $I(\boldsymbol{\theta}, \mathbf{y})$ stating the data $\mathbf{y}$ and a particular model $\boldsymbol{\theta}$ is then the sum of the lengths of the assertion and the detail, namely

$$I(\boldsymbol{\theta}, \mathbf{y}) = I(\boldsymbol{\theta}) + I(\mathbf{y}|\boldsymbol{\theta}). \qquad (3)$$

The MML principle of model selection advocates choosing the model $\boldsymbol{\theta}$ that minimises the length (3) of the hypothetical two-part message. Although several possible approximations to the codelength $I(\boldsymbol{\theta}, \mathbf{y})$ exist in the literature, the Wallace–Freeman approximation and the MMLD approximation are the most popular in practice.

2.1   The Wallace–Freeman Approximation

The Wallace-Freeman, or MML87 codelength approximation [9, 7] for a model $\boldsymbol{\theta} \in \boldsymbol{\Theta} \subset \mathbb{R}^k$ and data $\mathbf{y} = (y_1, \ldots, y_n)'$ is

$$I_{87}(\mathbf{y}, \boldsymbol{\theta}) = \underbrace{-\log \pi(\boldsymbol{\theta}) + \frac{1}{2} \log |\mathbf{J}_{\boldsymbol{\theta}}(\boldsymbol{\theta})| + \frac{k}{2} \log \kappa_k + \frac{k}{2}}_{I_{87}(\boldsymbol{\theta})} \underbrace{- \log p(\mathbf{y}|\boldsymbol{\theta})}_{I_{87}(\mathbf{y}|\boldsymbol{\theta})} \quad (4)$$

where $\pi(\cdot)$ denotes a prior distribution over the parameter space $\boldsymbol{\Theta}$, $\mathbf{J}_{\boldsymbol{\theta}}(\boldsymbol{\theta})$ is the Fisher information matrix, and κ_k is the normalised second moment of an optimal quantising lattice in k-dimensions. Model selection by the the Wallace–Freeman approximation proceeds by finding the model $\hat{\boldsymbol{\theta}}_{87}(\mathbf{y})$ that minimises (4). The MML87 codelength approximation allows for both model selection and parameter estimation within the same Bayesian framework. Unlike the commonly used maximum a posteriori estimates, the MML87 estimates obtained by minimising (4) are invariant under one-to-one re-parameterisation of the parameter space $\boldsymbol{\Theta}$. To date, the MML87 estimator has been successfully applied to a wide range of statistical models, including factor analysis [13] and mixture models [14], among others.

The Wallace–Freeman approximation is derived under several critical assumptions that may not be satisfied in some statistical models (see pp. 226–227, [7]). In particular, the approximation requires that: (1) the log-likelihood is approximately quadratic around the maximum, (2) the Fisher information matrix is positive definite over the entire parameter space $\boldsymbol{\Theta}$, and (3) the prior distribution $\pi(\cdot)$ is locally continuous and 'slowly' varying in the region determined by $\mathbf{J}_{\boldsymbol{\theta}}(\boldsymbol{\theta})$; note, this region is often referred to as the *uncertainty* region.

The Wallace–Freeman assumptions are generally not satisfied in multilayer perceptron networks. The Fisher information matrix is known to be singular if any of the following three conditions hold [15]:

1. $\exists j > 0,\ v_j = 0$
2. $\exists j > 0,\ \mathbf{w}_j = (0, 0, \ldots, 0)'$
3. $\exists j_1, j_2 > 0,\ (\mathbf{w}_{j_1}, w_{0j_1}) = \pm(\mathbf{w}_{j_2}, w_{0j_2})$

where v_j and w_j denote the network bias and weight parameters respectively (see Section 1). The aforementioned conditions imply that the Fisher information will be singular if the MLP contains redundant hidden neurons. In practice, it is quite rare that any of the three conditions hold exactly. However, MLP networks for which some of the above conditions are 'almost' satisfied are relatively common. In this case, the MLP network exhibits a nearly singular Fisher information matrix which creates problems for the Wallace–Freeman approximation. The main issue here is not due to the (near) singularity of the Fisher information matrix but in the size of the uncertainty region; the uncertainty region grows unbounded as one gets closer to the singularity point which causes a breakdown in the Wallace–Freeman codelength formula. The reader is referred to [16] for a detailed analysis of the Wallace–Freeman approximation applied to model selection of MLPs.

2.2 The MMLD Approximation

A recent alternative to the Wallace–Freeman approximation is Dowe's MMLD codelength approximation [5–7]. The MMLD approximation does not explicitly use the Fisher information matrix in the assertion alleviating some of the afore-mentioned issues when computing codelengths for models like MLPs, where the matrix is generally ill-conditioned. Let $\Omega(\mathbf{y}) \subset \mathbb{R}^k$ denote a region in the parameter space Θ whose size and geometry explicitly depend on the observed data $\mathbf{y}$. The MMLD codelength for a model $\boldsymbol{\theta} \in \Omega(\mathbf{y})$ and data $\mathbf{y}$ is:

$$I_D(\mathbf{y}, \boldsymbol{\theta}) = -\log\left(\int_{\Omega(\mathbf{y})} \pi(\boldsymbol{\theta})d\boldsymbol{\theta}\right) - \frac{1}{\int_{\Omega(\mathbf{y})} \pi(\boldsymbol{\theta})d\boldsymbol{\theta}} \int_{\Omega(\mathbf{y})} \pi(\boldsymbol{\theta}) \log p(\mathbf{y}|\boldsymbol{\theta})d\boldsymbol{\theta}. \quad (5)$$

In practice, computing the MMLD codelength amounts to solving an optimi-sation problem to determine the uncertainty region Ω. If no prior assumptions are made about the geometry of Ω, determining the uncertainty region is a non-trivial task especially in high dimensional parameter spaces. Furthermore, even if the shape of the region Ω is known a priori, the integrals required to estimate the MMLD codelength are often not analytically tractable. The next section introduces an algorithm for computing MMLD codelengths, henceforth referred to as MML07, that is applicable to many commonly used statistical models.

3   A General Algorithm for Computing MMLD Codelengths

3.1   Spherical Uncertainty Region

It is possible to construct an efficient algorithm for the computation of MMLD codelengths if some assumptions are made about the geometry of the uncertainty region $\Omega(\mathbf{y})$. To illustrate the general idea, assume first that the uncertainty region is a hypersphere with radius $r > 0$. In order to compute the MMLD codelength, one requires the parameter estimate corresponding to the centre of the hypersphere as well as the hypersphere radius. The hypersphere radius can be determined from, say, the Wallace–Freeman codelength by noting that the volume, $V(\Omega)$, of the region Ω is approximately:

$$V(\Omega) = \kappa_k^{-k/2}|\mathbf{J}_{\boldsymbol{\theta}}(\hat{\boldsymbol{\theta}})|^{-1/2} \quad (6)$$

and the volume of a k-dimensional hypersphere, S, with radius $r > 0$ is:

$$V(S) = \frac{\pi^{k/2}}{\Gamma\left(\frac{k}{2}+1\right)}r^k. \quad (7)$$

While the optimal value for κ_k is only known for some $k > 0$, Zador [17] has derived a sphere-based lower bound

$$\kappa_k \approx \left(\frac{1}{(k+2)\pi}\right)\Gamma\left(\frac{k}{2}+1\right)^{2/k} \quad (8)$$

which is sufficiently accurate for this example. Substituting (8) for κ_k and solving $V(S) = V(\Omega)$ for r yields [7]:

$$r \approx \frac{\sqrt{k+2}}{|\mathbf{J}_\theta(\hat{\theta})|^{1/(2k)}}. \qquad (9)$$

The centre of the hypersphere $\hat{\theta}$ may be taken as the maximum likelihood estimate or the maximum a posteriori estimate. Near singularities in the Fisher information matrix in (9) lead to a large hypersphere radius r and are no longer an issue in estimating codelengths since the assertion and detail are computed by numerical integration. The MMLD codelength can now be computed using, for example, cubature formulae for approximate integration over a k-dimensional ball [18].

MMLD codelengths computed in this fashion will only be reasonable if there is little correlation between the parameters resulting in a diagonal Fisher information matrix. This is not the case in many statistical models, including MLP networks, and an anisotropic region of integration that can capture correlations in the parameter space should instead be utilised.

3.2   Ellipsoidal Uncertainty Region

A much improved approximation to MMLD codelengths can be obtained if one opts for a (hyper-)ellipsoidal uncertainty region instead of the spherical region discussed in the previous section. Uncertainty regions of ellipsoidal geometry are able to capture varying levels of parameter correlation, including little to no correlation, rendering the resulting codelength approximation usable in many popular statistical models. Assume, as before, that the maximum likelihood or the maximum a posteriori estimate is selected as the centre of the uncertainty region. In order to compute MMLD codelengths, one must determine the size and orientation of the k principal axes of the ellipsoid. This is in contrast to the spherical uncertainty region where only the radius of the sphere is a unknown.

In order to determine the geometry of the uncertainty region, one may again use the Hessian matrix or the Fisher information matrix of the log-likelihood function. The spectral decomposition of the matrix $\mathbf{J}_\theta(\theta)$ is

$$\mathbf{J}_\theta(\theta) = \sum_{j=1}^{k} \lambda_j \mathbf{u}_j \mathbf{u}_j' \qquad (10)$$

where $\boldsymbol{\lambda} = (\lambda_1, \lambda_2, \ldots, \lambda_k)$ and $\mathbf{U} = (\mathbf{u}_1, \mathbf{u}_2, \ldots, \mathbf{u}_k)$ denote the eigenvalues and the corresponding eigenvectors of $\mathbf{J}_\theta(\theta)$, respectively. Let $\mathbf{r} = (r_1, r_2, \ldots, r_k)'$ and $\mathbf{A} = (\mathbf{a}_1, \mathbf{a}_2, \ldots, \mathbf{a}_k)$ denote the radii and principal axes of the ellipsoid. The orientation and size of the principal axes can be obtained from the aforementioned eigenvalues and eigenvectors. In particular, we set

$$r_j = \lambda_j^{-1/2}, (j = 1, 2, \ldots, k) \qquad (11)$$

$$\mathbf{A} = \mathbf{U}. \qquad (12)$$

The uncertainty region is therefore of the same orientation as the eigenvectors of $\mathbf{J}_\theta(\boldsymbol{\theta})$ with radii set to the inverse of the singular values of $\mathbf{J}_\theta(\boldsymbol{\theta})$.

The radii $\mathbf{r}$ computed in this fashion will rarely minimise the codelength (5) and may need to be perturbed to obtain a more accurate estimate of the MMLD codelength. A method that works well in practice is to multiply all the radii by a proportionality constant, say, $t > 0$, where t is allowed to vary until the codelength (5) is minimum for a given $\hat{\boldsymbol{\theta}}$ and data $\mathbf{y}$.

Recall that the MMLD criterion requires integration over the uncertainty region which is in general not analytically tractable. Given an uncertainty region $\Omega(\mathbf{y})$, the MML07 algorithm estimates the integrals required in (5) with the Monte Carlo method. Alternative approaches based on cubature formulae are also possible but are not pursued further in this paper. Monte Carlo integration requires uniform samples from the uncertainty region which can be obtained by a simple two-step procedure: (1) sample uniformly from a k-dimensional unit sphere, and (2) linearly transform the sphere into the hyperellipsoid defined by $\hat{\boldsymbol{\theta}}$, (11) and (12). MML07 uses an efficient algorithm for uniform sampling from a unit k-sphere [19] which only requires samplers from the uniform and normal distributions.

Algorithm 1. MML07 algorithm for estimating MMLD codelengths

Require: proportionality constant t, number of samples $B > 0$
1: Compute parameter estimates $\hat{\boldsymbol{\theta}}$

$$\hat{\boldsymbol{\theta}} = \arg\max_{\boldsymbol{\theta} \in \Theta} \left\{ \log \pi(\boldsymbol{\theta}) p(\mathbf{y}|\boldsymbol{\theta}) \right\} \tag{13}$$

2: Compute $\mathbf{J}_\theta(\hat{\boldsymbol{\theta}})$, the Fisher information matrix or the Hessian matrix
3: Compute uncertainty region radii $\mathbf{r}$ and axes orientation $\mathbf{A}$; see eqn. (11) and (12)

4: Sample B vectors from the interior of a k-dimensional unit hypersphere centred at $\hat{\boldsymbol{\theta}}$

$$S = \{\boldsymbol{\theta}_1, \boldsymbol{\theta}_2, \ldots, \boldsymbol{\theta}_B\} \tag{14}$$

5: Transform samples S into samples E from the uncertainty region Ω

$$E = \{\mathbf{A}\mathrm{diag}(t\mathbf{r})\boldsymbol{\theta}_1, \mathbf{A}\mathrm{diag}(t\mathbf{r})\boldsymbol{\theta}_2, \ldots, \mathbf{A}\mathrm{diag}(t\mathbf{r})\boldsymbol{\theta}_B\} \tag{15}$$

6: Estimate MMLD codelength (5) by Monte Carlo integration using samples E

Algorithm 1 summarises the steps necessary to compute MMLD codelengths with MML07 for a given a proportionality constant t. In Step 2, it is possible to replace the Fisher information matrix or the Hessian matrix by an approximate Hessian matrix obtained by, say, Richardson's extrapolation. This may be useful in cases where the Fisher information is difficult to compute. Steps 4–5 are necessary for integration by Monte Carlo and may not be required if alternate numerical integration methods are employed. In particular, even if the Monte Carlo approach is used, it is possible to replace the uniform sampling step with sampling from the prior density $\pi(\cdot)$. In this paper, the proportionality constant t is determined by numerical optimisation where the objective function is the MMLD codelength. In practice, a numerical optimisation procedure based on the binary search algorithm converges in relatively few steps as the optimisation function is concave and well-behaved.

An alternative method for estimating MMLD codelengths is the MMC algorithm [6, 20]. Briefly, MMC requires samples from the posterior distribution of the parameter space which are then used with the boundary rule (pp. 171–173, [7]) to estimate the uncertainty region, and hence the MMLD codelength. The posterior distribution of multilayer perceptrons is complex and highly multi-modal with large regions of flat curvature. While algorithms for sampling from such posteriors exist, see [21], these generally require a significant amount of computational resources and time. Furthermore, MMC requires grouping of MLPs based on the Kullback–Leibler (KL) metric [22] once posterior samples have been computed. This is highly inefficient and computationally demanding.

3.3   A Simple Example: Univariate Normal Distribution

The MML07 algorithm is now demonstrated on a simple problem where MML87 is known to be well-behaved facilitating an easy comparison between the MML07 and MML87 codelengths. For this experiment, $n = \{10, 50, 100, 250, 500, 1000\}$ samples of data were generated from a univariate normal distribution with mean $\mu = 20$ and variance $\tau = 49$. The prior distributions for the mean and the variance parameters were identical in both codelength formulae and are not relevant to the accompanying discussion. Following the data generation step, codelengths of the data were computed using both the MML87 and the MML07 formulae. The maximum a posterior estimate was used as the centre point of the uncertainty region in MML07. The MML07 and MML87 codelengths were virtually identical in all the experiments even for small amounts of data; for example, given a data set of $n = 10$ samples, the difference in MML07 and MML87 codelengths was approximately 0.2 of a nit.

4   MMLD Inference of Multilayer Perceptrons

We next examine MMLD model selection of fully-connected, single hidden layer MLP networks for regression problems. In order to compute MMLD codelengths for such MLP networks, one requires a likelihood function and a prior density over the parameter space (see Section 4.1). In addition, a prior density over the architecture of the network is required since the MMLD codelength will be used to select between candidate networks of varying sizes. This is discussed in Section 4.2.

From (1), the MLP negative log-likelihood of a data set $\mathcal{D}$ (2) is

$$-\log p(\mathbf{y}|\boldsymbol{\theta}, \tau) = \frac{1}{2\tau} \sum_{i=1}^{n} (y_i - f(\boldsymbol{\theta}; \mathbf{x}_i))^2 + \frac{n}{2} \log 2\pi\tau \qquad (16)$$

where $\boldsymbol{\theta} \in \mathbb{R}^k$ denotes the k network weight (and bias) parameters.

The Fisher information matrix (or Hessian matrix) required for the MML07 algorithm is readily available in the literature (see, for example, [23]) and is efficiently computed using Pearlmutter's algorithm [24]. The next section discusses a suitable prior density for MLP networks.

4.1   Prior Density for the Model Parameters

The prior distribution for the noise variance τ is chosen to be the log-uniform prior $\pi_\tau(\tau) \propto 1/\tau$ defined over some compact set, say $[e^{-6}, e^6]$; the range of the support for this prior density does not affect model selection and is omitted from further discussion. This commonly used prior density is invariant to the measurement scale used for the data and is thus a sensible choice. Selecting the prior density for the network weights and biases is a nontrivial task as these parameters have no interpretable meaning. Following Neal [21], we choose a zero-mean, spherical Gaussian prior with a variance hyperparameter α which advocates smaller weights and hence 'smooth' functions. The complete prior density over the variance parameter and all the network parameters is then

$$\pi(\boldsymbol{\theta}, \tau) \propto \frac{1}{\tau}\left[\left(\frac{1}{\sqrt{2\pi\alpha}}\right)^k \exp\left(-\frac{\boldsymbol{\theta}'\boldsymbol{\theta}}{2\alpha}\right)\right]. \tag{17}$$

The variance hyperparameter $\alpha > 0$ can be set to a fixed value or chosen based on the observed data. If the data set is scaled to a have zero mean and unit variance, a fixed value for the hyperparameter works relatively well in practice. In this paper, we set the hyperparameter α as in the automatic relevance determination framework [25]. Briefly, the hyperparameter value is estimated based on the Laplace approximation to the posterior distribution of $\boldsymbol{\theta}$ resulting in a computationally efficient rule for updating the hyperparameter as the network is trained. The update formula is a simple implicit equation

$$\frac{1}{\alpha} = \frac{\boldsymbol{\theta}'\boldsymbol{\theta}}{\gamma}. \tag{18}$$

Here, γ is usually referred to as the effective number of parameters and is

$$\gamma = \sum_{j=1}^{k} \frac{\lambda_j}{\lambda_j + \alpha} \tag{19}$$

where $\boldsymbol{\lambda} = (\lambda_1, \lambda_2, \ldots, \lambda_k)'$ are the eigenvalues of the Hessian matrix, or the Fisher information matrix. Strictly, the hyperparameter α should also be stated in the hypothetical two-part message for the MMLD criterion to be valid. However, since this hyperparameter is common to all networks being compared, one may code α assuming an asymptotically efficient code of order $O(\log k)$ [26] thereby eliminating the effect of the hyperparameter on model selection.

4.2   Prior Density for the Network Architecture

A slight modification to the MMLD codelength (5) is necessary to allow for automatic selection of the MLP network architecture. The modification involves adding a codelength for stating the number of hidden neurons in the network and has no impact on the MML07 algorithm. The total codelength for an MLP network with k_h hidden neurons is now

$$I(\boldsymbol{\theta}, \mathbf{y}; \mathcal{M}_{k_h}) = I_D(\boldsymbol{\theta}) + I_D(\mathbf{y}|\boldsymbol{\theta}) + I_D(\mathcal{M}_{k_h}) \tag{20}$$

where $I_D(\mathcal{M}_{k_h})$ denotes a prior density over the number of hidden layer neurons.

In this paper, we have chosen the geometric distribution for the number of hidden neurons yielding a codelength

$$I_D(\mathcal{M}_{k_h}) = -(k_h - 1)\log(1 - \xi) - \log \xi \quad (0 \leq \xi \leq 1) \tag{21}$$

where ξ determines the strength of the penalty for larger networks; for the experiments in Section 5, we set $\xi = 1/5$ implying that, on average, one expects the inferred MLP network to have around five hidden neurons. In practice, the codelength $I_D(\mathcal{M}_{k_h})$ makes little difference to model selection and could also be omitted.

5   Discussion and Results

The performance of the MML07 algorithm is now examined using artificially generated data as well as a real data set. In the following experiments, all MLPs were trained using the Levenberg–Marquardt algorithm on the MATLAB numerical computing platform and comprised a single hidden layer of nonlinear neurons. For tests with artificial data, input-output data pairs were generated from the following three test functions [27–29]:

$$y_1 = \sin(5x) + \sin(15x) + \sin(25x) + \epsilon_1, \quad x \in (0,1)$$
$$y_2 = 4.26\left(e^{-x} - 4e^{-2x} + 3e^{-3x}\right) + \epsilon_2, \quad x \in (0,2)$$
$$y_3 = 10\sin(\pi x_1 x_2) + 20(x_3 - 0.5)^2 + 10x_4 + 5x_5 + \epsilon_3, \quad x_i \in (0,1).$$

The input and output variables were standardised to have zero mean and unit variance. Training data sets with sample sizes $n = \{100, 400, 700, 1000\}$ were used for all three test functions. Gaussian noise was added to the target function with the signal-to-noise ratio (SNR) in the set $\{1, 4, 8, 16\}$. For the MML07 algorithm, the maximum a posteriori estimate was used as the centre of the uncertainty region (see Section 3). Each experiment was repeated for 1000 iterations. For each iteration, the prediction errors for the criteria were estimated based on an independently generated test set of size $n = 10^4$.

The performance of the MML07 algorithm for computation of MMLD codelengths was measured in terms of the complexity of the selected MLP (that is, the number of hidden neurons) and the mean squared prediction error on the

Table 1. Mean squared prediction errors for data generated from functions y_1, y_2, y_3 when signal-to-noise ratio (SNR) is 1

Training Sample		Model Selection Criteria				
		MML07	AIC	AIC_c	BIC	MDL
	100	1.380	116.9	110.7	1.328	1.417
	400	1.118	3.513	1.066	1.062	1.114
y_1	700	1.125	1.031	1.031	1.028	1.086
	1000	1.004	1.014	1.014	1.016	1.039
	100	1.155	1.267	1.251	1.174	1.174
	400	1.018	1.056	1.056	1.037	1.037
y_2	700	1.022	1.031	1.031	1.027	1.028
	1000	1.013	175.4	175.4	1.013	1.014
	100	1.650	6.073	4.631	4.435	2.008
	400	1.068	1.278	1.228	1.068	1.073
y_3	700	1.052	1.127	1.126	1.052	1.045
	1000	1.056	1.104	1.104	1.042	1.048

test set. The MML07 algorithm was compared against the AIC [30], AIC_c [31], BIC [32] and MDL criteria [33]. A new AIC-like criterion, referred to as the network information criterion (NIC), developed specifically for MLP networks [34] was initially included in all experiments. However, this criterion required the evaluation of the inverse of the Fisher information matrix which is often (nearly) singular in MLP models. In preliminary experiments, NIC showed highly variable performance especially when used with larger neural networks where many parameters are redundant. This has made it difficult to interpret the underlying behaviour of the criterion and NIC was consequently not included in the empirical comparisons.

Table 1 depicts the mean squared prediction errors when SNR=1 for the five criteria considered in this paper using data generated from functions y_1, y_2 and y_3. As the SNR was increased, the ranking of the criteria considered in the paper remained unchanged. The results presented in Table 1 are therefore representative of the complete experiment. The MML07 criterion performed well in terms of prediction error and often selected a simpler MLP network in contrast to the other criteria in a majority of the conducted experiments. The performance of the AIC-type criteria was highly variable for small training sets and high levels of noise. Both AIC and AIC_c tended to select more complex models in contrast to the other criteria for all three functions considered in the paper. The BIC and MDL criteria resulted in MLPs with similar prediction performance to MML07. For small amounts of data, MLP networks selected by MML07 often had the lowest prediction error amongst all the criteria considered and never resulted in unreasonable models. As the amount of training data was increased, the BIC, MDL and MML07 criteria inferred virtually identical MLP networks in all the experiments considered. For a more detailed analysis of the MML07 algorithm, see [16].

We also briefly examined the performance of the MML07 algorithm on the 'nelson' data set [35] which comprised two inputs and one real target variable. The total data set size was $n = 128$, from which 64 samples were used for training while the remaining 64 samples were used for testing. The experiment was repeated for 100 iterations. Here, the AIC, AIC_c and BIC criteria selected MLP networks of three hidden neurons as optimal. In contrast, both the MDL and MML07 criteria preferred a simpler MLP with one or two hidden neurons. The MML07 algorithm obtained the best prediction score for this experiment from all the criteria considered. A more detailed empirical comparison of the MML07 criterion is available in [16].

References

1. Hornik, K., Stinchcombe, M., White, H.: Multilayer feedforward networks are universal approximators. Neural Networks 2(5), 359–366 (1989)
2. Daniels, H., Kamp, B.: Application of MLP networks to bond rating and house pricing. Neural Computing and Applications 8(3), 226–234 (1999)
3. Cardinaux, F., Sanderson, C., Marcel, S.: Comparison of MLP and GMM classifiers for face verification on XM2VTS. In: Kittler, J., Nixon, M.S. (eds.) AVBPA 2003. LNCS, vol. 2688, pp. 911–920. Springer, Heidelberg (2003)
4. Duch, W., Adamczak, R., Grabczewski, K., Jankowski, N., Zal, G.: Medical diagnosis support using neural and machine learning methods. In: International Conference on Engineering Applications of Neural Networks (EANN 1998), Gibraltar, pp. 292–295 (1998)
5. Dowe, D.L.: Foreword re C. S. Wallace. The Computer Journal 51(5), 523–560 (2008)
6. Fitzgibbon, L.J., Dowe, D.L., Allison, L.: Univariate polynomial inference by Monte Carlo message length approximation. In: Proceedings of the Nineteenth International Conference on Machine Learning (ICML 2002), pp. 147–154 (2002)
7. Wallace, C.S.: Statistical and Inductive Inference by Minimum Message Length, 1st edn. Information Science and Statistics. Springer (2005)
8. Wallace, C.S., Boulton, D.M.: An information measure for classification. Computer Journal 11(2), 185–194 (1968)
9. Wallace, C.S., Freeman, P.R.: Estimation and inference by compact coding. Journal of the Royal Statistical Society (Series B) 49(3), 240–252 (1987)
10. Solomonoff, R.J.: A formal theory of inductive inference. Information and Control 7(2), 1–22, 224–254 (1964)
11. Kolmogorov, A.N.: Three approaches to the quantitative definition of information. Problems of Information Transmission 1(1), 1–7 (1965)
12. Chaitin, G.J.: A theory of program size formally identical to information theory. Journal of the Association for Computing Machinery 22(3), 329–340 (1975)
13. Wallace, C.S., Freeman, P.R.: Single-factor analysis by minimum message length estimation. Journal of the Royal Statistical Society (Series B) 54(1), 195–209 (1992)
14. Wallace, C., Dowe, D.L.: MML mixture modelling of multi-state, Poisson, von Mises circular and Gaussian distributions. In: Proceedings of the 6th International Workshop on Artificial Intelligence and Statistics, Ft. Lauderdale, Florida, U.S.A, pp. 529–536 (1997)
15. Fukumizu, K.: A regularity condition of the information matrix of a multilayer perceptron network. Neural Networks 9(5), 871–879 (1996)

16. Makalic, E.: Minimum Message Length Inference of Artificial Neural Networks. PhD thesis, Clayton School of Information Technology, Monash University (2007)
17. Zador, P.: Asymptotic quantization error of continuous signals and the quantization dimension. IEEE Transactions on Information Theory 28(2), 139–149 (1982)
18. Stroud, A.H.: Approximate calculation of multiple integrals. Prentice-Hall (1971)
19. Petersen, W.P., Bernasconi, A.: Uniform sampling from an n-sphere: Isotropic method. Technical Report TR-97-06, Swiss Center for Scientific Computing, Zürich, Switzerland (1997)
20. Fitzgibbon, L.J., Dowe, D.L., Allison, L.: Bayesian posterior comprehension via message from Monte Carlo. In: Proc. 2nd Hawaii International Conference on Statistics and Related Fields. Springer (June 2003)
21. Neal, R.M.: Bayesian learning for neural networks. Lecture Notes in Statistics. Springer (August 1996)
22. Kullback, S., Leibler, R.A.: On information and sufficiency. Annals of Mathematical Statistics 22(1), 79–86 (1951)
23. Scarpetta, S., Rattray, M., Saad, D.: Natural gradient matrix momentum. In: Ninth International Conference on Artificial Neural Networks (ICANN 1999), pp. 43–48 (1999)
24. Pearlmutter, B.A.: Fast exact multiplication by the hessian. Neural Computation 6(1), 147–160 (1994)
25. MacKay, D.J.C.: Comparison of approximate methods for handling hyperparameters. Neural Computation 11(5), 1035–1068 (1999)
26. Makalic, E., Schmidt, D.F.: Minimum message length shrinkage estimation. Statistics & Probability Letters 79(9), 1155–1161 (2009)
27. Lendasse, A., Simon, G., Wertz, V., Verleysen, M.: Fast bootstrap methodology for regression model selection. Neurocomputing 64(2), 537–541 (2005)
28. Alippi, C.: FPE-based criteria to dimension feedforward neural topologies. IEEE Transactions on Circuits and Systems – I: Fundamental Theory and Applications 56(8), 962–973 (1999)
29. Friedman, J.H.: Multivariate adaptive regression splines. The Annals of Statistics 19(1), 1–67 (1991)
30. Akaike, H.: A new look at the statistical model identification. IEEE Transactions on Automatic Control 19(6), 716–723 (1974)
31. Hurvich, C.M., Tsai, C.L.: Model selection for extended quasi-likelihood models in small samples. Biometrics 51(3), 1077–1084 (1995)
32. Schwarz, G.: Estimating the dimension of a model. The Annals of Statistics 6(2), 461–464 (1978)
33. Small, M., Tse, C.K.: Minimum description length neural networks for time series prediction. Physical Review E (Statistical, Nonlinear, and Soft Matter Physics) 66(6), 066701 (2002)
34. Murata, N., Yoshizawa, S., Ichi Amari, S.: Network information criterion-determining the number of hidden units for an artificial neural network model. IEEE Transactions on Neural Networks 5(6), 865–872 (1994)
35. Nelson, W.: Analysis of performance-degradation data. IEEE Transactions on Reliability 2(2), 149–155 (1981)

An Optimal Superfarthingale and Its Convergence over a Computable Topological Space

Kenshi Miyabe

Research Institute for Mathematical Sciences, Kyoto University

Abstract. We generalize the convergenece of the corresponding conditional probabilities of an optimal semimeasure to a real probability in algorithmic probability by using game-theoretic probability theory and the theory of computable topology. Two lemmas in the proof give as corollary the existence of an optimal test and an optimal integral test, which are important from the point of view of algorithmic randomness. We only consider an SCT$_3$ space, where we can approximate the measure of an open set. Our proof of almost-sure convergence to the real probability by a superfarthingale indicates why the convergence in Martin-Löf sense does not hold.

1 Introduction

Algorithmic probability [11,9] gives a formal theory of inductive inference. Its underlying space is the space of sequences over a finite alphabet and the main tool is a semimeasure. In this setting, Solomonoff's [19,20] central result is explained as follows. Given a finite string, each semimeasure induces a subjective probability of the next symbol. There exists an optimal semimeasure. Then the probability induced by the optimal semimeasure converges to the real computable probability almost surely.

In this paper, we make a first step to generalize algorithmic probability to a general space. The underlying space will be a space of sequences over a topological space. Our main results (Theorems 5 and 6) can be informally described as follows. We want the probability that the next point falls in a subset of the space given a finite sequence of points. There exists an optimal function and the function induces the probability. Then the probability induced by the function converges to the real probability almost surely.

A semimeasure is essentially an equivalent notion to a supermartingale in algorithmic randomness [3,13]. Algorithmic randomness over a general space is studied by some researchers [5,8,12]. The generalization uses computable topology studied by [22,23]. To obtain the desired result, we require condition SCT$_3$, which is a computable separation axiom studied in [24]. We use a superfarthingale [2,21], which is a prequential version of a supermartingale in game-theoretic probability theory [17]. The effectivization of game-theoretic probability theory is a generalization of algorithmic probability. In this setting we prove the

D.L. Dowe (Ed.): Solomonoff Festschrift, LNAI 7070, pp. 273–284, 2013.

existence of an optimal superfarthingale. We also prove convergence to a real probability.

With lemmas developed in the proof of the existence of an optimal superfarthingale, we prove Theorem 3 and Theorem 4 as corollaries. These are important from the point of view of algorithmic randomness.

Theorem 3 says that there exists an optimal test over an SCT$_3$ space. Hoyrup and Rojas [8,7] proved the existence of an optimal test over a computable metric space and it is known that a computable metric space can be constructed from an SCT$_3$ space [6]. We give another more direct proof here.

Theorem 4 says that there exists an optimal integral test over an SCT$_3$ space with a computable measure. The existence of an optimal integral test over Cantor space is well-known [11]. Hoyrup and Rojas [8] proved the existence of an optimal integral test over a computable metric space with a computable probability measure. We will prove the existence of an optimal integral test over a SCT$_3$ space with a computable measure. Note in particular that our proof does not use the distance function.

In Section 3 we introduce a notion of approximation. Then we prove the existence of an optimal test. In Sections 4 and 5 we prove the existence of an optimal integral test and an optimal superfarthingale respectively and discuss when and to which measure the prediction converges.

2   Preliminaries

We recall relevant results from various fields, as some of the terminology and notations are not standard. Results in algorithmic probability and algorithmic randomness are for comparison to our results.

We assume that the readers are familiar with computability theory [18,14,15] on natural numbers. A subset of $\mathbb{N}$ is *c.e.* if there exists a computable function such that the set is the domain of the function. A function $f : X \to \mathbb{R}$ is *c.e.* if $\{q \in \mathbb{Q} : q < f(x)\}$ is *c.e.* uniformly in $x \in X$. If X is countable, the meaning of the definition is clear. If X is a topological space, we refer the reader to Section 2.4 for details. A function $f : X \to \mathbb{R}$ is *computable* if f and $-f$ are c.e.

2.1   Algorithmic Probability

For details see [11,9]. Here we only consider binary sequences. The set of finite binary strings is denoted by 2^*. A *semimeasure* is a function $\mu : 2^* \to \mathbb{R}$ such that $\mu(\lambda) \leq 1$ and $\mu(\sigma) \geq \mu(\sigma 0) + \mu(\sigma 1)$ for all $\sigma \in 2^*$ where λ is the empty string. If the equalities hold, then μ is called a *probability measure*. A c.e. semimeasure μ_0 is *optimal*[1] if, for all c.e. semimeasure μ, there exists a constant $c > 0$ such that for all $\sigma \in 2^*$, we have $\mu_0(\sigma) \geq c \cdot \mu(\sigma)$. There exists an optimal c.e. semimeasure. For $\sigma \in 2^*$, σ_n is the n-th bit of σ, $\sigma_{t:n} = \sigma_t \sigma_{t+1} \cdots \sigma_{n-1} \sigma_n$ and $\sigma_{<n} = \sigma_{1:n-1}$. We also let $\mu(\sigma_n | \sigma_{<n}) = \mu(\sigma_{1:n})/\mu(\sigma_{<n})$.

---

[1] The terminology "universal" is more common.

Theorem 1. *Let μ_0 be an optimal c.e. semimeasure and μ be a computable probability measure. Then*

$$\frac{\mu_0(\sigma_n|\sigma_{<n})}{\mu(\sigma_n|\sigma_{<n})} \to 1 \ as \ n \to \infty \tag{1}$$

with μ-probability 1.

The convergence in difference is Solomonoff's [20] celebrated convergence result. The above theorem is the convergence in ratio, which has first been derived by Gács [11]. Informally speaking $\mu_0(\sigma_n|\sigma_{<n})$ is the prediction induced from μ_0. If the sequence is sampled by the measure space with computable μ, then the prediction converges to the real probability almost surely.

2.2   Algorithmic Randomness

For details see [13,3]. *Cantor space* 2^ω (the set of infinite sequences) is equipped with the topology generated by cylinders $[\![\sigma]\!] = \{A \in 2^\omega : \sigma \prec A\}$ where $\sigma \prec A$ means that σ is a prefix of A. An open set U in 2^ω is c.e. if $U = \bigcup\{[\![\sigma]\!] : \sigma \in S\}$ where S is a c.e. set of binary strings. Let μ be the uniform measure on 2^ω.

A μ-*Martin-Löf test* is a sequence $\{U_n\}$ of uniformly c.e. open sets with $\mu(U_n) \leq 2^{-n}$. A sequence $\alpha \in 2^\omega$ is μ-*Martin-Löf random* if $\alpha \notin \bigcap_n U_n$ for all μ-Martin-Löf tests. A μ-Martin-Löf test $\{U_n\}$ is *optimal* if, for any other μ-Martin-Löf test $\{V_n\}$, there exists c such that $V_{n+c} \subseteq U_n$ for all n. Let M be an optimal semimeasure. Then a sequence α is μ-Martin-Löf random iff there is a constant c such that $M(\alpha_{1:n}) \leq c \cdot \mu(\alpha_{1:n})$ for all n. The set of μ-Martin-Löf random sequences has μ-measure 1. By Theorem 1 the set of sequences satisfying (1) also has μ-measure 1. Remarkably, the latter set does not contain the former set in general. We will consider this problem in Section 5.2.

Theorem 2 (Hutter and Muchnik [10]). *There exists an optimal semimeasure M and a computable measure μ and μ-Martin-Löf random sequence α such that*

$$M(\alpha_n|\alpha_{<n}) - \mu(\alpha_n|\alpha_{<n}) \not\to 0 \ for \ n \to \infty.$$

2.3   Game-Theoretic Probability

Game-theoretic probability theory [17] is influenced by Dawid's prequential principle [1], which says that our evaluation of the quality of the forecasts $p_1, p_2 \ldots$ in light of the observed outcomes $x_1, x_2 \ldots$ should not depend on Forecaster's model even if it exists and is known. In view of this a (super)farthingale was introduced in [2].

Let X be a topological space and $\mathcal{M}$ be a space of probability measures on X. Let $\Pi = (\mathcal{M} \times X)^\infty$ and $\Pi^\diamond = (\mathcal{M} \times X)^*$. For $\pi = (p_1, x_1, p_2, x_2, \ldots) \in \Pi$, let $\pi^n = (p_1, x_1, \ldots, p_n, x_n) \in \Pi^\diamond$.

Definition 1 (superfarthingale). *A farthingale is a function* $V : \Pi^\diamond \to$ $[-\infty, \infty]$ *satisfying*

$$V(p_1, y_1, \ldots, p_{n-1}, y_{n-1}) = \int_X V(p_1, y_1, \ldots, p_{n-1}, y_{n-1}, p_n, x) dp_n \qquad (2)$$

for all n, *all* $(p_1, y_1, p_2, y_2, \ldots) \in \Pi$. *If we replace "=" by "$\geq$" in the equation* (2), *we get the definition of a* superfarthingale.

Game-theoretic probability assumes that a (super)farthingale V is bounded almost surely. So a property stemming from the boundedness holds almost surely. Such a theorem can be easily converted to a theorem in measure-theoretic probability.

In [21], the case $X = \{0, 1\}$ is considered and the existence of an optimal superfarthingale is shown. Furthermore a game-random sequence is defined as a sequence π such that $\sup_n V(\pi^n) < \infty$ for all c.e. superfarthingales V. The game-randomness is a generalization of Martin-Löf randomness. To define optimality of a superfarthingale, we need the definition that a superfarthingale is c.e.

2.4   Computable Topology

We mainly refer to [23,24] for computable topology. Let Σ^* and Σ^ω be the sets of the finite and infinite sequences, respectively, of symbols from a finite alphabet. A function mapping finite or infinite sequences of symbols from Σ is computable if it can be computed by a Type-2 machine. A representation of M is a surjective function $\gamma :\subseteq Y \to M$ where $Y \in \{\Sigma^*, \Sigma^\omega\}$. An object x is γ-computable if it has a computable representation p such that $\gamma(p) = x$. A sequence $p \in \{\Sigma^*, \Sigma^\omega\}$ can be seen as a sequence of strings. We use $v \ll p$ to mean that v is one of strings in the sequence; see [23] for the detail.

A computable topological space is a 4-tuple $\mathbf{X} = (X, \tau, \beta, \nu)$ such that (X, τ) is a topological T_0-space, $\nu :\subseteq \Sigma^* \to \beta$ is a notation of a base β of τ, dom(ν) is computable and $\nu(u) \cap \nu(w) = \bigcup \{\nu(w) : (u, v, w) \in S\}$ for all $u, v \in$ dom(ν) for some c.e. set $S \subseteq (\mathrm{dom}(\nu))^3$. For the finite union of base sets, we use representation $\bigcup \nu^{\mathrm{fs}}$ to mean $\bigcup \nu^{\mathrm{fs}} = W \iff (\forall v \ll w) v \in \mathrm{dom}(\nu), W = \bigcup \{\nu(v) : v \ll w\}$. For the points, the open sets and the closed sets, we use representations δ, θ and ψ^- that are defined as follows. For $p \in \Sigma^\omega$ and $x \in X$, $\delta(p) = x$ iff p is a list of all $u \in \mathrm{dom}(\nu)$ such that $x \in \nu(u)$, $\theta(p)$ is the union of all $\nu(u)$ where u is listed by p, and $\psi^-(p) = X \backslash \theta(p)$.

An example of a computable topological space is $\overline{\mathbf{R}}^+ = (\overline{\mathbb{R}}^+, \tau_<, \beta_<, \nu_<)$ where $\overline{\mathbb{R}}^+$ is the set of non-negative reals and $+\infty$, $\tau_<$ is the lower topology, $\beta_<$ is the set

$$\{[0, +\infty]\} \cup \{(q, +\infty] : q \in \mathbb{Q}^+\},$$

$\mathbb{Q}^+$ is the set of non-negative rationals, and $\nu_<$ is a computable notation of $\beta_<$. The representation δ of points in $\overline{\mathbf{R}}^+$ is denoted by $\overline{\rho}_<$.

Computable separations are studied in [24] in detail but we use only SCT$_3$.

Definition 2 (SCT$_3$). *There are a c.e. set $R \subseteq \text{dom}(\nu) \times \text{dom}(\nu)$ and a computable function $r :\subseteq \Sigma^* \times \Sigma^* \to \Sigma^\omega$ such that for all $u, w \in \text{dom}(\nu)$, $\nu(w) = \bigcup\{\nu(u) : (u, w) \in R\}$ and $(u, w) \in R \Rightarrow \nu(u) \subseteq \psi^- \circ r(u, w) \subseteq \nu(w)$.*

For computability of measures we refer to [12]. One can find an equivalent representation in Schröder [16]. Let $\mathcal{M}(X)$ be the space of finite non-negative Borel measures on X. The following sets form a countable subbase of the A-topology on $\mathcal{M}(X)$: $\{\mu : \mu(G) > q\}$, $\{\mu : \mu(X) < q\}$ where G is the finite union of base sets and $q \in \mathbb{Q}$. Let β_A denote the base generated from the above subbase and ν_A denote a natural computable notation of the base β_A. Then the 4-tuple $\mathbf{M} = (\mathcal{M}(X), \tau_A, \beta_A, \nu_A)$ is a computable topological space. The representation δ of points in $\mathcal{M}(X)$ is denoted by δ_A. If U is an open set, then $\mu(U)$ is approximated from below by a δ_A-representation of μ and a θ-representation of U. If V is an closed set, then $\mu(V)$ is approximated from above by a δ_A-representation of μ and a ψ^--representation of V.

3   Optimal Test

In this section we give a proof of Lemma 1, which states an important property of a SCT$_3$ space with a computable measure and plays a central role in the proof of Theorem 5. As a corollary we obtain the existence of an optimal test over a SCT$_3$ space.

3.1   Approximation

Let $\mathbf{X} = (X, \tau, \beta, \nu)$ be a computable topological space. Let μ be a measure on $\mathbf{X}$. Note that μ need not be computable.

We give an approximation of the measure of an open set. An approximation is usually a sequence of rationals or sometimes a sequence of computable reals. However, the following approximation may be neither and carries a weaker notion.

Definition 3 (Approximation). *A μ-approximation of an open set $U \subseteq X$ is a sequence (U_n, a_n) such that U_n is the finite union of base sets, $U_n \uparrow U$, a_n is a rational, $\mu(U_n) \leq a_n$ and $a_n - \mu(U_n) \leq 2^{-n}$ for each n.*

We say that a μ-approximation (U_n, a_n) is uniformly $(\bigcup \nu^{\text{fs}}, \rho)$-computable if U_n is uniformly $\bigcup \nu^{\text{fs}}$-computable and a_n is uniformly ρ-computable.

To state lemmas and propositions clearly and concisely, we introduce the notion of γ-relativeness for a representation γ.

Definition 4 (Relative computability). *Let $\mathbf{X}_i = (X_i, \tau_i, \beta_i, \nu_i)$ be computable topological spaces for $i = 1, 2$. A point $x_2 \in X_2$ is δ_2-computable δ_1-relative to $x_1 \in X_1$ if there exists a (δ_1, δ_2)-computable function $f :\subseteq X_1 \to X_2$ such that $f(x_1) = x_2$.*

Relative computability of open sets, closed sets and functions are similarly defined. For example, an open set $U_2 \subseteq X_2$ is θ_2-computable δ_A-relative to $\mu_1 \in \mathcal{M}(X_1)$ iff there exists a (δ_A, θ_2)-computable function $f :\subseteq \mathcal{M}(X_1) \to \tau_2$ such that $f(\mu_1) = U_2$.

Lemma 1. *Let $\mathbf{X}$ be a SCT_3 space. For an open set U we can uniformly construct a μ-approximation that is $(\bigcup \nu^{\mathrm{fs}}, \rho)$-computable (θ, δ_A)-relative to (U, μ).*

Proof. At first we show the lemma in the case that U is a base set $\nu(w)$. Let R and r be the c.e. set and the computable function for SCT_3 from Definition 2. Let $\{u_i\}$ be a computable enumeration of the c.e. set $\{u \in \mathrm{dom}(\nu) : (u, w) \in R\}$.

For each m, let $U_m = \bigcup_{i=1}^{m} \nu(u_i)$ and $V_m = \bigcup_{i=1}^{m} \psi^- \circ r(u_i, w)$. Note that U_m is open and V_m is closed. Then $U_m \subseteq V_m \subseteq \nu(w)$ and $U_m \uparrow \nu(w)$. It follows that $\mu(U_m) \to \mu(\nu(w))$ and $\mu(V_m) - \nu(U_m) \to 0$ as $m \to \infty$.

Note that the measure $\mu(U_m)$ is approximated from below and $\mu(V_m)$ from above δ_A-relative to μ. Then we can compute m_n from a representation of μ such that $\mu(V_{m_n}) - \nu(U_{m_n}) \leq 2^{-n}$.

Let $\mu(U_{m_n})[s]$ and $\mu(V_{m_n})[s]$ be an approximation of rationals. Let s_n be the first stage such that $\mu(V_{m_n})[s_n] - \nu(U_{m_n})[s_n] \leq 2^{-n}$. Let $a_n = \mu(V_{m_n})[s_n]$. Then a_n is uniformly ρ-computable δ_A-relative to μ. Note that $\mu(U_{m_n})[s_n] \leq \mu(U_{m_n}) \leq \mu(V_{m_n}) \leq \mu(V_{m_n})[s_n] = a_n$. It follows that $a_n - \mu(U_{m_n}) \leq 2^{-n}$. Hence (U_{m_n}, a_n) is a μ-approximation.

For a general open set $U = \bigcup_k \nu(w_k)$, construct U_m^k and V_m^k for each k. Let $U_m = \bigcup_{k=1}^{m} U_m^k$ and $V_m = \bigcup_{k=1}^{m} V_m^k$. Then $U_m \subseteq V_m \subseteq U$ and $U_m \uparrow U$. By a similar argument with above, we have a μ-approximation of U. □

3.2   Existence of an Optimal Test

Definition 5. *Let μ be a computable measure over $\mathbf{X}$. A μ-test is a sequence $\{V_n\}$ of uniformly θ-computable sets with $\mu(V_n) \leq 2^{-n}$. A μ-test $\{W_n\}$ is optimal if, for each μ-test $\{V_n\}$, there exists c such that $V_{n+c} \subseteq W_n$ for each n.*

Theorem 3. *Let $\mathbf{X}$ be a SCT_3 space and μ be a computable measure on $\mathbf{X}$. Then there exists an optimal μ-test over $\mathbf{X}$.*

Proof. There exists a computable enumeration $V_{m,n}$ of θ-computable sets. For each $V_{m,n}$, there exists a μ-approximation (U_s, a_s) by Lemma 1, which is uniformly $(\bigcup \nu^{\mathrm{fs}}, \rho)$-computable. Let $\widetilde{V}_{m,n} = U_{\sup\{s : a_s < 2^{-n}\}}$. Then

$$\mu(\widetilde{V}_{m,n}) = \mu(U_{\sup\{s : a_s < 2^{-n}\}}) = \sup\{a_s : a_s < 2^{-n}\} \leq 2^{-n}.$$

Hence $\{\widetilde{V}_{m,n}\}_n$ is a μ-test for each m.

Suppose $\mu(V_{m,n}) < 2^{-n}$. Then there exists s_0 such that $\mu(V_{m,n}) + 2^{-s} < 2^{-n}$ for all $s \geq s_0$. For such s we have $a_s \leq \mu(U_s) + 2^{-s} \leq \mu(V_{m,n}) + 2^{-s} < 2^{-n}$. Hence $\widetilde{V}_{m,n} = V_{m,n}$.

Let $W_n = \bigcup_m \widetilde{V}_{m,n+m+1}$. We claim that $\{W_n\}$ is an optimal μ-test. Note that $\mu(W_n) \leq \sum_m 2^{-n-m-1} \leq 2^{-n}$. Hence $\{W_n\}$ is a μ-test.

Let A_n be a μ-test. Then $\{B_n\}_n = \{A_{n+1}\}_n$ is also a μ-test with $\mu(B_n) \leq 2^{-n-1}$. Hence there exists m such that $B_n = V_{m,n}$. It follows that $W_n \supseteq V_{m,n+m+1} = B_{n+m+1} \supseteq A_{n+m+2}$ for each n. Then $\{W_n\}$ is optimal.   □

4 Optimal Integral Test

The goal in this section is to establish the existence of an optimal integral test over a SCT_3 space. The key of the proof is Lemma 2. As in Section 3, this lemma is also the key to proving Theorem 5 in the next section.

4.1 Computable Bound

In the previous section we gave an approximation of an open set. With this we give an approximation of a $(\delta, \overline{\rho}_<)$-continuous function.

Lemma 2. *Let $f : X \to \mathbb{R}^+$ be a total function and c be a ρ-computable real. Then there exists a $([\delta \to \overline{\rho}_<], \delta_A, [\delta \to \overline{\rho}_<])$-computable function b_c such that*

(i) $\int b_c(f, \mu) d\mu \leq c$,
(ii) $\int f d\mu < c \Rightarrow b_c(f, \mu) = f$.

Proof. Let $\mathbb{Q}^+$ be the set of all non-negative rationals. Let $Q_n = \{q_i : i \leq n\}$ where $\{q_i\}$ is a computable enumeration of $\mathbb{Q}^+$. Then $Q_n \uparrow \mathbb{Q}^+$. Let $s(n, i)$ be the index of $\min\{r \in Q_n : r > q_i\}$. If q_i is the maximum element in Q_n and the set is empty, then $s(n, i) = \infty$. Intuitively $q_{s_n(q)}$ is the least element in Q_n larger than q or ∞ if such an element does not exist. Then

$$\mu(f) = \int_X f d\mu = \lim_{n \to \infty} \sum_{i \leq n} q_i \cdot \mu(\{x : f(x) > q_i\} \setminus \{x : f(x) > q_{s(n,i)}\})$$

where $q_\infty = \infty$.

Let $U^i = \{x : f(x) > q_i\}$. Note that U^i is a θ-computable open set. Then it has a μ-approximation (U_n^i, a_n^i) satisfying the condition in Lemma 1. Note that there exists a computable function $b : \mathbb{N} \to \mathbb{N}$ such that $\sum_{i=0}^{\infty} q_i \cdot 2^{-b(i)} \leq 1$. Let

$$V_n^i = U_{n+b(i)}^i \setminus U_{n+b(s(n,i))}^{s(n,i)}.$$

Then $\mu(V_n^i) \to \mu(U^i \setminus U^{s(n,i)})$. Note that $\mu(f) \leq \sum_{i=0}^{n} q_i \cdot \mu(V_n^i)$ for each n and

$$\mu(f) = \lim_{n \to \infty} \sum_{i=0}^{n} q_i \cdot \mu(U_{n+b(i)}^i \setminus U_{n+b(s(n,i))}^{s(n,i)}) = \lim_{n \to \infty} \sum_{i=0}^{n} q_i \cdot \mu(V_n^i).$$

Let $c(n, i) = a_{n+b(i)}^i - a_{n+b(s(n,i))}^{s(n,i)}$. Then

$$a_{n+b(i)}^i - 2^{-(n+b(i))} \leq \mu(U_{n+b(i)}^i) \leq a_{n+b(i)}^i$$

for each n and i. It follows that

$$a^i_{n+b(i)} - a^{s(n,i)}_{n+b(s(n,i))} - 2^{-(n+b(i))} \le \mu(U^i_{n+b(i)} \setminus U^{s_n(q)}_{n+b(s(n,i))}),$$

$$\mu(U^i_{n+b(i)} \setminus U^{s_n(q)}_{n+b(s(n,i))}) \le a^i_{n+b(i)} - a^{s(n,i)}_{n+b(s(n,i))} + 2^{-(n+b(s(n,i)))}.$$

Hence

$$c(n,i) - 2^{-(n+b(i))} \le \mu(V^i_n) \le c(n,i) + 2^{-(n+b(s(n,i)))}.$$

We construct $b = b(f, \mu)$ as the limit of functions b_n. We define b_n inductively on n. Let $b_0(x) = 0$ for all x. If

$$\sum_{i \le n} q_i \cdot (c(n,i) + 2^{-(n+b(s(n,i)))}) < c,$$

then let $b_n(x) = \max\{q_i : x \in U^i_{n+b(i)}\}$, otherwise $b_n = b_{n-1}$.

Since U^i_n is increasing on n, $b_n(x) \ge b_{n-1}(x)$ for all n and x. Note that

$$\int b_n d\mu = \sum_{i \le n} q_i \cdot \mu(V^i_n) \le \sum_{i \le n} q_i \cdot (c(n,i) + 2^{-(n+b(s(n,i)))}) < c.$$

It follows that $\int b d\mu = \int \lim_n b_n d\mu = \lim_n \int b_n d\mu \le c$.

Suppose $\int f d\mu < c$. Then $\int f d\mu + 2^{-n+1} < c$ for a large n. Then for such n,

$$c > \sum_{i \le n} q_i \cdot \mu(V^i_n) + 2^{-n+1} \ge \sum_{i \le n} q_i \cdot c(n,i) - 2^{-n} + 2^{-n+1}.$$

Combining the previous two results, we obtain

$$\sum_{i \le n} q_i \cdot (c(n,i) + 2^{-(n+b(s(n,i)))}) \le \sum_{i \le n} q_i \cdot c(n,i) + 2^{-n} < c.$$

It follows that $b(x) = \lim_n b_n(x) = \sup\{q : f(x) > q\} = f(x)$ for all x.   □

4.2   Computable Enumeration

Now it suffices to show that we have a computable enumeration of $(\delta_X, \overline{p}_<)$-computable functions.

Lemma 3. *There is a computable enumeration of $(\delta_X, \overline{p}_<)$-computable functions $f_n : X \to \overline{\mathbb{R}}^+$.*

To prove this, we use the following representation.

Definition 6 ($\overrightarrow{\delta}_4$-representation; see [24]). *Define a multi-representation $\overrightarrow{\delta}_4$ of the set $CP(X_1, X_2)$ of all partial continuous functions $f :\subseteq X_1 \to X_2$ as follows:*

$$f \in \overrightarrow{\delta}_4(p) \iff \begin{cases} (w \ll p \Rightarrow (\exists u \in \mathrm{dom}(\nu_1), \ v \in \mathrm{dom}(\nu_2))w = \langle u, v \rangle) \\ \text{and } f^{-1}[\nu_2(v)] = \bigcup_{\langle u,v \rangle \ll p} \nu_1(u) \cap \mathrm{dom}(f). \end{cases}$$

Proof (Proof of Lemma 3). Let p be a $\overrightarrow{\delta_4}$-representation of a partial continuous function $f :\subseteq X \to \overline{\mathbb{R}}^+$. Then there exists only one total continuous function $f' : X \to \overline{\mathbb{R}}^+$ in $\overrightarrow{\delta_4}(p)$. Hence $\overrightarrow{\delta_4}$ is also a representation of the set $C(X, \overline{\mathbb{R}}^+)$ of all total continuous functions. The function represented by p is determined by the set $\{w \in \Sigma^* : w \ll p\}$. Then there is a computable enumeration of all computable $\overrightarrow{\delta_4}$-representations. $\square$

4.3   The Existence of an Optimal Integral Test

Definition 7. *A μ-integral test on $\mathbf{X}$ is a $(\delta, \overline{\rho}_<)$-computable function $f : X \to \overline{\mathbb{R}}^+$ δ_A-relative to μ such that $\mu(f) \leq 1$. A μ-integral test f_0 is optimal if, for each μ-integral test f, there exists c such that $f(x) \leq c \cdot f_0(x)$ for all $x \in X$.*

Theorem 4. *Let $\mathbf{X}$ be a SCT_3 space. For an arbitrary measure μ on $\mathbf{X}$, there exists an optimal μ-integral test. Furthermore we can construct an optimal μ-integral test uniformly from δ_A-representation of μ.*

Proof. By Lemma 3 there exists a computable enumeration $f_n : X \to \overline{\mathbb{R}}^+$ of $(\delta_X, \overline{\rho}_<)$-computable functions. Let $f = \sum_{n=0}^{\infty} 2^{-n-1} b_1(f_n, \mu)$ where b_1 is in Lemma 2. Then $\int b_1(f_n, \mu) d\mu \leq 1$ and $\int f d\mu \leq 1$. Hence f is an integral test.

If $\int f_n d\mu < 1$, then $b_1(f_n, \mu) = f_n$ and $f_n(x) \leq 2^n \cdot f(x)$ for all $x \in X$. Suppose $\int f_n d\mu = 1$. Then there exists m such that $f_n(x) = 2 f_m(x)$ for all x. It follows that $\int f_m d\mu = 1/2$ and $f_n(x) = 2 f_m(x) \leq 2^{m+1} \cdot f(x)$ for all $x \in X$. Hence f is optimal. $\square$

5   Optimal Superfarthingale

5.1   Effectivization of Game-Theoretic Probability

In the following we often use a $([\delta_A, [\delta \to \overline{\rho}_<], \delta]^*, \delta_A, \delta, \overline{\rho}_<)$-computable superfarthingale. For simplicity we call it a c.e. superfarthingale. Let $\mathcal{V}$ be the class of all non-negative c.e. superfarthingales V with $V(\Lambda) = 1$.

Definition 8. *A non-negative c.e. superfarthingale V is optimal if, for any superfarthingale $V' \in \mathcal{V}$, there exists a constant c such that, for any $\sigma \in \Pi^\circ$, $cV(\sigma) \geq V'(\sigma)$.*

Theorem 5. *If $\mathbf{X}$ is a SCT_3 space, then there is an optimal superfarthingale.*

Definition 9. *A superfarthingale V is strict if the equation (2) in Definition 1 holds as a strict inequality ("$>$") for all n.*

Lemma 4. *For a non-negative superfarthingale V, there exists a strict superfarthingale V' such that $2V' \geq V$.*

Proof. Let $V'(\pi^n) = \frac{2^n}{2^{n+1}-1} \cdot V(\pi^n)$. Then $2V' > V$ and

$$\int_X V'(\pi^{n-1}, p_n, x)dp_n = \int_X \frac{2^n}{2^{n+1}-1} \cdot V(\pi^{n-1}, p_n, x)dp_n$$

$$\leq \frac{2^n}{2^{n+1}-1} \cdot V(\pi^{n-1})$$

$$= \frac{2^n}{2^{n+1}-1} \cdot \frac{2^n-1}{2^n-1} \times \frac{2^{n-1}}{2^n-1} \cdot V(\pi^{n-1})$$

$$= \frac{2^{2n}-2^n}{2^{2n}-2^{n-1}} \times V'(\pi^{n-1}) < V'(\pi^{n-1}).$$

$\square$

Lemma 5. *There exists a computable enumeration $\{V_m\} \subset \mathcal{V}$ such that each non-negative c.e. strict superfarthingale with $V(\Lambda) = 1$ appears in the enumeration.*

Proof. Let $V'(\pi^n) = \sup_{q<V'(\pi^{n-1})} b_q(V(\pi^n), p_n)$ for all $n \geq 1$ and $V'(\Lambda) = 1$. Then $\int_X V'(\pi^{n-1}, p_n, x)dp_n \leq V'(\pi^{n-1})$. Hence $V' \in \mathcal{V}$.

Suppose that V is strict. We prove $V'(\pi^n) = V(\pi^n)$ inductively on n. Suppose that $V'(\pi^{n-1}) = V(\pi^{n-1})$. Then $\int_X V(\pi^{n-1}, p_n, x)dp_n < q \Rightarrow b_q(V(\pi_n), p_n) = V(\pi_n)$. Hence $\int_X V(\pi_{n-1}, p_n, x)dp_n < V'(\pi_{n-1}) \Rightarrow V'(\pi_n) = V(\pi_n)$. By the strictness of V and the assumption, $V'(\pi^n) = V(\pi^n)$. $\square$

Proof (Proof of Theorem 5). Let V_n be a computable enumeratation of strict superfarthingales. Let $V = 2^{-n-1}V_n$. We prove that V is optimal. Let V' be a superfarthingale. Then by Lemma 4 and Lemma 5 there exists n and c such that $cV_n \geq V'$. Then $c \cdot 2^n V \geq c \cdot 2^n 2^{-n} V_n \geq V'$. $\square$

5.2   Convergence to a Measure

We will prove a generalized version of Theorem 1. Let ν_n be the measures induced by the optimal superfarthingale V, that is, $\nu_n(A) = \int_A \overline{V}(\pi^{n-1}, p_n, x)dp_n$ where $\overline{V}(\pi^n) = \frac{V(\pi^n)}{V(\pi^{n-1})}$. We discuss what is the limit of the measures $\nu_n(A)$.

Fix $\pi = (p_1, y_1, p_2, y_2, \dots) \in \Pi$. Let W be a non-negative c.e. farthingale and μ_n be the measures induced by W. The Hellinger distance is defined by

$$h_n = \int_X \left(\sqrt{\overline{V}(\pi^{n-1}, p_n, x)} - \sqrt{\overline{W}(\pi^{n-1}, p_n, x)} \right)^2 dp_n$$

Let $N_n = \int_X \sqrt{\overline{V}(\pi^n)\overline{W}(\pi^n)}dp_n$. Then $N_n \leq 1 - \frac{h_n}{2} \leq \exp(-\frac{h_n}{2})$. The first inequality follows from $h_n = \int_X \overline{V}(\pi^n)dp_n + \int_X \overline{W}(\pi^n)dp_n - 2N_n \leq 2 - 2N_n$. The second inequality follows from $1 - x \leq e^{-x}$. Then $N_n \exp(\frac{h_n}{2}) \leq 1$.

There exists a superfarthingale Y such that

$$Y(\mu_1, y_1, \mu_2, y_2, \dots) = \sqrt{\frac{V(\pi^n)}{W(\pi^n)}} \cdot \exp(\frac{1}{2}\sum_{i=i}^{n} h_i),$$

because

$$\frac{\int_X Y(\pi^n)d\mu_n}{Y(\pi^{n-1})} = \int \sqrt{\frac{\overline{V}(\pi^n)}{\overline{W}(\pi^n)}} d\mu_n \exp(\frac{h_n}{2})$$

$$= \int \sqrt{\overline{V}(\pi^n)\overline{W}(\pi^n)} dp_n \exp(\frac{h_n}{2}) = N_n \exp(\frac{h_n}{2}) \le 1.$$

Theorem 6. *If* $\sup_n Y < \infty$ *then* $\sum_n h_n < \infty$. *In particular* $\sup_n Y < \infty$ *implies* $h_n \to 0$ *as* $n \to \infty$.

Proof. By optimality of V there exists $c > 0$ such that $V(\pi^n) \ge c \cdot W(\pi^n)$ for all π. If $\sum_{i=1}^{\infty} h_i = \infty$, then $V(\pi^n)/W(\pi^n) \to 0$, this is a contradiction. Also recall h_i is non-negative. □

Hence we conclude that $h_n \to 0$ as $n \to \infty$ almost surely. By Theorem 2, Y is not c.e. in general. This is because h_i is not. To obtain the convergence on a random sequence, we need a stronger randomness notion such as 2-randomness or difference randomness [4].

Acknowledgement. The author thanks Akimichi Takemura for encouragements and comments. This work was partly supported by GCOE, Kyoto University.

References

1. Dawid, A.P.: Statistical theory: the prequential approach (with discussion). Journal of the Royal Statistical Society A 147, 278–292 (1984)
2. Dawid, A.P., Vovk, V.: Prequential probability: principles and properties. Bernoulli 5, 125–162 (1999)
3. Downey, R., Hirschfeldt, D.R.: Algorithmic Randomness and Complexity. Springer, Berlin (2010)
4. Franklin, J.N.Y., Ng, K.M.: Difference randomness. Proc. Amer. Math. Soc. 139, 345–360 (2011)
5. Gács, P.: Uniform test of algorithmic randomness over a general space. Theoretical Computer Science 341, 91–137 (2005)
6. Grubba, T., Schröder, M., Weihrauch, K.: Computable metrization. Mathematical Logic Quaterly 53(4-5), 381–395 (2007)
7. Hoyrup, M., Rojas, C.: An Application of Martin-Löf Randomness to Effective Probability Theory. In: Ambos-Spies, K., Löwe, B., Merkle, W. (eds.) CiE 2009. LNCS, vol. 5635, pp. 260–269. Springer, Heidelberg (2009)
8. Hoyrup, M., Rojas, C.: Computability of probability measures and Martin-Löf randomness over metric spaces. Information and Computation 207(7), 830–847 (2009)
9. Hutter, M.: Universal artificial intelligence: Sequential decisions based on algorithmic probability. Springer (2005)
10. Hutter, M., Muchnik, A.: On semimeasures predicting Martin-Löf random sequences. Theoretical Computer Science 382, 247–261 (2007)

11. Li, M., Vitányi, P.: An introduction to Kolmogorov complexity and its applications, 3rd edn. Graduate Texts in Computer Science. Springer, New York (2009)
12. Miyabe, K.: Algorithmic randomness over general spaces (submitted)
13. Nies, A.: Computability and Randomness. Oxford University Press, USA (2009)
14. Odifreddi, P.: Classical Recursion Theory, vol. 1. North-Holland (1990)
15. Odifreddi, P.: Classical Recursion Theory, vol. 2. North-Holland (1999)
16. Schröder, M.: Admissible Representations for Probability Measures. Mathematical Logic Quarterly 53(4-5), 431–445 (2007)
17. Shafer, G., Vovk, V.: Probability and Finance: It's Only a Game! Wiley (2001)
18. Soare, R.I.: Recursively enumerable sets and degrees. Perspectives in Mathematical Logic. Springer, Berlin (1987)
19. Solomonoff, R.J.: A formal theory of inductive inference I, II. Information and Control 7, 1–22, 224–254 (1964)
20. Solomonoff, R.J.: Complexity-based induction systems: Comparisons and convergence theorems. IEEE Transaction on Information Theory IT 24, 422–432 (1978)
21. Vovk, V., Shen, A.: Prequential randomness and probability. Theoretical Computer Science 411, 2632–2646 (2010)
22. Weihrauch, K.: Computable Analysis: an introduction. Springer, Berlin (2000)
23. Weihrauch, K., Grubba, T.: Elementary Computable Topology. Journal of Universal Computer Science 15(6), 1381–1422 (2009)
24. Weihrauch, K.: Computable Separation in Topology, from T_0 to T_3. In: CCA (2009)

Diverse Consequences of Algorithmic Probability

Eray Özkural

Computer Engineering Department, Bilkent University, Ankara, Turkey

Abstract. We reminisce and discuss applications of algorithmic probability to a wide range of problems in artificial intelligence, philosophy and technological society. We propose that Solomonoff has effectively axiomatized the field of artificial intelligence, therefore establishing it as a rigorous scientific discipline. We also relate to our own work in incremental machine learning and philosophy of complexity.

1 Introduction

Ray Solomonoff was a pioneer in mathematical Artificial Intelligence (AI), whose proposal of Algorithmic Probability (ALP) has led to diverse theoretical consequences and applications, most notably in AI. In this paper, we try to give a sense of the significance of his theoretical contributions, reviewing the essence of his proposal in an accessible way, and recounting a few, seemingly unrelated, diverse consequences which, in our opinion, hint towards a philosophically clear world-view that has rarely been acknowledged by the greater scientific community. That is to say, we try to give the reader a glimpse of what it is like to consider the consequences of ALP, and what ideas might lie behind the theoretical model, as we imagine them.

Let M be a reference machine which corresponds to a universal computer[1] with a prefix-free code. In a prefix-free code, no code is a prefix of another. This is also called a self-delimiting code, as most reasonable computer programming languages are. Solomonoff inquired the probability that an output string x is generated by M considering the whole space of possible programs. By giving each program bitstring p an a priori probability of $2^{-|p|}$, we can ensure that the space of programs meets the probability axioms (by the extended Kraft inequality [2]). In other words, we imagine that we toss a fair coin to generate each bit of a random program. This probability model of programs entails the following probability mass function (p.m.f.) for strings $x \in \{0,1\}^*$:

$$P_M(x) = \sum_{M(p)=x*} 2^{-|p|} \tag{1}$$

which is the probability that a random program will output a prefix of x. $P_M(x)$ is called the *algorithmic probability* of x for it assumes the *definition* of program based probability. We use P when M is clear from the context to avoid clutter.

---

[1] Optionally, it can be probabilistic to deal with general induction problems, i.e., it has access to a random number generator [1, Section 4].

D.L. Dowe (Ed.): Solomonoff Festschrift, LNAI 7070, pp. 285–298, 2013.

2   Solomonoff Induction

Using this probability model of bitstrings, one can make predictions. Intuitively, we can state that it is impossible to imagine intelligence in the absence of any prediction ability: purely random behavior is decisively non-intelligent. Since, P is a universal probability model, it can be used as the basis of universal prediction, and thus intelligence. Perhaps, Solomonoff's most significant contributions were in the field of AI, as he envisioned a machine that can learn anything from scratch. Reviewing his early papers such as [3,4], we see that he has established the theoretical justification for machine learning and data mining fields. Few researchers could ably make claims about universal intelligence as he did. Unfortunately, not all of his ideas have reached fruition in practice; yet there is little doubt that his approach was the correct basis for a *science* of intelligence.

His main proposal for machine learning is inductive inference [5,6] circa 1964, for a variety of problems such as sequence prediction, set induction, operator induction and grammar induction [7]. Without much loss of generality, we can discuss sequence prediction on bitstrings. Assume that there is a *computable* p.m.f. of bitstrings P_1. Given a bitstring x drawn from P_1, we can define the conditional probability of the next bit simply by normalizing (1) [7]. Algorithmically, we would have to approximate (1) by finding short programs that generate x (the shortest of which is the most probable). In more general induction, we run all models in parallel, quantifying fit-to-data, weighed by the algorithmic probability of the model, to find the best models and construct distributions [7]; the common point being determining good models with high a priori probability. Finding the shortest program in general is *undecidable*, however, Levin search [8] can be used for this purpose. There are two important results about Solomonoff induction that we shall mention here. First, Solomonoff induction converges very rapidly to the real probability distribution. The convergence theorem shows that the expected total square error is related only to the algorithmic complexity of P_1, which is independent from x. The following bound [9] is discussed at length in [10] with a concise proof:

$$E_P \left[\sum_{m=1}^{n} (P(a_{m+1} = 1|a_1a_2...a_m) - P_1(a_{m+1} = 1|a_1a_2...a_m))^2 \right] \leq -\frac{1}{2} \ln P(P_1))$$

(2)

This bound characterizes the divergence of the ALP solution from the real probability distribution P_1. $P(P_1)$ is the a priori probability of P_1 p.m.f. according to our universal distribution P_M. On the right hand side of (2), $-\ln P_M(P_1)$ is roughly $k \ln 2$ where k is the Kolmogorov complexity of P_1 (the length of the shortest program that defines it), thus the total expected error is bounded by a constant, which guarantees that the error decreases very rapidly as example size increases. Secondly, there is an optimal search algorithm to approximate Solomonoff induction, which adopts Levin's universal search method to solve the problem of universal induction [8,11]. Universal search procedure time-shares all candidate programs according to their a priori probability with a clever watchdog policy to avoid the practical impact of the undecidability of the halting problem [11]. The search procedure starts with a time limit $t = t_0$, in its iteration tries all candidate programs c with a time limit of $t.P(c)$, and while a solution is not found, it doubles the time limit t. The time $t(s)/P(s)$ for a solution program s taking time $t(s)$ is called the Conceptual Jump Size (CJS), and it is easily shown that Levin Search terminates in at most 2.CJS time. To obtain alternative solutions, one may keep running after the first solution is found, as there may be more probable solutions that need more time. The optimal solution is computable only in the limit, which turns out to be a desirable property of Solomonoff induction, as it is *complete* and uncomputable [12, Section 2]. An explanation of Levin's universal search procedure and its application to Solomonoff induction may be found in [8,11,13].

3   The Axiomatization of Artificial Intelligence

We believe in fact that Solomonoff's work was seminal in that he has single-handedly *axiomatized* AI, discovering the minimal necessary conditions for any machine to attain general intelligence (based on our interpretation of [1]).

Informally, these axioms are:

AI0. AI must have in its possession a universal computer M (Universality).
AI1. AI must be able to learn any solution expressed in M's code (Learning recursive solutions).
AI2. AI must use probabilistic prediction (Bayes' theorem).
AI3. AI must embody in its learning a principle of induction (Occam's razor).

While it may be possible to give a more compact characterization, these are ultimately what is necessary for the kind of general learning that Solomonoff induction achieves. ALP can be seen as a *complete* formalization of Occam's razor (as well as Epicurus's principle) [14] and thus serve as the foundation of universal induction, capable of solving all AI problems of significance. The axioms are important because they allow us to assess whether a system is capable of general intelligence or not.

Obviously, AI1 entails AI0, therefore AI0 is redundant, and can be omitted entirely, however we stated it separately only for historical reasons, as one of the landmarks of early AI research, in retrospect, was the invention of the universal computer, which goes back to Leibniz's idea of a universal language (characteristica universalis) that can express every statement in science and mathematics, and has found its perfect embodiment in Turing's research [15,16]. A related achievement of early AI was the development of LISP, a universal computer based on lambda calculus (which is a functional model of computation) that has shaped much of early AI research.

See also a recent survey about inductive inference [17] with a focus on Minimum Message Length (MML) principle introduced in 1968 [18]. MML principle is also a formalization of induction developed within the framework of classical information theory, which establishes a trade-off between model complexity and fit-to-data by finding the minimal message that encodes both the model and the data [19]. This trade-off is quite similar to the earlier forms of induction that Solomonoff developed, however independently discovered. Dowe points out that Occam's razor means choosing the simplest single theory when data is equally matched, which MML formalizes perfectly (and is functional otherwise in the case of inequal fits) while Solomonoff induction maintains a mixture of alternative solutions [17, Sections 2.4 & 4]. On the other hand, the diversity of solutions in ALP is seen as desirable by Solomonoff himself [12], and in a recent philosophical paper which illustrates how Solomonoff induction dissolves various philosophical objections to induction [14]. Nevertheless, it is well worth mentioning that Solomonoff induction (formal theory published in 1964 [5,6]), MML (1968), and Minimum Description Length [20] formalizations, as well as Statistical Learning Theory [21] (initially developed in 1960), all provide a principle of induction (AI3). However, it was Solomonoff who first observed the importance of universality for AI (AI0-AI1). The plurality of probabilistic approaches to induction supports the importance of AI3 (as well as hinting that diversity of solutions may be useful). AI2, however, does not require much explanation. Some objections to Bayesianism are answered using MML in [22]. Please also see an intruging paper by Wallace and Dowe [23] on the relation between MML and Kolmogorov complexity, which states that Solomonoff induction is tailored to prediction rather than inference, and recommends non-universal models in practical work, therefore becomes incompatible with the AI axioms (AI0-AI1). Ultimately, empirical work will illuminate whether our AI axioms should be adopted, or more restrictive models are sufficient for universal intelligence; therefore such alternative viewpoints must be considered. In addition to this, Dowe discusses the relation between inductive inference and intelligence, and the requirements of intelligence as we do elsewhere [17, Section 7.3]. Also relevant is an adaptive universal intelligence test that aims to measure the intelligence of any AI agent, and discusses various definitions of intelligence [24].

4   Incremental Machine Learning

In solving a problem of induction, the aforementioned search methods suffer from the huge computational complexity of trying to compress the entire input. For instance, if the complexity of the p.m.f. P_1 is about 400 bits, Levin search would take on the order of 2^{400} times the running time of the solution program, which is infeasible (quite impossible in the observed universe). Therefore, Solomonoff has suggested using an *incremental* machine learning algorithm, which can re-use information found in previous solutions [13].

The following argument illustrates the situation more clearly. Let P_1 and P_2 be the p.m.f.'s corresponding to a training sequence of two induction problems (any of them, not necessarily sequence prediction, to which others can be reduced easily) with data $< d_1, d_2 >$. Assume that the first problem has been solved (correctly) with universal search. It has taken at most $2.\text{CJS}_1 = 2.t(s_1)/P(s_1)$ time. If the second problem is solved in an *incremental* fashion, making use of the information from P_1, then the running time of discovering a solution s_2 for

d_2 reduces, depending on the success of *information transfer* across problems. Here, we quantify how much in familiar probabilistic terms.

In [10], Solomonoff describes an information theoretic interpretation of ALP, which suggests the following entropy function:

$$H^*(x) = -\log_2 P(x) \tag{3}$$

This entropy function has perfect sub-additivity of information according to the corresponding conditional entropy definition:

$$P(y|x) = \frac{P(x,y)}{P(x)} \tag{4}$$

$$H^*(y|x) = -\log_2 P(y|x) \tag{5}$$

$$H^*(x,y) = H^*(x) + H^*(y|x) \tag{6}$$

This definition of entropy thus does not suffer from the additive constant terms as in Chaitin's version. We can instantly define mutual entropy:

$$H^*(x:y) = H^*(x) + H^*(y) - H^*(x,y) = H^*(y) - H^*(y|x) \tag{7}$$

which trivially follows.

A KUSP machine is a universal computer that can store data and methods in additional storage. In 1984, Solomonoff observed that KUSP machines are especially suitable for incremental learning [11]. In our work [25] we found that, the incremental learning approach was indeed useful (as in the preceding OOPS algorithm[26]). Here is how we interpreted incremental learning. After each induction problem, the p.m.f. P is updated, thus for every new problem a new probability distribution is obtained. Although we are using the same M reference machine for trial programs, we are referring to *implicit* KUSP machines which store information about the experience of the machine so far, in subsequent problems. In our example of two induction problems, let the updated P be called P', naturally there will be an update procedure which takes time $t_u(P, s_1)$. Just how much time can we expect to save if we use incremental learning instead of independent learning? First, let us write the time bound $2.t(s)/P(s)$ as $t(s).2^{H^*(s)+1}$. If s_1 and s_2 are not algorithmically independent, then $H^*(s_2|s_1)$ is smaller than $H^*(s_2)$. Independently, we would have $t(s_1).2^{H^*(s_1)+1} + t(s_2).2^{H^*(s_2)+1}$, together, we will have, in the best case $t(s_1).2^{H^*(s_1)+1} + t(s_2).2^{H^*(s_2|s_1)+1}$ for the search time, assuming that recalling s_1 takes no time for the latter search task (which is an unrealistic assumption). Therefore in total, the latter search task can accelerate $2^{H^*(s_1:s_2)}$ times, and we can save $t(s_2).2^{H^*(s_2)+1}(1 - 2^{-H^*(s_1:s_2)}) - t_u(P, s_1)$ total time in the best case (only an upper bound since we did not account for recall time). Note that the maximum temporal gain is related to both how much mutual information is discovered across solutions (thus P_i's), and how much time the update procedure takes. Clearly, if the update time dominates overall, incremental learning is in vain. However, if updates are effective and efficient, there is enormous potential in incremental machine learning.

During the experimental tests of our Stochastic Context Free Grammar based search and update algorithms [25], we have observed that in practice we can realize fast updates, and we can still achieve actual code re-use and tremendous speed-up. Using only 0.5 teraflop/sec of computing speed and a reference machine choice of R5RS Scheme [27], we solved 6 simple deterministic operator induction problems in 245.1 seconds. This running time is compared to 7150 seconds without any updates. Scaled to human-level processing speed of 100 teraflop/sec, our system would learn and solve the entire training sequence in 1.25 seconds, which is (arguably) better than most human students. In one particular operator induction problem (fourth power, x^4), we saw actual code re-use: (define (pow4 x) (define (sqr x) (* x x)) (sqr (sqr x))), and an actual speedup of 272. The gains that we saw confirmed the incremental learning proposals of Solomonoff, mentioned in a good number of his publications, but most clearly in [11,13,1]. Based on our work and the huge speedup observed in OOPS for a shorter training sequence [26], we have come to believe that incremental learning has the epistemological status of an additional AI axiom:

AI4. AI must be able to use its previous experience to speed up subsequent prediction tasks (Transfer Learning).

This axiom is justified by observing that many universal induction problems are completely unsolvable by a system that does not have the adequate sort of *algorithmic* memory, regardless of the search method.

The results above may be contrasted with inductive programming approaches, since we predicted deterministic functions. One of the earliest and most successful inductive programming systems is ADATE, which is optimized for a more specific purpose. ADATE system has yielded impressive results in an ML variant by user supplied primitives and constraining candidate programs [28]. Universal representations have been investigated in inductive logic programming as well [29], however U-learning unfortunately lacks the extremely accurate generalization of Solomonoff induction. It has been shown that incremental learning is useful in the inductive programming framework [30], which supports our observation of the necessity of incremental machine learning. Another relevant work is a typed higher-order logic knowledge representation scheme based on term representation of individuals and a rich representation language encompassing many abstract data types [31]. A recent survey on inductive programming may be found in [32].

We should also account our brief correspondence with Solomonoff. We expressed that the prediction algorithms were powerful but it seemed that memory was not used sufficiently. Solomonoff responded by mentioning the potential stochastic grammar and genetic programming approaches that he was working on at the time. Our present research was motivated by a problem he posed during the discussions of his seminars in Turing Days '06 at Bilgi University, Istanbul: "We can use grammar induction for updating a stochastic context free grammar, but there is a problem. We already know the grammar of the reference machine.". We designed our incremental learning algorithms to address this particular problem[2]. Solomonoff has also guided our research by making a valuable suggestion, that it is more important to show whether incremental learning works over a sequence of simpler problems than solving a difficult problem. We have in addition investigated the use of PPM family of compressors following his proposal, but as we expected, they were not sufficient for guiding LISP-like programs, and would require too many changes. Therefore, we proceeded directly to the simplest kind of guiding p.m.f. that would work for Scheme, as we preferred not to work on assembly-like languages for which PPM might be appropriate, since, in our opinion, high-level languages embody more technological progress (see also [33] which employs a Scheme subset). Colorfully speaking, inventing a functional form in assembly might be like re-inventing the wheel. However, in general, it would not be trivial for the induction system to invent syntax forms that compare favorably to LISP, especially during preliminary training. Therefore, much intelligence is already present in a high-level universal computer (AI0) which we simply take advantage of.

5   Cognitive Architecture

Another important discussion is whether a cognitive architecture is necessary. The axiomatic approach was seen counter-productive by some leading researchers in the past. However, we think that their opinion can be expressed as follows: the minimal program that realizes these axioms is not automatically intelligent, because in practice an intelligent system requires a good deal of algorithmic information to take off the ground. This is not a bad argument, since obviously, the human brain is well equipped genetically. However, we cannot either rule out that a somewhat compact system may achieve human-level general intelligence. The question therefore, is whether a simply described system like AIXI [34] (an extension of Solomonoff induction to reinforcement learning) is sufficient *in practice*, or there is a need for a modular/extensible cognitive architecture that has been designed in particular ways to promote certain kinds of mental growth and operation. Some proponents of general purpose AI research think that such a cognitive architecture is necessary, e.g., OpenCog [35]. Schmidhuber has suggested the famous Gödel Machine which has a mechanical model of machine consciousness [36]. Solomonoff himself has proposed early on in 2002, the design of Alpha, a generic AI architecture which can ultimately solve free-form time-limited optimization problems [13]. Although in his later works, Solomonoff has not made much mention of Alpha and has instead focused on the particulars of the required basic induction and learning capability, nonetheless his proposal remains as one of the most extensible and elegant self-improving AI designs.

---

[2] We occasionally corresponded via e-mail. Before the AGI-10 conference, he had reviewed a draft of my paper, and he had commented that the "learning programming idioms" and "frequent subprogram mining" algorithms were interesting, which was all the encouragement I needed. The last e-mail I received from him was on 11/Oct/2009. I regretfully learnt that he passed away a month later. His independent character and true scientific spirit will always be a shining beacon for me.

Therefore, this point is open to debate, though some researchers may want to assume another, entirely optional, axiom:

AI5. AI must be arranged such that self-improvement is feasible in a realistic mode of operation (Cognitive Architecture).

It is doubtful for instance whether a combination of incremental learning and AIXI will result in a practical reinforcement learning agent. Neither is it well understood whether autonomous systems with built-in utility/goal functions are suitable for all practical purposes. We anticipate that such questions will be settled by experimenters, as the complexity of interesting experiments will quickly overtake theoretical analysis.

We do not consider human-like behavior, or a robotic body, or an autonomous AI design, such as a goal-driven or reinforcement-learning agent, essential to intelligence, hence we did not propose autonomy or embodiment as an axiom. Solomonoff has commented likewise on the preferred target applications [37]:

> To start, I'd like to define the scope of my interest in A.I. I am not particularly interested in simulating human behavior. I am interested in creating a machine that can work very difficult problems much better and/or faster than humans can – and this machine should be embodied in a technology to which Moore's Law applies. I would like it to give a better understanding of the relation of quantum mechanics to general relativity. I would like it to discover cures for cancer and AIDS. I would like it to find some very good high temperature superconductors. I would not be disappointed if it were unable to pass itself off as a rock star.

6   Philosophical Foundation and Consequences

Solomonoff's AI theory is founded on a wealth of philosophy. Here, we shall briefly revisit the philosophical foundation of ALP and point out some of its philosophical consequences. In his posthumous publication, Solomonoff mentions the inspiration for some of his work: Carnap's idea that the state of the world can be represented by a finite bitstring (and that science predicts future bits with inductive inference), Turing's universal computer (AI0) as communicated by Minsky and McCarthy, and Chomsky's generative grammars [12]. The discovery of ALP is described by Solomonoff in quite a bit of detail in [38], which relates his discovery to the background of many prominent thinkers and contributors. Carnap's empiricism seems to have been a highly influential factor in Solomonoff's research as he sought to find how science is carried out, rather than particular scientific findings; and ALP is a satisfactory solution to Carnap's program of inductive inference [14].

Let us then recall some philosophically relevant aspects of ALP discussed in the most recent publications of Solomonoff. First, the exact same method is used to solve both mathematical and scientific problems. This means that there is no fundamental epistemological difference between these problems; our interpretation is that, this is well founded only when we observe that mathematical problems themselves are computational or linguistic problems, in practice mathematical problems can be reduced to particular computational problems, and here is why the same method works for both kinds of problems. Mathematical facts do not preside over or precede physical facts, they themselves are solutions of physical problems ultimately (e.g., does this particular kind of machine halt or not?). And the substance of mathematics, the lucid sort of mathematical language and concepts that we have invented, can be fully explained by Solomonoff induction, as those are the kinds of *useful programs*, which have aided an intellect in its training, and therefore are retained as *linguistic* and *algorithmic* information. The subjectivity and diversity aspects of ALP [12, Sections 3 & 4] fully explain why there can be multiple and almost equally productive foundations of mathematics, as those merely point out somewhat equally useful formalisms invented by different mathematicians. There is absolutely nothing special about ZFC theory, it is just a formal theory to explain some useful procedures that we perform in our heads, i.e., it is more like the logical explanation of a set module in a functional programming language than anything else, however, the operations in a mathematician's brain are not visible to their owner, thereby leading to useless Platonist fantasies of some mathematicians owing to a dearth of philosophical imagination. Therefore, it does not matter much whether one prefers this or that formalization of set theory, or category theory as a foundation, unless that choice restricts success in the solution of future scientific problems. Since, such a problematic scientific situation does not seem to have emerged yet (forcing us to choose among particular formalizations), the diversity principle of ALP forces us to retain them all. That is to say, subscribing to the ALP viewpoint has the unexpected consequence that we abandon both Platonism and Formalism. There is a meaning in formal language, in the manner which improves future predictions, however, there is not a single a priori fact, in addition to empirical observations, and no such fact is ever needed to conduct empirical work, except a proper realization of axioms A1–A3 (and surely no sane scientist would accept that there is a unique and empty set that exists in a hidden order of reality). When we consider these axioms, we need to understand the universality of computation, and the principled manner in which we have to employ it for reliable induction in our scientific inquiries. The only physically relevant assumption is that of the computability of the distributions which generate our empirical problems (regardless of whether the problem is mathematical or scientific), and the choice of a universal computer which introduces a *necessary* subjectivity. The computability aspect may be interpreted as *information finitism*, all the problems that we can work with should have finite entropy. Yet, this restriction on disorder is not at all limiting, for it is hardly conceivable how one may wish to solve a problem of actually infinite complexity. Therefore, this is not much of an assumption for scientific inquiry, especially given that both quantum mechanics and general relativity can be described in computable mathematics (see for instance [39] about the applicability of computable mathematics to quantum mechanics). And neither can one hope to find an example of a single scientifically valid problem in any textbook of science that requires the existence of distributions with infinite complexity to solve.

With regards to general epistemology, ALP/AIT may be seen as largely incompatible with non-reductionism. Non-reductionism is quite misleading in the manner it is usually conveyed. Instead, we must seek to understand irreducibility in the sense of AIT, of quantifying algorithmic information, which allows us to reconcile the concept of irreducibility with physicalism (which we think every empiricist should accept) [40]. In particular, we can partially formalize the notion of knowledge by mutual information between the world and a brain. Our paper proposed a physical solution to the problem of determining the most "objective" universal computer: it is the universe itself. If digital physics were true, this might be for instance a particular kind of graph automata, or if quantum mechanics were the basis, then a universal quantum computer could be used; however, for many tasks using such a low-level computer might be extraordinarily difficult. We also argued that extreme non-reductionism leads to arguments from ignorance such as ontological dualism, and information theory is much better suited to explaining evolution and the need for abstractions in our language. It should also be obvious that the ALP solution to AI extends the two main tenets of logical positivism, which are verificationism and unified science, as it gives a finite cognitive procedure with which one can conduct all empirical work, and allows us to develop a private language with which we can describe all of science and mathematics. However, we should also mention that this strengthened positivism does not require a strict analytic-synthetic distinction; a spectrum of analytic-synthetic distinction as in Quine's philosophy seems to be acceptable [41]. We have already seen that according to ALP, mathematical and scientific problems have no real distinction, therefore like Quine, ALP would allow revising even mathematical logic itself, and we need not remind that the concept of universal computer itself has not appeared out of thin air, but has been invented due to the laborious mental work of scientists, as they abstracted from the mechanics of *performing mathematics*; at the bottom these are all empirical problems [42]. On the other hand, a "web of belief" as in Quine, by no means suggests non-reductionism, for that could be true only if indeed there were phenomena that had unscathable (infinite) complexity, such as Turing oracle machines which were not proposed as physical machines, but only as a hypothetical concept [16]. Quine himself was a physicalist; we do not think that he would support the later vendetta against reductionism which may be a misunderstanding of his holism. Though, it may be argued that his obscure version of Platonism, which does not seem much scientific to us, may be the culprit. Today's Bayesian networks seem to be a good formalization of Quine's web of belief, and his instrumentalism is consistent with the ALP approach of maintaining useful programs. Therefore, on this account, psychology ought to be reducible to neurophysiology, as the concept of life to molecular biology, because these are all ultimately sets of problems that overlap in the physical world, and the relation between them cannot hold an infinite amount of information; which would require an infinitely complex local environment, and that does not seem consistent with our scientific observations. That is to say, discovery of bridge disciplines is possible as exemplified by quantum chemistry and molecular biology, and it is not different from any other kind of empirical work. Recently, it has been perhaps better understood in the popular culture that creationism and non-reductionism are almost synonymous (regarding the claims of "intelligent design" that the flagella of bacteria are too complex to have evolved). Note that ALP has no qualms with the statistical behavior of quantum systems, as it allows non-determinism. Moreover, the particular kind of irreducibility in AIT corresponds to weak emergentism, and most certainly contradicts with strong emergentism which implies supernatural events. Please see also [17, Section 7] for a discussion of philosophical problems related to algorithmic complexity.

7   Intellectual Property towards Infinity Point

Solomonoff has proposed the infinity point hypothesis, also known as the singularity, as an exponentially accelerating technological progress caused by human-level AI's that complement the scientific community, to accelerate our progress ad infinitum within a finite, short time (in practice only a finite, but significant factor of improvement could be expected) in 1985 [43] (the first paper on the subject). Solomonoff has proposed seven milestones of AI development: A: modern AI phase (1956 Dartmouth conference), B: general theory of problem solving (our interpretation: Solomonoff Induction, Levin Search), C: self-improving AI (our interpretation: Alpha architecture, 2002), D: AI that can understand English (our interpretation: not realized yet), E: human-level AI, F: an AI at the level of entire computer science (CS) community, G: an AI many times smarter than the entire CS community.

A weak condition for the infinity point may be obtained by an economic argument, also covered in [43] briefly. The human brain produces 5 teraflops/watt roughly. The current incarnation of NVIDIA's General Purpose Graphics Programming Unit architectures called Fermi achieves about 6 gigaflops/watt [44]. Assuming 85% improvement in power efficiency per year (as seen in NVIDIA's projections), in 12 years, human-level energy efficiency of computing will be achieved. After that date, even if mathematical AI fails due to an unforeseen problem, we will be able to run our brain simulations faster than us, using less energy than humans, effectively creating a bio-information based AI which meets the basic requirement of infinity point. For this to occur, whole brain simulation projects must be comprehensive in operation and efficient enough [45]. Otherwise, human-level AI's that we will construct should match the computational efficiency of the human brain. This weaker condition rests on an economic observation: the economic incentive of cheaper intellectual work will drive the proliferation of personal use of brain simulations. According to NVIDIA's projections, thus, we can expect the necessary conditions for the infinity point to materialize by 2023, after which point technological progress may accelerate very rapidly. According to a recent paper by Koomey, the energy efficiency of computing is doubling every 1.5 years (about 60% per year), regardless of architecture, which would set the date at 2026 [46].

Assume that we are progressing towards the hypothetical infinity point. Then, the entire human civilization may be viewed as a global intelligence working on technological problems. The practical necessity of incremental learning suggests that when faced with more difficult problems, better information sharing is required. If no information sharing is present between researchers (i.e., different search programs), then, they will lose time traversing overlapping program subspaces. This is most clearly seen in the case of *simultaneous inventions* when an idea is said to be "up in the air" and is invented by multiple, independent parties on near dates. If intellectual property (IP) laws are too rigid and costly, this would entail that there is minimal information sharing, and after some point, the global efficiency of solving non-trivial technological problems would be severely hampered. Therefore, to utilize the infinity point effects better, knowledge sharing must be encouraged in the society. Maximum efficiency in this fashion can be provided by free software licenses, and a reform of the patent system. Our view is that no single company or organization can (or should) have a monopoly on the knowledge resources to attack problems with truly large algorithmic complexity (monopoly is mostly illegal presently at any rate). We tend to think that sharing science and technology is the most efficient path towards the infinity point. Naturally, free software philosophy is not acceptable to much commercial enterprise, thus we suggest that as technology advances, the overhead of enforcing IP laws are taken into account. If technology starts to advance much more rapidly, the duration of the IP protection may be shortened, for instance, as after the AI milestone F, the bureaucracy and restrictions of IP law may be a serious bottleneck.

8   Conclusion

We have mentioned diverse consequences of ALP in axiomatization of AI, philosophy, and technological society. We have also related our own research to Solomonoff's proposals. We interpret ALP and AIT as a fundamentally new world-view which allows us to bridge the gap between complex natural phenomena and positive sciences more closely than ever. This paradigm shift has resulted in various breakthrough applications and is likely to benefit the society in the foreseeable future.

Acknowledgements. We thank anonymous reviewers, David Dowe and Laurent Orseau for their valuable comments, which substantially improved this paper.

References

1. Solomonoff, R.J.: Progress in incremental machine learning. Technical Report IDSIA-16-03, IDSIA, Lugano, Switzerland (2003)
2. Chaitin, G.J.: A theory of program size formally identical to information theory. J. ACM 22, 329–340 (1975)

3. Solomonoff, R.J.: An inductive inference machine. Dartmouth Summer Research Project on Artificial Intelligence (1956) A Privately Circulated Report
4. Solomonoff, R.J.: An inductive inference machine. In: IRE National Convention Record, Section on Information Theory, Part 2, New York, USA, pp. 56–62 (1957)
5. Solomonoff, R.J.: A formal theory of inductive inference, part i. Information and Control 7(1), 1–22 (1964)
6. Solomonoff, R.J.: A formal theory of inductive inference, part ii. Information and Control 7(2), 224–254 (1964)
7. Solomonoff, R.J.: Three kinds of probabilistic induction: Universal distributions and convergence theorems. The Computer Journal 51(5), 566–570 (2008); Christopher Stewart Wallace, memorial special issue (1933-2004)
8. Levin, L.A.: Universal sequential search problems. Problems of Information Transmission 9(3), 265–266 (1973)
9. Solomonoff, R.J.: Algorithmic probability: Theory and applications. In: Dehmer, M., Emmert-Streib, F. (eds.) Information Theory and Statistical Learning, pp. 1–23. Springer Science+Business Media, N.Y. (2009)
10. Solomonoff, R.J.: Complexity-based induction systems: Comparisons and convergence theorems. IEEE Trans. on Information Theory IT-24(4), 422–432 (1978)
11. Solomonoff, R.J.: Optimum sequential search. Technical report, Oxbridge Research, Cambridge, Mass., USA (1984)
12. Solomonoff, R.J.: Algorithmic Probability – Its Discovery – Its Properties and Application to Strong AI. In: Randomness Through Computation: Some Answers, More Questions, pp. 149–157. World Scientific Publishing Company (2011)
13. Solomonoff, R.J.: A system for incremental learning based on algorithmic probability. In: Proceedings of the Sixth Israeli Conference on Artificial Intelligence, Tel Aviv, Israel, pp. 515–527 (1989)
14. Rathmanner, S., Hutter, M.: A philosophical treatise of universal induction. Entropy 13(6), 1076–1136 (2011)
15. Davis, M.: The Universal Computer: The Road from Leibniz to Turing. W. W. Norton & Company (2000)
16. Turing, A.M.: On computable numbers, with an application to the entscheidungsproblem. Proceedings of the London Mathematical Society s2-42(1), 230–265 (1937)
17. Dowe, D.L.: MML, hybrid Bayesian network graphical models, statistical consistency, invariance and uniqueness. In: Handbook of the Philosophy of Science (HPS). Philosophy of Statistics, vol. 7, pp. 901–982. Elsevier (2011)
18. Wallace, C.S., Boulton, D.M.: A information measure for classification. Computer Journal 11(2), 185–194 (1968)
19. Wallace, C.S.: Statistical and Inductive Inference by Minimum Message Length. Springer, Berlin (2005)
20. Barron, A., Rissanen, J., Yu, B.: The minimum description length principle in coding and modeling (invited paper), pp. 699–716. IEEE Press, Piscataway (2000)
21. Vapnik, V.: Statistical Learning Theory. John Wiley and Sons, NY (1998)
22. Dowe, D.L., Gardner, S., Oppy, G.: Bayes not bust! why simplicity is no problem for bayesians. The British Journal for the Philosophy of Science 58(4), 709–754 (2007)
23. Wallace, C.S., Dowe, D.L.: Minimum message length and kolmogorov complexity. The Computer Journal 42(4), 270–283 (1999)
24. Hernndez-Orallo, J., Dowe, D.L.: Measuring universal intelligence: Towards an anytime intelligence test. Artificial Intelligence 174(18), 1508–1539 (2010)

25. Özkural, E.: Towards heuristic algorithmic memory. In: Schmidhuber, J., Thórisson, K.R., Looks, M. (eds.) AGI 2011. LNCS, vol. 6830, pp. 382–387. Springer, Heidelberg (2011)
26. Schmidhuber, J.: Optimal ordered problem solver. Machine Learning 54, 211–256 (2004)
27. Kelsey, R., Clinger, W., Rees, J.: Revised5 report on the algorithmic language scheme. Higher-Order and Symbolic Computation 11(1) (1998)
28. Olsson, J.R.: Inductive functional programming using incremental program transformation. Artificial Intelligence 74, 55–83 (1995)
29. Muggleton, S., Page, C.: A learnability model for universal representations. In: Proceedings of the 4th International Workshop on Inductive Logic Programming, vol. 237, pp. 139–160. Citeseer (1994)
30. Ferri-Ramírez, C., Hernández-Orallo, J., Ramírez-Quintana, M.J.: Incremental learning of functional logic programs. In: Kuchen, H., Ueda, K. (eds.) FLOPS 2001. LNCS, vol. 2024, pp. 233–247. Springer, Heidelberg (2001)
31. Bowers, A., Giraud-Carrier, C., Lloyd, J., Sa, E.: A knowledge representation framework for inductive learning (2001)
32. Kitzelmann, E.: Inductive programming: A survey of program synthesis techniques. In: Schmid, U., Kitzelmann, E., Plasmeijer, R. (eds.) AAIP 2009. LNCS, vol. 5812, pp. 50–73. Springer, Heidelberg (2010)
33. Looks, M.: Scalable estimation-of-distribution program evolution. In: Proceedings of the 9th Annual Conference on Genetic and Evolutionary Computation (2007)
34. Hutter, M.: Universal algorithmic intelligence: A mathematical top→down approach. In: Goertzel, B., Pennachin, C. (eds.) Artificial General Intelligence. Cognitive Technologies, pp. 227–290. Springer, Heidelberg (2007)
35. Goertzel, B.: Opencogprime: A cognitive synergy based architecture for artificial general intelligence. In: Baciu, G., Wang, Y., Yao, Y., Kinsner, W., Chan, K., Zadeh, L.A. (eds.) IEEE ICCI, pp. 60–68. IEEE Computer Society (2009)
36. Schmidhuber, J.: Ultimate cognition à la Gödel. Cognitive Computation 1(2), 177–193 (2009)
37. Solomonoff, R.J.: Machine learning - past and future. In: The Dartmouth Artificial Intelligence Conference, pp. 13–15 (2006)
38. Solomonoff, R.J.: The discovery of algorithmic probability. Journal of Computer and System Sciences 55(1), 73–88 (1997)
39. Bridges, D., Svozil, K.: Constructive mathematics and quantum physics. International Journal of Theoretical Physics 39, 503–515 (2000)
40. Özkural, E.: A compromise between reductionism and non-reductionism. In: Worldviews, Science and Us: Philosophy and Complexity. World Scientific Books (2007)
41. Quine, W.: Two dogmas of empiricism. The Philosophical Review 60, 20–43 (1951)
42. Chaitin, G.J.: Two philosophical applications of algorithmic information theory. In: Calude, C.S., Dinneen, M.J., Vajnovszki, V. (eds.) DMTCS 2003. LNCS, vol. 2731, pp. 1–10. Springer, Heidelberg (2003)
43. Solomonoff, R.J.: The time scale of artificial intelligence: Reflections on social effects. Human Systems Management 5, 149–153 (1985)
44. Glaskowsk, P.N.: Nvidia's fermi: The first complete gpu computing architecture (2009)
45. Sandberg, A., Bostrom, N.: Whole brain emulation: A roadmap. Technical report, Future of Humanity Institute, Oxford University (2008)
46. Koomey, J.G., Berard, S., Sanchez, M., Wong, H.: Implications of historical trends in the electrical efficiency of computing. IEEE Annals of the History of Computing 33, 46–54 (2011)

An Adaptive Compression Algorithm in a Deterministic World

Kristiaan Pelckmans

SysCon, Box 337, Information Technology, Uppsala University, 75105, Sweden
kp@it.uu.se
http://www.it.uu.se/katalog/kripe367

Abstract. Assume that we live in a deterministic world, we ask ourselves which place the device of randomness still may have, even in case that there is no philosophical incentive for it. This note argues that improved accuracy may be achieved when modeling the (deterministic) residuals of the best model of a certain complexity as 'random'. In order to make this statement precise, the setting of adaptive compression is considered: (1) accuracy is understood in terms of codelength, and (2) the 'random device' relates to Solomonoff's Algorithmic Probability (ALP) via arithmetic coding. The contribution of this letter is threefold: (a) the proposed adaptive coding scheme possesses interesting behavior in terms of its regret bound, and (b) a mathematical characterization of a deterministic world assumption is given. (c) The previous issues then facilitate the derivation of the Randomness- Complexity (RC) frontier of the given algorithm.

Keywords: Adaptive Compression, Online Learning, Regret Analysis, Algorithmic Probability.

1 Introduction

Traditional Algorithmic Probability (ALP) distinguishes between model definition and the evidence of using this model to explain or predict data. Specifically, the model is expressed in terms of the shortest program M describing the model, as well as the evidence S_n of using this model to describe the n samples. This leads to the definition of the 'figure of merit' of a program M on a sequence, given as $-|M| \ln S_n$. This distinction however vanishes when considering adaptive protocols where M is build up based on the previously observed data. Specifically, one does not need to encode the program explicitly, but it is in an implicit way constructed while receiving data. Conceptually however, a complexity term proportional to $|M|$ remains a governing factor of the performance as given in the regret analysis of such adaptive algorithm, see e.g. [2] for a survey.

This realization prompts to what degree this complexity interacts with the size of the remainders. It is only intuitive that proper choice of this trade-off can result in increased performances: given a perfect - but large program, there is no need whatsoever to spend effort into modeling the remainders as 'random'.

D.L. Dowe (Ed.): Solomonoff Festschrift, LNAI 7070, pp. 299–305, 2013.

However in that case it is very difficult to build up this program incrementally. On the other hand when building up a program of low complexity, a convenient way to model the remainders is in terms of 'randomness', implying increased codelengths. As such, such optimal trade-off decides on what part of the data is to be modeled explicitly as a function of the side information, and what part to model using the device of 'randomness'. Conversely, this defines 'randomness' in the data as too complex deterministic behavior.

This work builds on the large body of results as described in [3,7,9,4,2] and citing works. It differs from traditional coding theoretic results (such as on MDL [8], MML [11,5], ...) in terms of the deterministic world assumption we build on. A detailed mapping of the presented ideas to their respective contexts will be given in the extended version of this abstract. This abstract basically collects standard ideas of adaptive filters and adaptive coding schemes together with regret bounds (next section), and uses results to show how this procedure comes with surprising theoretical guarantees (third section). We conclude with some interesting upcoming challenges for this problem.

2   Adaptive Compression

The following setting is considered. Let $y^n = (y_1, y_2, \ldots, y_n)$ be a sequence of n symbols in an alphabet of size m denoted as $\Sigma = \{\sigma_1, \ldots, \sigma_m\}$. Assume that each symbol $y_t \in \Sigma$ is a consequence of the state of the world x_t right before time t, where $x_t \in \mathcal{F}_t$. For example, if y_t denotes the 1th character in Hamlet, $\mathcal{F}_t$ denotes the state of the world before Shakespeare actually wrote down this character. For example x_t can include the sequence $\{y_1, \ldots, y_{t-1}\}$. This concept relates closely to the concept of filtrations in martingale theory. The deterministic world assumption asserts intuitively that there exists a fixed (but unknown) mapping $f_0 : \cup_k \mathcal{F}_k \to \Sigma$ such that one has $y_t = f_0(x_t)$ for all $t = 1, \ldots, n$. In order to make our discourse more accessible, phrase x_t as a countable infinite vector $\mathbf{x}_t \in \mathbb{R}^\infty$ such that there exists a vector $\mathbf{w}_0 \in \mathbb{R}^\infty$ and

$$y_t = f_0(x_t) = \mathbf{w}_0^T \mathbf{x}_t, \ \forall t = 1, \ldots, n. \tag{1}$$

In Def. (2) we characterize the deterministic world assumption more precisely for the considered model. If $\mathbf{x}_t$ could be measured, and $\mathbf{w}_0$ were known, the progression of history would be trivial. In our example, Hamlet could be compressed simply as a number representing the length of the work. In order to fix the setting, consider the following 'probability assigning function'.

Definition 1 (Prediction Model). *For given* $\mathbf{x} \in \mathbb{R}^{|S|}$ *and* $\mathbf{W} \in \mathbb{R}^{m \times |S|}$, *the vector valued function* $\mathbf{p_W} : \mathbb{R}^{|S|} \to [0, 1]^m$ *is defined as*

$$\mathbf{p_W}(\mathbf{x}) = \frac{\exp(\mathbf{W}\mathbf{x})}{\sum_{k=1}^m \exp(\mathbf{W}_k\mathbf{x})}, \tag{2}$$

where we have $\exp(\mathbf{y})_k = \exp(\mathbf{y}_k)$ *for all* $\mathbf{y} \in \mathbb{R}^m$ *and* $k = 1, \ldots, m$. *such that for all* $\mathbf{W}, \mathbf{x}$ *one has that* $1_m^T \mathbf{p_W}(\mathbf{x}) = 1$ *and* $\mathbf{p_W}(\mathbf{x}) \geq 0_m$. *The derivative of*

$\ln \mathbf{pw}(\mathbf{x})_k$ *with respect to* $\mathbf{W}$ *for any* $k = 1, \ldots, m$ *is given as*

$$\frac{d\ln \mathbf{pw}(\mathbf{x})_k}{d\mathbf{W}} = \mathbf{e}_k \mathbf{x}^T - \mathbf{pw}(\mathbf{x})\mathbf{x}^T, \tag{3}$$

where $\mathbf{e}_k = (0, \ldots, 1, \ldots 0)^T \in \{0,1\}^m$ *is the* k*th unit vector.*

Then the Gradient Descent (GD) update formula becomes

$$\mathbf{W}_t = \mathbf{W}_{t-1} + \gamma \frac{d\ln \mathbf{pw}(\mathbf{x}_t)_{y_t}}{d\mathbf{W}}\Big|_{\mathbf{W}=\mathbf{W}_{t-1}}. \tag{4}$$

Now in the coding setup one tries to transfer the sequence y_n from sender to a receive through a channel. Adaptive coding en- and decodes the symbols in an intelligent way based on the previous experience, as well as on available side information. The protocol implemented both into sender and receiver, and properly synchronized are given in Alg. (1) and Alg. (2).

Algorithm 1. Adaptive Coding: Sender

Require: Given S and $\gamma > 0$. Initiate $\mathbf{W}_0 = 0_m 0_d^T$
    for t=1,...,n **do**
      (1) Collect the side information $\mathbf{x}_t^S \in \mathbb{R}^{|S|}$.
      (2) Compute the corresponding $\mathbf{pw}_{t-1}(\mathbf{x}_t^S)$.
      (3) Evaluate $y_t \in \Sigma$.
      (4) Send the symbol ξ_t encoding y_t using $-\ln \mathbf{pw}_{t-1}(\mathbf{x}_t^S)_{y_t}$ bits.
      (5) Update $\mathbf{W}_{t-1} \to \mathbf{W}_t$ using eq. (4).
    end for

The encoding using $-\ln p$ bits can e.g. be performed using arithmetic coding which ensures that one deals properly with non-integer valued numbers of bits for the encoding (i.e. without a large excess of the resulting full code), see e.g. [3,4]. At the receiving end of the channel the following algorithm is implemented. Again, decoding can be performed using arithmetic decoding.

Algorithm 2. Adaptive Coding: Receiver

Require: Given S and $\gamma > 0$. Initiate $\mathbf{W}_0 = 0_m 0_{|S|}^T$
    for t=1,...,n **do**
      (1) Collect the side information $\mathbf{x}_t^S \in \mathbb{R}^{|S|}$.
      (2) Compute the corresponding $\mathbf{pw}_{t-1}(\mathbf{x}_t^S)$.
      (3) Receive the symbol ξ_t.
      (4) Decode ξ_t into y_t using the vector $\mathbf{pw}_{t-1}(\mathbf{x}_t^S)$.
      (5) Update $\mathbf{W}_{t-1} \to \mathbf{W}_t$ using eq. (4).
    end for

---

3   Excess and the RC-Frontier

This protocol, however simple, comes with the following performance guarantee.

Lemma 1 (Regret Bound). *Given $n < \infty$. Given a set S of $|S| < \infty$ indices of $\mathbf{x}$ which are relevant to the problem at hand, and define $\mathbf{x}_t^S \in \mathbb{R}^{|S|}$ corresponding. Let $\bar{\mathbf{W}} \in \mathbb{R}^{m \times |S|}$ be any matrix, and let $\max_t \|\mathbf{x}_t^S\|_\infty \le R_x < \infty$, then there exists a $\gamma > 0$ such that the sender/receiver protocols yield a code with length bounded as*

$$-\sum_{t=1}^{n} \ln \mathbf{p}_{\mathbf{w}_{t-1}}(\mathbf{x}_t^S)_{y_t} \le -\sum_{t=1}^{n} \ln \mathbf{p}_{\bar{\mathbf{W}}}(\mathbf{x}_t^S)_{y_t} + c'\sqrt{n|S|}\|\bar{\mathbf{W}}\|_F R_x, \qquad (5)$$

with $c' > 0$ an appropriate constant.

This result goes entirely along the lines as set out in [1]. This result can be refined in many ways. For example use of the log-loss hints towards strengthening results as in [2], Ch.9. and cited works. For example, the $\sqrt{n}$ dependence is highly suboptimal compared to the $\ln(n)$ dependence of the minimax regret for such algorithms. This bound has however an (implicit) $\sqrt{m}$ dependence via $\|\bar{\mathbf{W}}\|_F$, while one typically has $O(m)$ dependence for other algorithms. The $\sqrt{|S|}$ dependence seems not to be achievable directly via the covering number approach as discussed in [2], Ch.9.9. Another improvement of this result can be made towards the case where the horizon n is not fixed a priori, see e.g. [2], Ch.2. The present algorithm seems not to be covered explicitly in the literature before, and precise derivations of the above results remain to be given. Such GD algorithms in practice need only to find a proper gain $\gamma > 0$ in order to achieve the theoretical bounds (the regret bounds state existence). This gain is often set in practice by trial and error.

Now, the left hand side of eq. (5) trades off two terms. On the one hand, one can make $-\sum_{t=1}^{n} \ln \mathbf{p}_{\bar{\mathbf{W}}}(\mathbf{x}_t^S)_{y_t}$ arbitrary small as the code sequence is assumed to be deterministic. This however requires possibly very large sets S as well as large norms $\|\bar{\mathbf{W}}\|_F$. On the other hand one can control the term $\sqrt{n|S|}\|\bar{\mathbf{W}}\|_F R_x$ by keeping $|S|$ and $\|\bar{\mathbf{W}}\|_F$ small, but then the coding protocol pays a price in the sense that it has to model the more complex behaviors of the sequence as random, resulting in a waste of coding bits. Now we address the question how this trade-off can be made optimally, that is, until what threshold does it pay off to capture the effects as deterministic while treating the 'remainders' as 'random' effects. In order to make this trade-off more explicit, let us introduce the following assumption:

Definition 2 (Deterministic World Assumption). *Let $y = (y_1, \ldots, y_n) \in \Sigma^n$ be any sequence, let $0 < c < \infty$ be any number and let S be any set. Then assume that there exists a $\bar{\mathbf{W}} \in \mathbb{R}^{m \times |S|}$ such that $\sqrt{|S|}\|\bar{\mathbf{W}}\|_F \le c$ and*

$$\sum_{t=1}^{n} -\ln \mathbf{p}_{\bar{\mathbf{W}}}(\mathbf{x}_t^S)_{y_t} \le \frac{q(n)}{c}, \qquad (6)$$

where $q : \mathbb{N} \to \mathbb{R}_0^+$ is a positive increasing function interpolating between $O(n)$ and $O(\sqrt{n})$.

It should be kept in mind that this is a mere technical assumption, but one which is in many cases not too far from reality. It states that asymptotically when $c \to \infty$, no 'randomness' is needed.

The factor $1/c$ is motivated as follows. If sorting the features of the problem at hand in decreasing relevance to the coding problem, it is not too unreasonable that it will be less and less beneficial to the coding problem to include the next one, or to increase the complexity of the function.

The factor $q(n)$ is motivated as follows. Suppose we have a sequence of length l which consists of a fair share of the possible codes. If applying a nonadaptive coding protocol using a fixed $\bar{\mathbf{W}}$ in our algorithm as in eq. (2), on all $\lfloor n/l \rfloor$ identical blocks, one has an encoding of length $\lfloor n/l \rfloor$ times of what can be achieved on one block. Hence one would expect a proportional factor n. However, since we have this result for any $\bar{\mathbf{W}}$ with appropriate norm, and we are allowed to concentrate on the one which happened to perform best on the given series y, the rate will often be improved from n to $q(n)$. Two common choices are $q(n) = n$ and $q(n) = \sqrt{n}$. The choice between either depends on how well the structure of the sequence as well as the side information is adapted to the model (2). If $q(n) = \sqrt{n}$, then one has that one already advances to a deterministic regime using models of relatively small complexity.

Proposition 1. *Let $a, b > 0$ be constants, then*

$$\inf_{\xi > 0} \frac{a}{\xi} + \xi b = 2\sqrt{ab}. \tag{7}$$

This is seen by choosing $\xi = \sqrt{\frac{a}{b}}$, obtained by equating the derivative to zero. Combining the above results yields the main result of this paper.

Theorem 1 (Optimal Trade-off). *Under the deterministic world assumption of eq. (6), there exists a set S and $\gamma > 0$ such that*

$$-\sum_{t=1}^{n} \ln \mathbf{p}\mathbf{w}_{t-1}(\mathbf{x}_t^S)_{y_t} \leq O\left(\sqrt{q(n)\sqrt{n}R_x}\right), \tag{8}$$

and this is achieved by using a proper S such that there exists a $\bar{\mathbf{W}}$ such that $\sqrt{|S|}\|\bar{\mathbf{W}}\|_F \leq O(\sqrt{q(n)/\sqrt{n}}R_x)$ and eq. (6) is satisfied.

In other words, the behavior which is encoded as 'random' when using the algorithm with such S and fixed $\bar{\mathbf{W}}$ is lying beyond the RC-Frontier. If $q(n) = n$, then the upperbound reduces to $O(n^{3/4})$. This occurs when taking a set S such that there exists a $\bar{\mathbf{W}}$ satisfying (6) and such that $\sqrt{|S|}\|\bar{\mathbf{W}}\|_F \leq O(\sqrt{n})$. If $q(n) = \sqrt{n}$, then the above bound is $O(\sqrt{n})$ by choosing S such that there exists a $\bar{\mathbf{W}}$ satisfying (6) and with $\sqrt{|S|}\|\bar{\mathbf{W}}\|_F \leq O(1)$.

This is a surprising result: If $q(n) \geq O(\sqrt{n})$ the excess of the adaptive coding algorithm is essentially at least as good as in case we were to know the best $\bar{\mathbf{W}}$ in advance (i.e. there is no regret term here!). In the common case that $q(n) > \sqrt{n}$, the adaptive coding strategy results in an order of magnitude smaller excess than if we were to use a - however as good - nonadaptive strategy.

Another way of formulating the result is to say that 'the frontier between deterministic modeling and random modeling is given as the maximal complexity which is allowed before degrading the worst-case performance'. In the present case this is achieved by a S and corresponding $\bar{\mathbf{W}}$ satisfying the deterministic world assumption and such that $|S| \|\bar{\mathbf{W}}\|_F^2 = O(\sqrt{nq(n)}/R_x)$. This is of course a statement relative to the deterministic world assumption, as well as to the adaptive algorithm that we implement.

4   Discussion

The above derivations gives a glimpse of a more general line of results: the validness of such derivations appears not to be tied to the precise algorithm, nor to the application setting. This prompts the following challenges:

- Note that the RC-frontier is given in terms of the regret of the algorithm, and that there exists a minimax version of such regret bound, see e.g. [2]. That is, we can quantify the worst case regret which is achieved with the best prediction strategy possible. This implies that this frontier can be made universal, i.e. independent of the algorithm. The term $\ln n$ in the minimax bound would give rise to a $O(\sqrt{q(n)\ln(n)})$ RC-frontier.
- The present trading off of learnability and randomness - or the bias-variance trade-off in this context - is not tied to the adaptive compression setting only. Similar derivations can be made for most online learning settings. In order to make such work as here, one needs to find an analogues to the deterministic world assumption in the new setting. It may be argued that this line of thinking remains valid in the batch learning setting as well, where an algorithm is asked to induce a model based on all observed data. Optimal trading complexity of a model while controlling variability has been a main theme in inductive inference, see e.g. the context of penalized learning and regularization, see e.g. [6] and citations.
- This derivation suggests that for increasing n, one could consider a sequence of model structures having increasing $|S|$. The latter however has to increase at a proper, lower pace in order to guarantee efficiency. In case $q(n) = O(\sqrt{n})$, the derivation suggests that it is not directly useful to let $|S|$ grow as the benefit of such would not outweigh the consequent increased regret. This is compatible with the lines set out in [10] where the author discusses an incremental learning strategy for learning increasingly more difficult concepts.

The line of thinking as set out in this abstract indicates that the twilight zone between randomness and deterministic assumptions gives a fertile area for novel conceptual ideas, based on standard theoretical derivations. I am indebted to the work of R. Solomonoff which indicated how to create new ideas based on mathematical results.

References

1. Cesa-Bianchi, N.: Analysis of two gradient-based algorithms for on-line regression. Journal of Computer and System Sciences 59(3), 392–411 (1999)
2. Cesa-Bianchi, N., Lugosi, G.: Prediction, Learning, and Games. Cambridge University Press (2006)
3. Cover, T.M., Thomas, J.A.: Elements of Information Theory. Springer (1991)
4. Csiszár, I., Shields, P.C.: Information theory and statistics: A tutorial. Now Publishers Inc. (2004)
5. Dowe, D.L.: MML, hybrid Bayesian network graphical models, statistical consistency, invariance and uniqueness. In: Handbook of Philosophy of Science. Handbook of Philosophy of Statistics, vol. 7, pp. 901–982. Elsevier (June 2011)
6. Györfi, L., Kohler, M., Krzyzak, A., Walk, H.: A distribution-free theory of nonparametric regression. Springer (2002)
7. Li, M., Vitányi, P.: An introduction to Kolmogorov complexity and its applications. Springer (1997)
8. Rissanen, J.: Modelling by shortest data description. Automatica 14, 465–471 (1978)
9. Shafer, G., Vovk, V.: Probability and finance: it's only a game! Wiley Interscience (2001)
10. Solomonoff, R.J.: Progress in incremental machine learning. In: NIPS Workshop on Universal Learning Algorithms and Optimal Search, Whistler, BC, Canada, p. 27 (December 2002)
11. Wallace, C.S., Boulton, D.M.: An information measure for classification. Computer Journal 11(2), 185–194 (1968)

Toward an Algorithmic Metaphysics

Steve Petersen

Department of Philosophy
Niagara University
Niagara University, NY 14109 USA
steve@stevepetersen.net

Abstract. There are writers in both metaphysics and algorithmic information theory (AIT) who seem to think that the latter could provide a formal theory of the former. This paper is intended as a step in that direction. It demonstrates how AIT might be used to define basic metaphysical notions such as *object* and *property* for a simple, idealized world. The extent to which these definitions capture intuitions about the metaphysics of the simple world, times the extent to which we think the simple world is analogous to our own, will determine a lower bound for basing a metaphysics for *our* world on AIT.

Keywords: metaphysics, formal metaphysics, computational metaphysics, algorithmic metaphysics, algorithmic information theory, real patterns.

Both philosophers and mathematicians have flirted with the idea that algorithmic information theory (AIT) could provide some foundation for basic notions in metaphysics. The main inspiration for this paper is one such hint from the philosophy side: in Daniel Dennett's sketch of a metaphysics based on "real patterns", he explicitly appeals to incompressibility, and offhandedly mentions the work of AIT theorist Gregory Chaitin in this connection.[1] Meanwhile AIT theorists since Andrey Kolmogorov frequently speak about, for example, the "information content" of *objects* generally, rather than of binary strings in particular. (Of course, "the original incentive to develop a theory of algorithmic information content of individual objects was *Ray Solomonoff's* invention of a universal a priori probability ..."[2])

This paper aims to help bridge this gap between metaphysics and AIT. As befits a philosophy paper, it contains little in the way of technical results, but some ruminations aiming to pave the way for technical results to come. And as is typical of work bridging discipline X to discipline Y, X theorists are likely to complain that the treatment of X is far too simplistic and sloppy, and that the treatment of Y engages trivial details—while Y theorists complain conversely.

---

[1] See [2] p. 32. Others have developed Dennett's metaphysics more fully than I have, most notably the "Rainforest Realism" of [9]. I think everything I say here is compatible with this work, while extending it to make more explicit the ties to AIT.

[2] [11] p. 333, my emphasis. Solomonoff's partially autobiographical (and posthumous) publication [13] lists [12] as the paper that started it all.

D.L. Dowe (Ed.): Solomonoff Festschrift, LNAI 7070, pp. 306–317, 2013.

I happily undertake that risk, with hope for some indulgence and patience from both.

My strategy is to construct an extremely simple toy world W, and give its metaphysics in terms of AIT. That is, using AIT I'll try to define key metaphysical notions for W such as *composite object* and *property*. These basics of synchronic metaphysics will be plenty to occupy this paper; in future work I hope to build on this foundation in order to model important diachronic metaphysical notions such as *persisting object, change,* and *cause.*

Eventually the goal is to connect these metaphysics to thriving programs in algorithmic *epistemology.* Work such as [8] and [7] extend Solomonoff's original insights for formalizing inductive reasoning. The Bayesian approach of [16] is closely related (as argued in [17]), and has demonstrated potential to characterize approximate truth [4] and perhaps more elusive philosophical fruit [3].

But first, the metaphysics. The extent to which these definitions seem to capture the intuitive metaphysics for the toy world W, times the extent to which we think the metaphysics for W are analogous to our own world, will determine an informal lower bound for the extent to which we think we might base a metaphysics for *our* world on AIT.

1   The Toy World W

W is built out of a finite set of n "objects" $\{w_1 \ldots w_n\}$ that we will consider unproblematically fundamental.[3] We'll need a fair number of them; one million would be plenty. These fundamental objects cannot be created or destroyed from one time to the next. In W there is one fundamental property, which each of these objects either has or does not have at any time. We can think informally of the w_is at a time as a row of life-game-like cells that wraps into a circle, each of which either possesses the fundamental property (represented as '■' on the cell, and encoded as '1'), or does not possess that property (represented as '□' on the cell, and encoded as '0').[4] We can think of W at the next time step as another circle of such cells just below. This W is, I hope, a very simple case for the kind of important features we seem to need to construct a metaphysics in our world: some unproblematically fundamental objects, one maximally simple fundamental property, and a succession of times.

More formally the $\{w_i\}$ form a finite cyclic group with a successor-like function, and W at a time t, or w_t, is a function $w_t : \{w_i\} \to \{0, 1\}$. W, in turn,

---

[3] This does not require that they be just-plain *fundamental*; if Ladyman and Ross are right that objects are always patterns, "all the way down", they still allow for fundamental objects in the context of a fixed resolution.

Also, the use of "build" here and elsewhere in the paper is meant to echo the wide sense proposed by [1]; one of my many hopes for algorithmic metaphysics is that it can characterize the important commonalities among the "building relations" she discusses.

[4] We want the cells to wrap into a circle basically because we do not want cells to the "left" to be simpler, in the AIT sense, than cells to the "right".

can be seen as a function from discrete possible times ($t \in \mathbf{N}$) to such functions; we could write the composite function as $w_{t,i}$. Let L, the *locations*, be the set of intervals on $\{w_i\}$.[5]

In W the w_i gain or lose their properties by the action of a fixed universal prefix Turing machine U. This machine has a unidirectional binary input tape, a bidirectional read-write binary work tape (including a blank symbol), and a write head on the w_i. This head can add or remove the fundamental property at its current cell or can move to the cell's successor. We'll abbreviate the first operations as '■' (for adding the property) and '□' (for removing the property), and the successor movement as 'S'. So that U does not have an unfair bias, we can suppose U is (or is one of) the "simplest" universal prefix Turing machine(s) to meet these specifications (on whatever chosen measure of simplicity for Turing machines); this is thought by AIT theorists to be the rough equivalent to a maximally uninformative prior.

Now consider any interval (location) $l \in L$, and let x_l represent the function w_t as restricted to that interval. An x_l is thus an ordering of zeroes and ones—in effect, a binary string.[6] Let X be the set of all such binary strings up to the maximal length n, and for $x \in X$ let the standard notation $\mathrm{K}_U(x)$ designate the Kolmogorov complexity of x relative to U—that is to say, $\mathrm{K}_U(x)$ is the length of the shortest input required to cause our fixed U, when starting at the "left" end of the interval, to output x and then halt. Finally, let the idiosyncratic notation $x^\sharp$ designate the length of the shortest program required to output x "literally"— that is, the length of x plus some small constant for the computational overhead to print any given string.

2   Things in W

One of the main potential advantages of Dennett's "real patterns" approach to metaphysics is that it can make sense of *composition*—that special, mysterious way a bunch of things can come together to form a new thing, as when atoms can make up a molecule, or molecules can make up a brick, or bricks can make up a house. Peter van Inwagen calls this the *special composition question*: the question of when it is true that some objects compose a new object—when it is true that "$\exists y$ the xs compose y."[7] This is a classic philosophical question at least in the sense that it looks like the answer should be obvious, but reflection shows just about any consistent answer to be counterintuitive. At least for the simple W, though, I think AIT can provide a relatively intuitive answer to this vexed

---

[5] That is, given the cyclic ordering relation $\langle x, y, z \rangle$, the interval $[a, b]$ is defined as all x such that $x = a$ or $x = b$ or $\langle a, x, b \rangle$.

[6] I will sometimes conflate the function w_t over interval l, the set of ordered pairs associated with that function, and the resulting ordered binary string. I think (and hope) that nothing hangs on this conflation.

[7] [15] p. 30. Note that, at least for W, I am happy to use 'thing' and 'object' interchangeably.

question.[8] This definition of composite objects will serve as a kind of lynchpin for the synchronic metaphysics that follow.

In W, an object is composed of other objects when the objects together form a "real pattern"—that is, the arrangement of the objects and their properties is easier to specify, computationally, than simply giving the complete details at the fundamental level. A simple, standard example (adapted for W) is when many of the fundamental objects (cells) in a row all possess the fundamental property. If the string of ■s is sufficiently long, a program equivalent to "for i = 1 to 10,000, ■S" will be much shorter than the literal-print "■S■S ... ■S." It is natural to see such a sufficiently long string of ■s amidst an otherwise chaotic jumble of squares as an object in its own right.

I propose this definition for identifying the non-fundamental things in W.

Definition 1. x_l is a **composite object** if and only if

1. $\mathrm{K}_U(x_l) < x_l^{\sharp}$ (the **compressible clause**)
2. There is no partition of l into intervals $\{l_1 \ldots l_n\}$ such that $\sum_i \mathrm{K}_U(x_{l_i}) \leq \mathrm{K}_U(x_l)$ (the **minimal clause**)
3. There is no interval l' containing l such that $\mathrm{K}_U(x_{l'}) \leq \mathrm{K}_U(x_l)$ (the **maximal clause**)

Does this definition adequately capture what we might call (non-fundamental) "objects" in W? Since none of us has any experience in W, it might be hard to tell what we could reasonably call a composite object there. Still, this definition has intuitive features in W that would, if they were carried over into our world, provide some grip on major challenges in metaphysics.

2.1   Composition and Division

One central challenge for any account of composition is to negotiate both the Scylla of *universalism*, according to which any mereological sum of objects is another object, and the Charybdis of *nihilism*, according to which the only objects are the fundamental ones. Universalists implausibly claim that "my desk plus the Eiffel tower" is a genuine object in its own right, while nihilists implausibly claim that desks and towers do not literally exist. They are driven to these extremes basically because it is hard to find a principled line to draw between them. Dennett's "real patterns" approach promises to provide just such a line.

The first clause of Definition 1 already implies that universalism is false for W, for most binary strings are not compressible and thus not objects. Some of the problem that motivated universalism remains, however. Let o_1 be 10,000 ■s in a row, and let o_2 be a binary representation of the first 10,000 decimal digits of π at a location immediately adjacent, and finally let $o_3 = o_1 \cup o_2$. This o_3 looks suspiciously like an arbitrary mereological sum such as "my desk plus the Eiffel tower", and yet it is easily compressible. It is not an object, though, because of the minimal clause; it possesses a natural decomposition into o_1 and o_2, where

---

[8] One I hope more intuitive than van Inwagen's answer for our world; he claims that no composite objects exist except for living beings.

$K_U(o_1) + K_U(o_2) \leq K_U(o_3)$. In summary, there is no simplicity *gain* in treating the two objects as one—and so, on the real patterns metaphysics, no ontological gain either.

It may seem that the minimal clause will overgenerate, and likewise rule out o_1 as a genuine object, since that long string of ■s can apparently be decomposed into other compressible objects. For example, split o_1 into two longish substrings; call them o_{1L} and o_{1R} (for "left" and "right"). Each would be compressible on their own, and their union is just o_1—so o_1 seems to run afoul of the minimal clause, and thus of objecthood. This would be W's analog to the Charybdis of nihilism, since if anything is a composite object in W, surely o_1 is!

But the unified o_1 is different from the chimera o_3 in an important respect. The programs for each of o_{1L} and o_{1R} will look very like the program for o_1, and summing them will double the computational overhead. In this way o_1 gains in simplicity over the sum of its substrings, and so is a genuine object by Definition 1. Similar considerations presumably apply to any substrings of o_2.

Still, substrings o_{1L} and o_{1R} seem to be objects in their own right; they surely would be if they were "on their own." If they are objects, though, we face a dilemma. On the one hand, if we say that o_{1L} and o_{1R} compose o_1, we must also say the same for a great number of other such partitions into sufficiently long substrings. o_1 is thus "composed" of way more overlapping "objects" than would be intuitive. On the other hand, if we say that o_{1L} and o_{1R} do not compose o_1, then we must say that o_1 is identical to the union of two objects, but not composed of those objects.

I think the best solution is simply to deny object status to substrings o_{1L} and o_{1R}, as the maximal clause does. Both o_{1L} and o_{1R} are subsets of o_1, and $K_U(o_1) = K_U(o_{1L}) = K_U(o_{1R})$, so substrings o_{1L} and o_{1R} are not objects in their own right.[9]

The maximal clause has a natural analog in our world, since it prohibits the flipside of arbitrary summation—namely, arbitrary division. Just as in our world it is intuitive to say there is no such "object" as the northern half, northern third, or northern 3/17ths of my desk, so too in W our string o_1 does not have its many compressible substrings as genuine parts, according to Definition 1. The natural motivation here is that a part that is more complex than its whole—because, say, it depends in some way on a description of the whole to be specified—is not an object in good standing on its own. (Definition 1 thus denies what [14] calls the "Doctrine of Arbitrary Undetached Parts".)

---

[9] Actually this is complicated by the fact that, for example, the binary specification of 10,000 in an instruction like "`for i = 1 to 10,000`" will take more bits than if it were 1,000 instead. Thus strictly speaking the 1,000-length substrings are *not* part of a longer string with equal or lower complexity; their minimal generating programs will be slightly shorter. I do not think this is a deep problem, though I can only think of a few kludgy fixes for it—for example, we could require the inequality not hold within the logarithm of the length difference between the containing and contained string, or perhaps set up the Turing machine so that it has typed registers for such purposes that always take the maximal possible bits.

But note that Definition 1 *does* allow for composing objects out of other composites; there just needs to be some complexity savings in so composing. For adjacent composite objects $\{o_i\}$ to compose o, we just need it to be the case that $K_U(o) < \sum_i K_U(o_i)$, and that $K_U(o_i) < K_U(o)$ for each i. In other words, the super-composite must be simpler than the sum of its parts, but not as simple as any individual one. Suppose, for example, that w_t has a streak of 5,000 ■s, followed by 3,000 □s, and then another 5,000 ■s, followed by another 3,000 □s, and so on, so that the black-white stripe alteration pattern is repeated (say) six times. In this case we can write one loop around the loops required for each stripe, and so we have a compressing program for the whole that is longer than the compression for each natural part, but shorter than the sum of each. Each stripe is an object on its own, and together those stripes compose the object that is the larger stripe pattern. No two of those stripes taken together is an object, though—and if we had only two stripes in a row like that, without the repeating pattern, then they would each be a single object that do not compose a new one together. This, I think, is an intuitively pleasing result.

2.2   Scattered Objects

The examples so far have concentrated on intuitively connected objects, but notice that Definition 1 allows for something like scattered objects too. Just as a cloud may count as one thing even without close bonds among the water molecules, or a jigsaw puzzle might count as one thing even when it is in pieces, so too a set of cells over an interval may count as one thing even when there is a good deal of random noise over the interval, scattering the pattern. Consider, for example, a large interval over which the odd-indexed cells are all ■s, while it is random whether the even-numbered cells in between have the property. Such a string would count as an object despite a certain intuitive lack of internal cohesion. Minimally interesting objects in W (but most common, in the sense of most probable to occur) will be long-enough strings where the preponderance of one property over another is just sufficient to allow compression. These objects will be, in some sense, maximally scattered.[10]

---

[10] One odd consequence of Definition 1 is that whether such scattered bits of order in the chaos count as one object or not will depend on *exactly* how spread out they are. At some point a slight preponderance of order mixed in a lot of chaos no longer gains enough simplicity advantage to make up the overhead required for the compressing calculation. In our world it's fairly natural to say that a group of water molecules with sufficient average distance no longer constitute a cloud, and jigsaw pieces sufficiently removed from each other are no longer that original puzzle—if, say, some pieces are in a box in the basement, and some in a landfill across town. On the other hand it is not so intuitive that there is a precise boundary here; the mere movement of one extra millimeter could hardly make the difference, but in W just one extra bit of noise can be enough. Insisting on lack of such precision when determining whether an object exists, however—insisting, in other words, that it is *vague* whether some object exists or not—has its own very serious problems. See, for example, [5] for a classic, one-page case against, and [19] for a much more extended

Another consequence to consider is that scattered objects, in our world any-way, allow for interpenetrability—a kite can fly through a cloud, but that does not intuitively destroy the kite in favor of a kite-cloud, for example. This leads us to the complicated topic of spatial overlap and coincidence for objects in W.

2.3   Object Overlap and Coincidence

The possibility of building new objects out of more fundamental ones gives rise to another standard metaphysical puzzle: that of *constitution*. For (worn) example, a sculptor forms a lump of clay into an elegant statue. Intuitively, the lump of clay has not disappeared; it has just been reshaped. And intuitively, the statue did not exist before the lump gained that shape. Thus many are tempted to say there are now two things (the lump of clay and the statue) where there was once one—two material things that occupy exactly the same location, so are coincident in at least this sense. The fairly neutral description of the case is that the lump of clay *constitutes* the statue, and the puzzle is in explaining just what this relation of "constitution" amounts to.[11] Our toy world W has an analogous puzzle, I think, and AIT provides at least some leverage against it.

As a warmup, consider first the issue of object *overlap*, without exact spatial coincidence. Suppose Lafayette Avenue and Grant Street intersect. That inter-section is intuitively part of both streets; after all, you do not suddenly abandon Lafayette while crossing Grant, nor vice-versa. If so, that rough square of pave-ment belongs to both Lafayette Avenue and Grant Street, even though the two roadways are not the same thing. The two roads overlap.

Here is what I take to be an analogous situation in our one-dimensional W: consider a long string in w_t that represents the first 11,806 binary digits in the decimal expansion of π; call it o_π. As it happens, this string ends in sixteen $\Box$s.[12] But now suppose that those sixteen $\Box$s are also followed by a great many more $\Box$s in a row, to make 10,000 overall, and call that string o_0. Of course o_π and o_0 overlap, in the sense that their location intervals on w_t intersect. To see that both are objects, consider each clause of Definition 1:

Compressible. Each is clearly compressible to shorter than their literal printings.

Minimal. Neither is decomposable into substrings that would save in complex-ity over the whole. Though o_π might look like it has a natural division, there is no complexity savings in so doing; it is better to have a π-calculating loop for 11,806 rounds then to have the same π calculation for 11,790 rounds and then a separate "repeat $\Box$ 16 times" loop.

Maximal. Neither object is part of a bigger object on a containing interval. The union of o_π and o_0 would have two reasonable compressing programs (into "π for 11,806, then $\Box$ for 9,984" or "π for 11,790, then $\Box$ for 10,000")

---

treatment of problems associated with vagueness at the metaphysical level. For a defense of vague identity, see [15].

[11] See [18].

[12] Thank you, http://www.befria.nu/elias/pi/binpi.html !

but neither such program would be shorter than those for o_π or o_0 on their own.

Thus it seems W can have overlapping objects. Perhaps now it is clear that it is *also* possible in W to have one object entirely contained by another, as a yolk is contained by an egg in our world. Consider, for example, the first compressible stretch of 0's in a very long expansion of π. Again, I think this captures intuitions.

Object coincidence, however, appears to be a different matter; while the story of the statue and the clay makes it seem at least an open possibility in our world, Definition 1 in effect stipulates against it for W, since it individuates objects by their locations. This is a problem, and I have two possible responses to it.

Here, I think, is a rough equivalent in W to the story of the clay and the statue: o_c (the "clay") is a long string built out of a random mix of the short strings '111', '0010', and '011010'. This fact makes o_c compressible. The string o_s (the "statue"), on the other hand, is made out of the same substrings, but their succession follows some identifiable (if somewhat arcane) pattern. This string is compressible in the same way o_c was, but also in an even more efficient way that encodes the pattern of the component strings. In this sense, the "clay" of o_c is still there, but with a further pattern layered on top of it. (Note it is not a case of object composition, though, since the short substrings are not objects.)

One way to capture our metaphysical intuitions for such a case would be to alter our definition slightly: identify objects in W not with (the equivalent of) compressible binary strings, but instead with the compressing *programs* for U that could generate such strings. Very roughly speaking, we might say objects are individuated by their Aristotelian formal causes, and not their material ones. Since (at least) either of two different compressing programs could potentially produce the same string o_s over the same interval, there are then (at least) two objects in that location.

Another possible option is to keep our definition and say that there is indeed at most one object in any location, but the object has two compatible *properties*: in our W example, the object both has the property of being a mix of three certain substrings, and has the property of having those substrings arranged in such-a-way. In the real world analog, there is one thing on the table, and it has both the relatively important property of being a statue, and the compatible property of being a lump of clay.

This approach worries many, because it requires the lump and statue to be identical, but only contingently; the clay lump might not have been a statue, even though the clay lump had to have been a clay lump. In other words the lump and statue have different modal properties, and that is at least odd if the lump is the same thing as the statue. How problematic this is depends on how we construe modal properties, but I suspect AIT has good prospects for modeling the "counterpart theory" approach of [10].

At least when it comes to AIT metaphysics in W, my working hunch is that not much hangs on the difference between these two options. To see why, though, we need to discuss how AIT might pick out *properties* in W, and their relation to *algorithmic sufficient statistics*.

3   Properties in W

Properties in W built out of the fundamental are most naturally thought of as sets of *possible* objects for W; they are in this sense *intensional* rather than extensional. This allows for the possibility of uninstantiated properties; it may be that for some P no object in P ever actually appears in W. I am okay with this if the serious metaphysicians are. (Are they?) Since we want to be able to talk about real patterns of such "abstract" sets that might not be realized in w_i concreta, programs causing U to output to cells in W will not be sufficient. Instead, we treat the objects in question as functions from $l \in L$ to $\{0, 1\}$, encode such functions into binary strings in a standard way, and encode sets of such strings into a new binary string in a standard way.[13] Thus we can speak of the Kolmogorov complexity of such a set as the program required to output the string encoding the set on U's work tape.

It may be tempting to consider any such set of objects S that is compressible (that is, a set where $K_U(S) < S^\sharp$) a property. This is no good, however; for example, a set of m-length blocks at various locations (for sufficiently large m) plus one long representation of π digits will count as a property, on this view, even though this set seems unnaturally gerrymandered. The challenge, then, is to carve the total set of possible objects into its natural joints, whatever "natural" means here.

I think—with somewhat less confidence than before—that the best approach is to follow the same technique that was used for defining objects. Just as we want "real" objects to be simple relative to the sum of their parts, and not arbitrary sums or divisions, so we want "real" properties to be simple relative to the sum of their objects, and not arbitrary disjunctions or conjunctions.

Definition 2. *Let O be the set of all possible objects in W. Then $P \subseteq O$ is a* **property** *if and only if*

1. $K_U(P) < \sum_{o \in P} K_U(o)$ *(compressible)*
2. *There is no partition of P into $\{P_1 \ldots P_n\}$ where $\sum_i K_U(P_i) \leq K_U(P)$ (minimal)*
3. *There is no $P' \subseteq O$ such that $P \subset P'$ and $K_U(P') \leq K_U(P)$ (maximal)*

I think Definition 2 does a respectable job capturing intuitions about properties.

First, any P satisfying it must have a relatively short program to generate it, and thus a relatively short description—which seems to imply a relative naturalness to it. The minimal clause rules out arbitrary disjunctive properties; generating the set of all objects that are either solid blocks or π representations is no more simple than generating the set of blocks and then the set of π representations. The maximal clause rules out arbitrary conjunctive properties; the set of all sufficiently long blocks that terminate before $w_{55,510}$ is not a proper

---

[13] In some sense the set of *possible* objects should include ones bigger than those possible in W, including (perhaps) infinite ones, or ones with more than one fundamental property, *etc.* I don't consider possibility in this sense here.

property, I think, though I think the set of all sufficiently long blocks is, and maybe the set of all objects that terminate before $w_{55,510}$ is too.[14]

One intriguing feature of Definition 2 I have only begun to explore is its tie to *algorithmic sufficient statistics*.[15] An algorithmic sufficient statistic for x is a finite set S such that

$$\mathrm{K}_U(x) = \mathrm{K}_U(S) + \log|S| + c$$

The c is a fixed constant—namely, the length of the program U requires, when given any set-generating program and index, to output the set element at that index. The idea is that generating a set containing x and then locating x in that set is as efficient as the minimal program for x. Note that for *any* S containing x, $\mathrm{K}_U(x)$ will always be less than or equal to $\mathrm{K}_U(S) + \log|S| + c$, since once given S one can always find x by simply enumerating its elements. Sets that are algorithmic sufficient statistics for x are "optimal" for x in the intuitive sense that important information about x is already captured by its membership in set S, so that no further point of substance can then identify x within S. It is thus natural to think of S as a model for x, while providing its index in S is like setting the parameters of the model.

Theorem. *If $S \subset O$ is an algorithmic sufficient statistic for some $o \in S$, and if it is maximal in the sense of Definition 2 (i.e. there is no $S' \subseteq O$ such that $S \subset S'$ and $\mathrm{K}_U(S') < \mathrm{K}_U(S)$), then S is a property.*

Proof. Compressible clause: Since S is optimal for o, we know $\mathrm{K}_U(S) < \mathrm{K}_U(o)$ (by $\log|S| + c$), and $\mathrm{K}_U(o) < \sum_{x \in S} \mathrm{K}_U(x)$, so $\mathrm{K}_U(S) < \sum_{x \in S} \mathrm{K}_U(x)$.

Minimal clause: Suppose for contradiction that there is some partition $\{S_i\}$ of S such that $\sum_i \mathrm{K}_U(S_i) \leq \mathrm{K}_U(S)$, and consider $S_j \ni o$. Then as for any set containing o,

$$\mathrm{K}_U(o) \leq \mathrm{K}_U(S_j) + \log|S_j| + c$$

And since S is optimal for o, that means in turn that

$$\mathrm{K}_U(S) + \log|S| + c \leq \mathrm{K}_U(S_j) + \log|S_j| + c$$

By supposition $\sum_i \mathrm{K}_U(S_i) \leq \mathrm{K}_U(S)$, so in particular $\mathrm{K}_U(S_j) < \mathrm{K}_U(S)$. Thus

$$\mathrm{K}_U(S_j) + \log|S| + c < \mathrm{K}_U(S_j) + \log|S_j| + c$$

This implies $\log|S| < \log|S_j|$, where $S_j \subset S$—a contradiction.

Maximal clause: By supposition. □

---

[14] I confess whether "objects terminating before w_i" is a property by this definition has stumped me, for now; it is certainly difficult to generate all objects so placed, since that would require a way to recognize objects, and that would in turn require computing Kolmogorov complexity. But generating such a set *given O* is, I think, pretty straightforward, and maybe that's the proper standard.

[15] See [11] p. 406, or [6] p. 29.

I suspect the connection between Definition 2 and algorithmic sufficient statistics may run deeper, though I have been unable to demonstrate as much in time to complete this paper. For example, I thought perhaps all *minimal* sufficient statistics for all $o \in O$ would be properties, but haven't been able to prove it, and now doubt it. I also cannot yet prove anything interesting in the other direction.

At any rate, sufficient statistics are about summarizing the "meaningful information" in data; they provide as much information as the data set itself for picking the best model out of a given model class. (In AIT this model class is very wide—the set of all computable models.) This notion of separating out the meaningful information from the happenstance details has natural connections to the notion of a real property of an object, since we can think of properties as fundamentally a matter of *abstraction*; to say that two non-identical objects share a property is to neglect some information in each in order to highlight substantive information they share.

Intuitively one can abstract from an abstraction to get another genuine property, and Definition 2 allows for these more abstract properties in the same way that Definition 1 allows for super-composed objects. If $P \subset O$ has a partition into properties $\{P_i\}$ where all $\mathrm{K}_U(P_i) < \mathrm{K}_U(P)$, and $\mathrm{K}_U(P) < \sum_i \mathrm{K}_U(P_i)$, then intuitively P summarizes something important that the P_i have in common. Thus consider for example these three sets:

- All blocks of ■s exactly 1,017 long (abstracting only from the location of the object)
- All blocks of ■s long enough to compress (abstracting from both location and block length)
- All blocks repeating any pattern short enough to be repeated often enough to be compressed (abstracting from location, length, and pattern to repeat)

The program to generate each of these sets will be short, but longer than the one before, and so each will (I think) meet both their minimal and maximal requirements.[16]

Thus our "statue" o_s from section 2.3 has two properties that are both—if I understand correctly—algorithmic sufficient statistics. We could identify an object with its sufficient statistic and index (the abstract specification and its "realization"?), or we could simply think of these as interesting properties of one object.

References

1. Bennett, K.: Construction area (no hard hat required). Philosophical Studies 154(1), 79–104 (2011)
2. Dennett, D.C.: Real patterns. The Journal of Philosophy 88(1), 27–51 (1991)

---

[16] Such successively abstract properties stand to each other roughly as *blue* stands to *colored*—both first-order properties of objects. But blue, the property, intuitively itself possesses a property: it is a color. The need to refer to higher-order properties can be accommodated easily enough, I think; they should be compressible, minimal, and maximal sets of properties of the order below.

3. Dowe, D.L.: MML, hybrid Bayesian network graphical models, statistical consistency, invariance and uniqueness. In: Bandyopadhyay, P.S., Forster, M.R. (eds.) Philosophy of Statistics, Handbook of the Philosophy of Science, vol. 7, pp. 901–982. Elsevier Science & Technology (2011)

4. Dowe, D.L., Gardner, S., Oppy, G.: Bayes not bust! Why simplicity is no problem for Bayesians. British Journal for the Philosophy of Science 58(4), 709–754 (2007)

5. Evans, G.: Can there be vague objects? Analysis 38(4), 208 (1978)

6. Grünwald, P., Vitányi, P.: Shannon information and Kolmogorov complexity (September 2004), http://de.arxiv.org/abs/cs.IT/0410002 (last accessed June 7, 2010)

7. Grünwald, P.D.: The Minimum Description Length Principle. MIT Press (2007)

8. Hutter, M.: Universal Artificial Intelligence. Springer (2005)

9. Ladyman, J., Ross, D., Spurrier, D., Collier, J.: Everything Must Go: Metaphysics Naturalized. Oxford University Press, Oxford (2007, 2009)

10. Lewis, D.: On the Plurality of Worlds. Blackwell, Oxford (1986)

11. Li, M., Vitányi, P.: An Introduction to Kolmogorov Complexity and Its Applications, 3rd edn. Springer, New York (2008)

12. Solomonoff, R.: A preliminary report on a general theory of inductive inference. Tech. Rep. V-131, Zator Co. and Air Force Office of Scientific Research, Cambridge, Mass. (February 1960)

13. Solomonoff, R.: Algorithmic probability – Its discovery – Its properties and application to strong AI. In: Zenil, H. (ed.) Randomness Through Computation: Some Answers, More Questions, pp. 1–23. World Scientific Publishing Company (2011)

14. van Inwagen, P.: The doctrine of arbitrary undetached parts. Pacific Philosophical Quarterly 62, 123–137 (1981)

15. van Inwagen, P.: Material Beings. Cornell University Press, Ithaca (1990, 1995)

16. Wallace, C.S.: Statistical and Inductive Inference by Minimum Message Length. Springer (2005)

17. Wallace, C.S., Dowe, D.L.: Minimum message length and Kolmogorov complexity. The Computer Journal 42(4), 270–283 (1999)

18. Wasserman, R.: Material constitution. In: Zalta, E.N. (ed.) The Stanford Encyclopedia of Philosophy (Spring 2009)

19. Williamson, T.: Vagueness. Routledge (1994, 1996)

Limiting Context by Using the Web to Minimize Conceptual Jump Size

Rafal Rzepka, Koichi Muramoto, and Kenji Araki

Graduate School of Information Science and Technology, Hokkaido University, S
Kita-ku, Kita 14, Nishi 8, Sapporo, Japan
{kabura,koin,araki}@media.eng.hokudai.ac.jp
http://arakilab.media.hokudai.ac.jp

Abstract. In this paper we introduce our ideas on how experiences from real situations could be processed to decrease what Solomonoff called "Conceptual Jump Size". We introduce applications based on commonsense knowledge showing that vast corpora are able to automatically confirm the validity of the output, and also replace a "trainer", which could lead to decreasing human influence and speeding up the process of finding solutions not provided by such a "trainer" or by real world descriptions. Following this idea, we also suggest a shift toward combining natural languages with programming languages to smoothen transitions between layers of Solomonoff's "Concept net" leading from primitive concepts to a problem solution.

Keywords: Conceptual Jump Size, artificial trainers, Wisdom of (Web) Crowd, Natural Language Processing.

1 Introduction

In his work on Algorithmic Probability (ALP), Solomonoff often underlined that his approach, strongly influenced by the works of Turing, was to build algorithms that are more universal and independent from human influence[1][2], differing from the approaches as of Lenat[3] or Newell[4]. We share his belief that acquiring concepts of learning on different levels is a shortcut to commonsense reasoning, which constitutes a base for more complicated, high level problem solutions and realizing Artificial General Intelligence (AGI). However, we chose a more real-world data-driven approach.

1.1 Common Sense Knowledge as a Contextual Filter

From the beginning of A.I. history, we have been told that people have commonsense while computers do not. From early childhood, human beings acquire various types of knowledge: about the physical world, social rules, and abstract concepts. When it comes to using these experiences, although being bombarded with large amounts of information while perceiving the world around us, we are able to shadow out the irrelevant data and focus on the situation we face.

D.L. Dowe (Ed.): Solomonoff Festschrift, LNAI 7070, pp. 318–326, 2013.

Today we know that Broca's area, a part of our brain responsible for language understanding, also plays an important role in ignoring irrelevant input[5]. We can notice the importance of this context fixation when evaluating commonsense knowledge. The human judges opinions vary depending on how rich their imagination or experiences are. However, in real life situations without much time for elaborate thinking, context awareness limits possibilities to the required minimum. When you see Laika sitting inside Sputnik, your association that *a dog can be used to defend your house* becomes shadowed out and the *dogs can be used for experiments* set becomes stronger, while *cats can be used for catching mice* is kept "switched off". Our minds seem to prioritize related domains and avoid irrelevant areas of knowledge. For this reason, after several unsuccessful attempts to use commonsense knowledge effectively and evaluate it fairly, we decided to use contextual restraints for retrieving concepts by limiting them to situations. We chose "house" (rooms, kitchen, bathroom, etc.) as an experimental environment, furniture and utensils as objects, and family members (plus a robot) as actors. We then performed an experiment for automatic discovery of common and uncommon behaviors. It appears that limiting context can easily prevent oversized Concept Jumps[1] (as explained in subsection 1.3) by decreasing the number of strings to be searched. In this paper, we briefly introduce our trials, showing that vast linguistic resources can be used for *training* as Solomonoff predicted[1]. We also take a step further, suggesting that natural language might be the key to faster concept creation and a faster learning process.

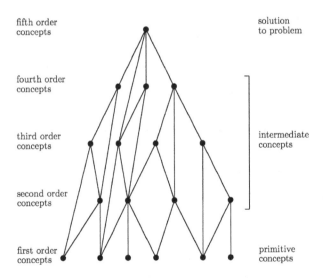

Fig. 1. Simple Concept net introduced by Solomonoff. Our idea is to combine MIT ConceptNet and our Web-based Commonsense Knowledge to smoothen the net processing - its automatic generation and concept manipulation. Preferably by creating some new paradigm which combines natural language based concepts and object-oriented programming language (see Section 3).

1.2   Subjectivity

Solomonoff did not agree with an opinion that subjectivity is "evil" and should not appear in science[2]. He treated finite sample size and model selection error as important sources of error in statistics. In ALP, subjectivity occurs in the latter, which is the choice of "reference" – a universal computer or universal computer language. In the end of his life, Solomonoff was working on an intelligent machine mechanisms that are also visible also in a human infant – born with certain capabilities that assume certain a priori characteristics of its environmenttobe.

> It expects to breathe air, its immune system is designed for certain kinds of challenges, it is usually able to learn to walk and converse in whatever human language it finds in its early environment. As it matures, its a priori information is modified and augmented by its experience.

Each time such a system solves a problem or fails, it updates the part of its a priori information that is relevant to problem solving techniques. It resembles a maturing human being and its a priori information grows as the life experience of the system grows. Solomonoff underlines that the subjectivity of algorithmic probability is a necessary feature that enables an intelligent system to incorporate experience of the past into techniques for solving problems of the future. Also in our experiments, especially on language[6] and knowledge acquisition[7] using inductive learning [8], we are driven by similar observations and we often alternate models to see how system's learning performance changes. Output clearly depends not only on the data (environment) it is exposed to but also the choices a researcher makes. Different algorithms, programming languages, users and their behavior always produce different output and this variety of output can lead to the best models but the main problem is that they must be found automatically. To achieve this goal we decided to use large real-world data and mimic what Damasio calls "primordial feelings"[9], an emotion that is a system regulator and the base for rational choices of an universal algorithm. One of he biggest challenges in this stage of our project is the task of limiting context to achieve the shortest possible knowledge testing time.

1.3   What is Conceptual Jump Size

In [1], Solomonoff describes how he uses Levin's search algorithm[10] to deal with the "exponential explosion" problem. Assuming that p_i is the probability of success of the ith trial string of concepts and t_i is the time needed to generate and test that trial, by using the t_i/p_i ordering it is found that for one approximate p_i it is impossible to know t_i before the ith trial, so we cannot make trials in the exact t_i/p_i order. However, it is possible to obtain the t_i/p_i order by selecting a small time limit T, and testing all strings, spending at most a length of time p_iT on the ith string. When a solution is found, the algorithm stops. If not, T is doubled and exhaustive testing is repeated. The process of doubling and testing continues until a solution is found. Solomonoff writes: "It is easy to estimate the total search time needed to discover a particular known solution to a problem.

If p_j is the probability assigned to a particular program, A_j , that solves a problem and it takes time t_j to generate and test that program, then this entire search procedure will take a time less than $2t_j/p_j$ to discover A_j. We call t_j/p_j the "Conceptual Jump Size" (CJS) of A_j"[1]. By using this method we can discover if a machine is practically able to find a particular solution to a problem at a particular state of its development. It is said that CJS is a critical parameter in the design of training sequences and in the overall operation of a system. We hypothesized that using context filtering and Web-based "semantic self-check" could minimize searching time by prioritizing the most obvious clues when a solution is to be found immediately. We introduce some of our experiments, suggesting that this could be a useful shortcut.

2   Our Trials with Commonsense Knowledge

In our research we define "commonsense" quite broadly, by including not only common knowledge of the physical or social world, but also shared beliefs on history, geography or culture. Therefore we allow our programs to retrieve knowledge on famous people or popular events, which is useful especially for dialog systems, when e.g.,a task-oriented mode is suddenly changed by the user's behavior[11]. In the following subsections, we show how such a system can eliminate its semantically erroneous utterances and then how similar ideas can improve the system's handling and generation of concepts.

Self-correcting Universal Dialog System. Non-task oriented dialog systems, usually called chatterbots or chatbots, can be used as free conversational partners that allow the gathering of linguistic information or knowledge about a user for further machine learning, or as a means for dealing with users who have lost their interest in a task of, for example, an automatic information kiosk. The first such conversational system we developed was Modalin, described in detail in [12]. Modalin is a free-topic keyword-based conversational system for Japanese that automatically extracts sets of words related to a conversation topic from Web resources, which was proved to outperform classic ELIZA-like[13] dialog systems and became a successful base for chatbots using emotions[11], humor[14] or causal knowledge[15]. The basic idea of Modalin is simple – after the search engine results extraction process, it generates an utterance, adds modality, and verifies the semantic reliability of the generated phrase before uttering it. Over 80% of the extracted word associations were evaluated as being correct, which was mostly due to an automatic self-correcting process. When a proposition including adjectives, nouns and verbs was created, the system searched for a newly created string on the Internet. If there were only a few such combinations, it discards the candidate and generates a new string with different words. With current search engines operating within seconds it, becomes much easier to avoid "exponential explosion" of meaningless word combinations. However, to search for concepts needed for finding possible solutions, a simple keyword search is not sufficient.

Toward Concept Search and Manipulation. For trials with automatic Shankian-like script retrievals or dialog agents like [16] and [12], the context and usualness are not particularly important, but when it comes to Ambient Intelligence[17] or Machine Ethics[7], the context and unambiguity of results become crucial. For instance, the act of *killing a person* is perceived differently depending on factors like how emotionally close the victim was to the observer, if it happened during a war, or who the victim was to a given society. Solomonoff's "strings" become numerous, long and complicated as they include more elaborate explanations of specific situations. Although the Web is the biggest text resource that exists, there are many problems with retrieving clean and credible knowledge, as many sites use colloquial language which causes noise and makes frequency weights[1] improper. Therefore, we decided to experiment with ConceptNet[18] using the Japanese OMCS[19] database, which is based not on WWW raw data, but on manual input from volunteers. We performed two small experiments to check if a) existing concepts can produce richer and less ambiguous new ones; b) limiting context can help eliminate errors and improve the efficiency of automatic naturalness evaluation of automatically generated concepts.

Generating Chains of Concepts. We tried to generate chains of concepts as follows. First, a random noun is input to ConceptNet, retrieving related concepts. For example, if the input is "a cook", we retrieve *AtLocation*(cook, restaurant), which means that you can nd a cook at a restaurant. Next, "restaurant" is sent back to ConceptNet, and we acquire *AtLocation*(restaurant, department store), as one usually finds restaurants inside department stores in Japan. Finally, we can use this knowledge to create a statement saying one can find a cook inside a department store, or more specifically "at a restaurant inside a department store". We call these combined concepts $Chains(x)$, where x is a number of inputs to ConceptNet. We soon realized that $x = 2$ is probably the maximum which can be useful for joining order levels in Solomonoff's Concept net (see Fig. 1) but often creates nonsense as assumed earlier. To show the scale of the inadequate generation problem, the authors performed a simple evaluation experiment.

Evaluating Concept Triplets. We retrieved pairs of Relations and Concepts using random nouns from the OMCS database for Japanese. From this set we randomly chose one hundred related concepts and evaluated them with a simple scale: "natural", "uncommon" and "unnatural". Only 49% of entries were agreed to be natural relations, 22% were uncommon and 29% unnatural. After an analysis of the data and discussion between evaluators, we agreed that there are at least eight reasons why people label a triplet as "uncommon" or "unnatural".

– Evaluators are not sure about mutual relationship: *AtLocation*(tanker, sea) + *AtLocation*(sea, Yamashita Park). This park is a famous place by the sea,

---

[1] These weights can be a base for calculating probabilities needed by ALP.

but couples use it for romantic dates and it is not likely you will see heavy ships passing nearby.

- Something is not impossible, but difficult to be evaluated as "natural" by all evaluators. For example $InstanceOf$(salmon, sh) + $AtLocation$(sh, on ship): if the input is "salmon", one rather expects "the sea", or "a plate" or "a fridge" as a natural location for this kind of fish.
- Concepts are obviously related, but the relationship is weak. $PartOf$ (accelerator, car) + $HasProperty$(car, runs on gasoline) would probably score higher if the dependency between using the accelerator and consuming the gasoline was mentioned.
- The OMCS data input by volunteers are not always correct. $PartOf$ (Kunashiri, Japan) + $HasProperty$(Japan, crowded) suggests that there is no conflict regarding whether the disputed island belongs to Russia or Japan. Kunashiri Island also cannot be considered as crowded, as there are very few inhabitants. Only 22% of random triplets were evaluated as "natural", because the more specific the concepts are, the higher the possibility of exceptions.
- Evidently wrong mutual relationship:
  $CapableOf$(goose, swim) + $HasSubevent$(swim, wearing swimsuit) suggests that geese swim in clothes.

The analysis showed that 54% of the patterns that scored low were related to context. Therefore we decided to test our ideas about context by narrowing the semantic environment and increasing its density.

Limiting Context. As mentioned in the Introduction, when creating a set of context descriptors we chose a "house" as we are interested in housekeeping robots and such places are often used for commonsense grounding research. We assumed that a machine could name all significant places (we picked up 9 nouns), items (37 nouns) and actions (21 verbs). We designed an algorithm for creating random acts from places, objects and actions. Its basic output was "ACTION with ITEM at PLACE", and this set was sent to Yahoo Japan Blog Search Engine, together with shorter queries, "ACTION in a PLACE" and "ACTION with a TOOL", in order to find frequencies of particular n-grams. The differences between them were used to find the most uncommon semantic components of an action (e.g., eating ice-creams is natural but uncommon if eaten in a bathroom). For this experiment we created the set of context descriptors by hand, but we are currently working on automatic generation of such sets by web-mining techniques supported by knowledge stored in WordNet[20] and ConceptNet. Context is not being labeled (e.g. as house, shop, conference or street); rather, it is based on the top ten semantically significant keywords (actors, place nouns, also description adjectives) and actions that are strongly associated with these keywords. So if an utterer inputs e.g. "That was the best tennis tournament I've ever seen", the context-limiting module retrieves sets of actors (players, spectators, referees, etc.), physical items (balls, rockets, seats, etc.), descriptions (fast, amazing, high-level, etc.) and actions (to play, to watch, to win, etc.) using words from the utterance as queries.

Experiment and Its Results. First, the system itself evaluated permutations of places, items and actions and randomly chosen 100 natural and 100 unnatural self-evaluation outputs, which were shown to three graduate school student evaluators. The self-scoring was done by comparing web frequencies of exact matches. It appeared that the three human evaluators agreed with the system's judgment in 77.08% of cases, showing that context limitation significantly increases accuracy in usualness evaluation.

3   Object-Oriented Programming between Artificial and Natural Languages

The more we work with concepts, the more we realize that they may become instances for joining two realms of language - that is, combining programming and natural languages. If objects, functions, modules or classes were phrases, sentences, instructional stories, etc., the borderline between both worlds could become blurred and Solomonoff's suggestions about training would become easier to realize. As he mentions in [1]:

> Perhaps the most important kind of training sequence is one that teaches the system to understand English text. By "understand" we mean able to correctly answer questions (in English) about the text. This understanding need not be at all complete, but should be good enough so that ordinary English texts can be a useful source of training for the system. This "training" sequence will involve formal languages of increasing complexity. The first examples of English text will cover a field that the system will already be familiar with – so that it will only have to learn the relationship of the syntax to facts it already knows.

In our opinion, smoother translation between written natural language and computer-readable logical structures should be faster achieved thanks to enormously growing data[2], which, though seen as very noisy, can help to eliminate a large part of the noise due to its coverage. Engineers from the field of Natural Language Processing (NLP) are making more and more progress in dealing with vast text resources and automatic understanding of these. There are tools (many being improved every month) that help to deal not only with morphological or dependency analysis (at the lexical level) but also with synonyms, homonyms, exceptions, emotive load, usualness and other tasks of the semantic realm. We think that with help of the algorithm community, language engineers could become very helpful for realizing Artificial General Intelligence. NLP is often associated with machine translation, summarization or question answering, which are not associated with simulating mental processes, but the techniques used by these tasks can be easily extended and used for enhancing concept learning and training as Solomonoff proposed.

---

[2] Nowadays it its mostly text, but one can imagine objects containing videos, sounds or smells.

4   Conclusions

We have described the idea of Conceptual Jump Size as introduced by Solomonoff, and suggested how it can be minimized by vast raw corpora such as World Wide Web textual resources. We introduced algorithms (dialog system and concept generators) where the training process is made by the WWW instead of humans, and showed improvements in their accuracy after using a Web-based self-correcting process. Although there are other research projects on commonsense knowledge enrichment, and also for specified context[21], the main difference is that we aim at universality; i.e., the same system must be able to limit any context in any situation with any kind of agents, objects or places. Finally, we briefly suggested that object-oriented programming and concepts could become a key for creating an intermediate instance between natural and programming languages. We have not introduced any particular algorithm for minimizing Conceptual Jump Size yet, but we believe that our thoughts and experiences on how the lack of settled context makes it difficult to work with common sense knowledge, and how to deal with this problem, may give some clues that may help researchers unfamiliar with NLP to get familiar with a different approach to achieving this goal. With this short introduction of our ideas and latest NLP capabilities, we want to encourage formal language-oriented specialists to cooperate with web-mining and language engineers in the way that agricultural machinery designers work together with soil specialists who know not only different kinds of soil, but also know how to prepare loam. We believe such co-research tendencies could help make Solomonoff's dream of realizing universally intelligent machines[2] become reality.

References

1. Solomonoff, R.: A system for incremental learning based on algorithmic probability. In: Proceedings of the Sixth Israeli Conference on Artificial Intelligence, Computer Vision and Pattern Recognition, Tel Aviv, Israel, pp. 515–527 (1989)
2. Solomonoff, R.: Algorithmic Probability – Its Discovery – Its Properties and Application to Strong AI. In: Zenil, H. (ed.) Randomness Through Computation: Some Answers, More Questions, ch. 11, pp. 149–157. World Scientific Publishing Company (2011)
3. Lenat, D.: Theory Formation by Heuristic Search – The Nature of Heuristics II: Background and Examples. Artificial Intelligence 21(1-2), 31–59 (1983)
4. Newell, A., Simon, H.: GPS, a program that simulates human thought. In: Feigenbaum, E., Feldman, J. (eds.) Computers and Thought, pp. 279–293. McGraw–Hill, New York (1963)
5. Haxby, J.V., Horwitz, B., Ungerleider, L.G., Maisog, J., Ma., P.P., Grady, C.L.: The functional organisation of human extrastriate cortex: a PET-rCBF study of selective attention to faces and locations. J. Neurosci. IR, 6336–6353 (1994)
6. Hasegawa, D., Rzepka, R., Araki, K.: Connectives Acquisition in a Humanoid Robot Based on an Inductive Learning Language Acquisition Model. Humanoid Robots, I-Tech Education and Publishing, Vienna (2009), http://www.intechopen.com/download/pdf/pdfs_id/6235

7. Rzepka, R., Komuda, R., Araki, K.: Bacteria Lingualis In The Knowledge Soup – A Webcrawler With Affect Recognizer For Acquiring Artificial Empathy. In: Proceedings of The AAAI 2009 Fall Symposium on Biologically Inspired Cognitive Architectures (BICA 2009), Washington, D.C., USA, p. 123 (2009)
8. Araki, K., Tochinai, K.: Effectiveness of natural language processing method using inductive learning. In: Proceedings of IASTED International Conference Artificial Intelligence and Soft Computing, Mexico, pp. 295–300 (2001)
9. Damasio, A.: Self Comes to Mind: Constructing the Conscious Brain. Pantheon (2010)
10. Levin, L.A.: Universal Search Problems. Problemy Peredaci Informacii 9, 115–116 (1973); Translated in Problems of Information Transmission 9, 265–266.
11. Rzepka, R., Higuchi, S., Ptaszynski, M., Dybala, P., Araki, K.: When Your Users Are Not Serious – Using Web-based Associations, Affect and Humor for Generating Appropriate Utterances for Inappropriate Input. Transactions of the Japanese Society for AI 25(1), 114–121 (2010)
12. Higuchi, S., Rzepka, R., Araki, K.: A Casual Conversation System Using Modality and Word Associations Retrieved from the Web. In: Proceedings of The 2008 Conference on Empirical Methods on Natural Language Processing (EMNLP 2008), Honolulu, USA, pp. 382–390 (2008)
13. Weizenbaum, J.: ELIZA – A computer program for the study of natural language communication between man and machine. Commun. ACM 9(1), 36–45 (1966)
14. Dybala, P., Ptaszynski, M., Rzepka, R., Araki, K.: Activating Humans with Humor – A Dialogue System that Users Want to Interact With. IEICE Transactions on Information and Systems Journal, Special Issue on Natural Language Processing and its Applications E92-D(12), 2394–2401 (2009)
15. Fujita, M., Rzepka, R., Araki, K.: Evaluation of Utterances Based on Causal Knowledge Retrieved from Blogs. In: Proceedings of the International Conference Artificial Intelligence and Soft Computing (ASC 2011), pp. 294–299 (2011)
16. Rzepka, R., Ge, Y., Araki, K.: Naturalness of an Utterance Based on the Automatically Retrieved Common Sense. In: Proceedings of IJCAI 2005 – Nineteenth International Joint Conference on Artificial Intelligence, Edinburgh, Scotland (2005), http://www.ijcai.org/papers/post-0490.pdf
17. Rzepka, R., Araki, K.: What About Tests In Smart Environments? On Possible Problems With Common Sense In Ambient Intelligence. In: Proceedings of 2nd Workshop on Artificial Intelligence Techniques for Ambient Intelligence (IJCAI 2007), Hyderabad, India, pp. 92–96 (2007)
18. Havasi, C., Speer, R., Alonso, J.: ConceptNet 3: a Flexible, Multilingual Semantic Network for Common Sense Knowledge. In: Proceedings of Recent Advances in Natural Languages Processing, pp. 277–293 (2007)
19. Singh, P.: Open Mind Common Sense: Knowledge Acquisition from the General Public. In: Meersman, R., Tari, Z. (eds.) CoopIS/DOA/ODBASE 2002. LNCS, vol. 2519, pp. 1223–1237. Springer, Heidelberg (2002)
20. Fellbaum, C.: WordNet: An Electronic Lexical Database. MIT Press, Cambridge (1998)
21. Gupta, R., Kochenderfer, M.K.: Commonsense data acquisition for indoor mobile robots. In: McGuinness, D.L., Ferguson, G. (eds.) AAAI, pp. 605–610. AAAI Press / The MIT Press (2004)

Minimum Message Length Order Selection and Parameter Estimation of Moving Average Models

Daniel F. Schmidt

Centre for MEGA Epidemiology, The University of Melbourne
Carlton VIC 3053, Australia
dschmidt@unimelb.edu.au

Abstract. This paper presents a novel approach to estimating a moving average model of unknown order from an observed time series based on the minimum message length principle (MML). The nature of the exact Fisher information matrix for moving average models leads to problems when used in the standard Wallace–Freeman message length approximation, and this is overcome by utilising the asymptotic form of the information matrix. By exploiting the link between partial autocorrelations and invertible moving average coefficients an efficient procedure for finding the MML moving average coefficient estimates is derived. The MML estimating equations are shown to be free of solutions at the boundary of the invertibility region that result in the troublesome "pile-up" effect in maximum likelihood estimation. Simulations demonstrate the excellent performance of the MML criteria in comparison to standard moving average inference procedures in terms of both parameter estimation and order selection, particularly for small sample sizes.

1 Introduction

Moving average models are one of the fundamental building blocks in linear time series analysis. A time series of length n, $\mathbf{y} = (y_1, \ldots, y_n)' \in \mathbb{R}^n$, is generated by a q^*-th order moving average model with coefficients, $\boldsymbol{\eta}_{q^*}^* = (\eta_1^*, \ldots, \eta_{q^*}^*)'$, if

$$y_t = \sum_{j=1}^{q^*} \eta_j^* v_{t-j} + v_t, \tag{1}$$

where $v_t \sim N(0, \tau^*)$ are the independently and identically distributed normal innovations with variance τ^*. The moving average model describes a time series as being composed of a linear combination of q^* unobserved random variables from the series v_t. In general, only the time series $\mathbf{y}$ is available for observation, and the order and parameters must be estimated on the basis of the data alone. A common approach to this problem is to combine maximum likelihood estimation of the parameters with an information criterion based order selection procedure.

D.L. Dowe (Ed.): Solomonoff Festschrift, LNAI 7070, pp. 327–338, 2013.

Let $\boldsymbol{\theta}_q = (\boldsymbol{\eta}_q', \tau)'$ denote the full parameter vector of a q-th order moving average. To estimate a moving average model using an information criterion one solves

$$\hat{q} = \underset{q \in \{0, \dots, Q\}}{\arg\min} \left\{ -\log p_q(\mathbf{y}|\hat{\boldsymbol{\theta}}_q) + \alpha(q, n) \right\}, \qquad (2)$$

where $p_q(\mathbf{y}|\boldsymbol{\theta}_q)$ is the likelihood of data $\mathbf{y}$ under a moving average model with parameters $\boldsymbol{\theta}_q$,

$$\hat{\boldsymbol{\theta}}_q = \underset{\boldsymbol{\theta}_q \in \Lambda_q \times \mathbb{R}_+}{\arg\max} \left\{ p_q(\mathbf{y}|\boldsymbol{\theta}_q) \right\}$$

is the maximum likelihood estimator of the parameters, and $\alpha(q, n)$ is a complexity penalty function; common choices include $\alpha(q, n) = q$ (Akaike's information criterion [1]) and $\alpha(q, n) = (q/2)\log n$ (the Bayesian information criterion [2]). The set Λ_q is the invertibility region for a q-th order moving average model, i.e., the set of all coefficients $\boldsymbol{\eta}_q$ for which the roots of the characteristic polynomial $1 + \sum_{j=1}^{q} \eta_j z^{-j}$ lie completely within the unit circle.

This paper examines the problem of estimating moving average models using the information theoretic minimum message length (MML) principle [3]. The MML principle has previously been applied to the problem of order selection of moving average models in [4] by Sak et al. Unfortunately, their derivation of the Fisher information matrix contains a serious mistake, and the resulting message lengths are based on a quantity that is neither the exact nor the asymptotic Fisher information. The main contribution of this paper, which is based in part on unpublished work presented in the author's PhD thesis [5], is the derivation of a correct message length formula for moving average models that is based on the asymptotic Fisher information matrix. The details of this new criterion, and some important properties, are discussed in Section 2, and its performance is compared against several moving average inference procedures in Section 3.

1.1   The Minimum Message Length Principle

The MML principle is based on the intimate connection between statistical inference and data compression and has close links to deep concepts such as Solomonoff's algorithmic information theory [6]. Under the MML principle, the explanation that most concisely describes the data is considered the *a posteriori* most likely; as the compression of the data must be decodable, the details of the model used to compress the data must also be included in the description. The length of the compressed data, usually expressed terms of base-e digits, or *nits*, acts as a universal measure of a model's goodness-of-fit that naturally takes into account both the capability and the complexity of the model. While calculation of the exact message length is in general an NP-hard problem [7], the Wallace–Freeman MML87 approximation [8] offers a tractable alternative under some regularity conditions involving the likelihood function and prior distribution (see pp. 226–227, [3]). Let $\omega \in \Omega$ denote a model class in a set of candidate model classes Ω. The MML87 message length for data $\mathbf{y}$ compressed using a fully specified model $\boldsymbol{\theta}_\omega \in \Theta_\omega$, with k_ω continuous parameters, is given by

$$I_{87}(\mathbf{y}, \boldsymbol{\theta}_\omega, \omega) = -\log p_\omega(\mathbf{y}|\boldsymbol{\theta}_\omega) + \frac{1}{2}\log|\mathbf{J}(\boldsymbol{\theta}_\omega)| - \log \pi(\boldsymbol{\theta}_\omega, \omega) + c(k_\omega), \qquad (3)$$

where $\pi(\cdot)$ is a joint prior distribution over the parameter space Θ_ω and the set of candidate model classes Ω, $\mathbf{J}(\cdot)$ is the Fisher information matrix, and

$$c(k) = -\frac{k}{2}\log(2\pi) + \frac{1}{2}\log(k\pi) + \psi(1) \tag{4}$$

where $\psi(\cdot)$ is the digamma function. Inference is performed by seeking the pair $(\hat{\boldsymbol{\theta}}_{\hat{\omega}}^{87}, \hat{\omega}^{87})$ that minimises the message length (3); in contrast to the information criterion approach, there is no need to appeal to different principles for parameter estimation and order selection.

2   Message Lengths of Moving Average Models

The ingredients required to evaluate the MML87 message length (3) are the likelihood function, a prior distribution over the continuous and structural parameters, and the Fisher information matrix. Data arising from model (1) can be exactly characterised as being generated by an n-dimensional multivariate normal distribution with zero mean and a special covariance matrix $\tau \boldsymbol{\Gamma}(\boldsymbol{\eta}_q)$, with entries $\Gamma_{i,j}(\boldsymbol{\eta}_q) = \mathbb{E}\left[y_i y_j\right]/\tau = \gamma_{|i-j|}(\boldsymbol{\eta}_q)$, where

$$\gamma_k(\boldsymbol{\eta}_q) = \begin{cases} \sum_{j=0}^{q-k} \eta_j \eta_{j+k} & k \leq q \\ 0 & k > q \end{cases}, \tag{5}$$

with $\eta_0 = 1$ [9]. The negative log-likelihood of a time series, $\mathbf{y}$, given a parameter vector $\boldsymbol{\theta}_q = (\boldsymbol{\eta}_q', \tau)'$, is

$$-\log p_q(\mathbf{y}|\boldsymbol{\theta}_q) = \left(\frac{n}{2}\right)\log(2\pi\tau) + \frac{1}{2}\log|\boldsymbol{\Gamma}(\boldsymbol{\eta}_q)| + \left(\frac{1}{2\tau}\right)\mathbf{y}'\boldsymbol{\Gamma}^{-1}(\boldsymbol{\eta}_q)\mathbf{y}. \tag{6}$$

Direct evaluation of (6) involves $O(n^3)$ operations, and therefore becomes infeasible for large sequences. An alternative, and computational efficient approach, is to evaluate the likelihood using the Kalman filter, which involves only $O(n)$ operations; see, e.g., [10] for details[1].

The prior distribution for the moving average coefficients is taken to be uniform over the invertibility region Λ_q (as in [11,4,5]), the prior distribution for the innovation variance τ is taken to be scale-invariant over some suitable interval (τ_0, τ_1), and the prior distribution for the model order is taken to be uniform over the set $\{0, \ldots, Q\}$, i.e.,

$$\pi(\boldsymbol{\eta}_q, \tau, q) = \pi(\boldsymbol{\eta}_q)\pi(\tau)\pi(q), \tag{7}$$

$$\pi(\boldsymbol{\eta}_q) = \frac{1}{\mathrm{vol}(\Lambda_q)},$$

$$\pi(\tau) \propto \frac{1}{\tau},$$

$$\pi(q) \propto 1.$$

---

[1] There is a minor typographical error in the initialisation algorithm in [10] in which the second matrix $\mathbf{T}$ is incorrectly transposed in Equation 12.

As the bounds (τ_0, τ_1), and the maximum order Q, appear only as constants in the final message length expression their values have no effect on order selection or parameter estimation and may be safely ignored. For completeness, the algorithm [12] for computing $\mathrm{vol}(\Lambda_q)$ is presented in Appendix A.

2.1 Fisher Information Matrix

By exploiting the fact that the moving average model is a multivariate Gaussian distribution, the exact, finite sample, Fisher information matrix $\mathbf{J}_n(\boldsymbol{\theta}_q)$ may be found using standard formulae. Unfortunately, there are two problems with the exact information matrix: (i) even using fast algorithms, such as the one in [9], computation of the exact information matrix is slow, requiring $O(n^2)$ operations (except in the special case that $q = 1$ [13]), and (ii) the exact information matrix is singular at the boundaries of the invertibility region. The latter problem arises from identifiability issues in the moving average model and can lead to serious violations of the regularity conditions under which the MML87 approximation was derived. Instead, we consider the asymptotic information matrix

$$\mathbf{J}(\boldsymbol{\theta}_q) = n \cdot \lim_{n \to \infty} \left\{ \frac{\mathbf{J}_n(\boldsymbol{\theta}_q)}{n} \right\}.$$

The entries of the asymptotic information matrix are given by Whittle's asymptotic formula [14], and in the case of moving average models they are straightforward to calculate. Define the auxilliary autoregressive process

$$x_t + \sum_{j=1}^{q} \eta_j x_{t-j} = u_t, \tag{8}$$

where $u_t \sim N(0, 1)$ are independently and identically distributed normal innovations. The asymptotic information matrix is then given by

$$\mathbf{J}(\boldsymbol{\theta}_q) = n \cdot \begin{pmatrix} \boldsymbol{\Phi}(\boldsymbol{\eta}_q) & 0 \\ 0 & \dfrac{1}{2\tau^2} \end{pmatrix} \tag{9}$$

where $\boldsymbol{\Phi}(\boldsymbol{\eta}_q)$ is a $(q \times q)$ matrix with entries $\Phi_{i,j}(\boldsymbol{\eta}_q) = \mathbb{E}\left[x_t x_{t+|i-j|}\right]$, which do not depend on the innovation variance τ. This is expected, given that the signal-to-noise ratio of a moving average model is also independent of τ. The asymptotic information matrix for a moving average model is therefore equivalent to the asymptotic information matrix for an autoregressive model with coefficients $\boldsymbol{\eta}_q$. This implies that $|\mathbf{J}(\boldsymbol{\eta}_q)| \geq n^q$ for all $\boldsymbol{\eta}_q \in \Lambda_q$, and that $|\mathbf{J}(\boldsymbol{\eta}_q)| \to \infty$ as the coefficients approach the boundary of the invertibility region. The entries of the autocovariance matrix $\boldsymbol{\Phi}(\boldsymbol{\eta}_q)$ can be computed using the formulae presented in [9]; however, in Section 2.2, a simplified expression for the message length is presented in which there is no need to explicitly compute the autoregressive autocovariance matrix. This results in significant increases in both numerical stability and computational efficiency.

2.2   Minimising the Message Length

The minimum message length estimates are the values of the parameters $\boldsymbol{\theta}_q$ that minimise the MML87 message length. Due to the difficulty in maximising the likelihood, these estimates must be found by a numerical search. The invertibility region, Λ_q, which defines the set of permissible moving average coefficients, forms a complex polyhedron for $q \geq 3$, making a constrained numerical search difficult. An alternative, and convenient, reparameterisation is in terms of reflection coefficients or partial autocorrelations. There exists a one-to-one transformation between partial autocorrelations, $\boldsymbol{\rho}$, in the invertibility region, and moving average coefficients $\boldsymbol{\eta}_q(\boldsymbol{\rho})$ [15]. In partial autocorrelation space the invertibility region, P_q, reduces to the interior of a hyper-cube

$$P_q = \{\boldsymbol{\rho} : |\rho_j| < 1, j = 1, \ldots, q\},$$

considerably simplifying the constrained minimisation problem. A further benefit to performing the numerical minimisation in partial autocorrelation space is that the determinant of the *coefficient-space* asymptotic Fisher information matrix, (9), is given by the simple expression

$$|\mathbf{J}(\boldsymbol{\theta}_q)| = \left(\frac{n^{q+1}}{2\tau^2}\right)\left(\prod_{j=1}^{q}\frac{1}{(1 - \rho_j^2(\boldsymbol{\eta}_q))^j}\right), \tag{10}$$

where $\boldsymbol{\rho}(\boldsymbol{\eta}_q) = (\rho_1(\boldsymbol{\eta}_q), \ldots, \rho_q(\boldsymbol{\eta}_q))'$ are the q partial autocorrelations corresponding to the coefficients $\boldsymbol{\eta}_q$. In contrast to direct evaluation of $|\mathbf{J}(\boldsymbol{\theta}_q)|$ in coefficient space, this expression involves only $O(q)$ operations and does not require the direct computation of the autocovariances of the auxilliary autoregressive process (8). Using (6), (7) and (10) in (3) yields the following expression for the MML87 message length, $I_{87}(\mathbf{y}, \boldsymbol{\eta}_q, \tau, q)$,

$$-\log p_q(\mathbf{y}|\boldsymbol{\eta}_q, \tau) + \frac{q}{2}\log n - \frac{1}{2}\sum_{j=1}^{q}j\log(1 - \rho_j^2(\boldsymbol{\eta}_q)) + \log \text{vol}(\Lambda_q) + c(q+1)$$

$$+\frac{1}{2}\log\left(\frac{n}{2}\right) + \log\left[(Q+1)\log\left(\frac{\tau_1}{\tau_0}\right)\right], \tag{11}$$

where $c(\cdot)$ is given by (4). The last two terms of (11) are constant with respect to q and $\boldsymbol{\theta}_q$, and therefore have no effect on parameter estimation or order selection, and may be ignored if we are only considering moving average models to be possible explanations of the data. The above expression easily handles the case that $q = 0$ by simply dropping the second through fourth terms. It is important to note that (11) gives an expression for the message length in terms of the coefficients $\boldsymbol{\eta}_q$; the corresponding partial autocorrelations, $\boldsymbol{\rho}(\boldsymbol{\eta}_q)$, are only used because they make evaluating and minimising this expression significantly easier. The MML87 estimate of the innovation variance, $\hat{\tau}^{87}(\boldsymbol{\eta}_q)$, conditional on a coefficient vector $\boldsymbol{\eta}_q$, is the same as the maximum likelihood estimate,

$$\hat{\tau}^{87}(\boldsymbol{\eta}_q) = \frac{\mathbf{y}'\boldsymbol{\Gamma}(\boldsymbol{\eta}_q)\mathbf{y}}{n},$$

which itself may be calculated efficiently through the use of the same Kalman filter recurrence relations used to calculate the negative log-likelihood. The MML87 parameter estimates, $\hat{\boldsymbol{\eta}}_q^{87}$, are found by searching for the partial autocorrelations that solve

$$\hat{\boldsymbol{\rho}}^{87} = \underset{\boldsymbol{\rho} \in P_q}{\arg\min} \left\{ I_{87}(\mathbf{y}, \boldsymbol{\eta}_q(\boldsymbol{\rho}), \hat{\tau}^{87}(\boldsymbol{\eta}_q(\boldsymbol{\rho})), q) \right\},$$

and transforming them to coefficient space, i.e., $\hat{\boldsymbol{\eta}}_q^{87} \equiv \boldsymbol{\eta}_q(\hat{\boldsymbol{\rho}}^{87})$. The MML estimate of the order, $\hat{q}^{87}$, may then be found by solving

$$\hat{q}^{87} = \underset{q \in \{0,\dots,Q\}}{\arg\min} \left\{ I_{87}(\mathbf{y}, \hat{\boldsymbol{\eta}}_q^{87}, \hat{\tau}^{87}(\hat{\boldsymbol{\eta}}_q^{87}), q) \right\}.$$

An interesting result is that evaluation of the MML87 message length (11) involves only $O(q)$ additional operations over evaluation of the negative log-likelihood, and thus the minimum message length estimates are theoretically as quick to find numerically as the maximum likelihood estimates. In fact, experiments suggest that the extra "regularisation" introduced by the presence of the asymptotic Fisher information term acts to significantly improve convergence of the search procedure for MML estimates in comparison to maximum likelihood estimation, which is well known to be problematic for moving average models.

2.3   Properties of the MML87 Estimator

The MML87 estimate of order, $\hat{q}^{87}$, is a strongly consistent estimate of q^*. To see this, rewrite the message length (11) as

$$- \log p_q(\mathbf{y}|\boldsymbol{\eta}_q, \tau) + \frac{q}{2} \log n + O(1),$$

where $O(1)$ denotes terms that are constant with respect to n. Thus, the MML87 message length (11) asymptotically coincides with the Bayesian information criterion (BIC), and from the arguments in [16], $\hat{q}^{87}$ is a strongly consistent estimate of q^*. Further, the MML87 estimates of the coefficients and innovation variance asymptotically coincide with the maximum likelihood estimates. This implies that when $q \geq q^*$ the MML87 parameter estimates are also strongly consistent [17]. The MML87 estimates of the moving average coefficients also possess an interesting finite sample property.

Property 1. *For all datasets, $\mathbf{y}$, of all finite sample sizes n, the partial autocorrelations corresponding to the MML87 estimates of the coefficients, $\hat{\boldsymbol{\eta}}^{87}$, satisfy*

$$||\boldsymbol{\rho}(\hat{\boldsymbol{\eta}}^{87})||_\infty < 1,$$

where $|| \cdot ||_\infty$ denotes the ℓ_∞ norm.

Proof. The MML estimates minimise the sum of the negative log-likelihood and the half log-determinant of the Fisher information matrix, as given in (11).

The negative log-likelihood is bounded from below for finite n for all $\boldsymbol{\eta}_q \in \mathbb{R}^q$; in contrast, the half log-determinant of the Fisher information matrix is unbounded from above as $||\boldsymbol{\rho}(\boldsymbol{\eta}_q)||_\infty \to 1$. Thus, the message length will be finite if and only if $||\boldsymbol{\rho}(\hat{\boldsymbol{\eta}}^{87})||_\infty < 1$, implying that the parameter estimates that minimise (11) must satisfy $||\boldsymbol{\rho}(\hat{\boldsymbol{\eta}}^{87})||_\infty < 1$.   □

This result implies that $\hat{\boldsymbol{\eta}}^{87} \in \Lambda_q$, and therefore the MML87 estimates of the moving average coefficients do not suffer from the so-called "pile-up" phenomenon [18], in which coefficients are estimated to lie exactly on the boundary of the invertibility region; this problem is well known to affect the maximum likelihood estimates. The removal of the troublesome pile-up effect is attributable to the "regularisation" introduced by the Fisher information terms, which also corroborates the empirical observations that the message length surface is better behaved than the likelihood surface when performing numerical optimisation.

3   Evaluation

Two measures of "closeness" to the true, generating moving average process were used to assess the competing estimators: (i) normalized expected one-step-ahead squared prediction error; and (ii) the directed Kullback–Leibler divergence. The expected one-step-ahead squared prediction error is defined as the expected squared difference between the true conditional mean and the predicted conditional mean for the next sample if the q previous innovations were available, and assesses the closeness of the estimated moving average model in ideal conditions. Given a true model, $\boldsymbol{\eta}^*$, and estimated model, $\hat{\boldsymbol{\eta}}$, this is equal to

$$\text{SPE}_1(\boldsymbol{\eta}^*, \hat{\boldsymbol{\eta}}) = \left(\frac{1}{\gamma_0(\boldsymbol{\eta}^*)} \right) (\boldsymbol{\eta}^* - \hat{\boldsymbol{\eta}})'(\boldsymbol{\eta}^* - \hat{\boldsymbol{\eta}}), \tag{12}$$

where $\gamma_0(\boldsymbol{\eta}^*)$ is the zero-order autocovariance of the generating process (found using (5)), and the two parameter vectors are made to be the same dimension by appending a suitable number of zero elements to the shorter vector. The scaling by the inverse of the zero-order autocovariance of the generating process renders the resulting quantity unitless, and is done to ensure that the value of the error metric is comparable between different generating processes. This is essential if simulations involve sampling a large number of generating models from the invertibility region, with correspondingly different signal-to-noise ratios. The second error metric used was the Kullback–Leibler (K–L) divergence [19]. This is an important, parameterisation-invariant measure of the "distance" between distributions, with strong information theoretic interpretations. The *per sample* K–L divergence between a true, generating moving average process, $\boldsymbol{\theta}^*$, and an approximating moving average process, $\hat{\boldsymbol{\theta}}$, for n data points is

$$\frac{1}{2} \log \left(\frac{\hat{\tau}}{\tau^*} \right) + \left(\frac{1}{2n} \right) \log \left(\frac{|\boldsymbol{\Gamma}(\hat{\boldsymbol{\eta}})|}{|\boldsymbol{\Gamma}(\boldsymbol{\eta}^*)|} \right) + \left(\frac{1}{2n} \right) \text{Tr} \left(\boldsymbol{\Gamma}(\boldsymbol{\eta}^*) \boldsymbol{\Gamma}^{-1}(\hat{\boldsymbol{\eta}}) \right) - \frac{1}{2}, \tag{13}$$

where $\boldsymbol{\Gamma}(\cdot)$ is an $(n \times n)$ autocovariance matrix as in (5). The choice of the size of the autocovariance matrix is essentially arbitrary and the use of the sample size,

n, reflects the fact that the sequence $\mathbf{y}$ can be regarded as a randomly generated vector from the n-dimensional multivariate normal distribution characterised by $\tau^* \boldsymbol{\Gamma}(\boldsymbol{\eta}^*)$. Thus, the Kullback–Leibler divergence measures the closeness of the estimated n-dimensional multivariate distribution to the distribution that generated the sample.

3.1   Parameter Estimation

The parameter estimation performance of the MML87 estimator was compared against two standard procedures from the literature: (i) the maximum likelihood (ML) estimator, and (ii) the modified Durbin estimator (ARMASA) [20,21] which exploits the duality between moving average and autoregressive models. Given our choice of a uniform prior distribution for the moving average coefficients, the maximum likelihood estimator also coincides with the maximum a posteriori (MAP) estimator. As we know that the mean of the generating moving average process is zero, we chose not to demean the data before estimation by ARMASA to allow for a fair comparison with MML87 and ML.

The simulation setup was as follows: (i) sample an invertible moving average model $\boldsymbol{\eta}_{q^*}$ uniformly from Λ_{q^*} (using the algorithm described in [22]); (ii) sample a time series of length n from the process defined by $\boldsymbol{\eta}_q^*$, with $\tau^* = 1$; (iii) estimate coefficients from the time series using MML87, maximum likelihood, the ARMASA procedure, and compute appropriate measures of closeness to the generating model. This was repeated for 10^3 iterations, for $q = \{1, 4, 7, 10\}$, with sample sizes $n = k(3q + 1)$, where $k = \{1, 2, 4\}$.

The results are presented in Table 1. Median expected one-step-ahead squared error, (12), and median per sample Kullback–Leibler divergences, (13), were used instead of arithmetic means as the tails of the empirical distributions of these error measures were significantly heavier than would be expected for a normal distribution. The results clearly show the strong performance of the MML87 estimator, which is superior in terms of both squared prediction errors, and Kullback–Leibler divergence, for every combination of sample size and true order. For the smallest sample sizes the maximum likelihood/MAP estimator uniformly performed the worst, often by a large margin; this can be attributed to the "pile-up" effect as well as the tendency of the maximum likelihood estimator to overestimate the magnitude of the zeros of the underlying process when the sample size is small. In contrast, observations suggested that the MML87 estimates tended to underestimate the magnitudes of the zeros in comparison to the maximum likelihood estimates, and the distributions of the estimates appeared unimodal, showing no sign of any "pile-up" type effect. For larger sample sizes, the modified Durbin's method generally performed worse than the maximum likelihood estimator in terms of squared errors. Of course, the true models used in the simulations have been sampled from the prior distribution used by the MML87 estimator, which makes direct comparisons with maximum likelihood and the modified Durbin's method somewhat problematic. However, even taking this into account, the results demonstrate that the MML87 estimator is clearly superior to the usual Bayesian MAP estimator which utilises the same prior information.

Table 1. Parameter estimation experiment results

Order	n	Squared Prediction Error			Kullback–Leibler Divergence		
		MML87	ML	ARMASA	MML87	ML	ARMASA
1	4	**0·071**	0·143	0·085	**0·139**	0·182	0·152
	8	**0·032**	0·055	0·051	**0·089**	0·105	0·090
	16	**0·015**	0·022	0·025	**0·040**	0·048	0·048
4	13	**0·158**	0·297	0·238	**0·182**	0·313	0·236
	26	**0·070**	0·102	0·111	**0·096**	0·147	0·120
	52	**0·031**	0·038	0·053	**0·048**	0·063	0·066
7	22	**0·164**	0·320	0·266	**0·210**	0·382	0·261
	44	**0·077**	0·116	0·126	**0·108**	0·173	0·132
	88	**0·033**	0·041	0·058	**0·052**	0·070	0·068
10	31	**0·172**	0·315	0·294	**0·209**	0·390	0·278
	62	**0·079**	0·117	0·123	**0·111**	0·185	0·133
	124	**0·035**	0·043	0·058	**0·051**	0·075	0·069

One point of particular note is that despite the fact that the message length formula (11) is based on the *asymptotic* Fisher information matrix, the MML87 estimates perform very well in the small sample regime. This suggests that further refinements of the message length formula to make use of the finite sample Kullback–Leibler divergence, such as the new message length formulae discussed in [5] (pp. 30–34) could lead to further performance improvements for small samples. This issue, along with a more complete characterisation of the behaviour of the MML87 moving average estimates, are interesting topics for future research.

3.2 Order Selection

The ability of the MML87 criterion to estimate a moving average model of unknown order from finite samples was compared against six standard procedures from the literature: the Akaike information criterion (AIC) [1], the corrected AIC (AIC$_c$) [23], the symmetric Kullback–Leibler divergence criterion (KIC) [24], the corrected KIC (KIC$_c$) [25] and the ARMAsel procedure [26]. The BIC, AIC, KIC and their corrected variants use maximum likelihood estimates, while the ARMAsel procedure uses modified Durbin estimates (without zero meaning the data, as previously discussed).

The simulation setup was as follows: (i) sample an invertible moving average model η_{q^*} uniformly from Λ_{q^*}; (ii) sample a time series of length n from the process defined by η_q^*, with $\tau^* = 1$; (iii) ask all criteria to estimate q^* along with estimates of the moving average coefficients, and compute appropriate measures of closeness to the generating model. This was repeated one thousand times for each true model order $q^* = \{0, \ldots, 10\}$, for a total of 11,000 iterations per sample size $n = \{10, 20, 50, 100\}$. At each iteration, all candidate models in $q = \{0, \ldots, r\}$ were considered by the model selection criteria, with $r = 4$ for $n = 10$, $r = 7$ for $n = 20$, and $r = 10$ for $n > 20$. These simulations were designed to mimic real data situations in which the true, underlying process

Table 2. Order estimation experiment results

n	Measure	Model Selection Criteria						
		MML87	BIC	AIC	AIC_c	KIC	KIC_c	ARMASA
10	SPE_1	**0·387**	0·412	0·414	0·426	0·414	0·444	0·405
	KL	**0·220**	0·247	0·258	0·246	0·242	0·255	0·239
	$\#\{\hat{q} = q^*\}$	1534	1607	**1670**	1390	1499	1250	1481
20	SPE_1	**0·245**	0·284	0·292	0·287	0·284	0·309	0·268
	KL	**0·175**	0·206	0·236	0·206	0·206	0·207	0·186
	$\#\{\hat{q} = q^*\}$	2341	2292	**2487**	2186	2292	2032	2243
50	SPE_1	**0·065**	0·093	0·109	0·091	0·086	0·090	0·086
	KL	**0·084**	0·114	0·138	0·117	0·111	0·113	0·094
	$\#\{\hat{q} = q^*\}$	**4343**	3912	4235	4281	**4343**	3978	4192
100	SPE_1	**0·022**	0·028	0·037	0·033	0·028	0·027	0·036
	KL	**0·036**	0·047	0·056	0·052	0·046	0·045	0·047
	$\#\{\hat{q} = q^*\}$	**6227**	5799	5584	5817	6200	6178	5997

may be considerably more complex than any model that the data will allow us to realistically consider.

The median expected one-step-ahead squared prediction error, (12), median per sample Kullback–Leibler divergence, (13), and the number of times a criteria correctly estimated the true model order are presented in Table 2. In terms of squared prediction errors, and Kullback–Leibler divergence, the MML87 criterion is uniformly the best for all sample sizes. For $n = 10$ and $n = 20$, the ARMAsel procedure performed similar to MML87, although for $n > 20$ it performed noticeably poorer. In terms of correct order selections, for all but $n = 50$ the AIC and/or KIC perform amongst the best of all the methods. Not too much should be made of this fact, however, as it is well known that as n grows these criteria are inconsistent and will tend to overfit with non-vanishing probability. Interestingly, for smaller sample sizes, despite performing the best in terms of predictive measures (squared error and Kullback–Leibler divergence) the MML87 criterion does not, in general, perform the best at selecting the true generating order. We believe this is because MML, and related compression based methods, make no assumptions about the existence of a "true" model; rather, they are designed to select a good, *plausible* explanation about the data generating source from the available candidates.

3.3   The Southern Oscillation Index Time Series

Finally, we conclude this section with a brief experiment on a real time series. The Southern Oscillation Index (SOI) is a time series of monthly measurements of fluctuations in air pressure difference between Tahiti and Darwin. The SOI is commonly used to study and predict *El Niño* phenomena. The time series analysed contained $n = 1,619$ monthly measurements taken from January, 1876 through to December, 2010, and was obtained from the Australian Government Bureau of Metereology website. The first $1,000$ samples in the series were used as a training sample, and the remaining 619 samples were used for validation

Table 3. Southern Oscillation Index Experiment

Measure	Model Selection Criteria						
	MML87	BIC	AIC	AIC$_c$	KIC	KIC$_c$	ARMASA
SPE$_1$	**59·129**	59·166	59·740	59·740	59·740	59·740	59·792
NLL	**2490·1**	2490·5	2492·3	2492·3	2492·3	2492·3	2491·4
Order	13	13	14	14	14	14	14

of the estimated models. All criteria were asked to estimate a suitable moving average model from the training data, with a maximum candidate order of $q = 20$. The evaluation measures were mean squared prediction error and negative log-likelihood obtained on the validation sample, conditional on the training sample. These were computed by running the Kalman filter on the complete time series using the models estimated from the training sample; this automatically produces predictions of the mean and variance for all data points in the time series, and these may be used to compute the squared error and negative log-likelihood of the validation sample (i.e., the last 619 samples).

The mean squared error and negative log-likelihood scores are presented in Table 3, along with the order of the moving average model selected by each of the criteria. All criteria perform similarly, with MML87 obtaining a slight improvement in squared prediction error. The two main points of interest are: (i) even for this large sample ($n = 1,000$), the MML87 criteria has selected a slightly lower order model ($\hat{q}^{87} = 13$) than all other criteria except BIC; and (ii) the MML87 estimates of coefficients for the $q = 13$ moving average model still differ slightly from the maximum likelihood estimates used by BIC, despite the high ratio of data-to-parameters.

Appendix A

For completeness we present the equations (taken from [12]) to calculate the volume of the invertibility region, Λ_q, for a q-th order moving average process. Define $M_1 = 2$ and $M_k = ((k-1)/k)M_{k-2}$. Let $V_q \equiv \mathrm{vol}(\Lambda_q)$, with $V_1 = 2$; for $q > 1$, $V_q = \prod_{k=0}^{q/2-1} M_{2k+1}^2$ for q even and $V_q = V_{q-1}M_q$ for q odd.

References

1. Akaike, H.: A new look at the statistical model identification. IEEE Transactions on Automatic Control 19(6), 716–723 (1974)
2. Schwarz, G.: Estimating the dimension of a model. The Annals of Statistics 6(2), 461–464 (1978)
3. Wallace, C.S.: Statistical and Inductive Inference by Minimum Message Length, 1st edn. Information Science and Statistics. Springer (2005)
4. Sak, M., Dowe, D., Ray, S.: Minimum message length moving average time series data mining. In: Proceedings of the ICSC Congress on Computational Intelligence Methods and Applications (ACFM 2005), Istanbul, Turkey (2005)

5. Schmidt, D.F.: Minimum Message Length Inference of Autoregressive Moving Average Models. PhD thesis, Clayton School of Information Technology, Monash University (2008)
6. Solomonoff, R.J.: A formal theory of inductive inference. Information and Control 7(2), 1–22, 224–254 (1964)
7. Farr, G.E., Wallace, C.S.: The complexity of strict minimum message length inference. Computer Journal 45(3), 285–292 (2002)
8. Wallace, C.S., Freeman, P.R.: Estimation and inference by compact coding. Journal of the Royal Statistical Society (Series B) 49(3), 240–252 (1987)
9. Porat, B., Friedlander, B.: Computation of the exact information matrix of Gaussian time series with stationary random components. IEEE Transactions on Acoustics, Speech and Signal Processing 34(1), 118–130 (1986)
10. Gardner, G., Harvey, A.C., Phillips, G.D.A.: Algorithm AS 154: An algorithm for exact maximum likelihood estimation of autoregressive-moving average models by means of Kalman filtering. Applied Statistics 29(3), 311–322 (1980)
11. Fitzgibbon, L.J., Dowe, D.L., Vahid, F.: Minimum message length autoregressive model order selection. In: Proceedings of the International Conference on Intelligent Sensing and Information Processing (ICISIP), pp. 439–444 (2004)
12. Piccolo, D.: The size of the stationarity and invertibility region of an autoregressive moving average process. Journal of Time Series Analysis 3(4), 245–247 (1982)
13. Makalic, E., Schmidt, D.F.: Fast computation of the Kullback-Leibler divergence and exact Fisher information for the first-order moving average model. IEEE Signal Processing Letters 17(4), 391–393 (2009)
14. Whittle, P.: The analysis of multiple stationary time series. Journal of the Royal Statistical Society, Series B (Methodological) 15(1), 125–139 (1953)
15. Barndorff-Nielsen, O., Schou, G.: On the parametrization of autoregressive models by partial autocorrelations. Journal of Multivariate Analysis 3, 408–419 (1973)
16. Haughton, D.M.A.: On the choice of a model to fit data from an exponential family. The Annals of Statistics 16(1), 342–355 (1988)
17. Rissanen, J., Caines, P.E.: The strong consistency of maximum likelihood estimators for ARMA processes. The Annals of Statistics 7(2), 297–315 (1979)
18. Davidson, J.E.H.: Problems with the estimation of moving average processes. Journal of Econometrics 16(3), 295–310 (1981)
19. Kullback, S., Leibler, R.A.: On information and sufficiency. The Annals of Mathematical Statistics 22(1), 79–86 (1951)
20. Durbin, J.: Efficient estimation of parameters in moving-average models. Biometrika 46(3/4), 306–316 (1959)
21. Broersen, P.M.T.: Autoregressive model orders for Durbin's MA and ARMA estimators. IEEE Transactions on Signal Processing 48(8), 2454–2457 (2000)
22. Jones, M.C.: Randomly choosing parameters from the stationarity and invertibility regions of autoregressive-moving average models. Applied Statistics 36(2), 134–138 (1987)
23. Hurvich, C.M., Tsai, C.L.: Regression and time series model selection in small samples. Biometrika 76(2), 297–307 (1989)
24. Cavanaugh, J.E.: A large-sample model selection criterion based on Kullback's symmetric divergence. Statistics & Probability Letters 42(4), 333–343 (1999)
25. Seghouane, A.K., Bekara, M.: A small sample model selection criterion based on Kullback's symmetric divergence. IEEE Transactions on Signal Processing 52(12), 3314–3323 (2004)
26. Broersen, P.M.T.: Automatic spectral analysis with time series models. IEEE Transactions on Instrumentation and Measurement 51(2), 211–216 (2002)

Abstraction Super-Structuring Normal Forms: Towards a Theory of Structural Induction

Adrian Silvescu and Vasant Honavar

Department of Computer Science, Iowa State University, Ames, IA, USA

Abstract. Induction is the process by which we obtain predictive laws or theories or models of the world. We consider the structural aspect of induction. We answer the question as to whether we can find a finite and minimalistic set of operations on structural elements in terms of which any theory can be expressed. We identify *abstraction* (grouping *similar* entities) and super-structuring (combining topologically e.g., spatio-temporally close entities) as the essential structural operations in the induction process. We show that only two more structural operations, namely, *reverse abstraction* and *reverse super-structuring* (the duals of abstraction and super-structuring respectively) suffice in order to exploit the full power of Turing-equivalent generative grammars in induction. We explore the implications of this theorem with respect to the nature of hidden variables, radical positivism and the 2-century old claim of David Hume about the principles of *connexion* among ideas.

1 Introduction

The logic of induction, the process by which we obtain predictive laws, theories, or models of the world, has been a long standing concern of philosophy, science, statistics and artifical intelligence. Theories typically have two aspects: structural or qualitative (corresponding to concepts or variables and their relationships, or, in philosophical parlance, *ontology*) and numeric or quantitative (corresponding to parameters e.g., probabilities). Once the qualitative aspect of a certain law is fixed, the quantitative aspect becomes the subject of experimental science and statistics. Induction is the process of inferring predictive laws, theories, or models of the world from a stream of observations. In general, the observations may be passive, or may be the outcomes of interventions by the learning agent. Here, we limit ourselves to induction from passive observation alone.

Under the *computationalistic assumption* (i.e., the Church-Turing thesis, which asserts that any expressible theory can be described by a Turing Machine [18]), one way to solve the induction problem is to enumerate all the Turing machines (and run them in parallel - dovetailing in order to cope with the countably infinite number of them) and pick one that strikes a good balance between the predictability (of the finite experience stream) and size (complexity) [16], [17], [15], [20] or within a Bayesian setting, using a weighted vote among the predictions of the various models [7] (see [2] and references therein). In the general

D.L. Dowe (Ed.): Solomonoff Festschrift, LNAI 7070, pp. 339–350, 2013.

setting, a priori the number of types of possible structural laws that can be postulated is infinite. This makes it difficult to design general purpose induction strategy. We ask whether a finite and minimalistic set of fundamental structural operations suffice to construct *any* set of laws. In this case such a set will render induction more tractable because at any step the learner will have to pick from a small *finite* set of possible operations as opposed to an infinite one.

Because Turing machines are rather opaque from a structural standpoint, we use the alternative, yet equivalent, mechanism of generative grammars[1]. This allows us to work with theories that can be built recursively by applying structural operations drawn from a finite set. The intuition behind this approach is that induction involves incrementally constructing complex structures using simpler structures (e.g., using super-structuring, also called *chunking*), and simplifying complex structures when possible (e.g., using abstraction). Such a compositional approach to induction offers the advantage of increased transparency over the enumerate-and-select approach pioneered by Solomonoff [16], [17]. It also offers the possibility of reusing intermediate structures as opposed to starting afresh with a new Turing machine at each iteration, thereby replacing enumeration by a process akin to dynamic programming or its heuristic variants such as the A* algorithm.

We seek laws or patterns that explain a stream of observations through successive applications of operations drawn from a small finite set. The induced patterns are not necessarily described solely in terms of the input observations, but may also use (a finite number of) additional internal or hidden (i.e., not directly observable) entities. The role of these internal variables is to simplify explanation. The introduction of internal variables to aid the explanation process is not without perils [12][2]. One way to preclude the introduction of internal variables is to apply the following *demarcation criterion*: If the agent cannot distinguish possible streams of observations based on the values of an internal variable, then the variable is non-sensical (i.e., independent of the data or "senses") [3]. The direct connection requirement restricts the no-nonsense theories to those formed out empirical laws [1] (i.e., laws that relate only measurable quantities). However several scientists, including Albert Einstein, while being sympathetic to the positivist's ideas, have successfully used in their theories, hidden variables that have at best indirect connection to observables. This has led to a series of revisions of the positivist's doctrine culminating in Carnap's attempt to accommodate hidden variables in scientific explanations [3]. The observables and the internal variables in terms of which the explanation is offered can be seen as the

---

[1] See [10] for a similarly motivated attempt using *Lambda calculus*.

[2] Consider for example, a hidden variable which stands for the truth value of the sentence: "In heaven, if it rains, do the angels get wet or not?"

[3] This is a radical interpretation of an idea that shows up in the history of Philosophy from Positivism through the empiricists and scholastics down to Aristotle's *"Nihil est in intellectu quod non prius fuerit in sensu"* (There is nothing in the mind that was not previously in the senses).

ontology[4] - i.e., the set of concepts and their interrelationships found useful by the agent in theorizing about its experience. In this setting, structural induction is tantamount to ontology construction.

The rest of the paper is organized as follows: Section 2 introduces Abstraction Super-structuring Normal Forms that correspond to a general class of Turing-equivalent generative grammars that can be used to express theories about the world; and shows that: *abstraction* (grouping *similar* entities) and super-structuring (combining topologically e.g., spatio-temporally close entities) as the essential structural operations in the induction process; Only two more structural operations, namely, *reverse abstraction* and *reverse super-structuring* (the duals of abstraction and super-structuring respectively), suffice in order to exploit the full power of Turing-equivalent generative grammars in induction. Section 3 interprets the theoretical results in a larger context the nature of hidden variables, radical positivism and the 2-century old claim of David Hume about the principles of *connexion* among ideas. Section 4 concludes with a summary.

2 Abstraction Super-Structuring Normal Forms

We start by recapitulating the definitions and notations for generative grammars and the theorem that claims the equivalence between Generative Grammars and Turing Machines. We then draw the connections between the process of induction and the formalism of generative grammars and motivate the quest for a minimalistic set of fundamental structural operations. We then get to the main results of the paper: a series of characterization theorems of two important classes of Generative Grammars: Context-Free and General Grammars, in terms of a small set of fundamental structural operations.

2.1 Generative Grammars and Turing Machines

Definitions (Grammar). A (generative) grammar is a quadruple (N, T, S, R) where N and T are disjoint finite sets called NonTerminals and Terminals, respectively, S is a distinguished element from N called the start symbol and R is a set of rewrite rules (a.k.a. production rules) of the form $(l \rightarrow r)$ where $l \in (N \cup T)^* N (N \cup T)^*$ and $r \in (N \cup T)^*$. Additionally, we call l the left hand side (LHS) and r the right hand side (RHS) of the rule $(l \rightarrow r)$. The language generated by a grammar is defined by $L(G) = \{w \in T^* | S \overset{*}{\rightarrow} w\}$ where $\overset{*}{\rightarrow}$ stands for the reflexive transitive closure of the rules from R. Furthermore $\overset{+}{\rightarrow}$ stands for the transitive (but not reflexive) closure of the rules from R. We say that two grammars G, G' are equivalent if $L(G) = L(G')$. The steps contained in a set of transitions $\alpha \overset{*}{\rightarrow} \beta$ is called a derivation. If we want to distinguish between derivations in different grammars we will write $\alpha \overset{*}{\rightarrow}_G \beta$ or mention it explicitly. We denote by ϵ the empty string in the language. We will sometimes use the

---

[4] The ontology in this case is not universal as it is often the case in philosophy; it is just a set of concepts and interrelations among them that afford the expression of theories.

shorthand notation $l \rightarrow r_1|r_2|...|r_n$ to stand for the set of rules $\{l \rightarrow r_i\}_{i=1,n}$. See e.g., [13] for more details and examples.

Definition (Grammar Types). Let $G = (N, T, S, R)$ be a grammar. Then

1. G is a **regular grammar (REG)** if all the rules $(l \rightarrow r) \in R$ have the property that $l \in N$ and $r \in (T^* \cup T^*N)$.
2. G is **context-free grammar (CFG)** if all the rules $(l \rightarrow r) \in R$ have the property that $l \in N$.
3. G is **context-sensitive grammar (CSG)** if all the rules $(l \rightarrow r) \in R$ have the property that they are of the form $\alpha A \beta \rightarrow \alpha \gamma \beta$ where $A \in N$ and $\alpha, \beta, \gamma \in (N \cup T)^*$ and $\gamma \neq \epsilon$. Furthermore if ϵ is an element of the language one rule of the form $S \rightarrow \epsilon$ is allowed and furthermore the restriction that S does not appear in the right hand side of any rule is imposed. We will call such a sentence an $\epsilon - Amendment$.
4. G is **general grammar (GG)** if all the rules $(l \rightarrow r) \in R$ have no additional restrictions.

Theorem 1. *The set of General Grammars is equivalent in power with the set of Turing Machines. That is, for every Turing Machine T there exists a General Grammar G such that $L(G) = L(T)$ and vice versa.*

Proof. This theorem is a well known result. See for example [13] for a proof[5]. $\square$

2.2   Structural Induction, Generative Grammars and Motivation

Before proceeding with the main results of the paper we examine the connections between the setting of generative grammars and the problem of structural induction. The terminals in the grammar formalism denote the set of observables in our induction problem. The NonTerminals stand for internal variables in terms of which the observations (terminals) are explained. The "explanation" is given by a derivation of the stream of observations from the initial symbol $S \xrightarrow{*} w$. The NonTerminals that appear in the derivation are the internal variables in terms of which the surface structure given by the stream of observations w is explained. Given this correspondence, structural induction aims to find an appropriate set of NonTerminals N and a set of rewrite rules R that will allow us to derive (explain) the input stream of observations w from the initial symbol S. The process of Structural Induction may invent a new rewrite rule $l \rightarrow r$ under certain conditions and this new rule may contain in turn new NonTerminals (internal variables) which are added to the already existing ones. The common intuition is that l is a simpler version of r, as the final goal is to reduce w to S. The terminals constitute the input symbols (standing for observables), the NonTerminals constitute whatever additional "internal" variables that are needed, the

---

[5] Similar results of equivalence exist for transductive versions of Turing machines and grammars as opposed to the recognition versions given here (See e.g., [2] and references therein). Without loss of generality, we will assume the recognition as opposed to the transductive setting.

rewrite rules describe their interrelationship and altogether they constitute the ontology. The correspondence between the terms used in structural induction and generative grammars is summarized in Table 1.

Table 1. Correspondence between Structural Induction and Generative Grammars

Structural Induction	Generative Grammar
Observables	Terminals T
Internal Variables	NonTerminals N
Law / Theory	production rule(s) $l \rightarrow r$
Ontology	Grammar G
Observations Stream	word w
Explanation	Derivation $S \xrightarrow{*} w$
Partial Explanation	Derivation $\alpha \xrightarrow{*} w$

Thus, in general, structural induction may invent any rewrite rule of the form $l \rightarrow r$, potentially introducing new NonTerminals, the problem is that there are infinitely many such rules that we could invent at any point in time. In order to make the process more well defined we ask whether it is possible to find a set of fundamental structural operations which is finite and minimalistic, such that all the rules (or more precisely sets of rules) can be expressed in terms of these operations. This would establish a normal form in terms of a finite set of operations and then the problem of generating laws will be reduced to making appropriate choices from this set without sacrificing completeness. In the next subsection we will attempt to decompose the rules $l \rightarrow r$ into a small finite set of fundamental structural elements which will allow us to design better structure search mechanisms.

2.3   ASNF (Abstraction SuperStructuring Normal Form) Theorems

Issue ($\epsilon - Construction$). In the rest of the paper we will prove some theorems that impose various sets of conditions on a grammar G in order for the grammar to be considered in a certain Normal Form. If $\epsilon \in L(G)$ however, we will allow two specific rules of the grammar G to be exempted from these constraints and still consider the grammar in the Normal Form. More exactly if $\epsilon \in L(G)$ and given a grammar G' such that $L(G') = L(G \backslash \{\epsilon\})$ and $G' = (N', T, S', R')$ is in a certain Normal Form then the grammar $G = (N \cup \{S\}, T, S, R = R' \cup \{S \rightarrow \epsilon, S \rightarrow S'\})$ where $S \notin N'$ will also be considered in that certain Normal Form despite the fact that the two productions $\{S \rightarrow \epsilon, S \rightarrow S'\}$ may violate the conditions of the Normal Form. These are the only productions that will be allowed to violate the Normal Form conditions. Note that S is a brand new NonTerminal and does not appear in any other productions aside from these two. Without loss of generality we will assume in the rest of the paper that $\epsilon \notin L(G)$. This is because if $\epsilon \in L(G)$ we can always produce using the above-mentioned construction a grammar G'' that is in a certain Normal Form and $L(G'') = L(G')$ from a grammar G' that is in that Normal Form and satisfies $L(G') = L(G\backslash\{\epsilon\})$. We will call the procedure just outlined the $\epsilon - Construction$. We will call the following statement the $\epsilon - Amendment$: Let $G = (N, T, S, R)$ be a grammar, if ϵ is an element of the language $L(G)$ one rule of the form $S \to \epsilon$ is allowed and furthermore the restriction that S does not appear in the right hand side of any rule is imposed.

First we state a weak form of the Abstraction SuperStructuring Normal Form for Context Free Grammars.

Theorem 2 (Weak-CFG-ASNF). *Let* $G = (N, T, S, R)$, $\epsilon \notin L(G)$ *be a Context Free Grammar. Then there exists a Context Free Grammar* G' *such that* $L(G) = L(G')$ *and* G' *contains only rules of the following type:*

1. $A \to B$
2. $A \to BC$
3. $A \to a$

Proof. Since G is a CFG it can be written in the Chomsky Normal Form [13]. That is, such that it contains only productions of the forms 2 and 3. If $\epsilon \in L(G)$ then a rule of the form $S \to \epsilon$ is allowed and S does not appear in the RHS of any other rule ($\epsilon - Amendment$). Since we have assumed that $\epsilon \notin L(G)$ we do not need to deal with $\epsilon - Amendment$ and hence the proof. □

Remarks.

1. We will call the rules of type 1 Renamings (REN).
2. We will call the rules of type 2 SuperStructures (SS) or compositions.
3. The rules of the type 3 are just convenience renamings of observables into internal variables in order to uniformize the notation and we will call them Terminal (TERMINAL).

We are now ready to state the the Weak ASNF theorem for the general case.

Theorem 3 (Weak-GEN-ASNF). *Let* $G = (N, T, S, R)$, $\epsilon \notin L(G)$ *be a General (unrestricted) Grammar. Then there exists a grammar* G' *such that* $L(G) = L(G')$ *and* G' *contains only rules of the following type:*

1. $A \to B$
2. $A \to BC$
3. $A \to a$
4. $AB \to C$

Proof. See Appendix of [19].

Remark. We will call the rules of type 4 Reverse Super-Structuring (RSS).

In the next theorem we will strengthen our results by allowing only the renamings (REN) to be non unique. First we define what we mean by uniqueness and then we proceed to state and prove a lemma that will allow us to strengthen the Weak-GEN-ASNF by imposing uniqueness on all the productions safe renamings.

Definition (*strong-uniqueness*). We will say that a production $\alpha \to \beta$ respects *strong-uniqueness* if this is the only production that has the property that it has α in the LHS and also this is the only production that has β on the RHS.

Lemma 2. *Let $G = (N, T, S, R)$, $\epsilon \notin G$ a grammar such that all its productions are of the form:*

1. $A \rightarrow B$
2. $A \rightarrow \zeta$, $\zeta \notin N$
3. $\zeta \rightarrow B$, $\zeta \notin N$

Modify the the grammar G to obtain $G' = (N', T, S', R')$ as follows:

1. *Introduce a new start symbol S' and the production $S' \rightarrow S$.*
2. *For each $\zeta \notin N$ that appears in the RHS of one production in G let $\{A_i \rightarrow \zeta\}_{i=1,n}$ all the the productions that contain ζ in the RHS of a production. Introduce a new NonTerminal X_ζ and the productions $X_\zeta \rightarrow \zeta$ and $\{A_i \rightarrow X_\zeta\}_{i=1,n}$ and eliminate the old productions $\{A_i \rightarrow \zeta\}_{i=1,n}$.*
3. *For each $\zeta \notin N$ that appears in the LHS of one production in G let $\{\zeta \rightarrow B_j\}_{j=1,m}$ all the the productions that contain ζ the LHS of a production. Introduce a new NonTerminal Y_ζ and the productions $\zeta \rightarrow Y_\zeta$ and $\{Y_\zeta \rightarrow B_j\}_{j=1,m}$ and eliminate the old productions $\{\zeta \rightarrow B_j\}_{j=1,m}$.*

Then the new grammar G' generates the same language as the initial grammar G and all the productions of the form $A \rightarrow \zeta$ and $\zeta \rightarrow B$, $\zeta \notin N$ respect strong-uniqueness. Furthermore, if the initial grammar has some restrictions on the composition of the $\zeta \notin N$ that appears in the productions of type 2 and 3, they are respected since ζ is left unchanged in the productions of the new grammar and the only other types of productions introduced are renamings that are of neither type 2 nor type 3.

Proof. See Appendix of [19].

By applying Lemma 2 to the previous two Weak-ASNF theorems we obtain strong versions of these theorems which enforce *strong-uniqueness* in all the productions safe the renamings.

Theorem 4 (Strong-CFG-ASNF). *Let $G = (N, T, S, R)$, $\epsilon \notin L(G)$ be a Context Free Grammar. Then there exists a Context Free Grammar G' such that $L(G) = L(G')$ and G' contains only rules of the following type:*

1. $A \rightarrow B$
2. $A \rightarrow BC$ - *and this is the only rule that has BC in the RHS and this is the only rule that has A in the LHS (strong-uniqueness).*
3. $A \rightarrow a$ - *and this is the only rule that has a in the RHS and this is the only rule that has A in the LHS (strong-uniqueness).*

Proof. Apply Lemma 2 to the grammar converted into Weak-CFG-ASNF $\square$

Theorem 5 (Strong-GEN-ASNF). *Let $G = (N, T, S, R)$, $\epsilon \notin L(G)$ be a general (unrestricted) grammar. Then there exists a grammar G' such that $L(G) = L(G')$ and G' contains only rules of the following type:*

1. $A \rightarrow B$
2. $A \rightarrow BC$ - and this is the only rule that has BC in the RHS and this is the only rule that has A in the LHS (strong-uniqueness).
3. $A \rightarrow a$ - and this is the only rule that has a in the RHS and this is the only rule that has A in the LHS (strong-uniqueness).
4. $AB \rightarrow C$ - and this is the only rule that has C in the RHS and this is the only rule that has AB in the LHS (strong-uniqueness).

Proof. Apply Lemma 2 to the grammar converted into Weak-GEN-ASNF   □

Remark. After enforcing strong uniqueness the only productions that contain choice are those of type 1 - renamings (REN).

In the light of this theorem we proceed to introduce the concept of abstraction and prove some additional results.

2.4   Abstractions and Reverse Abstractions

Definitions (Abstractions Graph). Given a grammar $G = (N, T, S, R)$ which is in an ASNF from any of the Theorems 1 - 4 we call an *Abstractions Graph of the grammar* G and denote it by $AG(G)$ a Directed Graph $G = (N, E)$ whose nodes are the NonTerminals of the grammar G and whose edges are constructed as follows: we put a directed edge starting from A and ending in B iff $A \rightarrow B$ is a production that occurs in the grammar. Without loss of generality, we can assume that the graph has no self loops, i.e., edges of the form $A \rightarrow A$; If such self-loops exist, the corresponding productions can be eliminated from the grammar without altering the language. In such a directed graph a node A has a set of outgoing edges and a set of incoming edges which we refer to as out-edges and in-edges respectively. We will call a node A along with its out-edges the *Abstraction at* A and denote it $ABS(A) = \{A, OE_A = \{(A, B)|(A, B) \in E\}\}$. Similarly, we will call a node A along with its in-edges the *Reverse Abstraction at* A and denote it $RABS(A) = \{A, IE_A = \{(B, A)|(B, A) \in E\}\}$.

2.5   Grow Shrink Theorem

Theorem 6. *Let* $G = (N, T, S, R)$, $\epsilon \notin L(G)$ *be a General Grammar. Then we can convert such a grammar into the Strong-GEN-ASNF i.e., such that all the productions are of the following form:*

1. $A \rightarrow B$
2. $A \rightarrow BC$ - *and this is the only rule that has* BC *in the RHS and this is the only rule that has* A *in the LHS. (strong-uniqueness)*
3. $A \rightarrow a$ - *and this is the only rule that has* A *on the LHS and there is no other rule that has* a *on the RHS. (strong uniqueness)*
4. $AB \rightarrow C$ - *and this is the only rule that has* C *in the RHS and this is the only rule that has* AB *in the LHS. (strong-uniqueness)*

And furthermore for any derivation w *such that* $\gamma \overset{*}{\rightarrow} w$, *in* G, $\gamma \in N^+$ *there exists a derivation* $\gamma \overset{*}{\rightarrow} \mu \overset{*}{\rightarrow} \nu \overset{*}{\rightarrow} w$ *such that* $\mu \in N^+$, $\nu \in N^*$ *and* $\gamma \overset{*}{\rightarrow} \mu$

contains only rules of type 1 and 2 (REN, SS), $\mu \xrightarrow{*} \alpha$ *contains only rules of the type 1, more particularly only Reverse Abstractions and type 4 (REN(RABS), RSS) and* $\nu \xrightarrow{*} w$ *contains only rules of type 3 (TERMINAL).*

Proof. See Appendix of [19].

We have therefore proved that for each General Grammar G we can transform it in a Strong-GEN-ASNF such that the derivation (explanation in structural induction terminology) of any terminal string w can be organized in three phases such that: Phase 1 uses only productions that grow (or leave unchanged) the size of the intermediate string; Phase 2 uses only productions that shrink (or leave unchanged) the size of the intermediate string; and Phase 3 uses only TERMINAL productions[6]. In the case of grammars that are not in the normal form as defined above, the situation is a little more complicated because of successive applications of grow and shrink phases. However, we have shown that we can always transform an arbitrary grammar into one that in the normal form. Note further that the grow phase in both theorems use only context free productions.

We now proceed to examine the implications of the preceeding results in the larger context including the nature of hidden variables, radical positivism and the David Hume's principles of *connexion* among ideas.

3   The Fundamental Operations of Structural Induction

Recall that our notion of structural induction entails: Given a sequence of observations w we attempt to find a theory (grammar) that explains w and simultaneously also the explanation (derivation) $S \xrightarrow{*} w$. In a local way we may think that whenever we have a production rule $l \rightarrow r$ that l explains r. In a bottom up - data driven way we may proceed as follows: First introduce for every observable a a production $A \rightarrow a$. The role of these productions is simply to bring the observables into the realm of internal variables. The resulting association is between the observables and the corresponding internal variables unique (one to one and onto) and hence, once this association is established, we can forget about the existence of observables (Terminals). Since establishing these associations is the only role of the TERMINAL productions, they are not true structural operations. With this in mind, if we are to construct a theory in the GEN-ASNF we can postulate laws of the following form:

1. $A \rightarrow BC$ - Super-structuring (SS) which takes two internal variables B and C that occur within proximity of each other (adjacent) and labels the compound. Henceforth, the shorter name A can be used instead for BC. This is the sole role of super-structuring - to give a name to a composite structure to facilitate shorter explanations at latter stages.

---

[6] At first sight, it may seem that this construction offers a way to solve the halting problem. However, this is not the case, since we do not answer the question of deciding when to stop expanding the current string and start shrinking, which is key to solving the halting problem.

2. $A \rightarrow B|C$ - Abstraction (ABS). Introduces a name for the occurrence of either of the variables B or C. This allows for compactly representing two productions that are identical except that one uses B and the uses C by a single production using A. The role of Abstraction is to give a name to a group of entities (we have chosen two only for simplicity) in order to facilitate more general explanations at latter stages which in turn will produce more compact theories.

3. $AB \rightarrow C$ - Reverse Super-structuring (RSS) which introduces up to two existing or new internal variables that are close to each other (with respect to a specified topology) that together "explain" the internal variable C.

4. $A \rightarrow C, B \rightarrow C$ - Reverse Abstraction (RABS) which uses existing or new internal variables A and B as alternative explanations of the internal variable C (we have chosen two variables only for simplicity).

3.1 Reasons for Postulating Hidden Variables

Recall that are at least two types of reasons for creating Hidden Variables:

1. (**OR** type) - [multiple alternative hidden causes] The OR type corresponds to the case when some visible effect can have multiple hidden causes $H1 \rightarrow Effect, H2 \rightarrow Effect$. In our setting, this case corresponds to Reverse Abstraction. One typical example of this is: The grass is wet, and hence either it rained last night or the sprinkler was on. In the statistical and machine learning literature the models that use this type of hidden variables are called mixture models [9].

2. (**T-AND** type) - [multiple concurrent hidden causes] The T-AND type, i.e., topological AND type, of which the AND is a sepcial case. This corresponds to the case when one visible effect has two hidden causes both of which have to occur within proximity of each other (with respect to a specified topology) in order to produce the visible effect. $H1H2 \rightarrow Effect$. In our setting, this corresponds to Reverse Super-structuring. In the Statistical / Graphical Models literature the particular case of AND hidden explanations is the one that introduces edges between hidden variables in the dependence graph [5], [9], [11].

The preceding discussion shows that we can associate with two possible reasons for creating hidden variables, the structural operations of Reverse Abstraction and Reverse Super Structuring respectively. Because these are the only two types of productions that introduce hidden variables in the GEN-ASNF this provides a characterization of the rationales for introducing hidden variables.

3.2 Radical Positivism

If we rule out the use of RSS and RABS, the only operations that involve the postulation of hidden variables, we are left with only SS and ABS which corresponds to the radical positivist [1] stance under the computationalist assumption. An explanation of a stream of observations w in the Radical Positivist theory of the world is mainly a theory of how the observables in the world are grouped into classes (Abstractions) and how smaller chunks of observations are tied together into bigger ones (Super-Structures). The laws of the radical positivist theory are truly empirical laws as they only address relations among observations.

However, structural induction, if it is constrained to using only ABS and SS, the class of theories that can be induced is necessarily a subset of the set of theories that can be described by Turing Machines. More precisely, the resulting grammars will be a strict subset of Context Free Grammars, (since CFG contain SS, and REN(ABS+RABS)). Next we will examine how any theory of the world may look like from the most general perspective when we do allow Hidden Variables.

3.3   General Theories of the World

If structural induction is allowed to take advantage of RSS and RABS in addition to SS and ABS, the resulting theories can make use of hidden variables. Observations are a derivative byproduct obtained from a richer hidden variable state description by a reduction: either of size - performed by Reverse SuperStructuring or of information - performed by Reverse Abstraction. Note that, while in general, structural induction can alternate several times between REN+SS and RABS+RSS, we have shown that three phases suffice: a growth phase (REN+SS); a shrink phase (RABS+RSS); and a Terminal phase. Whether we can push all the RABS from the first phase into the second phase and make the first phase look like the one in the radical positivist stance (only ABS+SS) remains an open question (See Appendix of [19] for a Conjecture to this effect).

3.4   Hume's Principles of Connexion among Ideas

We now examine, against the backdrop of GEN-ASNF theorem, a statement made by philosopher David Hume more that 2 centuries ago: *"I do not find that any philosopher has attempted to enumerate or class all the principles of association [of ideas]. ... To me, there appear to be only three principles of connexion among ideas, namely, Resemblance, Contiguity in time or place, and Cause and Effect" [6]*. If we substitute Resemblance with Abstraction (since abstraction is triggered by resemblance or similarity), Contiguity in time or place with Super-Structuring (since proximity, e.g., spatio-temporal proximity drives Super-Structuring) and Cause and Effect with the two types of explanations that utilize hidden variables, it is easy to see that the GEN-ASNF theorem is simply a precise restatement of Hume's claim under the computationalist assumption.

4   Summary

We have shown that *abstraction* (grouping *similar* entities) and super-structuring (combining topologically e.g., spatio-temporally close entities) as the essential structural operations in the induction process. A structural induction process that relies only on abstraction and super-structuring corresponds to the radical positivist stance. We have shown that only two more structural operations, namely, *reverse abstraction* and *reverse super-structuring* (the duals of abstraction and super-structuring respectively) (a) suffice in order to exploit the full power of Turing-equivalent generative grammars in induction; and (b) operationalize two rationales for the introduction of hidden variables into theories of the world. The GEN-ASNF theorem can be seen as simply a restatement, under the computationalist assumption, of Hume's 2-century old claim regarding the principles of connexion among ideas.

References

1. Ayer, A.J.: Language, Truth, and Logic, 2nd edn. Gollancz, London (1936, 1946)
2. Burgin, M.: Super-Recursive Algorithms. Springer (2005)
3. Carnap, R.: An introduction to the Philosophy of Science. Basic Books (1966)
4. Chomsky, N.: Syntactic Structures. Mouton, The Hague (1957)
5. Elidan, G., Friedman, N.: Learning Hidden Variable Networks: The Information Bottleneck Approach. Journal of Machine Learning Research (JMLR) 6, 81–127 (2005)
6. Hume, D.: An Enquiry Concerning Human Understanding. Hackett Publ. Co. (1993)
7. Hutter, M.: Universal Artificial Intelligence: Sequential Decisions based on Algorithmic Probability. EATCS. Springer (2005)
8. Kuroda, S.-Y.: Classes of languages and linear-bounded automata. Information and Control 7(2), 207–223 (1964)
9. Lauritzen, S.L.: Graphical Models. Clarendon Press, Oxford (1996)
10. Oates, T., Armstrong, T., Harris, J., Nejman, M.: On the Relationship Between Lexical Semantics and Syntax for the Inference of Context-Free Grammars. In: Proceedings of the 19th National Conference on Artificial Intelligence (AAAI), pp. 431–436 (2004)
11. Pearl, J.: Probabilistic Reasoning in Intelligent Systems. Morgan Kaufmann Publishers (1988)
12. Popper, K.R.: The Logic of Scientific Discovery, English ed. Basic Books (1934, 1959)
13. Salomaa, A.: Computation and Automata. Cambridge University Press (1985)
14. Savitch, W.: How to make arbitrary grammars look like context-free grammars. SIAM Journal on Computing 2, 174–182 (1973)
15. Schmidhuber, J., Zhao, J., Wiering, M.: Shifting Bias with Success Story Algorithm. Machine Learning 28, 105–130 (1997)
16. Solomonoff, R.: A Formal Theory of Inductive Inference, Part I. Information and Control 7(1), 1–22 (1964)
17. Solomonoff, R.: A Formal Theory of Inductive Inference, Part II. Information and Control 7(2), 224–254 (1964)
18. Turing, A.: On computable numbers with an application to the Entscheuidungsproblem. Proc. Lond. Math. Soc. 2(42), 230–265 (1936)
19. Silvescu, A., Honavar, V.: Abstraction Super-structuring Normal Forms: Towards a Computationalist Theory of Structural Induction. Technical Report. Department of Computer Science. Iowa State University (2011), http://arxiv.org/abs/1107.0434
20. Wallace, Dowe: Minimum Message Length and Kolmogorov complexity. Computer Journal (1999)

Locating a Discontinuity in a Piecewise-Smooth Periodic Function Using Bayes Estimation

Alex Solomonoff

Camberville Research Institute, Somerville, Mass., 02143

Abstract. A method is presented for locating a jump discontinuity in an otherwise-smooth function from its first few Fourier coefficients. It is based on a statistical model for otherwise-smooth functions and Bayes estimation, similar to and based on the work in [3]. Numerical results are presented, showing respectable performance, and comparing it to the jump locating algorithm of [1].

Fig. 1. Ray Solomonoff at his home in Arlington, Mass., USA, June 2008, a few days after cataract surgery. The fez was a gift, received on a visit to the North Lebanon campus (in Koura) of Notre Dame University in Lebanon, in March 2008. Ray was invited to visit NDU by Fouad Chedid.

1 Introduction

This paper studies the problem of determining the location of a discontinuity in a function $f(x)$ with, say $f : [-1, 1] \to \mathbb{R}$, when several of $f(x)$'s Fourier coefficients are known. This problem has been addressed before by Gelb and Tadmor[1][2]. Here we present a quite different approach to the problem, based on Bayesian/statistical ideas.

Many phenomena of interest to mathematics and science involve functions that are only piecewise smooth, and it is not uncommon for our information

D.L. Dowe (Ed.): Solomonoff Festschrift, LNAI 7070, pp. 351–365, 2013.

about them to consist of Fourier coefficients. The problem that motivated this work is numerically approximating equations of supersonic gas flow using spectral methods[9]. The function might be density or temperature of the air vs. position in space, and the jumps are shock waves. Another example is CAT scanning of a medical patient, where the information measured by the scanner is closely related to Fourier coefficients and every boundary between one type of tissue and another is a jump discontinuity.

In either case, the function $f(x)$ to be reconstructed is smooth and simple, except for small number of jump discontinuities. If $f(x)$ were completely smooth without discontinuities, then it could be easily approximated from a few of its Fourier coefficients by the partial sum

$$f(x) \approx f_N(x) = \sum_{k=-N}^{N} \hat{f}_k e^{ik\pi x}. \tag{1}$$

This partial sum converges to $f(x)$ rapidly as N increases *if $f(x)$ is smooth*. But if $f(x)$ has any jump discontinuities, then *no matter how smooth and simple it is away from the jumps*, $f_N(x)$ converges to $f(x)$ very slowly, see [9], section 2.2.

And yet, if $f(x)$ is smooth and simple except for a small number of jumps, the total complexity of it is small, and intuitively one would expect that an accurate way of reconstructing $f(x)$ from a few Fourier coefficients must exist. But equation (1) is not it.

Approaches for doing this reconstruction have been developed by Gottlieb, Gelb and others, for example [11]. In 1992, I developed a system [3] for doing this reconstruction using Bayes estimation, which was quite successful. The current work is based on this.

Two Kinds of Probability. In the more familiar kind of probability, an object comes from some random source, and each type of object has some probability of emanating from the source.

In the second, the situation is deterministic, but only partly known to the observer. Here, a probability distribution for an event is a description of the observer's knowledge of the situation. The canonical example is the weather report. When it says there is a 40% chance of rain today, there is no randomness to the weather. A 40% chance means that if the weatherman were a betting man, he would accept a bet that it would rain if and only if the odds were 3 to 2 or higher.

Probabilities in the shock locating system are of the second type. Bayesian analysis can be done on events with either type of probability. In the second case, a "correct" probability distribution is any one that contains most or all of the observer's knowledge of the system, and in some way does not make any further assumptions.

If all or most of the observer's information can be encoded in the mean and variance of the probability distribution, then a Gaussian distribution is attractive, because of the "no further assumptions" issue. In [10] it is proven that among probability distributions having a given mean and variance, the Gaussian distribution has the largest entropy. This can be interpreted as saying that a Gaussian makes the fewest "further assumptions".

Relationship to Algorithmic Probability. Ray Solomonoff's [12] Algorithmic Probability theory is based on a somewhat similar foundation, in that the events or observations being predicted by AP are deterministic, not random. The Universial A Priori Probability Distribution employed in AP is derived from a belief that the universe has structure and can be described by rules, *not* derived from frequencies of events.

Function Reconstruction. In the function reconstruction algorithm of [3] the observations were the first n Fourier coefficients of $f(x)$, the approximate function source $\mathcal{S}'$ was an infinite-dimensional Gaussian distribution, and the thing to be estimated was $f(x)$ itself. $\mathcal{S}'$ was constructed so that typical functions drawn from it were smooth everywhere except at one specified point. Then $f(x)$ was estimated in the usual Bayes way as the conditional expectation of $f(x)$ given the Fourier coefficients, under the probability distribution of $\mathcal{S}'$.

This approach is familiar, even trivial in the world of statistics and probability, (see, for example[5]) but much less familiar in the world of numerical analysis.

It worked quite well for estimating a function. The computations were somewhat laborious, but not conceptually difficult. They consisted mostly of standard matrix operations – products, inverses, etc, and were nicely carried out by LAPACK subroutines.

The fact that the location of the singularity needed to be known a priori was a nagging detail that reduced it's usefulness. This paper presents a method for locating the discontinuity that builds on that previous work.

Conceptually the method is simple:

1. Instead of a single Gaussian distribution, a mixture of Gaussians is used, each identical except that the discontinuity is in a different location.
2. When the distribution is conditioned on the Fourier coefficients, each Gaussian member of the mixture has an a posteriori probability.
3. This posterior probability is a probability distribution for the location of the discontinuity.

Function reconstruction using a system such as [3] or [11] can then be done. The simplest way to proceed is to pick the point most likely to be the discontinuity, and use existing function reconstruction methods based on this assumption. More subtle ways of working with the posterior will not be considered here.

We are only considering the situation where the function to be considered is periodic, has *exactly* one jump discontinuity and is smooth otherwise. Gelb and Tadmor's technique had the advantage of not requiring exactly one jump, but that is a topic for another paper. Like their work, we assume that the first k Fourier coefficients of the function are known.

Table of Contents

2   Mathematical Preliminaries

Random Functions

We will work with random sources of objects. Some sources dispense scalars, others vectors, still others functions $f : \mathbb{R} \to \mathbb{R}$. Let $\mathcal{S}$ be such a random source. **Notation:** The operation of getting a (particular) function from $\mathcal{S}$ is written as $f \leftarrow \mathcal{S}$. The notation $f \sim \mathcal{S}$ means that f is a random variable taken from $\mathcal{S}$.

$\mathrm{cov}(f) = \mathrm{cov}(\mathcal{S})$ is the covariance matrix of $\mathcal{S}$, defined as the (infinite) matrix (or linear operator) $\mathrm{cov}(f) = E\left((f - \bar{f})(f - \bar{f})^H\right)$. The mean of f is $\bar{f} = E(f)$.

The probability, or probability density of a particular function f being dispensed by $\mathcal{S}$ is written $\mathcal{S}(f)$ or $p(\mathcal{S}, f)$. If $\mathcal{S}$ depends on some parameters we write $\mathcal{S}(\alpha, \beta, \ldots)$ and $\mathcal{S}(f; \alpha, \beta, \ldots)$ for the probability.

Finite Set vs. Density Function vs. Measure. In the case of a source from a finite set, each element of the set has some generally-positive probability. For a source from a finite-dimensional vector space, there is a probability density function. For a source of functions or infinite-dimensional vectors, it is a measure. To keep from diluting the focus of the paper, most functional-analysis-related issues will be ignored. In that respect the presentation will be very casual.

2.1   Gaussian Distributions

A finite-dimensional Gaussian distribution $\mathcal{N}(\mu, C)$ with mean μ and covariance matrix C has the well-known [5] probability density

$$p(x) = \mathcal{N}(x; \mu, C) \equiv \frac{1}{\sqrt{(2\pi)^n \det C}} \exp\{-\frac{1}{2}(x - \mu)^t C^{-1}(x - \mu)\}. \qquad (2)$$

It can be shown fairly simply that for any matrix M, if $p(x) = \mathcal{N}(x, \mu, C)$, and $y = Mx$ then

$$p(y) = \mathcal{N}(y; M\mu, M^t CM). \qquad (3)$$

2.2   Gaussian Random Functions

Consider a smooth, nonperiodic function $f(x)$ defined on (say) the interval $[-1, 1]$. It has Legendre coefficients

$$\tilde{f}_m = (\mathcal{L}f)_m = \int_{-1}^{1} P_m(x)f(x)dx,$$

where $P_m(x)$ is the m-th Legendre polynomial (See [8] chapter 22.) and we call $\mathcal{L}$ the Legendre transform operator. Since $f(x)$ is smooth, these coefficients decay to zero rapidly. (See, for example [9], chapter 2.)

If f satisfies some extremely mild smoothness conditions then $f(x)$ can be written in terms of $\tilde{f}$:

$$f(x) = \left(\mathcal{L}^{-1}\tilde{f}\right)(x) = \sum_{m=0}^{\infty} \tilde{f}_m P_m(x).$$

A reasonable way of specifying a probability distribution for smooth functions would be to say that the Legendre coefficients are independent Gaussian random variables, and that each has zero mean and a specified variance σ_m. The smoothness of these functions can be expressed by making the variances decay rapidly to zero as m increases.

Then such a random function is constructed by

$$\tilde{f}_m \leftarrow \mathcal{N}(0, \sigma_m), \quad f(x) = \sum_{m=0}^{\infty} \tilde{f}_m P_m(x).$$

This can be written in a more all-at-once way as

$$\tilde{f} \sim \mathcal{N}(0, C),$$

where C is the diagonal matrix $C = \text{diag}\left(\{\sigma_m\}_{m=0}^{\infty}\right)$.

We need to choose C somehow. The choice

$$\sigma_m = \alpha^m, \quad \text{for some } 0 < \alpha < 1,$$

corresponds to functions that are analytic, and the distance between $[-1, 1]$ and the nearest singularity in the complex plane is some function of α. See [9], sections 2.11 and 2.13 for more details.

Diagonal Covariance Matrix. The intuition behind using a diagonal covariance matrix comes from the Proper Orthogonal Decomposition. If random functions are expanded in terms of the eigenfunctions of their covariance matrix, the convergence of the expansion is faster than any other set of basis functions, and the coefficients of the expansion are uncorrelated.

If the random functions are expanded in the fastest-known-converging set of basis functions, and the coefficients are *still* correlated, then there is another basis set, possessing even faster convergence. By assumption, this basis set is unknown, and so using a covariance matrix that is not diagonal violates the "no further assumptions" rule.

Circular Domain: There are two different ways the domain interval $[-1, 1]$ can be considered. In the first, -1 and 1 are at the opposite ends of the domain, and functions from the probability above are smooth. Call this domain $\mathcal{I}$. In the other, we wrap the interval around a circle so that -1 and 1 touch each other at the back of the circle, and connect them together there. Now the functions from the probability above are *periodic*, and smooth except for a discontinuity at ± 1. Call this version of the domain $\mathcal{C}$. So if $f(1) = f(-1)$ then f is continuous in $\mathcal{C}$.

2.3   Matrices

Suppose we have the (infinite vector of) Legendre coefficients $\tilde{f}$ of the function $f(x)$, and the vector of Fourier coefficients $\hat{f}$ of the same function is needed. There is an infinite matrix A_∞ such that $\hat{f} = A_\infty \tilde{f}$.

A_∞ is a unitary matrix. If we want only the first few Fourier coefficients of $f(x)$ then we use a finite strip of A_∞ corresponding to only the $-n, \ldots, n$ Fourier modes:

$$\hat{f}_N = A\tilde{f}.$$

The matrix A was examined at length in [3]. Its elements are

$$A_{km} = \int_{-1}^{1} P_m(x) e^{i\pi k x} dx = i^m \sqrt{\frac{m + 1/2}{k}} J_{m+\frac{1}{2}}(\pi k),$$

where $k \in -N, \ldots, N$ and $m \in 0, \ldots, \infty$. $J_n(x)$ is a Bessel function of the first kind, (See for example, [8] chapter 10.)

So if the Gaussian probability for the Legendre coefficients of a random function is

$$p(\tilde{f}) = \mathcal{N}(\tilde{f}, 0, C),$$

then by (3) the probability for the Fourier coefficients is

$$p(\hat{f}_N = A\tilde{f}) = \mathcal{N}(\hat{f}_N, 0, ACA^H).$$

2.4   Periodic Functions and Rotation

Let R_d be the linear operator that rotates a function a distance d around $\mathcal{C}$ so

$$(R_d f)(x) = f(x - d).$$

By "rotating around in $\mathcal{C}$" is meant that if $x - d$ is outside the interval $[-1, 1]$ then we wrap around to the other side of the domain:

$$r(x, d) = \begin{cases} x - d - 2 & \text{if } x - d > 1 \\ x - d + 2 & \text{if } x - d < -1 \\ x - d & \text{otherwise} \end{cases} \tag{4}$$

so more precisely

$$(R_d f)(x) = f\big(r(x, d)\big).$$

This operator has an analog in Fourier space:

$$\hat{R}_d \hat{f} = \{\omega^{dk} \hat{f}_k\}_k,$$

where $\omega^d = e^{i\pi d}$. So $\hat{R}_d$ is an (infinite) diagonal matrix

$$\hat{R}_d = \text{diag}(\{\omega^{dk}\}_k).$$

The point of this section is that if

$$p(\hat{f}_N = A\tilde{f}) = \mathcal{N}(\hat{f}; 0, ACA^H)$$

is the probability for the Fourier coefficients of otherwise-smooth periodic functions with a discontinuity at ± 1, *then* by (3) the probability for the Fourier coefficients of functions with a discontinuity at some other location $r(1, d)$ is

$$p(\hat{R}_d\hat{f}_N) = \mathcal{N}(\hat{R}_d\hat{f}_N; 0, \hat{R}_d ACA^H \hat{R}_d^H).$$

Mixtures of Gaussians. A mixture is a source whose probability is a linear combination of the probabilities of some set of other sources.

Suppose have a set of random sources of functions $\{S_d\}_d$, where d ranges over some index set K. and a separate random source N of indices from K. Then the probability of the mixture $\mathcal{M}(\{S_d\}, N)$ is

$$\mathcal{M}(f; \{S\}, N) = \sum_{d \in K} S_d(f)N(d).$$

Dispensing a function $f \leftarrow \mathcal{M}$ is a two-step process: 1) $d \leftarrow N$,   2) $f \leftarrow S_d$.

Mixture for the Shock Locator. The particular mixture of interest is where S_d is a random source of periodic functions that are smooth except for a jump at $x = d$ and N is a random source of points d in the circle $\mathcal{C}$.

Distribution of d: Given a function f drawn from $\mathcal{M}(\{S_d\}, N)$, the probability that a given value of d occurred during the drawing is given by Bayes rule:

$$p(d|f, \mathcal{M}) = \frac{p(f|d)p(d)}{\sum_{d'} p(f|d')p(d')}.$$

If we are only interested in the most likely d, then the normalizing factor in the denominator can be ignored, giving

$$d_{\text{most likely}} = \arg\max_d p(f|d)p(d) = \arg\max_d S_d(f)N(d). \tag{5}$$

3   The Shock Locating Algorithm

Our source for Legendre vector of a random function with a discontinuity at ± 1 is $\mathcal{N}(0, C)$. The Fourier coefficients of the same functions come from the random Gaussian source $\mathcal{N}(0, ACA^H)$. The Fourier coefficients of functions with a discontinuity at $r(1, d)$ come from the Gaussian source $S_d = \mathcal{N}(0, \hat{R}_d ACA^H \hat{R}_d^H)$.

The random function source we want is the mixture

$$\mathcal{M}(\{S_d\}_{d \in \mathcal{C}}, \mathcal{K}),$$

where $\mathcal{K}$ is some source of random points on the circle. (uniform in the simplest case)

Then from Bayes rule, the likelihood that a function with Fourier coefficients $\hat{f}_N$ came from a smooth function with a discontinuity at $r(1, d)$ is

$$p(d|\hat{f}_N) = \frac{1}{Z}\mathcal{N}(\hat{f}_N;\ 0,\ \hat{R}_d ACA^H \hat{R}_d^H)p(d), \qquad (6)$$

where Z is the normalizing factor from Bayes Rule. $p(d)$ is a prior probability that the discontinuity occurred at a location $r(1, d)$. This is a user-supplied quantity. Assuming a uniform probability distribution for d gives

$$p(d|\hat{f}_N) = \frac{1}{Z}\mathcal{N}(\hat{f}_N;\ 0,\ \hat{R}_d ACA^H \hat{R}_d^H).$$

As noted before,

$$\mathcal{N}(\hat{f}_N; 0, M) = \frac{1}{\sqrt{(2\pi)^n \det M}}\exp\{-\frac{1}{2}\hat{f}_N^H M^{-1}\hat{f}_N\},$$

where $M = \hat{R}_d ACA^H \hat{R}_d^H$. Note that $\det M$ does not depend on d because R_d is unitary and $\det R_d M R_d^H = \det M R_d^H R_d = \det M$. So $p(d|\hat{f}_N)$ can be written as

$$p(d|\hat{f}_N) = \frac{1}{Z_2}\exp\{-\frac{1}{2}\hat{f}_N^H(\hat{R}_d ACA^H \hat{R}_d^H)^{-1}\hat{f}_N\}.$$

As a further simplification, $\hat{R}_d$ is invertible and $\hat{R}_d^{-1} = \hat{R}_d^H$, so

$$p(d|\hat{f}_N) = \frac{1}{Z_2}\exp\{-\frac{1}{2}(\hat{R}_d^H \hat{f}_N)^H(ACA^H)^{-1}(\hat{R}_d^H \hat{f}_N)\}. \qquad (7)$$

If we just want to find the most likely location for the shock, then exponential in 7 can be ignored, which gives us

$$x_{most\ likely} = \arg\min_d(\hat{R}_d^H \hat{f}_N)^H(ACA^H)^{-1}(\hat{R}_d^H \hat{f}_N)\}. \qquad (8)$$

This is the the point of most likely rotation, but the actual shock is on the opposite side of the circle, which gives the *statistical shock locater* (SSL)

$$x_{SSL} = r\left(\arg\min_d(\hat{R}_d^H \hat{f}_N)^H(ACA^H)^{-1}(\hat{R}_d^H \hat{f}_N), 1\right). \qquad (9)$$

Given $(ACA^H)^{-1}$, it takes $O(n^2)$ operations to evaluate $p(d|\hat{f}_N)$ for each value of d, and many evaluations would be needed to locate the most likely d. This is rather a lot, but faster methods seem possible and are a topic of future work.

Noise and Ill-Conditioning. It may happen that the input/observed Fourier coefficients of f have been contaminated with noise. It may also happen that the matrix (ACA^H) is badly conditioned. A modification of our algorithm can deal with both problems.

Let $\hat{f}_N = \hat{n} + \hat{f}_{clean}$. The covariance matrix of $\hat{f}_{clean}$ is (ACA^H). The noise $\hat{n}$ has its own covariance matrix, and if the noise is independent of the function, the covariance matrix for the sum $\hat{f}_N$ is just the sum of the covariance matrices. So

$$\text{cov}(\hat{f}_N) = ACA^H + \text{cov}(\hat{n}).$$

The simplest characterization of the noise is $\text{cov}(\hat{n}) = \epsilon^2 I$. If the eigenvalues of ACA^H are $\{\lambda^2\}_i$, and some of the λ are tiny, then the corresponding eigenvalues of the inverse matrix $\text{cov}(\hat{f}_N)^{-1}$ are $1/(\lambda^2 + \epsilon^2)$, which can greatly relax the ill-conditioning of $\text{cov}(\hat{f}_N)$ if it is ill-conditioned.

4   Experimental Results

The first test function is one heavily used by Gelb & Tadmor in [1][2]:

$$f_a(x) = \begin{cases} \sin \frac{\pi}{2}(x+1) & x \in [-1,0) \\ \sin \frac{\pi}{2}(3x-1) & x \in (0,1] \end{cases}$$

Note that this function, in addition to having a discontinuity at $x = 0$, also has a jump in the derivative at $x = \pm 1$. As such it does not fully obey the single-discontinuity assumption that our work depends on, and our shock locater is less likely to work well than a fully-smooth function.

Figure 2. In this picture we have used 19 Fourier modes (10 cosine + 9 sine), and a diagonal, exponentially-decaying covariance matrix for the Legendre modes — $C_{mm} = \alpha^m$, suitable for analytic functions; the precise degree of smoothness is controlled by α. We have used $\alpha = 0.9$, a number picked somewhat at random. We have assumed that a bit of noise was added to the Fourier coefficients, with $\text{cov}(\hat{n}) = 10^{-10} I$. but no noise was actually added to $\hat{f}_N$. All computations were done using double precision arithmetic. Linear algebraic computations were done using LAPACK[6]. Bessel functions were computed using the Gnu Scientific Library[7].

Gelb's function f_a was used as a test function, after rotating it a bit to bring both discontinuities into the interior of the domain. The probability of discontinuity was scaled so the maximum value was 1.0.

In the figure we can see that the shock locator's computed probability has a single, fairly narrow spike, whose peak is quite close to the actual discontinuity. The most likely location was calculated to be $x = 0.695$, and the actual discontinuity was at $x = 0.7$. This error is much smaller than the width of oscillations (about 0.1) in the Fourier approximation of f_a. The width of the peak – about 0.015 – is also much smaller than the width of the Fourier oscillations. Note that the error in shock location is comparable to the width of the peak.

So in this case we have excellent performance, in spite of the assumption-violating presence of the secondary discontinuity.

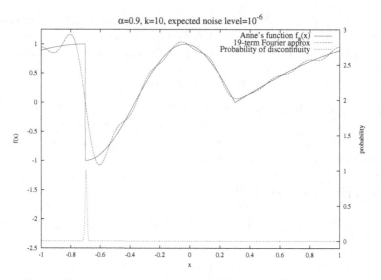

Fig. 2. Test function and calculated likelihood of discontinuity

Figure 3: Convergence. The test function

$$f_{\arctan}(x) = \tan^{-1}\left(a(x - b)\right)$$

has a shear layer of width $O(1/a)$ at $x = b$, and a jump discontinuity at $x = \pm 1$, so the distance between the shear layer and the discontinuity is $|1 - |b||$.

This picture examines the convergence of the most likely jump location to the true location as k is increased. $k = 10, 20, 40.$ were used. The purpose of these values was that there should be enough information in the Fourier coefficients to reconstruct the test function with reasonable accuracy.

Figure 3 shows that, as k increases, the accuracy of shock location increases fairly rapidly, but it is not clear exactly how fast. For small b it seems faster than polynomial and for b near 1 it seems slower than polynomial. Averaging over b, it seems that doubling k gives about a 10-fold reduction in error, which is approximately $\text{err} = O(k^{-3.2})$.

Conjecture 1: If there are enough Fourier coefficients to resolve the function with reasonable accuracy, then the shock locater works well, giving fairly rapid convergence to the true shock location, and is not too sensitive to the smoothness parameter α. But, if there are *not* enough Fourier coefficients to resolve the function, then the shock locater still works, but convergence is slower, and it is intolerant of any poor choice of α.

Conjecture 2: If k is small, then the shock locater is not fussy about the choice of α, but as k increases, it becomes more particular.

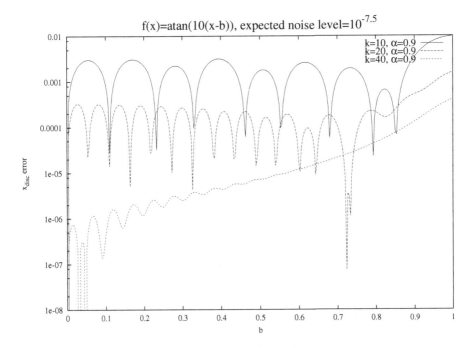

Fig. 3. Error in jump location for the shear layer function f_{arctan} as b and k vary

5   The Concentration Shock Locater

In [1] and [2] Gelb and Tadmor developed methods of estimating the *jump function* of a function from its truncated Fourier series. The jump function was defined as

$$(Jf)(x) = \lim_{\epsilon \to 0} f(x + \epsilon) - f(x - \epsilon).$$

At points of continuity $Jf(x) = 0$ and at jump discontinuities $Jf(x)$ is the height of the jump. Suppose we write $J_k f$ as the estimated jump function, using the $-k, \ldots, k$ Fourier coefficients. They converted this into a jump locater by simply taking the point of largest value of the estimated jump function:

$$x_{\mathrm{shock}} = \arg \max_x |(J_n f)(x)|$$

or, if multiple jumps were expected, by taking all the points at which the estimated jump function exceeded a preset threshold:

$$\{x_{\mathrm{shock}}\} = \{x : |(J_n f)(x)| > \tau\}.$$

They considered several different approximate jump functions, all of the form

$$J_n f(x) = \sum_{k=1}^{N} \sigma_k \big(c_k \sin(k\pi x) + s_k \cos(k\pi x) \big),$$

where c_k and s_k are the Fourier coefficients:

$$f(x) = c_0 + \sum_{k=0}^{\infty} c_k \cos(k\pi x) + \sin(k\pi x).$$

They called approximate jump functions of this type *concentration filters*, since the emphasis was that the energy of the filtered function was to be concentrated near the jump.

The σ_k were a set of carefully-scaled and generally increasing-with-k coefficients. They examined many choices of σ_k, but one of the better-performing choices was simply

$$\sigma_k = \frac{k}{N},$$

which is simply the Fourier spectral approximation of the derivative. The coefficients have to be scaled carefully to get the correct size of the jump, but for simply locating the jump, the scaling does not matter.

This gives the *Concentration Shock Locater* (CSL)

$$x_{CSL} = \arg\max_x |\frac{d}{dx}\mathcal{F}_N f(x)|, \qquad (10)$$

where $\mathcal{F}_N f$ is the N-Fourier-term approximation of f.

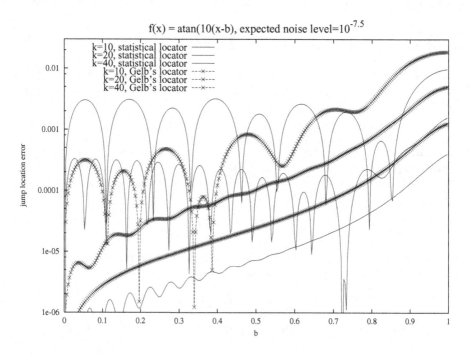

Fig. 4. Error in jump location for the shear layer function f_{arctan} as b and k vary. Both the statistical and concentration locater are shown

5.1   Experimental Comparison of the CSL and SSL

I expected the SSL to perform much better than Gelb and Tadmor's very simple locater. This did not happen, which was disappointing. Cases where the SSL was better do exist, but it required a bit of parameter tweaking to find them .

Convergence to the correct shock location for the SSL as $k \to \infty$ appears faster than the CSL, but for small k and difficult functions, the CSL locater is better.

It may be a resolution issue. If there isn't enough information in the Fourier coefficients to resolve the function, the SSL is not as good as the CSL. If it isn't resolving the function, then it can't really tell what is a shock and what isn't. The CSL somehow avoids this problem.

Figure 4. This picture displays the accuracy of shock location for a function with a moderate-thickness shear layer, $f(x) = \tan^{-1}(10(x - b))$. We show both the statistical locater and CSL for $k = 10, 20, 40$, to give some picture of the convergence behavior. The picture is rather busy, but

1. For small k, the concentration shock locater is better.
2. The statistical locater converges more quickly than the CSL, and for larger k it is better.
3. As the shear layer moves towards the shock (b increasing) the statistical locater gets better compared to the concentration locater.

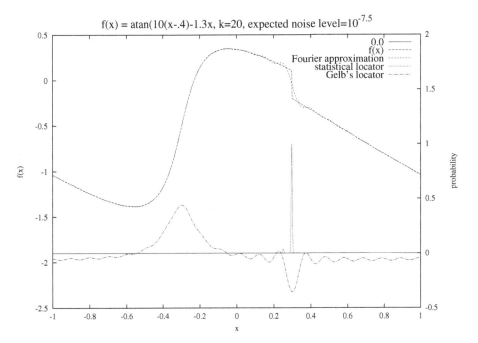

Fig. 5. Shock locater output for the troublesome function. Both the statistical and concentration locater are shown.

4. Both shock locator's get worse, in absolute terms, as the shear layer moves towards the shock.
5. Neither locater is dramatically better than the other.

Figure 5. One test function which I expected to give the CSL problems was a function with a tall thin shear layer and a much tinier jump discontinuity:

$$f_{\text{trouble}}(x) = \tan^{-1}(a(x - b)) - cx, \tag{11}$$

with c chosen to cancel most, but not all of the jump discontinuity at $x = \pm 1$. Figure 5 examines a function which fools the concentration shock locater but not the statistical one. The function source smoothness parameter was set at $\alpha = 0.9$. A certain amount of parameter tweaking was needed to achieve this case.

6   Discussion and Conclusions

Peak Widths and Scaling. For the CSL, the minimum width of a peak of $|\mathcal{F}_N f(x)|$ is $O(1/N)$. A reasonable conclusion to jump to would be that the typical error in the predicted jump location would also be $O(1/N)$. But this is not the case; the error is much smaller. It is clearly true that the CSL could not possibly deal with two sharp features that were closer than $O(1/N)$ apart, because of the minimum peak width. It is also clearly true that the peak width and the error of predicted shock location are unrelated. The peak width cannot be used as an error estimator.

For the SSL, the width of a peak of $p(d|\hat{f}_N)$ is often much narrower than $O(1/N)$. There is no intrinsic limit to the narrowness of the peak. In addition, at least some of the time, the peak width is comparable to the error of the predicted jump location, and so the peak width *can* be used as an error estimator.

Resolution of the Function. I have conjectured that if the function is "resolved" then the statistical shock locater works well, and if it is not resolved it works less well, but I haven't said what that means. Presumably if there are n Fourier coefficients, and the function can be reconstructed accurately enough by n terms of a Legendre polynomial expansion (with the domain properly rotated around the jump), then it is "resolved". Or it is resolved if the statistical filter[3] can accurately reconstruct the function from n Fourier coefficients.

I conjectured that if the function was not resolved, then the statistical shock locater was fussy about requiring the correct value of α. The intuition behind this this is that α is a piece of information relevant to the function, in addition to the Fourier coefficients. If the Fourier coefficients have "enough" information, then α is not used very much. If not, α is used more, and if it is wrong, the output of the locater is wrong.

Gelb and Tadmor's shock locater does not seem to require that the function be resolved in any way. Why not? This seems like an advantage.

Final Conclusions. We have presented a method of locating a jump in an otherwise-smooth function. It works reasonably well and surpasses the CSL in some situations, but does not clearly surpass it overall.

It is based on the ideas of the statistical filter[3] and since it works reasonably well, this makes the statistical filter itself look more plausible and interesting than it would otherwise.

References

1. Gelb, A., Tadmor, E.: Detection Of Edges in Spectral Data. Applied And Computational Harmonic Analysis 7, 101–135 (1999)
2. Gelb, A., Tadmor, E.: Detection Of Edges in Spectral Data II. Nonlinear Enhancement. SIAM J. Numer. Anal. 38, 1389–1408 (2000)
3. Solomonoff, A.: Reconstruction of a Discontinuous Function From a Few Fourier Coefficients Using Bayesian Estimation. J. Sci. Comput. 10(1) (1995)
4. Golub, G.H., Van Loan, C.F.: Matrix Computations, 2nd edn. Johns Hopkins University Press (1989)
5. Duda, R.O., Hart, P.E.: Pattern Classification And Scene Analysis. Wiley Interscience (1973)
6. Anderson, E., Bai, Z., Bischof, C., Blackford, S., Demmel, J., Dongarra, J., Du Croz, J., Greenbaum, A., Hammarling, S., McKenney, A., Sorensen, D.: LAPACK Users' Guide, 3rd edn. SIAM, Philadelphia (1999)
7. Galassi, M., et al.: GNU Scientific Library Reference Manual, revised 2nd edn., www.gnu.org/software/gsl/
8. Abramovitz, M., Stegun, I.A. (eds.): Handbook Of Mathematical Functions. Dover Publications (1964)
9. Boyd, J.P.: Chebyshev and Fourier Spectral Methods, revised 2nd edn. Dover Publications (2001)
10. Cover, T.M., Thomas, J.A.: Determinant Inequalities Via Information Theory. SIAM J. Matrix Anal. Appl. 9(3), 384–392 (1988)
11. Gottlieb, D., Shu, C.-W.: On the Gibbs Phenomenon IV: Recovering Exponential Accuracy in a Subinterval from a Gegenbauer Partial Sum of a Piecewise Analytic Function. Mathematics of Computation 64, 1081–1095 (1995)
12. Solomonoff, R.: The Application of Algorithmic Probability to Problems in Artificial Intelligence. In: Kochen, M., Hastings, H.M. (eds.) Advances in Cognitive Science. AAAS Selected Symposium Series, pp. 210–227 (1988)

On the Application of Algorithmic Probability to Autoregressive Models

Ray J. Solomonoff and Elias G. Saleeby

Alfaisal University, Riyadh, Saudi Arabia
esaleeby@yahoo.com

Abstract. Typically, the first step in carrying out predictions is to develop an inductive model. In many instances, the best model is used, and it is often selected based on certain relevant criteria that may possibly ignore some of the model uncertainties. The Bayesian approach to model selection uses a weighted average of a class of models thereby overcoming some of the uncertainties associated with selecting the best model. This approach is referred to in the literature as the Bayesian Model Averaging (BMA) approach. It turns out that this approach has significant overlap with the theory of Algorithmic Probability (ALP) developed by R. J. Solomonoff in the early 1960s. The purpose of this article is to first highlight this connection by applying ALP to a set of nested stationary autoregressive time series models, and to give an algorithm to compute "relative weights" of models. This reveals, although empirically, a model weight that can be compared with the Schwarz Bayesian Selection criterion (BIC or SIC). We then develop an elementary algorithm of the Monte Carlo type to evaluate multidimensional integrals over stability domains, and use it to compute what we call the "trimmed weights".

Keywords: algorithmic probability, predictive probability, model weights, information criteria, autoregressive time series, Monte Carlo method.

1 Introduction

A general problem that we are interested in is this: given a data sequence of reals, $x_1 x_2 \cdots x_n$, generated by a stationary source, which could be either linear or nonlinear, we would like to try to predict its continuation using linear models only. Often linear models are defined by their coefficients only. They give a prediction, but no probability distribution. We do not intend to use models of this sort. Note that when a nonlinear source is considered, the approximating family of models will not contain the true generator of the data. More specifically, we are interested in the question: will summing over linear models (as in ALP), give better prediction than using the "best" linear model (say as selected by Akaike's AIC, Schwarz's BIC, or Wallace's MML)?

We do not address these problems fully in this report, instead, we focus on developing an algorithm that would be useful later on in answering the prediction problem with some degree of confidence. We would like to mention that when

D.L. Dowe (Ed.): Solomonoff Festschrift, LNAI 7070, pp. 366–385, 2013.

we initially started working on this project, neither of us was aware of the large body of work available on BMA (see [9], [13]) — where problems of this sort are addressed to different extents. Furthermore, the order estimation problem has been recently addressed by information theoretic approaches (see for example [14],[7]). Despite the overlap with BMA, we think that our presentation includes some novel aspects that are not emphasized elsewhere.

Before presenting our development, we give a brief introduction to ALP and discuss its significance to model selection. In the 1960s (see [23] & [24]), Ray J. Solomonoff considered the probability that a universal computer outputs some string x when fed with a program chosen at random. This probability was called "Algorithmic Probability" (ALP), which is also known as the Universal *a Priori* Probability or the Universal Distribution. It turned out that this probability plays a central role in the theory of inductive inference. ALP is based on the philosophical principles of Occam's razor of simplicity and Epicurus' principle of multiple explanations. Using Bayes's Rule and Universal Turing machines, R.J. Solomonoff unified these principles in an algorithmic way. This probability was a precursor to the definition and the quantification of Algorithmic Complexity that was introduced later on by Kolmogorov (see [15],[26],[8],[28]).

To carry out prediction, one needs inductive models — and there are several types. In prediction one makes an estimate of what to occur in the future, and assigns a probability to express the level of confidence in the prediction. Suppose an inductive model or an algorithm gives a probability for each symbol in a sequence as a function of the previous symbols. One measure of "Merit" of this induction algorithm is the probability that it assigns to the entire data set. This will be the product of the probabilities assigned to each of the symbols: $S = \prod p_i$. For good prediction, we would like to have as large a value of S as possible (clearly $0 \leq S \leq 1$). Suppose R_i is an inductive algorithm. R_i predicts the probability of an symbol a_j in a sequence $a_1, a_2, \cdots, a_n$ by looking at the previous symbols, i.e., it is the conditional distribution of the unobserved quantity based on previous symbols. Put

$$p_j = R_i(a_j | a_1, a_2, \cdots, a_{j-1})$$

where a_j is the symbol for which we want the probability. The value of a_j can vary over the entire "alphabet" of symbols that occur in the sequence. Then we have that

$$S_n = \prod_{j=1}^{n} p_j = \prod_{j=1}^{n} R_i(a_j | a_1, a_2, \cdots, a_{j-1}).$$

Now we define the universal distribution for sequential prediction. Define the function $P_M(a_{n+1} | a_1, a_2, \cdots, a_n)$ — the weighted sum probability assigned by ALP to the $(n+1)^{th}$ symbol of the sequence (in view of the previous parts of the sequence) by all the models. That is,

$$P_M(a_{n+1} | a_1, a_2, \cdots, a_n) = \sum_{i=1}^{\infty} 2^{-|R_i|} S_i R_i(a_{n+1} | a_1, a_2, \cdots, a_n).$$

In other words, the ALP inductive model uses all possible models in parallel for prediction with weights $2^{-|R_i|}S_i$ dependent on the figure of merit of each model, $|R_i|$. $2^{-|R_i|}$ is something like the a-priori probability assigned to the model R_i, S_i is the probability assigned by the R_i (the ith model) to the known data, R_i is the probability assigned by the ith model to the predicted $(n + 1)^{th}$ symbol of the sequence (see [26] for more details). In contrast, recall that the "Maximum Likelihood" (ML) method of model selection uses S only to decide a model. First a set of models is chosen by the statistician based on an educated guess, then the model within that set having maximum S value is selected. More refined selection criteria for best models, that incorporate the principle of Occam's razor or parsimony, were developed later on by Wallace and Boulton ([27]), Akaike ([1],[2]), Schwarz ([21]), Rissanen ([20]) and others (see [3] for more details).

2   Model Probabilities and Weights

In this section, we develop expressions for "relative probabilities" or "relative weights" (for short we call weights) — in practice, probability ratios are of interest (see [25]. First, we set some notation. Let X_i be the data sequence up to and including x_i, i.e., $X_i = x_1 \cdots x_{i-1}x_i$. $R(y; X_n)$ is the probability density at y for the element following x_n , as a function of X_n (as given by model R). For small Δ, R says that the probability that x_{n+1} will be between y and $y + \Delta$ is $R(y; X_n) \cdot \Delta$. A linear model with $m + 1$ coefficients will be of the form

$$L_\Theta(y; X_n) = \left(\sqrt{2\pi\sigma^2}\right)^{-1} \exp\left(-\frac{\left(y - \left(a_0 + \sum_{j=1}^{m} a_j x_{n-j}\right)\right)^2}{2\sigma^2}\right). \quad (1)$$

This L_Θ is defined by $m + 2$ parameters, $a_0 \cdots a_m$ and σ^2. Θ denotes those $m + 2$ parameters.

Consider the model R. Define

$$S_R(x_1 \cdots x_n) = \prod_{i=1}^{n} R(x_i; X_{i-1}). \quad (2)$$

This is the probability of the data $(x_1 \cdots x_n)$ given by model R. Recall that ALP says to sum over all models, using weights proportional to the a priori probability of each model, multiplied by probability of the known data as given by that model — this is also the posterior probability. Since the parameters of the models are all continuous, we will integrate instead of sum. We will give below two different derivations to carry out the process of integration to derive the "weights".

Note that the integrand is

$$C \cdot S_{L_\Theta}(x_1 \cdots x_n) \cdot L_\Theta(y; X_n). \tag{3}$$

For now, we will consider deriving the models' weights when the $m+1$ parameters $a_0, \cdots, a_m$ have integration limits from $-\infty$ to $+\infty$. The σ^2 parameter will have integration limits 0 to $+\infty$. The "C" factor tells us that the $m+1$ parameter models have the same a priori probability. We present two approaches for this integration (which in fact are not that much different) to derive the weights. We call the first approach the indirect method as we will not be integrating (3) directly.

Consider a nested model space, and assume that the maximal number of lags a model can have is p. For comparison purposes, it is desirable that all the models use the same data.

Since $S_{L_\Theta}(x_{p+1} \cdots x_n) \cdot L_\Theta(y, \mathbf{X}_n) = S_{L_\Theta}(x_{p+1} \cdots x_n, y)$, we will first integrate $S_{L_\Theta}(x_{p+1} \cdots x_n)$ — then we obtain the integral of $S_{L_\Theta}(x_{p+1} \cdots x_n, y)$ as a special case of $S_{L_\Theta}(x_{p+1} \cdots x_n)$. Expanding $S_{L_\Theta}(x_{p+1} \cdots x_n)$, we get

$$\prod_{i=p+1}^{n} \left[(2\pi\sigma^2)^{-\frac{1}{2}} \exp(-\frac{(x_i - (a_0 + \sum_{j=1}^{m} a_j x_{i-j}))^2}{2\sigma^2}) \right]$$

$$= (2\pi\sigma^2)^{-\frac{n-p}{2}} \exp\left[-\frac{\sum_{i=p+1}^{n}(x_i - (a_0 + \sum_{j=1}^{m} a_j x_{i-j}))^2}{2\sigma^2} \right], \tag{4}$$

the conditional probability density function given that the first p values remain fixed. To simplify, let $\sigma^2 = V$ and $\frac{1}{n-p}\sum_{i=p+1}^{n}(x_i - (a_0 + \sum_{j=1}^{m} a_j x_{i-j}))^2 = f(\Theta)$. So (4) becomes

$$(2\pi)^{-\frac{n-p}{2}} V^{-\frac{n-p}{2}} \exp(-\frac{(n-p) f(\Theta)}{2V}) = (2\pi)^{-\frac{n-p}{2}} (V e^{\frac{f(\Theta)}{V}})^{-\frac{n-p}{2}}. \tag{5}$$

$f(\Theta)$ has a minimum equal to the mean square error of σ_0^2, when $\Theta = \widehat{\Theta}$. The minimum of $V e^{\frac{f(\Theta)}{V}}$ (and the maximum of (2)) occurs when $\Theta = \widehat{\Theta}$ and $V = f(\widehat{\Theta}) = \sigma_0^2$.

To integrate with respect to the a_i components of $\widehat{\Theta}$, we will move the origin to $\hat{a}_0 \cdots \hat{a}_m$, then rotate the system so f_Θ becomes of the form $f_0 + \sum_{j=0}^{m} \lambda_i^2 b_i^2$, $b_0 \cdots b_m$ being the rotated coordinates. First centering the $a_0 \cdots a_m$ coordinates at the origin: Let $a_i' = a_i - \hat{a}_i$ $(i = 0, \cdots, m)$. So

$$f(\Theta) = \sum_{j=0}^{m}\sum_{k=0}^{m} A_{j,k}\, a_j'\, a_k' + \sigma_0^2, \tag{6}$$

where the $A_{0,0} = 1$, $A_{0,k} = A_{k,0} = \frac{1}{n-p}\sum_{i=p+1}^{n} x_{i-k}, k > 0$, and $A_{j,k} = A_{k,j} = \frac{1}{n-p}\sum_{i=p+1}^{n} x_{i-j}x_{i-k}$ for $j, k > 0$, and $\sigma_0^2 = f(\widehat{\Theta})$, the minimum mean square value of $f(\Theta)$. The matrix A is a symmetric and positive definite, since $f(\Theta)$ is at its minimum. So we can rotate coordinates $a_i's$ to get the $b_i's$. The λ_i^2 are the eigenvalues of the matrix A, and are positive and real. Substituting back into (5), we obtain

$$(2\pi)^{-\frac{n-p}{2}} \, V^{-\frac{n-p}{2}} \exp\left(-\frac{(n-p)\,(\sigma_0^2 + \sum_{i=0}^{m} \lambda_i^2 \, b_i^2)}{2V}\right). \tag{7}$$

Integrating each of $b_0 \cdots b_m$ from $-\infty$ to $+\infty$, we have for $n > p$,

$$\int \exp\left(-\frac{(n-p)\sum_{i=0}^{m} \lambda_i^2 \, b_i^2}{2V}\right) db = \left(\left(\frac{V}{n-p}\right)^{\frac{m+1}{2}} \cdot (2\pi)^{\frac{m+1}{2}} \cdot \prod_{i=0}^{m} \frac{1}{\lambda_i}\right). \tag{8}$$

Define $D =$ determinant of matrix $A : D^{-\frac{1}{2}} = \prod_{i=0}^{m} \lambda_i^{-1}$. Then from (8), the integral of (7) can be written as

$$D^{-\frac{1}{2}} (2\pi)^{\frac{-n+p+m+1}{2}} (n-p)^{-\frac{m+1}{2}} \left(V^{\frac{-n+p+m+1}{2}} \cdot e^{-\frac{\sigma_0^2(n-p)}{2V}}\right). \tag{9}$$

Integrate (9) from 0 to ∞, with respect to V, we get

$$\frac{1}{2} D^{-\frac{1}{2}} (n-p)^{\frac{-n+p+2}{2}} \pi^{\frac{-n+p+m+1}{2}} \sigma_0^{-n+p+m+3} \, \Gamma\left(\frac{n-p-m-3}{2}\right). \tag{10}$$

As we mentioned, the probability associated with equation (10) is for the sequence $x_{p+1}, \cdots, x_n$. To obtain the equivalent expression for $x_{p+1}, \cdots, x_n, y$; n becomes $n+1$, $m+1$ remains the same, but σ_0 changes in a more complex way. We want $S_{L\Theta}(x_{p+1} \cdots x_n, y)$ as a function of y. To get the associated distribution function and its variance, let

$$\delta = y - (\text{predicted value of } x_{n+1}) = y - \left(\hat{a}_0 + \sum_{j=1}^{m} \hat{a}_j \, x_{n+1-j}\right).$$

The first $n - p$ prediction errors are of mean zero, because $\hat{a}_0$ was adjusted to make it so. The mean of all of the $n - p + 1$ prediction errors will be

$$((n - p) \cdot 0 + \delta)/(n - p + 1) = \delta/(n - p + 1).$$

The mean square error is the mean of the squares minus square of mean

$$\frac{(n-p)\sigma_0^2 + \delta^2}{n-p+1} - \left(\frac{\delta}{n-p+1}\right)^2 = \frac{(n-p)\,\sigma_0^2}{n-p+1} \left(1 + \frac{\delta^2}{(n-p+1)\,\sigma_0^2}\right).$$

Since $n \to n + 1$, the power of σ_0^2 in equation (10) becomes $\frac{-n+p+m+2}{2}$. We take our modified σ_0^2 to this power to obtain

$$\left(\frac{n-p}{n-p+1}\,\sigma_0^2\right)^{\frac{-n+p+m+2}{2}} \cdot \left(1+\frac{\delta^2}{(n-p+1)\,\sigma_0^2}\right)^{\frac{-n+p+m+2}{2}}.$$

If $\frac{\delta^2}{(n-p+1)\,\sigma_0^2} << 1$, the second factor is $\exp\left(-\frac{(n-p-m-2)\,\delta^2}{2(n-p+1)\sigma_0^2}\right)$, which is a normal distribution of variance $\sigma_0^2\,\frac{n-p+1}{n-p-m-2}$. Define

$$\sigma_{final}^2 = \sigma_0^2\,\frac{n-p+1}{n-p-m-2}.$$

σ_{final}^2 is *not* exact, but be made more exact if need be.

Omitting factors involving only constants and functions of n and p only, (10) becomes

$$D^{-\frac{1}{2}}\,\pi^{\frac{m}{2}}\,\Gamma\left(\frac{n-p-m-2}{2}\right)\,\sigma_0^{-n+p+m+2}\left(\frac{n-p}{n-p+1}\right)^{\frac{m}{2}}\frac{\sigma_0\left(2\pi\sigma_{final}^2\right)^{-\frac{1}{2}}}{\sqrt{n-p-m-2}}\,e^{-\frac{\delta^2}{2\sigma_{final}^2}}.$$
(11)

If $m << 2n$ then $\left(\frac{n-p}{n-p+1}\right)^{\frac{m}{2}}\frac{1}{\sqrt{n-p-m-2}}$ cancel to first order in $\frac{m}{n}$. This gives for (11)

$$D^{-\frac{1}{2}}\,\pi^{\frac{m}{2}}\,\Gamma\left(\frac{n-p-m-2}{2}\right)\,\sigma_0^{-n+p+m+3}\left(2\pi\sigma_{final}^2\right)^{-\frac{1}{2}}\,e^{-\frac{\delta^2}{2\sigma_{final}^2}}.$$
(12)

Next, consider $\Gamma\left(\frac{n-p-m-2}{2}\right)$. Rewrite using n in place of $n-p$, and look at $\left(\frac{n+2}{2}\right)!\,\left(\frac{n-m-4}{2}\right)!\,/\,\left(\frac{n+2}{2}\right)!$ We neglect the first $\left(\frac{n+2}{2}\right)!$ because it is canceled by normalization. Now

$$\frac{\left(\frac{n-m-4}{2}\right)!}{\left(\frac{n+2}{2}\right)!} = \left[\left(\frac{n-m-4}{2}+1\right)\left(\frac{n-m-4}{2}+2\right)\cdots\frac{n+2}{2}\right]^{-1},$$
(13)

If $\frac{m}{2}$ is small, we employ a simple approximation. The product

$$\left(\frac{n-m-4}{2}+1\right)\left(\frac{n-m-4}{2}+2\right)\cdots\left(\frac{n+2}{2}\right)$$
(14)

contains $\frac{m+4}{2}$ factors. The (arithmetic) mean of the factors is $\frac{n}{2}-\frac{m}{4}$; and a rough approximation to (14) is then $\left(\frac{n}{2}-\frac{m}{4}\right)^{\frac{m+4}{2}}$. For $m << n$ this is

$$\left(\frac{n}{2}\right)^{\frac{m+4}{2}}\cdot\left(1-\frac{m}{2n}\right)^{\frac{m+4}{2}} \approx \left(\frac{n}{2}\right)^2\cdot\left(\frac{n}{2}\right)^{\frac{m}{2}}\cdot e^{-\frac{m(m+4)}{4n}}.$$
(15)

Discarding the $\left(\frac{n}{2}\right)^2$ factor and noting that we need the reciprocal of (14) we obtain

$$n^{-\frac{m}{2}} \cdot 2^{\frac{m}{2}} \cdot e^{\frac{m^2}{4n}+\frac{m}{n}} \qquad (16)$$

Replacing n by $n - p$, and substituting this for $\left(\frac{n-m-4}{2}\right)!$ in (12), we obtain

$$e^{\frac{m^2}{4(n-p)}+\frac{m}{(n-p)}} D^{-\frac{1}{2}} (2\pi)^{\frac{m}{2}} (n-p)^{-\frac{m}{2}} \sigma_0^{-n+p+m+3} \left(2\pi\sigma_{final}^2\right)^{-\frac{1}{2}} e^{-\frac{\delta^2}{2\sigma_{final}^2}}. \qquad (17)$$

Now we define what we call the "weight" for a model with m-lags as

$$w(m) = e^{\frac{m^2}{4(n-p)}+\frac{m}{(n-p)}} D^{-\frac{1}{2}} (2\pi)^{\frac{m}{2}} (n-p)^{-\frac{m}{2}} \sigma_0^{-n+p+m+3}. \qquad (18)$$

We note here that we can also obtain, more directly, a derivation of an equivalent of (10), which makes use of the so called General Gaussian Integral (see, http://web.mit.edu/jaimevrl/www/Quantum/QFT/Gaussian%20Integrals.pdf)

$$Z(\mathbf{A}, \mathbf{b}) = \int_{\mathbf{R}^n} \exp\left(-\sum_{i,j=1}^{n} \frac{1}{2} x_i A_{ij} x_j + \sum_{i=1}^{n} b_i x_i\right) d^n x$$

$$= (2\pi)^{\frac{n}{2}} (\det \mathbf{A})^{-\frac{1}{2}} \exp\left(\sum_{i,j=1}^{n} \frac{1}{2} b_i \Delta_{ij} b_j\right),$$

where $\mathbf{\Delta} = \mathbf{A}^{-1}$. This integral is also obtained by orthogonal diagonalization of the matrix A and a translation based on the minimum of the quadratic form in the exponential. The integral of (4)

$$(2\pi\sigma^2)^{-\frac{n-p}{2}} \int \exp\left[-\frac{\sum_{i=p+1}^{n}(x_i - (a_0 + \sum_{j=1}^{m} a_j x_{i-j}))^2}{2\sigma^2}\right] d\mathbf{a}_0,$$

where $\mathbf{a}_0 = (a_0, a_1, \cdots, a_m)^t$, can be written as

$$(2\pi\sigma^2)^{-\frac{n-p}{2}} \exp\left(-\frac{\sum_{i=p+1}^{n} x_i^2}{2\sigma^2}\right) \int \exp\left(\frac{-\mathbf{a}_0^t \mathbf{A}_0 \mathbf{a}_0}{2\sigma^2} + \frac{\mathbf{S}_0^t \mathbf{a}_0}{\sigma^2}\right) d\mathbf{a}_0, \qquad (19)$$

where

$$\mathbf{A}_0 := \begin{bmatrix} \sum_{i=p+1}^{n} 1 & \sum_{i=p+1}^{n} x_{i-1} & \sum_{i=p+1}^{n} x_{i-2} \\ \sum_{i=p+1}^{n} x_{i-1} & \sum_{i=p+1}^{n} x_{i-1}^2 & \sum_{i=p+1}^{n} x_{i-1} x_{i-2} \\ \sum_{i=p+1}^{n} x_{i-2} & \sum_{i=p+1}^{n} x_{i-1} x_{i-2} & \sum_{i=p+1}^{n} x_{i-2}^2 & \cdots \\ & \vdots & & \end{bmatrix}_{(m+1)\times(m+1)},$$

and

$$\mathbf{S}_0 := \left[\sum_{i=p+1}^{n} x_i \quad \sum_{i=p+1}^{n} x_{i-1} x_i \quad \sum_{i=p+1}^{n} x_{i-2} x_i \quad \cdots\right]^t.$$

Now upon integrating (19), making use of the normal equations, and noting that $\mathbf{A}_0^{-1}\mathbf{S}_0 = \widehat{\mathbf{a}}_0$, we obtain

$$
(2\pi\sigma^2)^{-\frac{n-p}{2}}\left[\frac{\sigma^{m+1}(2\pi)^{\frac{m+1}{2}}}{(\det \mathbf{A}_0)^{\frac{1}{2}}}\right]\exp\left(\frac{-\sum_{i=p+1}^{n} x_i^2}{2\sigma^2}\right)\exp\left(\frac{\mathbf{S}_0^t\widehat{\mathbf{a}}_0}{2\sigma^2}\right). \tag{20}
$$

Next, let $V := \sigma^2$ (as we did above). Then (2.20) becomes

$$
\frac{(2\pi)^{\frac{-n+m+p+1}{2}}}{(\det \mathbf{A}_0)^{\frac{1}{2}}}V^{\frac{-n+m+p+1}{2}}e^{\frac{-\sum_{i=p+1}^{n} x_{i+1}^2+\mathbf{S}_0^t\widehat{\mathbf{a}}_0}{2V}}. \tag{21}
$$

Setting $A = \frac{-n+m+p+1}{2}$ and $B = \frac{-\sum_{i=p+1}^{n} x_i^2+\mathbf{S}_0^t\widehat{\mathbf{a}}_0}{2}$, then (21) reduces to

$$
(\det \mathbf{A}_0)^{-\frac{1}{2}}(2\pi)^A V^A e^{-\frac{B}{V}}. \tag{22}
$$

Integrating (22) over V from 0 to ∞, and making use of the integral $B^{A+1}\int_0^\infty U^{-A-2}e^{-U}dU = B^{A+1}\Gamma(-A-1)$, we obtain

$$
(\det \mathbf{A}_0)^{-\frac{1}{2}}(2\pi)^{\frac{-n+m+p+1}{2}}\left(\frac{\sum_{i=p+1}^{n} x_i^2 - \mathbf{S}_0^t\widehat{\mathbf{a}}_0}{2}\right)^{\frac{-n+m+p+3}{2}}\Gamma\left(\frac{n-m-p-3}{2}\right).
$$

Hence, after discarding the constants that are not function of m or of the data, we get

$$
wt(m) = \pi^{\frac{m}{2}}(\det \mathbf{A}_0)^{-\frac{1}{2}}\left(\sum_{i=p+1}^{n} x_i^2 - \mathbf{S}_0^t\widehat{\mathbf{a}}_0\right)^{\frac{-n+m+p+3}{2}}\Gamma\left(\frac{n-m-p-3}{2}\right).
$$

$$\tag{23}$$

Note that (23) is given in terms of total square error — that is, without the normalizing constant $n - p$. This constant will not make a difference when we compute weights.

3   Weight Trimming

In our analysis so far we have assumed that the a priori distribution of the coefficients is uniform, and it does not change as we use models of higher order. However, if we know that the time series is "stable" (and often it is), then we know that the roots of the associated characteristic polynomial must all be within the unit circle; and correspondingly, the coefficients must lie in the so called "stability domains" in parameter space. This suggests that weights (relative probabilities) of prediction models should be modified to take into account this additional information. To use this, we have to know that the maximum modulus of the roots is less than one before we see the data — to make it legitimate a priori information. Of course, we are aware of the objection that it may not be possible to know for certain that the time series is stable before looking at the data. It may be possible to deal with this issue by looking at part of the data to determine whether the maximum modulus is less than one for the whole data, and then use this as a priori information for the remaining part. However, at this point in our development, we will address the computational issues in finding the weights assuming that the time series given is stationary.

In order to evaluate the integrals over the stability domains, we develop in this section a Monte Carlo type method. We begin by showing how this method works for computing the hypervolumes $V(k)$ for the stability domains D_k. We start with $S = 0$. From the origin of the $k-$dimensional coefficient space, we draw a random ray outward until it hits the "wall". The "wall" is where the largest root modulus is 1. If the length of this ray from the origin to the wall is R, we then do

$$S = S + \int_0^R \frac{2\pi^{\frac{k}{2}} x^{k-1}}{(\frac{k}{2} - 1)!} dx. \tag{24}$$

If we select this random ray N times and update S each time, then, if N is large, the hypervolume is about S/N.

Now suppose we have a multivariate distribution. With each ray we choose, the distribution will be some function of x, the distance from the origin. Say this function is $M(x)$ along a particular ray — then our updating equation is

$$S = S + \int_0^R \frac{2\pi^{\frac{k}{2}} x^{k-1}}{(\frac{k}{2} - 1)!} M(x) dx. \tag{25}$$

As before, the final integral approximation will be S/N.

Now we describe a somewhat *ad-hoc* procedure on how to evaluate (25). At this stage, this procedure should be considered experimental. First, $u_i, 1 \leq i \leq k$, random variables were generated from the normal distribution with mean zero and variance one. Divide $u_i, 1 \leq i \leq k$, by the square root of the sum of squares to obtain $(u_1^s, \cdots, u_k^s)$. These vectors are uniformly distributed on the unit sphere (see [12], Ch.3). We then multiply these vectors by a constant h to obtain a vector of coefficients $\mathbf{c} = (c_1, \cdots, c_k) = h(u_1^s, \cdots, u_k^s)$. We call this factor h the "tuning factor". h was determined empirically in order for us to obtain a fairly accurate estimate of the volume. This is possible as we know in advance the volumes of the stability domains, and so we can "shoot" to get close to the exact value of the volume. This shooting process seems to be necessary as the method expressed in (25) is somewhat rigid, and one cannot expect a good estimate for $h = 1$ by using relatively small size samples (see Table 2 below). This is so, as in dimension two say, we are trying to capture the area of a triangle as the average area of a covering by a certain set of discs. It turns out, an appropriate value of h can be determined that enables us to obtain an approximate value for $V(k)$, and integrals over this volume, using a single run (or a single shot) if there is a need. We mention here that we have tried other schemes (of the acceptance/rejection type) for generating the $\mathbf{c}$/s. These $\mathbf{c}$/s were only perhaps approximately uniformly distributed on a sphere with a suitable radius chosen to reduce the rejection rate — yet we were still able to carry out the shooting successfully with a value of $h \simeq 1$. Now, a recurrence formula for $V(k)$ was obtained by Fam ([6], see also [18])

$$V(2k+1) = \frac{2kV(2k)V(2k-1)}{(2k+1)V(2k-2)}, \quad V(2k) = \frac{V^2(2k-1)}{V(2k-2)},$$

$k = 2, 3, \cdots$, under the initial conditions $V(1) = 2, V(2) = 4$, and $V(3) = 16/3$. D. Piccolo ([19]) (cited in [FDV]) also have given a recursion to compute $V(k)$.

Now we describe how the values of R in (24) and (25) were determined. Take one of the vectors $\mathbf{c}$ generated above and call it $\mathbf{c}^1$. Solve the characteristic polynomial with coefficients $\mathbf{c}^1$ for all roots. Determine the maximum modulus value of the roots and denote it by r_1. Multiplying each c_i by r^i scales the zeros of a polynomial by r. Pick a constant r_t (typically > 1) and generate another k-dimensional vector $\mathbf{c}^2$, where $c_i^2 = c_i^1 r_t^i$. Note that the calculations were not sensitive to the value r_t chosen. Now solve the characteristic polynomial associated with $\mathbf{c}_2$, then find the maximum modulus of its roots and denote it by r_2. Then employ linear interpolation/extrapolation to find the value of $r_p := 1 + (1 - r_1)\frac{r_t-1}{r_2-r_1}$. Compute $r_r = \sum_{i=1}^{k}(c_i^1 r_p^i)^2$ and take $R = \sqrt{r_r}$ (i.e., we are using the Euclidean norm). As a further check, and to guard against not expected performance of the root solver, the result was verified by solving the characteristic polynomial associated with $\mathbf{c}^3$, where $c_i^3 = c_i^1 r_p^i$, to confirm that we have gotten a root with maximum modulus equal to 1 to within a tolerance of 10^{-9}. The rejection rate of vectors not satisfying this criterion was zero or extremely low ($\leq$ to 1 in 2000). This tolerance can be relaxed considerably, say to 10^{-3}, with no significant effects. It is known that the D_k's are contractible along curves (and thus are simply connected). The D_k's are not convex for $k > 2$ (see [6]), and the bounding hypersurfaces are ruled surfaces (see [22]). Only the domain contractiblity property was necessary. We remark that it may be possible to refine the process of determining R and to employ an automated procedure to determine an appropriate value of h. Note that h is not a correction factor for the volume itself, and that h can be tuned to allow us to obtain accurate values of the stability domains volumes for relatively low number of sample points. The optimal number of sample points necessary to use for each k need to be investigated further.

Table 1 shows the results for computing one estimate of the stability domains volumes, V_k, using j vectors; and one estimate of Gaussian type integrals J_k given by (25) with $M(x) = e^{-\frac{x^2}{2}}$ using m_c points (for each j). As a further check, the last column I_k gives the one-shot estimate of (25) obtained by employing the recursion expression derived in Appendix A using j vectors. The values of J_2 and J_3 check reasonably well against those obtained by quadrature methods over V_2 and V_3 (= 2.652 8 and 3.379 7, respectively). All the results were obtained from a single shooting-type run for the value of h shown. The values of h were found by trial and error, and are shown to give an idea of the scaling needed. However, the values of h in this instance depend on the seed values used for the pseudo-random data generator and the number of vectors **c**. One way to find an appropriate value of h is to initially choose the seeds at random, but then to hold them fixed while tuning to determine a value of h that allow us to hit the targeted volume. Notice that the rough estimates found for the values of the integrals are not available to us by other means for $k > 3$.

Table 1. Estimates of volumes and Gaussian integrals by shooting
$$(j = m_c = 5000)$$

k	$V(k)$	h	V_k	J_k	I_k
2	4	1.26	3.990	2.664	2.670
3	5.333	1.25	5.337	3.281	3.271
4	7.111	1.555	7.114	3.916	3.890
5	7.585	1.599	7.610	4.064	4.027
6	8.091	1.652	8.098	4.115	4.081
7	7.397	1.695	7.401	3.777	3.746
8	6.763	1.585	6.774	3.190	3.161

Next, we examine the performance of the method a bit further. Table 2 shows the results obtained by doing shooting-on-average to find estimates. We give results for $k = 3$ and $k = 6$ from 25 different runs of the program. The notations is as above, but mean values are reported. The subscript var indicates the variance of the estimated quantity. No significant changes in the results were observed after generating an orthogonal random matrix (one for each run) to multiply each of the generated vector c_i within that run. It was observed that the average values of estimates are almost independent of the number of vectors **c** employed. Tables 3 and 4, are similar to Table 2, but with different values of j and m_c. Shooting on the average is more time consuming, and it actually becomes harder to tune as the values of k increase. Perhaps automating the tuning process would be very desirable. However, we observed that it is possible to use smaller j and m_c values when shooting on average.

Table 2. Average values for volumes and and Gaussian integrals
$$(j = 5000, mc = 1000)$$

k	$V(k)$	h	$\overline{V}_k$	$V_{k,var}$	$\overline{I}_k$	$I_{k,var}$	$\overline{J}_k$	$J_{k,var}$
3	5.333	1	4.697	0.00094	3.040	0.00107	3.053	0.00703
3	5.333	1.45	5.344	0.01198	3.287	0.00161	3.291	0.00438
6	8.091	1	4.925	0.04567	2.807	0.00246	2.816	0.02153
6	8.091	1.64	8.099	0.07614	4.044	0.00434	4.053	0.04682

Table 3. $j = 5000, mc = 500$

k	$V(k)$	h	$\overline{V}_k$	$V_{k,var}$	$\overline{I}_k$	$I_{k,var}$	$\overline{J}_k$	$J_{k,var}$
3	5.333	1.45	5.313	0.00967	3.272	0.00100	3.292	0.01325
6	8.091	1.64	8.099	0.07614	4.044	0.00432	4.038	0.09623

Table 4. $j = 2000, mc = 500$

k	$V(k)$	h	$\overline{V}_k$	$V_{k,var}$	$\overline{I}_k$	$I_{k,var}$	$\overline{J}_k$	$J_{k,var}$
3	5.333	1.46	5.327	0.01687	3.278	0.00192	3.293	0.01229
6	8.091	1.615	8.101	0.04203	4.036	0.01713	4.031	0.10723

Similar results for $j = 10000$ or 15000 were obtained. Occasionally, it was noticed that for certain repeat runs of the program, or upon a small change in h, one of the volumes (out of 25) could become untypically large - what can be characterized as an "outlier estimate". This problem appears to be originating sometimes from the root-solver for the characteristic polynomial (and it was observed for the higher k values). The root solver employed the Jenkins-Traub algorithm that may not in certain instances be able to find all the roots. Therefore, one has to guard against these exceptional cases and remove them. Changing the initial seed values helped to solve the problem in the trials we did. Perhaps a more refined implementation of the algorithm, or running the program on a machine with a higher precision platform, may help reduce the variances of the estimates obtained further.

Now we give the derivation of the trimmed weights. Let $a_j = c_j a_1, j = 2, \cdots, m$, $c_1 := 1$. Then from (4), the term $\sum_{i=p+1}^{n}(x_i - (a_0 + \sum_{j=1}^{m} a_j x_{i-j}))^2$ can be written, for $m \geq 1$, after expansion and completing squares, as

$$Q_1 \left(a_1 - \frac{Q_2}{Q_1}\right)^2 - Q_1 \left(\frac{Q_2}{Q_1}\right)^2 + Q_3,$$

where

$$Q_1(m) = \sum_{i=p+1}^{n} \left(c_0^2 + 2c_0 \sum_{j=1}^{m} c_j x_{i-j} + \sum_{j=1}^{m} c_j^2 x_{i-j}^2 + 2 \sum_{j=2}^{m} c_{j-1} x_{i-j+1} \sum_{k=j}^{m} c_k x_{i-k}\right)$$

$$Q_2(m) = \sum_{i=p+1}^{n} x_i \left(c_0 + \sum_{j=1}^{m} c_j x_{i-j}\right), \text{ and } Q_3 = \sum_{i=p+1}^{n} x_i^2.$$

So (4) can be written as

$$S_{L_\theta} = (2\pi\sigma^2)^{-\frac{n-p}{2}} \exp\left[-\frac{1}{2\sigma^2}\left(Q_1\left(a_1 - \frac{Q_2}{Q_1}\right)^2 - Q_1\left(\frac{Q_2}{Q_1}\right)^2 + Q_3\right)\right]. \quad (26)$$

First, we integrate (26) over σ^2 from 0 to ∞. Let $B = \frac{1}{2}\left(Q_1\left(a_1 - \frac{Q_2}{Q_1}\right)^2 - Q_1\left(\frac{Q_2}{Q_1}\right)^2 + Q_3\right)$, $A = -\frac{n-p}{2}$, and $V = \sigma^2$. Let $U = \frac{B}{V}$, and so $dV = -\frac{B}{U^2}dU$.
Then we obtain

$$\int_0^\infty S_{L_\theta} d\sigma^2 = (2\pi)^A \int_0^\infty V^A e^{-\frac{B}{V}} dV = (2\pi)^{\frac{-n+p}{2}} B^{\frac{-n+p+2}{2}} \Gamma\left(\frac{n-p-2}{2}\right).$$

Therefore, the integral over the coefficient space, representing the trimmed weight (un-normalized), can be expressed as

$$Q(m)Q_5 \int_0^R \frac{a_1^{m-1}}{\left[Q_1\left(a_1 - \frac{Q_2}{Q_1}\right)^2 + Q_4\right]^{\frac{n-p-2}{2}}} da_1, \tag{27}$$

where $Q_4(m) = Q_3 - Q_1\left(\frac{Q_2}{Q_1}\right)^2$, $Q_5 = \pi^{\frac{-n+p}{2}}\Gamma\left(\frac{n-p-2}{2}\right)$, and $Q(m) = \frac{\pi^{\frac{m}{2}}}{\left(\frac{m}{2}-1\right)!}$.
Using Integral Tables, it is possible to represent (27) in terms of some closed form expressions, some of which involve finite sums. However, the resulting expressions seems to be complex and a recurrence like that given in Appendix A does not appear to be easy to derive. Therefore, at this point, these expressions seem to offer no advantages over evaluating (27) directly.

4   Numerical Example

In this section we demonstrate how to compute the weights described above by considering an example. We generated a long enough stationary time series form the linear model

$$x_{n+1} = 0.2x_n + 0.1x_{n-1} + 0.5x_{n-2} + 1.0 * [noise \sim i.i.d. N(0,1)]. \tag{28}$$

with initial conditions: $x_1 = x_2 = x_3 = 0$. We discarded the first 200 points to reduce the effect of the initial conditions. We fixed a bound on the order of the models — $p = 7$ in this example, and took $n = 100$. We fitted seven linear autoregressive models $1 \le m \le p$, each has $m + 1$ coefficients and m lags. We found the best fit coefficients using the maximum likelihood method (or least squares) and found the corresponding mean square error for each of the models. To compute the weights $wt(m)$, we used (23) with $n \to n + 1$, coupled with a recursion procedure to find the normalized weights. In implementing this recursion procedure, we had to compute the ratio of determinants for two successive models. In particular, we observed that the matrix $\mathbf{A}(m)$ is obtained from $\mathbf{A}(m+1)$ by deleting the $(m+1)^{th}$ row and the $(m+1)^{th}$ column, and so we have the ratio

$$\frac{\det(\mathbf{A}(m))}{\det(\mathbf{A}(m+1))} = b_{(m+1),(m+1)},$$

where $b_{(m+1),(m+1)}$ is the $(m+1) \times (m+1)$ element of the inverse matrix of $\mathbf{A}$. Note that this element has already been computed when we found the coefficients — we employed an LU-decomposition to find the inverse matrix. In other words, we can compute the weights without computing determinants. To complete this recursion procedure, the following equation can be used to compute the ratio of gamma functions to a sufficient accuracy

$$(x + 0.5)! \simeq x! \left(x + 0.75 + \frac{1}{32x} \right)^{\frac{1}{2}}.$$

For comparison purposes, we computed for each model the Akaike Information Criterion (AIC) and its correction (AICC) (which performs better for small n), and the Schwarz Bayesian Criterion (BIC). Sample results are shown in Table 5. The normalized weights, $Wt_n(m)$ and $W_n(m)$ are based on (23) and (18), respectively.

Next we describe ALP relative weight for model selection. We used empirical evidence to define ALP and to make comparisons with BIC. Consider again the expression for $w(m)$ given in (18). For convenience we drop p.

$$w(m) = e^{\frac{m^2 + 4m}{4n}} D^{-\frac{1}{2}} (2\pi)^{\frac{m}{2}} n^{-\frac{m}{2}} \sigma_0^{-n+m+3}. \tag{29}$$

First we note that the term $e^{\frac{m^2 + 4m}{4n}} \approx 1$ when $m \ll n$. Then based on the results from the analysis of data from example (28), we first observe that $\det(A(m + 1)) \approx \det(A(m))S(m)$, where $S(m)$ is the total square error. We also observed that $\det(A(m))/(S(m))^m$ is approximately a constant times m for $m > 1$. So $D^{-\frac{1}{2}} \cdot \sigma_0^m$ is approximately a constant times $\sqrt{m}$. Based on these observations, the weight in (29) reduces to the form

$$\left(\frac{n}{2\pi} \right)^{-\frac{m}{2}} m^{\frac{c}{2}} \sigma_0^{-n+3},$$

where c is a constant. We also observed that σ_0 varied little between contested models, and so we can neglect the σ_0^3 factor. Consequently, we arrived at what we have called in the Tables 5 below the ALP relative weights. After writing k in place of m, we obtain

$$ALP = n \ln \left(\sigma^2 \right) + k \ln \left(\frac{n}{2\pi} \right) + c \ln (k). \tag{30}$$

Recall that $AIC = n \ln \left(\sigma^2 \right) + 2k$, $AICC = n \ln \left(\sigma^2 \right) + \frac{2kn}{n-k-1}$, and $BIC = n \ln \left(\sigma^2 \right) + k \ln (n)$ (see [3]). Other criteria, the minimum message length MML (see [27],[28]), and the minimum description length MDL (see [20]), can be considered as derivative of ALP (see [25]). MDL in the large-sample limit is equivalent to BIC. Both MDL and MML have good properties but differ from ALP in that they select the best model from a space of computable models instead of a weighted sum of models (see [26]). The study in [7] shows good performance of an MML estimator when applied to stationary and non-stationary autoregressive models. The value of the constant c in (30) was determined empirically and for our example, it can be taken to be either 1, or equally well, it can be chosen equal to $\frac{1}{2}$. It was observed that $c \ln (k)$ varies relatively slowly, and thus it was possible to drop this term from expression of ALP in (30). So we end up with

$$ALP = n \ln \left(\sigma^2\right) + k \ln \left(\frac{n}{2\pi}\right). \tag{31}$$

From (31) we see that the ALP-weight becomes equivalent to BIC selection, but with n divided by 2π in the second term. Recall also that BIC is consistent. This suggests that ALP weights could give consistent choices of model orders. We observe from looking at other examples, that BIC, ALP and the normalized weights $Wt_n\left(m\right)$ and $W_n\left(m\right)$, tend to select a lower order model more often than AIC does. ALP seems to favor a more complex model than BIC does (as expected from its form). Recall however that the idea of choosing a best model is not what ALP advocates. In generating the data in Table 5, we set $k = m+2$ ($m+1$ coefficients and σ^2, m = number of lags), and replaced n by $n-p$. Some authors/programs use $k = m+1$ — the number of fitted parameters. The ALP column in Table 5 is based on (31).

Now, assuming "stability", we take the $V\left(k\right)$'s as a set of probabilistic weights and divide the probabilities of the models by $V\left(k\right)$. This is possible as we only use a finite number of them, and moreover, the normalization constant would be irrelevant in most practical applications. We start out with equation (2.13) of Fam (see [6]) that gives an approximation for $V\left(k\right)$. The approximation has 11.6%, -3.3% and 4.9% error for $k = 1, 2$ and 3 respectively, and the error is less than 1% for $k > 13$. Changing to base e, Fam's equation becomes

$$V\left(k\right) = 0.5419005k^{-\frac{k}{2}-\frac{1}{4}} e^{1.415735k}. \tag{32}$$

Using (31), then ALP over $V\left(k\right)$ is given by $ALPV = \sigma^{-n} \left(\frac{0.37023k}{n}\right)^{\frac{k}{2}} k^{\frac{1}{4}}$, or equivalently as

$$ALPV = n \ln(\sigma^2) - k \ln \left(\frac{0.37033k}{n}\right) - \frac{1}{2} \ln k. \tag{33}$$

If we make use of (30), it may be possible to drop the last term from (33) as well. The results from (33) are also shown in Table 5.

Table 5. Information selection criteria and ALP relative weights, for $n = 100$

lags	AIC	AICC	BIC	ALP	Wt_n	W_n	ALPV
1	4.8409	5.1106	12.4386	6.9251	0.00195	0.00209	11.5744
2	6.4696	6.9241	16.5999	9.2485	0.00061	0.00067	14.3362
3	−8.7851	−8.0954	3.8779	−5.3115	0.56549	0.56401	−0.0058
4	−6.9136	−5.9368	8.2820	−2.7452	0.15790	0.15902	2.25974
5	−5.9410	−4.5233	11.8872	−0.9779	0.06392	0.06471	4.2483
6	−8.8725	−7.1582	11.3883	−3.3147	0.16484	0.16403	1.6621
7	−6.9908	−4.8221	15.8026	−0.7382	0.04528	0.04546	3.8717

Next, we compute and present the normalized trimmed weights based on (27), with $n \to n+1$, and utilizing the MC method described in Section 3. Note that no parameter estimation was needed to compute these relative weights. We use the same notation as in Section 3. j was fixed at 5000 points for each lag.

Note that the dimension of the stability domain used exceeds the number of lags by 1 — to account for the intercept a_0. The estimates of values of the normalized trimmed weights obtained are shown in Table 6. Column '$Twt.1$' was computed using $m_c = 5000$, while column '$Twt.2$' was computed with $m_c = 1000$. Note that by a simple change of variable in (27), the m_c points used to evaluate the integral over any ray need only be generated once from the uniform distribution on $[0, 1]$. Thus the estimates of these relative weights are not so sensitive to the value of m_c used. All the estimates in Table 6 were obtained using a single-shot calculation, and can be considered as rough estimates. These rough estimates are perhaps potentially good enough estimates for preliminary model selection and model screening purposes.

Table 6. Normalized trimmed weights estimates, for $n = 100$

lags	$Twt.1$	$Twt.2$
1	0.00906	0.00931
2	0.00305	0.00343
3	0.79711	0.79493
4	0.14202	0.14311
5	0.03158	0.03163
6	0.01349	0.01386
7	0.00370	0.00373

From Tables 5 and 6, we see that the trimmed weights are sharper than the weights derived over the whole coefficient space. For this example we have that all the selection and weight criteria are in unison — but this is not always the case. For large values of n, the multivariate distribution gets narrower, so one would expect that the integration limits to infinity become better and better approximations. Of course it would be of interest to carry out a simulation study that would give the frequency of selection, or order identification, of the data generator by each of these criteria over a large number of models.

5   Final Remarks

As was mentioned in the introduction, our ultimate goal is to study predictions. The next step then would be to compute for each of the models a probability $L_{\hat{\Theta}_m}(x_{n+1}, \mathbf{X}_n)$, the probability, in view of $L_{\hat{\Theta}_m}$, that the value following $\mathbf{X}_n$ will be x_{n+1}. Then obtain a "Combination Model Probability" for x_{n+1} (and x_{n+2}, etc.) using the associated normalized weights. This is much like what has been done in BMA, where the distribution of future observations is expressed as a mixture model in which the model specific distributions are weighted by the posterior probabilities that measure the support that the data gives to each model. It is well known that there are a number of estimation algorithms for ARMA processes in the literature. However, it appears that there are no definitive consensus in the literature on the issue of accuracy of these estimation procedures for model selection purposes (see [5]). Thus before making predictions, the parameter estimation method for the class of models used have to be carefully examined — some comments are given in ([7]). The method for computing the trimmed weights proposed above should be viewed as experimental at this point. Further investigation is necessary to determine the accuracy and the efficiency of computing these trimmed weights more precisely. A standard issue with Monte Carlo type methods is to devise an appropriate distribution of the sample over the domain of the integrand. This is also an important issue for us. To begin with, a detailed study of the empirical distribution of R and its relationship to the size of the initial sphere about the origin (or any other "box"), and its relationship to the distribution type put on such a sphere, need to be carried out. It seems that once a good procedure is established to compute the volumes accurately, estimates of the other integrals can be evaluated with some confidence. From the limited number of trials that we have carried out, it appears that the mean value of the Gaussian type integrals were less sensitive to the parameters in the procedure than the average value of the stability domain volume itself. In addition, it is important to understand better how to characterize stationarity using a small training sample from the data.

Finally, we would like to point out a representation of the AR model in the space of the reflection coefficients (also known as the partial autocorrelation coefficients), which are encountered in the Durbin-Levinson estimation procedure (see [4],[16] cited in [22], and [17]). The stability region in reflection coefficient space is an n-dimensional hypercube obtained via an invertible continuous mapping given in terms of a recurrence relationship. The generation of uniform samples from the stationary region is discussed in [11]. It would be of interest to examine the use of this approach to compute the trimmed weights, and to compare its performance with the more direct semi-stochastic shooting MC method we have suggested above.

Tribute and Acknowledgement. The second author was privileged to meet and work with Ray on this project and is honored to be his coauthor — but with great sadness as he is no longer with us today. Ray was a true scholar with a very gentle and warm personality and a very kind heart. It was a pleasure to work with him. The work with Ray on this project started in the spring of 2008. Ray sent his last message to the second author on Nov. 17, 2009. During that time, although the authors were burdened by other commitments, they have managed to complete the material of sections 1 & 2, and start the work on sections 3 & 4. Ray was very enthusiastic about this work and led the research effort while he was alive. The main goal of Ray was to use ALP to investigate predictions. Ray was very creative and very generous with his ideas and remained very sharp until the end. At the time I met Ray at Notre Dame University (NDU), Lebanon, I also met his wonderful wife Grace. I was fortunate to spend a few memorable evenings socializing with them. Later on, we communicated and socialized by email, and both Ray and Grace often inquired about my office cats Vivo and Nutnoot. I owe much to Grace for her friendship, and for her support and encouragement to finish this article. I owe also a special thanks to Ray's nephew, Dr. Alex Solomonoff, for several helpful suggestions on the first draft of this article. Last but not least, I would like to thank Prof. David Dowe and the referees for their time and helpful suggestions.

References

1. Akaike, H.: A new look at statistical model identification. IEEE Trans. Aut. Control 19, 716–723 (1974)
2. Akaike, H.: Information measures and model selection. Bull. of Int. Stat. Inst. 50, 277–290 (1983)
3. Burnham, K.P., Anderson, D.R.: Model selection and multimodel inference: a practical information-theoretical approach, 2nd edn. Springer, N.Y. (2002)
4. Brandoff-Nielsen, O., Schou, G.: On the parametrization of autoregressive models by partial autocorrelations. J. Multivar. Anal. 3, 408–419 (1973)
5. Chen, C., Davis, R.A., Brockwell, J.P., Bai, Z.D.: Order determination for autoregressive processes using resampling method. Stat. Sinica 3, 481–500 (1993)
6. Fam, A.T.: The volume of the coefficient space stability domain of monic polynomials. In: IEEE Int. Symp. Circuits and Systems, Portland, Oregon, vol. 2, pp. 1780–1783 (1989)
7. Fitzgibbon, L.J., Dowe, D., Vahid, F.: Minimum message length autoregressive model order selection. In: Palanaswami, M., Chandra Sekhar, C., Kumar Venayagamoorthy, G., Mohan, S., Ghantasala, M.K. (eds.) International Conference on Intelligent Sensing and Information Processing (ICISIP), Chennai, India, January 4-7, pp. 439–444 (2004)
8. Hutter, M.: Algorithmic information theory. Scholarpedia 2(3), 2519 (2007)
9. Hoeting, J.A., Madigan, D., Raftery, A.E., Volinsky, C.T.: Bayesian Model Averaging: A Tutorial. Statistical Science 14, 382–401 (1999)
10. Hurvich, C.M., Tsai, C.-L.: Regression and time series model selection in small samples. Biometrika 76, 297–397 (1989)
11. Jones, M.C.: Randomly choosing parameters from the stationary and invertibility regions of autoregressive-moving average models. J. Roy. Stat. Soc., Series C (Appl. Stat.) 36, 134–138 (1987)
12. Knuth, D.: The art of computer programming, Volume 2: Seminumerical Algorithms, 3rd edn. Addison-Wesley (1997)
13. Kass, R.E., Raftery, A.E.: Bayes Factors. J. Amer. Stat. Assoc. 90, 773–795 (1995)
14. Liang, F., Barron, A.: Minimax strategies for predictive density estimation, data compression, and model selection. IEEE Trans. Info. Th. 50, 2708–2726 (2004)
15. Li, M., Vitányi, P.: An introduction to Kolomogorov complexity and its applications. Springer, N.Y. (1997)
16. Makhoul, J.: Linear prediction: a tutorial review. Proc. IEEE 63, 561–580 (1975)
17. Monahan, J.F.: A note on enforcing stationarity in autoregressive-moving average models. Biometrika 71, 403–404 (1984)
18. Nikolaev, Y.P.: The multidimensional asymptotic stability domain of linear discrete systems: Its symmetry and other properties. Aut. and Rem. Control 62, 109–120 (2001)
19. Piccolo, D.: The size of the stationarity and invertibility region of an autoregressive-moving average process. J. of Time Series Analysis 3, 245–247 (1982)

20. Rissanen, J.: Modeling by the shortest data description. Automatica 14, 465–471 (1978)
21. Schwarz, G.: Estimating the dimension of a model. Ann. of Stat. 6, 461–464 (1978)
22. Shlien, S.: A Geometric description of stable linear predictive coding digital filters. IEEE Trans. Info. Th. 31, 545–548 (1985)
23. Solomonoff, R.J.: A preliminary report on general theory of inductive inference (1960)
24. Solomonoff, R.J.: A formal theory of inductive inference. Inform. and Control, Part I, 1-22, Part II 7, 224–254 (1964)
25. Solomonoff, R.J.: The discovery of algorithmic probability. J. Comp. & Sys. Sci. 55, 73–88 (1997)
26. Solomonoff, R.J.: Algorithmic Probability: Theory and Applications, Revision of article. In: Emmert-Streib, F., Dehmer, M. (eds.) Information Theory and Statistical Learning, pp. 1–23. Springer Science+Business Media, N.Y. (2009)
27. Wallace, C.S., Boulton, D.M.: An information measure for classification. Comput. J. 11, 185–194 (1968)
28. Wallace, C.S., Dowe, D.L.: Minimum Message Length and Kolmogorov Complexity. Computer J. 42, 270–283 (1999)

Appendix A. In this appendix we give a recursion formula that is helpful in computing certain Gaussian type integrals. We are interested in the integral

$$I_k = \int_0^R x^k exp(-\frac{(x-a)^2}{2\sigma^2})dx.$$

Let $y = x - a$, so $x = y + a$, $dx = dy$, then $I_k = \int_{-a}^{R-a}(y+a)^k exp(-\frac{y^2}{2\sigma^2})dy$.
Let $z^2 = \frac{y^2}{2\sigma^2}$, so $z = \frac{y}{\sigma\sqrt{2}}$, $y = z\sigma\sqrt{2}$, $y + a = z\sigma\sqrt{2} + a$, $dy = dz\sigma\sqrt{2}$, then
$I_k = \int_{\frac{-a}{\sigma\sqrt{2}}}^{\frac{R-a}{\sigma\sqrt{2}}}(z + \frac{-a}{\sigma\sqrt{2}})^k(\sigma\sqrt{2})^{k+1}e^{-z^2}dz$. Let $b = \frac{a}{\sigma\sqrt{2}}$, then

$$I_k = (\sigma\sqrt{2})^{k+1}\int_{\frac{-a}{\sigma\sqrt{2}}}^{\frac{R-a}{\sigma\sqrt{2}}}(z+b)^k e^{-z^2}dz.$$

Let's look at $\int(z+b)^k e^{-z^2}dz$, with "integration by parts" in mind: $d(FG) = FdG + GdF$ so $FG = \int FdG + \int GdF$. Let $F = \frac{(z+b)^{k+1}}{k+1}$ and $G = e^{-z^2}$, so

$$\frac{(z+b)^{k+1}}{k+1}e^{-z^2} = \frac{-2}{k+1}\int(z+b)^{k+1}z\, e^{-z^2}dz + \int(z+b)^k e^{-z^2}dz$$

We note that

$$\frac{-2}{k+1}(z+b)^{k+1}z\, e^{-z^2} = \frac{2}{k+1}(z+b)^{k+2}e^{-z^2} - \frac{2}{k+1}(z+b)^{k+1}b\, e^{-z^2}$$

Substituting this value of $\frac{-2}{k+1}(z+b)^{k+1}z\, e^{-z^2}$ into the previous equation and multiplying by e^{z^2}, we can obtain that

$$\frac{(z+b)^{k+1}}{k+1} - \frac{e^{z^2} b^{k+1}}{k+1} = \frac{-2}{k+1} H(z, k+2) + \frac{2b}{k+1} H(z, k+1) + H(z, k),$$

where

$$H(z, k) = e^{z^2} \int_0^z (\varepsilon + b)^k e^{-\varepsilon^2} d\varepsilon, H(z, 0) = e^{z^2} \int_0^z e^{-\varepsilon^2} d\varepsilon = \frac{1}{2} \sqrt{\pi} e^{z^2} erf(z),$$

and

$$H(z, 1) = e^{z^2} \int_0^z (\varepsilon + b) e^{-\varepsilon^2} d\varepsilon = -\frac{1}{2} + \frac{1}{2} e^{z^2} \left(b \sqrt{\pi} erf(z) + 1 \right).$$

As we are after $I_k = \left(\sigma \sqrt{2} \right)^{k+1} \int_{\frac{-a}{\sigma\sqrt{2}}}^{\frac{R-a}{\sigma\sqrt{2}}} \left(\varepsilon + \frac{a}{\sigma\sqrt{2}} \right)^k e^{-\varepsilon^2} d\varepsilon$, we see that

$$I_k = \left(\sigma \sqrt{2} \right)^{k+1} \left[e^{-\left(\frac{R-a}{\sigma\sqrt{2}} \right)^2} H\left(\left(\frac{R-a}{\sigma\sqrt{2}} \right), k \right) - e^{-\left(\frac{-a}{\sigma\sqrt{2}} \right)^2} H\left(\frac{-a}{\sigma\sqrt{2}}, k \right) \right].$$

Picture: Elias receiving a certificate from Ray for completing a course that Ray gave at NDU in March of 2008.

Principles of Solomonoff Induction and AIXI

Peter Sunehag[1] and Marcus Hutter[1,2]

[1] Research School of Computer Science, Australian National University, Canberra,
ACT, 0200, Australia
[2] Department of Computer Science, ETH Zurich, Switzerland
{Peter.Sunehag,Marcus.Hutter}@anu.edu.au

Abstract. We identify principles characterizing Solomonoff Induction
by demands on an agent's external behaviour. Key concepts are rationality, computability, indifference and time consistency. Furthermore, we
discuss extensions to the full AI case to derive AIXI.

Keywords: Computability, Representation, Rationality, Solomonoff
induction.

1   Introduction

Ray Solomonoff [17] introduced a universal sequence prediction method that in
[19,6,11] is argued to solve the general induction problem. [5] extended Solomonoff
induction to the full AI (general reinforcement learning) setting where an agent
is taking a sequence of actions that may affect the unknown environment to
achieve as large amount of reward as possible. The resulting agent was named
AIXI. Here we take a closer look at what principles underlie Solomonoff induction and the AIXI agent. We are going to derive Solomonoff induction from four
general principles and discuss how AIXI follows from extended versions of the
same.

Our setting consists of a reference universal Turing machine (UTM), a binary
sequence (produced by an environment program (not revealed) on the reference
machine) fed incrementaly to the agent and a loss function (or reward structure).
We give the agent in question the task of choosing a program for the reference
machine so as to minimize the loss. The loss is in general defined to be a function from a pair of programs, an environment program and an agent program,
to real numbers. The loss function can be such that it is only the prediction (for
a certain number of bits) produced by the program that matters or it can care
about exactly which program was presented. A loss function of the latter kind
leads to the agent performing the task of prediction, which is what Solomonoff
induction is primarily concerned with while the latter can be viewed as identifying an explanatory hypothesis, which is more closely related to the minimum
message length principle [23,24,22,3] or the minimum description length principle [12,4,13]. Solomonoff induction is using a mixture of hypothesis to achieve
the best possible prediction. Note that the fact that we pick one program does
not rule out that the choice is internally based on a mixture. In the case when

D.L. Dowe (Ed.): Solomonoff Festschrift, LNAI 7070, pp. 386–398, 2013.

the loss only cares about the prediction, the program is only a representation of that prediction and not really a hypothesis.

The principles are designed to avoid stating what the internal workings of the agent should be and instead derive those as a consequence of the demands on the behaviour. Thus we demand rationality instead of stating explicitly that the agent should have probabilistic beliefs and we demand time consistency instead of explicitly stating probabilistic conditioning. The computability principle is avoiding saying that the agent should have a hypothesis class that consists of all computable environments by instead demanding that it deliver a computation procedure (a program for our reference machine) that produces its prediction for the next few bits.The indifference principle states what the initial preferences of the agent must be, i.e. a demand for how the initial decision should be taken. The choice is based on symmetry with respect to a chosen representation scheme for sequences, e.g. programs on a reference machine. In other words we do not allow the agent to be biased in a certain sense that depends on our reference machine. Informally we state the principles as follows:

1. **Computability:** If we are going to guess the future of a sequence, we should choose a computation procedure (a program for the reference machine) that produces the predicted bits

2. **Rationality:** We should choose our predicted sequence such that the dependence on the priorities (formalized by a reward (or loss) structure) is consistent.

3. **Indifference:** The initial choice between programs only depends on their length and the priorities (again formalized by reward (or loss))

4. **Time Consistency:** The choice of program does not change by a new observation if the program's output is consistent with the oberservation and the reward structure is still the same and concerned with the same bits

Our reasoning leading from external behavioural principles to a completely defined internal procedure can be summarized as follows; The rationality principle tells us that we need to have probabilistic beliefs over some set of alternatives; The computability principle tells us what the alternatives are, namely programs; The indifference principle leads to a choice of the original beliefs; The time-consistency principle leads to a simple procedure for updating the beliefs that the second principle tells us must exist, namely conditioning. In total it leads to Solomonoff Induction.

We can not remove any of the principles without losing the complete specification of a procedure. The first property is part of the set up of what we ask the agent to do. Without the second we lose the restriction that we take decisions based on maximum expected utility with respect to probabilistic beliefs and one could then have an agent that always chose the same program (e.g. a very short one). Without the third principle we could have any apriori beliefs and without the fourth the agent could after a while change its mind regarding what beliefs it started with.

1.1   Setup

We are considering a setting where we give an agent a task that is defined by a reference machine (a UTM) , a reward structure (or loss function if we negate) and a binary sequence that is presented one bit at a time. The binary sequence is generated by a program for the reference machine.

The agent must (as stated by the first principle) chose a program (whose output must be consistent with anything that we have seen in case we have made observations) for the reference machine and then use its output (which can be of finite or infinite length) as a prediction. If we want to predict at least h bits we have to restrict ourself to machines that output at least h bits. We will consider an enumeration of all programs T_i. We are also going to consider a class of reward structures $R_{i,j}$. The meaning is that if we guess that the sequence is (as the output of) T_i and the actual sequence is T_j, then we receive reward $R_{i,j}$. Note that for any finite string there are always Turing machines that computes it. We will furthermore suppose that $\forall i$, $R_{i,j} \to 0$ as $j \to \infty$. This means that we consider it to be a harder and harder task to guess T_j as j gets really large. This assumption is not strictly necessary as we will discuss later.

1.2   Outline

Section 2 provides background on Solomonoff induction and AIXI. In Section 3 we deal with the first two principles mentioned above about rationality and computability. In Section 4, we discuss the third principle which defines a prior from a (Universal Turing Machine) representation. Section 5 describes the sequence prediction algorithm that results from adding the fourth principle to what has been achieved in the previous sections. Section 6 extends our analysis to the case where an agent takes a sequence of actions that may affect its environment. Section 7 concerns equivalence between our beliefs over deterministic environments and beliefs over a much larger class of stochastic environments.

2   Background

2.1   Sequence Prediction

We consider both finite and infinite sequences from a finite alphabet $\mathcal{X}$. We denote the finite strings by $\mathcal{X}^*$ and we use the notation $x_{1:t} := x_1, x_2, ..., x_t$ for the first t elements in a sequence x. A function $\rho : \mathcal{X}^* \to [0,1]$ is a probability measure if

$$\rho(x) = \sum_{a \in \mathcal{X}} \rho(xa) \ \forall x \in \mathcal{X}^* \tag{1}$$

and $\rho(\epsilon) = 1$ where ϵ is the empty string. Such a function describes a priori probabilistic beliefs about the sequence. If the equality in (1) is instead $\geq$ and $\rho(\epsilon) \leq 1$ then we have a semi-measure. We define the probability of seeing the string a after seeing x as being $\rho(a|x) := \rho(xa)/\rho(x)$. If we have a loss function $L : \mathcal{X} \times \mathcal{X} \to \mathbb{R}$, we ([6]) choose, after seeing the string x, to predict

$$\operatorname*{argmin}_{a \in \mathcal{X}} \sum_{b \in \mathcal{X}} L(a,b)\rho(b|x). \tag{2}$$

More generally, if we have an alphabet $\mathcal{Y}$ of actions we can take and a loss function $L : \mathcal{Y} \times \mathcal{X} \to \mathbb{R}$ we make the choice

$$\operatorname*{argmin}_{a \in \mathcal{Y}} \sum_{b \in \mathcal{X}} L(a,b)\rho(b|x). \tag{3}$$

2.2   The Solomonoff Prior

Ray Solomonoff [17] defined a set of priors that only differ by a multiplicative constant. We call them Solomonoff priors. To define them we need to first introduce some notions about Turing machines [21].

A *monotone Turing machine* T (which we will just call Turing machine and whose exact technical definition can be found in [8]) is a function from a set of (binary) strings to binary sequences that can either be finite or infinite. We demand that it be possible to describe the function as a machine with unidirectional input and output tapes, read/write heads, a bidirectional work tape and a finite state machine that decides the next action of the machine given the symbols under the head on the input and work tape. The input tape is read only and the output tape is write only. We write that $T(p) = x*$ if output of T starts with x when given input (*program*) p.

A *universal Turing machine* is a Turing machine that can emulate all other Turing machines in the sense that for every Turing machine T there is at least one prefix p, such that when px is fed to the universal Turing machine, it computes the same output as T would when fed x (See [8,5] for further details).

A sequence is called *computable* if some Turing machine outputs it, or in other words, if for every universal Turing machine there is a program p that leads to this sequence being the output.

We can also define what we will call a *computable environment* from a Turing machine. A computable environment is something which you (an agent) feed an action to and the environment outputs a string which we call a perception. We can for example have a finite number of possible actions and we put one after another on the input tape of the machine. We wait until the previous input has been processed and one of finitely many outputs has been produced. The machine might halt after a finite number of actions have been processed or it might run for ever.

Definition 1 (Semi-measure from Turing Machine). *Given a Turing machine T, we let*

$$\lambda_T(x) := \sum_{p:T(p)=x*} 2^{-l(p)} \tag{4}$$

where $l(p)$ is the length of the program (input) p and $T(p) = x*$ means that T starts with outputting x when fed p, though it might continue and output more afterwards.

If the Turing machine T in Definition 1 is universal we call λ_T a Solomonoff distribution. Solomonoff induction is defined by letting ρ in Section 2.1 be the Solomonoff prior for some universal Turing machine. If U is a universal Turing machine and T is any Turing machine there exists a constant $c > 0$ (namely $2^{-l(q)}$ where q is the prefix that encodes T in U) such that

$$\lambda_U(x) \geq c\lambda_T(x) \; \forall x \in \mathcal{X}^*. \tag{5}$$

The set $\{\lambda_T \mid T \text{ Turing}\}$ can be identified with [8] with all lower semi-computable semi-measures (see [8] for definitions and proofs). The property expressed by (5) is called universality (or dominance) and is the key to proving the strong convergence results of Solomonoff Induction [18,8,5,6].

2.3   AIXI

In the active case where an agent is taking a sequence of actions to achieve some sort of objective, we are trying to determine the best *policy* π, defined as a function from a history $a_1 q_1, ..., a_t q_t$ of actions a_t and perceptions q_t to a choice of the next action a_{t+1}. The function ρ from the sequence prediction case is in the active case of the form $\rho(q_1, ..., q_t | a_1, ..., a_t)$ and represent the probability of seing $q_1, ..., q_t$ given that we have chosen actions $a_1, ..., a_t$. We can again define a "learning" algorithm by conditioning on what we have seen to define

$$\rho(q_{t+1}, ..., q_{t+k} | q_1, ..., q_t, a_1, ..., a_{t+k}) := \frac{\rho(q_1, ..., q_{t+k} | a_1, ..., a_{t+k})}{\rho(q_1, ..., q_t | a_1, ..., a_t)}. \tag{6}$$

If $a_t = \pi(a_1 q_1, ..., a_{t-1} q_{t-1}) \; \forall t$ and $q = q_1, q_2, ...$, then we also write $\rho(q|\pi)$ for the left hand side in (6).

Suppose that we have an enumerated set of policies $\{\pi_i\}$ to choose from. Given a definition of reward $R(q)$ for a sequence of percepts $q = q_1, q_2, ...$ that can for example be defined as in reinforcement learning by splitting q_t into observation o_t and reward r_t and using a discounted reward sum $\sum_t \gamma^t r_t$ [15,5], then we can define

$$R(\pi) := \mathbb{E}_\rho R(q) := \sum_q R(q)\rho(q|\pi) \tag{7}$$

and make the choice

$$\pi^* := \operatorname*{argmax}_\pi R(\pi). \tag{8}$$

If we have a class of environments $\{T_j\}$ (say the computable environments) and if ρ is defined by saying that we assign probability p_j to T_j being the true environment, then we let $R_{i,j} = R(q)$ if q is the sequence of perceptions resulting from using policy π_i in environment T_j. Then $R(\pi_i) = \sum_j p_j R_{i,j}$ and we choose the policy with index

$$\operatorname*{argmax}_i \sum p_j R_{i,j}. \tag{9}$$

As outlined in [5], one can choose a Solomonoff distribution also over active environments. The resulting agent is referred to as AIXI.

3   Choosing a Program

In this section we describe the setup of the second principle mentioned in the introduction, namely rationality. The section is much briefer than what is suitable for the topic and we refer the reader to our companion paper [16] for a more compherensive treatment. Rationality is meant in the sense of internal consistency [20], which is how it has been used in [9] and [14]. We set up simple axioms for a rational decision maker, which implies that the decisions can be explained (or defined) from probabilistic beliefs. The approach to probability by [10,1] is interpreting probabilities as fair betting odds. There is an intuitive similarity between our setup to the idea of explaining/deriving probabilities as a bookmaker's betting odds as done in [1] and [10].

Before we consider the question regarding which program we want to choose we will first consider the question if we are prepared to accept guessing T_i for a given $R = \{R_{i,j}\}$ (i.e. accepting this bet). We suppose that the alternative is to abstain (reject) and receive zero reward. We introduce rationality axioms and prove that we must have probabilistic beliefs over the possible sequences. Note that for any given i, we have a sequence $R_{i,j}$ in c_0 (the space of real valued sequences that converge to 0). We will set up some common sense rationality axioms for the way we make our decisions. We will demand that a decision can be taken for any reward structure r ($R_{i,j}$ with fixed i) from c_0. If r is acceptable and $\lambda \geq 0$ then we want λr to be acceptable since this is simply a multiple of the same. We also want the sum of two acceptable reward structures to be acceptable. If we cannot lose (receive negative reward) we are prepared to accept while if we are guaranteed to gain we are not prepared to reject it. We cannot remove any axiom without losing the conclusion.

Definition 2 (Rationality). *Suppose that we have a function $z : c_0 \rightarrow \{-1,1,0\}$ defining the decision reject/accept/either $(-1/1/0)$ and $Z = \{r \in c_0 \mid z(r) \in \{0,1\}\}$.*

1. *$z(r) \in \{0,1\}$ if and only if $z(-r) \in \{-1,0\}$*
2. *$r, s \in Z$, $\lambda, \gamma \geq 0$ then $\lambda r + \gamma s \in Z$*
3. *If $r_k \geq 0 \ \forall k$ then $r \in Z$ while if $r_k > 0 \ \forall k$ then $z(r) = 1$.*

The following theorem connects our Rationality axioms with the Hahn-Banach theorem [7] and concludes that rational decisions can be described with a positive continuous linear functional on the space of reward structures. The Banach space dual of c_0 is ℓ_1 which gives us a probabilistic representation of underlying beliefs.

Theorem 1 (Linear Separation). *Given the assumptions in Definition 2 there exists a positive continuous linear functional* $f : c_0 \to \mathbb{R}$ *defined by* $f(r) = \sum_j r_j p_j$ *where* $r = \{r_j\}$, $p_j \geq 0$ *and* $\sum_j p_j < \infty$, *such that*

$$\{x \mid f(r) > 0\} \subseteq Z \subseteq \{r \mid f(r) \geq 0\}. \tag{10}$$

Proof. The second property tells us that Z and $-Z$ are convex cones. The first and third property tells us that $Z \neq \mathbb{R}^m$. Suppose that there is a point r that lies in both the interior of Z and of $-Z$. Then the same is true for $-r$ according to the first property and for the origin. That a ball around the origin lies in Z means that $Z = \mathbb{R}^m$ which is not true. Thus the interiors of Z and $-Z$ are disjoint open convex sets and can, therefore, be separated by a hyperplane (according to the Hahn-Banach theorem) which goes through the origin (since according to the first and third property $z(0) = 0$). The first property tell us that $Z \cup -Z = \mathbb{R}^m$. Given a separating hyperplane (between the interiors of Z and $-Z$), Z must contain everything on one side. This means that Z is a half space whose boundary is a hyperplane that goes through the origin and the closure $\bar{Z}$ of Z is a closed half space and can be written as $\{r \mid f(r) \geq 0\}$ for some f in the Banach space dual $c_0' = \ell_1$ of c_0. The third property tells us that f is positive.

Theorem 1 also leads us to how to choose between different options. If we consider picking T_i over T_k we will do (accept) that if $R_{i,\cdot} - R_{k,\cdot}$ is accepted. This is the case if $\sum p_j R_{i,j} > \sum p_j R_{k,j}$. The conclusion is that if we are presented with $R_{i,j}$ and a class $\{T_j\}$ and we assign probability p_j to T_j being the truth, then we choose

$$\operatorname*{argmax}_i \sum_j R_{i,j} p_j. \tag{11}$$

Remark 1. If we replace the space c_0 by ℓ_∞ as the space of reward structures in Theorem 1, the conclusion (see [16]) is instead that f is in the Banach space dual ℓ'_∞ of ℓ_∞ which contains ℓ_1 (the countably additive measures) but also functions that cannot be written on the form $f(r) = \sum_j r_j p_j$. ℓ'_∞ is sometimes called the ba space [2] and it consists of all finitely additive measures.

4   Representation

In this section we will discuss how indifference together with a representation leads to a choice of prior weights. The representation will be given in terms of codes that are strings of letters from a finite alphabet and it tells us which distinctions we will apply our indifference principle to. Choosing the first bit can be viewed as choosing between two propositions, e.g. x is a vegetable or x is a fruit. More choices follow until a full specification (a code word for the given reference machine) is reached. The section describes the usual material on the Solomonoff distribution (see [8]) in a way that highlights in what sense it is based on indifference. The indifference principle itself is an external behavioural principle.

Definition 3 (Indifference). *Given a reward structure for two alternative out-comes of an event where we receive R_1 or R_2 depending on the outcome, then if we are indifferent we accept this bet if $R_1 + R_2 > 0$. For an agent with proba-bilistic beliefs that maximize expected utility this means that equal probability is assigned to both possibilities.*

We will discuss examples that are based on considering the set {apple, orange, carrot} and the representation that is defined by first separating fruit from veg-etables and then the fruits into apples and oranges.

Example 1. We are about to open a box within which there is either a fruit or a vegetable. We have no other information (except possibly, a list of what is a fruit and what is a vegetable).

Example 2. We are about to open a box within which there is either an apple, or an orange or a carrot. We have no other information.

Consider a representation where we use binary codes. If the first digit is a 0 it means a vegetable, i.e. a carrot. No more digits are needed to describe the object. If the first digit is a 1 it means a fruit. If the next digit after the 1 is a 0 its an apple and if it is a 1 its an orange. In the absence of any other background knowledge/information and given that we are going to be indifferent for this choice, we assign uniform probabilities for each choice of letter in the string. For our examples this results in probabilities $Pr(\text{fruit}) = Pr(\text{vegetable}) = 1/2$. After concluding this we consider the next distinction and conclude that $Pr(\text{apple}|\text{fruit}) = Pr(\text{orange}|\text{fruit}) = 1/2$. This means that the decision maker has the prior beliefs $Pr(\text{carrot}) = 1/2$, $Pr(\text{apple}) = Pr(\text{orange}) = 1/4$.

An alternative representation would be to have a trinary alphabet and give each object its own letter. The result of this is $Pr(\text{apple}) = Pr(\text{orange}) = Pr(\text{carrot}) = 1/3$, $Pr(\text{fruit}) = 2/3$ and $Pr(\text{vegetable}) = 1/3$.

The following formalizes the definition of a code and a prefix free code. Since we are assuming that the possible outcomes are never special cases of each other we need our code to be prefix free. Furthermore, Kraft's inequality says that $\sum_{c \in \mathcal{C}} 2^{-length(c)} \leq 1$ if the set of codes $\mathcal{C}$ is prefix free.

Definition 4 (Codes). *A code for a set $\mathcal{A}$ is a set of strings $\mathcal{C}$ of letters from a finite alphabet $\mathcal{B}$ and a surjective map from $\mathcal{C}$ to $\mathcal{A}$. We say that a code is prefix-free if no code string is a proper prefix of another.*

Definition 5 (Computable Representation). *We say that a code is a com-putable representation if the map from code-strings to outcomes is a Turing machine.*

In the definition below we provide the formula for how a binary representation of the letters in an alphabet leads to a choice of a distribution. It is easily extended to non-binary representations.

Definition 6 (Distribution from representation). *Given a binary prefix-free code for $\mathcal{A}$ (our possible outcomes), the expression*

$$w_a = \sum_{c \text{ code for } a} 2^{-length(c)}, \ a \in \mathcal{A}$$

defines a measure over $\mathcal{A}$.

Though the formula in Definition 6 uniquely determines the weights given a representation, there is still a very wide choice of representations. We are going to deal with this concern to restrict ourself to the class of universal representations with the property that given any other computable representation, the universal weights are at least a constant times the weights resulting from the other representation. See [17,8,5] for a more extensive treatment. These universal representations are defined by having a universal Turing machine (in our case the given reference machine) as the map from codes to outcomes.

Definition 7 (Universal Representation). *If a universal Turing machine is used for defining the map from codes to outcomes we say that we have a universal (computable) representation.*

The weights that result from using a universal representation w_a^U satisfy the property that if w_a are the resulting weights from another computable representation, then there is $C > 0$ such that $w_a^U \geq C w_a \ \forall a \in \mathcal{A}$. This follows directly from the universality of the Turing machine, which means that any other Turing machine can be simulated on the universal one by adding an extra prefix (interpreter) to each code. That is, feeding ic to the universal machine gives the same output as feeding c to the other machine. The constant C is $2^{-length(i)}$.

Theorem 2. *Applying Definition 6 together with a representation of finite strings based on a universal Turing machine gives us the Solomonoff semi-measure.*

Proof. Given a universal Turing machine U we create a set of codes $\mathcal{C}$ from all programs that generate an output of at least h bits. We let the code $c \in \mathcal{C}$ represent the finite string $x \in \mathcal{X}^*$ with $l(x) = h$ if $U(c) = x*$. We show below that this representation together with Definition 6 leads to the Solomonoff distribution for the next h bits. By considering all $h \geq 1$ we recover the Solomonoff semi-measure over $\mathcal{X}^*$.

Formally, given $x \in \mathcal{X}^*$ we let (in Definition 6) $a = x$ and we define $\rho(x) := w_a$ and conclude that

$$\rho(x) = \sum_{U(p)=x*} 2^{-length(p)}$$

which is the Solomonoff semi-measure.

Remark 2 (Unique Representation). Given a universal Turing machine, we could choose to let only the shortest program that generates a certain output represent that output, and not all the programs that generate this output. The length of the shortest program p that gives output x is called the Kolmogorov complexity $K(x)$ of x. Using only the shortest program leads to the slightly different weights

$$w_x = 2^{-K(x)}$$

compared to Definition 6. Both weighting schemes are, however, equivalent within a multiplicative constant [8].

5   Sequence Prediction

We will in this section summarize how Solomonoff Induction as described in [6] follows from what we have presented in Section 3 and Section 4 together with our fourth principle of time consistency. Consider a binary sequence that is revealed to us one bit at a time. We are trying to predict the future of the sequence, either one bit, several bits or all of them. By combining the conclusions of Section 3 and 4, we can define a sequence prediction algorithm which turns out to be Solomonoff Induction. The results from Section 3 tells us that if we are going to be able to make rational guesses about which computable sequence we will see, we need to have probabilistic beliefs.

If we are interested in predicting a finite number of bits we need to design the reward structure in Section 3 to reflect what we are interested in. If we want to predict the next bit we can let $R_{i,j} = 1$ if T_i and T_j have the same next bit and $R_{i,j} = -1$ otherwise. This leads to (a weighted majority decision to) predicting 1 if $\sum_{j|T_j \text{ produces } 1} p_j > \sum_{j|T_j \text{ produces } 0} p_j$ and 0 if the reverse inequality is true. The reasoning and result generalizes naturally to predicting finitely many bits and we can interpret this as minimizing the expected number of errors.

5.1   Updating

Suppose that we have observed a number of bits of the sequences. This result in contradictions with many of the sequences and they can be ruled out. We next formally state the fourth principle from the introduction.

Definition 8 (Time-consistency). *Suppose that we are observing a sequence* $x_1, x_2, \ldots$ *one bit at a time (x_t at time t). Suppose that we (at time t) want to predict the next h bits of a sequence and our decisions (for any t and h) are defined by a function z_h^t from the set of all reward structures ($\mathbb{R}^{m \times m}$ where $m = 2^h$ in the binary case) to the set of strings of length h.*

Suppose that if $z_{h+1}^t(r) = y$ and y starts with x_{t+1}. If it then follows that $z_h^{t+1}(r') = y$ where r' is the restriction of r to the strings that start with x_{t+1} (and we identify such a string of length $h + 1$ with the string of length h that follow the first bit) and if this implication is true for any t, r, h we say that we have time-consistency.

Theorem 3. *Suppose that we have a semi-measure $\rho : \mathcal{X}^* \to [0, 1]$ and that we at time 0 (given any loss L) predict the next h bits according to*

$$\underset{y_1 \in \mathcal{X}^h}{\operatorname{argmin}} \sum_{y_2 \in \mathcal{X}^h} L(y_1, y_2) \rho(y_2). \tag{12}$$

If we furthermore assume time-consistency and observe $x \in \mathcal{X}^*$, then we predict

$$\operatorname*{argmin}_{y_1 \in \mathcal{X}^h} \sum_{y_2 \in \mathcal{X}^h} L(y_1, y_2) \rho(xy_2|x). \qquad (13)$$

Proof. Suppose that there are y_1, y_2 and x such that $\frac{\rho(xy_1|x)}{\rho(xy_2|x)} \neq \frac{\rho(xy_1)}{\rho(xy_2)}$. This obviously contradicts time-consistency. In other words, time-consistency implies that relative beliefs in strings that are not yet contradicted remains the same. Therefore, the decision function after seeing x can be described by a semi-measure where the inconsistent alternatives have been ruled out and the others just renormalized. This is what (13) is describing. The only remaining point to make is that we have expressed (12) and (13) in terms of loss instead of reward though it is simply a matter of changing the sign and max for min.

6   The AIXI Agent

In this section we discuss extensions to the case where an agent is choosing a sequence of actions that affect the environment it is in. We will simply replace the principle that says that we predict computable sequences by one that says that we predict computable environments. The environments are such that the agent takes an action that is fed to the environment and the environment responds with an output that we call a perception. There is a finite alphabet for the action and one for the perception.

Our aim is to choose a policy for the agent. This is a function from the history of the actions and perceptions that has appeared so far, to the action which the agent chooses next. Suppose that a class $\{\pi_i\}$ of policies, a class of (all) computable environments $\{T_j\}$ and a reward structure $R_{i,j}$ which is the total reward for using policy π_i in environment T_j. To assume the property that $\lim_j R_{i,j} = 0 \; \forall i$, would mean that we assume that the stakes are lower in the environments of high index. This somewhat restrictive and there are alternatives to making this assumption (that the reward structure is in c_0) and we investigate the result of assuming that we instead have the larger space ℓ_∞ (see Remark 1) in a separate article [16] on rationality axioms and conclude that the difference is that we get finite additivity instead of countable additivity for the probability measure but that we can get back to countable additivity by adding an extra monotonicity assumption. The arguments in Section 3 imply (given c_0 reward structure) that we must assign probabilities $\{p_j\}$ for the environment being T_j and choose a policy with index

$$\operatorname*{argmax}_i \sum_j R_{i,j} p_j. \qquad (14)$$

This is what the AIXI agent described in [5] is doing. The AIXI choice of weights p_j correspond to the choice $2^{-K(\nu)}$ (as in Remark 2), but for the class of lower semi-computable ν discussed below in Section 7.

The same updating technique as in Section 5, where we eliminate the environments which are inconsistent with what has occurred, is being used. This is deduced from the same time-consistency principle as for sequence prediction, just stating that the relative belief in environments that are still consistent will remain unchanged. This leads to the AIXI agent from [5].

7   Remarks on Stochastic Lower Semi-computable Environments

Having the belief that the environment is computable does seem like a restrictive assumption though we will here argue that it is in an interesting way equivalent to having beliefs over all lower semi-computable stochastic environments. The Solomonoff prior is based on having belief $2^{-l(p)}$ in having input program p defining the environment. We can (proven up to a multiplicative factor in [8] and exact identity in [25]), however, rewrite this prior as a mixture $\sum_\nu w_\nu \nu$ over all lower semi-computable environments ν where $w_\nu > 0$ for all ν. Therefore, acting according to our Solomonoff mixture over computable enviroments is identical to acting according to beliefs over a much larger set of environments where we have randomness.

8   Conclusions

We defined four principles for universal sequence prediction and showed that Solomonoff induction and AIXI are determined from them. These principles are computability, rationality, indifference and time consistency. Computability tells us that Turing machines are the explanations we consider for what we are seeing. Rationality tells us that we have probabilistic beliefs over these. Time-consistency leads to the conclusion that we update these beliefs based on conditional probability and the principle of indifference tells us how to chose the original beliefs based on how compactly the various Turing machines can be implemented on the reference machine.

Acknowledgement. This work was supported by ARC grant DP0988049.

References

1. de Finetti, B.: La prévision: Ses lois logiques, ses sources subjectives. In: Annales de l'Institut Henri Poincar, Paris, vol. 7, pp. 1–68 (1937)
2. Diestel, J.: Sequences and series in Banach spaces. Springer (1984)
3. Dowe, D.L.: MML, hybrid bayesian network graphical models, statistical consistency, invariance and uniqueness. In: Handbook of the Philosophy of Science, HPS. Philosophy of Statistics, vol. 7, pp. 901–982 (2011)
4. Grünwald, P.: The Minimum Description Length Principle. MIT Press Books, The MIT Press (2007)
5. Hutter, M.: Universal Artificial Intelligence: Sequential Decisions based on Algorithmic Probability. Springer, Berlin (2005)

6. Hutter, M.: On universal prediction and Bayesian confirmation. Theoretical Computer Science 384, 33–48 (2007)
7. Kreyszig, E.: Introductory Functional Analysis With Applications. Wiley (1989)
8. Li, M., Vitányi, P.: Kolmogorov Complexity and its Applications. Springer (2008)
9. Neumann, J., Morgenstern, O.: Theory of Games and Economic Behavior. Princeton University Press (1944)
10. Ramsey, F.: Truth and probability. In: Braithwaite, R.B. (ed.) The Foundations of Mathematics and other Logical Essays, ch. 7, pp. 156–198. Brace & Co. (1931)
11. Rathmanner, S., Hutter, M.: A philosophical treatise of universal induction. Entropy 13(6), 1076–1136 (2011)
12. Rissanen, J.: Modeling By Shortest Data Description. Automatica 14, 465–471 (1978)
13. Rissanen, J.: Minimum description length principle. In: Sammut, C., Webb, G. (eds.) Encyclopedia of Machine Learning, pp. 666–668. Springer (2010)
14. Savage, L.: The Foundations of Statistics. Wiley, New York (1954)
15. Sutton, R., Barto, A.: Reinforcement Learning: An Introduction (Adaptive Computation and Machine Learning). The MIT Press (March 1998)
16. Sunehag, P., Hutter, M.: Axioms for rational reinforcement learning. In: Kivinen, J., Szepesvári, C., Ukkonen, E., Zeugmann, T. (eds.) ALT 2011. LNCS, vol. 6925, pp. 338–352. Springer, Heidelberg (2011)
17. Solomonoff, R.: A Preliminary Report on a General Theory of Inductive Inference. Report V-131, Zator Co., Cambridge, Ma. (1960)
18. Solomonoff, R.J.: Complexity-based induction systems: comparisons and convergence theorems. IEEE Transactions on Information Theory 24, 422–432 (1978)
19. Solomonoff, R.J.: Does algorithmic probability solve the problem of induction? In: Proceedings of the Information, Statistics and Induction in Science Conferece (1996)
20. Sugden, R.: Rational choice: A survey of contributions from economics and philosophy. Economic Journal 101(407), 751–785 (1991)
21. Turing, A.M.: On Computable Numbers, with an application to the Entscheidungsproblem. Proc. London Math. Soc. 2(42), 230–265 (1936)
22. Wallace, C.S.: Statistical and Inductive Inference by Minimum Message Length. Information Science and Statistics. Springer (2005)
23. Wallace, C.S., Boulton, D.M.: An information measure for classification. Computer Journal 11, 185–194 (1968)
24. Wallace, C.S., Dowe, D.L.: Minimum message length and Kolmogorov complexity. Computer Journal 42, 270–283 (1999)
25. Wood, I., Sunehag, P., Hutter, M. (Non-) Equivalence of universal priors. In: Proc. of Solomonoff Memorial Conference, Melbourne, Australia (2011)

MDL/Bayesian Criteria
Based on Universal Coding/Measure

Joe Suzuki

Department of Mathematics, Osaka University, Japan
suzuki@math.sci.osaka-u.ac.jp

Abstract. In the minimum description length (MDL) and Bayesian criteria, we construct description length of data $z^n = z_1 \cdots z_n$ of length n such that the length divided by n almost converges to its entropy rate as $n \to \infty$, assuming z_i is in a finite set A. In model selection, if we knew the true probability P of $z^n \in A^n$, we would choose a model F such that the posterior probability of F given z^n is maximized. But, in many situations, we use $Q : A^n \to [0, 1]$ such that $\sum_{z^n \in A^n} Q(z^n) \le 1$ rather than P because only data z^n are available. In this paper, we consider an extension such that each of the attributes in data can be either discrete or continuous. The main issue is what Q is qualified to be an alternative to P in the generalized situations. We propose the condition in terms of the Radon-Nikodym derivative of P with respect to Q, and give the procedure of constructing Q in the general setting. As a result, we obtain the MDL/Bayesian criteria in a general sense.

Keywords: Bayesian/MDL, universal coding/measure, Markov order estimation, feature selection.

1 Introduction

Consider feature selection: suppose we wish to estimate a set of random variables on which another random variable depends from data actually emitted by them. More precisely, for random variables $X^{(1)}, \cdots, X^{(m)}$ and Y, we wish to estimate the minimal $F \subseteq \{1, \cdots, m\}$ such that $P(Y|X^{(1)}, \cdots, X^{(m)}) = P(Y|\{X^{(j)}\}_{j \in F})$ from n data[1] $z^n := \{(x_i^{(1)}, \cdots, x_i^{(m)}, y_i)\}_{i=1}^n \in \{X^{(1)}(\Omega) \times \cdots \times X^{(m)}(\Omega) \times Y(\Omega)\}^n$.

If we knew the probability $P(z^n, F)$ of each pair of data z^n and a subset F, then we would be able to calculate the posterior probability $P(F|z^n)$ of F given z^n. However, in many practical situations, only data z^n are available. So, we need to consider an alternative $Q : Z^n(\Omega) \to [0, 1]$ with $\sum_{z^n} Q(z^n) \le 1$ (not depending on P) to the true probability P. If we can prepare such a Q, we only choose F such that $-\log \pi(F) - \log Q(z^n|F)$ is minimized, or equivalently, one such that $\pi(F)Q(z^n|F)$ is maximized, where the a prior probability $\pi(F)$ of each

---

[1] Throughout the paper, by $X(\Omega)$ we mean the range of random variable $X : \Omega \to \mathbb{R}$, where Ω is the sample space.

D.L. Dowe (Ed.): Solomonoff Festschrift, LNAI 7070, pp. 399–410, 2013.

subset F is assumed to be available. We refer those evaluations to the minimum description length (MDL) [10] and Bayesian criteria, respectively[2]

Fortunately, if each z_i in $z^n = (z_i)_{i=1}^n$ takes a value in a finite set $A := Z(\Omega)$, then such $Q : A^n \to [0,1]$ with $\sum_{z^n} Q(z^n) \leq 1$ have been developed for compression without assuming the knowledge of the true probability such as Lempel-Ziv codes, adaptive arithmetic codes [5] which are currently used extensively in internet communications. In fact, any data z^n can be compressed into at most $-\log Q(z^n)$ plus one bits, where the logarithm base is two, and it is known that the quantity $-\frac{1}{n} \log Q(z^n)$ almost surely converges to the entropy that is the lower limit of the compression ratio when we encode z^n using the knowledge of P.

The idea of replacing the true P by such a Q to obtain a Bayesian solution has been used thus far. Wray Buntine considered its application to construction of classification trees [2], Cooper and Herskovits estimated Bayesian network structures using such a Q [4], and modification to the MDL principle and its application to a Bayesian version of the Chow-Liu algorithm were considered in [14]. Since then, many authors reported applications using similar techniques thus far.

However, if some attributes take continuous values, it is hard to construct such a Q in order to identify the F given z^n. Some might consider to quantize the continuous data to take care of only discrete data. However, this only leads to an approximation, and we do not know how to decide the sizes of the quantized cells only from data: overestimation and underestimation may occur if the cell sizes are too small and too large, respectively[3].

In this paper, we propose how to choose an optimal F given z^n in the sense of MDL/Bayesian criteria, without assuming that the data are either discrete or continuous. The main issue is what Q is qualified to be an alternative to P in more general settings. We will give an answer to the problem in terms of the Radon-Nikodym derivative [3] of P with respect to Q at the data z^n.

The theory developed in this paper is partially due to Boris Ryabko's density estimation [11]. The idea is to prepare many histograms nested each other: one histogram is a refinement of another; for each histogram, the quantity like $Q(z^n)$ is computed and divided by the cell volume (Lebesgue measure) of dimension n; and the final estimation is given by weighting those estimated density functions. Ryabko proved the estimation is consistent [11].

Our contribution to theory is to remove the constraint that the density function should exist for universal coding. Obviously, just because a random variable is not finite does not mean that its density function exists. For example, if the distribution function is given by

$$F_X(x) = \begin{cases} 0 & x < -1, \\ \frac{1}{2}, & -1 \leq x < 0 \\ \frac{1}{2} + \frac{1}{2}\int_0^x h(t)dt, & 0 \leq x \end{cases}$$

---

[2] The two-part message scheme of Bayesian minimum message length (MML) [6,7] precedes MDL by many measures.

[3] Wallace et.al [7,16,17] considered a similar idea first (strict MML), but this is for estimating stochastic parameters.

with $\displaystyle\int_0^\infty h(x)dx = 1$, then there exists no density function f_X such that $F_X(x) = \displaystyle\int_{-\infty}^x f_X(t)dt$.

As a result, the idea can be applied to many situations in estimation. In fact, this paper proposes the general notion of the MDL/Bayesian criteria even if coding is not possible. Besides the feature selection problem introduced above, we illustrate how to estimate the order of Markov ergodic sources given data sequence even if the random variables are continuous.

Section 2 introduces the notion of universal coding for finite sources. Section 3 gives two illustrative examples by which we specify the scope of the MDL/Bayesian criteria in this paper. Section 4 extends the notion of universal coding for general sources. Section 5 generalizes the MDL/Bayesian criteria using the discussion in Sections 3 and 4. Section 6 summarizes the obtained results and state future works.

2   Universal Coding

As preliminaries, we introduce the notion of universal coding which will play an important role in this paper.

2.1   Coding

Let A be a finite set, and $n \in \mathbb{N} := \{1, 2, \cdots\}$. We denote the set of binary sequences of finite length by $\{0, 1\}^*$, and write $|y| = m$ if $y \in \{0, 1\}^m$ for $y \in \{0, 1\}^*$. We define coding c and its length l_c by any mapping $A^n \to \{0, 1\}^*$ and $x^n \in A^n \mapsto |c(x^n)| \in \mathbb{N}$, respectively. We say that coding $c : A^n \to \{0, 1\}^*$ is *uniquely decodable* if the map $(n, x^n) \in \mathbb{N} \times A^n \mapsto c(x^n) \in \{0, 1\}^n$ is one-to-one.

We say that map $l : A^n \to \mathbb{N}$ satisfies *Kraft's inequality* if $\displaystyle\sum_{x^n \in A^n} 2^{-l(x^n)} \leq 1$.

It is known [5] that if $c : A^n \to \{0, 1\}^*$ is uniquely decodable, then l_c satisfies Kraft's inequality, and that if $l : A^n \to \mathbb{N}$ satisfies Kraft's inequality, then there exists a uniquely decodable $c : A^n \to \{0, 1\}^*$ such that $l = l_c$.

Let $Q^n(x^n) := 2^{-l(x^n)}$. Then, the problem of coding reduces to specifying $Q^n : A^n \to [0, 1]$ such that $\sum_{x^n \in A^n} Q^n(x^n) \leq 1$.

2.2   Sources

We say a sequence $\{X_i\}_{-\infty}^\infty$ (*source*) of random variables X_i to be *finite* if the range $A := X_i(\Omega)$ of X_i is finite, and that it is *stationary* if for each $k \in \mathbb{N}$ and $i \in \mathbb{Z} := \{\cdots, -1, 0, 1, \cdots\}$, $P(X_{i-k} \cdots X_{i-1}) = P(X_{i-k+1} \cdots X_i)$. For example, for $X^n := \{X_i\}_{i=1}^n$, if X^n is i.i.d (independently and identically distributed), then $P(X^n) = \displaystyle\prod_{i=1}^n P(X_i)$ and if X^n depends on a finite number of latest random variables, then $P(X^n|X_{-\infty}, \cdots, X_0) = \prod_{i=1}^{n} P(X_i|X_{i-k} \cdots X_{i-1})$, where we say the source is *Markov* of order k if k is the minimal value satisfying the above equation.

On the other hand, if $\{X_i\}_{-\infty}^{\infty}$ is stationary, there exists the limit (*entropy*) $H := \lim_{n\to\infty} -\frac{1}{n} \sum_{x^n \in A^n} P^n(x^n) \log P^n(x^n)$. We only deal with stationary ergodic sources, where for the definition of ergodicity in a general sense, see [3] for example.

2.3   Universal Coding for i.i.d. Sources

If the probability P^n is known, then $H \leq E[-l_c(X^n)]$ for any uniquely decodable c, and $l_c(x^n) := \lceil -\log P^n(x^n) \rceil$ (round-up) satisfies $E[l_c(X^n)] < H+1$. However, if P^n is not known, those facts are not available. Instead, we can construct $Q^n : A^n \to [0,1]$ such that $\sum_{x^n \in A^n} 2^{-l(x^n)} \leq 1$, and

$$-\frac{1}{n} \log Q^n(x^n) \to H \tag{1}$$

for any stationary ergodic P^n with probability one as $n \to \infty$ (*universal coding*).

In fact, suppose P^n is i.i.d. with unknown stochastic parameters. Let $m := |A|$ and denote by $c_n[x]$ the number of occurrences of $x \in A$ in $x^n \in A^n$, where hereafter we write the cardinality of set S by $|S|$. Then, we can check that [8]

$$Q^n(x^n) := \prod_{i=1}^{n} \frac{c_{i-1}[x_i] + \frac{1}{2}}{i-1+\frac{m}{2}} = \frac{\Gamma(\frac{m}{2}) \prod_{x \in A} \Gamma(c_n[x] + \frac{1}{2})}{\Gamma(n+\frac{m}{2})\Gamma(\frac{1}{2})^m} \tag{2}$$

satisfies (1), where $\Gamma(x) := \int_0^{\infty} t^{x-1} e^{-t} dt = (x-1)\Gamma(x-1)$ is the Gamma function.

On the other hand, from the Shannon-McMillan-Breiman theorem [5], we have $-\frac{1}{n} \log P^n(x^n) \to H$ for any stationary ergodic P^n with probability one as $n \to \infty$, which together with (1) means

$$\frac{1}{n} \log \frac{P^n(x^n)}{Q^n(x^n)} \to 0 . \tag{3}$$

3   MDL/Bayesian Criteria

Universal coding is used not just for data compression but also for estimation of sources: the rule with which data can be described shortest explains the nature of the data best.

3.1   Markov Order Identification

Suppose that the source P^n is ergodic Markov with known order k and unknown parameters. Let $S := A^k$ be the set of states of a Markov source, and $c_n[x, s]$ the number of occurrences of $(x_{i-k} \cdots x_{i-1}, x_i) = (s, x) \in S \times A$ in $x^n \in A^n$. Then, (2) is generalized as

$$Q^n(x^n|k) := \prod_{i=1}^{n} \frac{c_{i-1}[x_i, s_i] + \frac{1}{2}}{\{\sum_{x \in A} c_{i-1}[x, s_i]\} + \frac{m}{2}} = \prod_{s \in S} \frac{\Gamma(\frac{m}{2}) \prod_{x \in A} \Gamma(c_n[x, s] + \frac{1}{2})}{\Gamma(n + \frac{m}{2})\Gamma(\frac{1}{2})^m} . \quad (4)$$

Similarly, we can show $\dfrac{L(x^n)}{n} = -\dfrac{1}{n} \log Q^n(x^n|k) \to H$ with probability one as $n \to \infty$.

Next, suppose that the Markov order k is unknown and only actually emitted examples $x^n \in A^n$ are available. The problem is to identify the Markov order k given $x^n \in A^n$. To this end, we count $c_n[x, s]$ of occurrences of each $x \in A$ for each $s \in S$ in $x^n \in A^n$ and obtain the value of (4) for each $k = 0, 1, \cdots$.

Let $\pi(k)$ be the a prior probability of each Markov order $k = 0, 1, \cdots$. If we choose k such that $-\log \pi(k) - \log Q^n(x^n|k)$ is minimized, equivalently, such that $\pi(k)Q^n(x^n|k)$ is maximized, then we obtain a solution based on the MDL/Bayesian criteria.

3.2   Conditional Probabilities

Let X, Y be random variables, and $X(\Omega), Y(\Omega)$ their ranges with $|Y(\Omega)| < \infty$. We specify the conditional probability $P(Y|X)$ by defining equivalent classes of $X(\Omega)$ as follows: $x \sim x' \iff P(y|x) = P(y|x'), y \in Y(\Omega)$. Let $[x]$ be the class including $x \in X(\Omega)$, and $S := \{[x]|x \in X(\Omega)\}$ the set of equivalent classes (*equivalence relation*), where we assume $|S| < \infty$.

Example 1 (feature selection). Suppose that the random variable X is expressed by a vector $X = (X^{(1)}, \cdots, X^{(m)})$ consisting of m random variables $X^{(1)}, \cdots, X^{(m)}$, and that $s \in S$ is unique given the values of random variables $\{X^{(j)}\}_{j \in F}$. Then, we say the minimal subset F satisfying this property to be a *feature set*. On the other hand, if we select F (*feature selection*), then the equivalent relation S can be decided by $S := \prod_{j \in F} X^{(j)}(\Omega)$.

The problem is to identify the equivalent relation S given n pairs of examples $\{(x_i, y_i)\}_{i=1}^{n} \in X(\Omega) \times Y(\Omega)$. To this end, we count the number $c_n[y, s]$ of occurrences of each $y \in Y(\Omega)$ for each $s \in S$ in $\{(x_i, y_i)\}_{i=1}^{n}$, and obtain the value of

$$Q^n(y^n|x^n, S) := \prod_{s \in S} \frac{\Gamma(\frac{m}{2}) \prod_{y \in Y(\Omega)} \Gamma(c_n[y, s] + \frac{1}{2})}{\Gamma(n + \frac{m}{2})\Gamma(\frac{1}{2})^m}$$

for each S. Let $\pi(S)$ be the prior probability of S. If we choose S such that $-\log\pi(S) - \log Q^n(y^n|x^n, S)$ is minimized, or equivalently, such that $\pi(S)Q^n(y^n|x^n, S)$ is maximized, then we obtain a solution based on the MDL/Bayesian criteria.

4   Universal Coding in a General Sense

In this section, we construct a universal measure rather than a universal coding in order to extend the notion to general sources because coding is available only for finite sources.

4.1   Estimation of Density Functions

Let $\{X_i\}_{i=1}^n$ be stationary ergodic with density function f^n, which means that the source $\{X_i\}_{i=1}^n$ is not finite. Let $\{A_k\}_{k=0}^\infty$ be such that $A_0 := \{X_i(\Omega)\}$, and A_{k+1} is a refinement of A_k.

Example 2. Suppose $X_i(\Omega) = [0, 1)$, and that we consider the following sequence:
$A_0 = \{[0, 1)\}$
$A_1 = \{[0, 1/2), [1/2, 1)\}$
$A_2 = \{[0, 1/4), [1/4, 1/2), [1/2, 3/4), [3/4, 1)\}$
$\cdots$

$A_k = \{[0, 2^{-k}), [2^{-k}, 2 \cdot 2^{-k}), \cdots, [(2^k - 1)2^{-k}, 1)\}$
$\cdots$.

Then $m = 2^k$, and if the source is i.i.d., we have $Q_k^n(s_k(x^n)) :=$

$$\frac{\Gamma(\frac{m}{2}) \prod_{a \in A_k} \Gamma(c_n[a] + \frac{1}{2})}{\Gamma(n + \frac{m}{2})\Gamma(\frac{1}{2})^m}$$, where $c_n[a]$ is the number of occurrences of $a \in A_k$ in

$s_k(x^n) \in A_k^n$. The Lebesgue measure is $\lambda(s_k(x)) = 2^{-k}$ for $x \in X_i(\Omega)$.

Let $s_k : X_i(\Omega) \to A_k$ be the projection, i.e. $s_k(x) = a$ if $x \in a \in A_k$. Similarly, we write $s_k(x^n) = a^n$ if $x^n \in a^n \in A_k^n$. Let $\lambda : \mathcal{B} \to \mathbb{R}$ be the Lebesgue measure, i.e. $\lambda(a) = d - c$ if $a = [c, d]$ with $c \leq d$. Similarly, we write $\lambda^n(a^n) = \prod_{i=1}^n \lambda(a_i)$ for $a^n \in \mathcal{B}^n$, where $\mathcal{B}$ is the Borel set field of the entire real $\mathbb{R}$.

For each $k = 1, 2, \cdots$, let P_k^n be the probability measure of $s_k(X^n)$ with alphabet A_k. Then, there exists $Q_k^n : A_k^n \to [0, 1]$ such that $\sum_{a^n \in A_k^n} Q_k^n(a^n) \leq 1$ and $\frac{1}{n} \log \frac{P_k^n(s_k(x^n))}{Q_k^n(s_k(x^n))} \to 0$ for any stationary ergodic f^n with probabilities as $n \to \infty$ (see (3)).

Let $g_k^n(x^n) := \frac{Q_k^n(s_k(x^n))}{\lambda^n(s_k(x^n))}$ and $\{\omega_k\}_{k=1}^\infty$ be such that $\sum \omega_k = 1$, $\omega_k > 0$.

Suppose we estimate f^n by g^n as $g^n(x^n) := \sum_{k=1}^\infty \omega_k g_k^n(x^n)$.

Let $f_k^n(x^n) := \dfrac{P_k^n(s_k(x^n))}{\lambda^n(s_k(x^n))}$, and define the *differential entropy* by

$$h(f) := \lim_{n \to \infty} \int -f(x^n) \log f(x_n | x_1, \cdots, x_{n-1}) dx^n . \tag{5}$$

Proposition 1 (Ryabko, 2009 [11]). With probability one as $n \to \infty$,

$$\frac{1}{n} \log \frac{f^n(x^n)}{g^n(x^n)} \to 0 \tag{6}$$

for any stationary ergodic f^n such that

$$h(f_k) \to h(f) \tag{7}$$

as $k \to \infty$.

Notice that Proposition 1 assumes the existence of a density function.

4.2   Conditional Probabilities

We say that a measure μ is *absolutely continuous* with respect to another measure ν and write $\mu \ll \nu$ if $\nu(A) = 0 \Longrightarrow \mu(A) = 0$ for each $A \in \mathcal{F}$, and that a measure ν is *σ-finite* if there exists $\{A_i\}$ such that $\cup_i A_i = \Omega$ and $\nu(A_i) < \infty$.
Let μ, ν be σ-finite.

Proposition 2 (Radon-Nikodym [3]). Then, $\mu \ll \nu$ if and only if there exists $\mathcal{F}$-measurable $g : \Omega \to \mathbb{R}$ such that $\mu(A) = \int_A g(\omega) d\nu(\omega), A \in \mathcal{F}$.

We write such a g by $\dfrac{d\mu}{d\nu}$.

Let X, Y be random variables. Then, $\mu(X \in D) = 0 \Longrightarrow \mu(X \in D, Y \in D') = 0$ for $D, D' \in \mathcal{B}$. From Proposition 2, for each $D' \in \mathcal{B}$, there exists $\mu(Y \in D' | \cdot) : \mathbb{R} \to \mathbb{R}$ such that $\mu(X \in D, Y \in D') = \int_D \mu(Y \in D' | x) d\mu(x)$ (the *conditional probability* of Y given X).

4.3   Kullback-Leibler Divergence

When $\mu \ll \nu$, we define the *Kullback-Leibler divergence* of μ with respect to ν by $D(\mu || \nu) := \int d\mu \log \dfrac{d\mu}{d\nu}$. Let $\mu(X \le x) := F_X(x)$. Then, $\mu \ll \lambda$ if and only if there exists $f_X = \dfrac{d\mu}{d\lambda} : \mathbb{R} \to \mathbb{R}$ such that $\mu(X \le x) = \int_{-\infty}^x f_X(t) d\lambda(t)$. In particular,

$$D(\mu || \lambda) = \int d\mu \log \frac{d\mu}{d\lambda} = \int d\mu \log f_X = \int_{-\infty}^{\infty} f_X(x) \log f_X(x) dx .$$

Let $\{X_i\}_{i=1}^n \sim \mu^n$ be stationary ergodic. Then, $\mu^{n-1}(X^{n-1} \in D^{n-1}) = 0 \Longrightarrow \mu^n(X^n \in D^n) = 0$ for $D^n \in \mathcal{B}^n$, so that there exists $\mu(X_n \in D_n | \cdot) : \mathbb{R}^{n-1} \to \mathbb{R}$

such that $\mu^n(X^n \in D^n) = \int_{D^{n-1}} \mu(X_n \in D_n|x^{n-1})d\mu^{n-1}(x^{n-1})$ (*conditional Probability* $\mu(X_n \in D_n|x^{n-1})$ of $X \in D_n$ given $x^{n-1} \in \mathbb{R}^{n-1}$).

Similarly, there exists $\nu(X_n \in D_n|\cdot) : \mathbb{R}^{n-1} \to \mathbb{R}$ as well for ν^n such that $\int_{x^n \in X^n(\Omega)} d\nu^n(x^n) \leq 1$. When $\mu^n \ll \nu^n$, write the Radon-Nikodym derivative at $x_n \in D_n$ by $\dfrac{d\mu}{d\nu}(x_n|x^{n-1})$, and define

$$D(\mu||\nu) := \lim_{n\to\infty} \int d\mu^n(x^n) \log \frac{d\mu}{d\nu}(x_n|x^{n-1})$$

In particular, from (5), when $\mu^n \ll \lambda^n$,

$$D(\mu||\lambda) = -h(f) . \tag{8}$$

4.4   Universal Coding for General Sources

In this paper, we extend the constructions of Q^n and g^n achieving (3) and (6), respectively, to that of the general measure without assuming to be either discrete or continuous [15].

Let $\{X_i\}_{i=1}^n$ be stationary ergodic with probability measure μ^n, and η^n be such that $\mu^n \ll \eta^n$. Let $\dfrac{d\nu_k^n}{d\eta^n}(x^n) := \dfrac{Q_k^n(s_k(x^n))}{\eta^n(s_k(x^n))}$ and $\{\omega_i\}_{k=0}^\infty$ such that $\displaystyle\sum_{k=0}^\infty \omega_k = 1$, $\omega_k > 0$.

We estimate $\dfrac{d\mu^n}{d\eta^n}(x^n)$ by $\dfrac{d\nu^n}{d\eta^n}(x^n) := \displaystyle\sum_{k=0}^\infty \omega_k \dfrac{d\nu_k^n}{d\eta^n}(x^n)$. Let $\dfrac{d\mu_k^n}{d\eta^n}(x^n) := \dfrac{\mu_k^n(s_k(x^n))}{\eta^n(s_k(x^n))}$.

Theorem 1. Let $\{A_k\}_{k=1}^\infty$ such that $A_0 := \{X_i(\Omega)\}$ and A_{k+1} is a refinement of A_k, and η a σ-finite measure. There exists ν^n such that $\int_{x^n \in X^n(\Omega)} d\nu^n(x^n) \leq 1$ and with probability one

$$\frac{1}{n} \log \frac{d\mu^n}{d\nu^n}(x^n) \to 0 \tag{9}$$

for any stationary ergodic μ^n such that $\mu^n \ll \eta^n$ and

$$D(\mu_k||\eta) \to D(\mu||\eta) \tag{10}$$

as $k \to \infty$.

(see proof of Theorem 1 for Appendix).

Remark 1. When $\eta = \lambda$, (9) and (10) become (6) and (7) (see (8)).

Example 3. Suppose $X_i(\Omega) = \{1, 2, \cdots\}$, and that the following sequence is given:

$A_0 = \{\{1, 2, \cdots\}\}$
$A_1 = \{\{1\}, \{2, \cdots\}\}$
$A_2 = \{\{1\}, \{2\}, \{3, \cdots\}\}$

$\cdots$

$A_k = \{\{1\}, \cdots, \{k\}, \{k+1, \cdots\}\}$

$\cdots$

Then $m = k + 1$, and if the source is i.i.d., $\nu_k^n(s_k(x^n)) :=$

$$\dfrac{\Gamma(n + \frac{m}{2})\Gamma(\frac{1}{2})^m}{\Gamma(\frac{m}{2}) \prod\limits_{a \in A_k} \Gamma(c_n[a] + \frac{1}{2})},$$ where $c_n[a]$ is the number of occurrences of $a \in A_k$

in $s_k(x^n) \in A_k^n$. If we set η as follows, then $\mu \ll \eta$: $\eta(\{j\}) := \dfrac{1}{j(j+1)}$ for

$j = 1, 2, \cdots$, and $\eta(\{k+1, \cdots\}) = \sum\limits_{j=k+1}^{\infty} \eta(\{j\}) = \dfrac{1}{k+1}$. Then, we can compute

$$\frac{d\nu_k^n}{d\eta^n} = \frac{\nu_k(s_k(x^n))}{\prod_{i=1}^{n} \eta(s_k(x_i))} \text{ to obtain } \frac{d\nu^n}{d\eta^n} = \sum\limits_{k=1}^{\infty} \omega_k \frac{d\nu_k^n}{d\eta^n}.$$

5 MDL/Bayesian Criteria in a General Sense

Let $\{X_i\}_{i=1}^{n} \sim \mu^n$ be stationary ergodic. Given n examples $x^n \in \prod_{i=1}^{n} X_i(\Omega)$, we estimate μ^n based on the following assumptions:

1. the true μ^n is known to be specified with some model in a countable set M and some parameters;
2. for each $m \in M$, there exists $\nu^n[m]$ such that with probability one

$$\frac{1}{n} \log \frac{d\mu^n[m]}{d\nu^n[m]}(x^n) \to 0$$

   for $\mu^n[m]$ with model m and arbitrary parameters; and
3. the a prior probability $\pi[m]$ of $m \in M$ is known.

By the MDL/Bayesian criteria, we mean to apply the following decision rule:

$$\frac{\pi[m]}{\pi[m']} \cdot \frac{d\nu^n[m]}{d\nu^n[m']}(x^n) > 1 \iff m \text{ is prefer to } m'.$$

5.1 Markov Order Identification for Continuous Sources

In general, by the Markov order of a stationary ergodic source $\{X_i\}_{i=-\infty}^{\infty}$ we mean the minimal k such that $\{X_i\}_{i=-\infty}^{0}$ and $\{X_i\}_{k+1}^{\infty}$ are conditionally independent given $\{X_i\}_{i=1}^{k}$.

Based on Theorem 1, for each $k = 0, 1, \cdots$, we can construct $\nu^n[k]$ such that $\int d\nu^n[k](x^n) \leq 1$, and $\frac{1}{n} \log \frac{d\mu^n[k]}{d\nu^n[k]}(x^n) \to 0$ with probability one for $\mu^n[k]$ with order k and arbitrary parameters.

Suppose we are given actually emitted n examples $x^n \in X^n(\Omega)$. Let $\pi[k]$: the a prior probability of k, and η such that $\mu[k] \ll \eta$, $k = 0, 1, \cdots$. Then, for each $k = 0, 1, \cdots$ we can construct $\frac{d\nu[k]}{d\eta}$, and choose k such that $\pi[k]\frac{d\nu[k]}{d\eta}(x^n)$ is maximized given the x^n.

5.2   Feature Selection Including Continuous Attributes

Consider again the feature selection problem discussed in Example 2, and give a solution to the problem raised in Introduction. Let $X = \{X^{(j)}\}_{j=1}^m$ and Y random variables with $|Y_i(\Omega)| < \infty$.

Based on Theorem 1, for each $F \subseteq \{1, \cdots, m\}$, construct $\nu^n_{XY}[F]$ and $\nu^n_X[F]$ such that $\int d\nu^n_{XY}[F](x^n, y^n) \leq 1$, $\int d\nu^n_X[F](x^n) \leq 1$ and

$$\frac{1}{n} \log \frac{d\mu^n_{XY}[F]}{d\nu^n_{XY}[F]}(x^n, y^n) \to 0 \ , \ \frac{1}{n} \log \frac{d\mu^n_X[F]}{d\nu^n_X[F]}(x^n) \to 0$$

for $\mu^n_{XY}[F]$ and $\mu_X[F]$ with feature set F and arbitrary parameters.

Suppose we are given actually emitted n examples $(x^n, y^n) \in X^n(\Omega) \times Y^n(\Omega)$ with $X^n(\Omega) = \prod_{i=1}^n \prod_{j=1}^m X_i^{(j)}(\Omega)$. Let $\pi[F]$: the a prior probability of $F \subseteq \{1, \cdots, m\}$, and η such that $\mu_X[F] \ll \eta$. Then, for $F \subseteq \{1, \cdots, m\}$, we can construct $\frac{d\nu_{XY}[F]}{d\eta}$ and $\frac{d\nu_X[F]}{d\eta}$, and choose F such that $\pi[F]\frac{d\nu_{XY}[F]}{d\eta}(x^n, y^n)/\frac{d\nu_X[F]}{d\eta}(x^n)$ is maximized given (x^n, y^n).

Example 4. Suppose $X^{(1)}(\Omega) = [0, 1)$, $X^{(2)}(\Omega) = \{0, 1\}$, $X^{(3)}(\Omega) = \{1, 2, \cdots\}$. We estimate $F \in \{\{\}, \{1\}, \{2\}, \{1, 2\}\}$ given $\{(x_i^{(1)}, x_i^{(2)}, x_i^{(3)})\}_{i=1}^n \in \{X^{(1)}(\Omega) \times X^{(2)}(\Omega) \times X^{(3)}(\Omega)\}^n$. Let $\{A_k^{(1)}\} := \{A_k\}$ be as in Example 3, let $A_0^{(2)} = \{\{0, 1\}\}$, $A_1^{(2)} = A_2^{(2)} = \cdots = \{\{0\}, \{1\}\}$, and $\{A_k^{(3)}\} := \{A_k\}$ in Example 4, respectively. Also, let $\eta^{(1)} := \eta$ in Example 3, $\eta^{(2)}(0) = \eta^{(2)}(1) = \frac{1}{2}$, and $\eta^{(3)} := \eta$ in Example 4, respectively. Let $B := X^{(3)}(\Omega)$.

For example, let $A := X^{(1)}(\Omega)$. We compute the value of $\frac{d\nu^n}{d\eta^n}(b^n|a^n)$ for $F = \{1\}$ and $a^n \in A^n$, $b^n \in B^n$. For each $k = 1, 2, \cdots$, let $A_k := A_k^{(1)} \times A_k^{(3)}$ with $m := 2^k(k+1)$, $c_n(a, b)$ the number of occurrences of $(a, b) \in A_k$ in $(a^n, b^n) \in A_k^n$, and

$$\nu^n_k(a^n, b^n) := \frac{\Gamma(\frac{m}{2}) \prod\limits_{(a,b) \in A_k} \Gamma(c_n(a, b) + \frac{1}{2})}{\Gamma(n + \frac{m}{2})\Gamma(\frac{1}{2})^m} \ .$$

Also, let $\eta(a, b) := \eta^{(1)}(a)\eta^{(3)}(b) = 2^{-k} \cdot \dfrac{1}{j(j+1)}$ for $(a, b) \in A_k$ if $b = \{j\}$, and

$\eta(a^n, b^n) := \prod_{i=1}^{n}\{\eta^{(1)}(a_i)\eta^{(3)}(b_i)\}$ for $(a^n, b^n) \in A_k^n$. We estimate $\dfrac{d\mu_k^n}{d\eta^n}$ and $\dfrac{d\mu^n}{d\eta^n}$

by $\dfrac{d\nu_k^n}{d\eta^n}(a^n, b^n) = \dfrac{\nu_k^n(a^n, b^n)}{\eta^n(a^n, b^n)}$ and $\dfrac{d\nu^n}{d\eta^n}(a^n, b^n) = \sum_{k=1}^{\infty} \omega_k \dfrac{d\nu_k^n}{d\eta^n}(a^n, b^n)$, respectively.

On the other hand, from Example 3, we immediately obtain estimation $\dfrac{d\nu^n}{d\eta^n}(a^n)$

of $\dfrac{d\mu^n}{d\eta^n}(a^n)$ for $a^n \in A^n$. Then, we obtain the value of

$$\frac{d\nu^n}{d\eta^n}(b^n | a^n) = \left[\frac{d\nu^n}{d\eta^n}(a^n, b^n)\right] / \left[\frac{d\nu^n}{d\eta^n}(a^n)\right]$$

for $F = \{1\}$. Similarly, we obtain the values of $\dfrac{d\nu^n}{d\eta^n}$ for $F = \{2\}, \{\}, \{1, 2\}$.
Finally, we choose the maximum value among the four to choose $F \in \{\{\}, \{1\}, \{2\}, \{1, 2\}\}$.

6 Concluding Remarks

We proposed the MDL/Bayesian criteria in a general sense, and illustrate the idea in the two examples:

- Markov order identification for continuous sources
- feature selection containing continuous attributes

We removed the constraint that each attribute should take a value in a finite set.

One could quantize continuous data to obtain the description length assuming each underlying model. However, the cell size in the partition should be optimized to obtain the correct MDL/Bayesian criteria: overestimation and underestimation may occur if the cell size is too small and too large, respectively. Intuitive speaking, our method utilizes weighting partitions to obtain more robust estimations compared with estimating only one partition.

Appendix: Proof of Theorem 1

Proof: for $k = 1, 2, \cdots$, $\dfrac{d\nu^n}{d\eta^n}(x^n) \geq \omega_k \dfrac{d\nu_k^n}{d\eta^n}(x^n)$, so that $\dfrac{d\mu^n}{d\nu^n}(x^n) \leq \dfrac{1}{\omega_k}\dfrac{d\mu^n}{d\nu_k^n}(x^n)$,

thus

$$\frac{1}{n}\log\frac{d\mu^n}{d\nu^n}(x^n) \leq -\frac{1}{n}\log\omega_k + \frac{1}{n}\log\frac{d\mu_k^n}{d\nu_k^n}(x^n) + \frac{1}{n}\log\frac{d\mu^n}{d\mu_k^n}(x^n)$$

with probability one. Note that for each $k = 1, 2, \cdots$, from (3), we have

$$\frac{1}{n}\log\frac{d\mu_k^n}{d\nu_k^n}(x^n) = \frac{1}{n}\log\frac{P_k(s_k(x^n))}{Q_k(s_k(x^n))} \to 0 .$$

Notice that $\int d\nu^n \leq 1$ and Proposition 3 imply $0 \leq D(\mu||\nu)$ and $D(\mu||\nu) \leq D(\mu||\mu_k)$ for $k = 1, 2, \cdots$, respectively. Since we assume $D(\mu||\mu_k) \to 0$ $(k \to \infty)$, $D(\mu||\nu) = 0$ is required, which implies Theorem 1. $\qquad \square$

Proposition 3 (Barron, 1985 [1]). With probability one as $n \to \infty$,

$$\frac{1}{\bullet n} \log \frac{d\mu^n}{d\nu^n}(x^n) \to D(\mu||\nu) \ .$$

References

1. Barron, A.R.: The Strong Ergodic Theorem for Densities: Generalized Shannon-McMillan-Breiman Theorem. Annals. Probability 13(4), 1292–1303 (1985)
2. Buntine, W.L.: Learning Classification Trees. Statistics and Computing 2, 63–73 (1991)
3. Billingsley, P.: Probability & Measure, 3rd edn. Wiley, New York (1995)
4. Cooper, G.F., Herskovits, E.: A Bayesian Method for the Induction of Probabilistic Networks from Data. Machine Learning 9, 309–347 (1992)
5. Cover, T.M., Thomas, J.A.: Elements of Information Theory, 2nd edn. Wiley, New York (1995)
6. Dowe, D.L.: Foreword re C. S. Wallace. Computer Journal 51(5), 523–560 (2008), Christopher Stewart WALLACE (1933-2004) memorial special issue
7. Dowe, D.L.: MML, hybrid Bayesian network graphical models, statistical consistency, invariance and uniqueness. In: Bandyopadhyay, P.S., Forster, M.R. (eds.) Handbook of the Philosophy of Science (HPS). Philosophy of Statistics, vol. 7, pp. 901–982. Elsevier (June 2011)
8. Krichevsky, R.E., Trofimov, V.K.: The Performance of Universal Encoding. IEEE Trans. Inform. Theory 27(2), 199–207 (1981)
9. Kullback, S., Leibler, R.A.: On information and sufficiency. Ann. Math. Statistics 22(1), 79–86 (1951)
10. Rissanen, J.: Modeling by shortest data description. Automatica 14, 465–471 (1978)
11. Ryabko, B.: Compression-Based Methods for Nonparametric Prediction and Estimation of Some Characteristics of Time Series. IEEE Trans. on Inform. Theory 55(9), 4309–4315 (2009)
12. Solomonoff, R.: A Formal Theory of Inductive Inference. Information and Control 22, 224–254 (1964)
13. Suzuki, J.: On Strong Consistency of Model Selection in Classification. IEEE Trans. on Inform. Theory 52(11), 4767–4774 (2006)
14. Suzuki, J.: A Construction of Bayesian Networks from Databases on an MDL Principle. In: The Ninth Conference on Uncertainty in Artificial Intelligence, vol. 7, pp. 266–273 (1993)
15. Suzuki, J.: The Universal Measure for General Sources and its Application to MDL/Bayesian Criteria. In: Data Compression Conference 2011, Snowbird, Utah (2011)
16. Wallace, C.S., Boulton, D.M.: An information measure for classification. Computer Journal 11(2), 185–194 (1968)
17. Wallace, C.S.: Statistical and Inductive Inference by Minimum Message Length. Springer (2005) ISBN: 0-387-23795-X

Algorithmic Analogies to Kamae-Weiss Theorem on Normal Numbers

Hayato Takahashi

The Institute of Statistical Mathematics, 10-3 Midori-cho, Tachikawa,
Tokyo 190-8562, Japan
hayato.takahashi@ieee.org

Abstract. In this paper we study subsequences of random numbers. In Kamae (1973), selection functions that depend only on coordinates are studied, and their necessary and sufficient condition for the selected sequences to be normal numbers is given. In van Lambalgen (1987), an algorithmic analogy to the theorem is conjectured in terms of algorithmic randomness and Kolmogorov complexity. In this paper, we show different algorithmic analogies to the theorem.

1 Introduction

In this paper we study subsequences of random numbers. A function from sequences to their subsequences is called selection function. In Kamae [5] selection functions that depend only on coordinates are studied, and their necessary and sufficient condition for the selected sequences to be normal numbers is given. In the following we call the theorem Kamae-Weiss (KW) theorem on normal numbers since a part of the theorem is shown in Weiss [15]. In van Lambalgen [13], an algorithmic analogy to KW theorem is conjectured in terms of algorithmic randomness and complexity [2,7,9,11]. In this paper we show two algorithmic analogies to KW theorem.

Let Ω be the set of infinite binary sequences. For $x, y \in \Omega$, let $x = x_1 x_2 \cdots$ and $y = y_1 y_2 \cdots$, $\forall i \; x_i, y_i \in \{0, 1\}$. Let $\tau : \mathbb{N} \to \mathbb{N}$ be a strictly increasing function such that $\{i \mid y_i = 1\} = \{\tau(1) < \tau(2) < \cdots\}$. If $\sum_i y_i = n$ then $\tau(j)$ is defined for $1 \leq j \leq n$. For $x, y \in \Omega$ let x/y be the subsequence of x selected at $y_i = 1$, i.e., $x/y = x_{\tau(1)} x_{\tau(2)} \cdots$. For example, if $x = 0011 \cdots$, $y = 0101 \cdots$ then $\tau(1) = 2, \tau(2) = 4$ and $x/y = 01 \cdots$. For finite binary strings $x_1^n := x_1 \cdots x_n$ and $y_1^n := y_1 \cdots y_n$, x_1^n/y_1^n is defined similarly. Let S be the set of finite binary strings and $|s|$ be the length of $s \in S$. For $s \in S$ let $\Delta(s) := \{s\omega | \omega \in \Omega\}$, where $s\omega$ is the concatenation of s and ω. Let $(\Omega, \mathcal{B}, P)$ be a probability space, where $\mathcal{B}$ is the sigma-algebra generated by $\Delta(s), s \in S$. We write $P(s) := P(\Delta(s))$.

In Kamae [5], it is shown that the following two statements are equivalent under the assumption that $\liminf \frac{1}{n} \sum_{i=1}^n y_i > 0$:

Theorem 1 (KW)
(i) $h(y) = 0$.
(ii) $\forall x \in \mathcal{N} \; x/y \in \mathcal{N}$,
where $h(y)$ is Kamae entropy [1,13] and $\mathcal{N}$ is the set of binary normal numbers.

D.L. Dowe (Ed.): Solomonoff Festschrift, LNAI 7070, pp. 411–416, 2013.

A probability p on Ω is called cluster point if there is a sequence $\{n_i\}$

$$\forall s \in S \; p(s) = \lim_{i \to \infty} \#\{1 \leq j \leq n_i \mid x_j \cdots x_{j+|s|-1} = s\}/n_i.$$

From the definition, the cluster points are stationary measures. Let $V(x)$ be the set of cluster points defined from x. From a standard argument we see that $V(x) \neq \emptyset$ for all x. Kamae entropy is defined by

$$h(x) = \sup\{h(p) \mid p \in V(x)\},$$

where $h(p)$ is the measure theoretic entropy of p. If $h(x) = 0$, it is called completely deterministic, see [5,15,16]. The part (i)$\Rightarrow$ (ii) is appeared in [15].

As a natural analogy, the following equivalence (algorithmic randomness version of Kamae's theorem) under a suitable restriction on y is conjectured in van Lambalgen [13],
(i) $\lim_{n \to \infty} K(y_1^n)/n = 0$.
(ii) $\forall x \in \mathcal{R} \; x/y \in \mathcal{R}$,
where K is the prefix Kolmogorov complexity and $\mathcal{R}$ is the set of Martin-Löf random sequences with respect to the uniform measure (fair coin flipping), see [8]. Note that $\lim_{n \to \infty} K(y_1^n)/n = h, P - a.s.$, for ergodic P and its entropy h, see [1].

2   Results

In this paper, we show two algorithmic analogies to KW theorem. The first one is a Martin-Löf randomness analogy and the second one is a complexity rate analogy to KW theorem, respectively. In the following, P on Ω is called computable if there is a computable function A such that $\forall s, k \; |P(s) - A(s, k)| < 1/k$. For $A \subset S$, let $\tilde{A} := \cup_{s \in A} \Delta(s)$. A recursively enumerable (r.e.) set $U \subset \mathbb{N} \times S$ is called (Martin-Löf) test with respect to P if 1) U is r.e., 2) $\tilde{U}_{n+1} \subset \tilde{U}_n$ for all n, where $U_n = \{s : (n, s) \in U\}$, and 3) $P(\tilde{U}_n) < 2^{-n}$. A test U is called universal if for any other test V, there is a constant c such that $\forall n \; \tilde{V}_{n+c} \subset \tilde{U}_n$. In [9], it is shown that a universal test U exists if P is computable and the set $(\cap_{n=1}^{\infty} \tilde{U}_n)^c$ is called the set of Martin-Löf random sequences with respect to P.

Our first algorithmic analogy to the KW theorem is the following.

Proposition 1. *Suppose that y is Martin-Löf random with respect to some computable probability P and $\sum_{i=1}^{\infty} y_i = \infty$. Then the following two statements are equivalent:*
(i) y is computable.
(ii) $\forall x \in \mathcal{R} \; x/y \in \mathcal{R}^y$,
where $\mathcal{R}^y$ is the set of Martin-Löf random sequences with respect to the uniform measure relative to y.

Proof: (i)$\Rightarrow$ (ii). Since $\sum_{i=1}^{\infty} y_i = \infty$ we have $\forall s \; \lambda\{x \in \Omega \mid s \sqsubset x/y\} = 2^{-|s|}$, where λ is the uniform measure. Let U be a universal test with respect to λ and $y(s) \subset S$ be a finite set such that $\{x \in \Omega \mid s \sqsubset x/y\} = \tilde{y}(s)$. Then $y(s)$ is computable from y and s, and hence $U^y := \{(n, a) \mid a \in y(s), s \in U_n\}$ is a test if y is computable. We have $x \in \tilde{U}^y_n \leftrightarrow x/y \in \tilde{U}_n$. (Intuitively U^y is a universal test on subsequences selected by y). Then

$$x \in \mathcal{R} \to x \notin \cap_n \tilde{U}^y_n \leftrightarrow x/y \notin \cap_n \tilde{U}_n \leftrightarrow x/y \in \mathcal{R}.$$

Since y is computable, $\mathcal{R}^y = \mathcal{R}$ and we have (ii).

Conversely, suppose that y is a Martin-Löf random sequence with respect to a computable P and is not computable. From Levin-Schnorr theorem, we have

$$\forall n \; Km(y^n_1) = -\log P(y^n_1) + O(1), \tag{1}$$

where Km is the monotone complexity. Throughout the paper, the base of logarithm is 2. By applying arithmetic coding to P, there is a sequence z such that z is computable from y and $y^n_1 \sqsubseteq u(z^{l_n}_1)$, $l_n = -\log P(y^n_1) + O(1)$ for all n, where u is a monotone function and we write $s \sqsubseteq s'$ if s is a prefix of s'. Since y is not computable, we have $\lim_n l_n = \infty$. From (1), we see that $\forall n \; Km(z^{l_n}_1) = l_n + O(1)$. We show that if $y \in \mathcal{R}$ then $\sup_n l_{n+1} - l_n < \infty$. Observe that if $y \in \mathcal{R}$ then $\forall n \; P(y^n_1) > 0$ and

$$\sup_n l_{n+1} - l_n < \infty \leftrightarrow \sup_n -\log P(y_{n+1} \mid y^n_1) < \infty \leftrightarrow \inf_n P(y_{n+1} \mid y^n_1) > 0$$

$$\leftrightarrow \liminf_n P(y_{n+1} \mid y^n_1) > 0.$$

Let $U_n := \{s \mid P(s \mid s^{|s|-1}_1) < 2^{-n}\}$. Then $P(\tilde{U}_n) < 2^{-n}$ and $U := \{(n, s) \mid s \in U_n\}$ is a r.e. set. Since $y \in \limsup_n \tilde{U}_n \leftrightarrow \liminf_n P(y_{n+1} \mid y^n_1) = 0$, if $y \in \mathcal{R}$ then $\sup_n l_{n+1} - l_n < \infty$. (If U is r.e. and $P(\tilde{U}_n) < 2^{-n}$ then $\mathcal{R} \subset (\limsup_n \tilde{U}_n)^c$, see [10].) Since $\forall n \; Km(z^{l_n}_1) = l_n + O(1)$ and $\sup_n l_{n+1} - l_n < \infty$, we have $\forall n \; Km(z^n_1) = n + O(1)$ and $z \in \mathcal{R}$. Since z is computable from y we have $z/y \notin \mathcal{R}^y$. □

Note that if y is computable then y is a Martin-Löf random sequence with respect to a computable measure that has positive probability at y.

In order to show the second analogy, we introduce another notion of randomness. We say that y has maximal complexity rate with respect to P if

$$\lim_{n \to \infty} \frac{1}{n} K(y^n_1) = \lim_{n \to \infty} -\frac{1}{n} \log P(y^n_1), \tag{2}$$

i.e., both sides exist and are equal. For example, y has maximal complexity rate with respect to the uniform measure (i.e., $P(s) = 2^{-|s|}$ for all s) if $\lim_{n \to \infty} K(y^n_1)/n = 1$. If y is Martin-Löf random sequences with respect to a computable ergodic P then from upcrossing inequality for the Shannon-McMillan-Breiman theorem [4], the right-hand-side of (2) exists (see also [14]) and from (1), we see that (2) holds i.e., y has maximal complexity rate w.r.t. P.

Proposition 2. *Suppose that y has maximal complexity rate with respect to a computable probability and $\lim_n \frac{1}{n} \sum_{i=1}^n y_i > 0$. Then the following two statements are equivalent:*
(i) $\lim_{n \to \infty} \frac{1}{n} K(y^n_1) = 0$.
(ii) $\forall x \; \lim_{n \to \infty} \frac{1}{n} K(x^n_1) = 1 \to \lim_{n \to \infty} \frac{1}{|x^n_1/y^n_1|} K(x^n_1/y^n_1 \mid y^n_1) = 1$.

Proof:

(i) $\Rightarrow$ (ii)

Let $\bar{y} := \bar{y}_1 \bar{y}_2 \cdots \in \Omega$ such that $\bar{y}_i = 1$ if $y_i = 0$ and $\bar{y}_i = 0$ else for all i. Since

$$|K(x_1^n) - K(x_1^n|y_1^n)| \leq K(y_1^n) + O(1)$$

and

$$K(x_1^n|y_1^n) = K(x_1^n/y_1^n, x_1^n/\bar{y}_1^n|y_1^n) + O(1),$$

if $\lim_{n \to \infty} K(y_1^n)/n = 0$ and $0 < \lim_n \frac{1}{n}\sum_{i=1}^n y_i < 1$ then we have

$$\lim_{n \to \infty} K(x_1^n)/n = 1$$

$$\Rightarrow \lim_{n \to \infty} \frac{1}{n} K(x_1^n/y_1^n, x_1^n/\bar{y}_1^n|y_1^n) = 1$$

$$\Rightarrow \lim_{n \to \infty} \frac{1}{n}(K(x_1^n/y_1^n|y_1^n) + K(x_1^n/\bar{y}_1^n|y_1^n)) = 1$$

$$\Rightarrow \lim_{n \to \infty} \frac{n_1}{n}\frac{1}{n_1} K(x_1^n/y_1^n|y_1^n) + \frac{n - n_1}{n}\frac{1}{n - n_1} K(x_1^n/\bar{y}_1^n|y_1^n) = 1$$

$$\Rightarrow \lim_{n \to \infty} \frac{1}{n_1} K(x_1^n/y_1^n|y_1^n) = 1 \text{ and } \lim_{n \to \infty} \frac{1}{n - n_1} K(x_1^n/\bar{y}_1^n|y_1^n) = 1.$$

where $n_1 = |x_1^n/y_1^n| = \sum_{i=1}^n y_i$. Similarly, if $\lim_{n \to \infty} K(y_1^n)/n = 0$ and $\lim_n \frac{1}{n}\sum_{i=1}^n y_i = 1$ then we have $\lim_{n \to \infty} \frac{1}{n_1} K(x_1^n/y_1^n|y_1^n) = 1$.

(ii) $\Rightarrow$ (i)

Suppose that

$$\lim_{n \to \infty} \frac{1}{n} K(y_1^n) = \lim_{n \to \infty} -\frac{1}{n} \log P(y_1^n) > 0, \tag{3}$$

for a computable P. Let l_n be the least integer greater than $-\log P(y_1^n)$. Then by considering arithmetic coding, there is $z = z_1 z_2 \cdots \in \Omega$ and a monotone function u such that $y_1^n \sqsubset u(z_1^{l_n})$. By considering optimal code for $z_1^{l_n}$ we have $Km(y_1^n) \leq Km(z_1^{l_n}) + O(1)$. From (3), we have $\lim_n Km(y_1^n)/l_n = \lim_n Km(z_1^{l_n})/l_n = 1$. For $l_n \leq t \leq l_{n+1}$, we have $Km(z_1^{l_n})/l_{n+1} \leq Km(z_1^t)/t \leq Km(z_1^{l_{n+1}})/l_n$. From (3), we have $\lim_n l_{n+1}/l_n = 1$, and hence $\lim_n Km(z_1^n)/n = \lim_n K(z_1^n)/n = 1$.

Since 1) $z_1^{l_n}$ is computable from y_1^n, 2) $\lim_n l_n/n > 0$ by (3), and 3) $\lim_n \frac{1}{n}\sum_{i=1}^n y_i > 0$, we have $\limsup_{n \to \infty} \frac{1}{|z_1^n/y_1^n|} K(z_1^n/y_1^n|y_1^n) < 1$. $\quad\square$

Example 1. Champernowne sequence satisfies the condition of the proposition and (i) holds, however its Kamae-entropy is not zero.

Example 2. If y is a Sturmian sequence generated by an irrational rotation model with a computable parameter [6,12] then y satisfies the condition of the proposition and (i) holds.

3   Discussion

Both proofs of Proposition 1 and 2 have similar structure, i.e., the part (i) →
(ii) are straightforward and in order to show the converse, we construct random
sequences (in the sense of Proposition 1 and 2, respectively) by compression.

We may say that Proposition 1 is a Martin-Löf randomness analogy and
Proposition 2 is a complexity rate analogy to KW theorem, respectively. These
results neither prove nor disprove the conjecture of van Lambalgen. However
Martin-Löf randomness and complexity rate randomness give different classes of
randomness, and a curious point of the conjecture is that it states equivalence
of statements described in terms of them.

As stated above we proved our propositions by constructing random sequences.
In [3] pp.962, a different direction is studied, i.e., a sequence that is not predicted
by MML with respect to finite order Markov processes is considered. Such a sequence is called *red herring sequence* [3] and considered to be a non-random
sequence with respect to MML and finite order Markov processes, in the sense
that MML cannot find a finite order Markov model for that sequence.

Acknowledgement. The author thanks Prof. Teturo Kamae (Matsuyama
Univ.) for discussions and comments.

References

1. Brudno, A.A.: Entropy and the complexity of the trajectories of a dynamical system. Trans. Mosc. Math. Soc. 44, 127–151 (1983)
2. Chaitin, G.J.: A theory of program size formally identical to information theory.
   J. ACM 22, 329–340 (1975)
3. Dowe, D.L.: MML, hybrid Bayesian network graphical models, statistical consistency, invariance and uniqueness. In: Bandyopadhyay, P.S., Foster, M. (eds.) Handbook of the Philosophy of Science. Philosophy of Statistics, vol. 7, Elsevier (2011)
4. Hochman, M.: Upcrossing inequalities for stationary sequences and applications.
   Ann. Probab. 37(6), 2135–2149 (2009)
5. Kamae, T.: Subsequences of normal numbers. Israel J. Math. 16, 121–149 (1973)
6. Kamae, T., Takahashi, H.: Statistical problems related to irrational rotations.
   Ann. Inst. Statist. Math. 58(3), 573–593 (2006)
7. Kolmogorov, A.N.: Three approaches to the quantitative definition of information.
   Probl. Inf. Transm. 1(1), 1–7 (1965)
8. Li, M., Vitányi, P.: An introduction to Kolmogorov complexity and Its applications,
   3rd edn. Springer, New York (2008)
9. Martin-Löf, P.: The definition of random sequences. Information and Control 9,
   602–609 (1966)
10. Shen, A.K.: On relations between different algorithmic definitions of randomness.
    Soviet Math. Dokl. 38(2), 316–319 (1989)
11. Solomonoff, R.J.: A formal theory of inductive inference, part 1 and part2. In-
    form. Contr. 7, 1–22, 224–254 (1964)

12. Takahashi, H., Aihara, K.: Algorithmic analysis of irrational rotations in a single neuron model. J. Complexity 19, 132–152 (2003)
13. van Lambalgen, M.: Random sequences. PhD thesis, Universiteit van Amsterdam (1987)
14. V'yugin, V.V.: Ergodic theorems for individual random sequences. Theor. Comp. Sci. 207, 343–361 (1998)
15. Weiss, B.: Normal sequences as collectives. In: Proc. Symp. on Topological Dynamics and Ergodic Theory. Univ. of Kentucky (1971)
16. Weiss, B.: Single Orbit Dynamics. Amer. Math. Soc. (2000)

(Non-)Equivalence of Universal Priors

Ian Wood[1], Peter Sunehag[1], and Marcus Hutter[1,2]

[1] School of Computer Science, The Australian National University,
Canberra ACT 0200 Australia
[2] Department of Computer Science, ETH Zürich, Switzerland

Abstract. Ray Solomonoff invented the notion of universal induction featuring an aptly termed "universal" prior probability function over all possible computable environments [9]. The essential property of this prior was its ability to dominate all other such priors. Later, Levin introduced another construction — a mixture of all possible priors or "universal mixture" [12]. These priors are well known to be equivalent up to multiplicative constants. Here, we seek to clarify further the relationships between these three characterisations of a universal prior (Solomonoff's, universal mixtures, and universally dominant priors). We see that the the constructions of Solomonoff and Levin define an identical class of priors, while the class of universally dominant priors is strictly larger. We provide some characterisation of the discrepancy.

1 Introduction

In the study of universal induction, we consider an abstraction of the world in the form of a binary string. Any sequence from a finite set of possibilities can be expressed in this way, and that is precisely what contemporary computers are capable of analysing. An "environment" provides a measure of probability to (possibly infinite) binary strings. Typically, the class $\mathcal{M}$ of enumerable semimeasures is considered. Given the equivalence between $\mathcal{M}$ and the set of monotone Turing machines (Lemma 1), this choice reflects the expectation that the environment can be computed by (or at least approximated by) a Turing machine.

Universal induction is an ideal Bayesian induction mechanism assigning probabilities to possible continuations of a binary string. In order to do this, a prior distribution, termed a universal prior, is defined on binary strings. This prior has the property that the Bayesian mechanism converges to the true (generating) environment for *any* environment μ in $\mathcal{M}$, given sufficient evidence.

There are three popular ways of defining a universal prior in the literature: Solomonoff's prior [9,12,4], as a universal mixture [12,4,5], or a universally dominant semimeasure [4,5]. Briefly, a universally dominant semimeasure is one that dominates every other semimeasure in $\mathcal{M}$ (Definition 8), a universal mixture is a mixture of all semimeasures in $\mathcal{M}$ with non-zero coefficients (Definition 7), and a Solomonoff prior assigns the probability that a (chosen) monotone universal Turing machine outputs a string given random input (Definition 6). These and other relevant concepts are defined in more detail in Section 2.

D.L. Dowe (Ed.): Solomonoff Festschrift, LNAI 7070, pp. 417–425, 2013.
© Springer-Verlag Berlin Heidelberg 2013

Solomonoff's and the universal mixture constructions have been known for many years and they are often used interchangeably in textbooks and lecture notes. Their equivalence has been shown in the sense that they dominate each other [12,4,7]. We extend this result in Section 3, showing that they in fact define exactly the same class of priors.

Further, it is trivial to see that both constructions produce universally dominant semimeasures. The converse is, however, not true. Universally dominant semimeasures are a larger class. We provide a simple example to demonstrate this in Section 4.

These results are relatively undemanding technically, however given their fundamental nature, that they have not to our knowledge been published to date, and the relevance to Ray Solomonoff's famous work on universal induction, we present them here.

The following diagram summarises these inclusion relations:

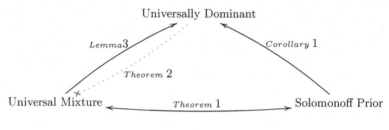

Fig. 1.

2   Definitions

We represent the set of finite/infinite binary strings as $\mathbb{B}^*$ and $\mathbb{B}^\infty$ respectively. ϵ denotes the empty string, xb the concatenation of strings x and b, $\ell(x)$ the length of a string x. A cylinder set, the set of all infinite binary strings which start with some $x \in \mathbb{B}^*$ is denoted Γ_x.

A string x is said to be a prefix of a string y if $y = xz$ for some string z. We write $x \sqsubseteq y$ or $x \sqsubset y$ if x is a proper substring of y (ie: $z \neq \epsilon$). We denote the maximal prefix-free subset of a set of finite strings $\mathcal{P}$ by $\lfloor \mathcal{P} \rfloor$. It can be obtained by successively removing elements that have a prefix in $\mathcal{P}$. The uniform measure of a set of strings is denoted $|\mathcal{P}| := \sum_{p \in \lfloor \mathcal{P} \rfloor} 2^{-\ell(p)}$. This is the area of continuations of elements of $\mathcal{P}$ considered as binary decimal numbers.

There have been several definitions of monotone Turing machines in the literature [7], however we choose that which is now widely accepted [9,12,4,7] and has the useful and intuitive property Lemma 1.

Definition 1. *A monotone Turing machine is a computer with binary (one-way) input and output tapes, a bidirectional binary work tape (with read/write heads as appropriate) and a finite state machine to determine its actions given input and work tape values. The input tape is read-only, the output tape is write-only.*

The definitions of a universal Turing machine in the literature are somewhat varied or unclear. Monotone universal Turing machines are relevant here for defining the Solomonoff prior. In the algorithmic information theory literature, most authors are concerned with the explicit construction of a single reference universal machine [4,7,9,11,12]. A more general definition is left to a relatively vague statement along the lines of "a Turing machine that can emulate any other Turing machine". The definition below reflects the typical construction used and is often referred to as *universal by adjunction* [2,3].

Definition 2 (Monotone Universal Turing Machine). *A monotone universal Turing machine is a monotone Turing machine U for which there exist:*

1. *an enumeration $\{T_i : i \in \mathbb{N}\}$ of all monotone Turing machines*
2. *a computable uniquely decodable self-delimiting code $I : \mathbb{N} \to \mathbb{B}^*$*

such that the programs for U that produce output coincide with the set $\{I(i)p : i \in \mathbb{N}, p \in \mathbb{B}^*\}$ of concatenations of $I(i)$ and p, and

$$U(I(i)p) = T_i(p) \quad \forall i \in \mathbb{N}, \ p \in \mathbb{B}^*$$

A key concept in algorithmic information theory is the assignment of probability to a string x as the probability that some monotone Turing machine produces output beginning with x given unbiased coin flip input. This approach was used by Solomonoff to construct a universal prior [9]. To better understand the properties of such a function, we will need the concepts of enumerability and semimeasures:

Definition 3. *A function or number ϕ is said to be* **enumerable** *or* **lower semicomputable** *(these terms are synonymous) if it can be approximated from below (pointwise) by a monotone increasing set $\{\phi_i : i \in \mathbb{N}\}$ of finitely computable functions/numbers, all calculable by a single Turing machine. We write $\phi_i \nearrow \phi$. Finitely computable functions/numbers can be computed in finite time by a Turing machine.*

Definition 4. *A* **semimeasure** *is a "defective" probability measure on the σ-algebra generated by cylinder sets in $\mathbb{B}^\infty$. We write $\mu(x)$ for $x \in \mathbb{B}^*$ as shorthand for $\mu(\Gamma_x)$. A probability measure must satisfy $\mu(\epsilon) = 1$, $\mu(x) = \sum_{b \in \mathbb{B}} \mu(xb)$. A semimeasure allows a probability "gap": $\mu(\epsilon) \leq 1$ and $\mu(x) \geq \sum_{b \in \mathbb{B}} \mu(xb)$. $\mathcal{M}$ denotes the set of all enumerable semimeasures.*

The following definition explicates the relationship between monotone Turing machines and enumerable semimeasures.

Definition 5 (Solomonoff semimeasure). *For each monotone Turing machine T we associate a semimeasure*

$$\lambda_T(x) := \sum_{\lfloor p:T(p)=x* \rfloor} 2^{-\ell(p)} = |T^{-1}(x*)|$$

where $\lfloor \mathcal{P} \rfloor$ indicates the maximal prefix-free subset of a set of finite strings $\mathcal{P}$, $T(p) = x*$ indicates that x is a prefix of (or equal to) $T(p)$ and $\ell(p)$ is the length of p. If there are no such programs, we set $\lambda_T(x) := 0$. [See [7] definition 4.5.4]

Note that this is the probability that T outputs a string starting with x given unbiased coin flip input. To see this, consider the uniform measure given by $\lambda(\Gamma_p) := 2^{-\ell(p)}$. This is the probability of obtaining p from unbiased coin flips. $\lambda_T(x)$ is the uniform measure of the set of programs for T that produce output starting with x, ie: the probability of obtaining one of those programs from unbiased coin flips. Note also that, since T is monotone, this set consists of a union of disjoint cylinder sets $\{\Gamma_p : p \in \lfloor q : T(q) = x* \rfloor\}$. By dovetailing a search for such programs and an lower approximation of the uniform measure λ, we can see that λ_T is enumerable. See Definition 4.5.4 (p.299) and Lemma 4.5.5 (p.300) in [7].

An important lemma in this discussion establishes the equivalence between the set of all monotone Turing machines and the set $\mathcal{M}$ of all enumerable semimeasures. It is equivalent to Theorem 4.5.2 in [7] (page 301) with a small correction: $\lambda_T(\epsilon) = 1$ for any T by construction, but $\mu(\epsilon)$ may not be 1, so this case must be excluded.

Lemma 1. *A semimeasure μ is lower semicomputable if and only if there is a monotone Turing machine T such that $\mu = \lambda_T$ except on $\Gamma_\epsilon \equiv \mathbb{B}^\infty$ and $\mu(\epsilon)$ is lower semicomputable.*

We are now equipped to formally define the 3 formulations for a universal prior:

Definition 6 (Solomonoff prior). *The Solomonoff prior for a given universal monotone Turing machine U is*

$$M := \lambda_U$$

The class of all Solomonoff priors we denote $\mathcal{U}_M$.

Definition 7 (Universal mixture). *A universal mixture is a mixture ξ with non-zero positive weights over an enumeration $\{\nu_i : i \in \mathbb{N}, \nu_i \in \mathcal{M}\}$ of all enumerable semimeasures $\mathcal{M}$:*

$$\xi = \sum_{i \in \mathbb{N}} w_i \nu_i \quad : \quad \mathbb{R} \ni w_i > 0 \, , \sum_{i \in \mathbb{N}} w_i \leq 1$$

We require the weights $w_{()}$ to be a lower semicomputable function. The mixture ξ is then itself an enumerable semimeasure, i.e. $\xi \in \mathcal{M}$. The class of all universal mixtures we denote $\mathcal{U}_\xi$.

Definition 8 (Universally dominant semimeasure). *A universally dominant semimeasure is an enumerable semimeasure δ for which there exists a real number $c_\mu > 0$ for each enumerable semimeasure μ satisfying:*

$$\delta(x) \geq c_\mu \mu(x) \quad \forall x \in \mathbb{B}^*$$

The class of all universally dominant semimeasures we denote $\mathcal{U}_\delta$.

Dominance implies absolute continuity: Every enumerable semimeasure is absolutely continuous with respect to a universally dominant enumerable semimeasure. The converse (absolute continuity implies dominance) is however not true.

3 Equivalence between Solomonoff Priors and Universal Mixtures

We show here that every Solomonoff prior $M \in \mathcal{U}_M$ can be expressed as a universal mixture (i.e.: $M \in \mathcal{U}_\xi$) and vice versa. In other words the class of Solomonoff priors and the class of universal mixtures are identical: $\mathcal{U}_M = \mathcal{U}_\xi$.

Previously, it was known [12,4,7] that a Solomonoff prior M and a universal mixture ξ are equivalent up to multiplicative constants

$$M(x) \leq c_1 \xi(x) \qquad\qquad \forall x \in \mathbb{B}^*$$
$$\xi(x) \leq c_2 M(x) \qquad\qquad \forall x \in \mathbb{B}^*$$

The result we present is stronger, stating that the two classes are exactly identical. Again we exclude the case $x = \epsilon$ as $M(\epsilon)$ is always one for a Solomonoff prior, but $\xi(\epsilon)$ is never one for a universal mixture ξ (as there are $\mu \in \mathcal{M}$ with $\mu(\epsilon) < 1$).

Lemma 2. *For any monotone universal Turing machine U the associated Solomonoff prior M can be expressed as a universal mixture. i.e. there exists an enumeration $\{\nu_i\}_{i=1}^{\infty}$ of the set of enumerable semimeasures $\mathcal{M}$ and computable function $w_{()} : \mathbb{N} \to \mathbb{R}$ such that*

$$M(x) = \sum_{i \in \mathbb{N}} w_i \nu_i(x) \quad \forall x \in \mathbb{B}^* \backslash \epsilon$$

with $\sum_{i \in \mathbb{N}} w_i \leq 1$ and $w_i > 0 \; \forall i \in \mathbb{N}$. In other words the class of Solomonoff priors is a subset of the class of universal mixtures: $\mathcal{U}_M \subseteq \mathcal{U}_\xi$.

Proof. We note that all programs that produce output from U are uniquely of the form $q = I(i)p$. This allows us to split the sum in (1) below.

$$\begin{aligned} M(x) &= \sum_{\lfloor q:U(q)=x* \rfloor} 2^{-\ell(q)} \\ &= \sum_{i \in \mathbb{N}} \sum_{\lfloor p:U(I(i)p)=x* \rfloor} 2^{-\ell(I(i)p)} \qquad\qquad (1) \\ &= \sum_{i \in \mathbb{N}} 2^{-\ell(I(i))} \sum_{\lfloor p:T_i(p)=x* \rfloor} 2^{-\ell(p)} \\ &= \sum_{i \in \mathbb{N}} 2^{-\ell(I(i))} \lambda_{T_i}(x) \end{aligned}$$

Clearly $2^{-l(I(i))} > 0$ and is a computable function of i. Since I is a self-delimiting code it must be prefix free, and so satisfy Kraft's inequality:

$$\sum_{i \in \mathbb{N}} 2^{-l(I(i))} \leq 1$$

Lemma 1 tells us that the λ_{T_i} cover every enumerable semimeasure if ϵ is excluded from their domain, which shows that $\sum_{i \in \mathbb{N}} 2^{-l(I(i))} \lambda_{T_i}(x)$ is a universal mixture. This completes the proof.   □

Corollary 1. *[12] The Solomonoff prior M for a universal monotone Turing machine U is universally dominant. Thus, the class of Solomonoff priors is a subset of the class of universally dominant lower semicomputable semimeasures:* $\mathcal{U}_M \subseteq \mathcal{U}_\delta$.

Proof. From Lemma 2 we have for each $\nu \in \mathcal{M}$ there exists $j \in \mathbb{N}$ with $\nu = \lambda_{T_j}$ and for all $x \in \mathbb{B}^*$:

$$M(x) = \sum_{i \in \mathbb{N}} 2^{-l(I(i))} \lambda_{T_i}(x)$$

$$\geq 2^{-l(I(j))} \nu(x)$$

as required.   □

Lemma 3. *Every universal mixture ξ is universally dominant. Thus, the class of universal mixtures is a subset of the class of universally dominant lower semicomputable semimeasures:* $\mathcal{U}_\xi \subseteq \mathcal{U}_\delta$.

Proof. This follows from a similar argument to that in Corollary 1.   □

Lemma 4. *For every universal mixture ξ there exists a universal monotone Turing machine and associated Solomonoff prior M such that*

$$\xi(x) = M(x) \quad \forall x \in \mathbb{B}^* \backslash \epsilon$$

In other words the class of universal mixtures is a subset of the class of Solomonoff priors: $\mathcal{U}_\xi \subseteq \mathcal{U}_M$.

Proof. First note that by Lemma 1 we can find (by dovetailing possible repetitions of some indicies) parallel enumerations $\{\nu_i\}_{i \in \mathbb{N}}$ of $\mathcal{M}$ and $\{T_i = \lambda_{\nu_i}\}_{i \in \mathbb{N}}$ of all monotone Turing machines, and lower semicomputable weight function $w_{()}$ with

$$\xi = \sum_{i \in \mathbb{N}} w_i \nu_i \quad , \quad \sum_{i \in \mathbb{N}} w_i \leq 1$$

Take a computable index and lower approximation $\phi(i,t) \nearrow w_i$:

$$w_i = \sum_t |\phi(i, t+1) - \phi(i,t)| \tag{2}$$

$$= \sum_j 2^{-k_{ij}} \tag{3}$$

$$i, j \mapsto k_{ij} \text{ computable} \tag{4}$$

The K-C theorem [6,8,1,2] says that for any computable sequence of pairs $\{k_{ij} \in \mathbb{N}, \tau_{ij} \in \mathbb{B}^*\}_{i,j \in \mathbb{N}}$ with $\sum 2^{-k_{ij}} \leq 1$, there exists a prefix Turing machine P and strings $\{\sigma_{ij} \in \mathbb{B}^*\}$ such that

$$\ell(\sigma_{ij}) = k_{ij} \ , \ P(\sigma_{ij}) = \tau_{ij} \tag{5}$$

Choosing distinct τ_{ij} and the existence of prefix machine P ensures that $\{\sigma_{ij}\}$ is prefix free. We now define a monotone Turing machine U. For strings of the form $\sigma_{ij}p$ for some i, j:

$$U(\sigma_{ij}p) := T_i(p) \tag{6}$$

For strings not of this form, U produces no output. U inherits monotonicity from the T_i, and since $\{T_i\}_{i \in \mathbb{N}}$ enumerates all monotone Turing machines, U is universal. The Solomonoff prior associated with U is then:

$$\lambda_U(x) = |U^{-1}(x*)| \tag{7}$$

$$= \sum_{i,j} 2^{-\ell(\sigma_{ij})} |T_i^{-1}(x*)| \tag{8}$$

$$= \sum_i \left(\sum_j 2^{-k_{ij}} \right) \lambda_{T_i}(x) \tag{9}$$

$$= \sum_i w_i \nu_i(x) \tag{10}$$

$$= \xi(x) \tag{11}$$

$$\square$$

The main theorem for this section is now trivial:

Theorem 1. *The classes $\mathcal{U}_M$ of Solomonoff priors and $\mathcal{U}_\xi$ of universal mixtures are exactly equivalent. In other words, the two constructions define exactly the same set of priors: $\mathcal{U}_M = \mathcal{U}_\xi$.*

Proof. Follows directly from Lemma 2 and Lemma 4.

4   Not All Universally Dominant Enumerable Semimeasures Are Universal Mixtures

In this section, we see that a universal mixture must have a "gap" in the semimeasure inequality greater than $c\,2^{-K(\ell(x))}$ for some constant $c > 0$ independent of x, and that there are universally dominant enumerable semimeasures that fail this requirement. This shows that not all universally dominant enumerable semimeasures are universal mixtures.

Lemma 5. *For every Solomonoff prior M and associated universal monotone Turing machine U, there exists a real constant $c > 0$ such that*

$$\frac{M(x) - M(x0) - M(x1)}{M(x)} \geq c\,2^{-K(\ell(x))} \quad \forall x \in \mathbb{B}^*$$

where the Kolmogorov complexity $K(n)$ of an integer n is the length of the shortest prefix code for n.

Proof. First, note that $M(x) - M(x0) - M(x1)$ measures the set of programs $U^{-1}(x)$ for which U outputs x and no more. Consider the set

$$\mathcal{P} := \{ql'p \,|\, p \in \mathbb{B}^*, \, U(p) \sqsupseteq x\}$$

where l' is a shortest prefix code for $\ell(x)$ and q is a program such that $U(ql'p)$ executes $U(p)$ until $\ell(x)$ bits are output, then stops.

Now, for each $r = ql'p \in \mathcal{P}$ we have $U(r) = x$ since $U(p) \sqsupseteq x$ and q executes $U(p)$ until $\ell(x)$ bits are output. Thus $\mathcal{P} \subseteq U^{-1}(x)$ and

$$|\mathcal{P}| \leq |U^{-1}(x)| \tag{12}$$

Also $\mathcal{P} = ql'U^{-1}(x*) := \{s = ql'p \,|\, p \in U^{-1}(x*)\}$, and so

$$|\mathcal{P}| = 2^{-\ell(ql')}|U^{-1}(x*)| \tag{13}$$

combining (12) and (13) and noting that $M(x) - M(x0) - M(x1) = |U^{-1}(x)|$ and $M(x) = |U^{-1}(x*)|$ we obtain

$$\begin{aligned}
M(x) - M(x0) - M(x1) &= |U^{-1}(x)| \\
&\geq |\mathcal{P}| \\
&= 2^{-\ell(ql')}|U^{-1}(x*)| \\
&= 2^{-\ell(q)}2^{-K(\ell(x))}M(x)
\end{aligned}$$

Setting $c := 2^{-\ell(q)}$ this proves the result. $\square$

Theorem 2. *Not all universally dominant enumerable semimeasures are universal mixtures:* $\mathcal{U}_\xi \subset \mathcal{U}_\delta$

Proof. Take some universally dominant semimeasure δ, then define $\delta'(\epsilon) := 1$, $\delta'(0) = \delta'(1) := \frac{1}{2}$, $\delta'(bx) := \frac{1}{2}\delta(bx)$ for $b \in \mathbb{B}$, $x \in \mathbb{B}^*\backslash\epsilon$. δ' is clearly a universally dominant enumerable semimeasure with $\delta'(0) + \delta'(1) = \delta'(\epsilon)$, and by Lemma 5 it is not a universal mixture. $\square$

5   Conclusions

One of Solomonoff's more famous contributions is the invention of a theoretically ideal universal induction mechanism. The universal prior used in this mechanism can be defined/constructed in several ways. We clarify the relationships between three different definitions of universal priors, namely universal mixtures, Solomonoff priors and universally dominant semimeasures. We show that the class of universal mixtures and the class of Solomonoff priors are exactly the same while the class of universally dominant lower semicomputable semimeasures is a strictly larger set.

We have identified some aspects of the discrepancy between Solomonoff priors/universal mixtures and universally dominant lower semicomputable semimeasures, however a clearer understanding and characterisation would be of interest.

Since universal dominance is all that is needed to prove convergence for universal induction [4,10] it is interesting to ask whether the extra properties of the smaller class of Solomonoff priors have any positive consequences for universal induction.

Acknowledgements. We would like to acknowledge the contribution of an anonymous reviewer to a more elegant presentation of the proof of Lemma 4. This work was supported by ARC grant DP0988049.

References

1. Chaitin, G.J.: A theory of program size formally identical to information theory. Journal of the ACM 22, 329–340 (1975)
2. Downey, R.G., Hirschfeldt, D.R.: Kolmogorov complexity of finite strings. In: Algorithmic Randomness and Complexity, pp. 110–153. Springer, New York (2010)
3. Figueira, S., Stephan, F., Wu, G.: Randomness and universal machines. Journal of Complexity 22(6), 738–751 (2006)
4. Hutter, M.: Universal artificial intelligence: Sequential decisions based on algorithmic probability. Springer (2005)
5. Hutter, M.: On universal prediction and Bayesian confirmation. Theoretical Computer Science 384(1), 33–48 (2007)
6. Levin, L.A.: Some Theorems on the Algorithmic Approach to Probability Theory and Information Theory. Phd dissertation, Moscow University, Moscow (1971)
7. Li, M., Vitányi, P.: An Introduction to Kolmogorov Complexity and Its Applications, 3rd edn. Springer (2008)
8. Schnorr, C.: Process complexity and effective random tests. Journal of Computer and System Sciences 7(4), 376–388 (1973)
9. Solomonoff, R.J.: A formal theory of inductive inference. parts I and II. Information and Control 7(2), 224–254 (1964)
10. Solomonoff, R.J.: Complexity-based induction systems: Comparisons and convergence theorems. IEEE Transactions on Information Theory 24(4), 422–432 (1978)
11. Turing, A.: On computable numbers, with an application to the Entscheidungsproblem. Proceedings of the London Mathematical Society 42(2), 230–265 (1936)
12. Zvonkin, A.K., Levin, L.A.: The complexity of finite objects and the development of the concepts of information and randomness by means of the theory of algorithms. Russian Mathematical Surveys 25(6), 83–124 (1970)

A Syntactic Approach to Prediction

John Woodward and Jerry Swan

Computer Science, The University of Nottingham UK
{john.woodward,jerry.swan}@nottingham.ac.uk
http://www.cs.nott.ac.uk/~jrw,~jps

Abstract. A central question in the empirical sciences is; given a body of data how do we best attempt to make predictions? There are subtle differences between current approaches which include Minimum Message Length (MML) and Solomonoff's theory of induction [24].

The nature of hypothesis spaces is explored and we observe a correlation between the complexity of a function and the frequency with which it is represented. There is not a *single* best hypothesis, as suggested by Occam's razor (which says prefer the simplest), but *a set* of functionally equivalent hypotheses. One set of hypotheses is preferred over another set because it is larger, thus giving the impression simpler functions generalize better. The probabilistic weighting of one set of hypotheses is given by the relative size of its equivalence class. We justify Occam's razor by a counting argument over the hypothesis space.

Occam's razor contrasts with the No Free Lunch theorems which state that it impossible for one machine learning algorithm to generalize better than any other. No Free Lunch theorems assume a distribution over functions, whereas Occam's razor assumes a distribution over programs.

Keywords: Bias, Conservation of Generalization, Induction, No Free Lunch (NFL), Occam's Razor, Complexity, Machine Learning, Genetic Programming.

1 Introduction

There are at least three approaches to the problem of induction; (1) compression (Kolmogorov Complexity), (2) probability (Algorithmic Complexity), and (3) minimum message length (Information Theory), each with similarities and subtle differences (see sections 1 of [4,24]). Turing machines feature in the first two, while a coding scheme features in the third. (1) and (3) look for an explanation (i.e. a single theory), while (2) takes a weighted sum over all hypotheses in order to make predictions (see section 8 of [24] and section 4 of [4]). While Solomonoff [22,23] laid the foundations for a predictive approach, and recently emphasized genetic programming [21]. One of the reasons being that it can embrace recursion, unlike some other methods. In addition, genetic programming readily lends itself to both explanation and prediction motives, in that genetic programming can either return a single program, or can make predictions based on the current population (so called ensemble methods). This paper examines induction from a genetic programming perspective.

D.L. Dowe (Ed.): Solomonoff Festschrift, LNAI 7070, pp. 426–438, 2013.

A hypothesis is an effective procedure mapping input data to output data. Induction is the process of being given a set of input–output pairs, finding a hypothesis which makes accurate predictions [2,13,14,22,23]. The process of generating hypotheses is largely done by scientists, but is now the focus of machine learning [14]. This is realized by defining a hypothesis space (program space or search space). A hypothesis space is the set of all instances of some representation (with some size limit imposed). It is then sampled, often using nature inspired methods, to find a hypothesis. The subject of this article is about the static nature of hypothesis spaces, rather than the dynamics of how they are sampled. Investigations into the nature of computational hypothesis spaces [10,12] leads to two key observations;

KEY OBSERVATION 1: Simple functions are represented more frequently in a hypothesis space, and complex functions are represented less frequently.

KEY OBSERVATION 2: Above a certain size of program, the frequency distribution of functions represented in a hypothesis space does not alter.

Occam's razor has been adopted by the machine learning community and has been taken to mean; *"The simplest explanation is best"* [2], echoed BY Einstein; "Make everything as simple as possible, but no simpler". It has been argued that simpler explanations are more likely to give better predictions on unobserved data. Kearns et. al. [9] state that Occam's razor has become a central doctrine of scientific methodology. Occam's razor is essentially a meta-hypothesis; it is a hypothesis about hypotheses. Why is a simpler hypothesis more likely to generalize to unseen data than a more complex hypothesis? Webb [25] states; *"Several attempts have been made to provide theoretical support for the principle of Occam's razor in the machine learning context. However, these amount to no more than proofs that there are few simple hypotheses and that the probability that one of any such small selection of hypotheses will fit the data is low"*. We also criticize these attempts in Section 3. While Webb's paper [25] suggests difficulties with Occam's Razor, Needham and Dowe [16] do cast doubt over this and suggest further investigation in needed.

The NFL theorems [20,26,27] state that over all functions, no learning algorithm has superior performance, negating Occam's razor [3,8]. We should therefore scrutinize the assumptions. NFL is argued in semantic terms (i.e. distributions over functions). We argue in syntactic terms (i.e. distributions over programs) to support Occam's Razor.

The remainder of this article is as follows; In Section 2, examples are given where multiple explanations of the observations are plausible, illustrating that hypotheses should only be falsified if they are shown to be incorrect. In Section 3, previous arguments for parsimony are examined. In Section 4, we examine the assumptions behind NFL theorems. In Section 5, formal definitions are given. Section 6 explores the nature of hypothesis spaces. In Section 7, Occam's razor

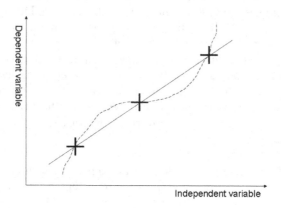

Fig. 1. What is the underlying trend which best explains the data? Two possibilities are shown here, a straight line and a curved line. An Occam's razor approach would prefer a simple straight line, compared to a more complicated curvy line, assuming that the straight line is simpler than the curved line. A NFL approach would say both lines are equally good descriptions of the observation, as all functions have equal probability. We will argue that the more complex wavy line is *a possible explanation* of the data, but with *a lower probability* than the simpler straight line.

is proved based on assumptions which have empirical support. The final Section summarizes this article.

2   Illustrative Examples

We give examples in which alternative hypotheses are equally consistent with observation. While a simpler hypothesis may be consistent with the data, we can never discard the possibility that a more complex hypothesis is isomorphic to the process which is responsible for what we observe. Empirically we cannot differentiate two hypotheses which are functionally equivalent on the observations. An experiment can never be constructed which distinguishes them. We can only make statements about the validity of a hypothesis at a semantic level, (i.e. regarding the predictions about input and output).

Imagine we have a computer program which generates the sequence ($< input, output >$ pairs) $< 1, 1 >, < 2, 2 >, < 3, 3 >$ and we are given the task of finding a function which describes the data. Given the data the following three hypothesis are all valid explanations;

$$H1 : y = x$$
$$H2 : y = x + e^{i\pi} + sin^2(x) + cos^2(x)$$
$$H3 : y = 0 \text{ if } x = 100 \text{ else } y = x$$

All three hypotheses are syntactically different. $H1$ is semantically equivalent to $H2$, and therefore make identical predictions (like Newton and Lagrange, see following paragraph). However $H1$ and $H2$ are semantically distinct from $H3$, which is observationally identical to $H1$ and $H2$ except at the point $x = 100$. The measurement at the point $x = 100$, and only this measurement, will allow us to distinguish between these hypotheses and discard either $H3$ or $H1$ and $H2$. No measurement will ever distinguish between $H1$ and $H2$. While $H1$ and $H2$ are trivially semantically equivalent, it maybe the case that a computer program equivalent to $H2$ is responsible for generating the observed data. We are not interested in inducing a program syntactically equivalent to the program responsible producing the data. We are interested in inducing a program semantically equivalent to the program producing the data. Note that in example, as in this paper, we have ignored noise.

Let us now take an example from physics. Newton's 2nd law of motion is a perfectly good description of "everyday mechanics", where the path of particles is determined by forces. An alternative formulation is Lagrangian mechanics, which determines the path a particle takes by minimizing a quantity based on kinetic and potential energies (i.e. the action functional is stationary). These two approaches are formally equivalent (while a Relativistic formulation of mechanics *is* different). Based on experimental observation, we cannot differentiate between these two theories. A similar situation exists in optics. Indeed (ignoring quantum mechanics and relativity for a moment), assuming the universe is a physical computer (i.e. hardware), we will never know if the software running on it is a Newtonian or Lagrangian program, we can only make observations which will never distinguish between them. Newton and Lagrange are analogous to $H1$ and $H2$ in the preceding paragraph.

3   Justifications and Criticisms of Occam's Razor

[14,19] provide similar arguments. They essentially reduce Occam's razor to the fact that there are fewer shorter hypotheses than longer ones. [19] states: "*There are far fewer simple hypotheses than complex ones, so that there is only a small chance that* any *simple hypothesis that is wildly incorrect will be consistent with all observations*". A simple hypothesis has fewer degrees of freedom, so if it is consistent with the training data, it is more likely to be consistent with validation data when compared to a more complex hypothesis.

[14] states; "*There are fewer short hypotheses than long ones (based on straightforward combinatorial arguments), it is less likely that one will find a short hypothesis that coincidentally fits the training data. In contrast there are often many very complex hypotheses that fit the current training data but fail to generalize correctly to subsequent data*". While this is true, it then raises the question that, while there are also many complex hypotheses that fit the data but will fail to generalize, there are also many complex hypotheses that do fit subsequent data. It still does not explain why we should choose a shorter hypothesis in preference to another one. We should not arbitrarily discard more

complex hypotheses which are consistent with the data. For example, in Section 2, we should not discard Lagrange over Newton on grounds of complexity.

There has also been empirical work for and against Occam's Razor. [3,15,25]. However, further investigations has revealed flaws in the experimental approach. For example, in the induction of decision tree, node cardinality was used as an interpretation of Occam's Razor [15]. However, the insightful work of Needham and Dowe, suggests a more sophisticated Minimum Message Length approach is needed (also see [4] section 4). And, as the title suggests from a paper, *"very simple classification rules perform well on most commonly used datasets"* [6].

4   No Free Lunch Theorems and Generalization

The NFL theorems are a collection of theorems, which broadly state that, any gain in performance regarding generalization on one problem, is reflected by a loss in performance on another problem, and clearly contradict Occam's Razor. These are referred to as NFL theorems [26,27], the law of Conservation of Generalization [20] and the Ugly Duckling theorems [5]. We will refer to these collectively as NFL as this is the more established term. Over a set of all problems (functions), the positive performance over some learning situations must be offset by an equal degree of negative performance in others, where the performance of a learning algorithm is measured in terms of its prediction of cases not included in the training set. For every problem a learner performs well on, there exists a problem on which the learner performs poorly. An alternative but equivalent statement is, generalization is a zero sum game. There are various ways of stating these theorems, but they are all essentially equivalent as one can be proved from another. All of these arguments for NFL are in purely semantic terms. That is, they are trying to prove a proposition about the distribution over function (semantics), by making assumptions about the probability distribution over functions (semantics). In section 7 we will assume a distribution over programs to prove Occam's razor.

5   Definitions

Definition 1 (Function). *A function is a mapping from one set to another.*

Definition 2 (Program). *A program is an implementation of a function.*

The semantic concept of "increment" is expressed in many different ways by a number of syntactically correct programs containing symbols from the set $\{x, +, 1, ; \}$, see figure 2. One semantic entity (function) can be expressed by many syntactic structures (programs). Functions correspond to semantic entities, and programs correspond to syntactic structures. A hypothesis corresponds to a program and a set of predictions corresponds to a function.

Definition 3 (Set of Base Functions). *A set of base functions (or primitives) is a finite set of functions $\{f_1, \ldots, f_n\}$ which can be used to generate new*

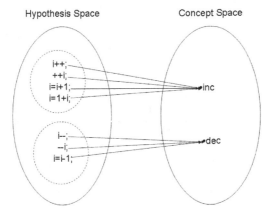

Fig. 2. The space of hypotheses (syntactic structures) maps to the space of concepts (semantic entities). For example, a set of programs maps to a set of functions. Many hypotheses can map to the same concept. The hypothesis space is partitioned into equivalence classes defined by the concepts they map onto. Two equivalence classes are shown by dotted ellipses. Programs representing the same function belong to the same equivalence class.

functions (e.g. a function h is constructed from f_1 and f_2; $h(x) = f_1(f_2(x))$). We are not concerned with how the base functions are implemented, which can be thought of as atomic black boxes. The set of base functions is the same as functions included in the function set of Genetic Programming, where the goal is to synthesize a target function from the base set [10].

Langdon [12]) uses different sets of base functions for example {NAND}, {AND, OR, NAND, NOR}, and $\{+, -, *, \%\}$, see Section 6 of this paper. Note that none of these sets are capable of expressing the computable functions.

Definition 4 (Size). *The size of a program is the total number of bits needed to express it. (However, we could use any reasonable definition of size. For example, in [12], the size is the number of nodes in the parse tree.)*

Definition 5 (Descriptive Complexity). *The descriptive complexity of a function, $c(f)$, is the size of the smallest program which expresses it, with respect to a set of base functions and data structure. This is the same definition as often used in Genetic Programming [28,29].*

If the set of base functions is capable of expressing the computable functions, and the definition of size is the number of bits, then this definition is equivalent to Kolmogorov Complexity [13]. The descriptive complexity of a function will in general depend on the set of base functions.

Definition 6 (Equivalence Class of Hypotheses). *An equivalence class of hypotheses contains all hypotheses mapping to the same function.*

For example, a hypothesis space of Java programs maps to a concept space of computable functions. This mapping is achieved by the Java Virtual Machine ($I(p) = f$, where p is a Java program, f is a computable function and I is the Java Virtual Machine). $I(p_i) = I(p_j)$ implies the programs p_i and p_j compute the same function and are semantically equivalent, while $p_i \neq p_j$ implies the programs are syntactically different. A hypothesis space is a set of programs and a concept space is a set of functions.

The hypothesis space is partitioned into equivalence classes of semantically equivalent hypotheses. For example the Java/C programs $\{y = x + 1;\}, \{y = 1 + x;\}, \{y = x + +;\}$, and $\{y = + + x;\}$ all belong to the same class called increment (figure 2). Newtonian and Lagrangian formulations of mechanics belong to the same equivalence class (called classical mechanics), while Special relativity falls into different class as it makes different predictions. During the process of induction, we are eliminating functions inconsistent with the data, and therefore discarding whole equivalence classes (sets of programs) which compute these functions. This leaves us with a set of equivalence classes, all of which are consistent with the data. We are going to argue that the largest equivalence class of this set is the most probable to contain the hypothesis which generalizes best.

Definition 7 (Bias). *Bias is any preference for choosing one concept (function) over another. Bias is a probability distribution over the set of functions expressed by the hypothesis space.*

Learning is the induction of a function which is (approximately) functionally equivalent to the underlying process. An unbiased learning system, by definition, is one where each function is equally likely to be produced. We state the definition given by [14]: *"Any basis for choosing one generalization over another, other than strict consistency with the observed training instances"*.

6   Exploring the Nature of Hypothesis Spaces

6.1   Koza's Lens Effect

Koza [10] considers the role of representation. He examines the probability of generating a solution to the even-3-parity problem with three different types of representation; lookup tables, parse trees and Automatically Defined Functions. For lookup tables, there is the uniform chance of generating a correct lookup table of 1 in 256. Such a representation has no bias as each function is as likely as any other function to be generated. Given the function set {AND, OR, NAND, NOR}, he generates 10^7 trees at random but finds no solutions. However, if two, two argument Automatically Defined Functions are used, 35 solutions are generated. Koza calls this difference in the probability of generating a function due to the representation *"the lens effect"* (we call it representational bias), and talks about the problem environment being viewed through "*the lens of a given type of representation*". The difference between the parse tree results and the Automatically Defined Functions results is due entirely to the representation.

6.2   Langdon's Program Spaces

Langdon [12] generates the hypothesis spaces for 2, 3, and 4 input programs using the function set {NAND} and plots the proportion of programs that represent different functions. With the 2 input function plots, the functions are in lexical order, and he points out that this is not the most convenient ordering, so in other plots they are presented in order of decreasing frequency. From the plots for 3 and 4 inputs, it can be seen that more complex functions occur with less frequency than simpler functions. All Boolean functions of 3 inputs are considered when using base functions of {AND, OR, NAND, NOR} and {AND, OR, NAND, NOR, XOR}. As a general rule, we can see from these two plots (figures 5 and 6 in [12]) that more complex functions are represented less frequently. As it is impractical to analyze such large program spaces generated by 6 input programs, Langdon concentrates on just two functions, namely the always-on-6 function and the even-6-parity function. In this set of figures, [12] plots the error but again a correlation between the error and frequency can be observed.

Langdon [12] uses a polynomial of degree 6 for function regression with a function set $\{+, -, *, \%\}$ (where $\%$ is divide, protected against division by zero) and a terminal set consisting of the input x and random constants. Plots of the mean error against the proportion of times that error is observed are presented for increasing program length. Again, similar to the situation with Boolean program spaces, there is a correlation between error and the proportion of programs.

The artificial ant problem is a standard benchmark problem in the genetic programming literature. In some ways this is more complex than the previous two domains of logic and arithmetic functions as it includes side effects and iteration, that is it is Turing Complete. A plot of fitness against program length against proportion is presented. Again there is a correlation between the fitness and the proportion of program corresponding to that fitness similar to that seen with the logical functions and symbolic regression.

7   Justification of Occam's Razor

A preference for one function over another is expressed as $p(f_1) > p(f_2)$ where, the $p(f_1)$ is the probability of function f_1. We denote the complexity of a function f as $c(f)$, and $c(f_1) < c(f_2)$ meaning, f_1 is less complex than f_2. We combine these to provide a statement of Occam's razor;

Theorem 1 (Occam's razor). $p(f_1) > p(f_2) \leftrightarrow c(f_1) < c(f_2)$

7.1   Occam's Razor, Uniform Sampling of Program Space

We begin by defining our notation. P is the hypothesis space (i.e. a set of programs). $|P|$ is the size of the space (i.e. the cardinality of the set of programs).

F is the concept space (i.e. a set of functions represented by the programs in P). $|F|$ is the size of the space (i.e. the cardinality of the set of functions). If two programs p_i and p_j map to the same function (i.e. they are interpreted as the same function, $I(p_i) = f = I(p_j)$), they belong to the same equivalence class (i.e. $p_i \in [p_j] \leftrightarrow I(p_i) = I(p_j)$). The notation $[p_i]$ denotes the equivalence class which contains the program p_i (i.e. given $I(p_i) = I(p_j)$,then $[p_i] = [p_j]$). The size of an equivalence class $[p_i]$ is denoted by $||[p_i]||$.

We make two assumptions. The first assumption is that we uniformly sample the hypothesis space, and therefore, the probability of sampling a given program is $1/|P|$. This assumption can be relaxed somewhat and in discussed later in this section. The second assumption is that there are fewer hypotheses that represent complex functions: $||[p_1]|| > ||[p_2]|| \leftrightarrow c(f_1) < c(f_2)$, where $I(p_1) = f_1$ and $I(p_2) = f_2$. Note that $||[p_1]||/|P| = p(I(p_1)) = p(f_1)$, that is $||[p_1]||/|P| = p(f_1)$ i.e. the probability of sampling a function is given by the ratio of the size of the equivalence class containing all the programs which are interpreted that function, divided by the size of the hypothesis space. Indeed, one can show that if there are many equivalent programs of the same length, then there must be a shorter equivalent program and a proof sketch of this assumption is given in [7].

Proof (Occam's Razor). We begin the proof by starting from the assumption;

$$||[p_1]|| > ||[p_2]|| \leftrightarrow c(f_1) < c(f_2)$$

Dividing the left hand side by $|P|$,

$$||[p_1]||/|P| > ||[p_2]||/|P| \leftrightarrow c(f_1) < c(f_2)$$

As $||[p_1]||/|P| = p(I(p_1)) = p(f_1)$, we can rewrite this as

$$p(f_1) > p(f_2) \leftrightarrow c(f_1) < c(f_2)$$

which is a statement of Occam's razor (theorem 1).

We take the probability distribution $p(f)$ to be the frequency with which the functions are represented in the hypothesis space (i.e. the size of the equivalence class). The assumption is $||[p_1]|| > ||[p_2]|| \leftrightarrow c(f_1) < c(f_2)$, where $p(I(p_1)) = p(f_1)$, which we have not proved but is reasonable based on empirical work in [12]. We have not explicitly assumed more complex functions are less likely, but rather, the size of equivalence classes are larger if they contain programs which represent simple functions. For further empirical work supporting this see [16].

7.2   Occam's Razor, Non-uniform Sampling of Program Space

Above we assumed the hypothesis space was uniformly sampled. Now we make a much milder assumption, and theorem 1 is still true for a large number of distributions, not just a uniform distribution over the hypothesis space.

The probability of sampling some function is $p(f)$. Let the probability of sampling some function, given a certain hypothesis size be $p(f, s)$, and we know

$p(f, s)$ is independent of size above some threshold [12]. Let the limiting distribution be $D(f)$. Thus, $p(f, s) = D(f)$, when $s > \theta$, where θ is the size threshold. S is the size of the largest hypotheses in the hypothesis space. Instead of uniformly sampling the search space, we weight hypotheses of size s with $w(s)$. The question becomes, what is the distribution of functions if we sample the hypothesis space with an arbitrary weighting over program size above the threshold.

Proof (Independence of Size). We begin the proof by stating the expression for the distribution of functions, weighted by $w(s)$

$$\sum_{s>\theta}^{S} p(f, s).w(s)$$

As $p(f, s) = D(f)$, when $s > \theta$,

$$p(f, s). \sum_{s>\theta}^{S} (w(s))$$

As $\sum_{s>\theta}^{S} (w(s)) = 1$, this reduces to $D(f)$. Therefore,

$$\sum_{s>\theta}^{S} p(f, s).w(s) = D(f)$$

As the distribution over functions is independent of program size (above a certain program size), if we take any distribution over any program size (above the threshold), we obtain the same limiting probability distribution.

This second proof is vital to the full story. The first proof says, if we uniformly sample a program space, we encounter more simple functions than complex functions. The second proof says, if we sample a program space given programs of the same size equal weight (but programs of different size may have different weight), then we observe the same distribution of functions as if we had sampled the program space uniformly. In addition, there are issues if we attempt to sample over an infinite sized space; however we can take the limit as the size of the space increases (and this limit appears to exist [12]).

8 Summary

Occam's razor was a criticism of theories which became more complex without a corresponding increase in predictive power. i.e. the added complexity was redundant. As we are trying to prove a theorem which is about probabilities over functions, we are not in a position to make assumptions about probabilities over functions. such arguments can always be accused of circularity. This leaves us with the approach of looking at probabilities over programs.

From the empirical work of [12] we make two key observations (see Section 1). Firstly, simple functions can be expressed in more ways than complex function, and that there are more programs that map to simple functions than programs that map to complex functions. This suggests dividing the program space up into equivalence classes, where members of each class represent the same function. We make the assumption that the larger the equivalence class, the smaller the smallest program is in that set. The larger the equivalence class, the smaller the complexity of the function represented by programs in that class. As these equivalence classes are different sizes, uniformly sampling the program space will translate into a non-uniform sampling of the function space (i.e. a bias).

Secondly, as the limit of the of the programs in the hypothesis space increases, the proportion of programs that correspond to different functions does not change. The probability distribution tends towards some limiting distribution. What is more, this convergence is fast. Thus, in many machine learning paradigms, while a hard limit on the size of the hypothesis space is imposed, this does not affect the frequency with which functions are represented, as long as the size of the hypothesis space is larger than a certain threshold.

Occam's razor states a simpler function is more likely to generalize than a more complex function. While we agree; we argue that the underlying reason is that the simpler function is represented more frequently in the hypothesis space than more complex functions and this is the reason it should be chosen. We should prefer the function for reasons of probability rather than reasons of complexity, as it is ultimately probabilities we are interested in. We restate Occam's razor: *the most probable function is the one which belongs to the largest class of functionally equivalent hypotheses, consistent with the observed data.*

The most probable function to generalize the observed data is the one that is most *frequently* represented in the hypothesis space. By making observations, we can discard individual functions, but we cannot discard individual programs as we can only discard a whole equivalence class of functionally identical programs. There are two points to be made relating to this restatement of Occam's razor. Firstly, this is closer to the induction process. Secondly, if we take Occam's razor as "prefer the simpler", this gives us no indication of statistical confidence. Our approach, allows us to do this by considering the ratio of the sizes of the equivalence classes to which functions belong.

Occam's razor and NFL are mutually exclusive. In the former case there is a bias toward simpler functions, and in the latter case there is no bias. The NFL results should come as no surprise to the reader. Paraphrasing the theorems; if we *assume a uniform distribution over a set of all functions,* and after making some observations, then *there is still a uniform distribution over the remaining functions consistent with observation,* and hence we cannot prefer one function over another. Initially, if there is no bias, then finally there is no bias. With Occam's razor, we start with a monotonically decreasing distribution over a set of functions ordered by increasing complexity, and the act of observation dismisses some functions, then *there is still a monotonically decreasing distribution* over the remaining consistent functions. There are situations where NFL is applicable, and situations where Occam's razor is applicable.

I suspect that many people who regard NFL as the holy grail (as Hutter [7] so eloquently puts it), have not understood the assumptions, or the reasons for an alternative i.e. Occam's Razor. We would not attempt to predict next week's lottery numbers based only on the sequence of past lottery numbers as this is effectively white noise. We could, however, in principle, given the initial state of the lottery number generating machine, predict precisely next week's lottery numbers, as this initial information uniquely determines future states of the system. While Solomonoff's theory cannot be applied in practice, approximations can and are applied through out the machine learning literature. NFL, on the other hand, fails to have a single application (to the author's best knowledge). Indeed, nobody cares about the optimum of a white noise (incompressible) function [7]. Nor do we care about the optimum of very simple functions (e.g. constants). As Langdon [11] states; "most functions are constants and the remainder are mostly parsimonious". There is however a Goldilock zone of interesting functions which are sensible to apply machine learning algorithms to (i.e. not too simple, not too complex). Physicists are largely interesting in continuous functions [18], rather than incompressible functions. In addition NFL is not valid for continuous functions [1] or in a number of machine learning contexts (genetic programming, neural networks, hyper-heuristics) [17].

References

1. Auger, A., Teytaud, O.: Continuous lunches are free plus the design of optimal optimization algorithms. Algorithmica 57(1), 121–146 (2010)
2. Cover, T.M., Thomas, J.A.: Elements of information theory. Wiley-Interscience, New York (1991)
3. Domingos, P.: The role of occam's razor in knowledge discovery. Data Min. Knowl. Discov. 3(4), 409–425 (1999)
4. Dowe, D.L.: MML, hybrid Bayesian network graphical models, statistical consistency, invariance and uniqueness. In: Handbook of the Philosophy of Science (HPS). Philosophy of Statistics, vol. 7, pp. 901–982 (2011)
5. Duda, R.O., Hart, P.E., Stork, D.G.: Pattern Classification, 2nd edn. Wiley-Interscience (November 2000)
6. Holte, R.C.: Very simple classification rules perform well on most commonly used datasets. In: Machine Learning, pp. 63–91 (1993)
7. Hutter, M.: A complete theory of everything (will be subjective). Algorithms 3(7), 360–374 (2010)
8. Hutter, M.: Universal Artificial Intelligence: Sequential Decisions based on Algorithmic Probability, 300 pages. Springer, Berlin (2004), http://www.idsia.ch/~marcus/ai/uaibook.htm
9. Kearns, M.J., Vazirani, U.V.: An introduction to computational learning theory. MIT Press, Cambridge (1994)
10. Koza, J.R.: Genetic Programming II: Automatic Discovery of Reusable Programs. The MIT Press, Cambridge (1994)
11. Langdon, W.B.: Scaling of program functionality. Genetic Programming and Evolvable Machines 10(1), 5–36 (2009)
12. William, B.: Langdon. Scaling of program fitness spaces. Evolutionary Computation 7(4), 399–428 (1999)
13. Li, M., Vitányi, P.: An introduction to Kolmogorov complexity and its applications, 2nd edn. Springer-Verlag New York, Inc., Secaucus (1997)
14. Mitchell, T.M.: Machine Learning. McGraw-Hill, New York (1997)
15. Murphy, P.M., Pazzani, M.J.: Exploring the decision forest: An empirical investigation of occams razor in decision tree induction. Journal of Artificial Intelligence Research, 257–275 (1994)

16. Needham, S.L., Dowe, D.L.: Message length as an effective ockham's razor in decision tree induction. In: Proc. 8th International Workshop on Artificial Intelligence and Statistics (AI+STATS 2001), Key West, Florida, U.S.A., pp. 253–260 (January 2001)
17. Poli, R., Graff, M., McPhee, N.F.: Free lunches for function and program induction. In: Proceedings of the Tenth ACM SIGEVO Workshop on Foundations of Genetic Algorithms (FOGA 2009), Orlando, Florida, USA, January 9-11, pp. 183–194. ACM (2009)
18. Rogers, H.: Theory of recursive functions and effective computability. McGraw-Hill series in higher mathematics. MIT Press (1987)
19. Russell, S.J., Norvig, P.: Artificial Intelligence: A Modern Approach. Pearson Education (2003)
20. Schaffer, C.: A conservation law for generalization performance. In: Proceedings of the Eleventh International Conference on Machine Learning, pp. 259–265. Morgan Kaufmann (1994)
21. Solomonoff, R.: Machine learning - past and future. In: The Dartmouth Artificial Intelligence Conference, AI@50, pp. 257–275. Dartmouth, N.H. (2006)
22. Solomonoff, R.J.: A formal theory of inductive inference. part i. Information and Control 7(1), 1–22 (1964)
23. Solomonoff, R.J.: A formal theory of inductive inference. part ii. Information and Control 7(2), 224–254 (1964)
24. Wallace, C.S., Dowe, D.L.: Minimum message length and kolmogorov complexity. Computer Journal 42, 270–283 (1999)
25. Webb: Generality is more significant than complexity: Toward an alternative to occam's razor. In: Australian Joint Conference on Artificial Intelligence (AJCAI) (1994)
26. Wolpert, D.H., Macready, W.G.: No free lunch theorems for search. Technical Report SFI-TR-95-02-010, Santa Fe, NM (1995)
27. Wolpert, D.H., Macready, W.G.: No free lunch theorems for optimization. IEEE Transactions on Evolutionary Computation 1(1), 67–82 (1997)
28. Woodward, J.R.: Complexity and cartesian genetic programming. In: Collet, P., Tomassini, M., Ebner, M., Gustafson, S., Ekárt, A. (eds.) EuroGP 2006. LNCS, vol. 3905, pp. 260–269. Springer, Heidelberg (2006)
29. Woodward, J.R.: Invariance of function complexity under primitive recursive functions. In: Collet, P., Tomassini, M., Ebner, M., Gustafson, S., Ekárt, A. (eds.) EuroGP 2006. LNCS, vol. 3905, pp. 310–319. Springer, Heidelberg (2006)

Developing Machine Intelligence within P2P Networks Using a Distributed Associative Memory

Amiza Amir[1,3], Anang Hudaya M. Amin[2], and Asad Khan[1]

[1] Clayton School of IT, Monash University, Melbourne, Australia
{amiza.amir,asad.khan}@monash.edu
[2] Multimedia University, Malaysia
anang.amin@mmu.edu.my
[3] Universiti Malaysia Perlis, Malaysia

Abstract. In this paper, we discuss machine intelligence for conducting routine tasks within the Internet. We demonstrate a technique, called the Distributed Associative Memory Tree (DASMET), to deal with multi-feature recognition in a peer-to-peer (P2P)-based system. Shared content in P2P-based system is predominantly multimedia files. Multi-feature is an appealing way to tackle pattern recognition in this domain. In our scheme, the information held at individual peers is integrated into a common knowledge base in a logical tree like structure and relies on the robustness of a well-designed structured P2P overlay to cope with dynamic networks. Additionally, we also incorporate a consistent and secure backup scheme to ensure its reliability. We compare our scheme to the Backpropagation network and the Radial Basis Function (RBF) network on two standard datasets, for comparative accuracy. We also show that our scheme is scalable as increasing the number of stored patterns does not significantly affect the processing time.

1   Introduction

Machine intelligence that can perform better than human intellect depends on the ability to recognize pattern regularities from given evidence which allows for better inference [1, 2]. With pervasiveness of the Internet, such intelligence can be provisioned using an in-network associative memory approach. This paper looks at a practical application of network intelligence for recognising content involving multi-feature information within a P2P system.

P2P-based systems encompass powerful capabilities but have become controversial due to copyright infringement issues and more recently for sensitive data leakage. P2P involves dealing with complex datasets such as image, audio, and video, hence significant effort is required to analyse these datasets. Doing so is infeasible owing to the computational complexity in automatic content recognition and the reluctance on the part of peers to share their private resources inordinately.

D.L. Dowe (Ed.): Solomonoff Festschrift, LNAI 7070, pp. 439–443, 2013.

Current approaches in pattern recognition [3–5] incur high computational complexity that inhibits their capability to scale up to handle a large number of features. This limits their ability to seamlessly and effectively perform recognition and classification involving complex datasets.

Multiple-feature implementations consider all significant features which represent a particular set of patterns from many modalities such as vision and sound. Therefore, the aim is to reduce the bias effect of selecting only a single feature for recognition. This is useful in the P2P domain where objects may be processed by different types of analyses and forms such as sound and vision at various locations.

In this paper, we demonstrate the implementation of a fully distributed associative memory for multi-feature recognition within P2P networks. Our underlying approach requires that all peers share their resources in recognizing objects or patterns. Each peer is responsible for sensing, interpreting and remembering patterns by working collaboratively with other peers to recognise an object. This forms a distributed recognition network which can continue to scale-up with increasing number of features in the input patterns. Some P2P networks may comprise hundreds of thousands or even to millions of peers. Such large-scale networks carry vast amount of information and the in-network computational resources for processing it through appropriately designed schemes that can effectively leverage the distributed content and resources.

2   The Distributed Associative Memory Tree (DASMET)

Our approach (called the Distributed Associative Memory Tree (DASMET) [6]) is adapted from the Hierarchical Graph Neuron (HGN) [7]. The HGN is an associative memory for wireless sensor environments. Other than its highly-parallel nature, the strength of this scheme is its lightweight processing and single cycle learning. However, the number of processing nodes and communication costs are significantly increased with an increase in number of features of this scheme.

The DASMET inherits the single cycle learning and accuracy characteristics of the HGN but significantly reduces the number of nodes and communications required by the HGN [6]. Each peer is only responsible to process a subset of features. Each distinct pattern that occurs at a peer is stored and assigned a unique index number. The most similar indices[1] are then sent to the parent node. The parent node then performs the same action based on the combined information from its children. These results are combined iteratively in a tree structure until these converge at the root. At the rootnode, the class label for each distinct index is stored during the training phase. The recall decision is made based on the majority class amongst the most similar indices. An increasing number of features may be easily handled by recruiting more peers[2] into

---

[1] It is possible to have several indices with the highest similarity.

[2] It is not a problem in most P2P systems which usually have in the order of hundred thousands of nodes.

the associative memory network. Since all subsets of features are processed simultaneously, the learning time remains low resulting in a scalable algorithm capable of handling high dimensional multi-feature datasets. Thus, DASMET is a fully distributed associative memory algorithm that facilitates accurate, efficient and scalable multi-feature pattern classification. Fig. 1 shows an example of a DASMET structure for 8 different feature sets. The number of leaves equals the number of distinct feature sets. It may also be set to the number of feature subsets which are split from the original set of features. This is done to reduce the dimensionality of the feature set.

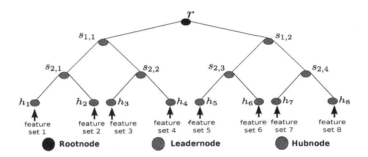

Fig. 1. Example of DASMET architecture for 8 different feature sets. The predefined maximum children of each node, φ is 2. Each feature set is assigned to a hubnode. It has 8 hubnodes and 6 leadernodes.

3   DASMET within a Dynamic Network

Inherent dynamics of a P2P system impede the system from working correctly. We rely on structured P2P overlays such as Kademlia [8] and Chord [9] to link peers. These overlays are well-designed to provide robustness. Furthermore, we create data redundancy across the network to ensure data availability and scheduled maintenance mechanism to maintain the availability of data. A peer may be responsible for a particular session before failure or may go offline and another peer will be able to replace it without a significant degradation to the system. In order to synchronise local replicas, consistent data update and control mechanisms are provided by byzantine fault tolerance replication protocols [10]. The DASMET network periodically recovers through a scheduled recovery mechanism. All nodes work collaboratively to detect any change to the system and perform a node's recovery if needed.

4   Experimental Result

For the purpose of ensuring the suitability of our scheme for P2P networks, we restricted the processing nodes in our simulations to a single machine with a limit of 2GB RAM. Owing to this resource restriction, we were unable to test large dataset for comparison with the BackPropagation network [4] and the Radial Basis Function (RBF) network [11] since these methods require large amount of memory to process large datasets. Therefore, to show the accuracy of our distributed scheme compared to the state-of-the-art neural networks which run on a single site, we made comparison with two smaller datasets. These were Adult and Spam datasets from UCI Data Mining Repository [12]. The Adult dataset consists of 14 features and the Spam dataset consists of 57 features. The results are presented in the Table 1 below.

Table 1. Accuracy comparison of DASMET with single site implementations of neural networks. Accuracy is the percentage of correct classification.

Methods	Accuracy (%)	
	Adult (14 features)	Spam (57 features)
Backpropagation Network	84	92
RBF Network	85	92
DASMET	79	98

Our distributed approach performs marginally less than the Backpropagation network and the RBF network for the Adult dataset. However, it provides better results for the Spam dataset. Note that it is not our intention to outperform other methods in this work but to show that our scheme can be easily distributed over a P2P network with comparable accuracy to a centralised scheme. More results related to accuracy with larger dataset can be found in [6].

We further tested the scalability of the scheme in two experiments involving 750 features and 1500 features. We stored up to 40, 000 patterns in the system in the both experiments. As shown in Fig. 2, our simulation result shows that the store time increases slowly with the increase in stored pattern reflecting the scalability of our scheme.

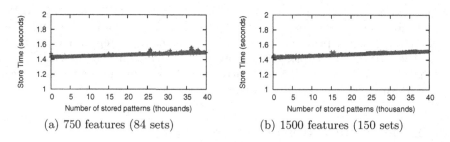

(a) 750 features (84 sets)   (b) 1500 features (150 sets)

Fig. 2. Store time per input pattern with increasing number of stored patterns

5   Conclusion

In this paper, we demonstrate the DASMET approach for multi-feature pattern recognition within a P2P network. A peer only computes a subset of feature from the feature set and this is performed separately in parallel by a group of peers. The recognition results from these peers are then combined iteratively in a tree structure. Thereby significantly reducing the computation complexity at a node in terms of space and time. The success of this preliminary work provides the first concrete steps toward achieving machine intelligence through a highly scalable associative memory resource that forms within the body of the network and allows rapid correlation of pattern data. Such a resource will provide a practical test bed for advanced applications built on Solomonoff's theory.

References

1. Hernández-Orallo, J., Dowe, D.L.: Measuring universal intelligence: Towards an anytime intelligence test. Artif. Intell. 174, 1508–1539 (2010)
2. Solomonoff, R.: A formal theory of inductive inference: Part II. Information and Control 7(2), 224–254 (1964)
3. Hopfield, J.J.: Neural networks and physical system with emergent collective computational properties, pp. 2554–2558 (1982)
4. Hecht-Nielsen, R.: Theory of the backpropagation neural network. In: International Joint Conference on Neural Networks, IJCNN, pp. 593–605 (1989)
5. Browne, M., Ghidary, S.S., Mayer, N.M.: Convolutional neural networks for image processing with applications in mobile robotics. In: Speech, Audio, Image and Biomedical Signal Processing using Neural Networks, pp. 327–349 (2008)
6. Amir, A., Muhamad Amin, A., Khan, A.: A multi-feature pattern recognition for P2P-based system using in-network associative memory. Technical Report 2011/265, Clayton School of IT, Monash University, Victoria, Australia (2011)
7. Nasution, B., Khan, A.I.: A hierarchical graph neuron scheme for real-time pattern recognition. IEEE Transactions on Neural Networks, 212–229 (2008)
8. Maymounkov, P., Mazières, D.: Kademlia: A peer-to-peer information system based on the XOR metric. In: Druschel, P., Kaashoek, M.F., Rowstron, A. (eds.) IPTPS 2002. LNCS, vol. 2429, pp. 53–65. Springer, Heidelberg (2002)
9. Stoica, I., Morris, R., Karger, D., Kaashoek, M.F., Balakrishnan, H.: Chord: A scalable peer-to-peer lookup service for internet applications. SIGCOMM Comput. Commun. Rev. 31, 149–160 (2001)
10. Castro, M., Liskov, B.: Practical byzantine fault tolerance and proactive recovery. ACM Transactions on Computer Systems (TOCS) 20(4), 398–461 (2002)
11. Buhmann, M.D.: Radial Basis Functions: Theory and Implementations. Cambridge University Press (2003)
12. Frank, A., Asuncion, A.: UCI machine learning repository (2010)

Author Index